Microeconomics

An Open Introduction

Richard Friberg

Routledge
Taylor & Francis Group
LONDON AND NEW YORK

Designed cover image: Paul Signac, "Les Andelys, Côte d'Aval", 1886. The Art Institute of Chicago. This information, which is available on the object page for each work, is also made available under Creative Commons Zero (CC0).

First published 2026
by Routledge
4 Park Square, Milton Park, Abingdon, Oxon OX14 4RN

and by Routledge
605 Third Avenue, New York, NY 10158

Routledge is an imprint of the Taylor & Francis Group, an informa business

British Library Cataloguing-in-Publication Data
A catalogue record for this book is available from the British Library

Library of Congress Cataloging-in-Publication Data
Names: Friberg, Richard, 1967- author
Title: Microeconomics : an open introduction / Richard Friberg.
Description: Abingdon, Oxon ; New York, NY : Routledge, 2026. |
Includes bibliographical references and index.
Identifiers: LCCN 2025027465 | ISBN 9781041034476 hardback |
ISBN 9781041034360 paperback | ISBN 9781003623854 ebook
Subjects: LCSH: Microeconomics--Textbooks
Classification: LCC HB172 .F745 2026
LC record available at https://lccn.loc.gov/2025027465

ISBN: 978-1-041-03447-6 (hbk)
ISBN: 978-1-041-03436-0 (pbk)
ISBN: 978-1-003-62385-4 (ebk)

DOI: 10.4324/9781003623854

Typeset in Times New Roman
by SPi Technologies India Pvt Ltd (Straive)

Access the Support Material: www.routledge.com/9781041034360

Contents

About the author xii
What is this book? xiii
Some notes for faculty thinking of assigning the book xiv
Note xv
Acknowledgments xvi

1 Introduction 1

1.1 An example to get our minds primed about the role of economics 1
1.2 Economics – The Wealth of Nations *3*
1.3 Scarcity – An underlying assumption 3
1.4 On the use of models in microeconomics 4
1.5 What we do in the book – And what we don't do 6
Notes 6

2 Supply and demand 8

2.1 Supply and demand – An introduction 8
2.2 Demand 10
2.2.1 Effect on demand of changes in... 11
2.2.2 Demand functions – Some additional aspects 15
2.3 Supply 16
2.3.1 Effect of changes on the supply curve 18
2.4 Combining supply and demand to find the market equilibrium 19
2.5 Shifts in the equilibrium 22
2.5.1 The slope of supply and demand curves and the effects of shocks 26
Notes 27

PART I
Where does supply come from? 31

3 From technology to costs 33

3.1 Setting the stage 33

3.2 Defining some key concepts 34
3.3 The production function 35
3.3.1 Varying one input while keeping other inputs fixed 36
3.3.2 Different ways of producing the same volume of output: Describing the technology 38
3.3.3 Production function and isoquants: A numerical example 43
3.4 Productivity 44
3.5 From technology to costs 48
3.5.1 Cost minimization and isocosts, some additional results 51
3.6 From cost minimization to a cost function 53
3.6.1 Average costs and marginal costs 54
3.7 Additional aspects of cost functions 57
3.7.1 Costs in the long and short run 57
3.7.2 Economies of scale 57
Notes 59

4 Supply by price-taking firms 61

4.1 Maximizing profit – An introduction 61
4.2 The supply of a price-taking firm: How much should be produced? 64
4.3 The supply of a price-taking firm: Should the good be produced at all? 68
4.4 Profits: Positive, negative, or zero? 69
4.5 From firm supply to the market supply 71
4.6 Free entry and profits 73
4.7 What do we mean by zero profit? 75
4.7.1 Opportunity cost 76
4.8 Supply in the long run 77
Notes 78

PART II
Where does demand come from? 79

5 Consumer choice 81

5.1 How can we model choice? 81
5.2 Preferences 82
5.2.1 Utility 85
5.3 Budget constraints 87
5.4 Maximization of utility subject to constraints 89
5.4.1 Example of optimal choices under different prices 91
5.5 Discussion of assumptions and framework 92
5.5.1 Where are the limits of the framework outlined? 92
5.6 Behavioral economics 94
5.6.1 Social preferences 95

5.6.2 *Behavioral biases* 96
5.6.3 *Lack of self-control* 96
5.6.4 *Cognitive limitations and biased information processing* 97
5.6.5 *Final words* 98
5.7 *Appendix – Solving for the optimal consumption basket* 99
Notes 101

6 Demand curves and elasticities 102

6.1 *From constrained optimization to demand curves* 103
6.1.1 *An example of the usefulness of linking preferences to demand* 105
6.2 *Effect of changes in income on demand* 106
6.3 *From individual to market-level demand* 109
6.4 *Elasticities* 110
6.4.1 *Own-price elasticity of demand* 110
6.4.2 *Cross-price elasticities of demand* 114
6.4.3 *Income elasticity of demand* 114
6.4.4 *Elasticities: A simple example* 115
6.5 *Income and substitution effects* 116
Notes 120

PART III
Efficiency and equity in a competitive market 123

7 Efficiency in partial equilibrium 125

7.1 *Efficiency of a competitive market* 125
7.2 *Consumer surplus* 125
7.2.1 *Changes in consumer surplus* 127
7.2.2 *Diamonds and water again* 127
7.3 *Producer surplus* 129
7.4 *Putting CS and PS together: Efficiency in partial equilibrium* 130
7.5 *Policy and deadweight loss* 132
7.5.1 *Price cap* 132
7.5.2 *Unit tax* 133
7.5.3 *Subsidies* 135
Notes 137

8 Efficiency in general equilibrium 138

8.1 *How resources are allocated in an economy* 138
8.2 *Efficiency in consumption* 142
8.3 *Efficient use of inputs* 150
8.4 *Efficient combination of goods* 152

8.5 Comparing different allocations: Equity 155
8.5.1 Normative and positive economics 156
8.5.2 Social welfare functions 157
8.6 Final words 159
Notes 160

PART IV
Imperfect competition 163

9 Monopoly and monopolistic competition 165

9.1 Quantity set by a monopolist 166
9.1.1 Profit maximization for a monopolist – A numerical example 167
9.1.2 Deadweight loss of a monopoly 169
9.1.3 Profit maximization for a monopolist – The general case 171
9.2 Why do monopolies exist? 173
9.2.1 Regulation 173
9.2.2 Natural monopoly 174
9.2.3 Control of an important input 174
9.2.4 Strategic behavior on the part of the incumbent 174
9.3 Monopolistic competition 175
9.3.1 Monopolistic competition when firms differ in productivity 177
9.3.2 Appendix 184
Notes 184

10 Oligopoly 186

10.1 Overview of oligopoly markets 186
10.2 Oligopoly with homogeneous products 187
10.2.1 Quantity competition: Cournot 187
10.2.2 Price competition: Bertrand 195
10.3 Oligopoly with differentiated products 198
10.3.1 Price competition with differentiated products 199
Notes 203

11 Games and strategies 205

11.1 Overview 205
11.2 Simultaneous games 206
11.2.1 Dominant strategies and the prisoner's dilemma 206
11.2.2 Nash equilibria 209
11.2.3 Cases where there are no equilibria in pure strategies 210
11.2.4 Nash Equilibria with continuous strategies 211

11.3 Repeated games 212
11.4 Sequential games 216
11.4.1 Credible commitments 219
11.4.2 Hold-up problems 221
11.5 Game theory – Some concluding thoughts 222
Notes 223

12 Price discrimination 225

12.1 Overview of price discrimination 225
12.1.1 Perfect price discrimination 226
12.1.2 Different prices to different customer groups based on observable criteria 228
12.1.3 Price discrimination under self-selection constraints 231
Notes 238

PART V
Market failures 239

13 Externalities 241

13.1 Externalities 241
13.1.1 Too much is produced when there is strong competition and negative externalities 242
13.1.2 Public policy to deal with externalities 246
13.1.3 Property rights and bargaining as a solution to externalities 250
13.2 Different types of goods 254
13.2.1 Common resource 255
13.2.2 Public goods 259
13.2.3 Club goods 261
Notes 262

14 Asymmetric information 265

14.1 Different forms of asymmetric information 265
14.2 Adverse selection 267
14.2.1 Examples of situations with scope for adverse selection 269
14.2.2 Ways of limiting effects of adverse selection 270
14.3 Moral hazard 274
14.3.1 Further examples of moral hazard 278
14.3.2 How to limit consequences of moral hazard 282
14.4 Concluding discussion 283
Notes 285

PART VI
Applications 287

15 Labor supply and demand 289

15.1 Firm-level demand for labor under perfect competition 290
15.2 Supply of labor 291
15.2.1 Bringing in the real world: The intensive and extensive margins of labor supply 296
15.3 Analysis of equilibria in labor markets 297
15.3.1 Market power on input markets: Monopsony 299
15.3.2 Market power on the supply side: Unions and wage bargaining 301
Notes 302

16 Uncertainty 304

16.1 States of the world, risk and uncertainty 305
16.2 Risk preferences 307
16.2.1 Risk neutrality and defining an increase in risk 308
16.2.2 Risk-averse preferences 309
16.2.3 Risk-loving preferences 311
16.3 Strategies for dealing with risk and uncertainty 313
16.3.1 Diversification 314
16.3.2 Insurance 315
16.3.3 Buffers 315
16.3.4 Flexibility 315
Notes 317

17 International trade 318

17.1 International trade – Some background 318
17.2 The mechanisms that drive trade – Three classes of models 319
17.2.1 Comparative advantage and the gains from trade – An example 319
17.2.2 Trade under perfect competition with specific factors 322
17.2.3 Trade with monopolistic competition 328
17.3 Trade policy 331
17.3.1 Partial equilibrium analysis of trade policy 332
17.3.2 The welfare effects from trade integration – A very brief overview of the evidence 335
Notes 336

18 Topics in digital markets 338

18.1 Digitalization 338
18.2 Platform markets 339

18.2.1 Issues when designing a platform 340
18.2.2 Competition issues raised by platforms 343
18.3 Auctions 345
18.3.1 Valuations and bids 346
18.3.2 Various auction formats 347
18.3.3 Evaluating the different auction formats 348
18.4 Appendix – Further details on profit maximization on a platform 350
18.5 Appendix – The revenue equivalence theorem 351
Notes 352

19 Mathematical appendix 354

19.1 Functions of one variable and their slopes 354
19.2 Finding the optimum of a function of one variable in the absence of constraints 358
19.3 Some rules of differentiation 359
19.4 Inverse functions 361
19.5 Functions of two variables 361
Notes 363

Bibliography 364
Index 371

About the author

Richard Friberg holds the Jacob Wallenberg professorship at the Stockholm School of Economics. He has been teaching microeconomics to undergraduate students (and industrial organization at the PhD level) for more than 20 years. His research interests span both applied theory and empirical work and he has published in leading journals such as *American Economic Review, Journal of Finance* and *Marketing Science*. He has been a visiting researcher at the economics departments of MIT, Princeton, and UC Berkeley and is affiliated with CEPR and NHH in Bergen, Norway. He is also a member of the Prize Committee for the Sveriges Riksbank Prize in Economic Sciences in Memory of Alfred Nobel. See richardfriberg.se for links to published and ongoing research.

What is this book?

This is a textbook suited for a first or second course in microeconomics at the university level. I have been teaching such a course at the Stockholm School of Economics for about 20 years, and the book is an outgrowth of the notes and examples that I have found worked well during those years. There are a large number of books that target the same audience and let me highlight a few distinguishing features:

- Many of us find it easier to understand a graph if it is drawn live, as we are following with some commentary, rather than just presented as a ready-made figure. For this reason I have posted short videos of many of the key figures on YouTube, and they are linked from within the book.
- I've surveyed many, and taught from several, microeconomics textbooks. The basic material of perfectly competitive markets (Chapters 2–8) is covered in very similar ways, and I'm mostly happy with these treatments. When it comes to the issues where markets run into problems, however, what we cover from Chapter 9 and onwards, I find that many textbooks get into a rather bewildering array of cases with surprisingly little thought on how best to convey the central ideas and link them to practice and empirical evidence. I hope that my ambition to do better here has been successful.
- I've included some topics that are becoming increasingly important but are traditionally left out in microeconomic textbooks: In particular, Chapter 9 includes models of competitive selection when firms have different marginal costs, and Chapter 18 examines topics of importance for digital markets: platforms and auctions.
- The digital version of the book is open source and free to download. Many of us like having a physical book as well, and this is published and marketed by Routledge. The text is identical in the digital and print versions.
- It tries to be succinct. A pedagogical adage is, "What is worth learning is worth learning well". Therefore, rather than present a very large number of different cases and applications, we focus on the key concepts in each topic. If you understand these well, you are well set to apply the concepts to other issues.
- Many of the key insights in microeconomics compare the costs and benefits of changing a variable – be it consumption, production or a tax. Many textbooks shy away from using mathematics and try to describe effects verbally and via rules of thumb. In my experience, most of us find it easier to instead understand these concepts using calculus, taking derivatives of functions. This is how we think of these concepts as professional economists, and it reflects how the tools were developed. We therefore rely on calculus in the book. We use the same limited set of tools over and over again in different situations, while explaining clearly what is going on. I have found this to work well.

Some notes for faculty thinking of assigning the book

A few words of background may be useful. The Stockholm School of Economics is a highly selective institution and is arguably the most prestigious university for students going into business and public administration in Sweden. Cohorts of 300 entering students have made their first university acquaintance with economics with the course in microeconomics from which this book has developed. This background is reflected in the book. We assume no prior knowledge of economics but move faster and deeper than what is common in an introductory text. Thus, the book is well suited also as a text for an intermediate class in microeconomics. I have been selected teacher of the year by the students twice, so I must have been doing something right.

As to my background, I first taught microeconomics at university as a TA using Hal Varian's marvelously clear books in both undergraduate and PhD-level courses in the early 1990s. During my PhD studies, I spent one year as a visiting Fulbright student at MIT with an all-star cast of teachers, including Holmström, Dornbusch, and Solow. In particular, the latter made a great impression on me – in his hands, a single equation could say so much, and his pedagogical style has been my role model ever since. Not surprisingly, my research is focused on topics in microeconomics, in particular empirical industrial organization. My interests are broad however, and I've published in both general interest journals such as *American Economic Review* and top journals in closely related fields such as *Journal of Finance* and *Marketing Science*. Widely dispersed research interests might not be the best strategy for maximizing professional impact, but for a textbook author, it may have its benefits, seeing questions from different angles.

Many of us who work as economists fondly look back to our first encounters with microeconomics. The magic of a set of simple tools that can be so useful in making sense of the world. Susan Athey, high-profile economist at Stanford, describes what attracted her to economics as follows (slightly edited for clarity): "What's going on? Why does the world work this way? It all feels like a morass and I can't understand. And then when you find a clear framework. Where it all makes sense. It's just great. . .once you've broken it down in a clear abstract way it's much more easy to figure out how to do something about it, how to change something".[1] This is the feeling that I hope that the book will inspire.

The book relies more on mathematical arguments and calculus than what is common for introductory, and to some extent, intermediate textbooks in microeconomics. A concept can be understood by students at different levels – ranging from an intuitive "that sounds reasonable" when someone else explains it to students having the ability to confidently work with problems. In his advice for how to build a model (and write a textbook), Hal Varian highlights a tip given to him (Varian, 2016, p. 89): "Get together the problems that you want your students to be able to solve after they've read your book – and then write the book that will teach them how to solve them." This book is written very much in that spirit. While problems are the key part of the learning process (my students have graded hand-in problem sets every week), including the problems in the book itself makes it a bit unwieldy. A set of problems are therefore available at the book's homepage on Routledge (https://www.routledge.com/Microeconomics-An-Open-Introduction/Friberg/p/book/9781041034476). In a perhaps useful analogy, the problems ensure that we are not just talking about riding a bike, students are learning to actually ride the bike.

The book contains frequent references to empirical work and surveys. These may be valuable to students who are particularly interested in a certain topic but are also meant to help faculty who want to refresh their background in an area to be able to provide more color and context in lectures. Clearly, since the ebook is available as open source, it may also be useful if you only want to use it as a basis for one or a few lectures on a particular topic.

Slides for the book are available for download at the same homepage as exercises and the full book and will also be linked from my personal homepage, richardfriberg.se

Note

1 The Mixtape with Scott, Interview with Susan Athey, June 16, 2022.

Acknowledgments

I'm grateful for valuable comments from Tommy Andersson, Emil Bustos, Luigi Butera, Anna Dreber Almenberg, Tore Ellingsen, Therese Hartman Liungman, Mark Sanctuary, Karol Szwagrzak, Björn Tyrefors, Ebbe Vestberg, Eva Forslund, and Robert Östling. I'm also grateful to Björn Ericsson, Ute Harris and Anna Kågedal of the library at Stockholm School of Economics for helping me navigate the world of textbook publication and financial support to contribute to the open access publication.

1 Introduction

Illustration 1.1 I got in! iStock by Getty Images, fizkes.

> Economics is a science of thinking in terms of models joined to the art of choosing models which are relevant to the contemporary world.
>
> John Maynard Keynes in a letter to Roy Harrod, July 4, 1938

In this chapter, we give a brief background on microeconomics as a topic of study and the scope of the present book.

1.1 An example to get our minds primed about the role of economics

If you're reading this textbook, you are presumably taking part in a university education. It is an example of a type of good or service that we are interested in studying in economics. Who should get to study what topic at what university? How should educational spots be financed? We can imagine a large number of different ways to solve this issue. First consider

DOI: 10.4324/9781003623854-1

a number of different selection mechanisms that are not directly linked to funding of the education:[1]

- Selection by aptitude tests, interviews, and references.
- Selection by grades from secondary education.
- Education is open to all prospective students, but popular educations will be oversubscribed; difficult exams limit the number of students that continue on.
- Selection by waiting lists. For really popular educations, your parents would have rushed to place you on the list while you were still just a toddler.
- Selection by queue. Like with tickets for a popular concert, some might be waiting for several days or weeks even – camping on the sidewalk to be one of the first 300 through the door. How many weeks would you be willing to camp on the sidewalk to get into Harvard?
- Selection by lottery.
- Selection by social class or the university your parents attended.

The previous examples share the feature that financing of education is not directly linked to the selection of who gets to study what. Alternatively, educational spots can be sold in different ways, thereby determining who gets to study what partly by who is willing and able to pay the price:

- All students pay the same yearly fee. Prices set high enough that not more students want to study than the number of available spots.
- Educational spots are auctioned off sequentially – the highest bidders get to study.

The previous mechanisms have all been used in some circumstances, and in many cases, several selection mechanisms are combined – many US universities for instance are largely financed by tuition fees but also select students based on aptitude tests and interviews. In addition, we may note that historically, many resources have been allocated by violence or threat of violence.

The different ways of allocating educational spots have different implications for who gets to study. They thereby have important ramifications for equality – and the extent to which they decouple selection from parents' incomes. They also differ in the incentives that they give to work hard on developing valuable skills. Some provide strong incentives to study hard in secondary school, whereas others do not. They also differ in their ability to generate revenue for the university. We may want to provide a systematic analysis of how the educational slots are allocated – what are the pros and cons of different ways of allocating slots? Microeconomics provides the tools to conduct a systematic analysis of questions regarding how to allocate a scarce resource, such as university education. Much of microeconomics examines the case where prices are used to allocate goods – hence reflecting individual choices that depend on the interaction of prices and incomes. The example of university education is nevertheless useful in highlighting that many other ways are also used to allocate goods or services and that the tools of economics are useful in studying such cases as well.

1.2 Economics – *The Wealth of Nations*

Who gets what, and the rules that govern how goods and services are created and divided, has clearly been given serious thought since the dawn of history. Nevertheless we often emphasize the Scottish economist Adam Smith, and his book *Wealth of Nations*, first published in 1776, as the beginning of economics as a field of analysis. The timing is no coincidence. Europe in the 1700s in earnest saw the shift away from largely self-sufficient farming communities to people interacting more widely via markets. Understanding how those markets worked became ever more important. Also today, the title of his book, *Wealth of Nations*, is useful in describing the aims and goals of economics. As we look around the globe, the conditions under which people work and live are vastly different and it is natural to ask what we can do to allow people to live happier and healthier lives.

An understanding of economics and how interactions take place in markets is so pervasive to our lives that it is easy to take the functioning of markets for granted. None of my breakfast is grown by myself or those close to me – instead, I have bought all the items in a store, relying on being able to purchase tea from Sri Lanka, orange juice from Spain, and bread and cheese from more nearby. I sell my services as an economist and purchase what I need from markets. Those markets are kept functioning by a huge number of different people working within firms and governments indirectly interacting in markets. These markets are partly supported by laws and public policy, and partly by norms, ways of conduct and trust that have developed over time. Economics studies how this whole system works and can be made to work even better. Within a first textbook in microeconomics, we take most of those laws and public policies as given and focus largely on the role of prices in directing resources in this system. This is not because it is the only question of great interest, but it sufficiently important and nontrivial that it will keep us busy for the next 17 chapters.[2]

1.3 Scarcity – An underlying assumption

One useful starting point for understanding the scope of economics is the following:

> Economics can be defined in a few different ways. It's the study of scarcity, the study of how people use resources and respond to incentives, or the study of decision-making. It often involves topics like wealth and finance, but it's not all about money. Economics is a broad discipline that helps us understand historical trends, interpret today's headlines, and make predictions about the coming years.[3]

Scarcity is indeed often taken as a foundation for the study of economics. By **scarcity** we mean that resources are limited, and we need to make choices about how to use them. It may be useful to start with an example that is not scarce – air for breathing.[4] If we are in a room, I'm not thinking that if you're taking more breaths, I need to take fewer breaths. I don't think about taking fewer breaths now to be able to take more breaths later. Simply put, how many breaths of air to take in a minute is not an economic question. In contrast, many resources are in limited supply, and we need to make decisions on how to use them. This is true for individuals, firms, countries, and the world as a whole.

Time is an example of a scarce resource from the perspective of an individual. A day has 24 hours, and if you live a relatively long life, you may experience some 30,000 days. How should you spend those? For every minute that you're doing something, there is something else that you're not doing. You can study microeconomics, work, hang out with new friends, old friends, play video games, binge-watch fantasy movies, play badminton, or practice your slackline skills. Time is limited and how you choose to spend it is an economic question. Similarly, for most of us, income is limited in that if we're buying more of one good or service, that implies buying less of something else. As we cover in Chapter 4, one implication of scarcity is that there is an opportunity cost of everything that we do; the cost of doing something can be seen as what we are giving up by not spending that time and those resources on an alternative use. This is sometimes summarized under the saying "there's no such thing as a free lunch".

Resources are scarce also at the more aggregate level. Electricity for instance, can be used for heating and cooling houses, for fueling manufacturing plants, for mining bitcoins, for fueling electrical vehicles and for lighting up the garden with reindeers and santas in the run-up to Christmas. More electricity spent on one use typically means less spent on other uses. More resources spent on military defense means less resources spent on other uses. Again, economics provides a structured way to analyze how those resources are best spent given the goals of an individual, firm or state.

1.4 On the use of models in microeconomics

If we want to compare different ways of allocating goods and services, like education, we can make different assumptions about how people choose. Do people follow "what is expected of them" based on social class and background only? Or are choices mainly reflecting chance? The microeconomic approach to this question is to assume that people make deliberate choices, and we then aggregate from the ground up. For instance, the total number of applicants to a university reflects the deliberate choices of a large number of potential students that try to do as well as possible, given the constraints that they face. Of course there will be some mistakes, and some people will just mindlessly follow what is expected of them, but the microeconomic starting point is that choices are deliberate. This allows us to in a natural way examine the effect of factors that we expect make university education more or less attractive: higher wages for university-educated students, student housing, and student loans are all potentially important factors.

When we say that people make deliberate choices, we need to operationalize that in some way. In the following chapters, we examine the baseline type of model that we use in economics – individuals maximize utility given the prices that they face, the income they have, and their preferences. Similarly, we assume that firms strive to maximize profits given the technology that they use and the prices of inputs. We use **models**, simplified versions of decision problems that firms, states, and individuals face, to make predictions and understand the trade-offs faced. The models are useful in that they allow us to check that our arguments are logically sound and allow us to examine various counterfactual scenarios. An old analogy states that a model is like a map. To be useful, a map needs to simplify – a map on the scale of 1:1 is hardly helpful. A saying sometimes attributed to Albert Einstein states, "A model should be as simple as possible, but not simpler than that". A useful model simplifies enough that we can work efficiently with it but is still rich enough to provide insights and predict well with regard to the key problems that we want to solve.

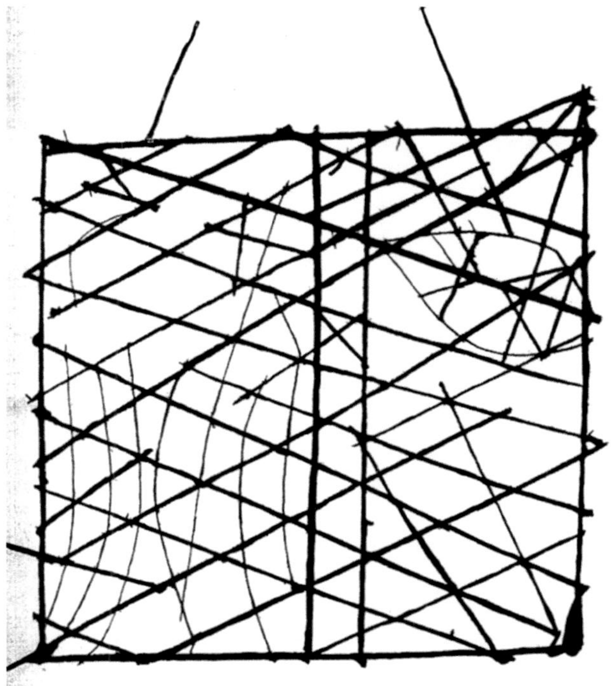

Figure 1.1 A stick chart. https://commons.wikimedia.org/wiki/File:Polynesian_navigation_device_showing_directions_of_winds,_waves_and_islands.jpg.

To me, the history of how Polynesians and other peoples populated the Pacific Ocean is one of the more fascinating of human history. Paying close attention to winds, stars, currents, and wave patterns, they were able to successfully navigate across the huge expanses of the Pacific Ocean, long before the advent of modern navigational tools. In some areas, such as the Marshall Islands, stick charts like the one depicted in Figure 1.1 were also used. Small shells were used to represent islands, and sticks were used to represent wave patterns, which reflect off of islands and are discernible to the initiated also from far away. To a trained mind, stick charts were a useful navigational tool. They do not provide a detailed image of the Pacific – they provide a highly stylized representation that was useful for navigation. Similarly, I like to think of models in economics as stick charts – useful simplifications.

As noted in the introductory quote by John Maynard Keynes,[5] the models assure us that our thinking is sound. But it is often not obvious which model is appropriate in what situation. In microeconomics, we typically use the same basic model (maximization of utility under constraints) but assumptions need to reflect key aspects of how a particular market works (regarding, e.g., number of sellers, information or product differentiation). Compare, for instance, demand for potatoes, education, addictive drugs, and human kidneys for donation. Demand for potatoes is likely to be importantly determined by price and be relatively straightforward – many producers grow potatoes, and we can relatively easily judge the quality. In cases where there is school choice, demand for a particular school is likely to be more complicated. In many countries, prices are low, or education is free, such that price is not a key factor. On the other hand, quality may be hard to judge and highly dependent on who the other students are. Price is then relatively unimportant for demand, and understanding of educational markets will need to focus on other aspects than the study of markets for potatoes. Turning to our third example, addictive drugs, they present thorny questions about the limits of what people should be allowed to do, hurting themselves and others. And as to our final example, humans have two kidneys and can donate one to others, which may save the life of the recipient. People may donate for altruistic reasons, typically to close family, but in almost all countries, the sale of kidneys is illegal, reflecting commonly held moral views on what kind of goods and services should be acceptable to exchange in return for money. One can come to different conclusions regarding the preferred type of regulation, but clearly, a serious analysis needs to reflect that trade in heroin or human kidneys poses very different questions than trade in potatoes.[6]

1.5 What we do in the book – And what we don't do

This book, as is common for courses in microeconomics, focuses on models. In practice, no question in economics should be decided on theory alone. All of the key classes of models that we examine have been used to understand how markets and individuals operate. The next chapter will open with an example from global rice markets, for instance, and any policy recommendation needs to be cognizant of the empirical work. A single textbook can't cover everything, however, and in keeping with how microeconomics is typically taught, this book focuses on theory. Theory gives us the indication of what data that empirical analysis should examine and provides hypotheses to guide the work.

The chapters in this book follow a standard curriculum of what is taught in microeconomics. Microeconomics studies how prices and quantities are set on markets, often focusing on one market at a time (e.g., the market for rice). It examines how markets work when they work as well as possible and some especially important cases when they run into problems, market failures.

Microeconomics is not only important in its own right; the tools that we learn in microeconomics are also used in other applications in economics. Macroeconomics is the other main building block of an economics curriculum. In macroeconomics, we focus on the economy as a whole, how the economy grows and on business cycles. Monetary (e.g., how should the central bank act) and fiscal (e.g., should governments stimulate the economy to counter a recession) policy are key areas of interest.

Similarly, many specialized courses are given at a more advanced level – for instance, public economics (focusing on the role of government), labor economics, and international economics. These typically rely on the type of framework that we study in microeconomics but dive deeper and relate the models to institutional details and data.

Thus microeconomics really is the foundation of further studies in economics.

Notes

1 These mechanisms are especially relevant in cases where university education is financed via taxes or donations. Indeed, the Stockholm School of Economics is mainly financed via donations that allow us to be a private university with no tuition for students from within the European Union.

2 I'm sometimes asked about suggested readings for such broader topics. New and good books appear continuously, but the following three are personal favorites that are profound and thought-provoking yet easy enough reads to keep your attention also on the beach: McMillan (2003), Rodrik (2015), Seabright (2010).

3 The quote is taken from the website of the American Economic Association, one of the key societies that organizes economists and conferences and publishes academic journals. Their website also has some resources targeted at students; for instance, the following one where the quote was taken from on March 15 2023: https://www.aeaweb.org/resources/students/what-is-economics.

4 Pollution can be seen as leading to an exception to this rule, but we hold off on that discussion until Chapter 13.

5 Keynes is one of the more impressive economists ever. His main contribution is in helping us understand the forces that shape business cycles (Keynes, 1936), but he also made profound contributions to our understanding of uncertainty (e.g., Keynes, 1921), made remarkably prescient observations regarding the dangers of the harsh conditions imposed on Germany in the post–World War I peace (Keynes, 1920), and was a dominant force in creating the framework for international cooperation in the aftermath of World War II. He actively engaged with artists, writers, and leading philosophers of his time. Out of many biographies, the one by Skidelsky (2009) is particularly comprehensive and readable.

6 One constraint on altruism as a source of human kidneys is that there may be no good match within a family – I may be willing to donate to you, but you may not be able to medically receive my kidney. Setting up donor chains – I give to your family, and your family gives to mine – can then be a way of realizing gains from trade and save lives also when prices are not used; see Roth (2007) for an overview.

2 Supply and demand

Illustration 2.1 The market. Pexels, Mark Dalton.

2.1 Supply and demand – An introduction

Figure 2.1 shows an index of the price of rice on global markets.[1] As typical of many agricultural products and minerals, prices exhibit large changes over time. A standout feature of the graph is the increase, and subsequent drop, in price in 2008. Rice is a key food for billions of people, and when prices more than double in a short period, this clearly has great repercussions for many poor across Asia in particular, but the price surge also led to riots in, for instance, Haiti. What causes such price changes? How can we understand them? How can we think of counterfactual scenarios? In this chapter, we will learn how the tools of supply and demand can be used to determine how prices and quantities are decided on markets. These are simple tools that are extremely powerful in thinking about

DOI: 10.4324/9781003623854-2

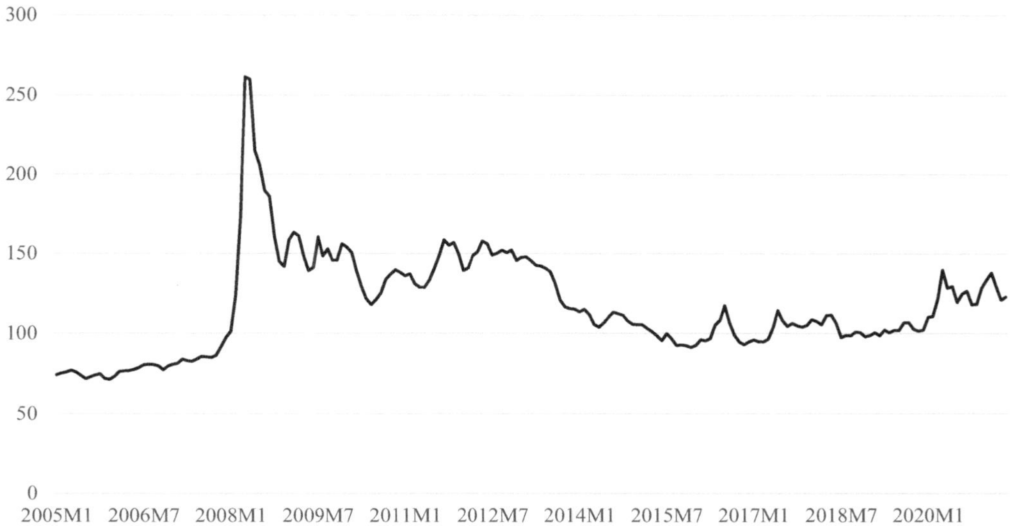

Figure 2.1 World market price of rice (index). https://www.imf.org/en/Research/commodity-prices.

markets. We will see how prices and quantities respond to changing conditions. In the case of rice markets, this clearly matters if we are producers of rice – what should we plan for – as well as if we are policymakers, investors, or any other interested party whose well-being is somehow tied to the price of rice.

We will also use the example of supply and demand to show how models are key to our ability to make sense of the world. For instance, it seems natural that price says something about value – a painting by Vincent Van Gogh sold for hundreds of millions is seen as more valuable than a painting by me that probably would carry a price of 0. But then consider what is sometimes known as the diamond-water puzzle: How can it be that water, which is so central to our life, typically has a very low price, whereas diamonds, that we can easily live without, typically have a very high price? We shall see that in terms of a supply and demand analysis, there is no puzzle at all – it is a natural outcome of such an analysis.[2]

When studying how prices and quantities are determined on a market, we first need to specify what we mean by a market. A **market** is a collection of buyers and sellers of a good or service. It is defined both by geography and by the product. The market for haircuts in Wellington New Zealand is a different market from the market for haircuts in Lima, Peru. In addition, the market for haircuts in Lima is different from the market for watermelons in Lima.[3]

In the following, we examine how market price and quantity is determined by **demand curves** (the quantities that buyers wish to purchase at different prices) and **supply curves** (the quantities that sellers are willing to provide at different prices). Strictly speaking, a number of assumptions are needed for us to be able to describe a market price and quantity as the outcome of a meeting of a supply curve and a demand curve. We will return with a discussion of these assumptions when we discuss how markets allocate resources and whether that allocation is "efficient" in Chapter 8. For now, note that the key assumptions for being able to analyze a market with supply and demand curves are the following:

- We assume that we can treat the product in question as a **homogeneous** product: The products from different suppliers are seen as equal in all dimensions. As a buyer, I do not care about which wheat farmer produced my wheat. In large centralized markets for commodities, this holds true, as I can buy, for instance, one ton of wheat for delivery in a month, which will bundle wheat grains from many different farmers. The quality of the wheat is determined by various standards, but individual producers are not kept track of. Goods traded on exchanges – in particular between large professional parties – can often be thought of in this way. Later on in the book, we will consider the case where different producers sell **differentiated** products, where, for instance, I as a consumer can choose between buying a bicycle with certain characteristics from one producer and buying one with slightly different characteristics from another producer.[4]
- There are *many buyers and sellers*, and each acts as if they have no impact on the market price – that is, they act as **price takers**. As an individual wheat farmer, I'm faced with many decisions, but when deciding how much wheat to plant, I do not take into account that if I plant more, I will affect the world market price of wheat.

2.2 Demand

We use a **demand function** to relate the quantity that buyers of the good or service want to purchase at different prices. Use Q^D to denote the total quantity demanded and p to denote price. Quantity is in some measure of units such as kilos of rice or number of rickshaw rides taken. The corresponding price is in some currency, such as 2 euros per kilo of rice or 50 rupees for a rickshaw ride of a particular duration. As we shall see later, market-level demand is the sum of demand from all buyers in the market.

To take a specific example, consider the market for strawberries in a small town. Assume that there are 10 people in the town and their willingness to pay is such that one person is willing to pay at most 9 euros for a liter of strawberries, one person is willing to pay at most 8 euros for one liter, one at most 7 euros, and so forth. To make our setting even simpler, assume that each person buys at most 1 liter. Thus, for instance, if the price is 8 euros, 2 liters will be demanded, and if the price is 7 euros, 3 liters will be demanded. We plot the relation in Figure 2.2. While demand in this case is discrete, that is, only whole liters will be sold, we typically simplify the analysis and assume that quantity is a continuous function of price such that, for instance, 2.586 liters can be bought. The relation between quantity and price can then in this case be described by the function

$$Q^D = 10 - p.$$

If we, for instance, plug in the price 7 euros, the demand function indicates that 3 liters will be sold. For the purposes of drawing demand, we typically rewrite the demand function so that it is stated with price as the dependent variable, on the left-hand side, as is indeed drawn in Figure 2.2. We term this the **inverse demand function**. Thus in this case, it is

$$p = 10 - Q^D.$$

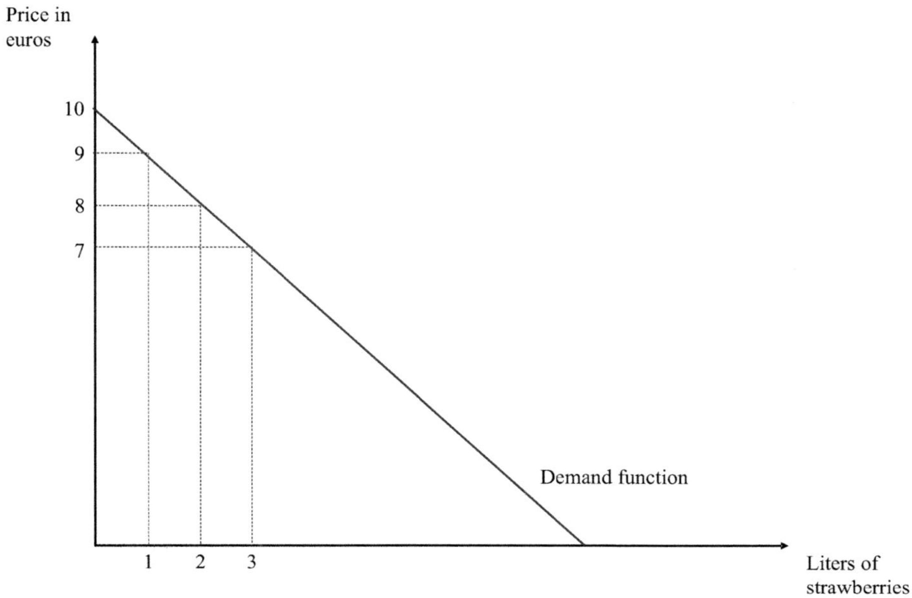

Figure 2.2 Demand – A simple example.

Applied to the current setting, a function is a mathematical relation between price and quantity. Give me a quantity, and the function gives me a price. Equivalently, give me a price, and the function gives me a quantity.[5]

2.2.1 *Effect on demand of changes in...*

One use of supply and demand analysis is to determine how price and quantity respond to various changes in the environment. Next, we present a list of some of the most common changes of interest. The list is not exhaustive, and depending on the market in question, other variables may also be of interest.

2.2.1.1 Changes in the price of the good

What is the effect of a change in the price of the good on the quantity demanded for the same good? The answer to this is given by the demand curve, which relates the quantity demanded of a product to the price of that same product. We move along the demand curve, as illustrated in Figure 2.3. For the example given earlier, $Q^D = 10 - p$. Plugging in different values of prices in this relation, we, for instance, find that quantity increases from 3 to 4 if price decreases from 7 to 6.

Typically, we expect demand curves to slope downward: The lower the price, the higher quantities are demanded. While in principle they can slope upward, a little introspection points out that this is likely to be a very unusual situation – it is a rare situation in which you demand more as prices go up.[6]

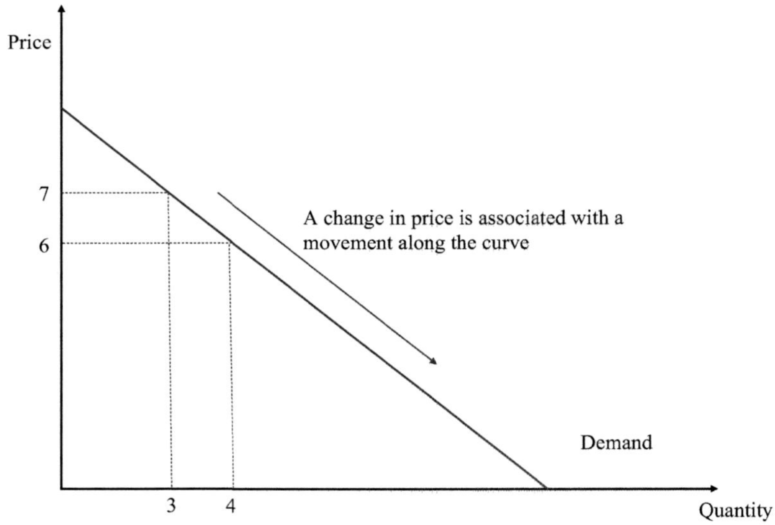

Figure 2.3 Demand: Movement along the demand curve.

Let us also point out a misunderstanding that sometimes appears. People might, for instance, make the observation that a branded T-shirt sells a lot of units, whereas a cheaper generic T-shirt sells much fewer units. Isn't this evidence that a higher price is associated with a higher demand in some cases? No. Remember that an assumption underlying the analysis is that we are examining homogeneous products, comparing apples to apples rather than apples to oranges. When Gucci lowers the price of their T-shirts during a temporary sale, they expect to sell more rather than less.[7]

2.2.1.2 *Changes in income*

How much of a good is demanded depends not only on price but also on a number of other variables. Is the group demanding the strawberries impoverished, or are we examining demand in a spot where billionaires thrive? Clearly, income does not explicitly figure in equation $Q^D = 10 - p$ but is subsumed in the intercept 10. For many goods, we expect higher incomes to be associated with higher demand, something that characterizes what we refer to as **normal goods**. As my income increase, I will demand more strawberries. How do we illustrate this in a diagram? The simplest way to think of it is the following: At a given price, will consumers demand more or less if income increases? If they demand more, demand will be given by a point further out in the diagram for that particular price. The same applies for any price when income increases for a normal good. We thus say that the demand curve *shifts outward*, as illustrated in Figure 2.4.

Another possible pattern is that demand shifts inward if income increases. For **inferior goods**, a higher income leads to a lower demanded quantity. Low-priced food items are common examples of such products; if incomes go up, we buy fewer instant noodles, as we can better afford more attractive alternatives. Figure 2.5 provides an illustration.

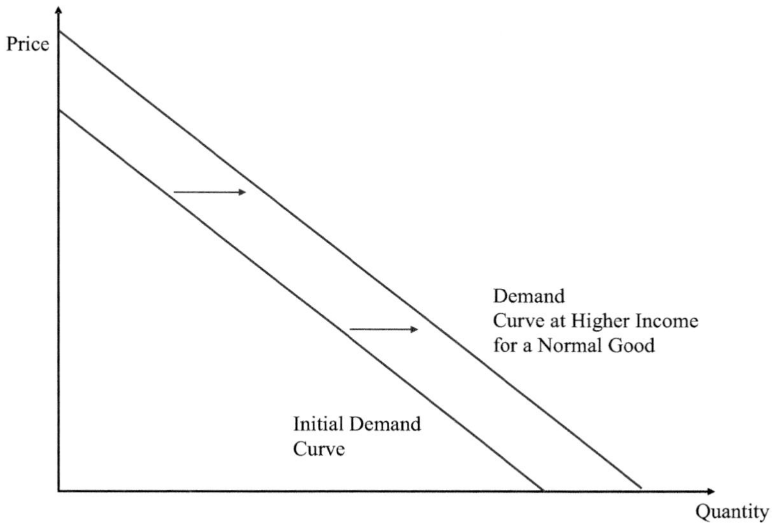

Figure 2.4 An outward shift in the demand curve as income increases (normal goods).

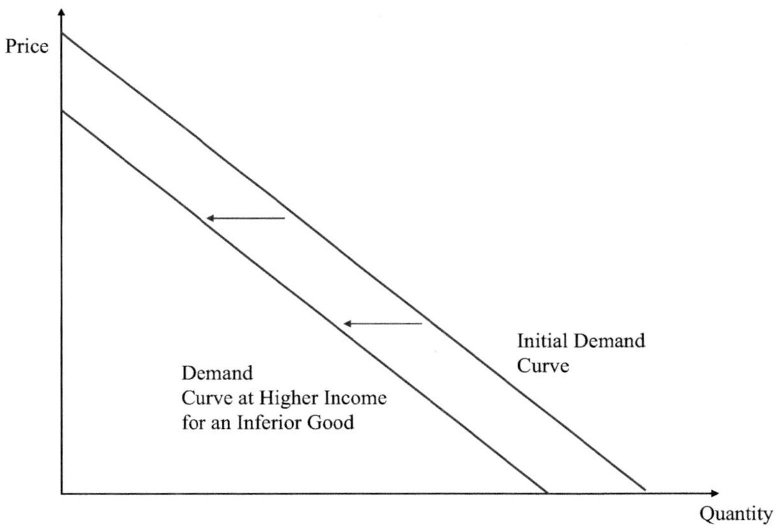

Figure 2.5 An inward shift in the demand curve as income increases (inferior goods).

2.2.1.3 Changes in the price of other goods

We examine the demand for one good, but clearly, the prices of many other goods have the potential to affect demand as well. As I'm standing in the store thinking of buying strawberries, there may be raspberries stacked up right next to the strawberries. In a lot of cases, I might envision consuming either strawberries or raspberries – on a cake or with some sugar and cream for desert. Again, the effect of the price of raspberries on the demand

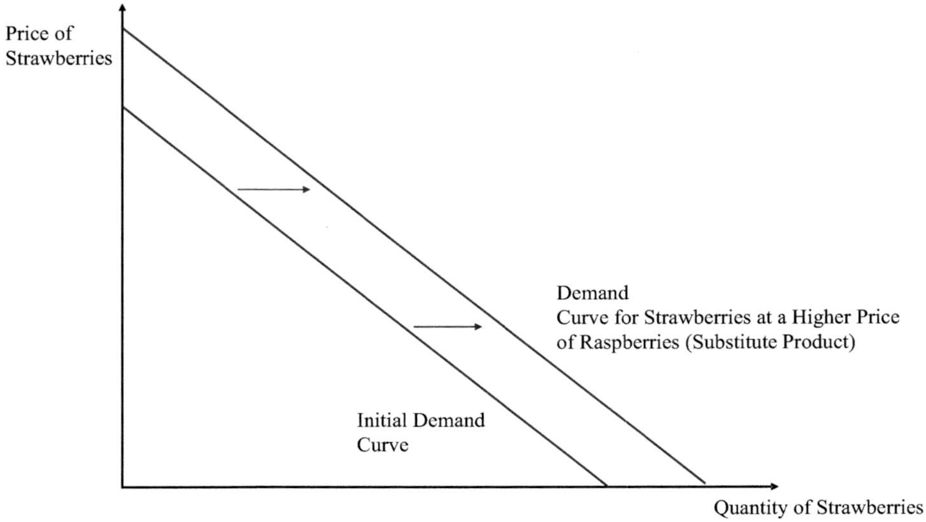

Figure 2.6 An outward shift in the demand curve as the price of a substitute product increases.

for strawberries is subsumed in the intercept, and a change in the price of raspberries would be associated with a shift in the demand curve for strawberries.

Again, we perform the simple thought experiment: At a given price, will consumers demand more or less if the price of another good increases? If the price of raspberries goes up, and consumers view raspberries as an alternative, demand for strawberries shifts outward. The formal term is that goods are **substitutes** if demand for good 1 increases when the price of good 2 increases. The substitute product just got more expensive, which implies that at least some consumers will opt for strawberries rather than raspberries, as illustrated in Figure 2.6.

There may also be inward shifts in demand as the price of another product increases. The formal term is goods are **complements** if demand for good 1 decreases when the price of good 2 increases. A typical example is products that are consumed together, such as milk and ready-to-eat cereal, such as Corn Flakes. We can think of the two products as a joint bundle, and if the price of one of the products goes up, than the joint bundle will become less attractive to buy. At a given price of strawberries, fewer strawberries will be demanded if the price of the complement goes up. Many like the combination of vanilla ice cream and strawberries; let us assume that the two goods are complements. So, if the price of vanilla ice cream goes up, fewer strawberries will be demanded, and the demand curve will shift inward, as illustrated in Figure 2.7.

2.2.1.4 *Other factors that shift demand functions*

A host of other variables can shift demand curves. At some level, a list of such variables can become almost metaphysical, and as the American saying goes, "everything but the kitchen sink" could have an effect. Of course, an analysis in which we considered hundreds of variables would become unwieldy, and in typical applications, we focus on a few variables that we expect to be particularly important. What those other variables are will

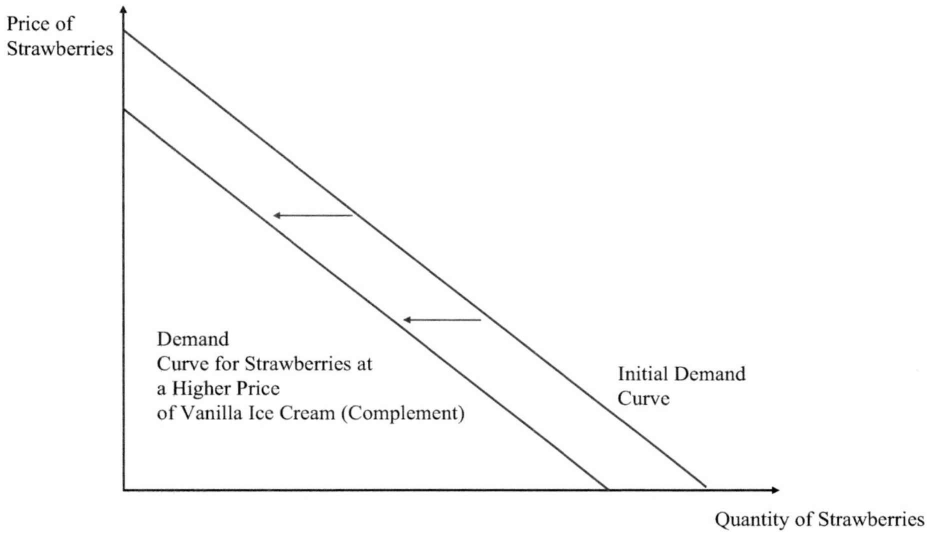

Figure 2.7 An inward shift in the demand curve as the price of a complement product increases.

be specific to the product and partly determined by applications of common sense, possibly complemented by statistical analysis. For instance, demand for ice cream will likely be affected by temperatures, and demand for ski passes at a snow resort will be affected by the snow cover. Expectations are another important variable in some markets. A standout example was in the early days of the COVID-19 pandemic when expectations that toilet paper would run out (a really odd expectation by the way) led to stockpiling in a lot of countries, with demand shifting out for a time period.

2.2.2 *Demand functions – Some additional aspects*

In the previous example, the demand function was linear. Simply put, it is a straight line, and when we shifted the demand curve, we simply stated that demand should shift in some direction. In the following section, we expand somewhat beyond those simplifying assumptions.

2.2.2.1 Demand: General form vs. specific form

Earlier, we showed a simple demand curve. We gave it a specific form: For every increase in price by 1 euro, 1 liter of strawberries less were demanded. We can also express the demand function in general form, just noting that quantity demanded of strawberries depends in some way on the price of strawberries. As discussed, in principle, many different circumstances could also affect the demand for strawberries: temperature (if its a warm day, a strawberry dessert may be more attractive), prices of a substitute like raspberries, and incomes of the demanders in the market. Using T to denote temperature, p_r to denote the price of raspberries, and I to denote income, we can then express demand for strawberries in a general form, such as

$$Q^D = f(p, T, p_r, I).$$

Thus quantity demanded of strawberries depends in some way, as specified by a function that we denote by f, on the four variables p, T, p_r, and I. In principle, we could think of a very long list of potential variables that affect demand for strawberries. In practice, we limit ourselves to what we believe to be the main variables that have an impact. In specific form, that is to say, the function takes a particular form, the relationship may, for instance, be expressed as

$$Q^D = 1 - p + T \times 0.25 + p_r \times 0.75 + I \times 0.5$$

The demand function $Q^D = 10 - p$ that we described earlier can then be seen as the relation between quantity demanded and price for specific values of the other variables. Thus for T=20 degrees, p_r=2 euros, and income I (in thousands) = 5 euros, the relation becomes

$$Q^D = 1 - p + \underbrace{20}_{T} \times 0.25 + \underbrace{2}_{p_r} \times 0.75 + \underbrace{5}_{I} \times 0.5 = 10 - p.$$

This may also be the place to point out a wording convention. In line with common practice, we essentially use the terms "demand function" and "demand curve" interchangably. Strictly speaking, there is a difference: The term demand function captures that demand is a mathematical function that potentially depends on several variables. The term "demand curve" is a graphical illustration of the relation between quantity demanded and price for that same good for a given set of values of other factors that influence demand.

2.2.2.2 *Demand: Different shapes*

Economists typically estimate demand functions based on observations of prices and quantities from markets. Covering how to do that would take us too far afield and is left for courses in statistics and econometrics. Let us nevertheless for illustration consider a case where we observe quantities purchased in a market at various prices. Assume that these different prices have been shifted because of changes in costs, rather than in response to developments in demand. Figure 2.8 presents a simple example where each black dot represents an observed combination of price and quantity. There is some randomness so that the dots do not perfectly line up on a single curve, but clearly, a fitted line such as the downward-sloping curve would provide a reasonable representation of the demand curve in a case such as this. Demand curves with this kind of curvature, where the lines become increasingly flat at lower prices are common in economics.[8] Note however that a linear demand curve provides a reasonable application at prices in the "middle." In practice, it is not uncommon to believe that a linear demand curve gives reasonable ballpark answers at middling observations, but special care is needed if we are to make inferences about what happens as either the number of units goes to 0 or as the price goes to 0.

Similarly, in Figure 2.8, we illustrated shifts in the demand curve as perfectly parallel shifts. In many applications, we could think of demand shifting more at certain price levels so that the demand curve, e.g., both shifts and becomes flatter.

2.3 Supply

Similarly, the **supply** curve for a good determines the amount of the good that sellers are willing to sell at different prices. The supply curve typically slopes upward: At higher prices,

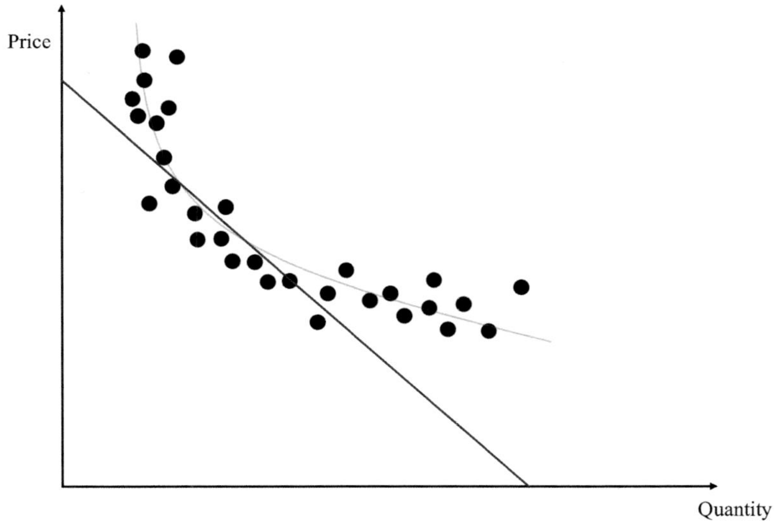

Figure 2.8 Demand: Different shapes.

suppliers are willing to supply more. While demand curves are typically a straightforward concept, it is not uncommon for students to find supply curves more complex and perhaps confusing. The key point to remember here is that firms whose decisions can be described by a supply curve are not setting the price, they are *price takers*. They determine how many strawberries to pick and bring to the market; they don't determine the price itself. If this still appears somewhat puzzling, worry not; we will provide a thorough walk-through of the supply curve in later chapters.

Many of the aspects that we discussed in connection to demand curves apply also to supply curves. They may be linear, but they may also have other shapes; for instance, they may increase at an increasing rate. Similarly, we can express them in general form, such as

$$Q^S = f(p)$$

or in specific form such as

$$Q^S = -2 + p. \tag{2.1}$$

We also typically draw the **inverse supply curve** (p as a function of Q) rather than Q as a function of p. Thus, rewriting supply from Equation (2.1) to have p as the dependent variable yields

$$p = 2 + Q^S. \tag{2.2}$$

The supply intercept of -2 in the supply function may look a bit puzzling in Equation (2.1) but is more intuitive when we express the supply relation as the inverse supply curve, as we do in Equation (2.2) and Figure 2.9. Price needs to be well above 0 before any producer is willing to supply the good.

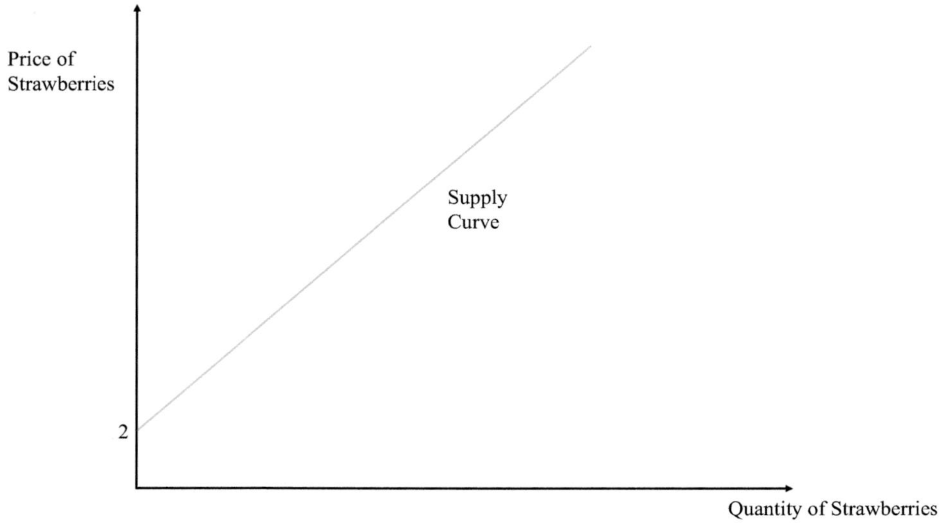

Figure 2.9 Supply curve: An example.

2.3.1 *Effect of changes on the supply curve*

2.3.1.1 *Changes in the Price*

Just as with the demand curve, the effect of changes in price on quantities supplied are given by the supply curve. As price changes, we move along the supply curve. With a supply curve given by $Q^S = -2+p$, the many firms that jointly make up supply are willing to supply 1 liter of strawberries if the price is equal to 3 euros and 2 liters as the price increases to 4 euros.[9]

2.3.1.2 *Changes in the price of inputs*

In Chapter 4, we formalize the idea that how much firms are willing to supply depends on their costs, which in turn depends on the price of the inputs that are used in production. For now, note that it is intuitive that if costs increase, firms will want a higher price to supply the same quantity. Or, another way to say the same thing, for a given price, a lower quantity will be supplied if cost increases. If wages or costs of transporting the strawberries to the market increase, this will lead to an inward shift in the supply curve, as illustrated in Figure 2.10. Similarly, if input costs decrease, the supply shifts outwards, and firms are willing to supply a greater quantity for the same price. Or, another way to say the same thing, firms are willing to supply the same quantity at a lower price.

2.3.1.3 *Other factors that shift supply functions*

Just as with demand curves, many other factors can affect the supply curve, and again, the question is if supply will increase or decrease at a given price. For instance, if a formerly closed local market opens up to foreign suppliers, this will shift the supply curve outward. Disruptions where some production units close because of accidents, extreme weather, or strikes are other prominent examples that would cause supply curves to shift inward.

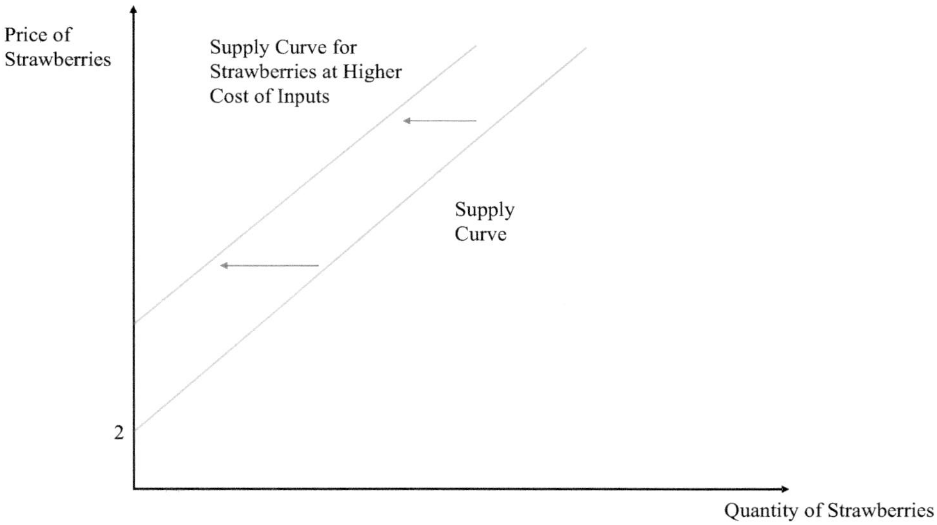

Figure 2.10 Supply curve: The effect of higher input prices.

2.4 Combining supply and demand to find the market equilibrium

We now combine supply and demand to establish how prices and quantities are determined on a market. We say that the market is in **equilibrium** when the price is such that quantity demanded equals the quantity supplied. Buyers buy all that they want at this prevailing market price, and sellers are able to sell all that they want at this price. We sometimes refer to the equilibrium price as the **market clearing price**, as the market "clears," sellers are not left with large piles of unsold stock, and buyers are able to buy as much as they want at the prevailing prices.

We can analyze the equilibrium price graphically as the price at which the supply and demand curves intersect. We can also solve for the equilibrium price using explicit functional forms for the supply and demand equations. Using the previous expressions, we have

$$Q^D = 10 - p \text{ and } Q^S = -2 + p$$

At the equilibrium price, quantity demanded is the same as the quantity supplied, and hence, we can set $Q^D = Q^S$. In this case, it implies that the equilibrium price is given by solving $10 - p = -2 + p$ for p

$$\begin{aligned} \underbrace{10 - p}_{Q^D} &= \underbrace{-2 + p}_{Q^S} \\ 12 &= 2p \\ p &= 6. \end{aligned}$$

Figure 2.11 illustrates and we see that the point of intersection happens at the price of 6 euros. To find the associated equilibrium quantity, we insert price into either the demand or the supply equation (they give the same answer) and find that $Q = 10 - 6 = 4$ liters.

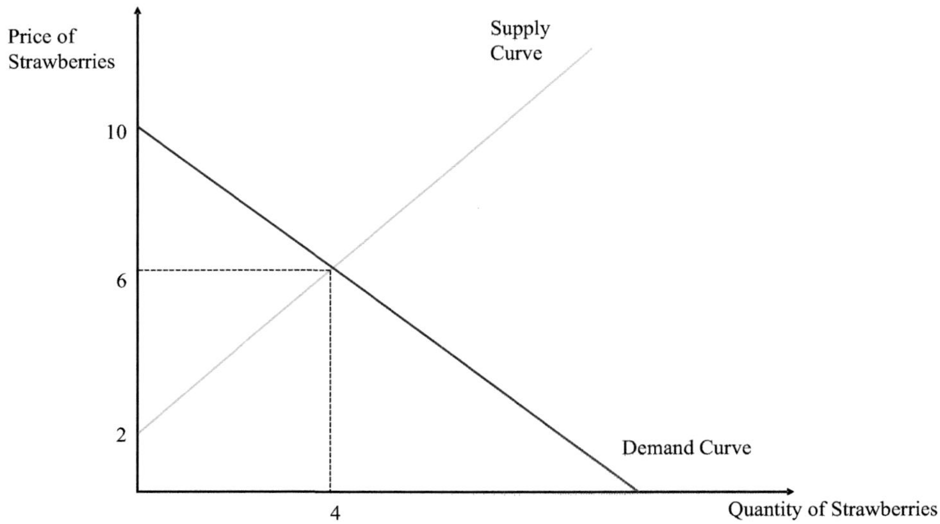

Figure 2.11 Market equilibrium. Video link for table: https://youtu.be/7_00TFu9RBc.

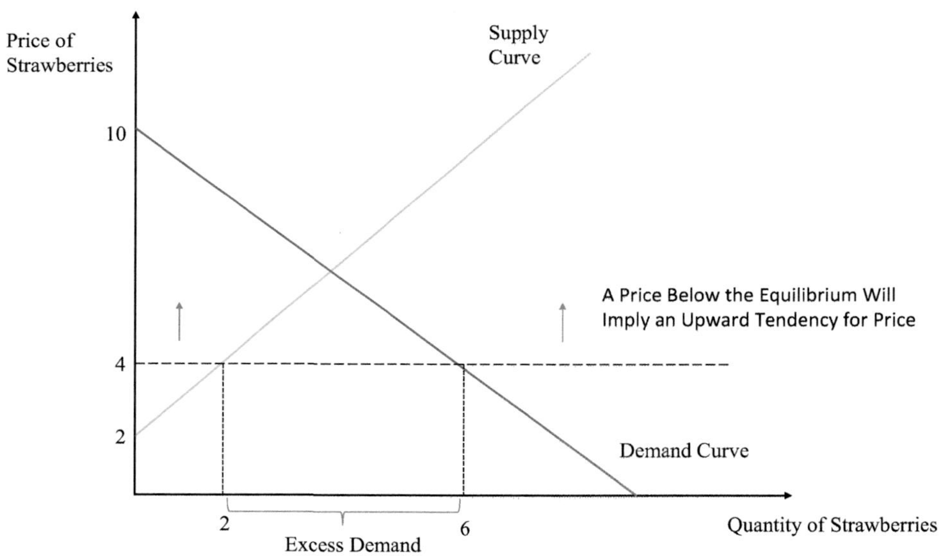

Figure 2.12 A price below the market equilibrium: Upward pricing pressure. Video link for table: https://youtu.be/2NcdivUfDzw.

What are the mechanisms that lead to the equilibrium price being established on a well-functioning market? First, let us consider what would happen if the price were below the equilibrium, as illustrated in Figure 2.12. For a moment, assume that the price was 4 euros. If we draw a line at this level in Figure 2.12, we find the quantity *supplied* at this price by reading off quantity at the point at which this price line intersects supply and the quantity

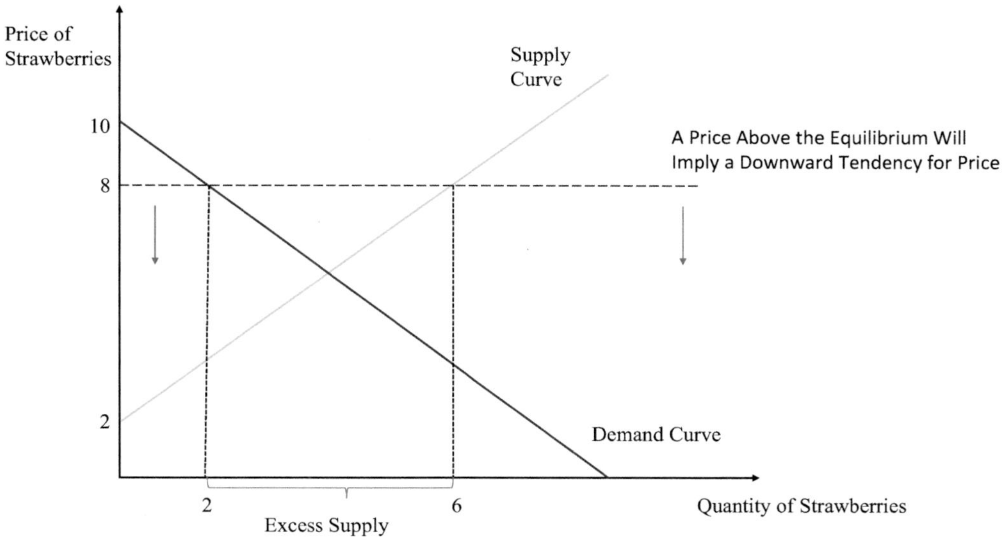

Figure 2.13 A price above the market equilibrium: Downward pricing pressure. Video link for figure: https://youtu.be/2NcdivUfDzw.

demanded at this price from the intersection of the price line with the demand curve. We can also calculate these by simply inserting the price 4 euros into supply and demand functions to determine how much is supplied and demanded at this price. Thus $Q^S = -2 + 4 = 2$ liters of strawberries are supplied, and $Q^D = 10 - 4 = 6$ liters of strawberries are demanded if $p = 4$. Thus, at this price, more is demanded than what is supplied; we then say that there is **excess demand**. In this particular case, there is excess demand of 4 liters (the difference between quantity demanded (6) and quantity supplied (2)).

We can think of excess demand as a situation where there are lines building up as people struggle to purchase the good. People are milling about looking for an opportunity to buy at this price. At this price, there are many buyers who are willing to purchase good, but they are not able to get their hands on any units of it. If the price is low because of a regulation, such as a price cap, we might expect a secondhand market where some of the lucky few who have been able to purchase some units resell at a higher price. In a well-functioning market, we would instead expect at least some sellers to sell for a higher price. At a slightly higher price than $p = 4$, there is no problem finding buyers; also at a price of 5 euros, for instance, there is unmet demand. We thus expect upward pressure on the price, as long as it is below the equilibrium.[10]

In contrast, if a price were to for some reason be above the equilibrium, we expect a downward pressure on price. Figure 2.13 illustrates a case where the price for some reason is equal to 8 euros, and hence above the equilibrium price of 6 euros. Again, we trace out a path at the level of the price and first hit the demand curve, the point of contact being associated with a demanded quantity of 2 liters of strawberries ($Q^D = 10 - 8 = 2$). Continuing rightward, we eventually reach the supply curve, and the point of contact is associated with a willingness to supply 6 liters ($Q^S = -2 + 8 = 6$). There is an **excess supply** if quantity demanded is lower than what sellers want to supply. In this case, there is an excess supply of 4 liters: the difference between the supply of 6 and the demand of 2. Here we can visually think of a situation where sellers at a village market are sitting in their stalls behind large piles of unsold strawberries. At least some of those will choose to sell for a lower price. Since goods are homogeneous; such a seller will have no problem attracting buyers and will diminish her pile of unsold strawberries. There will thus be downward pressure on prices as long as the price is above equilibrium.

One confusion that I sometimes meet in students is the following: How can there be excess demand or excess supply? Clearly, not more goods can be bought than are sold, so are demand and supply not always equal? The key to understand why supply curves and demand curves might not equate is that they determine how much buyers *want to* buy at a given price and how much sellers *want to* sell at a given price. For a price that is below the market price for some reason (because of a price cap or because concert tickets for some reason are sold below the market clearing price), it is true that not more goods can be bought than are offered. But at the actual price, buyers would want to buy much more – and the concept of excess demand is useful to understand why there is an upward pressure on price and to understand a secondhand market where, for instance, concert tickets are resold.

An important result is that *both demand and supply matter for the equilibrium price and quantity*. Cambridge economist Alfred Marshall produced a path-breaking textbook in economics, and his *Principles of Economics* (Marshall (1890)) noted that we might as well argue about whether it is the upper or the lower blade of a pair of scissors that cuts a piece of paper, as whether the equilibrium is determined by demand or supply. With this insight, we can also easily understand the puzzle, "Why is the price of diamonds, which we can live perfectly without, so high whereas the price of water, which we need for survival, so low?" There are several layers to this question, and we will return to it, but for now, note that the simple answer is that price is determined not only by demand but also by supply. If diamonds were as plentiful as water, rest assured that their price would be low, or even negative; we'd pay to get rid of them.

2.5 Shifts in the equilibrium

An important use for supply and demand analysis is to examine how changes affect markets. As with the case of rice that we used at the start of the chapter, there are many cases that may be of interest to firms, investors, consumers, or governments. With the price of rice as an example, governments have been toppled for less, and high prices may mean starvation for large groups of people.

The supply and demand analysis that we developed earlier, and that we will explore additionally in coming chapters, is a theoretical construct. Starting from a set of assumptions (for instance, price taking behavior by all agents in a market), a set of results follow by application of logic. Back in the real world, things are typically more messy than in the rarefied air of economic theorists, but for more than a hundred years, market participants, firms, journalists, and governments have found supply and demand analysis useful in analyzing market outcomes. As will be discussed at length later, we would not try to analyze the competitive situation in a market that is clearly dominated by a few firms or by firms that produce differentiated products in this way. But many agricultural products (such as cocoa, rice, wheat, potatoes), metals, and fuels are produced by many producers, and the products of different producers are more or less perfect substitutes. Such goods, often known as "commodities," are often traded on organized exchanges, and prices move by the day or sometimes by the minute, and supply and demand analysis is routinely used to analyze developments.[11]

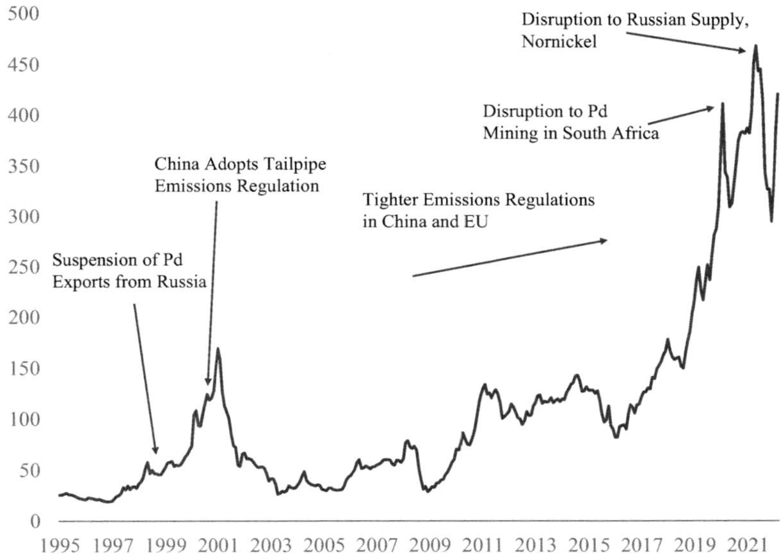

Figure 2.14 Price index for palladium (Pd), together with some supply and demand shocks. https://www.imf.org/en/Research/commodity-prices and https://www.sfa-oxford.com/.

An example of such a commodity is the metal palladium, and Figure 2.14 shows the development of price over a longer, particularly eventful period. Palladium has a number of industrial uses, for instance, in catalytic converters to lower emissions from cars, as well as in fuel cells, batteries, and electronics. What is driving these price developments? A simple answer would be "shocks to supply and demand," and in Figure 2.14, we have also indicated the timing of a set of supply and demand shocks to the palladium market as identified by a consultancy firm. We see that movements consistent with factors that can plausibly be thought of as affecting both supply and demand play a role – **for instance**, supply disruptions in South Africa and regulations affecting demand for catalytic converters. In the following, we present an analysis of how to analyze the impact of shocks on the market equilibrium.

Let us highlight a few important guidelines for analyzing the effect of shocks on the market equilibrium:

- First and foremost: Is primarily demand or primarily supply affected? In my experience, a beginner is likely to bring too many effects into the analysis and thinking in various ways through which there could be an effect. While there are cases where both supply and demand are affected, we would typically find that the major impact is on *either* supply *or* demand. Are incomes of consumers falling? This should be expected to primarily affect demand. Similarly, are prices of close substitutes changing? This should be expected to primarily affect demand. Some technology or regulatory changes can also be expected to affect demand, as in the case of palladium. Closings and disruptions at producers are shocks that primarily affect supply. Similarly, changes in the cost of inputs used in production primarily affect supply.

  The textbook by Alfred Marshall that we mentioned earlier was important for driving home the usefulness of this approach, focusing on what we believe to be the major impact of a change and disregarding secondary effects. Any major change is also likely to appear at the same time as other changes happen. Trying to analyze all possible changes at the same time will tend to produce a muddle. Following in the footsteps of Marshall[12] we therefore focus on the main effect, keeping "other things equal." We might return to those other things, but in the type of supply and demand analysis that we perform in the following, we look at one or two changes at a time. As economists, we often add this qualifier: If A happens, I expect the price of B to increase, **other things equal**. That is, we examine the impact on price of changing one factor that determines price while keeping other factors that determine price unchanged. The latin version of "other things equal," **ceteris paribus**, is also frequently used.

- To see the direction of change in supply or demand, it is useful to use the way of thinking that we introduced earlier: At a given price, do we expect a particular change to lead to higher or lower demand? At a given price, do we expect a particular change to lead to higher or lower supply?
- Also, don't jump directly to thinking, "What happens to price and quantity?" Keep the first stage: Is it primarily supply or demand that is affected, and if so in what direction? This in turn will give predictions for price and quantity. As you become used to this kind of analysis, your mind will probably jump to the price and quantity effects directly, but at the start, this is likely to confuse rather than clarify.

Thus let us exemplify how the analysis can be used and consider a shock in the form of tighter emissions regulations that lead to catalytic converters being installed in more cars. What is the effect of this on the market for palladium? First, is demand likely to be affected? Yes. At a given price of palladium, more catalytic converters would be installed, demand will be affected and shifted outward. Is there a direct effect on supply? No. In the long run, one could imagine new mines opening, additional efforts being directed at recycling, and so forth, but on impact, we expect the main impact to be an outward shift in demand. Figure 2.15 illustrates this. For shorthand, we use D_0 and S_0 to denote the initial demand and supply curves and the associated equilibrium price p_0 and quantity Q_0. Higher demand for palladium, because of more use of catalytic converters, shifts the demand curve outwards to D_1, and we reach a new equilibrium where price is p_1 and quantity Q_1. The producers respond to the increased demand by producing more. How much more? Well, that is given by the supply curve.

Before we move on, let me note that students sometimes find a comparison of the type in Figure 2.15 confusing. We compare two cases: one with a higher price and higher quantity (p_1, Q_1) and one with a lower price and lower quantity (p_0, Q_0). Doesn't this go against our expectation that demand curves slope down so that lower prices are associated with a higher quantity? No. The fundamental thing to remember is that *if demand curves shift, we are not moving along the demand curve*.

The assumption of "other things equal" does not preclude us from examining several changes at the same time – we just need to be clear about the changes that we are examining. Thus, in addition to the demand shock noted earlier, consider that at the same time a number of palladium mines are closed to flooding. This affects supply. At a given price, the exit of some producers should lead to lower quantities being supplied, thus supply shift inward. Figure 2.16 shows how we can analyze the joint effect of these two shocks where we have included the shift in the supply curve S_0 to S_2. The outward demand shift and inward supply shift both contribute to raising prices, which rise from p_0 to p_2 in the new equilibrium, given by the intersection of the new supply and demand curves. In the case illustrated,

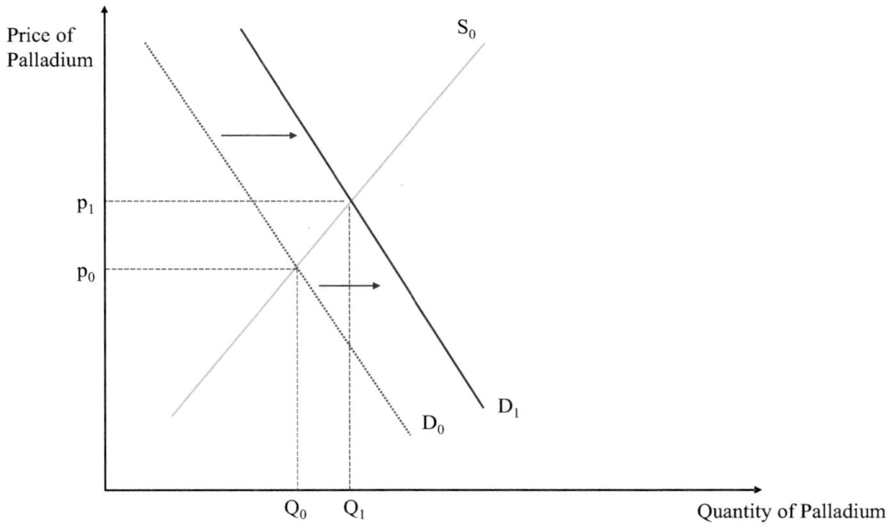

Figure 2.15 Change in equilibrium: An increase in demand.

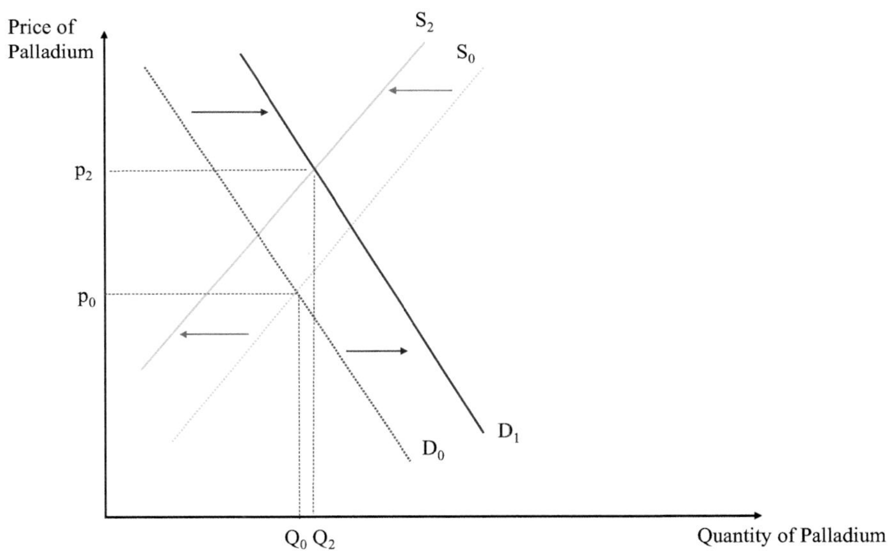

Figure 2.16 Change in equilibrium: An increase in demand and a decrease in supply. Video link for figure: https://youtu.be/YmZ175cTCyw.

quantity in the new equilibrium Q_2 is higher than in the original equilibrium Q_0. From visual inspection, it should be clear that while the effect of increasing prices from outward shifts in demand and inward shifts in supply are unambiguous, the effect on equilibrium quantities depend on the relative magnitude of the shifts. For instance, if supply had shifted more, we could end up in a situation where quantity was lower.

Let us also tie back to the introductory example with sharp increases in the price of rice in 2008–2009. How can those be explained? Economists who have looked closely at the events (e.g., Dawe and Slayton (2010)) see a combination of supply and demand shocks as responsible for the sharp increase in price. A number of important exporters, starting with India in late 2007, imposed restrictions on the export of rice. From the perspective of world markets, this clearly lowers supply.[13] As noted, expectations can also affect demand and a fear that export restrictions would spread and lead to even higher future prices prompted several importers like the Phillipines, Malaysia, and Nigeria to stockpile: "Buy now because tomorrow it will be even more expensive, or even difficult to purchase at any price." This is associated with an outward shift in demand; just as in the palladium example, we thus have two movements that combine to drive prices higher. Concerted efforts to reassure importing countries that markets would be open and a signaling of willingness to sell some stockpiles of rice in, e.g., Japan to keep prices down helped lower the prices in the later part of 2008. The financial crisis of 2008, which can be thought of as a negative demand shock, further contributed to lowering price levels.

2.5.1 *The slope of supply and demand curves and the effects of shocks*

Visual inspection of the previous figures indicate that two aspects are central for the quantitative impact of a demand shock on equilibrium prices and quantities: the *size* of the shift in demand and the *slope* of the supply curve. Likewise, the size of the shift in supply and the slope of the demand curve determine the quantitative impact of shocks to supply. Let us exemplify with a demand shock. First, consider the case of avocados and assume that a host of trends and new information that avocados are healthy shift demand outward. Assume that the supply curve of avocados is relatively steep, at least in the short run. It takes several years from the planting of an avocado tree until it bears avocados, so in the short run, the set of trees is fixed. Yield among existing trees can be increased by, for instance,

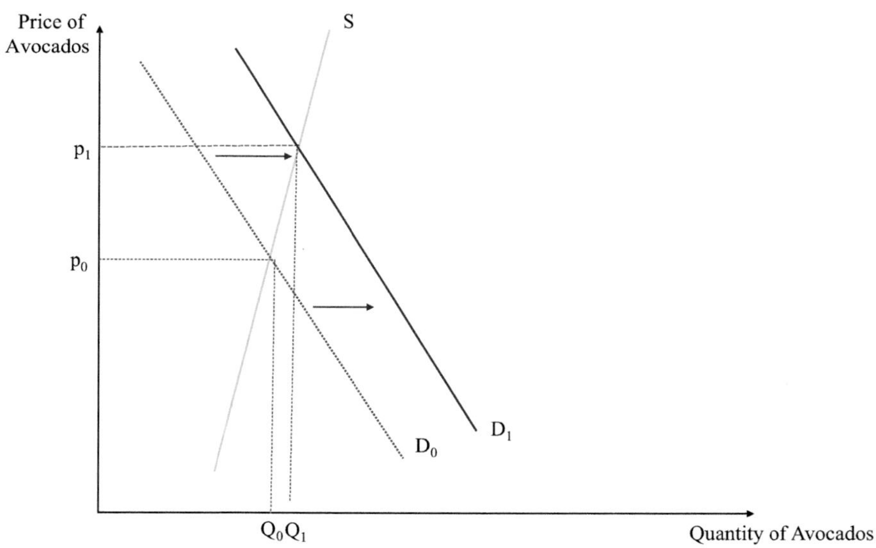

Figure 2.17 Change in equilibrium: A shift in demand when the supply curve is steep.

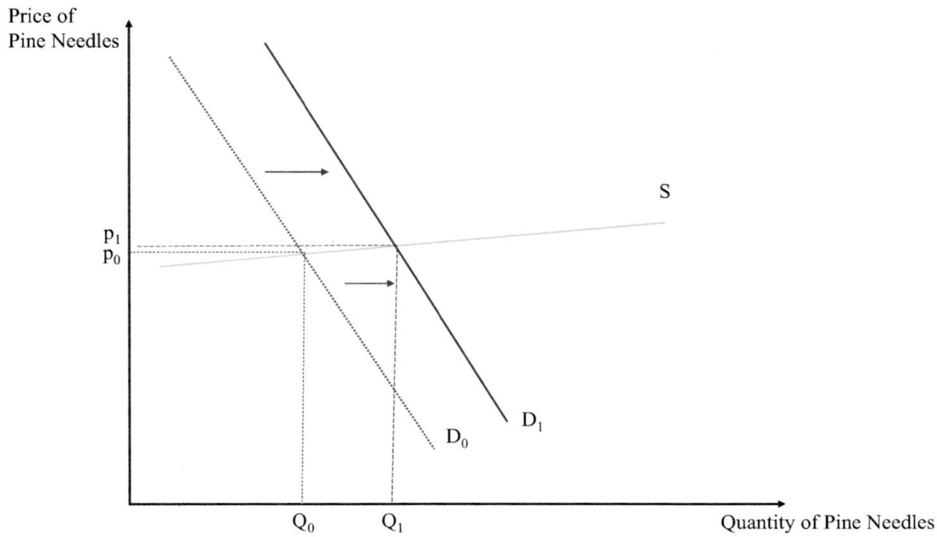

Figure 2.18 Change in equilibrium: A shift in demand when the supply curve is relatively flat.

having more pickers, taking greater care that fewer avocados are damaged in picking and transport, pampering the trees more, etc. These factors imply that the supply curve is less than vertical such that higher prices are associated with higher supply. The supply curve is, nevertheless, likely to be quite steep. The steepness ensures that large movements along the vertical price axis are associated with relatively small movements along the horizontal quantity axis. In a case such as this, an outward demand shock generates a large increase in price but only a limited expansion of quantity since it is difficult to expand production.

Contrast the case of avocados with one where the supply curve is rather flat. I am writing this in Sweden, a country where pine trees abound. Now consider the case where pine needles are used to make tea. Supply can come from any person who simply goes out and collects pine needles in the forest, and just a few pinches of pine needles are sufficient to generate a nice cup of pine-needle tea. At present, there is next to no harvesting of pine needles so that many potential needle pickers are likely to find an abundance of needles just within a short walk from their place of residence. A situation such as this suggests that if the price of pine needles were to increase, it could generate a large supply response – the supply curve is relatively flat, as illustrated in Figure 2.18. Here supply easily expands to meet the shift in demand; in consequence, prices do not rise much and quantity increases.

Notes

1 The data are from a website maintained by the International Monetary Fund, https://www.imf.org/en/Research/commodity-prices. This is a convenient and free source of data on prices of agricultural products and other commodities, such as metals.

2 Often, this puzzle is presented as one that philosophers from Aristotle and Plato onward, via Copernicus and Adam Smith, struggled with, and only with the development of supply and demand analysis in the 1800s did this question become resolved. I have a lot of sympathy for this view, but a substantial literature goes to great lengths to try to determine exactly in what sense the

ancient thinkers thought of it as a puzzle or paradox (see Ekelund and Thornton (2011)). Thus, for the purposes of this textbook, take it as a puzzle whose answer is not immediately obvious but that has a very simple answer and interpretation in the model that we are about to learn.

3 Time is another dimension that is relevant in defining a market. For a typical consumption good, the time is "now," but in, for instance, commodity markets, the price of a commodity delivered in one year's time can be seen as different market than the same commodity delivered tomorrow.

4 An aspect that sometimes confuses students is that similar physical goods can exist in both homogeneous and differentiated versions. The vast majority of wheat traded on global markets can be seen as homogeneous products. This does not necessarily conflict with the fact that an individual wheat farmer can sell boutique wheat from her farm at premium prices, where the location and story of the production help make it into a differentiated product. Similarly, tap water can be seen as a homogeneous product, which does not hinder some premium producers in successfully marketing high-priced bottled waters. We return to the distinction between homogeneous and differentiated products in Chapter 10.

5 For another example, consider the demand function $Q^D = 10 - 2p$. The inverse demand function is again found by solving for p, yielding $p = 5 - Q^D/2$. Two ways of expressing the same relationship.

6 Goods with an upward-sloping demand curve are termed "Giffen goods," after British journalist Robert Giffen, who allegedly made the observation that such a pattern held for demand for potatoes during the great famine in Ireland in the mid-1800s. Whether the demand curve for potatoes in Ireland during the famine was indeed upward sloping remains a debated issue, but such Giffen behavior has been documented, for instance, for rice among poor Chinese households (see Jensen and Miller, 2008). In Chapter 5, we examine Giffen goods in some detail. In simple terms, when the price of potatoes goes up, poor consumers forego whatever other foodstuffs that could enrich the diet and purchase more potatoes.

7 This is not to deny that in the long run, demand for a particular type of product can be shaped by perceptions of quality and social status associated with use of the product. Price can play a role there, but we have then left the standard analysis of the slope of demand curves way behind us.

8 A particularly common formulation is what is known as the constant elastic demand curve, for instance, expressed as $p = Q^{\frac{1}{\epsilon}}$, where the parameter ϵ determines the curvature of the inverse demand function.

9 You may find it unconvincing that many suppliers together only supply a handful of liters. I agree but have chosen to opt for simple numbers rather than realism in this dimension. If you want, you can think of quantity as thousands of liters, which solves the conundrum.

10 While this is intuitive, we should note that there could be seen to be some contradiction between the upward price pressure, which implies that at least some firms set prices, and the assumption that all firms are price takers. In theory, equilibrium is assumed to be reached by an agent who takes up information about supply and demand curves from all buyers and sellers and then proposes an equilibrium price, a "Walrasian auctioneer" (after Léon Walras, a French economist who in the 1800s made large contributions to the study of market equilibrium). In the early 1960s, Nobel laureate Vernon Smith was dissatisfied with this state of affairs and created a set of experiments where participants in the experiment where given valuations of a good, an identity as a seller or buyer, and then allowed to trade. The experiments consistently showed that the equilibrium price was relatively quickly reached, a finding that has been confirmed in many subsequent studies. Smith (1962) is the original reference, and an accessible discussion of the results is found in the motivation for the 2002 Nobel Prize in Economics at the Nobel foundation's website https://www.nobelprize.org/uploads/2018/06/advanced-economicsciences2002.pdf. Thus while theory relies on somewhat of a "trick" to establish the equilibrium price, the predictions seem to work well in the "laboratory" and ample evidence from the real-world market shows how prices are established and respond to new information in line with predictions of the supply and demand model. Let us also point out that, strictly speaking, the Sveriges Riksbank Prize in Economic Sciences in Memory of Alfred Nobel is not a Nobel Prize. It was not in the will of Alfred Nobel. It is funded by the Swedish central bank and was first awarded in 1969. Its standing as a Nobel Prize is a topic of perennial discussion in some circles. Nevertheless, it is awarded following similar procedures as the original Nobel Prize, and for simplicity, we refer to it as the Nobel Prize in Economics and the winners as Nobel laureates henceforward.

11 We might note that quality certification goes into the assignment of products as homogeneous. A trader can go to an organized exchange and purchase 1 ton of grade A quality of a particular good.
12 He did walk a lot. Summers were largely spent on foot, criss-crossing the Alps, as discussed in Keynes (1924).
13 On the other hand, within an exporting country that suddenly imposes a ban on exports, domestic supply of rice will increase, tending to keep price down, which is a typical motivation for such export bans.

Part I

Where does supply come from?

In the next two chapters, we will see where the supply curve comes from. Why does it have the slope that it does? Why does it differ across products? What precisely is the reason why supply curves shift when the price of inputs change? These are some of the questions that motivate us. We will also introduce a set of tools that we will apply again when we examine the determinants of demand in subsequent chapters.

Broadly speaking, we assume that supply comes from firms that want to make as much profit as possible given the constraints that they face. Getting from this broad characterization to a supply curve requires a number of steps and assumptions, as we describe in the following. We first describe technology and costs in Chapter 3 – how do firms decide on the way to produce and what are the costs that result from this? These tools are relevant for any firm, not just the firms that are faced with strong competition that we analyze in this first part of the book, but they can also be used to analyze, for instance, the relation between demand for labor and the increased capacities of artificial intelligence. Differences in cost structure are also a useful way to understand differences in the way that firms compete in different markets. Understand the cost structure of a market and you are well on the path of understanding that market.

In Chapter 4, we move from the costs to the supply of a firm faced with strong competition. This is directly applicapable to many markets, ranging from mineral extraction to container shipping. Again, the tools that we learn here are going to be useful also for understanding how, for instance, a monopolist sets prices later in the book.

DOI: 10.4324/9781003623854-3

3 From technology to costs

Illustration 3.1 Portrait of Dante. *Dante's Portrait*, Attilio Runcaldier, mid-1800s. Public domain, via Wikimedia Commons.

3.1 Setting the stage

If I were writing this in Florence in the 1300s, I'd be writing with a goose pen, and for you to have your own copy, you would need to manually copy the book. The invention of the printing press in the 1500s clearly drastically increased the possibility of producing books. And now a billion copies could easily be downloaded across the globe. This is just one example of how the output associated with the effort of my labor depends on the technology with which it is matched.

DOI: 10.4324/9781003623854-4

Even if we disregard the historical dimension, there are many different ways of producing a good. Put yourself in the shoes of a tomato grower. How much land should you use for growing tomatoes? Should you mostly rely on manual labor for watering and tending and picking, or should you rely on automation as far as possible, including the use of tomato-picking robots? Should you add artificial sunlight? All of these choices affect your costs of production: the costs that you have irrespective of volumes, as well as the costs of expanding the volume harvested. Taking this one step further, it seems plausible that your costs for producing and selling are important for how much you are willing to supply at different prices of tomatoes.

The following chapter will specify how we as economists model the first stage of the chain of reasoning just described: What is the link between how a firm chooses to produce and its cost?

3.2 Defining some key concepts

Let us now outline the basic building blocks used in economics to describe how goods and services are produced. Simply put, **goods** are physical products. Thus goods can be commodities, such as those studied in the previous chapter, but they can also be pharmaceutical products, bicycles, or small figurines of smurfs made out of porcelain. You name it. **Services** are activities provided by other people, such as a haircut, yoga instruction, a play at the theater, or the help of a consulting firm. In many cases, you pay for a combination of goods and services, as when you go to a restaurant. The food itself is a good, but the whole restaurant experience is bundled with the services of a waiter, and you don't have to do the dishes when you're done.

Thus, we are interested in describing how goods, services, or some combination of the two are produced. Someone is doing the production, choosing what to produce and how much, and in the following, we use the term **firm** about the decision-maker who decides what to produce and how. These can be firms as we think of them in daily language, such as Apple, Carlsberg, McDonalds, or McKinsey. The decision-maker could also be a publicly owned firm (such as a state-owned electricity producer), or a nonprofit organization such as a university or sports club. There are many interesting questions regarding how decisions are made within firms, much of it within economics, but at this stage, and for most of this book, we make the simplifying assumption that we can view the firm as one decision-maker with a clear objective.

The **factors of production** are the resources used to produce goods or services. Pretty much anything that we produce needs to have some time devoted to the production by humans, and we term this factor labor. Sometimes we distinguish between different types of labor (for instance, by specialization (e.g., barbers, economists, rocket scientists) or by education level (e.g., university educated or only primary school completed), but for many questions, we take an overarching view and lump all categories of labor together. **Capital** is used to denote resources that are used in the production but that are not spent. The buildings in which production takes place, computers, and machinery are some examples. We also talk of **intellectual capital**, such as patents, trademarks, or designs. Such intellectual capital (also referred to as intangible capital) is clearly highly important for many firms in, e.g., pharmaceutical markets or in the entertainment industry. **Land** is another factor of production that is often highlighted; clearly, it is crucial in agricultural production. We also use the term **inputs** as a synonym for factors of production. **Raw materials** are an important input for some goods; these are commodities of the type that we examined in the previous chapter, where, for instance, the metal palladium is used as an input in production of catalytic converters. Finally, let us also highlight **intermediate inputs**, manufactured products that are used in the production. A bicycle manufacturer, for instance, uses labor, capital, and a number of different intermediate inputs where it purchases gears from one supplier, brakes from another, and saddles from a third.

3.3 The production function

The firm combines inputs to produce output in terms of goods or services. **Output** is measured in the number of units of the good or service, Q. The set of inputs needed differ across firms, and we would typically have a long list of inputs. For pedagogical purposes, we focus on two inputs only, capital (typically denoted K since we want to use c to denote costs) and labor (typically denoted L). We use a **production function** to describe how the out put depends on the amount of inputs used in production. As with any function, we can express it in general form, such as

$$Q = f(K, L),$$

which simply says that the amount of L and K used gives some number of units of output Q for the firm. The relation between inputs and output is described by the function f. The production function can also take a specific form,[1] such as

$$Q = \sqrt{KL}.$$

A third way of describing a production function is with a matrix, as in Table 3.1. The matrix shows the number of units produced as dependent on the number of units of K used (1, 2, or 3 as measured by each row) and units of L (1, 2, or 3 as measured by each column) used. For instance, if 2 units of K and 1 unit L is used, 14 units are produced. For concreteness, we may think of this as a bakery that produces baguettes and the output during one day. The amount of machinery used is summarized by K. One needs an oven and some space, of course, but more capital could be added, as in having a larger oven or having more mechanical aids – there is a full range available from kneading the dough by hand to fully automated machines that perform all the tasks. L is the number of bakers who work a full day in the bakery. Other inputs are also needed in practice (flour, water, salt, and yeast), but for simplicity, we disregard those. Our purpose here is to bring out the intuition for some key properties of production functions, not to learn how to bake a baguette.

Table 3.1 A representation of a simple production function

		L		
		1	**2**	**3**
	1	10	14	16
K	**2**	14	20	24
	3	16	24	30

Table 3.2 A representation of a simple production function

		L		
		1	2	3
	1	10	14	16
K	2	14	20	24
	3	16	24	30

In the following, we will describe a number of aspects of the production function. Apologies that some of this may appear somewhat dry, but they do provide important building blocks for our later analysis.

3.3.1 Varying one input while keeping other inputs fixed

In the following, we rely on calculus to clarify the nature of some results. The appendix (very last chapter of this book) collects a number of results and details on notation that may be useful if your recollection is a bit rusty.

One potentially interesting thought experiment is to see what happens to the number of units produced if we change the amount of one input while keeping others fixed. In Table 3.2, we have marked the case where K is kept fixed at 2, and we just vary L. Thus as we move from 1 to 2 workers output increases by 6 baguettes (from 14 to 20), and as we move from 2 to 3 workers output increases by 4 baguettes (from 20 to 24).

This change in output produced is important for many questions in economics. Consider, for instance, the wage that the bakery would be willing to pay to the last worker hired. What is the cost of that worker? The wage. What is the increase in profit for the firm if it hires this additional worker? The price of baguettes times the increase in number of baguettes produced. The concept of the change in output as the amount of labor used increases by a small amount is important enough that we have given it a name: the **marginal product of labor**. A common shorthand for the marginal product of labor is MP_L, a notation that we will also use in this book.

Anytime we in economics use the term **marginal**, it refers to the change in something to a "small" change in something else. Small is in quotation marks as its magnitude differs somewhat across applications. Strictly speaking, we use it to refer to a derivative (or partial derivative), and small then refers to an infinitesimal change, as when we define derivatives. We can think of it as the slope of a function at a particular point, as the slope of a line tangent to the function. In many applications, we use the concept somewhat more loosely, however, and hence marginal product of labor might also refer to one more hour worked or the hiring of one more worker.

To explain further, consider again the following production function,

$$Q = \sqrt{KL}. \tag{3.1}$$

The marginal product of labor is the change in output from a small change in the amount of labor used, holding other inputs fixed. In other words, it is the partial derivative of the

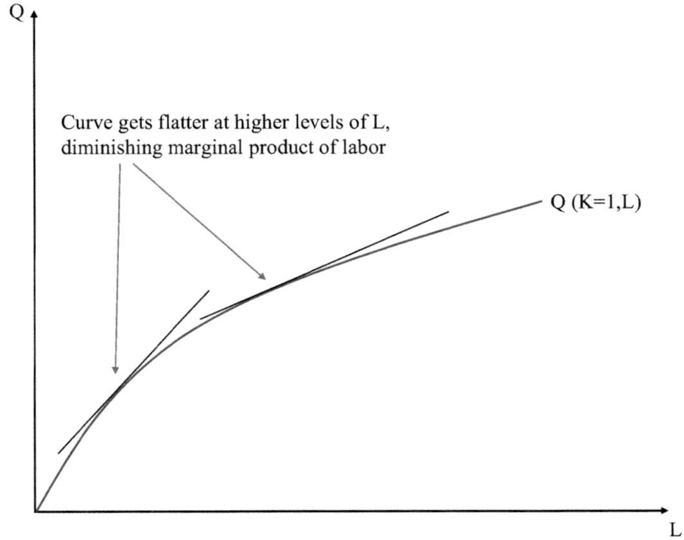

Figure 3.1 An example of a production function and the marginal product of labor.

production function with respect to labor, which we denote by $\frac{\partial Q(K,L)}{\partial L}$. Remembering that $\sqrt{A} = A^{\frac{1}{2}}$, using the rules of differentiation and that $A^{-B} = \frac{1}{A^B}$, we then easily establish that

$$\begin{aligned}\frac{\partial Q(K,L)}{\partial L} &= \frac{1}{2}L^{\frac{1}{2}-1}K^{\frac{1}{2}}\\ &= \frac{1}{2}L^{-\frac{1}{2}}K^{\frac{1}{2}}\\ &= \frac{1}{2}\sqrt{\frac{K}{L}}\end{aligned} \tag{3.2}$$

To provide some intuition, Figure 3.1 plots Q and MP_L for different values of L, using Equation (3.2) to describe the partial derivative. We assume that $K = 1$ in the graph. That is, we keep the amount of capital fixed and see what happens to output as we add more workers. We see that as more workers are added, more and more is produced. We also see that the curve is getting flatter the further right that we move in diagram. The curve is increasing, but at a decreasing rate, as indicated by the tangents to the curve that are illustrated at two points. Each additional worker adds less than the previous worker, a pattern that we term *diminishing marginal product of labor*. This is a common assumption in economics. It is important to note that diminishing *marginal product* is not the same as decreasing *product*.

While we often make assumptions that imply a diminishing marginal product, we can also have cases with increasing or constant marginal products. Of general importance is that anything that we term *marginal* in economics may differ depending on where we evaluate it. The slope at one point is not necessarily the same as the slope at another point. The marginal product of capital (or the marginal product of any other input) are defined analogously: What is the change in output from using slightly more capital whilst holding other inputs fixed?

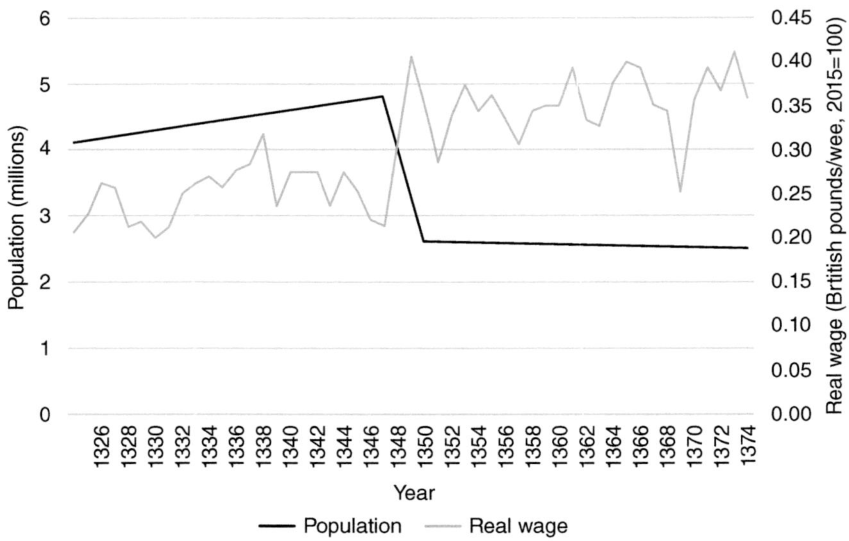

Figure 3.2 Real wages and population in England at the time of the Black Death in the 1300s. Thomas, R and Dimsdale, N (2017) "A Millennium of UK Data," Bank of England OBRA dataset, http://www.bankofengland.co.uk/research/Pages/onebank/threecenturies.aspx.

3.3.1.1 *Marginal products matter: An example from the Black Death*

Marginal product of labor might seem like a contrived theoretical construct that you need to know for an exam and can then safely forget. However, let us again note that marginal product matters greatly for wages following the previous arguments. An example that is often highlighted comes from the impact of the plague known as the Black Death that hit Europe in the late 1340s.[2] Think of an economy where there are two factors of production, land and labor. Assume that the amount of land is fixed. When population decreases sharply, as indeed happened during the Black Death, that means that each laborer is matched with more land; the marginal product of labor rises, which is reflected in real wages. A sharp fall in population and a sharp increase in real wages is indeed what we see in the data, as seen in Figure 3.2.[3]

3.3.2 *Different ways of producing the same volume of output: Describing the technology*

Earlier, we varied the amount of one input while keeping all other inputs fixed. We kept the same amount of capital (ovens, etc.) and only varied the number of bakers. Let us now instead consider different *combinations* of inputs. Table 3.3 shows the same baguette production example as noted earlier. We note that we can produce a given number of baguettes with different combinations of output. Fourteen baguettes can be produced with 2 units of K and 1 L or with 1 unit of K and 2 L. Similarly, 16 baguettes can be produced with 3 units of K and 1 L or with 1 unit of K and 3 L. Intuitively, we can produce baguettes with a lot of capital, with almost fully automated machines where one worker only needs to oversee the process and perhaps clean some parts. Alternatively, we can produce baguettes with very little capital, performing almost all tasks by hand.

Table 3.3 Different combinations of inputs that produce the same output

		L		
		1	**2**	**3**
K	**1**	10	14	16
	2	14	20	24
	3	16	24	30

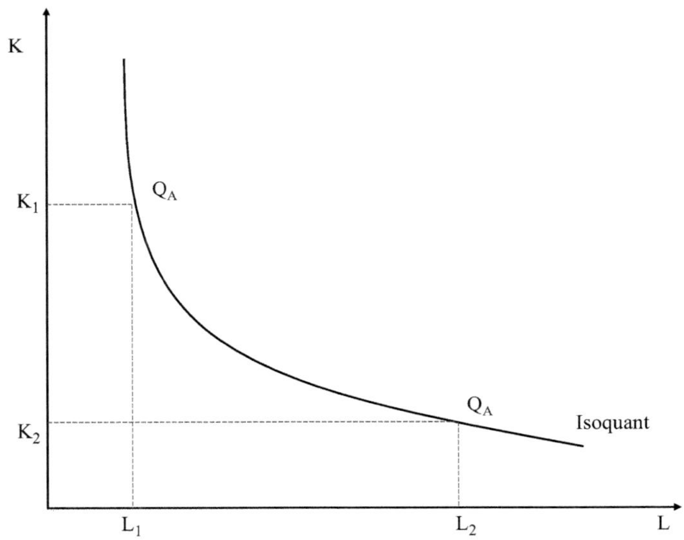

Figure 3.3 Different combinations of inputs that produce the same output.

We can also use a graph to illustrate the different combinations of inputs that give a certain output as in Figure 3.3. Measure the number of units of K used in production of a certain good on the vertical axis and the number of workers L on the horizontal axis. Q_A units of output can be produced by using K_1 units of K and L_1 units of L or by by using K_2 units of K and L_2 units of L. The curve represents different combinations of inputs that give the same output, and we term it **isoquant**. "Iso" comes to us from ancient Greek and means equal. We could equally well call it "same-quantity-curve," but isoquant is more crisp and scientific-sounding.[4]

The slope of the isoquant says something about how easy it is to substitute one input for another. Consider first the case in Figure 3.4 where the isoquant is a straight line. Here a given amount of output can be produced with 3 K and 1 L or equally well with 2 units of each input or with 1 K and 3 L. In this case, we can always substitute one baker for one unit of capital and still produce the same output. The combination doesn't matter; its only the total amount that matters. We say that in this case, the two inputs are **perfect substitutes**. They are perfectly substitutable.

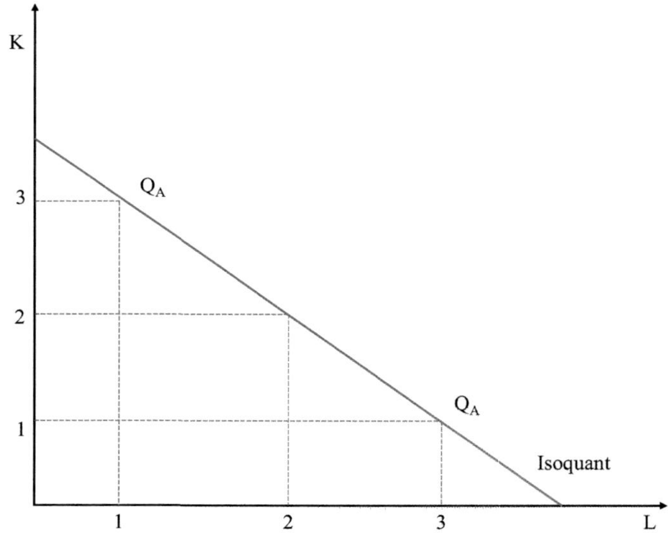

Figure 3.4 Isoquants for perfect substitutes. Video link for Figures 3.4–3.6: https://youtu.be/DXDfJBz5BG8.

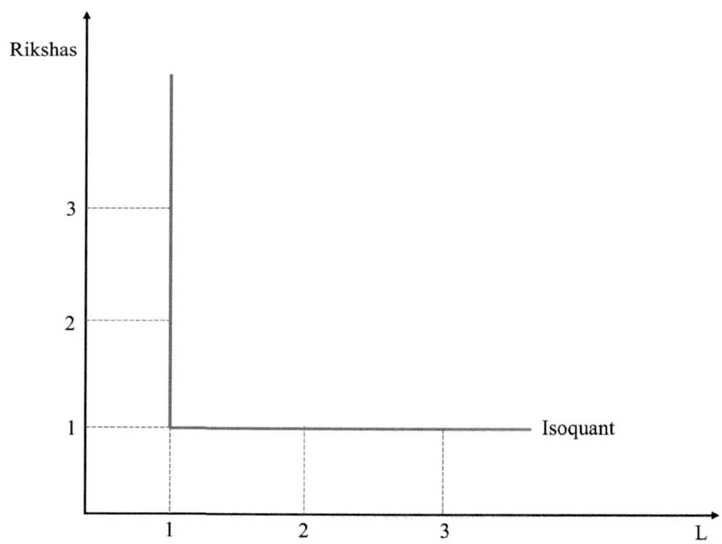

Figure 3.5 Isoquant for perfect complements. Video link for Figures 3.4–3.6: https://youtu.be/DXDfJBz5BG8.

In many cases, different inputs are not likely to be perfectly substitutable however. At the other extreme, inputs are not substitutable at all. Consider the case of rickshaws, a bike taxi. One rickshaw driver and one rickshaw can be used to deliver a certain number of trips during an afternoon. What happens if one more rickshaw is added? Nothing. A rickshaw

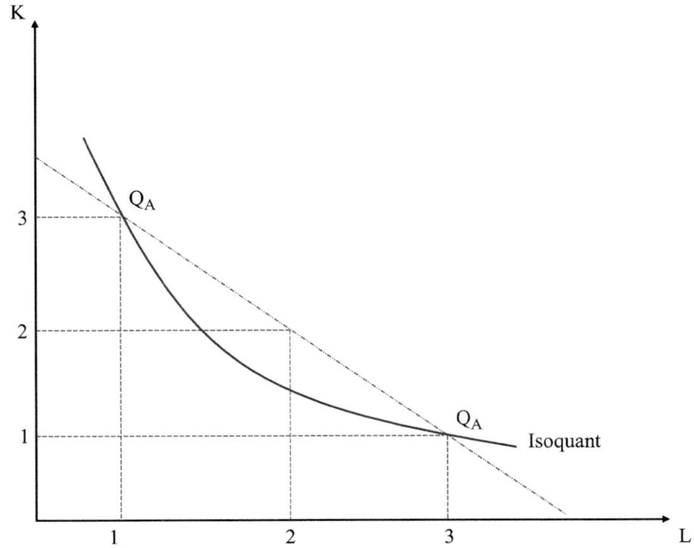

Figure 3.6 Isoquant for imperfect substitutes. Video link for Figures 3.4–3.6: https://youtu.be/DXDfJBz5BG8.

driver can only ride one rickshaw at a time, so with an additional rickshaw, the same number of trips can be delivered. Similarly, if one more driver is added, no more trips can be done. The two inputs are then **perfect complements**, and the isoquant is L-shaped.

Cases in between perfect complements and perfect substitutes are termed **imperfect substitutes**, and this is arguably the most common type of situation for the relation between inputs. The less of an input that we use, the more difficult is it then to substitute away from this input. Consider a bakery that is almost fully automated, to decrease the amount of people working even more will be difficult. We need to bring in machines that supervise the machines. Vice versa, with a hundred bakers crowding around 1 oven, we would not be indifferent between getting an extra oven or an extra worker. Figure 3.6 illustrates a case of imperfect substitutes.

Here, a given number of units can be produced with 3 K and 1 L or, vice versa, with 1 K and 3 L. If, however, we use more equal proportions, we can get away with using less of each input and still produce equally as much. Two bakers and 2 ovens produce more baguettes than 1 baker with 3 ovens or 3 bakers with 1 oven. Isoquants for imperfect substitutes will have the shape where they bow inward toward the origin. More formally, we would say that they are strictly convex; if we were to tie a string between two points on the function, the string would be above the function. Many production functions would have this form, and indeed a wish to avoid extremes has been a common point in philosophy and religion across the world: "Nothing in excess," as said at the temple of Apollon in Delphi in ancient Greece and argued by religious thinkers and philosophers at many points in history.

The convex shape can be given further context if we are willing to make use of some mathematics.

3.3.2.1 An aside in mathematics: Total differentiation

$Q = f(K, L)$ is a function of two variables, K and L. We might want to determine what happens to the quantity produced if we change both inputs somewhat. Use d to denote a change and (as noted earlier) use

$$\frac{\partial f(K, L)}{\partial K}$$

to denote the partial derivative of the production function with respect to K whilst keeping the amount of L fixed.[5] If we let "everything change," we perform an operation known as *total differentiation*. Thus

$$dQ = \frac{\partial f(K, L)}{\partial K} dK + \frac{\partial f(K, L)}{\partial L} dL.$$

What is the change in quantity as we change the inputs? Well, that depends on how much the inputs change (dK and dL) and on the effect of those changes on output (the partial derivatives). Where are we headed with this? Well, we want to say something profound about the slope of the isoquant. First, note that along the isoquant, $dQ = 0$. Quantity is the same along the isoquant, and hence the change in quantity is 0. Thus, along the isoquant,

$$\underbrace{dQ}_{=0} = \frac{\partial f(K, L)}{\partial K} dK + \frac{\partial f(K, L)}{\partial L} dL.$$

Move the first term on the right hand side over to the left to get

$$-\frac{\partial f(K, L)}{\partial K} dK = \frac{\partial f(K, L)}{\partial L} dL.$$

Divide by the partial derivative and dL to get

$$-\frac{dK}{dL} = \frac{\frac{\partial f(K,L)}{\partial L}}{\frac{\partial f(K,L)}{\partial K}}.$$

What is the term on the right? Well, we noted earlier that these partial derivatives are what we term the marginal products of labor and of capital, which we denote by MP_L and MP_K respectively.

$$-\frac{dK}{dL} = \frac{\frac{\partial f(K,L)}{\partial L}}{\frac{\partial f(K,L)}{\partial K}} = \frac{MP_L}{MP_K}.$$

So, as we are moving along the isoquant, the slope is equal to the marginal product of labor over the marginal product of capital, as we illustrate in Figure 3.7. At point A, the firm is using relatively much capital in relation to labor. We can think of it as a highly automated bakery where staff is watching monitors and supervising the robots. To see the slope at this point, we draw out the tangent – a line that just touches the isoquant at this point. The slope of that tangent gives the change in K over the change in L. At this point MP_L is relatively

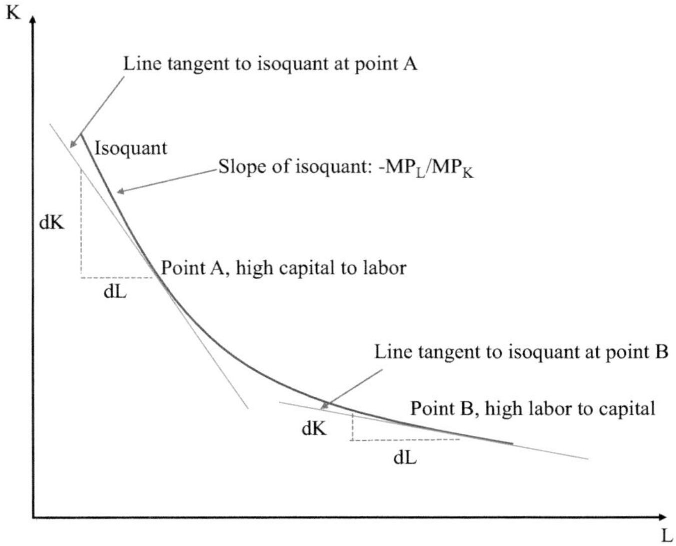

Figure 3.7 The slope of the isoquant. Video link for Figure 3.7 and derivation of the slope: https://youtu.be/nLJO3OZ4v84.

high in relation to MP_K. Each of the workers in the highly automated plant has a lot of capital to work with. The marginal contribution of a worker is therefore high.

As we move along the isoquant, the amount of capital that each worker is matched with decreases. Consider point B, where a lot is done manually, and many workers crowd around the ovens, bumping into each other and waiting their turn to use some of the scarce equipment. Here MP_L is low relative to MP_K. How will firms choose to produce? That is something that we turn to next, after having done a numerical example.

3.3.3 *Production function and isoquants: A numerical example*

So far, we have discussed production functions in general form ($Q = f(K, L)$), but let us now consider a specific example, $Q = K \times L$. Think of bicycle production. Twenty-five bikes can then be made by using 5 K and 5 L,

$$\underbrace{5}_{K} \times \underbrace{5}_{L} = \underbrace{25}_{bikes}.$$

But we can also produce 25 bikes by using 2.5 K and 10 L or 10 K and 2.5 L as illustrated in Figure 3.8. The isoquant in this case is all combinations of inputs that yield a production of 25 bikes. This is, of course, only one isoquant. Say that we instead examine a case of 6 K and 6 L being used, then 36 bikes are produced, and we have one point on another isoquant (where, for instance, 10 K and 3.6 also would be one point on this higher isoquant).

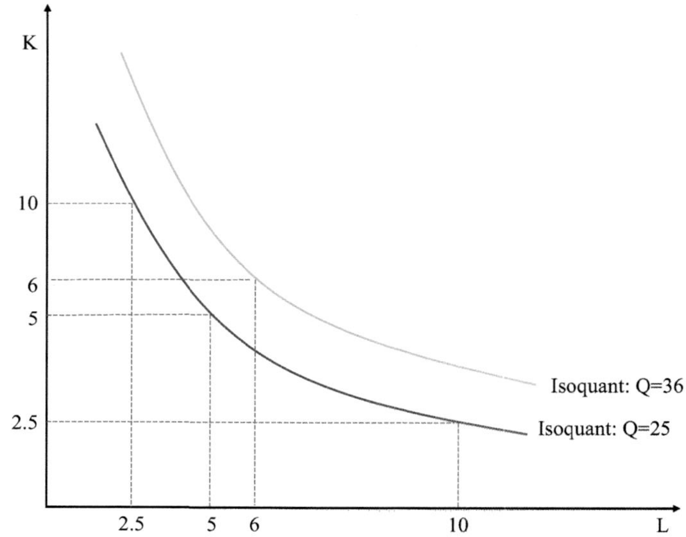

Figure 3.8 Two different isoquants. Video link for Figures 3.4–3.6: https://youtu.be/rHfKIen4NdQ.

3.4 Productivity

Earlier, we exemplified the marginal product of labor with agricultural production. Clearly, since the 1300s, there has been massive change in this, and this subsection dives deeper into such changes. If you're pressed for time, you can skip it, but for others, and those curious, it does provide a useful connection between the models that we cover and aspects of reality that are easy to relate to. The production function f relates output, Q, to the use of inputs such as capital (K) and labor (L). To capture that the production function itself can change over time and be different across different firms, we can introduce a parameter A, which shifts the production function.[6] Thus, in general form, we write

$$Q = Af(K, L).$$

A particularly interesting application to understand productivity concerns the production function in agriculture. Think of a simple production function for food with two inputs, land (J) and labor. If the amount of arable land is given, then if more people are working on the fields, the marginal product of labor is lower, as illustrated in Figure 3.9. The lower marginal product is also reflected in a lower average product.

While this may seem innocuous, the implications are profound if we are in an agriculturally dominated economy with little change in the production function – conditions that have been true for much of human history. As forcefully argued by British economist Thomas Malthus in the late 1700s, the implication is that if there is population growth, this translates into less output of food per person. To avoid this, there can be productivity gains; the production function can shift upward, as illustrated in Figure 3.10. There would then again be a decreasing marginal product of labor but at a higher level.

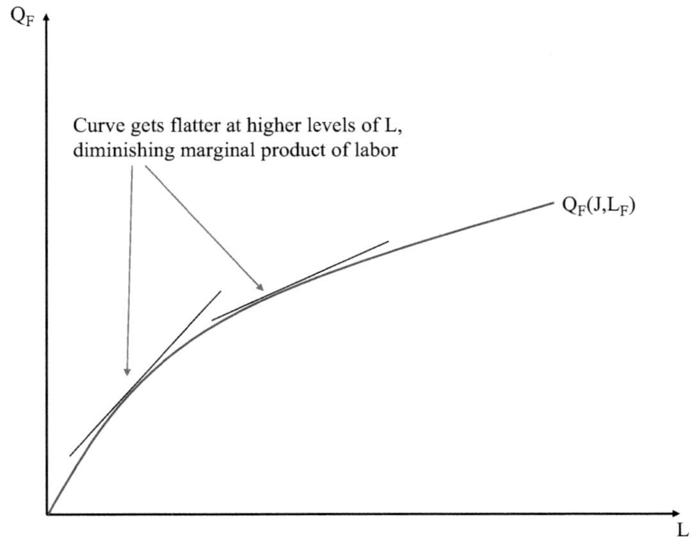

Figure 3.9 Diminishing marginal product in production of food.

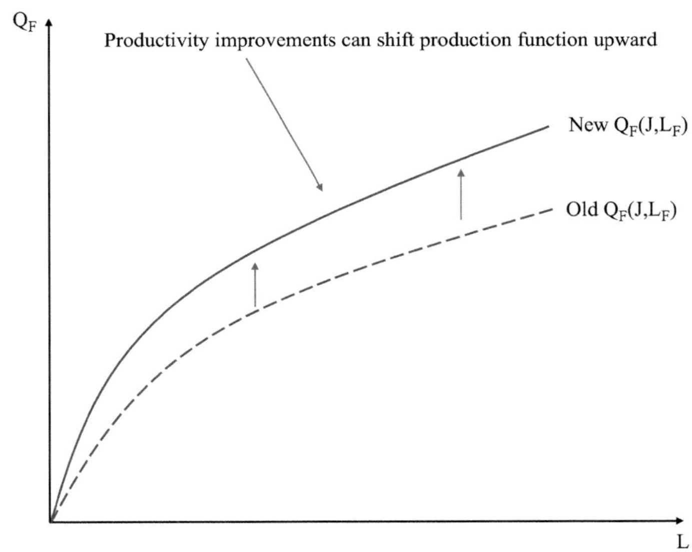

Figure 3.10 The effect of shifts in the production function. Video link for Figures 3.4–3.6: https://youtu.be/rHfKIen4NdQ.

Let us consider some of the changes that might lead to such productivity increases in agriculture. A better understanding of when to plant and to harvest and how to provide water and nourishment to crops is one example – indeed, the ancient growth of great civilizations in, e.g., Egypt and Mesopotamia was partly triggered by irrigation projects.

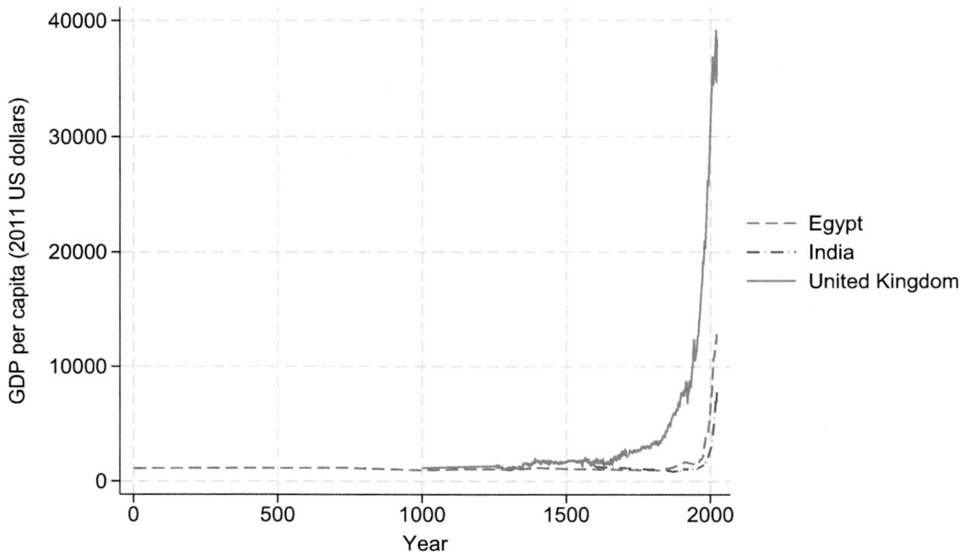

Figure 3.11 GDP per person over the last 2,000 years. Our World in Data/ economic growth. Bolt and van Zanden, Maddison project database 2023. The data is expressed in in international US dollars at 2011 prices.

Changes in the organization of the land – shifting from small dispersed plots to continuous land holdings can increase yields, as can new technologies, for instance moving from plows made of wood to plows made of iron.[7] New crops can also matter – the introduction of potatoes to Europe from the Americas, for instance, raised the ability to feed a given number of people on a given land area.[8]

In a nutshell, Malthus argued that societies needed to keep population growth down; if not, rapid population growth coupled with low productivity growth in agriculture could lead to starvation and catastrophes. For a long time, Malthus's reasoning seemed to provide a workable description of human history. Whatever small productivity gains that there were in agriculture tended to be neutralized by population increases, and growth in real incomes per capita were limited – a pattern that we sometimes refer to as the Malthusian trap. Figure 3.11 highlights how, until the technological changes that started with the Industrial Revolution, such dynamics ruled much of the development.[9]

In the more recent period, productivity increases in agriculture have been large, with increased mechanization, use of fertilizer, pesticides, and new crops. Under what is known as the green revolution, a concerted effort was made to raise agricultural productivity, with particularly successful results in Latin America and Asia. Other forms of employment have sprung up, and in many countries, only a small fraction of the population is working in agriculture – each worker in agriculture therefore combines with substantial capital and land such that decreasing marginal product of labor, as in Figure 3.9, is not the dominant dynamic. Figure 3.12 shows the development of labor productivity in Sweden – representative in that after a flat period, it shows a marked increase in the last half century or so.

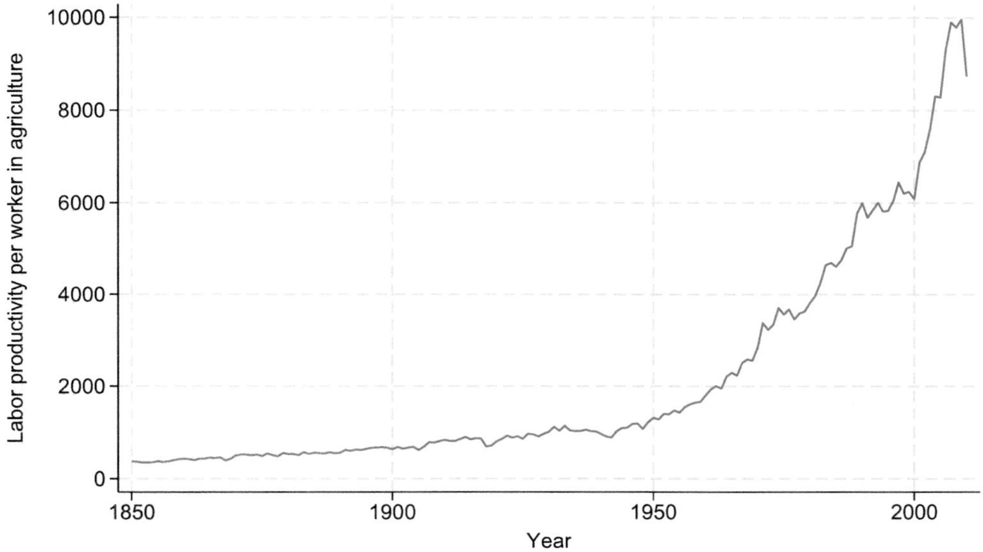

Figure 3.12 Labor productivity in agriculture, Sweden 1850–2010. https://ourworldindata.org/grapher/labor-productivity-agriculture-sweden. Schön and Krantz (2007, 2012, 2015). The ratio between value added in agriculture (SEK, constant 1910/1912 prices) and the number of people employed in agriculture.

This deep-dive into labor productivity in agriculture serves two purposes in this textbook. First, it provides some context to what we mean by productivity improvements and the marginal product of labor. Second, it illustrates that productivity developments can potentially be of great consequence to the human condition.[10]

Let us end this section with a perhaps more frivolous, but hopefully memorable, example. As noted, we think of technological progress in a broad sense – for instance, encompassing available technology (e.g., machinery, computers) and information (e.g., accurate weather reports, knowledge about processes) and how to organize the work. We can think of greater productivity as producing more output for a given set of inputs or, equivalently, as less inputs needed to produce a given output. Consider the case of the climbing route known as the Nose on El Capitan in Yosemite National Park, seen behind three legendary climbers in Illustration 3.2. The route was first established by a team lead by Warren Harding in 1958, with the final climb clocking in at 45 days. Gradually, the best teams became faster and faster, with the trio in Figure 3.2 being the first to do the route in a day in 1975. Spurred by a competitive spirit, a sequence of climbing profiles have then lowered times further, and at the time of writing, Tommy Caldwell and Alex Honnold hold the fastest time at 1 hour and 58 minutes for covering approximately 1,000 vertical meters of difficult climbing.[11] A combination of knowledge of the route, training, techniques to cover ground quicker, and technical equipment have made possible such productivity improvements.[12]

After this digression, let us now return to the main thrust of the story – taking us from choice of how to produce to a cost function. We return with some additional results on productivity in Chapter 9.

Illustration 3.2 Billy Westbay, Jim Bridwell, and John Long after the first one-day ascent of the Nose on El Capitan in 1975. Stone masters. https://commons.wikimedia.org/wiki/File:Stone_Masters_in_front_of_El_Capitan.jpg. Copyright 1979 Michael P White

3.5 From technology to costs

The isoquant describes different ways through which a firm can produce a given quantity. Where will the firm choose to operate? We assume that firms choose how to operate with the aim of minimizing costs – to produce a given quantity as cheaply as possible. How to formalize that choice is what we'll examine in the following. The starting point is very natural, a firm pays for the inputs that it uses. Labor is paid a wage per hour worked; a bakery pays a price per kilo of flour that it uses; a grocer pays rent for the store. Some of these costs, such as wages and the price of flour, present no conceptual difficulties, but a factor like capital is harder. What about a firm that owns its own premises? What about the price of a computer that was bought several years ago? To simplify the analysis in economics, we think of a firm as renting the capital it needs. We can think of it as a simplification, but at a deeper level, it also captures the concept of opportunity cost that we will explore in depth further in this chapter.

So think of a firm that uses labor and capital. The price for an hour of labor is w, and the rental rate for a unit of capital is r. Use C to denote cost, and the cost of using K and L units are then simply given by

$$C = wL + rK.$$

Different combinations of L and K that give the same cost are said to be on the same **isocost**.[13] We will later see how the firm decides on the optimal quantity to produce; for now, we consider the issue of how to produce a given quantity at the lowest possible cost. In formal terms, we say that the firm solves a cost minimization problem subject to the constraint that a certain quantity $\overline{Q}$ is produced. It solves the problem by choosing the amounts of inputs to use. So the minimization problem is the following

$$\min_{K,L} wL + rK \text{ subject to } f(K, L) = \overline{Q}.$$

This can be solved mathematically by, for instance, what is known as the Lagrange method. In the following, we focus on an intuitive graphical solution however. To solve this graphically, we want to be able to represent costs – that is, draw the isocost line – in the same diagram as the isoquant. If we have K on the vertical axis, we hence want to also reshuffle the isocost line to have K on the left-hand side

$$C = wL + rK,$$
$$rK = C - wL,$$
$$K = \frac{C}{r} - \frac{w}{r}L.$$

Figure 3.13 illustrates a cost-minimizing choice of inputs. The isoquant represents the desired quantity to produce, and then we have illustrated two isocost lines. The solution – the cost minimizing choices of K and L – must be such that the chosen K and L represent a point that is both on an isoquant and an isocost. Consider first the top isocost and the associated point defined by K_0 and L_0. Can this be a cost-minimizing point? No, isocosts

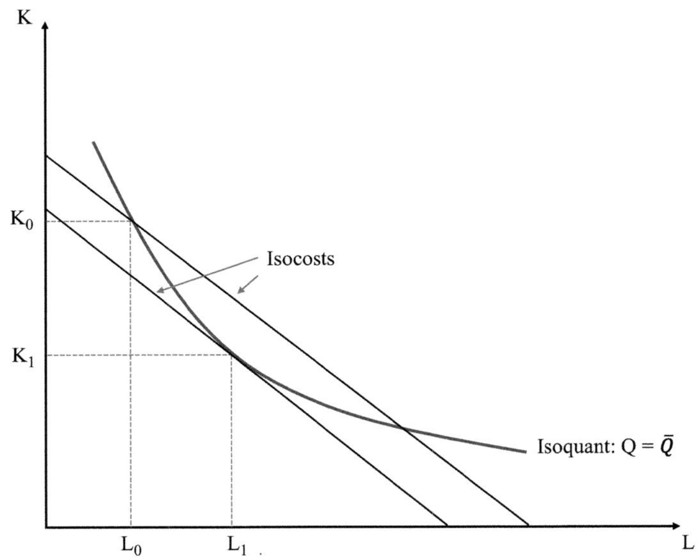

Figure 3.13 The cost-minimizing choice. Video link for Figure 3.13: https://youtu.be/UrFOYMYAJ1I.

that are closer to the origin represent lower costs. So in this case, by using less K and more L, the firm could produce at a lower cost. How long can the firm lower K and increase L and still be on the same isoquant? Well, until the two lines are just tangent at point K_1, L_1. The quantity can then not be produced in any cheaper way. We can think of the solution in several different ways:

- Graphically, we can think of the solution as the lowest possible isocost that we can reach for a given isoquant. This will represent the lowest cost.
- In Figure 3.13, the cost-minimizing point is one where the isocost is tangent to the isoquant. With some exceptions that we mention next, this will typically be the case.
- Somewhat more profoundly, we note that the slope of the isocost is w/r. This is the *relative price* of inputs: wages in relation to the cost of capital. We learned earlier that the slope of the isoquant is MP_L/MP_K, the ratio of marginal products. Hence, at the optimal combination of inputs

$$\frac{w}{r} = \frac{MP_L}{MP_K}.$$

Note that both the slope of the isocost and isoquant are negative; rather than point this out throughout and refer to the absolute value of the slope, I'm somewhat sloppy and refer to just w/r as the slope (rather than $-w/r$). As they are both negative, the minus signs cancel in the comparison ($-\frac{w}{r} = -\frac{MP_L}{MP_K}$ is the same condition as $\frac{w}{r} = \frac{MP_L}{MP_K}$).

Consider again the first point that we looked at, K_0 and L_0. At this point, the isocost was not tangent to the isoquant. At this point, with a lot of capital, the marginal product of labor is very high in relation to the marginal product of capital. Each worker has a lot of capital to work with, which gives her a high marginal product. But the isocost is relatively flat, meaning that the wage is not so high relative to the cost of capital. If the firm uses less capital and more labor, this will cost less – and it is relatively easy to replace capital with labor.

We can use the framework to consider how the production will respond to differences in wages and cost of capital. Consider, for instance, the case of a firm that makes shirts and has one plant in Japan and one in Bangladesh. For simplicity, assume that the technology is the same so that the isoquants in the two countries are the same, and assume further that the same quantity is to be produced in both plants. To further simplify, assume that the cost of capital is the same in both countries. We only assume one difference between the two locations: that wages are lower in Bangladesh than Japan. So, same quantity and same technology and same cost per unit of capital. Will the combination of inputs differ? Yes, because prices of one input factor differ.

Figure 3.14 illustrates the situation. As technology is assumed to be the same (in other words, the production function is the same, and thereby the isoquants are the same) the isoquant represents both countries. As noted earlier, the cost is minimized at the point where the isocost is tangent to the isoquant. The isocosts differ in their slope since wages differ; the isocost for Japan has slope $-w_{Japan}/r$, which is steeper than the isocost for Bangladesh that has slope $-w_{Bangladesh}/r$. Given the different slopes, the tangency for Japan will occur at a point where the firm uses more capital and less labor. The model is, of course, highly stylized but still gives insights into why factories in Japan tend to be highly automated, whereas you would see a lot of labor in the Bangladeshi garment industry. We can also compare the

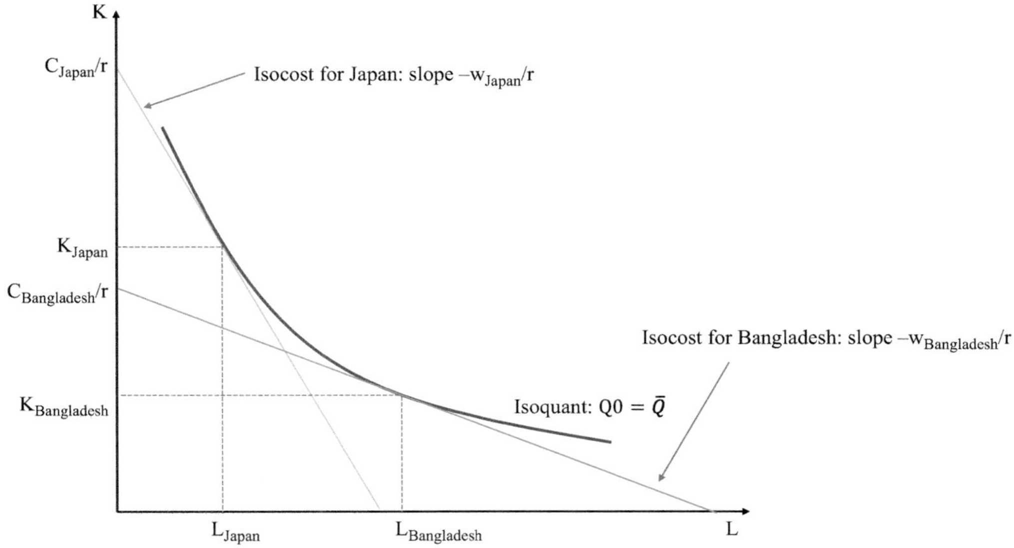

Figure 3.14 The cost-minimizing solution under two different levels of input costs. Video link for Figure 3.14: https://youtu.be/JaDdz9MsVV4.

overall costs. Since we've assumed that the cost of capital, r, is the same in both countries, we can, from the higher intercept of the isocost on the vertical axis, deduce that costs are higher in Japan. The lower wages in Bangladesh imply a lower cost of production there, and the firm would further adjusts its capital/labor ratio to minimize cost.

3.5.1 Cost minimization and isocosts, some additional results

This section presents some further detail and some interesting cases that expand the previous discussion. First, let us consider how changes in overall costs and in relative price of inputs shift the isocost. Remember that the isocost can be written as

$$K = \frac{C}{r} - \frac{w}{r}L.$$

Changes in wages, w, will shift the slope of the isocost. If only w changes, the intercept on the vertical axis will not change: If the firm only uses capital, its cost will not change, and in that case, the intercept is given by C/r. A lower r flattens the isocost, and a higher r makes it steeper, as illustrated in Figure 3.15. A higher cost, where w and r are unchanged, on the other hand, will be associated with a parallel shift outward, as also illustrated in Figure 3.15.

Earlier, we stated that, typically, the cost-minimizing combination of inputs will occur when the isocost is tangent to the isoquant. Mathematically, we term this an **interior** solution; we have a solution, a combination of inputs, that is not at any of the extremes but in the interior. The alternative case, that is sometimes relevant, is what we call a **corner** solution. This is the case where only one input is used. Let us examine such a situation closer. Figure 3.16 shows the isoquant for perfect substitutes. In a somewhat trivial, but perhaps

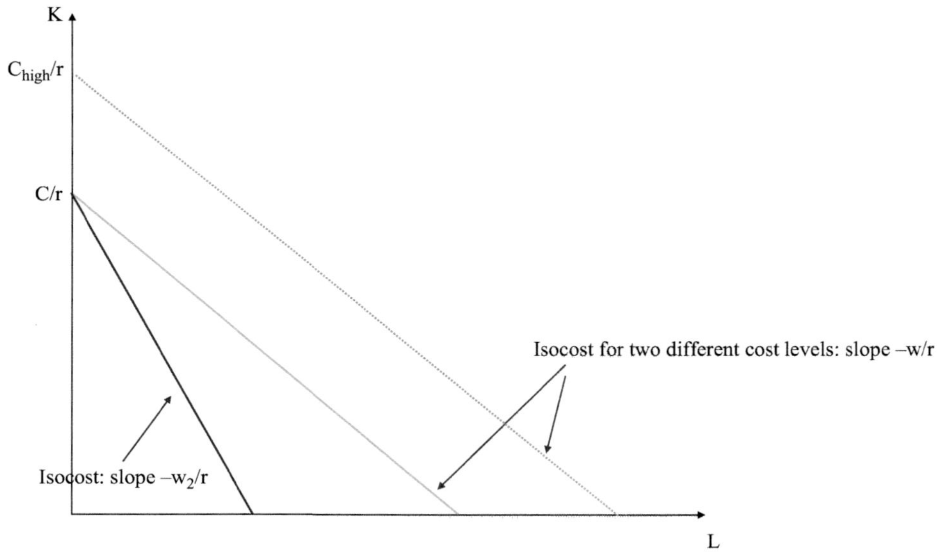

Figure 3.15 Changes in the isocost.

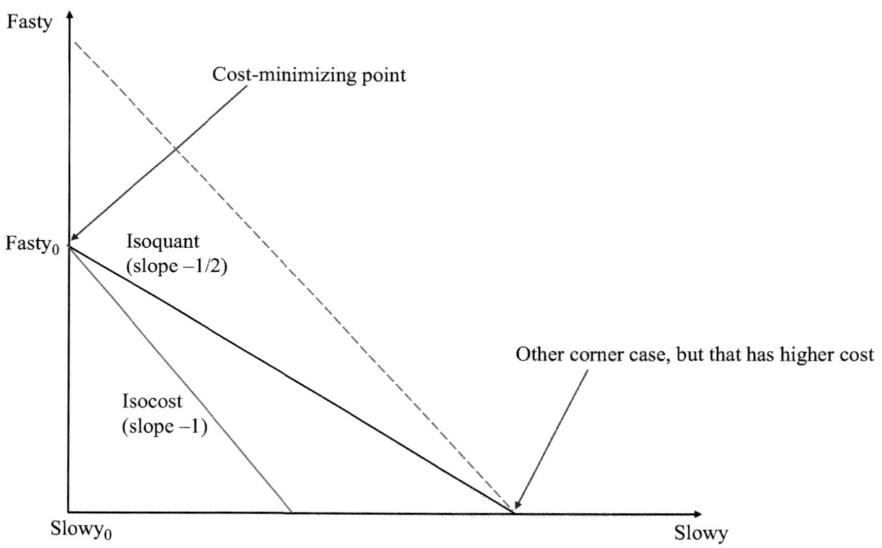

Figure 3.16 A corner solution. Video link for Figure 3.16: https://youtu.be/3QUDmZ_qQZQ.

enlightening, example, consider the case of a hair salon where consumers go to get haircuts. The only input is labor, but there are two types of labor: Fasties and Slowies. Fasties produce twice as many haircuts as Slowies per hour. Take a simple case of an isoquant representing 20 haircuts. If you need 5 Fasties to produce 20 haircuts, you would then need 10 Slowies to produce 20 haircuts. The isoquant thus has a slope of $-1/2$ (the intercept on the vertical axis being 5 and the intercept on the horizontal axis being 10). The barbers don't really interact, and hence the owner of the salon can always trade off one against the other; the owner can always replace 1 Fasty with 2 Slowies, irrespective of where on the isoquant that production takes place. Thus, there are no decreasing returns, and the MP_{Fasty}/MP_{Slowy} is constant. Now consider an isocost where the wages of Fasties and Slowies are equal. The isocost would then be

$$Fasties = \frac{C}{w_{Fasty}} - \frac{w_{Slowy}}{w_{Fasty}} Slowies,$$

where equal wages for the two factors give a slope of -1. Clearly, a line with a constant slope -1 is not going to be tangent to a line with a constant slope of $-1/2$. Instead, we use the logic of cost minimization to see what is the lowest isoquant that can be reached? Fasties are twice as fast but cost the same per worker: hence, the cost-minimizing solution is to only use Fasties. The firm is in a corner solution. Clearly, the other potential corner solution, to only use Slowies (indicated by the dashed line) would be associated with a higher cost of producing the same quantity.[14]

3.6 From cost minimization to a cost function

Different quantities are typically associated with different costs, as we illustrate in panel (a) of Figure 3.17. At a quantity of Q_1, the cost-minimizing choice of inputs implies an isocost that is associated with a cost of C_1. Likewise, at a quantity of Q_2, the cost-minimizing choice of inputs implies an isocost that is associated with a cost of C_2. In panel (b), we graph the resulting relation between quantity and cost. It is a cost function, and mathematically, we express it as $C(Q)$. The **cost function** describes the cost (in euros, dollars, or whatever currency we are using) of producing a certain number of units. Cost functions play a key

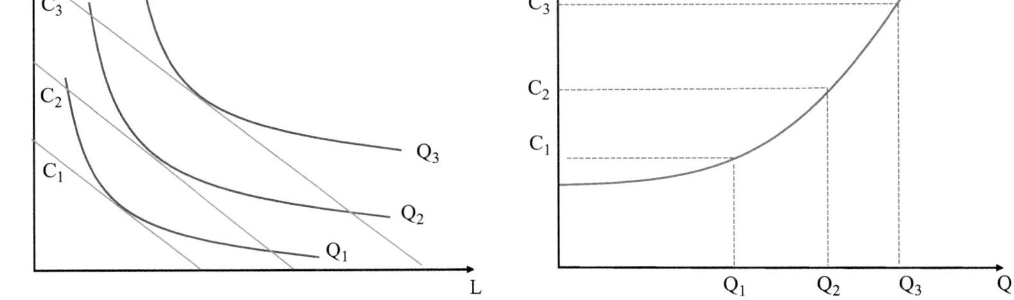

Figure 3.17 From cost minimization to a cost function. Video link for Figure 3.17: https://youtu.be/eCoXtmT7ycQ.

Table 3.4 An example of a cost function

In words	Quantity	Total cost	Average total cost	Marginal cost	Variable cost	Fixed cost	Average fixed cost
Standard abbreviation			ATC	MC	VC	FC	AFC
General form	Q	C(Q)	C(Q)/Q	dC/dQ	C(Q)-F	F	F/Q
Specific form (example)	Q	$30+Q^2$	$(30+Q^2)/Q$	2Q	Q^2	30	30/Q
	0	30			0	30	
	1	31	31	1	1	30	30
	2	34	17	3	4	30	15
	3	39	13	5	9	30	10
	4	46	11.5	7	16	30	7.5
	5	55	11	9	25	30	6
	6	66	11	11	36	30	5
	7	79	11.28	13	49	30	4.29
	8	94	11.75	15	64	30	3.75
	9	111	12.33	17	81	30	3.33

Video link for Table 3.4 and Figures 3.18 and 3.19: https://youtu.be/bUDgXbN9t24.

role in economics, and we will examine a number of questions related to cost functions in the following.

3.6.1 *Average costs and marginal costs*

In general form, the cost function is expressed as $C(Q)$. Take the example of an ice cream maker. The cost function might, for instance, state that her cost of making 20 ice creams is 40 euros, and the cost of making 30 ice creams is 50 euros. Give me a quantity and the cost function gives the total cost of producing that quantity. Different parts of the cost function will be of interest in different applications, and we use Table 3.4 to explain the different parts. The first column gives different quantities, and the second column gives an example of the cost of producing these units. In the case of Table 3.4, we assume that the cost function takes a specific form; in this case, $C(Q) = 30 + Q^2$. Thus, for instance, the cost of producing 3 units is $30 + 3^2 = 39$ euros, as illustrated in the table.

We can think of the cost function as aggregating two parts. One part are the **fixed costs**; these are costs that do not depend on how much is produced. They are unavoidable costs at the time horizon that is considered. For a retailer, it might, for instance, be the rent for the premises if it is locked into a rental agreement that expands some into the future. Even if the store is kept closed and nothing is sold, the rent needs to be paid. There are also **variable costs**, costs that vary with the quantity produced. For instance, for a retailer, the more that is sold, the more inputs are needed – to sell 100 sweaters, it must have at least 100 sweaters as input. In the specific case we are examining here, the variable cost is equal to Q^2. We could also express variable cost as total cost minus fixed cost since **total cost = fixed cost + variable cost**.

Next, **marginal cost** is the change in cost associated with producing slightly more. As with anything that we term "marginal" in economics, we are in essence measuring the slope of a curve at different points. The shorthand MC is often used to denote the marginal cost. Strictly speaking, the marginal cost refers to the derivative of the cost function. In the specific case here, with $C(Q) = 30 + Q^2$, the derivative $dC/dQ = 2Q$.[15] Thus the marginal cost, $2Q$, is upward sloping and depends on where we evaluate it. For instance, at Q = 2, the marginal cost is equal to 2 × 2 = 4, and at Q = 3, the marginal cost is equal to 2 × 3 = 6. Economists frequently use the term marginal cost somewhat more loosely, referring to a change of 1 (or a few) unit, as we indeed do in Table 3.4. The discrete change from 2 to 3 units is associated with going from a total cost of 34 to 39 euros. The change in cost is thus equal to 39 − 34 = 5 euros. As 5 is an average of the more precise measures of marginal costs when 2 are produced (MC = 4) and 3 (MC = 6), we see that it is an approximation.

We can also examine average costs. Sometimes students are a bit overwhelmed by different measures of costs, but remember to just think of what the name implies. For instance, **average total cost** is simply what it sounds like: the average total cost, with ATC as a common shorthand. So if it, as in the example, costs 55 euros to produce 5 units, the average total cost is equal to 55/5 = 11 euros. In general terms, average total cost is given by $C(Q)/Q$. It is not more complicated than thinking of average height in a group of individuals. **Average variable cost**, as well, is just what it sounds like: the variable costs divided by the number of units produced, and we often use AVC as a shorthand. And finally, **average fixed costs** is simply the fixed cost divided by the number of units.

Let us now analyze how these costs look in some more detail. First, just to get a visual impression, Figure 3.18 shows the total costs from the example in Table 3.4. The cost function is upward sloping; the more that is produced, the higher the total cost. We also see that slope of the curve is getting increasingly steep. The more the firm produces, the more it costs to produce additional units. If we were to draw tangents to the cost function, they would be increasingly steep. Of course, we have a name for those tangents – the tangent of the total cost curve is the marginal cost.

Figure 3.19 graphs the marginal cost. We also graph the average total cost. The figure is useful for highlighting the difference between average cost and marginal cost. The more

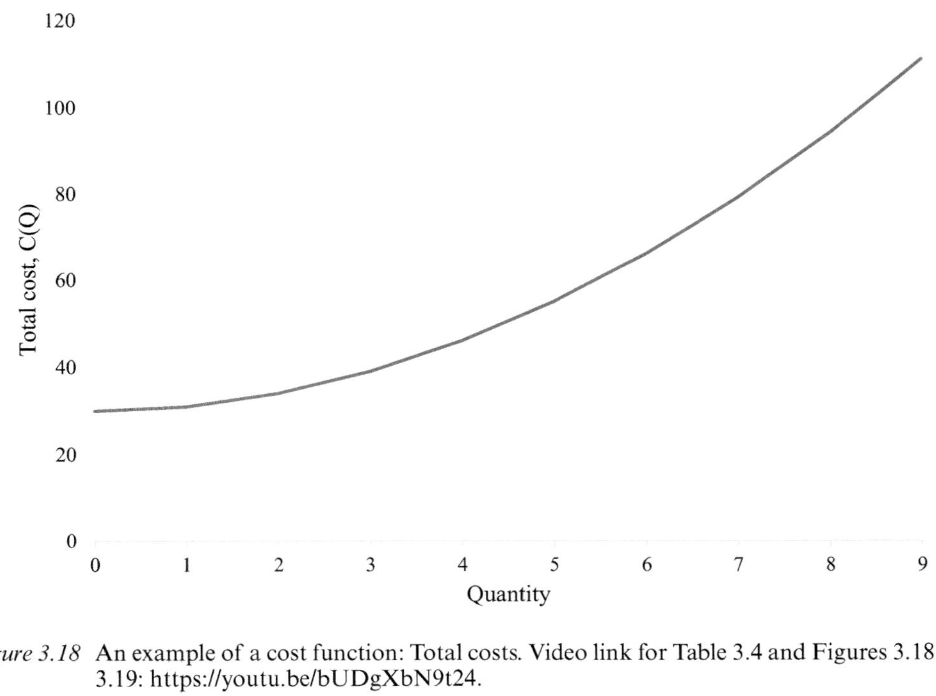

Figure 3.18 An example of a cost function: Total costs. Video link for Table 3.4 and Figures 3.18 and 3.19: https://youtu.be/bUDgXbN9t24.

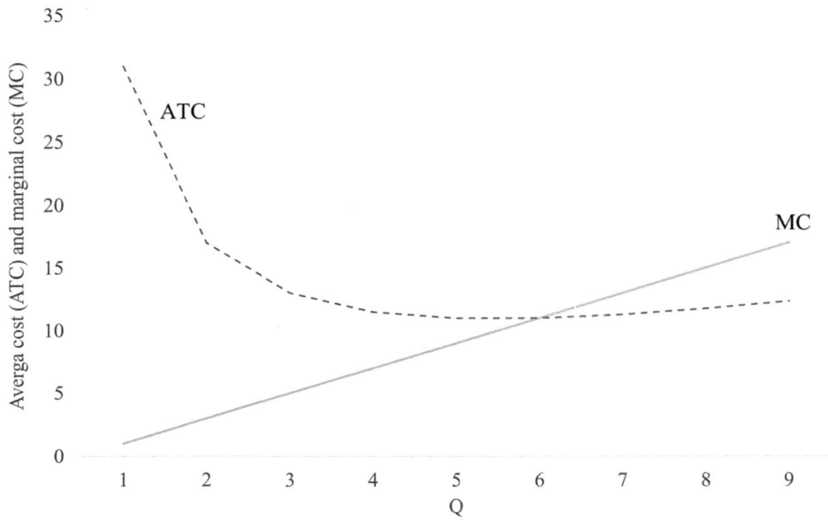

Figure 3.19 An example of a cost function: Marginal cost and average total cost. Video link for Table 3.4 and Figures 3.18 and 3.19: https://youtu.be/bUDgXbN9t24.

the firm produces, the more it costs to produce an additional unit in the case that we examine here. Such upward-sloping marginal costs are commonly observed and amount to a standard assumption when we work with simple illustrative models. We will return with a longer discussion of why that is the case when we discuss supply curves in the next chapter.

For now, let us instead highlight that average total costs look quite different from marginal costs. At first, average total costs are falling. No mystery here, we are spreading the fixed costs across more units, which means that the average costs are falling. To consider a simple intuitive example, note that an airplane manufacturer has tremendously high fixed costs of developing a new model, amounting to billions of euros. These costs are fixed and taken, no matter how many airplanes are produced. If Airbus only produced 3 planes of a certain type, the average fixed cost, the fixed cost spread on the number of planes produced would be very high. As more units are produced, the average cost is falling. However, we also noted that marginal costs are increasing. On the one hand, fixed costs are being spread on more units as we produce more; this is pulling average costs downward. On the other hand, the cost of producing additional units is increasing as we produce more. On the margin, each additional unit costs more to produce than the last. This leads to an upward pull on average costs. The combined influence of these two forces lead to the U-shaped pattern of the average total cost curve.

We can also note that the MC curve cuts the ATC curve at its lowest point. Intuitively, as long as we are adding units that are below the average, they help pull the average down. After the curves cross, we are instead adding units that are above the average and therefore pull the average up. To see the intuition, consider a group of people with an average height of 1.7 meters. Adding one person to the group who has a height of 1.6 meters will lower the average, whereas adding a person with a height of 1.8 meters will raise the average.

3.7 Additional aspects of cost functions

3.7.1 Costs in the long and short run

When we showed how the cost function was linked to cost minimization, we assumed that both K and L were variable. In many cases, we are interested in the short-run response of costs to changes in quantity produced – indeed, this is a typical application. In the short run, some factor of production may be hard to adjust, and economists often define the short run as the period during which one factor (typically capital) is fixed, rather than say that the short run is 1 year or 6 months. Intuitively, a bakery can relatively rapidly expand many inputs in response to a demand shock – to increase L, it can pay overtime and hire temporary staff, and typically, it can easily expand purchases of other variable inputs, such as flour and yeast on markets. Capital – the buildings and machinery – is likely to be much harder to adjust in a short time frame. This implies that the cost function in the short run (when capital is fixed) will differ from the cost function in the long run (when also capital can be adjusted). Figure 3.20 illustrates this and assumes that K is fixed at the level indicated by the horizontal line. It is similar to Figure 3.17, but now the isocosts that are relevant are the ones where the isoquant intersects the black horizontal bar rather than the point of tangency between isoquants and isocosts (apart from C_2, which is taken as a reference point). The, respective isocost is given by C_L, C_2, and C_H rather than the dashed alternative isocosts. Hardly surprising, costs are higher when the firm is not able to optimize in all dimensions, and thus the short-run costs are at least as high as the long-run costs. In other words, the long-run cost curve is flatter than the short-run cost curve.

3.7.2 Economies of scale

There are millions of rice growers in the world but only two producers of wide-bodied aircraft: Airbus and Boeing. In some industries, very many small firms seem to be operating

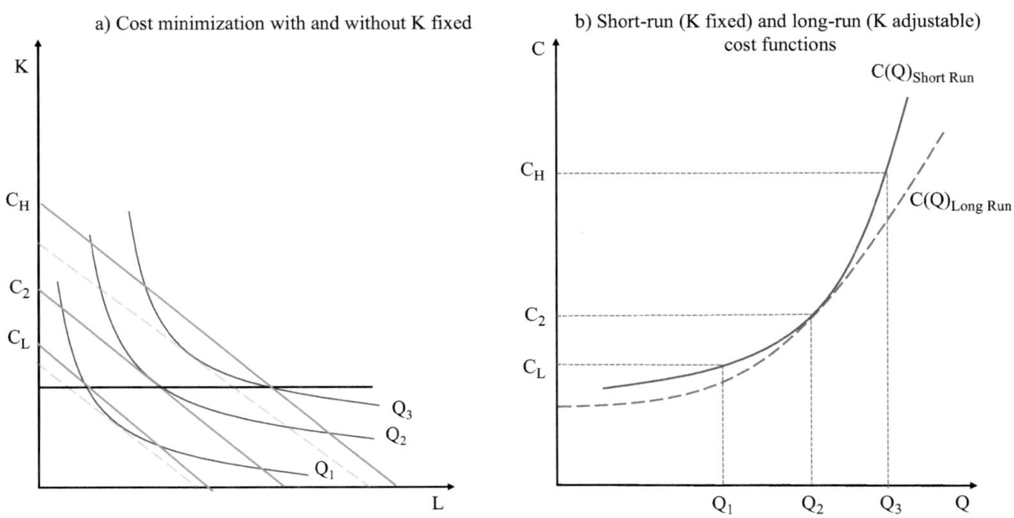

Figure 3.20 Cost function in the long and short run.

viably, whereas in other industries, there are strong forces that lead a few firms to completely dominate the market. One important aspect that helps explain such patterns concerns how the costs of production vary with the scale of production. We here focus on long-run costs, implying that input variables such as capital and labor can be adjusted. If the long-run average total cost curve is decreasing, this implies that a producer of larger volumes will have lower average costs. We refer to this as **economies of scale**.[16] As a large-scale producer will have lower costs than a smaller producer, the large-scale producer will have an advantage in competition. Markets where there are economies of scale therefore tend to become dominated by relatively few firms. Airplane production, pharmaceutical production, and car manufacturing are some examples that are commonly used. The cost advantage can come from the actual production technology (more about that later) but can also come from access to finance, from access to better terms from suppliers, or from better terms with customers and retailers that sell the product.

If the long-run average total cost is roughly flat, we say that there are **constant economies of scale**. If this is the case, smaller-scale producers are able to be competitive with larger-scale producers. Finally, **diseconomies of scale** refers to the case where average total costs are increasing when quantities produced increase. Here, large producers are at a disadvantage. Managerial difficulties in running very large organizations are an important reason for diseconomies of scale. Notably, the extent of economies of scale need not be the same across the whole range – the U-shape of average cost curves that we saw earlier is typical also for long-run average cost curves, as illustrated in Figure 3.21, but the minimum for something like airplane production is likely to come at a much higher quantity than for a business like Michelin-star level restaurants.

Closely related to the concept of economies of scale is the concept of **returns to scale**.[17] Returns to scale refers to the production function – what happens to *quantity produced* if the amount of inputs used change in the same proportion. If we double the amount of all inputs

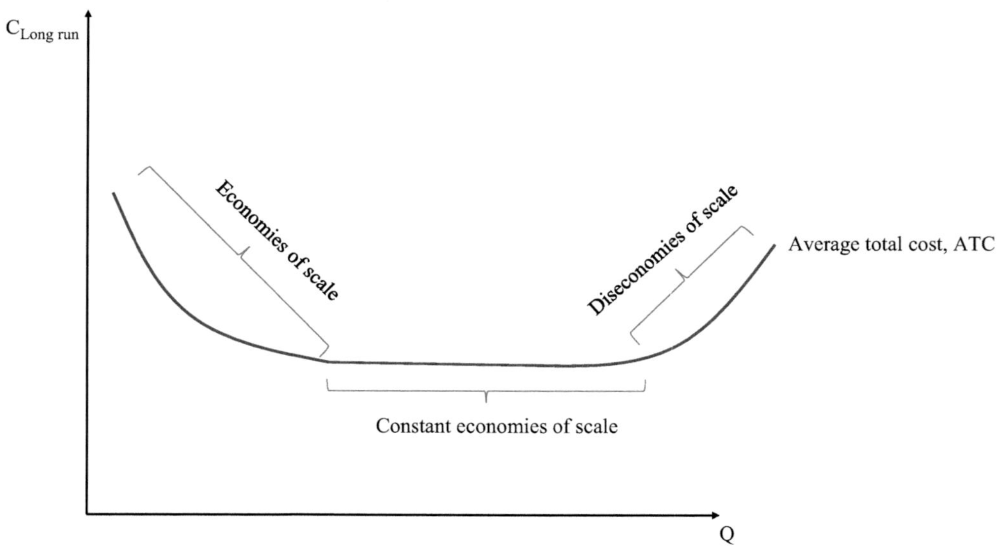

Figure 3.21 Economies of scale.

used and output also doubles, the technology has **constant returns to scale**. If we double the amount of all inputs used and output more than doubles, the technology has **increasing returns to scale**, and if output less than doubles, the technology has **decreasing returns to scale**. Clearly, the concepts of economies of scale and returns to scale are interlinked: If a firm scales up to a factory twice the size with twice the amount of people and output more than doubles (i.e., there are increasing returns to scale), it is likely that there also are economies of scale as long as input prices are not rising sharply or distribution runs into bottle-necks.

As a final point, it may be instructive to illustrate how we check what the returns to scale are for a particular production function. While the discussion relied on a doubling of inputs, the concept is more general than that, and we could replace "double" by a factor α (greek letter "alpha") that can be equal to 2 (as in the case of double) but also a lower number such as 1.1. Using the Cobb-Douglas production function from the start of this chapter that specified $Q(K, L) = \sqrt{KL}$, we can note that we have constant returns to scale if increasing both K and L with a factor α leads to an increase in Q by the same factor. If Q increases by more (less), we have increasing (decreasing) returns to scale. Using a subindex of 0 to denote a particular level of K and L, we can thus check if

$$\begin{aligned}
\alpha Q(K_0, L_0) &\overset{?}{=} Q(\alpha K_0, \alpha L_0)\\
\alpha Q(K_0, L_0) &\overset{?}{=} (\alpha L_0)^{\frac{1}{2}}(\alpha K_0)^{\frac{1}{2}}\\
\alpha Q(K_0, L_0) &\overset{?}{=} \alpha^{\frac{1}{2}+\frac{1}{2}}(L_0)^{\frac{1}{2}}(K_0)^{\frac{1}{2}}\\
\alpha Q(K_0, L_0) &= \alpha \underbrace{(L_0)^{\frac{1}{2}}(K_0)^{\frac{1}{2}}}_{Q(K_0,L_0)}
\end{aligned}$$

and conclude that $Q(K, L) = \sqrt{KL}$ exhibits constant returns to scale. Similarly, checking $Q(K, L) = K^2L^2$, we find that it exhibits increasing returns to scale since[18]

$$\begin{aligned}
\alpha Q(K_0, L_0) &\overset{?}{=} Q(\alpha K_0, \alpha L_0)\\
\alpha Q(K_0, L_0) &\overset{?}{=} (\alpha L_0)^2(\alpha K_0)^2\\
\alpha Q(K_0, L_0) &\overset{?}{=} \alpha^{2+2}L_0^2K_0^2\\
\alpha Q(K_0, L_0) &< \alpha^4 \underbrace{L_0^2K_0^2}_{Q(K_0,L_0)}.
\end{aligned}$$

Notes

1 The functional form where variables enter multiplicatively and are raised to the power of some exponent is known in economics as Cobb-Douglas.
2 See, e.g., Galor and Weil (2000).
3 A fixed amount of land and decreasing returns are key elements of the analysis of population developments following Thomas Malthus, as we will discuss later in this chapter.
4 This is the same iso as in isobars on weather maps, indicating areas with the same air pressure.
5 Another common form of notation would label the partial derivative as f_k.
6 There are many ways through which such shifts can be modeled – for instance, affecting labor more than capital. The simple way that we introduce it here – affecting all inputs in the same way – is a

common starting point and appropriate for an introductory course. In formal terms, we say that A captures Hicks-neutral technological change, named in honor of Sir John Hicks, who received the Nobel Prize in 1972.

7 We are thereby introducing additional production factors, capital in this case, and strictly speaking, we could formulate the production function as dependent on several production factors.

8 For a survey of productivity developments in agriculture, with a more modern focus, see, e.g., Ruttan (2002).

9 The source from which the graph is adapted provides a succinct and highly readable summary of the Malthusian trap, https://ourworldindata.org/breaking-the-malthusian-trap.

10 I also bring it up since I find Malthus a fascinating figure. In more recent treatments, he is often disparaged as a misanthropic preacher of doom who was obviously wrong in hindsight. I find him a thoughtful economist who inspired Charles Darwin and whose ideas are still useful in understanding the broad sweep of history (see, e.g., Galor and Weil 2000), as well as specific cases of Malthusian disasters, as covered in Diamond (2005). Notably, the person most identified with the green revolution, Norman Borlaug, emphasized the continued relevance of Malthus's ideas in his acceptance speech for the 1970 Nobel Peace Prize, https://www.nobelprize.org/prizes/peace/1970/borlaug/lecture/.

11 See, for instance, here: https://www.redbull.com/int-en/el-capitan-speed-climbing-records-history.

12 Arguably, related developments are even more impressive: In 1993, Lynn Hill became the first person to free climb the route – that is, using rope and gear only for protection, not for help in upward movement. In 2017, Alex Honnold free soloed an adjacent route not using rope or protective gear – the effort documented in the Oscar-winning movie *Free Solo*.

13 There's "iso" again – "same cost line."

14 One could also ask, What would the solution be if the wages were such that w_{fasty} was twice as high as w_{slowy}? The isocost would then have the same slope as the isoquant, and the solution would be indeterminate – any combination of Fasties and Slowies would then imply the same cost, and all combinations of workers would be equally attractive from the perspective of a cost-minimizing firm.

15 Another common form of notation is $C' = 2Q$.

16 Markets that are characterized by economies of scale often have some inputs that are not easily varied – such as a minimum level of research & development needed to be active in a market. Such discussions can become almost metaphysical, and we leave that for more advanced texts. Suffice it to say that Airbus and Boeing operate in a business where there seems to be large economies of scale – also when we allow firms to adjust factory size and the number of employees.

17 Indeed, it is not uncommon for textbooks to treat the two concepts as synonyms and present an intertwined intuition that can easily confuse; see Bell (1988) for a critique of this practice.

18 In the case of a Cobb-Douglas production function, we can simply check what the exponents on the inputs sum to: If they sum to 1, the production function has constant returns to scale; if they sum to more than 1, it has increasing returns to scale, and less than 1 implies decreasing returns to scale.

4 Supply by price-taking firms

Illustration 4.1 Finding the top of the hill. iStock by Getty Images, ahei.

4.1 Maximizing profit – An introduction

We continue our quest toward the goal of understanding how much will be supplied on the market. To do so, we will need to make some assumption about how firms behave. The standard assumption in economics is that firms want to maximize profit, and this is what we assume in the following. Let us first determine what we mean by that and then discuss some possible alternative stories and misunderstandings.

We define **profit** as the difference between revenue and costs. **Revenue** is whatever income is generated to the firm by selling goods and services. In its most basic form, revenue is simply the price of a good p times the quantity sold of that good, q. Costs can be direct outlays (as the cost associated with buying a particular input) but can also be more subtle cost associated with resources that are not used where they are most profitable. We will return with a deeper discussion of this, but for now, the term "cost" is used in the same way as it is used in everyday language.

We assume that firms want to maximize profit; they want the difference between revenue and costs to be as large as possible. Let us reflect on some different aspects of this.

DOI: 10.4324/9781003623854-5

- As we discussed in the introductory chapter, we want our theories to be "as simple as possible, but not simpler than that." In other words, we want models to capture the most important aspects of various situations, but we also want to keep them simple, transparent, and not more complicated than need be. Thus, in the models that we examine in this textbook, we mostly disregard time. In a setting with many time periods (as is common in more advanced applications), we would assume that the firm maximized the value of the firm, essentially the difference between revenue and cost but aggregated over many time periods. Making an investment today, and thus having a lower profit today, may be motivated by higher profits tomorrow.
- Could other decision variables be maximized? Of course. A foundation that owns a school might strive to maximize the educational attainment of the school only. A football club that is owned by members, like Real Madrid, might strive to win as many trophies as possible rather than to maximize profits. A winery might strive to maximize the prestige of its wines, rather than profits per se. In a market subject to strong competition, there will be a strong tendency for profit maximizing behavior to be rewarded; however, that is something we will discuss later in this chapter.
- Isn't the view of firms maximizing profits too narrow and cynical? One may note that successful founders of firms like Steve Jobs at Apple or Ingvar Kamprad at IKEA seem to be driven by passion to bring their products to the world and change how we live our lives. These passions are so much richer than just maximizing profits. This is true, but it is also worth emphasizing what we are after here. In our baseline models, we want to understand how much is produced and how prices are determined. Going back to the example of the rice market that we used at the start of Chapter 2, we want to understand the rice market in general, not the psychological motivations for founders. In terms of prices and quantities, the evidence is certainly in line with expectations of profit maximization. Similarly, top football players like Cristiano Ronaldo or Zlatan Ibrahimovic probably have loved playing and been driven by a passion for the game and for winning. But if we are looking at what deals they have signed and payments they have asked for, we're likely to get good predictive performance out of an assumption that they maximize profits.

  Let us also emphasize that there is a difference between what owners do with profit and what firms maximize. The Bill and Melinda Gates Foundation has given huge sums to help make the world a better place. But if we are to understand pricing at Microsoft (of which Gates is a large owner), an assumption of profit maximization is likely to get us far.
- What about corporate social responsibility, CSR? Is it showing that firms are more about doing good than just maximizing profits? Or is it just cynical window dressing on the part of firms? Putting small amounts of money on a save-the-dolphins campaign to motivate employees and customers while at the same time saving billions by tweaking the limits of tax planning? It is a topic that is worthy of a whole book, and while I at a personal level would love if high moral standards and a willingness to contribute were pervasive, I find it far too easy to find examples of firms acting in narrowly profit-maximizing self-interest for me to abandon the assumption of profit maximization as the starting point of our analysis of economics.

So without further ado, let us examine the profit maximization problem of the firm. To keep things as simple as possible for now, we assume that the firm produces one good only. Also for now, take it as a given that it wants to produce at least some of this good, and the question is, How much of the good should it produce? Denote quantity by q and assume that both $Revenue(q)$ and cost $C(q)$ are increasing in quantity produced. Standard notation in economics is to denote profits by π (greek letter "pi"). The profit is thus written as

$$\pi = Revenue(q) - C(q).$$

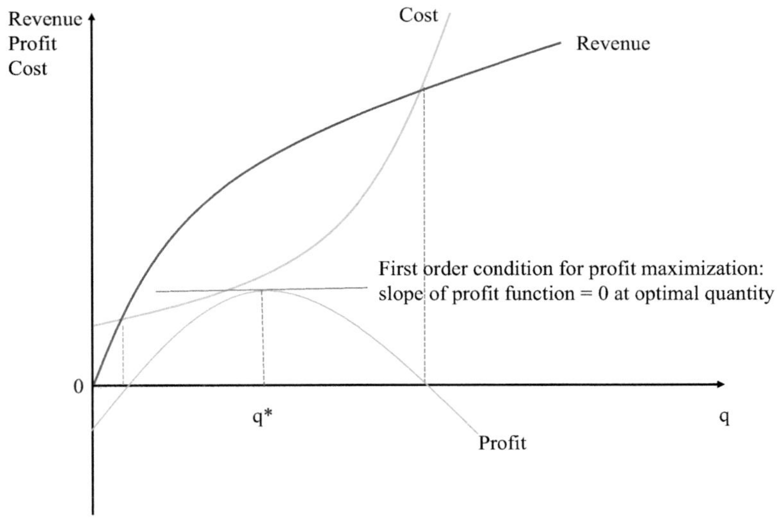

Figure 4.1 Profit maximization in the general case. Video link for Figure 4.1: https://youtu.be/I5ZQq5gioJE.

At what point are profits the highest? Figure 4.1 illustrates. We depict revenue, costs, and the difference between them, profit. Imagine that we are out hiking on the profit curve coming from the left. We are faced with an upward hike first, but after a while, we come to the summit; we're at the top of the hill, and if we continue further, we'll be walking downhill. Clearly, profits are the highest at the top of the hill, and that is associated with the quantity that we want to produce. How should we find this point? One way of doing is to use calculus – at what point is the slope of the profit function equal to zero? The slope of the profit function is equal to the derivative of the profit function with respect to quantity. In formal terms, we would say that the first-order condition for profit maximization is that the derivative of the profit function with respect to quantity is equal to zero. We thus use the rules of differentiation to find the quantity at which this holds. So the optimal quantity is given by the condition that

$$\frac{d\pi}{dq} = \underbrace{\frac{dRevenue}{dq}}_{\text{Marginal Revenue}} - \underbrace{\frac{dC(q)}{dq}}_{\text{Marginal Cost}} = 0,$$

or, in words, that

Marginal Revenue (MR) = Marginal Cost (MC).

Returning to Figure 4.1, we see that the slope of the marginal revenue is increasing at first and then becoming flatter and flatter. Similarly, the slope of the marginal cost curve is becoming steeper and steeper. The distance between the two curves (profits at the respective quantity) are increasing up to the point at which they have the same slope, after which, the distance between the two curves is decreasing. At the point where the distance is the greatest, the two curves have the same slope. A tangent to the revenue curve, the marginal revenue, then has the same slope as a tangent to the cost curve, the marginal cost. Marginal revenue equals marginal cost, or MR = MC, using widely adopted abbreviations. The actual slopes may, of course, differ across situations, as we shall see shortly, but the logic of MR = MC is pervasive in economics.

4.2 The supply of a price-taking firm: How much should be produced?

The decision for a profit-maximizing firm can be split into two parts. Should the firm produce the good at all, and if so, how much should it produce? We start with the second part of this decision. Assumptions that underlie what we do in the following are primarily two:

- There are many firms producing the good in question.
- The goods from different firms are seen as perfect substitutes by buyers.

The two assumptions are key for allowing us to draw a supply curve. These assumptions are often paired with additional ones to describe what we term a perfectly competitive market, but we save those for later when they become relevant for our conclusions.[1] Thus there are many producers that supply goods that are perfectly substitutable in the eyes of buyers. This means that if the firm were to set prices and would set a price higher than others, no one would buy from that firm. It can sell the quantity produced if it sells at the same price as others and would not sell more if it lowers the price further. We therefore say that the firm is a **price taker**. The firm acts as if its decisions on how much to produce does not affect market price. A farmer faces many decisions, but the market price of wheat in the world is not one of them. She would decide on a quantity to produce – how much wheat to sow and how intensively to cultivate, but note that the price is beyond her control.[2]

The revenue for a price taker is given by q times the *price* per unit. If 200 kilos of wheat are sold at a price of 0.5 euros per kilo, the revenue is $200 \times 0.5 = 100$ euros. As in the general case, we want to find the top of the profit hill, and the price-taking firm thus sets quantity to maximize

$$\pi = pq - C(q)$$

with the first-order condition for profit maximization given by

$$\frac{d\pi}{dq} = p - \underbrace{\frac{dC(q)}{dq}}_{MC} = 0.$$

If the firm acts as a price taker, it takes the price as a constant in the maximization problem, differentiating pq with respect to q yields p.[3] Thus the condition for the optimal choice of quantity is

$$p = MC.$$

Let us consider a specific example. Assume that costs are such that $C(q) = 10 + q^2$. Consider the case where $p = 12$. The profit maximization problem is thus

$$\max_q 12q - (10 + q^2).$$

Differentiating with respect to q yields

$$12 - 2q = 0$$

or simply rewriting

$$\underbrace{12}_{p} = \underbrace{2q}_{MC}.$$

We can now simply solve for the quantity at which $p = MC$ and use a * to denote the optimal quantity

$$12 = 2q,$$
$$q = \frac{12}{2},$$
$$q^* = 6.$$

We illustrate the case in Figure 4.2. The revenue is given by an upward-sloping curve with a slope of p; in this case, $p = 12$. For every additional unit produced, revenue increases by 12 euros. The cost curve has an intercept at 10; these are the fixed costs, and then the cost is quadratic in q since variable costs are equal to q.[2] The slope of the cost curve, the marginal cost, is thus given by $2q$. For instance, at $q = 3$ the marginal cost is equal to $2 \times 3 = 6$, and at $q = 4$, the marginal cost is equal to $2 \times 4 = 8$. At the point where quantity is equal to 6, the marginal cost is $2 \times 6 = 12$, and the slope of the cost curve is thus equal to the slope of the revenue curve, which is also 12. This determines the profit-maximizing quantity.

We can also use Figure 4.3 to illustrate the same case. Instead of having revenue and cost on the vertical axis, let us have price and marginal cost on the vertical axis. As before, we have quantity on the horizontal axis. Price is here represented by a horizontal line at $p = 12$,

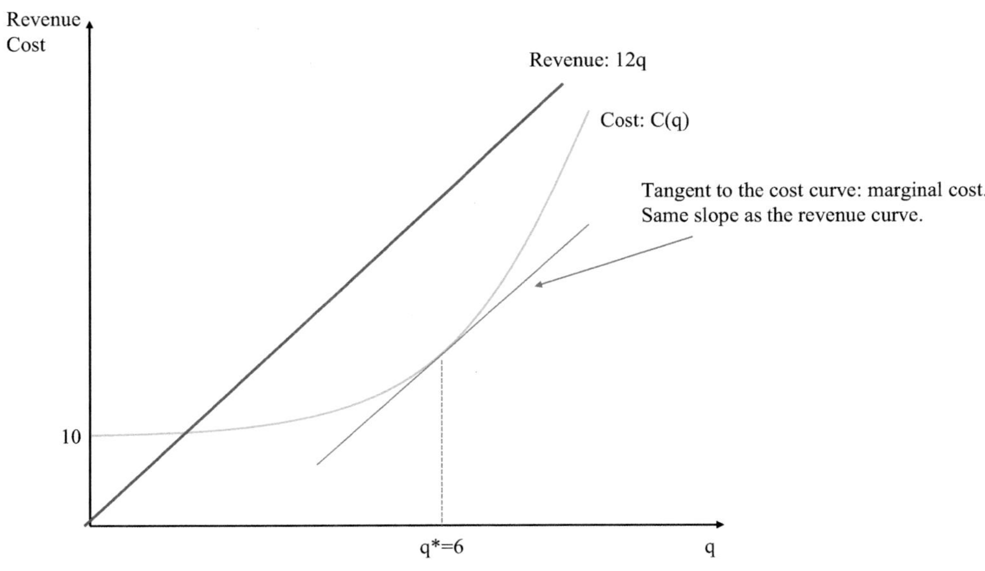

Figure 4.2 Profit maximization for a price taker: Example. Video link for Figures 4.2–4.4: https://youtu.be/_k7VZ-aWi5U.

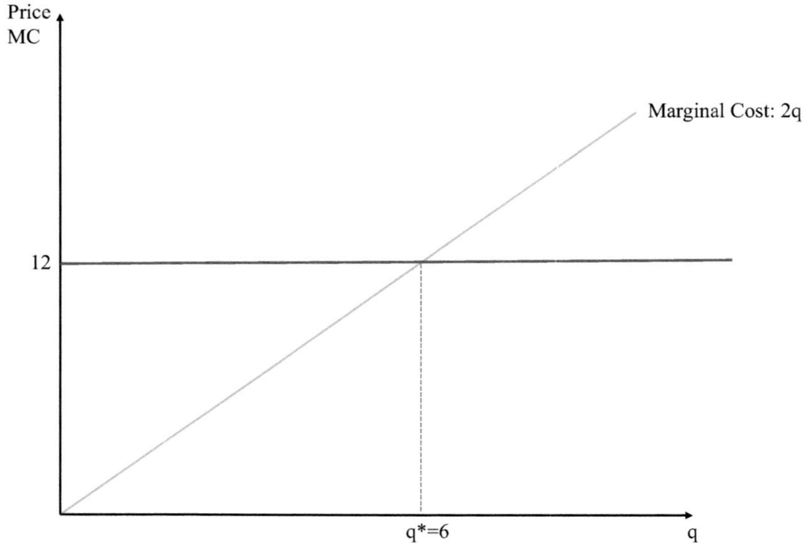

Figure 4.3 Profit maximization for a price taker: Example portrayed in another way. Video link for Figures 4.2–4.4: https://youtu.be/_k7VZ-aWi5U.

and the marginal cost curve is given by $2q$. This is another way to depict that $p = MC$ occurs at the quantity of 6 units.

So the quantity supplied is determined by the marginal cost curve and the price. We can easily see what happens at other prices. For instance, if price is equal to 10, the $p = MC$ condition in this case becomes $10 = 2q$, and thus at the price 10, the optimal quantity is 5. At a price of 14, the optimal quantity is equal to 7, and so forth. Different prices give different optimal quantities, as we illustrate in Figure 4.4. We said before that the supply curve of a firm determines how much the firm is willing to supply at different prices. We have here illustrated that *the supply curve of a price-taking firm is given by its marginal cost curve.*

Let us briefly explain why this is the case. Look again at Figure 4.4 and assume that price is equal to 12. The optimal quantity in this case is 6. What if the firm instead produces fewer than 6 units in this case? Well, price would then be above marginal cost, implying that if the firm increases production, revenue increases by more than costs do. This would clearly be beneficial for the firm. On the other side, if the firm were to produce more than 6 units when the price is 12, the last units produced would be associated with a greater increase in cost than in revenue. At $q = 8$, for instance, the increase in cost from producing more is given by $2 \times 8 = 16$ euros, whereas that additional unit only brings in a revenue of 12. Not good. The firm would then want to lower production, as profits in this case will increase if the firm produces less.

The example that we considered earlier has upward-sloping marginal costs. There are two reasons for this. First, it is often a realistic case. While marginal costs can also be decreasing, as well as constant, there are many cases where decisions are likely to be in a region where marginal costs are sloping upward. A second reason is that if the firm is a price taker, there will be no optimal quantity unless marginal costs are upward sloping at some point. We use Figure 4.5 to explain both of these points.

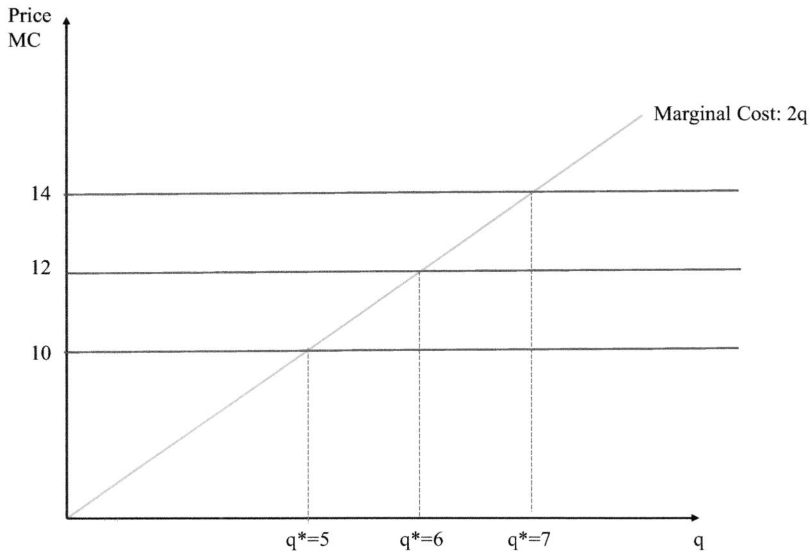

Figure 4.4 The supply of a price-taking firm is given by its marginal cost curve. Video link for Figures 4.2–4.4: https://youtu.be/_k7VZ-aWi5U.

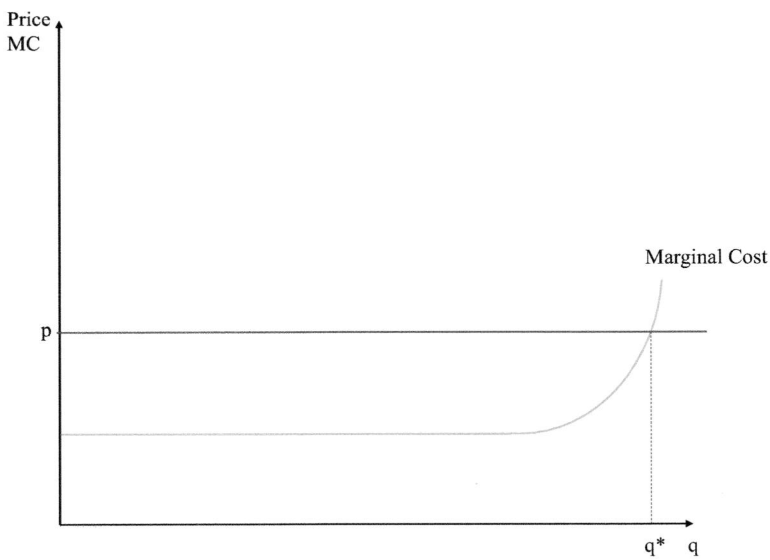

Figure 4.5 The shape of the marginal cost curve and profit-maximizing quantity.

Consider a firm that produces sugar in a factory. Major influencing factors of its marginal costs, such as the price of electricity and price of sugar canes used in the production, are likely to be constant over a wide range of quantities produced. We would therefore expect marginal cost to be roughly constant. Say, for instance, that each additional kilo produced leads to an increase in total costs of 2 euros. This is true for both the previous and the next kilo; in a case such as this, marginal costs are constant.[4] At some point, however, the factory is likely to start reaching capacity constraints, adding a night shift, pushing machines harder so that they require more maintenance, buying sugarcanes from suppliers further away, and so forth, all factors that lead the marginal cost curve to increase. For the second point, we just note that if the marginal cost curve was flat everywhere, the firm would want to produce more – continuing out into infinite quantities, as the marginal costs and prices would never intersect.[5]

4.3 The supply of a price-taking firm: Should the good be produced at all?

Should the good be produced at all? To answer that question, we need to examine profits as well. For the previous case, we can simply plug the optimal value of $q = 6$ into the profit function and find that

$$\pi = \underbrace{12}_{p} \times \underbrace{6}_{q*} - (10 + \underbrace{6^2}_{q*^2}) = 26.$$

It is also useful to illustrate the profit in a figure. A convenient way to do so notes that profit, in general form, is given by

$$\pi = pq - C(q).$$

A couple of simple operations where we first multiply the last term with q/q (which is like multiplying with 1) and then break out q allows us to write profit as price minus average total cost times quantity.

$$\pi = pq - C(q)\frac{q}{q}$$

$$\pi = \left(p - \underbrace{\frac{C(q)}{q}}_{ATC} \right) q.$$

Figure 4.6 adds the average total cost curve to the previous figure, and we can express profits as the shaded area. Profit is the difference between price and average cost times quantity. Average cost depends on how many units are produced, and clearly, the relevant quantity for our comparison is the profit-maximizing quantity of 6 units. So a price of 12 minus average cost at the quantity of 6 units $((10 + 6^2)/6)$ times 6 will again yield a profit of 26 euros.

Let us note a couple of points. First, many students have been exposed to some economics and perhaps seen expressions where $p = MC$ and been told that profits are zero. We'll come to the case when profits are zero later, but clearly, profits are not zero in the case that we have illustrated here. One might have the misconception that $p = MC$ sounds like that price equals cost and that in turn sounds like there are no profits. At this stage, we know better than that though. $p = MC$ means that the firm produces up to the point where $p = MC$. As long as $p > MC$, the firm is increasing profit as it increases production.

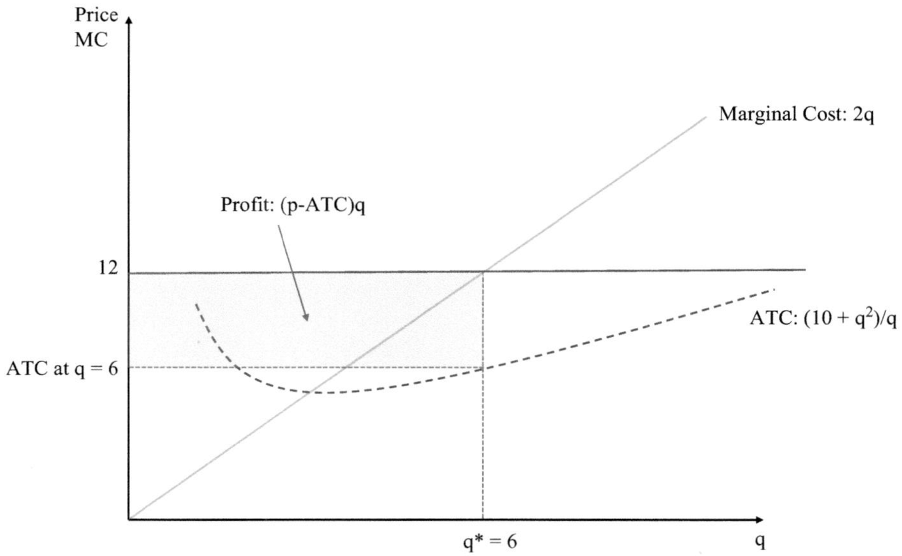

Figure 4.6 Profit at the profit maximizing quantity. Video link for Figure 4.6: https://youtu.be/s3m_qLAqMdc.

It might not make money on the very last unit that it produces, but it makes money on all the units leading up to that point.

A second point is that it can make profits at other quantities as well. At the quantity 5, for instance, profit would be $(12 - (10 + 5^2)/5) \times 5 = 25$ euros. So still a profit, but not as high as at the profit-maximizing volume of 6.

4.4 Profits: Positive, negative, or zero?

Earlier, we showed the case of positive profits. Profits can also be 0. In terms of Figure 4.6, we can think of this as the case where price falls to the point where it is equal to the average total cost at the point where $p = MC$, as illustrated in Figure 4.7.[6]

Profits might also be negative; consider, for instance, a case where the price is 12, as noted earlier, but fixed costs suddenly increased to 45 such that the cost function was instead given by $C(q) = 45 + q$.[2] The situation would look like the case in Figure 4.8. Given that the firm is producing, the profit-maximizing quantity is still given by the point where $p = MC$ and $q^* = 6$. At this point, the average cost is $(45 + 6^2)/6 = 13.5$, however, and higher than the price so that the profit is negative: $(12 - 13.5) \times 6 = -9$ euros.

Can it ever be profitable to produce at a loss in a case such as this? Yes, and here the distinction between fixed costs and variable costs becomes important. To consider a simple example, think of the case where a farmer has rented a field where pineapple plants have just been planted. The rental for the field is a fixed cost. Assume that after the lease is signed, something happens that forces the price of pineapples to fall sharply. At the time of signing, the farmer foresaw a regular year where she would at least be breaking even, but with the lower prices, she now foresees a loss if she continues taking care of the plants and harvests them. If she does so, she will face a number of variable costs where staff are needed for picking the pineapples and tending to the plants and fertilizer is needed to optimize the

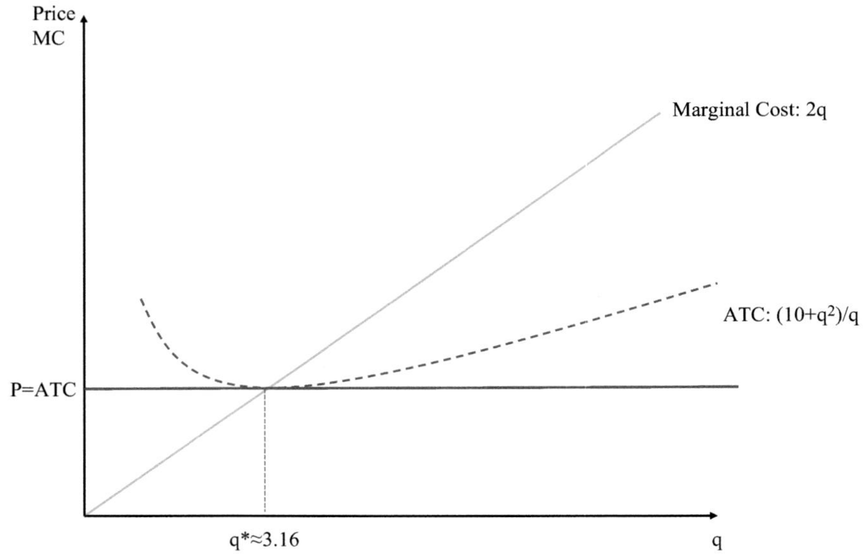

Figure 4.7 Zero profit. Video link for Figures 4.7 and 4.8: https://youtu.be/gxP_vDsWTrQ.

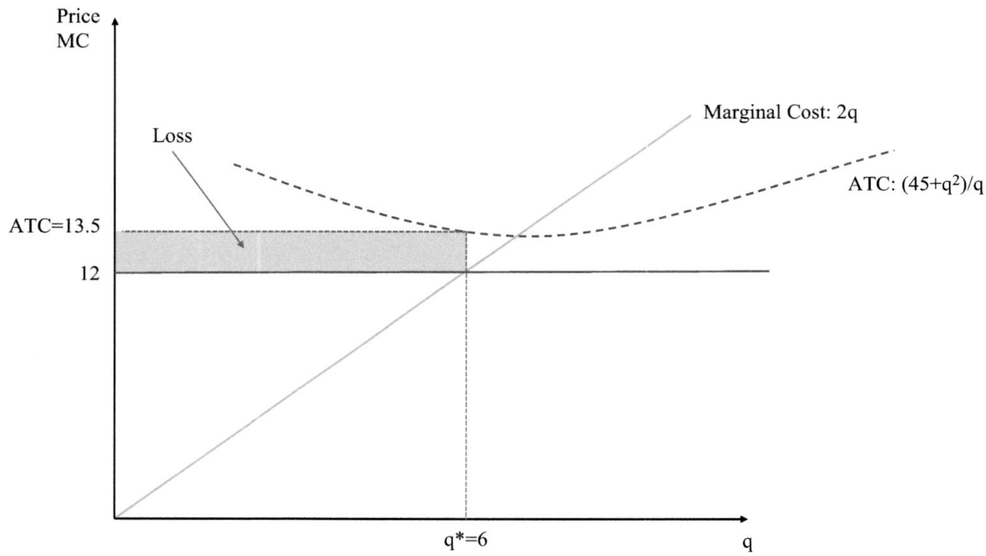

Figure 4.8 A loss. Video link for Figures 4.7 and 4.8: https://youtu.be/gxP_vDsWTrQ.

harvest.[7] These inputs can be varied according to how intensely the farmer wants to pamper the pineapples. Can it be worth it to bear these additional costs even if the operation as a whole makes a loss? Isn't it just throwing good money after bad money? Not necessarily. If revenue from continuing to tend to and harvest the pineapples is greater than the variable costs, the farmer will lower the loss by choosing to produce. Table 4.1 illustrates this. The

Table 4.1 Why a firm may produce at a loss

	No production	*Production*
Revenue	0	$p \times q$
Cost	Fixed cost	Fixed cost + variable cost
Profit	−Fixed cost	− Fixed cost + ($p \times q$ − variable cost)

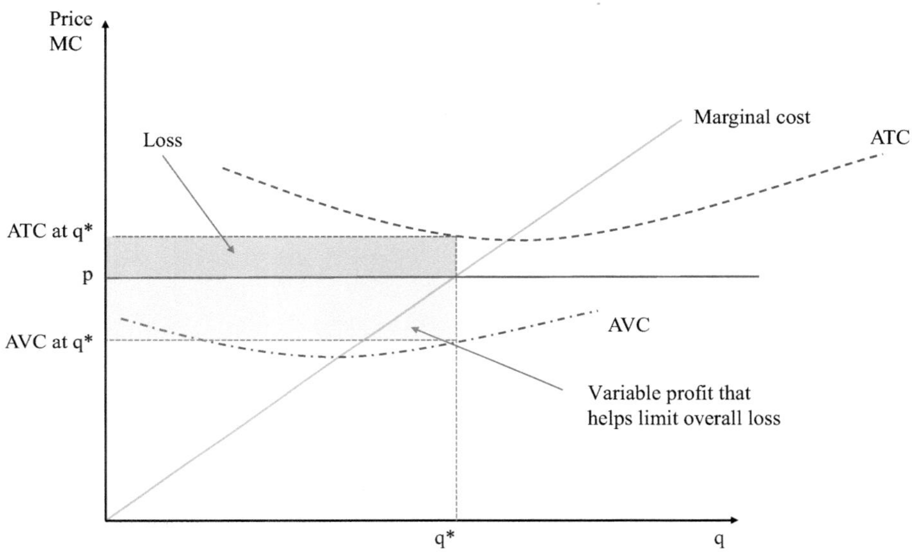

Figure 4.9 Operating at a loss in the short run.

fixed cost is lost anyway; the question is if the firm lowers the loss by continuing operations; if so, this is optimal in this simple setting. Clearly, this all hinges on the fixed cost being already commited to – had the pineapple grower foreseen that she would make a loss before she signed the rental contract, she would have abstained.

So the key question is if the firm covers the variable costs; sometimes the term **variable profit** is used to denote the difference between revenue and variable costs. Figure 4.9 illustrates the general case of a price taker that operates at a loss.[8]

4.5 From firm supply to the market supply

Putting together the results, we conclude that *a firm's supply curve is given by its marginal cost curve as long as price is above the average variable cost.* Figure 4.10 illustrates. This also makes it clear why factors that shift the marginal costs, such as changes in input prices, affect the supply.

Next, we turn to the **market supply curve**. At a given price, it is the sum of the quantities that all the firms together are willing to supply. We present an example with 3 firms, named A, B, and C, in Table 4.2. For instance, at the price of 3, only firm A is supplying. At the price of 4, market supply is higher for two reasons: Firm A is now willing to supply more at this higher price, and firm B is also willing to supply at this higher price.

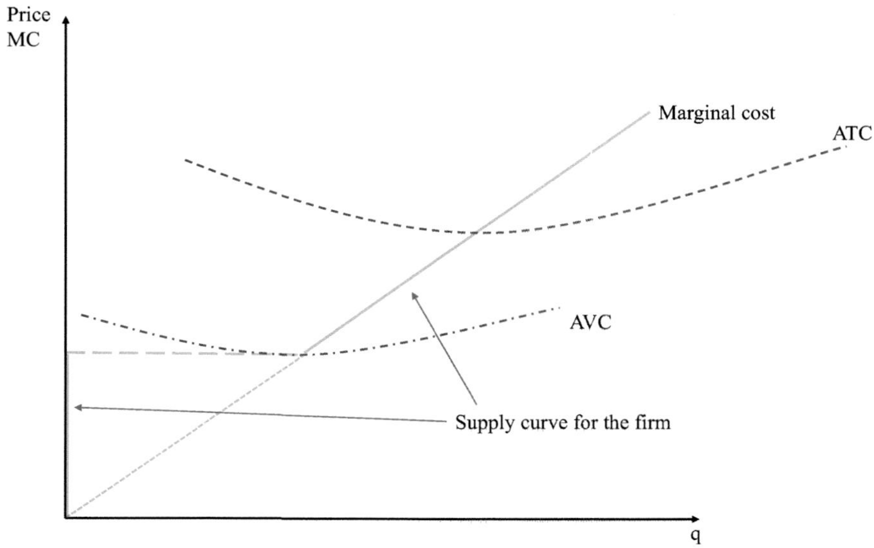

Figure 4.10 The supply curve for an individual firm.

Table 4.2 Market supply is the sum of individual firms' supply

price	*Firm A*	*Firm B*	*Firm C*	*Market supply (A+B+C)*
5	4	2	1	7
4	3	1	0	4
3	2	0	0	2
2	1	0	0	1
1	0	0	0	0

We can also show a graphical example. Consider two firms where supply for firm 1 is given by $q_1 = -2 + p$ and that of firm 2 by $q_2 = -4 + p$. Market supply is the sum of the quantities for the two firms, $Q = q_1 + q_2$. The summing of supply curves is straightforward, but we need to remember that the intercepts are different. A useful first step is to express the supply curves with price on the left-hand side and draw the curves. Thus for firm 1, we have $p = 2 + q_1$, and for firm 2, we have $p = 4 + q_2$, as we show in Figure 4.11. If the price is below 2, supply is 0. As the price is above 2 but below 4, only firm 1 supplies, and the market demand curve is equivalent to firm 1's supply.[9] Finally, if the price is 4 or above, the market supply is the sum of the two firms' supply curves: $Q = -2 + p - 4 + p$, which yields $Q = -6 + 2p$ or, if we rewrite, $p = 3 + Q/2$, which we draw in Figure 4.11 where market supply is marked in bold.

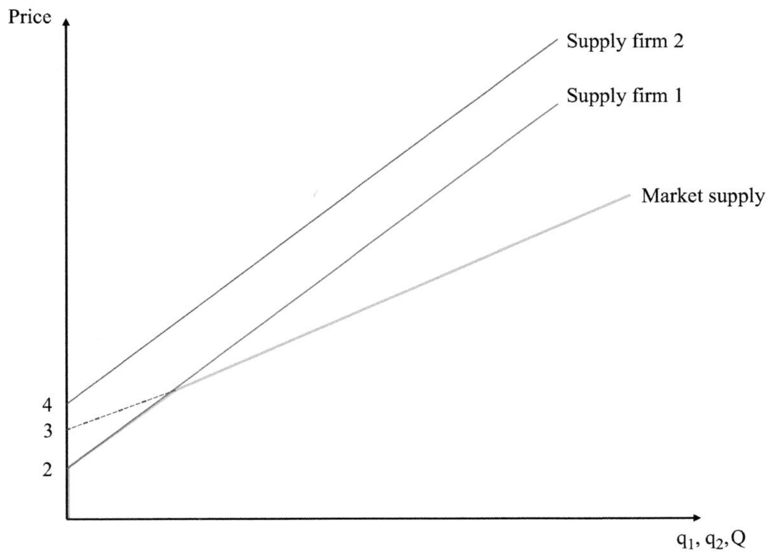

Figure 4.11 The market supply curve. Video link for Figure 4.11: https://youtu.be/XE7T8hFSlTc.

We can also express the market supply curve mathematically as follows.

$$Q(p) = \begin{cases} 0, & \text{if } p < 2 \\ -2 + p & \text{if } 2 \leq p < 4 \\ -6 + 2p & \text{if } p \geq 4 \end{cases} \tag{4.1}$$

The previous discussion may seem a bit dry. To connect back to the real world, let us illustrate with the market supply for electricity in Figure 4.12.[10] Different sources of electricity have very different marginal costs and hence very different supply curves. Electricity from wind and hydro have the lowest marginal cost, followed by nuclear power. Electricity generated by burning fossil fuel has the highest marginal cost. The steep slope of the supply curve at high quantities implies that swings in the demand can have very large effects on the prices. We also see that if demand could fall sufficiently to reach an intersection with supply without fossil fuel being used, the price could fall sharply.

4.6 Free entry and profits

A perfectly competitive market features many firms selling homogeneous products. An additional assumption behind perfectly competitive markets is that there is **free entry**; it is "easy" for new firms to enter the market and for old ones to exit. Farming is a good example. You need some time and capital to start a farm, but in most countries, you could rent some land, technology is widespread, and necessary inputs easily acquired in well established markets. It is relatively straightforward for new entrants to come into the market and start producing. It is also relatively easy to exit, you sell the land and the equipment. Contrast this with a case where you want to start competing with Airbus or Google. You need large

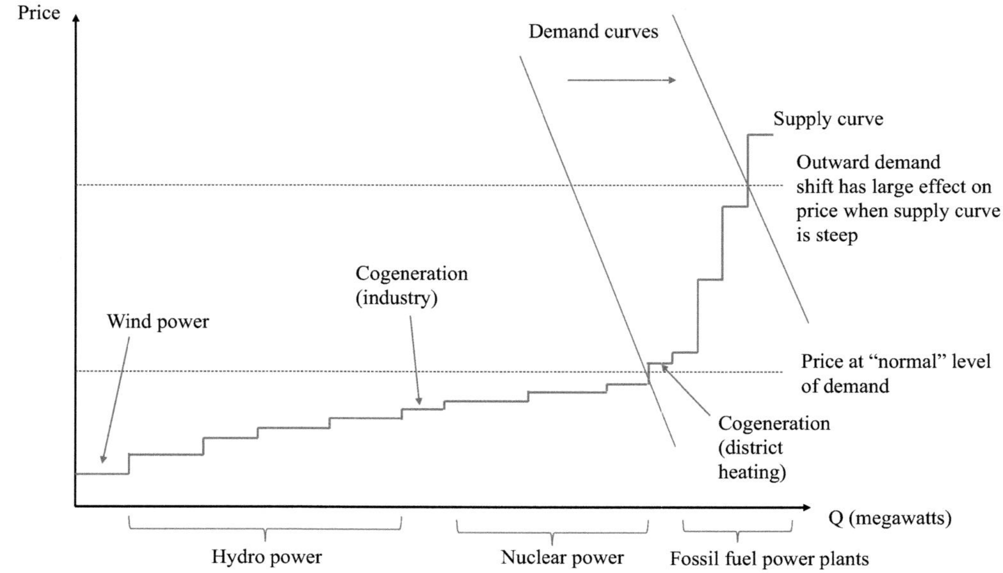

Figure 4.12 The market supply curve for electricity. Based on information from the Swedish Energy Markets Inspectorate: https://ei.se/konsument/el/elmarknaden.

amounts of capital and there are a multitude of legal and technological details that you as entrant don't have easy access to.

Let us examine the effect of free entry on equilibrium. Panel (a) of Figure 4.13 shows the supply and demand curves of a competitive market in equilibrium with price p_0 and quantity Q_0. Supply is made up of a large number of firms; for simplicity, assume that they are all the same, and panel (b) shows the situation for a representative firm that, faced with the price p_0, supplies q_0. As noted earlier, it supplies where $p = MC$, and we show a case where there are zero profits since $p = ATC$ at the profit-maximizing point.

Assume now that there is a positive demand shock for the product in question. Demand shifts to D_1, which drives prices up to p_1. How do firms respond to the increased demand? Well, the supply curve is given by their marginal cost curve, and the representative firm supplies more in response to the rise in demand. Quantity for the representative firm increases to q_1, as shown in Figure 4.14. As price increases, the firm makes a profit, as represented by the shaded area.

If there is free entry, we expect profits in an industry to attract entering firms. New firms will be entering, which in turn will be associated with a shift in the market supply curve. At a given price, more is supplied as additional firms are entering. How long can this occur? In principle, as long as there are profits to be had. Thus in a market where there is free entry, we expect that in the long run, profits are zero. In a perfectly competitive market, profit is zero because of free entry, not because quantity is set at a point where $p = MC$.

The zero profit condition is one that is subject to some misunderstandings; let us end this section with a discussion of costs and what are included in them. This might have been placed in the previous chapter that focused on costs, but I think it is easier to cover here where we are more motivated by context.

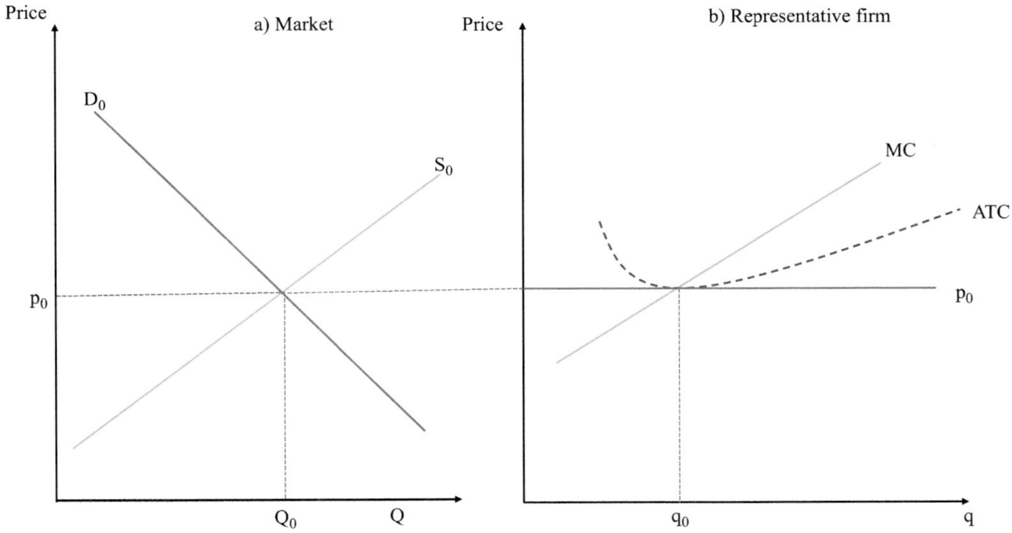

Figure 4.13 The relation between market supply and firm-level supply. Video link for Figures 4.13–4.15: https://youtu.be/tK-AM0T9OC4.

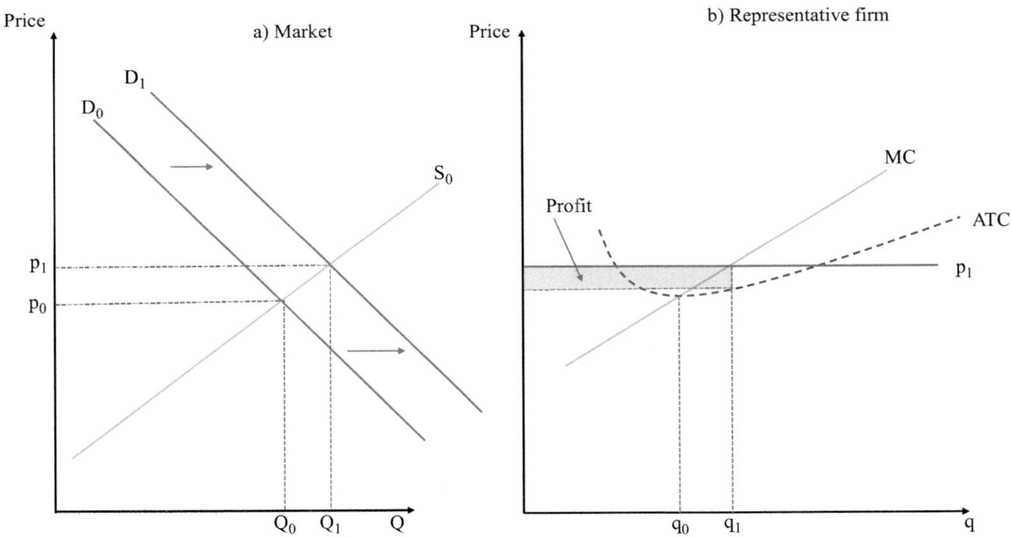

Figure 4.14 The relation between market supply and firm-level supply: Short-run response to a positive demand shock. Video link for Figures 4.13–4.15: https://youtu.be/tK-AM0T9OC4.

4.7 What do we mean by zero profit?

In the previous chapter, we examined costs. As noted, many costs are the same as when we discuss them in daily language. The cost of sugarcanes for a sugar producer is what it pays for them; the cost of labor is given by the wages paid, and so forth. We can call such direct

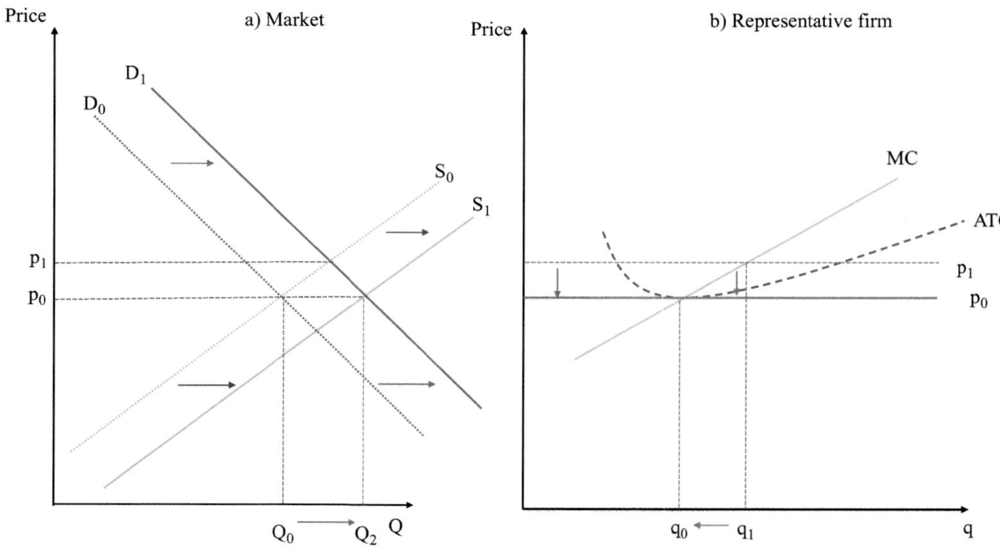

Figure 4.15 The relation between market supply and firm-level supply: The effect of entry. Video link for Figures 4.13–4.15: https://youtu.be/tK-AM0T9OC4.

outlays **accounting costs**. If we do the firm accounts, the firm's income statement will reflect all of these kinds of outlays.

4.7.1 Opportunity cost

Some other costs are more subtle. What about a saw mill that uses timber from its own forest in the production? And what about an entrepreneur who works in her own firm without withdrawing any remuneration from the firm? Or how should we think of her own savings that she has invested in the firm? Are all these free? No. A key concept in economics is **opportunity cost**, which is what you're giving up by using a resource – the payoff from the best alternative use of a resource. Colloquially, we as economists have many ways to express this. "There's no such thing as a free lunch," and "for everything that you do, there's something that you don't do" are but two of those classics. Clearly, we would want to take account of that in our decision-making.

Suppose that I happen to own land in a prime location in the Champagne region of France. A rough estimate shows that the grapes from one hectare can be sold for around 50,000 euros.[11] Say that instead of growing grapes and selling them for Champagne production, I grow apples on this land. There's nothing special about the price of apples in Champagne, so I would essentially be saying no to 50,000 euros for the pleasure of growing my own apples. Assume that this land has been inherited, and in this sense, I have no accounting costs for it. Should I treat the land as a free input into my apple production? No – the opportunity cost of using the land for growing apples is what I could gain from growing grapes on it in this case. Similarly, if I happened to own a part of Central Park in New York City, I might use it to grow wheat. The revenue I get from selling the wheat may be substantially higher than my direct outlays for labor, use of tractors and harvesters, but presumably, I can use the land for something more profitable.

Similarly, the opportunity cost of an entrepreneur's time is whatever she would be earning if she were engaging in the next best alternative. The opportunity cost of timber used in a saw mill is whatever the timber could be sold for on the market. The opportunity cost of capital[12] is whatever return that capital could earn if invested somewhere else.

When we talk of costs in economics, we want them to include opportunity costs, and when we want to be extra clear that this is what we mean, we use the term **economic cost**, which is defined as the sum of accounting costs and opportunity costs.[13]

Thus, there may at first appear to be a contradiction between our prediction that there are zero profits in equilibrium in an industry faced with free entry and observing accounting profits for lots of farmers and others in commodity markets. But then we are forgetting that zero profits refers to revenue minus *economic costs*. For instance, the capital that is used in a firm should be getting some return that is valued at the next best investment opportunity. Thus zero profit could be interpreted as zero profit when all factors of production have gained a market-level return.

Note also that opportunity cost as a concept can become almost metaphysical. A long chain of what-ifs could be linked, but that is not the way we think of it in practice. We want to catch the big fish here – not grow apples in Champagne without thinking of what the land could be used for instead and making sure that we don't forget that time and money used in a start-up could be used elsewhere. This is one reason why, for instance, a lot of firms are using internal prices (also known as transfer prices) when one branch of a firm (e.g., a saw mill) is using resources from another branch of the same firm (e.g., the forest management division).

Finally, note that *accounting profits* can differ a lot between firms in a market with free entry. To intuitively see why, let us return to the Champagne example. A hectare of wine-growing land in the Champagne region costs around 1 million euros, and the average size of a farm is around 3 hectares. So someone who has bought this with borrowed funds is going to have large interest payments that lower accounting profits, whereas someone who inherited the land is likely to make large accounting profits. We would say that there is zero profit in the actual wine-growing business but that there is a value to owning a scarce resource, in this case land in the Champagne region. We sometimes term the return to owning a scarce resource as **economic rent**.

4.8 Supply in the long run

We saw in this chapter how a demand shock triggered entry. In the case that we examined, the price returned to the original level as additional firms entered and shifted the supply curve. Another way to say the same thing then is that the long-run supply curve is horizontal in such a case. This is not a general result. The long-run supply curve can instead slope upward if it is hard for new firms to enter. The case of electricity that we examined earlier is one example; hydro power has low marginal costs, but there are a limited number of locations that can be used for hydro-electric dams. There is a limit to how new entrants can replicate what existing firms are doing. If an industry relies on a scarce input, and the price of this input is driven up by the demand increase, this will also result in an upward-sloping, long-run supply curve.

On the other hand, long-run supply curves can slope downward if there, for instance, is learning-by-doing; the case where it becomes cheaper to produce the more is produced. Such effects can take place at the level of the firm or the product and have been documented to be important in, for instance, airplane production (Benkard (2000)) and shipbuilding, where US shipbuilding of the so-called Liberty type of ships during World War II is a classic example of learning-by-doing (Thompson (2001)). Learning-by-doing can also be present at wider level of type of product, where large decreases in the cost of computing power by microprocessors over time is a prominent case – see, e.g., Irwin and Klenow (1994).

Notes

1 For the curious, or those who return to this point, the main assumptions are free entry, no informational asymmetries, and no externalities.
2 Again, we simplify; in reality, there is, of course, uncertainty regarding weather, and when making the decision on how much to sow, the market price at the time of harvest is unknown. Such issues can be incorporated into the model, but as economists, we first see how much mileage we can get out of a simple model where we have abstracted away from the time dimension. Similarly, a farmer may choose to differentiate her product (we cover product differentiation in Chapter 10) and try to market premium wheat to a few select customers. This is not key if we want to understand the global wheat market that is dominated by price-taking farmers producing homogeneous products.
3 Remembering the rules of differentiation, this is no different from that; if you differentiate $3x$ with respect to x, the resulting derivative is 3.
4 Note, it is not *costs* that are constant, just the *marginal cost* that is constant. This is the case if costs are increasing at a constant rate as more is produced.
5 At some point, well it would of course be a dominant supplier on the world market, and the price-taking assumption would no longer hold, but you get the point.
6 In this example, we can find the quantity, for instance, by using the fact that this occurs at the point where ATC and MC intersect. Hence, in this case, we can solve $(10 + q^2)/q = 2q$ for q and get $q = \sqrt{10} \approx 3.16$, and price in this case is approximately 6.32 (found by solving $p = 2q$).
7 The example is inspired by Sarpong (2002).
8 Here we have followed standard textbook cases and let average variable cost also follow a U-shape. This would be the case if marginal costs were initially quite high and then fell before leveling out and later increasing. In the numerical case that we examined earlier, the average variable cost would be an increasing straight line since average variable cost in that case is simply given by $q^2/q = q$.
9 You may wonder how this rhymes with our assumption that there are very many firms. It is just a simplified illustrative example; you could think of it as the supply of 20 firms instead.
10 The conceptual figure is based on the electricity supply on the Swedish electricity market and hence reflects the sources of electricity used there. Source https://ei.se/konsument/el/sa-har-fungerar-elmarknaden, accessed January 30, 2023.
11 Boundaries of the Champagne region are fixed, and the price of wine-growing land in the Champagne region is above 1 million euro per hectare, see for instance https://www.thedrinksbusiness.com/2020/08/champagne-agrees-dramatic-yield-reduction-for-2020-harvest/.
12 In this case, we're thinking of capital in the common language sense, "actual money" that is in a bank account or in some fund that invests in the stock market.
13 This is the most common definition. Some use the term "opportunity cost" as a synonym for economic cost and hence include accounting costs in opportunity costs. I can see the logic of doing that but find it more pedagogical to define it as above, and this is indeed the way that it is most commonly defined.

Part II

Where does demand come from?

The next two chapters are closely analogous to the previous two chapters. There we built from technology and costs to derive supply curves. The path that we pursue in these next two chapters is to build a model of how individuals choose and how we can aggregate those choices to a demand curve. We will see how many of the tools are very similar. Note also that whereas the last chapter explicitly focused on supply of homogeneous products, the tools of demand that we apply in the following can be directly applied to both homogeneous and differentiated products.

We assume that people try to do as well as possible. But how can we operationalize that? What does it take to generate a model that we can use to make predictions and use as a foundation for empirical work? In Chapter 5, we introduce the ingredients for that model, which by many are seen as the core of the rational choice model. We will also discuss some limitations of the framework. Chapter 6 then moves from optimal choice to a market-level demand curve and develops tools for measuring the effects of changes in prices and incomes on demand.

DOI: 10.4324/9781003623854-6

5 Consumer choice

Illustration 5.1 Choices, choices. iStock by Getty Images, Ranta Images.

5.1 How can we model choice?

We now turn to modeling rational choice by individuals. We assume that an individual faces constraints (e.g., in terms of income) and makes choices so as to do as well as possible, given the constraints. This, sounds almost tautological but we will see how we can put some structure into this statement.

As we build a demand system from the ground up, starting with individual choice, we rely on three basic premises:

- We know how we value things, and those valuations are stable. We use the term "preferences" to describe what we want and like.
- We face constraints in terms of, e.g., time and money.
- We try to do as well as possible given the constraints we are facing.

We will discuss these different building blocks in turn.

DOI: 10.4324/9781003623854-7

5.2 Preferences

How can we build a system that allows us to move from "what we like" to a demand curve? Clearly, we must make some formalization about what we like and try to be more precise than just say that I like kayaking and Granny Smith apples. We will be looking to examine choice between what we term different **bundles** of goods and services. A bundle is described by the goods and services that are contained in it, and how many of each. Studying business administration in Bangalore can be seen as choosing one bundle of goods and services. Studying engineering in New Delhi as another bundle. The model of choice that we build rests on the idea that individuals are able to rank different bundles. We know our **preferences**, how our tastes allow us to rank different bundles. In order to be able to build a consistent model of how individuals choose, we make two assumptions about those preferences.

- *Preferences are complete*. We can rank all bundles. Given two bundles A and B, we can say if we prefer A to B, B to A or whether we are indifferent between them.[1]
- *Preferences are transitive*. That is, they "hold in transit." If A is preferred to B and B is preferred to C, then transitive preferences imply that A is preferred to C. Thus if we know that Yoichi prefers Apples to Bananas, and Bananas to Cherries, the transitivity assumption allows us to infer that he prefers Apples to Cherries. Transitivity allows us to predict choice in a chain of comparisons.[2]

In addition, we often add an assumption that "more is preferred to less."[3] Goods and services are something that we like to have more of. I'd like to have more food, more entertainment, more leisure and so forth. This is not meant to imply that there is some crazy dash where whoever consumes the most is the happiest; it is more that interesting economic choices are concentrated in the area where you have to choose between different objectives. There is also the possibility of goods that you want less of: for instance pollution and noise. To simplify the analysis, we typically label such goods as "bads" and redefine the good as absence of pollution or noise.

In many applications, we will be interested in bundles that contain many goods and services but for illustration, we will focus on two, call them Food (denoted by F) and Entertainment (denoted by E). We describe some different bundles in Table 5.1.

Let us plot these different bundles in Figure 5.1. We measure units of entertainment on the vertical axis (think of it as hours spent watching theater plays or some other form of entertainment) and units of food on the horizontal axis (kilos of food that you put on your plate in a restaurant where you pay by weight if you want a visual image).

How can we rank these bundles? First, note that if we are willing to use the "more is better" assumption, then bundle D is preferred to bundle C. It contains more of both

Table 5.1 Examples of consumption bundles

Bundle	*Entertainment*	*Food*
A	4	2
B	8	2
C	3	3
D	6	5

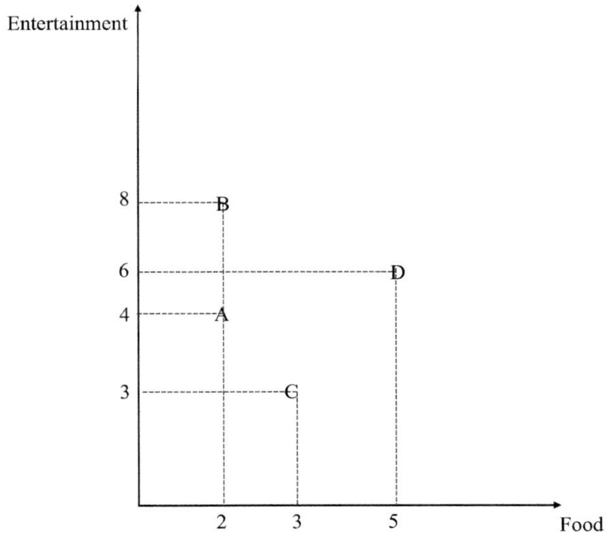

Figure 5.1 Some different bundles

goods.[4] How can we compare the other bundles? Compare *A* to *C* for instance: bundle A contains more entertainment (4 *E* rather than 3 *E*) but less food (2 *F* rather than 3 *F*) than what bundle C does. My ranking of these clearly depends on how hungry I am and how much I like entertainment. The assumption that more is better is not sufficient to compare these bundles.

How can we compare bundle A to C? To be able to compare bundles more generally, we introduce a new tool, **indifference curves**. An indifference curve connects all the bundles that a consumer views as equally attractive; she is indifferent between them. Indifference curves have a very close analogy to the isoquants that we studied earlier – both connect points in a diagram that are equivalent in some way. Indifference curves further from the origin are preferred to those closer to the origin. This follows from the more is better assumption. Figure 5.2 illustrates with two indifference curves. Assume that bundles *A* and *C* are on the same indifference curve, and hence the individual is indifferent between them. This also means that we can compare bundle *B* to *C*, for instance, and conclude that *B* is preferred to *C*. We can deduce this from indifference curves further from the origin being preferred – to additionally highlight why, consider the new point *G* in the figure. From "more is better," we know that *G* is preferred to *A*, and we know that the individual is indifferent between *G* and *B*. From transitivity, we can thus conclude that *B* is preferred to *C*. Any bundle is on some indifference curve (this follows from the completeness assumption), and we see that the framework allows us to establish the preference relation between any two bundles.

To continue the analogy with isoquants, note that while the slope of the isoquant represented how one input could be substituted for the other while maintaining the same quantity of production, the slope of the indifference curve represents how one good can be traded off against another with the consumer still equally well off. Just as with isoquants, we can think of different cases:

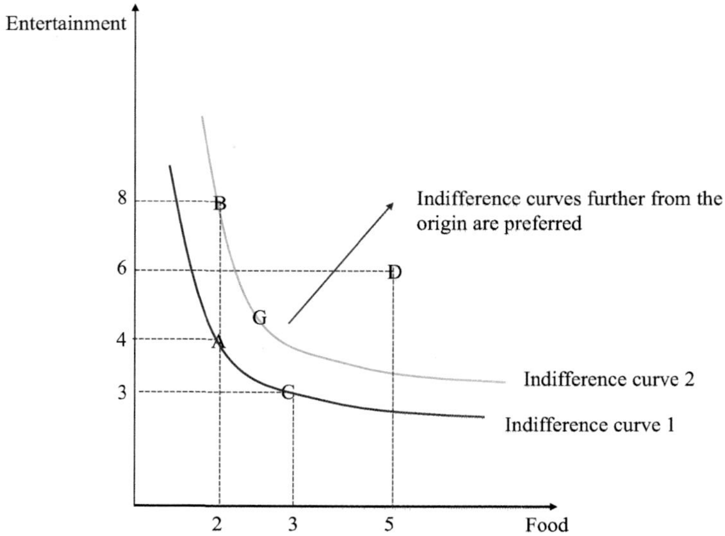

Figure 5.2 Ranking of bundles. Video link for figure: https://youtu.be/FHuqp1BTDyU.

- **Perfect complements.** These are goods that are consumed as a fixed combination. Left and right shoes is a classical example. Indifference curves for perfect complements are L-shaped. Consider the case where you have 2 left shoes and 2 (matching) right shoes. Adding more right shoes only will not make you better off, only if you receive one more shoe of each type will you be better off.
- **Perfect substitutes.** These are goods where the consumer is always willing to trade off one good against the other at a constant rate and be equally well off. Indifference curves are straight lines. We hardly use paper money anymore, but it presents an intuitive example. I'd always be willing to trade one 20 euro bill for four 5 euro bills and be equally well off.
- **Imperfect substitutes.** Preferences that are between the two extremes just mentioned. The individual is willing to trade off one good against the other but in what proportion depends on how much of the respective good she has in the bundle.

While most of us would probably subscribe to the preferences for shoes and bills presented earlier, it is important to note that indifference curves capture an *individual's* preferences, and these may well differ across individuals. It might even be that what for one person is a good is something that another person wants to avoid (a "bad"). Clearly, the indifference curve for a local Australian food like Vegemite will differ between a typical Australian and a typical Frenchman. Similarly, while a carnivore would get utility from meat, a vegetarian would not.

Let us examine the case of imperfect substitutes in some more detail in Figure 5.3. Assume that there are two products only: potato chips and soft drinks. You can think of this as your potential bundles for an evening of binge-watching, and the units are small bags for chips and small cans for the soft drinks. *If* the two goods were perfect substitutes, the indifference curve would be given by the dashed straight line. With perfect substitutes, you'd be indifferent between 4 bags of chips and no soft drinks, two of each or no chips

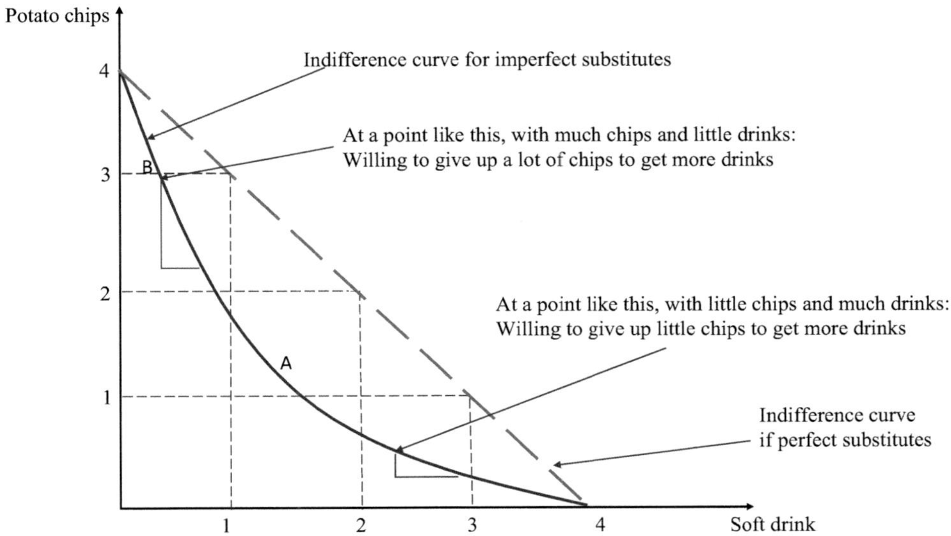

Figure 5.3 Indifference curve for imperfect substitutes. Video link for figure: https://youtu.be/3cNy93CS5QU.

and only soft drinks. You'd always be willing to trade one bag of chips for one soft drink, no matter how many of each that you have. The indifference curve would in that case have a constant slope of -1. But, if products are *im*perfect substitutes, your willingness to trade off one for the other depends on how many of each of the products that you have. A lot of us would like to have some combination of snacks and drinks, so we'd be willing to accept a bundle (like point A) that has less in total than the average of the two extremes with only chips or only soft drinks (the average can be thought of as a point on the dashed straight line). Point A is below the point on the dashed curve at 2 and 2. Just as with isoquants, we say that preferences are strictly convex if they have this shape where they are bowed toward the origin.

At a point like B, it is awfully dry in the mouth, and you'd be willing to give up quite a few chips to get just a few more drinks. The flip side being that in a case where you have few chips, you'd only be willing to part with some chips to get even more drinks. How you value something on the margin depends on where we are evaluating a potential change.

5.2.1 Utility

Indifference curves have a close relation to what we call **utility functions**. Economists in the 1800s started to work on rational choice and how we should view choices between different bundles. The concept of felicity or utility came to be seen as a useful concept. We use a utility function to assign values to different bundles. Taking E and F from earlier as an example, a utility function in general form could thus be expressed as $U = U(E, F)$ or in specific form as, for instance, $U = \sqrt{EF}$. Indifference curves that are further from the origin are associated with a higher utility. We could think of E and F as two axis that we lay out on the floor and a third axis, extending vertically, as capturing utility.

To provide an illustration, consider the case of perfect complements, left and right shoes, in Figure 5.4. On the floor are the two axis that measure the number of units of good

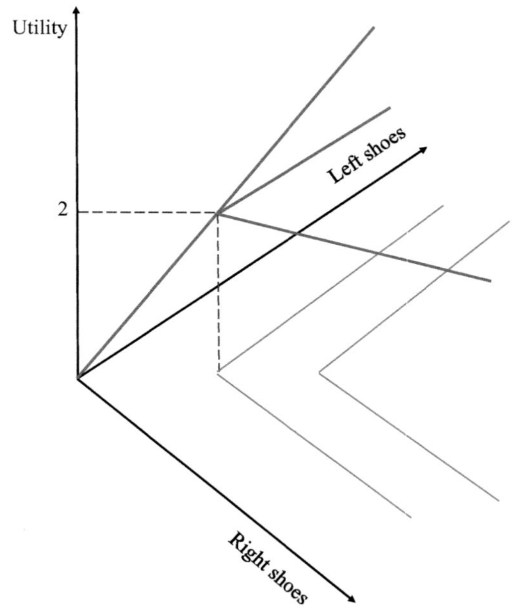

Figure 5.4 A utility function and indifference curves for perfect complements

(left and right shoes) and indifference curves. Each indifference curve is associated with one level on the third, vertical axis. In the case of 2 pairs of shoes, for instance, the utility level would be at a certain level, and we can think of the utility function as the edge of a pyramid.

Let us now return to imperfect substitutes and consider the specific utility function $U = \sqrt{EF}$. If we evaluate that at say $E = 2$ and $F = 8$, we have a utility level of 4 (since $\sqrt{2 \times 8} = 4$. Other combinations of goods that give the same utility level (e.g., $E = 4$ and $F = 4$; $E = 8$ and $F = 2$) are on the same indifference curve. Combinations that give a higher utility (such as $E = 5$ and $F = 5$ giving $U = \sqrt{5 \times 5} = 5$) are on a higher indifference curve. We use the numerical values of utility to rank different bundles, but we do not attach any quantitative meaning to the actual numbers beyond the ranking. Thus comparing a utility of 8 to one of 4, we do not say that one is double that of the other. The reason for this is that utility is not observable, and such statements would be meaningless. This is a difference from isoquants where a quantity of 4 bikes produced is half of that if 8 bikes are produced. We say that utility functions are **ordinal**, in that we care only about the ranking; only the order of ranking matters.[5]

We are now also in the position to say something more profound about the slope of the indifference curve. Here we essentially just repeat the exercise that we used to examine the slope of the isoquants. The utility function in general form is expressed as $U = U(E, F)$. *Total differentiation* yields

$$dU = \frac{\partial U(E,F)}{\partial E} dE + \frac{\partial U(E,F)}{\partial F} dF.$$

What is the change in utility as we change the amounts of goods consumed? Well, that depends on how much the consumption changes (dE and dF) and on the effect of those changes on utility (the partial derivatives). We note that along the indifference curve, utility is the same; hence, the change in utility along the indifference curve is equal to 0: $dU = 0$. Thus

$$\underbrace{dU}_{=0} = \frac{\partial U(E,F)}{\partial E} dE + \frac{\partial U(E,F)}{\partial F} dF.$$

Move the first term on the right-hand side over to the left to get

$$-\frac{\partial U(E,F)}{\partial E} dE = \frac{\partial U(E,F)}{\partial F} dF.$$

Divide by the partial and dF to get

$$-\frac{dE}{dF} = \frac{\frac{\partial U(E,F)}{\partial F}}{\frac{\partial U(E,F))}{\partial E}}.$$

The term on the right is the ratio between what we call **marginal utilities**. Just as the marginal products of inputs, these are frequently assumed to be diminishing. Holding the consumption of other goods fixed, each additional unit of a particular good gives me less and less additional utility. The first play that I go to in a week gives me more utility than the seventh in a week. The first beer of the evening gives me more utility than the second. Denote the marginal utility of entertainment and food MU_E and MU_F, respectively, to get

$$-\frac{dE}{dF} = \frac{\frac{\partial U(E,F)}{\partial F}}{\frac{\partial U(E,F)}{\partial E}} = \frac{MU_F}{MU_E}.$$

So, as we are moving along the indifference curve, its slope is equal to the marginal utility of food over the marginal utility of entertainment, as we illustrate in Figure 5.5. At point A, you're watching a lot of plays on an almost empty stomach. Your marginal utility of some additional food is high relative to the marginal utility of watching another play. To see the slope at this point, we draw out the tangent – a line that just touches the isoquant at this point. The slope of that tangent gives the change in E over the change in F. The slope of the indifference curve is prominent enough in economics that it has a specific name, the **marginal rate of substitution**, typically abbreviated MRS. As with the typical terms in microeconomics, it might not be very poetic, but it is usefully descriptive: How are we willing to substitute one good for the other on the margin?

5.3 Budget constraints

Our next step in the three-stage process of linking optimal choice to preferences is to model constraints. To do so, we use a **budget constraint**: how much we can purchase of different goods and services given prices and our income. Let income be denoted by I, the price of food by p_F, and the price of entertainment by p_E. These are all in a currency (such as euros), and prices are per unit. For instance, $p_F = 2$ would imply that 1 kilo of food costs 2 euros. If I buy 10 kilos, my outlays on food are hence $2 \times 10 = 20$ euros.

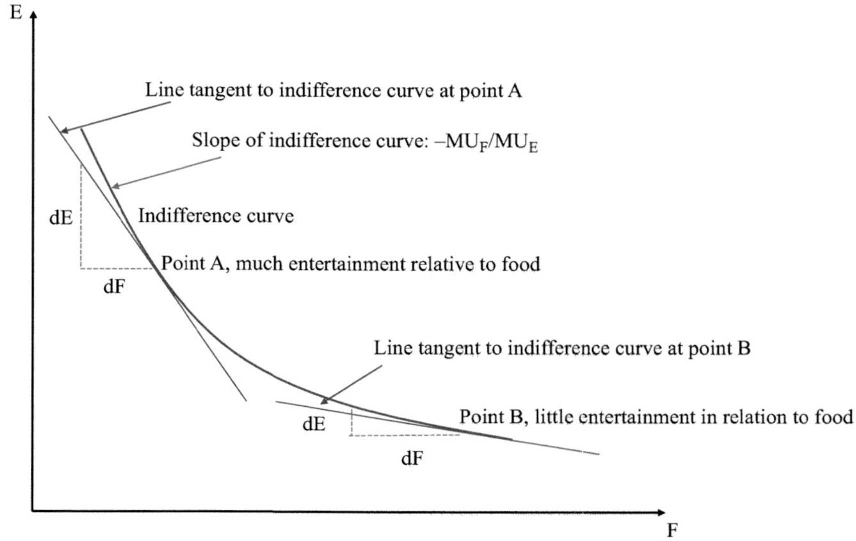

Figure 5.5 The slope of the indifference curve: Marginal rate of substitution (MRS). Video link for derivation of why MRS captures ratio of marginal utilities: https://youtu.be/sx1ytrEoiP8.

A consumer can purchase for no more than her income allows, and with these two goods, the budget constraint is thus

$$I = \underbrace{p_F F}_{\text{total outlay on food}} + \underbrace{p_E E}_{\text{total outlay on entertainment}} . \tag{5.1}$$

Budget constraints can be extended to many goods and can also be extended to include time so that a consumer might save in one period in order to consume more in future periods. To keep the presentation simple, we continue to focus on the simple case with two goods from earlier. There is a close analogy between budget constraints and the isocosts that we used when examining production. Just like in the case of production, we will want to draw the budget constraint in a diagram, as in Figure 5.6. We therefore solve Equation (5.1) for the amount of entertainment that can be purchased to get to Equation (5.2). The first term on the right-hand side in Equation (5.2) reflects that the higher the income and the lower the price of entertainment, the more entertainment I can purchase. If I only purchase entertainment, this is how much I can afford, and it thus gives the intercept on the vertical axis. If I also want to buy food, I will be able to afford less entertainment. How much less? That depends on the relative price, p_F/p_E.

$$E = \frac{I}{P_E} - \frac{p_F}{p_E}F \tag{5.2}$$

To be concrete, assume that I = 22, $p_F = 3$, and $p_E = 2$. The intercept is thus equal to $22/2 = 11$. If I also want to buy some F, I can afford less E. An affordable bundle would, for instance, be $E = 5$ and $F = 4$, and we can easily confirm that $2 \times 5 + 3 \times 4 = 22$. An other affordable bundle, also marked in Figure 5.6, would, for instance, be $E = 2$ and $F = 6$, and

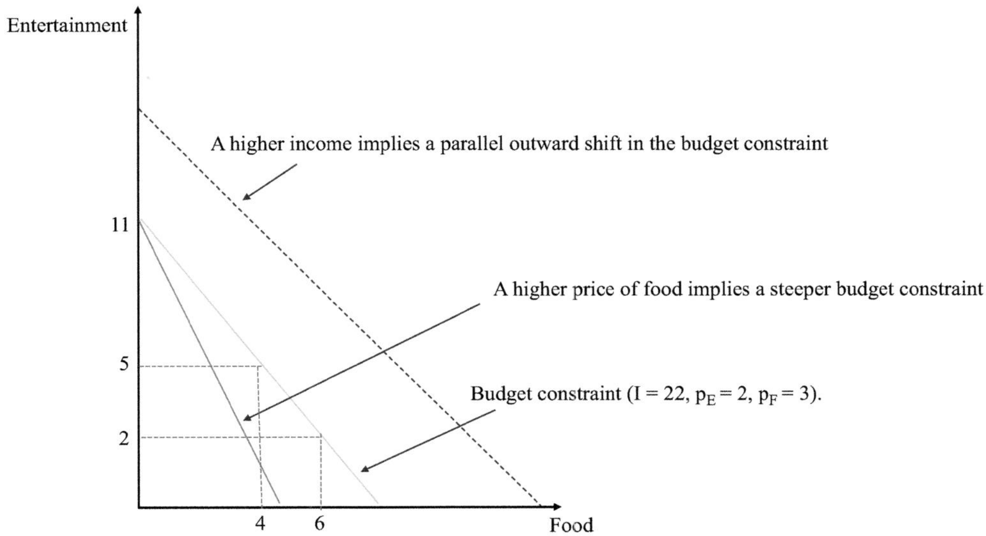

Figure 5.6 A budget constraint. Video link for figure: https://youtu.be/6d6ENXS40cM.

we can again easily confirm that $2 \times 2 + 3 \times 6 = 22$. It is also easily seen that changes in income are associated with parallel shifts in the budget constraint, whereas change in the price of one good relative to the other changes the steepness of the constraint. An increase in p_F while p_E is constant implies a steeper curve, as illustrated in Figure 5.6. For every E that I give up, I get less F in this case. A lower p_F, on the other hand, makes the budget constraint flatter.

5.4 Maximization of utility subject to constraints

We're now ready to put the pieces we've developed to work and operationalize our statement that individuals try to do as well as possible given the constraints that they face. We assume that individuals maximize utility, subject to the constraint that the chosen set of products satisfies the budget constraint. Mathematically, we can express the problem that individuals face as

$$\max_{E,F} U(E, F) \text{ subject to } p_E E + p_F F \leq I.$$

Given a specific functional form for the utility function, we can solve for the choices of E and F that maximize utility. We show an example in the appendix for the curious. Here however, we content ourselves with a graphical solution. We know that each indifference curve is associated with a utility level and that indifference curves further from the origin are associated with higher utility. We can therefore solve for the optimizing quantities by finding the "highest" indifference curve, given a particular budget constraint, as illustrated in Figure 5.7. Consider first indifference curve A and the consumption choices associated with E_A and F_A. They are clearly affordable, as they are on the budget constraint. But are they utility maximizing? No, at these prices and this income, the individual can achieve a higher utility by consuming less E and more F. The highest indifference curve that the individual can reach is that associated with choosing E^* and F^*.

At this point, you may ask yourself, What are we to do with all this? One curve is tangent to another, and this is associated with optimal choices. The key point, that we will revisit several times further in this chapter, is that even though utility functions (and indifference curves) are essentially unobservable, prices, incomes, and chosen quantities are observable. We can map choices to utility and hence make a number of statements regarding, for instance, how consumers can be compensated for various changes, how some reallocations of goods can increase utility for all, and, in the next chapter, how demand curves can be derived from the machinery that we've just covered. Foreshadowing what we do there, we simply note that changes in a price will be associated with changes in the quantity demanded: Voilà, we have a demand curve. We thus have a coherent machinery that links utility to observed choices in markets. It rests on a number of assumptions that we will discuss, but an important reason for the intellectual appeal of microeconomics, and why it is such an integral part of decision-making in public policy, is this intellectual coherence. You might even say beauty.

To provide one little glimpse into that beauty, we can prod a little deeper as to why point A is not optimal in Figure 5.7. At one level, we can say that the individual can reach a higher indifference curve by changing her consumption, and hence a point like A is not optimal. At a deeper level, we can utilize what we know about the slope of the indifference curve. It says how we value more of one good relative to the other, MU_F/MU_E. At point A, the marginal utility of F relative to E is relatively high. The individual consumes a lot of E in relation to F and at this point values more F highly at the margin. You've seen a lot of plays at the theater but are pretty hungry – your valuation of some more food at this point is high relative to your valuation of watching some more theater. But how can you trade off these two goods on the market? By prices. And at point A, the price of food relative

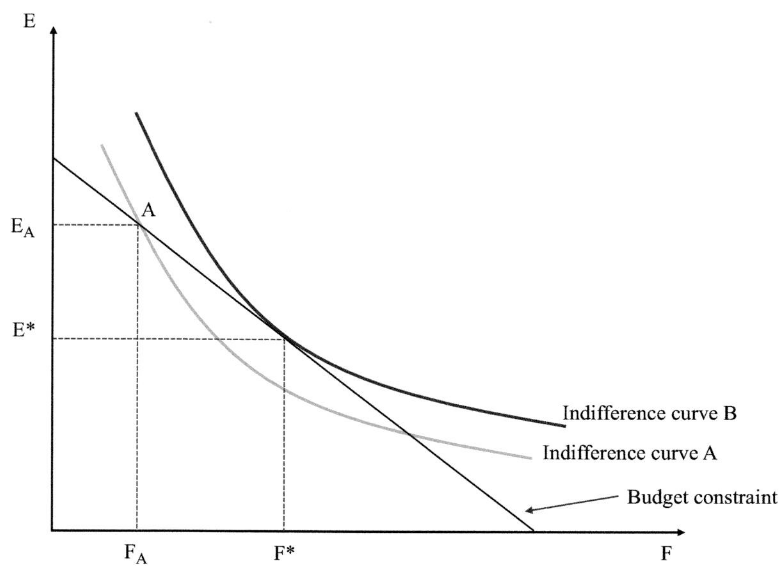

Figure 5.7 Utility maximization. Video link for figure: https://youtu.be/k2-alazhsxE.

to entertainment is not so high. So if you value food relative to entertainment more than what it is valued on the market (as reflected in prices), it makes sense to adjust your basket to consume more food and less entertainment. At the point where the indifference curve is tangent to the budget constraint, it holds that

$$\frac{MU_F}{MU_E} = \frac{p_F}{p_E}.$$

The slope of the indifference curve is also known as the marginal rate of substitution (MRS), and the slope of the budget constraint as the marginal rate of transformation (MRT) so the condition is sometimes known as MRS = MRT.

5.4.1 Example of optimal choices under different prices

Let us in the following look at examples of how the framework that we have developed can be used to understand how prices and preferences interact in determining choice. A number of years ago, the economist Stephen Levitt asked readers of his *Freakonomics* blog to send in suggested answers to the following question: "Why has the consumption of shrimp increased so much?" (per capita consumption had roughly tripled over the preceding 25 years).[6] The majority of answers, in particular from noneconomists, hypothesized that something had happened to demand. Explanations included that demand had shifted because of newly emphasized health benefits of shrimp, or a popular movie, or prominent chefs making shrimp consumption trendy. Such effects are clearly possible, but the framework of choice that we've developed emphasizes that shifts in incomes and prices are key determinants of choice. Consumption of meat increases as incomes grow. The falling price of one good relative to other goods increases demand for that product (indeed, Levitt's quick look at the evidence in his blog post points to a falling relative price of shrimp as the key driver of the increase in shrimp consumption).

A related examination is done by Dubois et al. (2014). They use detailed data on food consumption of a large number of French, British, and US households. Differences in consumption patterns between countries are marked, and on average, US households get a much larger share of their calories from carbohydrates than French households do. French households, on the other hand, tended to get a much larger share of their calories from fat than US households. Playing with national stereotypes, we can think of Americans eating more pizza and of French eating more duck confit (duck slowly prepared and cooked in its own fat). Do Americans simply like pizza and French like confit? Preferences, what we've grown to like over years as a reflection of our experiences and culture, clearly play a role. But Dubois et al. (2014) also document an important role for price differences. To highlight this pattern, think of a case where an individual in France has the exact same preferences as an individual in the United States – that is we can use the same indifference curve to represent her preferences. Think of two goods only, pizza and duck confit, with prices p_{pizza} and p_{duck}, respectively, and use superscripts F and US to reference the respective country.

Assume that the price of pizza is lower in the United States than in France and that the opposite holds for the price of duck confit. Figure 5.8 illustrates. First consider this individual facing US prices, choosing to consume $Pizza_{US}$ and $Duck_{US}$, given by the point of tangency between the budget constraint and the indifference curve. Now consider the choices by an individual with the exact same preferences but instead facing French relative prices and therefore a flatter budget line. The intercept on the vertical axis shifts down since

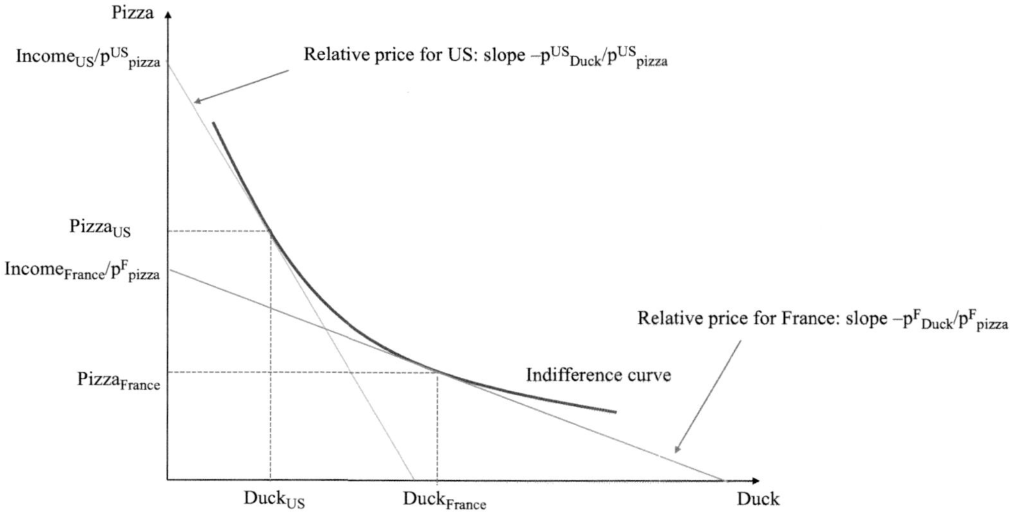

Figure 5.8 Different choice despite the same preferences

the French price of pizza is higher. To keep the individual on the exact same indifference curve, we may also have to adjust the income. If a French woman only purchases pizza, she can afford less than her US twin, but if she only consumes duck, she can afford more than her US twin (as seen by comparing the intercepts on the horizontal axis). Faced with French prices, this individual would consume less pizza and more duck. We have thus highlighted how differences in prices are an important determinant of differing choices. Even with identical preferences, individuals facing different prices will make different choices. The intuition behind the result is closely linked to the intuition surrounding different choices of inputs for production that we examined in Chapter 3.

5.5 Discussion of assumptions and framework

The previous framework forms the heart of the analysis of rational choice in economics. While it perhaps appears innocuous when presented earlier, the implications of the assumption that our choices are rational utility maximizing choices of individuals are far reaching. Should smoking be allowed? Should drug use be legal? In the following, we discuss some misconceptions and some challenges to the previous analysis.

5.5.1 Where are the limits of the framework outlined?

The previous example only considered an individual's own consumption into the utility function. More goods were always assumed to be better than fewer. The conclusion that one might draw is that selfish materialism is what economists prescribe as the goal to strive for. This is wrong; the framework assumes that *utility* should be maximized, not the amount of goods. There is nothing irrational in giving money to charity or valuing organic products more than a cheaper nonorganic product. The framework aims to link an individual's rational choices to that individual's preferences, and those preferences can differ across individuals. Indeed, pretty much any economics professor I could think of would be making a higher wage if occupied elsewhere. They choose to work in academia because their choices reveal that they are willing to give up some consumption of goods in order to teach and work with topics they find intellectually exciting. Nothing irrational there. In conclusion, we often model choice between different goods in a quite simplistic fashion. This is particularly true in a first textbook but also in more elaborate models. It is thus perhaps easy to see where the misperception comes from.

We might think of the framework of rational choice only weighing in utility of consumption outlined earlier as most straightforward to implement when we think of typical goods and services in our daily lives. Should I buy apples or oranges? Will I buy more or less bread if prices go up? That said, economists have also been remarkably successful in applying this kind of framework to wider issues, such as how many children to have. Gary Becker, winner of the 1992 Nobel Prize in Economics was a key influence in extending the domain of application of a rational choice framework to questions such as drug use, marriage patterns, and discrimination.

Consider fertility rates across different countries, as presented in Table 5.2, for instance. Why are there such large differences? Do people in Afghanistan like kids more than people in Spain? Thus is it preferences? We could also discuss whether it is a complex web of traditions, income levels, stages of development that together determine the outcomes. A stylized view of a Becker-style application of economics would be to assume that preferences are the same everywhere but that the costs and benefits of having children differ depending on conditions in different countries. Can kids be combined with dual careers? Are children key to being able to have a decent life in old age? If so, questions regarding, for instance, stability of a pension system and child mortality become important. The power of an economic analysis that relies on stable preferences and maximizing behavior is that almost anything can be analyzed, often with sharp and non-trivial predictions. In the words of Gary Becker (1976, p. 5),"The combined assumptions of maximizing behavior, market equilibrium, and stable preferences, used relentlessly and unflinchingly, form the heart of the economic approach."

That said, it is also easy to think of many examples of human behavior that are not easily explained by the kind of framework discussed earlier. Some of those are documented within what is known as "behavioral economics," which we will discuss next. More generally, I believe that it is important to recognize that **social norms** – the type of behavior that's expected in our society or group, our sense of belonging to a group with traditions and rituals – also matter for many types of behavior. For instance, consider voting in political

Table 5.2 Fertility rates in selected countries

Country	*Fertility rate*
South Korea	0.97
Spain	1.25
Sweden	1.73
Afghanistan	4.95
Mali	6.14

Average number of children born per woman over 2015–2022. Source: World Development Indicators https://databank.worldbank.org/source/world-development-indicators. (series SP.DYN.TFRT.IN)

elections. Voter turnout generally responds as you would expect from a framework such as the one described earlier – if the weather is awful (raising the "cost" of voting), voter turnout is lower, whereas it is higher in close elections, and people's voting is to some extent influenced by direct effects of policies on voters' household economy. If we push the framework even harder, note that a simplistic application of the most basic mechanisms from the type of cost-benefit framework outlined earlier leads to what is known as the "paradox of voting." It notes that in many elections, the probability that your vote will be decisive is close to zero, whereas the costs may be nontrivial. One could therefore argue that it would be irrational to vote. This may be a fruitful starting point for an investigation of why we vote, but as a prediction, it is clearly way off. Countless people have made huge sacrifices to fight for voting rights. Voting is just one of the things that we do that is not well captured by a narrow-minded comparison of selfish material costs and benefits. Similarly, many volunteer for military service at the risk of losing their lives. If we term such behavior irrational, I'd say we have too narrow a view of rationality. One definition of irrationality that I like comes from Gilboa (2009, p. 139) where "a mode of behavior is irrational for a given decision-maker if, when the decision-maker behaves in this mode and is then exposed to the analysis of her behavior, she feels embarrassed." I like the definition because it highlights a key element of irrationality that, when revisiting a decision and applying clearheaded thinking, you'd have wanted to act differently.

In closing this section, and on a related note, we highlight that J. M. Keynes (1924) once reflected (in a eulogy over Alfred Marshall Keynes) that

> The master-economist must possess a rare combination of gifts .... mathematician, historian, statesman, philosopher—in some degree. [They] must understand symbols and speak in words. He must contemplate the particular, in terms of the general, and touch abstract and concrete in the same flight of thought. He must study the present in the light of the past for the purposes of the future. No part of man's nature or his institutions must be entirely outside his regard.

I am in agreement with Keynes on this – but also note that we must not always bring these things to the table ourselves. Many questions will benefit also from input by experts with other backgrounds, such as sociology, anthropology, and psychology.[7]

5.6 Behavioral economics

There is a large literature within economics that focuses on deviations from the model that we introduced earlier (rational utility maximization only taking an individual's own consumption into account). The subfield is often referred to as behavioral economics. The contributions of this field are wide ranging, and different ways of slicing the cake are possible. Let us highlight three deviations from the simple framework described earlier. The first, what we term *social preferences*, does not rely on any deviation from rationality per se. It is emphasizing that we are social animals and that factors like pride, status, self-respect, and spite matter for our choices. Incorporating such factors into formal models makes the models more complex to work with, but they do not imply a lack of rationality per se. Some other important deviations from the simple framework, however, represent behavioral biases where people systematically deviate from rational behavior, and we cover two especially prominent classes of such deviations further in the next section.

5.6.1 Social preferences

The simple model of behavior presented earlier has each of us maximize utility of our own consumption – the actions and consumption of others do not matter per se. In contrast, there is ample evidence that humans care about issues such as belonging to a perceived group, as well as status and prestige that come from comparisons with others. Large amounts of research has been directed at documenting and understanding, for instance, **altruism** – acts in which the welfare of others is the primary concern (such as giving to charity) – and **fairness** (see, e.g., Charness and Rabin (2002) for evidence on some such preferences). Such behavior can be perfectly consistent with maximization of a utility function and thereby not irrational – it does, however, point out that the simplifying assumptions made if we only focus on our own material consumption are likely to miss important aspects in some situations. Fairness, in the words of Rabin (1993) – "People like to help those who are helping them, and to hurt those who are hurting them" – was, highlighted already by Adam Smith, by many regarded as the key founder of the study of economics. Smith is quoted in Ashraf et al. (2005) as stating, "Nature has implanted in the human breast [fairness]...to protect the weak, to curb the violent, and to chastise the guilty."

One class of experiments, known as the ultimatum game, has been highly influential in driving home the message about fairness to economists (the first such experiment was reported in Güth et al. (1982)). Typically, one participant in the experiment (the proposer) gets to propose a division of a pile of money made available by the researchers to another participant in the experiment (the responder). That other participant can choose to say yes to the division – in which case they each get as proposed. Say for instance that the first person proposes a division of 10 euros given within the experiment so that she keeps 6 euros and the responder gets 4 euros. If the responder says yes, they each get paid according to the proposal, but in the case that the responder says no, neither gets anything. Both parties are anonymous to each other. In a simple case, where people only care about their own consumption, the proposer would keep almost everything (say 9.9 euros), and the responder would say yes since 0.1 euro is still more than nothing. The experiment has been reproduced many times, in different variations, and the finding that proposers suggest a division much closer to 50/50 is extremely robust. In their summary of a large number of studies, Oosterbeek et al. (2004), for instance, find that on average, the proposer offers 40% of the pie to the responder. On average, 16% of the offers are rejected with a rejection rate that is lower for larger pie sizes and for larger shares offered. Henrich et al. (2001) run ultimatum game experiments in 15 different small-scale societies across the world, such as the Hadza hunter-gatherers cultures of Tanzania and traditional Lamelara whale hunting societies of Indonesia. Patterns across these groups correlate with expectations of how important cooperation is and other social norms (for instance, the groups with the highest average offers are societies from Papua New Guinea that are characterized as "competitive gift giving societies" – accepting a gift requires that you reciprocate by a greater gift in the future). Nevertheless, also across this highly diverse set of groups, the average share offered to the responder is never below 25%. Overall, these results emphasize that perceived fairness is highly important and that people are willing to take nontrivial costs to punish what they see as unfair behavior.

(a) (b)

Figure 5.9 Randomness vs. bias. Photo by author.

5.6.2 *Behavioral biases*

There is a large literature within economics and psychology that focuses on deviations from rational behavior, behavioral biases. Let's use the targets with darts in Figure 5.9 to illustrate. Panel (a) of Figure 5.9 is meant to illustrate a case where darts are randomly dispersed but still roughly centered on the bull's-eye. Metaphorically speaking, this corresponds to a case where people on average are rational (hit or are close to the bull's-eye), but there are random deviations. People make mistakes but not systematically so. In contrast, panel (b) shows a case where the arrows appear to be systematically off, upward from the bull's-eye. Metaphorically speaking, this corresponds to the case of a **behavioral bias**: systematic deviations from rational behavior. The research agenda was to a large extent shaped by early work by Daniel Kahneman and Amos Tversky, and you may, for instance, have come across the bestseller *Thinking, Fast and Slow* (Kahneman (2017)).[8]

The research agenda started by them has focused on documenting deviations from models of rationality, and the list of documented biases can become very long. There are different ways to present these and slice the cake, but arguably, the following are some of the most important.[9]

5.6.3 *Lack of self-control*

The rational decision-maker that we presented in the first part of this chapter maximizes utility over time – coolly weighing costs and benefits over the entire lifetime. While mistakes would occur also in a world where people on balance were fully rational, there is substantive evidence for systematic deviations from rationality in that humans are prone to do what gives satisfaction in the moment rather than what is consistent with maximization of long-term utility. People smoke, drink alcohol to excess, splurge on unhealthy foods, spend more time than wished for staring at their smartphones, don't save enough for pensions, and overspend on credit card debt. When such behavior is coupled with a wish to break these patterns, they are indicative of a lack of self-control: "I'll stop procrastinating tomorrow," as the quip has it.

A useful way of thinking about such issues has proven to be a model where we are guided by a conflict between two selves: a myopic *doer* that only cares about the present and a *planner* that weighs costs and benefits over time in a consistent way, as developed by Thaler and Shefrin (1981). The formalization has proven useful and has deep roots in historical views of human behavior – there is also supportive medical evidence that different parts of the brain are engaged in evaluating immediate and longer-term rewards (see, e.g., McClure et al. (2004)). More than 2,000 years ago, stoic philosophers emphasized the virtue of self-control, and the ability of small kids to resist the temptation of eating a marshmallow placed in front of them, as in the 1960s marshmallow experiments, is a vivid illustration of self-control issues (Mischel (2014)).[10] Again, this line of reasoning has been present in economics from the start and in the other (apart from *Wealth of Nations*) main book by Adam Smith, *The Theory of Moral Sentiments*, the struggle between the short-run "passions" and the "impartial spectator," who within us serves as the rational arbiter, is a central theme.[11]

Thus, self-control problems represent an important class of deviations from rational behavior. One set of responses, showing that this has long been recognized by policymakers, are legal and regulatory constraints on consumption and savings decisions. For instance, mandatory pension contributions, mandatory health insurance, and legal restrictions on use of alcohol, drugs, and gambling are all examples of such responses. Responses can also be at the personal level: Don't go shopping for food when you're hungry; don't keep cigarettes at home if you want to quit smoking, and tie yourself to the mast to avoid being lured by the sirens as Ulysses did in the 3,000-year old story. Making commitments public can also be a way of limiting self-control problems.[12]

5.6.4 Cognitive limitations and biased information processing

Economic models are simplified – even as we leave the stylized two-good models of an introductory textbook, we rely on simplifying assumptions. Just in thinking what to shop for dinner, we are faced with thousands of products as we enter a supermarket with different brands, prices, special offers; thoughts about what goes well with what; and so forth. Choices that lock you into different actions over time – such as education, marriage, children, what job to choose, and how to save and invest – can in principle involve gazillion parameters, many of which are uncertain. To deal with this, economic models simplify. Similarly, in human decision-making, we also simplify – there is ample evidence that we rely on various **heuristics**, or rules-of-thumb, in making decisions. Nobel laureate Herbert Simon was an early proponent of the idea that rather than tackle the highly complex problem of finding optimal solutions, we solve a simpler problem of satisfying a set of self-imposed constraints, stopping when we've reached something that is "good enough." In the words of Simon, we act as if we are **boundedly rational**.

As noted earlier, the work by Kahneman and Tversky has been key in driving this line of thinking, and many of the associated biases concern how we process information and what we use as a benchmark. For instance, when evaluating a risky choice, the standard economic model would evaluate the *level* of consumption or wealth. Kahneman and Tversky instead proposed a descriptive model, where it is *changes* relative to some reference point that are key.[13] There is a tendency to frame decisions in terms of gains and losses rather than in terms of levels, and losses are weighted stronger than gains: Such behavior implies that people are **loss-averse** – the disutility of giving up an object is greater than the utility associated with acquiring it. Such an individual tends to avoid change since the losses from a change are weighted more heavily than the gains, and we talk of a status-quo bias. In an often referred to experiment Kahneman et al. (1990) similarly show the impact of what they term the *endowment effect*: People are more likely to keep an object that they own than they are to acquire that same object when they do not own it. This contrasts with the rational behavior outlined at the start of this chapter where your utility of a good didn't include some reference to the history of ownership. Roughly speaking, in the experiment, half of the students were given Cornell University coffee mugs and the other half were not. Participants were then asked what they'd be willing to buy or sell the mug for. Since mugs were given out randomly, the average price of both selling and buying the mug would be expected to be close – there should be little or no correlation between your valuation of a coffee mug and whether you by chance happened to get one in the experiment. In contrast, the student who got a mug had a median valuation of the mug that was around 2 to 4 times higher than the median valuation of a student who didn't get one. A clear illustration of how reference points matter.

In decisions involving risk, we also need to have some estimates of the associated probabilities for different outcomes, and here as well there are systematic biases. The list of various biases can become long and somewhat bewildering, and for our purposes here, we may simply emphasize that how information is presented matters for the decisions that we make. To highlight one example of the impact of such **framing**, Tversky and Kahneman (1981) posed a question about which of two possible treatments a set of subjects would prefer. In their hypothetical scenario, a disease would kill 600 people unless treatments were undertaken. Subjects had to choose between two treatments. People were more likely to choose an alternative that lets one-third live over one that allows two-thirds to die, even though they are just two ways of expressing the same thing.

A bias that is particularly relevant for many economic decisions is that we have a tendency to be **overconfident**. There is a tendency to systematically have a view of reality that tends to be too optimistic and underestimate the effect of randomness on future realizations. This was emphasized already by Adam Smith who, in *Wealth of Nations*, noted, "The over-weening conceit which the greater part of men have of their own abilities, is an ancient evil remarked by the philosophers and moralists of all ages" (the quote is from Malmendier and Taylor (2015), which also provides an introduction to the broader evidence). To illustrate just one case, Cooper et al. (1988) asked some 3,000 entrepreneurs who had recently started or taken over a venture to rate their chances of success: 68% believed that they had a better chance than other businesses like theirs, and only 5% believed that they had a worse chance. More than 80% rated their chances of success as 7 or higher out of 10. Given the high failure rates of new firms, a lot of these respondents were going to be proved wrong.

5.6.5 Final words

In conclusion, the model of rational choice that we started with in this chapter, where preferences are stable and individuals make informed choices about how to be as well off as possible given the constraints that they face, has proven to be extremely useful in predicting and interpreting behavior in many situations. The rational model remains fundamental both for predicting behavior and as a benchmark for understanding any deviations from rational behavior. That said, applications need to be aware of behavioral biases and when they may be important. For instance, self-control problems imply that it is not unimportant if we examine demand for opiatic pain killers or for baking soda.

5.7 Appendix – Solving for the optimal consumption basket

In this chapter, we solved for the utility maximizing choices graphically and focused on the intuition. This is sufficient for most (if not all) introductory courses in microeconomics. You may nevertheless be curious – how can we calculate these numbers? In this appendix, we use a common method to do so, solving constrained optimization problems with the help of a Lagrange multiplier. The purpose of the example here is to show how it can be done – not to provide a comprehensive description of how to solve constrained optimization problems in general.

The utility maximization problem that we want the individual to solve is the following:

$$\max_{E,F} U(E, F) \text{ subject to } p_E E + p_F F \leq I.$$

In the chapter, we considered a Cobb-Douglas utility function (for instance, $U = E^{0.75} F^{0.25}$), and we could solve for optimal choices with that utility function. Just to highlight that there are many different shapes that a utility function may take, however, let us consider what is known as a constant elasticity of substitution ("CES") utility function – it is a strange looking animal but rather common in applications because it features, well, a constant elasticity of substitution between the goods – a concept explained in the next chapter. Thus, we parameterize the utility function as $U = \left(\sqrt{E} + \sqrt{F}\right)^2$ and the constrained maximization problem under these assumptions becomes

$$\max_{E,F} \left(\sqrt{E} + \sqrt{F}\right)^2 \text{ subject to } p_E E + p_F F \leq I. \tag{5.3}$$

Arguably, the most common way to solve constrained optimization problems in economics is to use the Lagrange method: We combine the function that is to be optimized (U in this case) and the constraint into one equation that we term the Lagrangian function, $\mathcal{L}$. A Lagrange multiplier λ interacts with the constraint, and we say that if $\lambda > 0$ the constraint binds, the constraint affects the solution. This is an optimization problem with 3 unknowns (E, F, and λ), and by setting the derivative of the Lagrange function equal to 0 for each of the variables, we get 3 equations that we can use to solve for the 3 unknowns.

$$\mathcal{L}(E, F, \lambda) = \left(\sqrt{E} + \sqrt{F}\right)^2 + \lambda \left(I - p_E E - p_F F\right). \tag{5.4}$$

Remembering that a variable $\sqrt{x}$ can equally well be written as $x^{0.5}$, and using the chain rule (the derivative of a composite function is given by the derivative of the outer function times the derivative of the inner function), we find that the first-order conditions for Equation (5.4) are

$$\frac{\partial \mathcal{L}}{\partial E} = 2\left(E^{0.5} + F^{0.5}\right)^1 \times 0.5 \times E^{-0.5} - \lambda p_E = 0, \tag{5.5}$$

$$\frac{\partial \mathcal{L}}{\partial F} = 2\left(E^{0.5} + F^{0.5}\right)^{1} \times 0.5 \times F^{-0.5} - \lambda p_F = 0, \tag{5.6}$$

$$\frac{\partial \mathcal{L}}{\partial \lambda} = I - p_E E - p_F F = 0. \tag{5.7}$$

Solve Equations (5.5) and (5.6) for λ and equate them to get

$$\left(E^{0.5} + F^{0.5}\right) \times \frac{1}{p_E E^{0.5}} = \left(E^{0.5} + F^{0.5}\right) \times \frac{1}{p_F F^{0.5}}. \tag{5.8}$$

The term $\left(E^{0.5} + F^{0.5}\right)$ cancels, and Equation (5.8) thus gives us

$$p_E E^{0.5} = p_F F^{0.5} \tag{5.9}$$

$$E^{0.5} = \frac{p_F}{p_E} F^{0.5} \tag{5.10}$$

$$E = \left(\frac{p_F}{p_E}\right)^2 F. \tag{5.11}$$

We have thus found how the optimal choice of E relates to the optimal choice of F. Use this to substitute for E in the constraint[14] to get

$$I - p_F F - \underbrace{p_E \left(\frac{p_F}{p_E}\right)^2 F}_{=E} = 0. \tag{5.12}$$

In the next chapter, we consider an example where $I = 90$, $p_E = 1$, and $p_F = 1$. Equation (5.12) then becomes

$$90 - F - \left(\frac{1}{1}\right)^2 F = 0, \tag{5.13}$$

which we solve to find the utility maximizing consumption of $F^* = 45$ (where we use a * to denote an optimal choice). Plugging this value of F into the constraint, we also immediately find that $E^* = 45$. Equation (5.12) can also be used for finding optimal consumption at other prices and another income. If p_F increases to 2, for instance ($I = 90$, $p_E = 1$ and $p_F = 2$), we find that

$$\begin{aligned} 90 - 2F - \left(\frac{2}{1}\right)^2 F &= 0 \\ 90 - 2F - 4F &= 0 \\ 6F &= 90 \\ F^* &= 15 \end{aligned}$$

and at these values

$$90 - 2 \times 15 - 1 \times E = 0$$

such that $E^* = 60$.

Notes

1 Note that we are keeping everything in the choice situation constant when spelling out the fundamental assumptions behind rational choice. Preferring an umbrella to sunglasses when it rains and sunglasses to an umbrella on a sunny day is not irrational.
2 If transitive preferences didn't hold, choice would be a mess and not internally consistent. Suppose that transitivity didn't hold and that again we know that Yoichi prefers Apples to Bananas, and Bananas to Cherries. If transivity didn't hold, Yoichi would give up an Apple to get a Cherry. But from the assumptions on preferences, he would give up the Cherry to get a Banana (since B is preferred to C) and then trade again to give up the Banana for an Apple (since A is preferred to B). But he just gave up an Apple for a Cherry. Are you confused yet? Transitivity avoids these kind of cycles. Under transitivity, Yoichi can give a straight answer to which good he prefers. If transitivity doesn't hold, he can't give a coherent answer to what he likes best.
3 A more formal way of saying this is that preferences are nonsatiated.
4 Note that when we're comparing bundles and using "more is better," we're not just adding the number of units. For instance, bundle B has $8 + 2 = 10$ units in total, but it need not be preferred to bundle *C* that has 3+3=6 units in total. Two bikes and 3 apples can be preferred to 1 bike and 28 apples.
5 The alternative case where numbers carry a quantitative meaning (beyond simply ordering) is known as cardinal.
6 https://freakonomics.com/2007/08/shrimponomics/.
7 By and large, I think it is fair to say that economists are skeptical of interdisciplinary work. Not rarely is there a sense that the sharp predictions of economics are watered down to pretentious nonsense. As chairman of the "Economic Club" in Stockholm, I had the privilege of having Nobel laureate Elinor Ostrom as a dinner companion – someone who had been organizing successful interdisciplinary research. I asked her what the secret to her success was. She noted that letting people really bring their various areas of expertise to the table and having a common research question were key. Clearly, the organization of multidisciplinary teams is outside the scope of an introductory microeconomics book, but I offer it as food for thought.
8 Kahneman was awarded the Nobel Prize in economics in 2002 – Tversky would almost surely have shared the prize but died early. The author Michael Lewis has a great gift for bringing economic stories to life – and the movies *Moneyball and The Big Short* both build on his books. In the *Undoing Project*, Lewis (2016) provides an inspirational view into their collaboration.
9 The way that I organize material is inspired by the scientific description of Thaler's 2017 Nobel Prize in Economics, https://www.nobelprize.org/uploads/2018/06/advanced-economicsciences2017-1.pdf
10 Walter Mischel ran tests with 4- and 5-year-olds in a Stanford nursery school telling kids that they can have one marshmallow now or two when he gets back later. Follow-up studies indicated that the kids with the willpower to wait did better in many aspects related to health and wealth in subsequent decades. The most recent evidence suggests that the link is not as clear as once thought (Benjamin et al. (2020)). More broadly however, substantial evidence indicates that a self-control is a useful trait in leading a long and prosperous life. Whether the ability to resist the temptation of eating one marshmallow immediately rather than waiting a little and getting two at the age of 4 or 5 is sufficient to capture this trait is less clear. I mention it here because it is a thought-provoking and often reported result.
11 Ashraf et al. (2005) provide an accessible reflection on how Smith's views on human behavior correspond to behavioral economics.
12 For fun, you may want to check out the website stickK.com, which tries to facilitate such commitments.
13 It is known as prospect theory; Kahneman and Tversky (1979) is the original reference, and Kahneman et al. (1991) provides an accessible discussion of some of the implications, as discussed in this section.
14 We could equally well have solved for *F*.

6 Demand curves and elasticities

Illustration 6.1 Testing the elasticity. *Trapeze Artist*, anonymous, British, 19th century (detail from). Public domain, Metropolitan museum of art.

DOI: 10.4324/9781003623854-8

6.1 From constrained optimization to demand curves

We saw in the previous chapter how optimal choices could be modeled depending on preferences, incomes, and prices. From this, it is a simple step to derive demand curves, but it is worth doing so in some detail. Thus again, consider the case where there are two goods, E and F. Assume initially that income is equal to 90 euros and that $p_E = 1$ and $p_F = 1$. Figure 6.1 presents the budget constraint in this case.

This line presents the affordable combinations of goods for this individual. Where will she end up consuming? Well, that depends on her preferences. In micro textbooks at this level, we usually do not solve for the actual quantities with the help of explicit functional forms. This text will be no exception – the important thing is to understand the principles involved and not the detailed derivations. Nevertheless, in my experience, some students are somewhat frustrated if curves just appear out of nowhere. Thus we now draw an indifference curve that is tangent to the budget constraint. If you want, you can think of it just like that. If you are of the type who will go, "Wait, wait, where did this come from?", you can check the appendix in the previous chapter where we show how we derive the optimal solution for the utility function that has the specific functional form[1] of $U = \left(\sqrt{E} + \sqrt{F}\right)^2$.

Thus, panel (a) of Figure 6.2 shows the budget constraint (with $I = 90$, $p_E = 1$ and $p_F = 1$), together with the indifference curve that is tangent to this budget constraint. The significance of this point of tangency is that it identifies the utility maximizing choices of E and F. In the case of the specific functional form that we examine, the optimal choices are $E = 45$ and $F = 45$, but as mentioned, feel free to think of this more loosely as the tangency for some form of utility function and thereby for some form of the indifference curve. Thus we see what is a key result for this chapter – utility maximization links preferences, income, and prices, on the one hand, to demand for individual goods, on the other hand. The budget

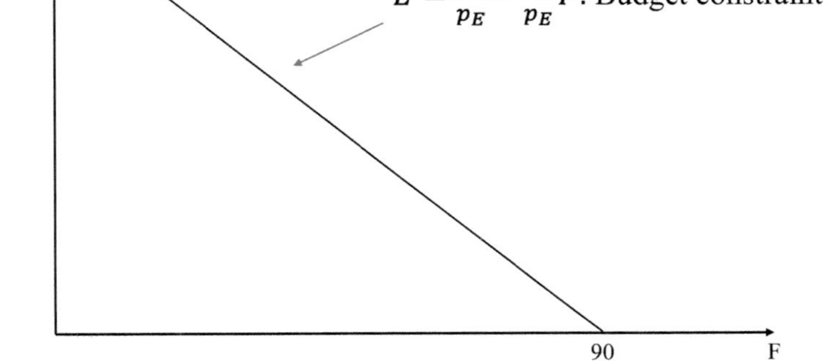

Figure 6.1 A budget constraint. Video link for Figures 6.1–6.4: https://youtu.be/8d2wh1SN2L8.

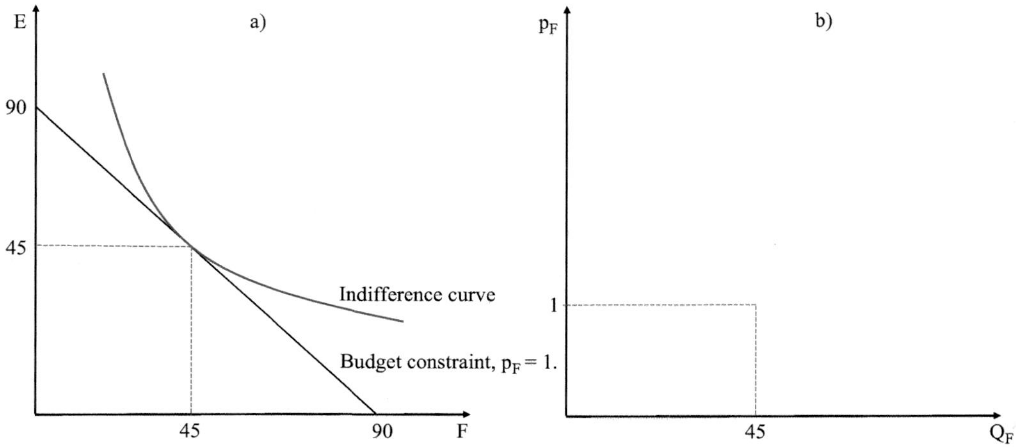

Figure 6.2 Optimal choice as a point on a demand curve – a first price. Video link for Figures 6.1-6.4: https://youtu.be/8d2wh1SN2L8.

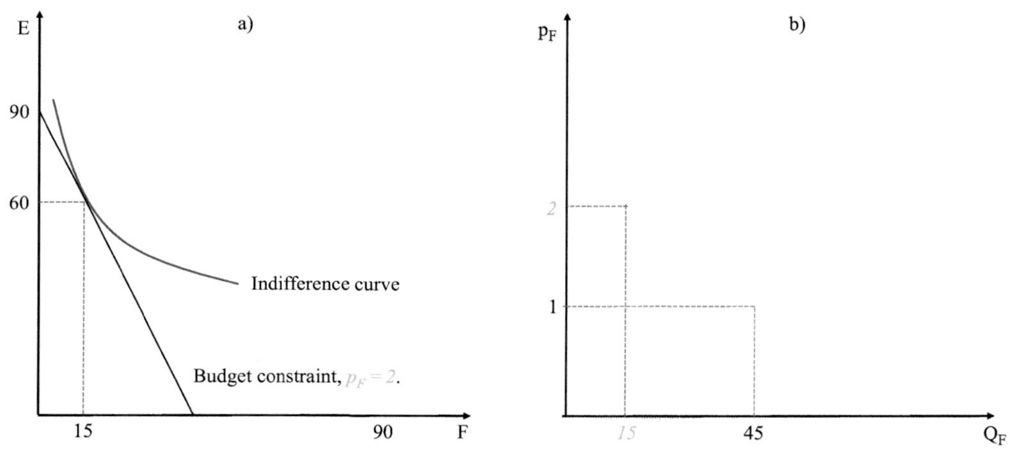

Figure 6.3 Optimal choice as a point on a demand curve – a higher price. Video link for Figures 6.1–6.4: https://youtu.be/8d2wh1SN2L8.

constraint is drawn for $p_F = 1$, and the optimal quantity is $F = 45$ units. Panel (b) in Figure 6.2 presents this relation, the link between the price of a good (F in this case) and the quantity demanded of this good. The optimal quantity of 45 at a price of food equal to 1 gives us one point on a demand curve for food.

To find other points on the demand curve, we simply examine optimal choices at other prices. In Figure 6.3, we consider the case where the price of F has increased to $p_F = 2$. At this higher price of p_F, the budget constraint is steeper. Since the price of E is unchanged (remember the standard assumption of "other things equal"), the intercept is unchanged, but for every unit of F that I want to buy, I have to give up more E when the price of F is higher. The optimal choice now involves buying less F and more E. In this particular

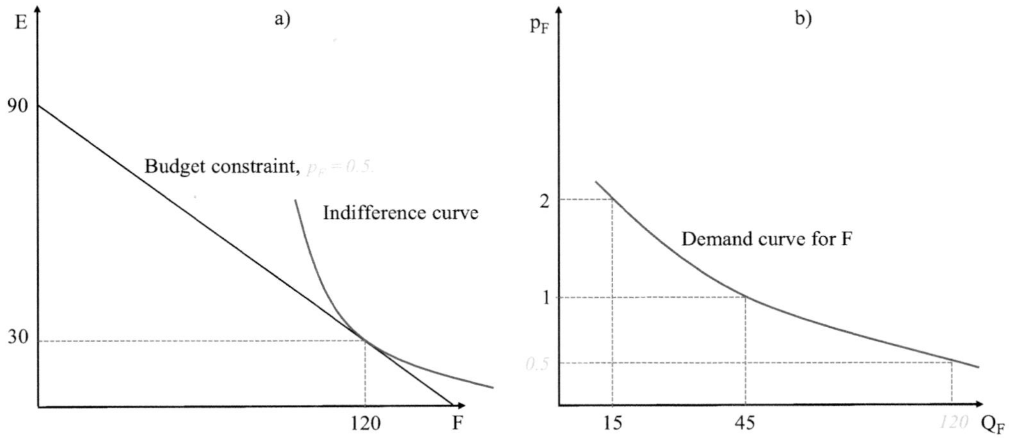

Figure 6.4 Optimal choice as a point on a demand curve – a lower price. Video link for Figures 6.1–6.4: https://youtu.be/8d2wh1SN2L8.

case, the point of tangency occurs where $F = 15$, and we thus have one more point on the demand curve ($p_F = 2$ yields $Q_F = 15$), as illustrated in panel (b) of Figure 6.3.

We can consider any price of F and find the optimal associated quantity. Panel (a) of Figure 6.4 represent the optimal choices when the price of F falls to $p_F = 0.5$ with the associated optimal quantity demanded for F being equal to 120 units. Panel (b) shows how this gives us a third point on the demand curve.

6.1.1 An example of the usefulness of linking preferences to demand

In this book, we only scratch the surface as to the potential uses of the framework that we introduced earlier. But the link between demand and utility can be useful in many types of analysis. Consider the following example, where for environmental reasons a government wants people to use less gasoline and implements this via a higher price of gasoline (for instance, via a tax on gasoline). At the level of the individual consumer, a higher price is associated with less demand for gasoline and a lower utility level (in the simple case where we disregard climate and other benefits in personal utility). We could also imagine compensating people in some way by giving money back, for instance, via a tax subsidy. If the government gives with one hand and takes back with the other, can this still affect demand? Yes, and let us show how such a question can be analyzed with the tools that we have available.

Earlier, we considered two goods. A useful simplification when examining a policy question is to think of the two goods as being the good of interests and "other goods." Thus, using G to denote gasoline and O to denote other goods, the budget constraint is given by $I = p_G G + p_O O$, and we draw this in Figure 6.5. A higher price of G makes the budget constraint steeper, and the individual responds by lowering consumption of gasoline from G_1 to G_2. The higher price is associated with a lower indifference curve; the one that is dashed in the figure.

Can we now compensate the individual and still affect choice? What would compensation do here? Consider a **lump sum**, a sum of money given to an individual (thus a sum of money,

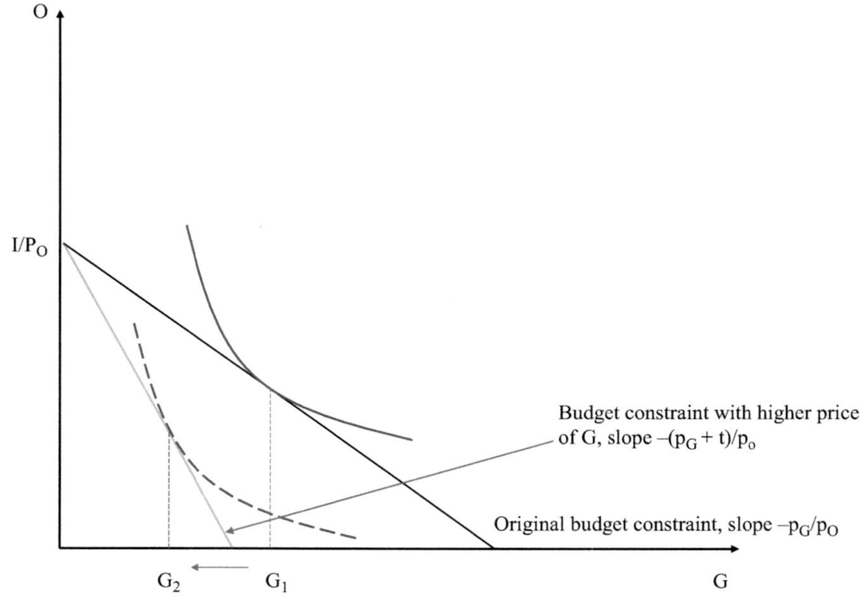

Figure 6.5 The effect of a higher price of gasoline on choices and indifference curve reached. Video link for Figures 6.5–6.6: https://youtu.be/dKcNiolFTMw.

not some subsidy that changes prices). This will affect the budget constraint, and using ΔI to denote the lump sum transfer, we illustrate the effect in Figure 6.6. The lump sum transfer shifts the budget constraint outward. Given that the new budget constraint still reflects the new price of gasoline relative to other goods, the budget constraint is steeper than the original constraint. The steeper budget constraint, reflecting that a consumer has to give up more of other goods to buy gasoline, implies that the optimal choice will involve less gasoline being bought (G_3 rather than G_1). The compensation can in principle be set high enough that the consumer is kept at the same indifference curve as before the change, as is indeed illustrated in Figure 6.6. It thus shows a case where the effect on utility of a change is "neutralized" by compensation but where the relative price change still affects demand. Implementing such policies are of course more difficult in practice than in the simple example that we examined here, but the underlying logic was an important part of policy responses to high energy prices in the aftermath of Russia's invasion of Ukraine in 2022 for instance.

6.2 Effect of changes in income on demand

Prices are of course only one factor that affect demand. As alluded to earlier, we can also examine the effect of changes in income on demand. A higher income, other things equal, will be associated with an outward parallel shift in the budget constraint, which will be associated with a new optimal quantity. In Figure 6.7, we illustrate the effect of a fall in income. Start from the same example provided earlier ($I = 90$, $p_E = 1$ and $p_F = 1$) but now let income fall to $I = 60$ euros. This will be associated with new optimal choices of E and

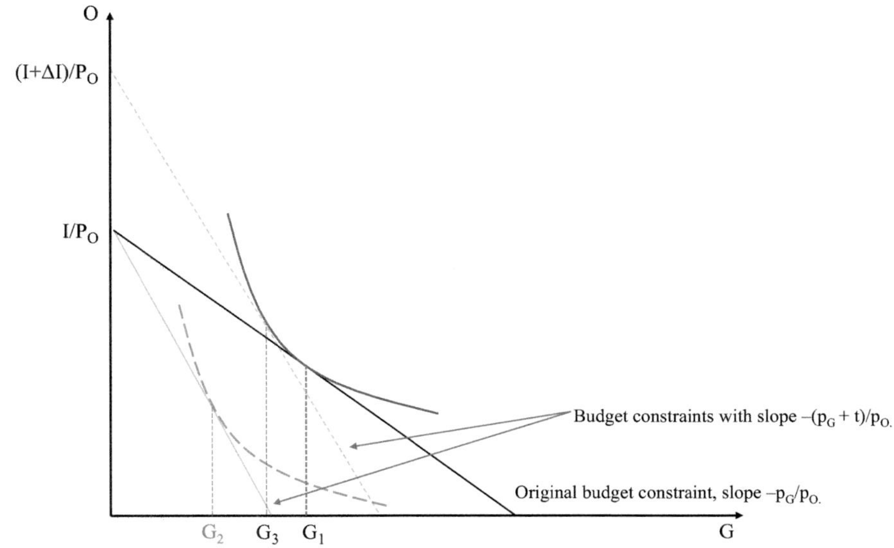

Figure 6.6 The effect of a higher price of gasoline on choices and the indifference curve reached with a lump-sum compensation. Video link for Figures 6.5–6.6: https://youtu.be/dKcNiolFTMw.

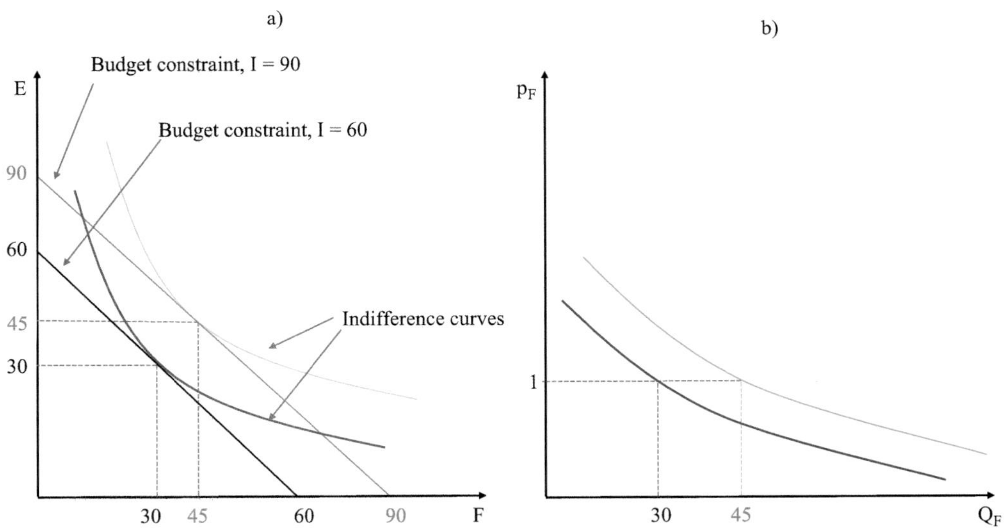

Figure 6.7 The effect of lower income on demand

F (30 of each in this case), and just as before, we can evaluate the effect of a large number of different prices of F to trace out the demand curve for F at this lower income. The figure also makes clear why we depicted changes in income as shifts in the demand function in Chapter 2.

The case illustrated shows one where a lower income is associated with lower quantities demanded. Or equivalently, one where higher incomes are associated with higher quantities demanded. Goods for which this is the case are termed **normal goods**. We can also have the case where quantities demanded decrease as incomes increase. These are termed **inferior goods**. Typical examples are products that are consumed at low incomes but that people tend to switch away from if their income increases. Instant noodles may, for instance, be consumed a lot when you're a student, but as you start working and income increases, you may likely switch to other food stuffs. Goods where we can think of several quality levels for similar goods are other prime examples (low-budget store brands at retailers).

It deserves to be pointed out that, as always, tastes vary by individuals so that a good may be inferior for one person but not for another. It is also the case that a good can be normal at low incomes and inferior at higher incomes. For instance, as a student traveling over part of the summer, I might stay more nights in hostels if I earn more on my summer job, but if my income were to increase even further, I'd switch to hotels. Figure 6.8 illustrates the situation with demand for nights in a hostel for a summer of interrailing. At the lowest income, H_L is demanded; at an intermediate income, the budget constraint shifts out, and demand for hostel nights is higher at H_M. Thus, at low incomes nights in hostel are a normal good for this person. At yet higher incomes demand for hostel nights falls back to H_H.

Next, we examine how the effect of incomes on demand can be measured and we also discuss applications. Before doing so, let us show how we move from individual demand to market-level demand.

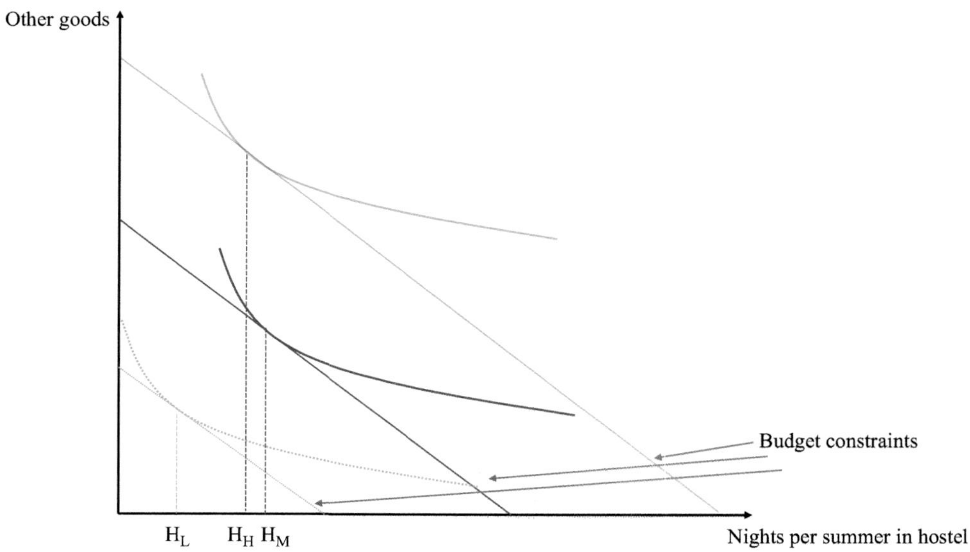

Figure 6.8 A good can be normal at low incomes and inferior at higher incomes

6.3 From individual to market-level demand

As with supply, market demand is the sum of individuals' demand. Market demand is the sum of the quantities that all consumers are willing to demand at a given price. We present an example with 3 individuals, named Anna, Boris, and Conrad, in Table 6.1. For instance, at the price of 4 euros, only Anna demands the good. As the price falls to 3 euros, market demand increases for two reasons: Anna demands more at this lower price, and Boris also starts demanding positive amounts as the price falls.

We can also illustrate the summing of demand curves graphically. Consider demand from two individuals, Highie (denote with H) and Lowie (denote with L). Demand from H is $q_H = 10 - p$ and from L is $q_L = 5 - p$. One might be tempted to just add demand curves, but we need to keep track of whether all individuals have positive demand at a particular price. For this reason, it is useful to first write the demand functions as inverse demand functions and draw them in a figure. For H, the inverse demand function is $p = 10 - q_H$ and for L $p = 5 - q_L$, as illustrated in Figure 6.9.

Table 6.1 Market demand is the sum of individuals' demand

Price	*Anna*	*Boris*	*Conrad*	*Market demand (A + B + C)*
5	1	0	0	1
4	2	0	0	2
3	3	1	0	4
2	4	2	1	7
1	5	3	2	10

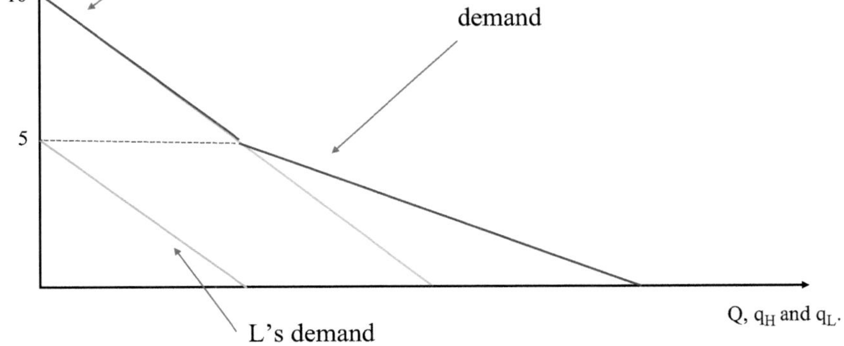

Figure 6.9 Adding of demand curves. Video link for Figure: https://youtu.be/dW1UhX_WnwI.

Thus if price is above 5, market demand is the same as demand from H, but if price is 5 or lower, both H and L demand the good. Thus, for a price not higher than 5, market demand, $Q = q_L + q_H$, is given by $Q = (10-p)+(5-p)$ or, collecting terms, as $Q = 15-2p$. To draw this in Figure 6.9, we rewrite as demand as an the inverse demand function with $p = 7.5 - Q/2$. So, the demand function can be expressed as

$$Q(p) = \begin{cases} 10 - p & \text{if } p > 5 \\ 15 - 2p & \text{if } p \leq 5. \end{cases} \tag{6.1}$$

As is typically the case, we see that market demand is flatter than individual demand. The total response of many to a change in price is greater than the response of one individual.

6.4 Elasticities

6.4.1 Own-price elasticity of demand

As we saw in Chapter 2, we are sometimes interested in the slope of demand curves. The extent to which demand responds to a price change will be important for how supply shocks affect markets, and it is also a key variable for determining profit-maximizing prices for firms that are not price takers. Figure 6.10 illustrates. Panel (a) shows a case where demand is relatively insensitive to price. Pharmaceuticals, with few substitutes, are a common example. Many consumers will be willing to pay whatever it costs to get their daily dose of a necessary medicine, and market demand is likely to shrink only little (from Q_0 to Q_1) as price increases from p_0 to p_1.

Panel (b) shows an opposite case, where demand is very sensitive to price. Also, a small change in price will be associated with a large change in quantity demanded in this case.

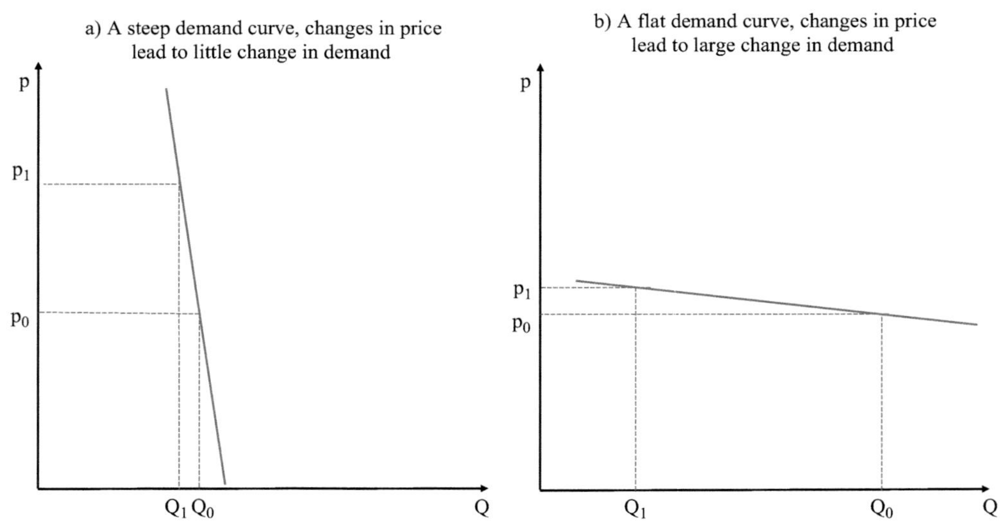

Figure 6.10 Slope of demand curves

Products with close substitutes are a key example: If consumers can readily switch to other products, the response to a price change will be large.

When we want to describe the slope of demand curves, we could in principle give the estimated equations, but such an approach is often cumbersome: Comparing data across time and countries would, for instance, require accounting for different market sizes. For example, consider the coefficient on a linear equation on demand for rice; quantity change to a price response will depend both on the currency, and the interpretation will depend on the size of the market: 1,000 tons less in purchases will not have the same interpretation in a large market such as Vietnam as in a small market like Bhutan. For many purposes, it will be useful with a measure of the price sensitivity of demand that is easily comparable across time and markets.

In economics, **elasticity** provides such a measure. It is the percentage change in one variable in response to the percentage change in another variable. While the concept is general, let us first examine the **price elasticity of demand**. This is the percentage change in quantity demanded in response to a percentage change in the price of the same good. Using Greek letter Δ (capital "Delta") to denote a change, we can thus express the elasticity of demand (E^D) as

$$E^D = \frac{\frac{\Delta Q}{Q} \times 100}{\frac{\Delta p}{p} \times 100}.$$

Use Table 6.2 to examine a simple example. Applying the formula for elasticities, we find that[2]

$$E^D = \frac{\frac{\Delta Q}{Q} \times 100}{\frac{\Delta p}{p} \times 100} = \frac{\frac{6-4}{6}}{\frac{1-2}{1}} = -\frac{1}{3}.$$

The formula is useful for many applications. To take a specific example, Allcott et al. (2019) estimate an own-price elasticity of sugar-sweetened beverages (sodas such as Coca-Cola) of −1.37 for the United States. For health reasons, soda consumption is a major policy issue in many countries, and an estimate of the impact of a price change (for instance because of a soda tax) on demand would clearly be useful for policymakers, as well as for firms active in these markets. So assume that price were to increase by 5%, by how much do we expect quantity to change if the demand elasticity is −1.37? The elasticity formula in general form is

$$E^D = \frac{\frac{\Delta Q}{Q} \times 100}{\frac{\Delta p}{p} \times 100},$$

Table 6.2 Elasticity, a simple example

	Before	*After*
Q	6	4
p	1	2

and plugging in what we know in this specific case yields

$$-1.37 = \frac{\frac{\Delta Q}{Q} \times 100}{5}$$

$$\frac{\Delta Q}{Q} \times 100 = -1.37 \times 5 = -6.85\%.$$

So, we predict that a 5% increase in price would lead to a decrease in quantity demanded of slightly less than 7% when the elasticity is −1.37. We can also use the elasticity formula to answer the related question: If we want to target a decrease in demand of 15%, by how much would price need to change? Again, we use the information that we have in the elasticity formula

$$-1.37 = \frac{-15}{\frac{\Delta p}{p} \times 100}$$

$$\frac{\Delta p}{p} \times 100 = \frac{-15}{-1.37} \approx 10.95\%$$

so that we expect that price would need to increase by around 11% for quantity to fall by 15%.[3]

Elasticities are used frequently enough that we also have names for different levels of elasticity, as outlined in Table 6.3.[4] Inelastic demand refers to the case where the percentage change in quantity is smaller than the percentage change in price. These are markets where demand curves are relatively steep (as in the left panel of Figure 6.10). Supply shocks in such markets are to a large extent going to affect prices. As mentioned, a useful aspect of elasticity estimates are that they are easily summarized and comparable. For instance, Boysen et al. (2023) survey the literature on demand for cocoa and find estimates for the price elasticities of world cocoa demand that range from −0.19 to −0.96. In their policy evaluations, they settle for a point estimate of −0.34, which was the most recent estimate at the time. Indeed, in a typical application, we use some figure for analysis but want to be sure that it is plausible in terms of the literature. To see the practical importance of such estimates, we note that a low elasticity of demand implies that supply shocks translate into large price changes, which clearly matter greatly for cocoa growers in large exporting countries like Ghana and Côte d'Ivoire. When demand is elastic, supply shocks are to a greater extent translating into quantity changes, something which clearly is of policy relevance as well.

Let us now mention some aspects of elasticities that are useful to know. First, given that demand elasticities are negative, it can be a bit confusing to talk of smaller or larger elasticities. The clearest is to talk of more or less elastic, but note that if we say a higher elasticity, we typically think of the absolute value of the elasticity, $|E^D|$. A second aspect

Table 6.3 Elasticities, naming conventions

Name	*Level of elasticity*
Inelastic	$-1 < E^D < 0$
Unit elastic	$-1 = E^D$
Elastic	$E^D < -1$

is that we often see elasticities also for differentiated products, such as soda, as discussed earlier. We can estimate elasticities at several levels, from disaggregated (for instance how does the demand for 250 ml bottles of Fanta Lemon respond to a price change) to more aggregated levels (summing all the soda sales and seeing how the aggregate sale responds to a change in the average price). Typically, elasticity at the more disaggregated level is more elastic since there are more close substitutes if the price increases, which leads to a larger response. Miller et al. (2021), for instance, estimate that, for beer in the United States, the median product-level demand elasticity is −4.74, whereas the median demand elasticity for beer overall is −0.60.

Finally, because of the ease of substitution, demand is typically less elastic in the short run than in the long run. In their survey of the literature, Labandeira et al. (2017), for instance, find an average estimated elasticity of electricity demand around −0.6 in the long run and −0.24 in the short run.[5] In the long run, consumers have greater scope to modify their behavior in response to a higher price, choose equipment that uses less electricity, and so forth.

Let us end this exposé of elasticities by commenting on functional forms and how elasticities are evaluated. One specific form of demand curves are those known as constant elastic. The demand function is then given by $Q = ap^{\epsilon}$, where ϵ is the elasticity of demand. It is commonly used in empirical estimation of demand functions, and, simply put, if we have random observations on a large number of prices, we can estimate the elasticity of demand from the following specification (where *ln* denotes the natural logarithm):

$$ln(Q) = ln(a) + \epsilon \times ln(p) + \text{error term}.$$

In this case, the elasticity is captured by the variable ϵ, irrespective of at what price it is evaluated. Say that we have estimated an $\epsilon = -1.2$ for apples, for instance. Then, with this demand curve, the elasticity would be −1.2 at both a price of 0.5 euros per kilo and a price of 5 euros per kilo. That is not always the case however, and for another type of demand function, linear demand functions, the elasticity depends on where we evaluate it. To see this, take the formula for elasticity

$$E^D = \frac{\frac{\Delta Q}{Q} \times 100}{\frac{\Delta p}{p} \times 100}$$

and rewrite in the following form:[6]

$$E^D = \frac{\Delta Q}{\Delta p} \times \frac{p}{Q}. \tag{6.2}$$

The first term in Equation (6.2), the change in quantity over the change in price, can be thought of as a derivative if we are considering a small change. For a linear demand function, this derivative is always the same, whereas the price and quantity at which we evaluate an elasticity will differ. To illustrate, let us consider the linear demand function $Q = 10 - 2p$. Using dQ/dp to denote the derivative of Q with respect to p, we thus have that

$$E^D = \frac{dQ}{dp} \times \frac{p}{Q}.$$
$$E^D = -2 \times \frac{p}{Q}.$$

An increase in price of 1 euro will always result in 2 units less being demanded. In percentage terms, this change will differ depending on where we evaluate it however. At $p = 2.5$, for instance, $Q = 10 - 2 \times 2.5 = 5$ so that

$$E^D = -2 \times \frac{2.5}{5} = -1$$

and at $p = 4$, $Q = 10 - 2 \times 4 = 2$ such that

$$E^D = -2 \times \frac{2}{2} = -2.$$

This illustrates how, for a linear demand curve, the elasticity depends on at what price it is evaluated. Demand is more elastic when price is higher: A given change in quantity will be a greater percentage change when quantities are lower, and a given change in price will be smaller in percentage terms when price is high.

6.4.2 *Cross-price elasticities of demand*

We are sometimes interested in how prices of other products affect demand – for instance, how is the quantity demanded for a particular brand of soda affected by the price of another brand of soda? How is the demand for apples affected by the price of pears? Again we use elasticities and the **cross-price elasticity of demand** measures the percentage change in demanded quantity for product A in response to a percentage change in the price of product B. If the cross-price elasticity is positive the two products are **substitutes** – if the price of a Heineken beer goes up this increases the demand for Carlsberg beer, the substitute product just got more expensive which induces more people to choose Carlsberg. The greater the cross-price elasticity, the closer substitutes are the two products. These effects are important for instance when we want to understand the competitive pressure of new products entering the market or when competition authorities evaluate mergers between firms.

If, on the other hand, the cross-price elasticity is negative the products are **complements**. If the price of smart phones increases, the demand for smart phone protective covers decreases. Summarizing the discussion we thus have:[7]

$$\text{If } E^{Cross-price} = \begin{cases} \dfrac{\frac{\Delta Q_A}{Q_A} \times 100}{\frac{\Delta p_B}{p_B} \times 100} > 0, & \text{products are substitutes} \\ \dfrac{\frac{\Delta Q_A}{Q_A} \times 100}{\frac{\Delta p_B}{p_B} \times 100} < 0, & \text{products are complements.} \end{cases} \tag{6.3}$$

6.4.3 *Income elasticity of demand*

The **income elasticity of demand** measures the percentage change in demand as incomes change. Depending on the application, income might be household or individual-level data but this can also refer to average incomes measured at for instance the municipality level.

We use the terms "normal goods" for goods whose demand increases when incomes increase and "inferior goods" for goods whose demand decreases as incomes increase.

$$\text{If } E^{Income} = \begin{cases} \frac{\frac{\Delta Q}{Q} \times 100}{\frac{\Delta I}{I} \times 100} > 0, & \text{normal goods} \\ \frac{\frac{\Delta Q}{Q} \times 100}{\frac{\Delta I}{I} \times 100} < 0, & \text{inferior goods.} \end{cases} \tag{6.4}$$

The income elasticity of demand is useful when making long term projections over what happens to demand as incomes change over time – for instance making projections of demand for health care or of household appliances in low income countries. Knowing how quantity demanded responds to changes in income is also useful for predicting how demand depends on the business cycle – demand for pharmaceuticals for instance is relatively unaffected by incomes and pharmaceutical companies are a common example of "defensive stocks," stocks that do comparatively well in economic downturns.

Some of the first more serious data work in economics was concerned with the relation between demand for food and incomes. In the 1800s Ernst Engel was prominent in the Prussian statistical office and took an interest in these issues. In his honor, we name a graphical relation between demand for a product and incomes for Engel curves.[8] With income on the horizontal axis and demand on the vertical axis, Engel curves have a positive slope for normal goods and a negative slope for inferior goods. What is sometimes termed "Engel's law" is also associated with Ernst Engel: It states that the share of income spent on food decreases as incomes increase. In other words, the income elasticity of food is less than 1.[9]

6.4.4 Elasticities: A simple example

The discussion of elasticities may still appear somewhat abstract, and it may be useful to briefly discuss an example. In my native Sweden, a question of policy interest has been that some consumers travel to neighboring Denmark to buy alcohol, taking advantage of lower prices of beer, wine, and spirits in Danish retail stores. To understand the effect of such cross-border shopping on demand for alcohol in Swedish retail stores, I, together with two co-authors, assembled and analyzed data from Sweden (Asplund et al. (2007)). Using statistical methods, we relate the sales per month (liter) per municipality of beer, wine, and spirits over a number of years. We relate this outcome variable to a price index of the respective product (generating an own-price elasticity), to average household income in the municipality (generating an income elasticity of demand), and to a price index of the respective product in Denmark (generating a cross-price elasticity of demand). Table 6.4 presents the results. We see, for instance, that demand for spirits – high-alcohol products such as vodka and whiskey – is elastic. An increase in the price index for spirits in Sweden of 1% generates a decrease in the number of liters sold of 1.3%. The cross-price elasticity of demand for spirits with respect to price in neighboring Denmark is positive; as expected, spirits bought in Denmark are a substitute for spirits bought at home.[10] The income elasticity of demand for spirits is 1.4, indicating that spirits are a normal good. The final row serves to illustrate that we can think of many other elasticities than the ones discussed earlier. Here we note that the number of Fridays differ across months, and weekends are likely to be high demand periods. Indeed, that hypothesis was confirmed; more Fridays in a month are associated with more sales.

Table 6.4 Elasticities – An example

	Spirits	*Beer*	*Wine*
Own-price elasticity	−1.3	−0.9	−0.2
Cross-price elasticity (price in Denmark)	0.3	0.5	0.2
Income elasticity	1.4	1.0	0.6
Elasticity with respect to number of Fridays per month	0.1	0.2	0.2

Excerpt from Table 3 in Asplund et al. (2007)

6.5 Income and substitution effects

In Figure 6.5, we showed how demand could be affected even if a consumer was fully compensated. This is a specific example of a more general topic of analysis – that of income and substitution effects, which we explore in this section. It is conceptually deeper than the material we have encountered so far and amounts to a "behind-the-scenes" examination of the mechanisms that shape the effect of price changes on demand. Consider again the case of two goods, *E* and *F* and assume that the price of *F* increases. If demand curves are downward sloping, we expect demand for *F* to decrease in response to that higher price. An analysis of income and substitution effects shows how the total quantity response to such a price change can be decomposed into two parts:

- An **income effect**: If p_F increases, it is as if the consumer's income has decreased. If the consumer were to purchase the same quantity as before the price change, she would now have less to spend on other goods. Just as with "regular" changes in income, this is positive for normal goods and negative for inferior goods.
- A **substitution effect**: If p_F increases, *F* becomes more expensive relative to other goods – the isolated effect of the substitution effect is that this relative price increase induces a consumer to substitute away from *F* (if goods are imperfect substitutes).

The analysis is useful to understand at a deeper level the forces that shape demand. Overall, we have that

Total effect of a price change on demand = income effect + substitution effect.

The substitution effect is always negative (or zero) – if the price of a good or service increases, consumers tend to lower consumption of that product, other things equal. The income effect can either reinforce this tendency (for normal goods) or counteract it (for inferior goods). If I live on a low income, consuming a lot of macaroni and then the price of macaroni goes up, I'd like to move away from buying macaroni and instead buy more of other products whose prices have not gone up. But with the price increase, its as if I had a lower income. If macaroni are an inferior good, this tends to limit the amount of switching. Let's use some figures to further clarify.

In Figure 6.11, we first show the effect of a price increase in *F*, from p_F^O to p_F^N. The intercept with the vertical axis (I/p_E) is unchanged, but the steeper slope of the budget constraint, due to the higher relative price of *F*, associates with a lower quantity demanded for *F*.

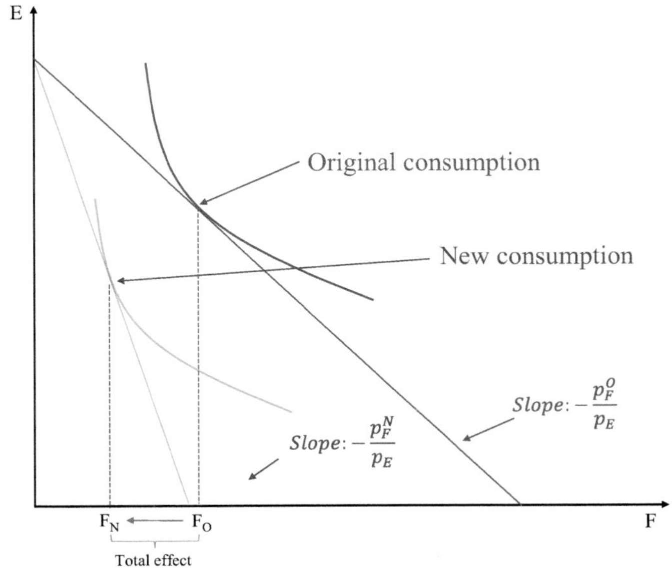

Figure 6.11 Demand for F at two different prices for F. Video link for Figures 6.11–6.13: https://youtu.be/SluLMYCjOak.

Now turn to the decomposition. First, consider the substitution effect. We operationalize this as the change in quantity demanded for F, letting the consumer face the new relative price but keeping utility fixed at the initial indifference curve.[11] We illustrate in Figure 6.12, where we can think of a hypothetical budget constraint where the individual is compensated so that she is able to reach the original indifference curve but, facing the new, steeper relative price p_F^N/p_E, would demand less F. In some cases (as in the example in Figure 6.5), a compensation is carried out, but typically, this is just a thought experiment. The substitution effect is the change in quantity from F_O to F_S.

The income effect then is the change in quantity that is associated with the parallel shift in this hypothetical budget constraint that is associated with the difference between the allocation chosen at the original and new prices; that is, the income effect is given by the difference between F_S and F_N in Figure 6.13. Here, for a normal good, the income effect reinforces the substitution effect. I buy less F since F has become more expensive relative to other goods (substitution effect), and because the price increase leaves me with less money, its as if I had a lower income, and for a normal good, I want to consume less (the income effect).

Now, we proceed to examine income and substitution effects for an inferior good. Assume that macaroni is an inferior good and consider the effects of a price increase in macaroni from p_M^O to p_M^N in Figure 6.14. We proceed by the same steps as before, first establishing a substitution effect from M_O to M_N, but now the income effect pulls in the opposite direction. I want to shift away from macaroni, but again, it's as if I had a lower income. With my lower income, demand for an inferior good tends to increase, which counterbalances, but does not fully make up for, the substitution effect. The end result is that for such a product, demand tends to be relatively unresponsive to price. The "more

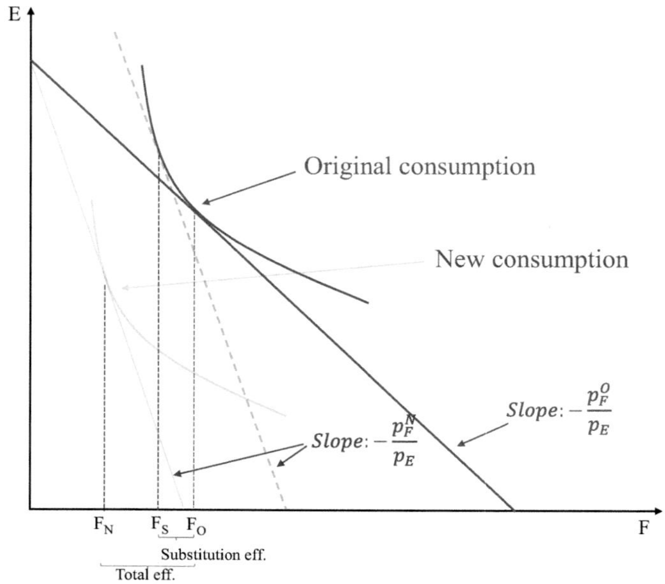

Figure 6.12 The substitution effect. Video link for Figures 6.11–6.13: https://youtu.be/SluLMYCjOak.

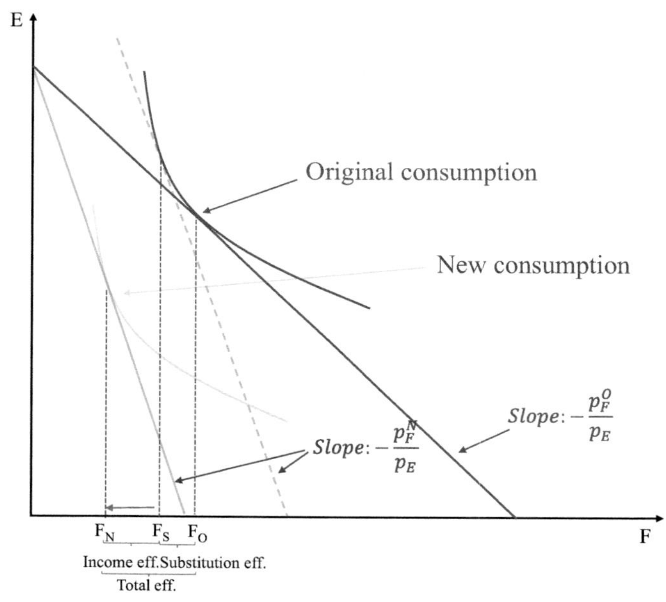

Figure 6.13 The income effect for a normal good. Video link for Figures 6.11–6.13: https://youtu.be/SluLMYCjOak.

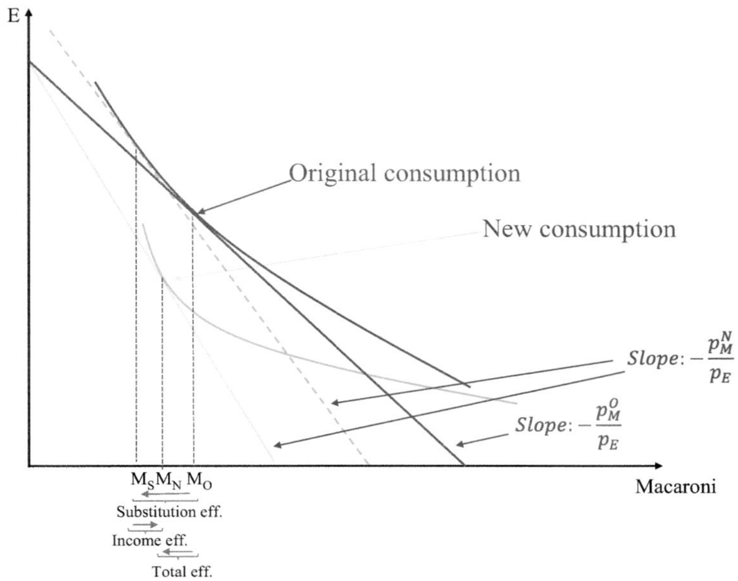

Figure 6.14 Income and substitution effects for an inferior good. Video link for Figure 6.14: https://youtu.be/R8nORhYHhIo.

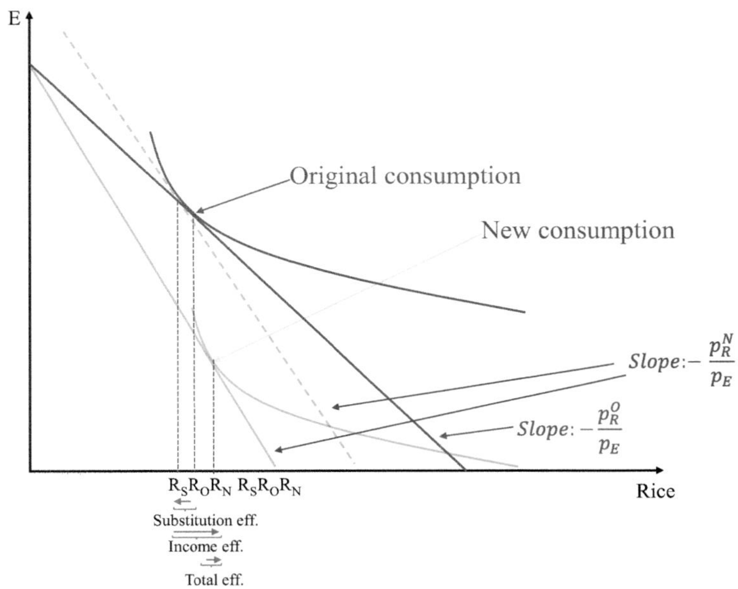

Figure 6.15 Income and substitution effects for a Giffen good. Video link for Figure 6.15: https://youtu.be/q5Jxu3GHa9o.

inferior" (the more negative the income elasticity of demand) and the lower the degree of substitutability, the less will demand shrink in response to a price increase.

This last observation also points to the case of **Giffen goods**. These are inferior goods where the income effect is strong enough to dominate the substitution effect. The case of potatoes in Ireland in the mid-1800s that gave the effect its name remains far from settled, but a more recent example concerns rice among poor households in China (Jensen and Miller (2008)). Figure 6.15 illustrates. The figure is also useful to illustrate that it is the shape of the indifference curves that generates the points of tangency with the budget constraints, and hence the relative size of effects. Here a low degree of substitutability is visible – when the price of rice goes up, these households find it very hard to substitute to anything else, only changing from R_O to R_S. The income effect is strong with this one and shifts demand from R_S to R_N – more than outweighing the substitution effect and leading to the result that as price increases, consumers demand more of the good. These are the cases where consumers will forego whatever protein they might otherwise have afforded; now they can "only afford rice."

Notes

1 While this may look like a pretty odd animal, it is a functional form that is fairly common in economic applications and is known as a constant elasticity of substitution utility function.

2 For simplicity, we use the quantity and price before the change as base. In applications, we typically use the midpoint as base (e.g., letting $\Delta Q/Q = (6-4)/(0.5 \times 6 + 0.5 \times 4)$, but the way we present it in this section is the simplest way to introduce the concepts.

3 Note how we use decimals in the calculations but round off to larger numbers in our discussion. While what you round off to is a matter of taste, it is often useful in economics to avoid using too many decimals so as not to give the impression of more precision than what is reasonable to work with. So many things are not kept constant in the real world that numbers like these are best thought of as ballpark numbers. Reporting that price needs to increase by 10.94890511 would give the wrong impression. You may have come across the quip, "How can you tell economists have a sense of humor? They use decimal points," which aims to target precisely this. This, of course, is in contrast to the case in some natural sciences where precision can really matter.

4 I am sometimes asked what we call a demand elasticity that is positive. There is no commonly used term for that, the reason being that a case where demand increases as prices increase is such an unusual situation that we discuss it in detail. It is known as Giffen goods, as discussed in the appendix to this chapter.

5 There is no standard definition of long run in these cases, but rather, it refers to a period when major adjustment in principle can take place, and arguably, a case of adjustment over say 2–5 years would be considered as long run, while short run could be over periods up to a year.

6 We here use the mathematical rule that $\frac{1}{\frac{a}{b}} = \frac{b}{a}$.

7 A third possibility is, of course, that the cross-price elasticity is 0. We then say that the demand for the products are independent. There is no effect of a change in the price of haircuts in Wellington, New Zealand, on demand for bicycles in Quito, Ecuador.

8 See Chai and Moneta (2010) for an accessible discussion of Engel's early work. Note that Ernst Engel is a different person that Friedrich Engels, who worked closely with Karl Marx.

9 Sometimes we refer to goods with income elasticities of demand between 0 and 1 as necessities. To take a simple example, the amount of toothpaste that you demand is likely to be relatively independent of your income. Goods with an elasticity greater than 1 are sometimes referred to as luxury goods.

10 The reported coefficient measures the effect in the municipality closest to Denmark; for the other municipalities (not reported here), we let the coefficient reflect distance to Denmark as well; the data confirm that the further from Denmark a municipality is located, the weaker the cross-price effect.

11 This way of calculating the substitution effect is associated with Sir John Hicks, and hence is sometimes known as the Hicksian substitution. An alternative, with much of the same intuition, is associated with Evgeny (often written as "Eugen") Slutsky and keeps the ability to afford the original consumption basket fixed. The hypothetical budget constraint then rotates around the original consumption point rather than around the indifference curve. The Hicks version is the one most commonly used.

Part III

Efficiency and equity in a competitive market

Thus far in the book, we have developed supply and demand under the assumption that all firms and consumers act as *price takers* with many producers of *homogeneous products*. We also saw how the *free entry* led to zero profits. Together, these are the key assumptions for what we term a **perfectly competitive market**.[1]

Perfectly competitive markets are often upheld as an ideal, and in the following two chapters, we present the background for that. Simply put, we can think of the question of how resources are allocated as encompassing two issues:

- Is the allocation efficient? That is, does it "make the pie as large as possible"'?
- Is the allocation fair? "How do we split the pie"?

Chapter 7 analyzes the efficiency of allocation studying one market at a time – what we term "partial equilibrium." We also show how we can quantify the effects of various policies on firms and consumers. Chapter 8 analyzes efficiency in a perfectly competitive economy where all markets interact and introduces some fundamental concepts regarding fairness of the resulting economy.

Note

1 Sometimes textbooks list additional assumptions, in particular that there are no information asymmetries (explored in Chapter 14) and that there are no costs of transacting. Creating long lists invites memorization, however, and that is the wrong message to take from this book. Hence, the focus on price-taking behavior and free entry, which are the key ingredients. We will provide a deeper discussion at the beginning of Chapter 8, but for clarity, you can think of the additional assumptions that imply a perfectly competitive market as boiling down to assuming that markets work as well as possible in making sure that prices reflect demand and the true costs associated with production of each good or service.

DOI: 10.4324/9781003623854-9

7 Efficiency in partial equilibrium

Illustration 7.1 How to split the cake? *Still Life with Cake* Raphaelle Peale. Public domain, Metropolitan Museum of Art.

7.1 Efficiency of a competitive market

Broadly speaking, we can think of efficiency as maximizing the value that is created in a market. How much satisfaction, joy, well-being, or utility is created among consumers? How much profit is generated among producers? We could imagine adding up some measure of efficiency in production with the sum of utilities of individuals. But how should we know what those utility levels are? How can we add them? Such an exercise would be extremely difficult. Economists have therefore instead come up with a measure, in money, that attempts to capture the value created to consumers of consuming a particular good at a particular price. We term this measure **consumer surplus**. It is a measure in euros, or whatever the relevant currency is, and it measures the difference between what consumers would be willing to pay for a good and what they actually pay.

7.2 Consumer surplus

To explain the concept of consumer surplus, let us consider an example. Figure 7.1 presents the demand for cups of coffee for me during one day. For clarity, we assume that the number of cups of coffee is a discrete variable (1, 2, etc, not 1.1145, for instance), and hence the

DOI: 10.4324/9781003623854-10

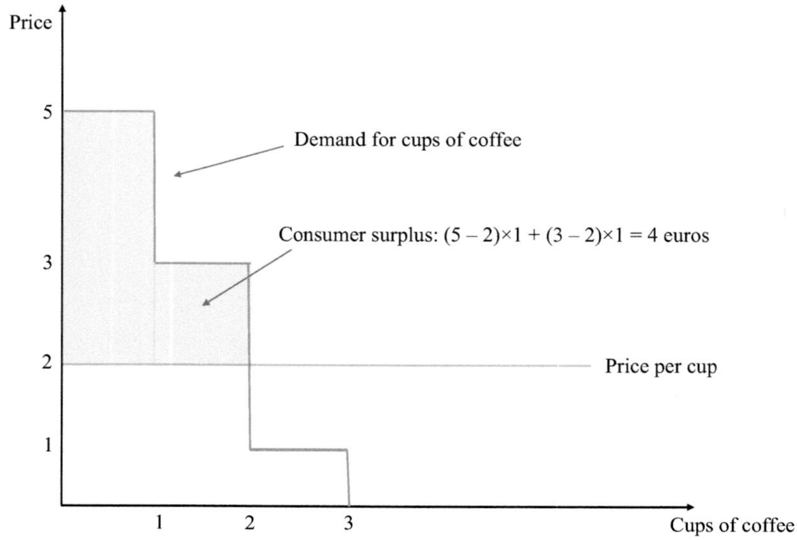

Figure 7.1 Consumer surplus for one individual.

jagged look of the demand curve. Assume that the price of coffee in this market is 2 euros per cup. For the first cup, I am willing to pay 5 euros (just an aside on nomenclature: the highest price that I'm willing to pay for a good is referred to as the **reservation price**). So I'm willing to pay 5 euros, but I only have to pay 2 euros for this first cup. The difference between what I'm willing to pay and what I actually pay is my consumer surplus, and hence, for the contribution of the first cup to consumer surplus is $5 - 2 = 3$ euros. For a second cup, I'm willing to pay less, in this case 3 euros (as I've already satisfied my craving for caffeine), and this second cup adds $3 - 2 = 1$ euro to the consumer surplus. The total consumer surplus of my coffee consumption for one day is therefore $3 + 1 = 4$ euros.

For the intuition behind the measure, think of participating in an auction for buying a small apartment. Assume that you are willing to offer at most 50,000 euros for the apartment. If you then are able to buy it for 49,000 euros, you're likely to be glad that you got it but a lot less content than what you would be if the difference between your maximum willingness to pay and what you actually pay were greater. If you got the apartment for only 10,000 euros, you'd in all likelihood be much more content. From the figure, we can also note that the consumer surplus equals the area bounded by the demand curve and the prices that are paid for each unit.

These monetary measures of surplus can be added across individuals. The consumer surplus for the market is simply the area between the market demand curve and the price line, as illustrated in Figure 7.2. This implies a simple way to implement a calculation of consumer surplus. We can estimate the demand curve using data from a market. Say that the estimated demand function is given by $p = 5 - Q$, where Q is measured in hundreds of cups. The consumer surplus would thus be given by the area of the triangle bounded by 5 (the intercept) and 2 (the price) and the quantity demanded (300). Remembering

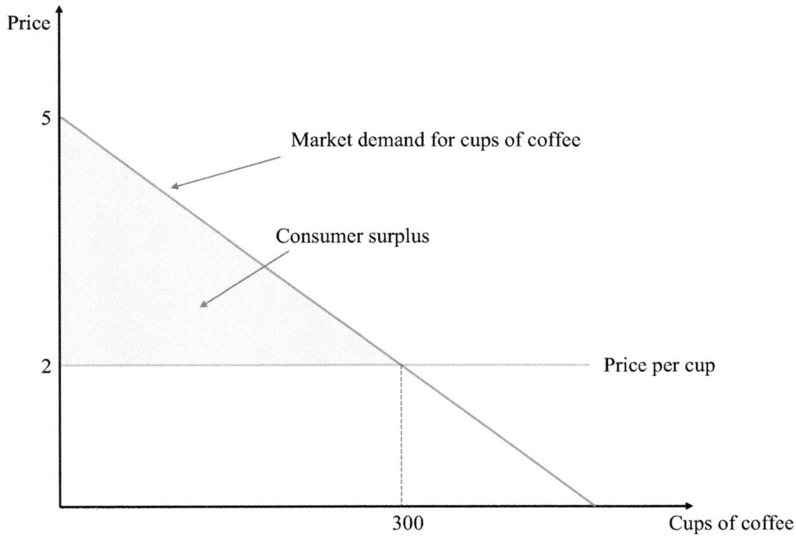

Figure 7.2 Consumer surplus for the market.

that the area of a triangle is given by base × height divided by 2, we immediately find that

$$\text{Consumer Surplus} = \frac{(5-2)\times 300}{2} = 450 \text{ euros.}$$

7.2.1 *Changes in consumer surplus*

A frequent application of the current framework examines how consumer surplus responds to a change in price. We can distinguish two effects, as illustrated in Figure 7.3. Consider the market for buses going to the beach in a small town. If price increases from p_0 to p_1, consumer surplus decreases partly because the bus trips that are taken also at this higher price leave less surplus between the willingness to pay (as captured by the demand curve) and the price. So consumer surplus decreases by the beige area, bounded by p_0, p_1 and Q_1. Consumer surplus also decreases by the trips not taken at this higher price, trips between Q_1 and Q_0. These trips, with their joy of swimming and hanging out at the beach, are not taken at this higher price. This forgone consumption is an additional loss to consumer surplus.

7.2.2 *Diamonds and water again*

In Chapter 2, we noted that it was sometimes expressed as a puzzle that the price of diamonds is high and the price of water in most cases low, despite the latter being crucial for survival. If we think of the price of something as the sole measure of value, this might indeed seem disconcerting. Here we note how consumer surplus can help give intuitive results on the valuation of different goods. While price is determined by the intersection of supply and demand, we typically value the first units of water very highly, which impacts

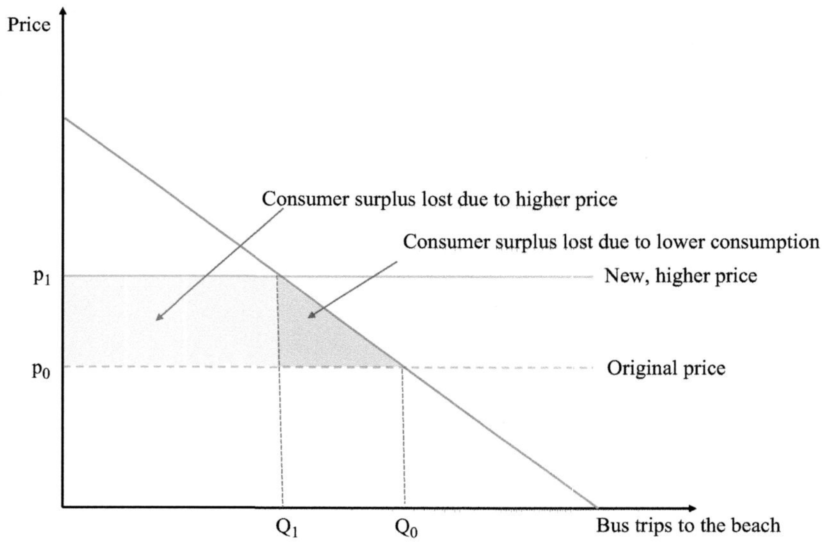

Figure 7.3 Effects of a higher price on consumer surplus.

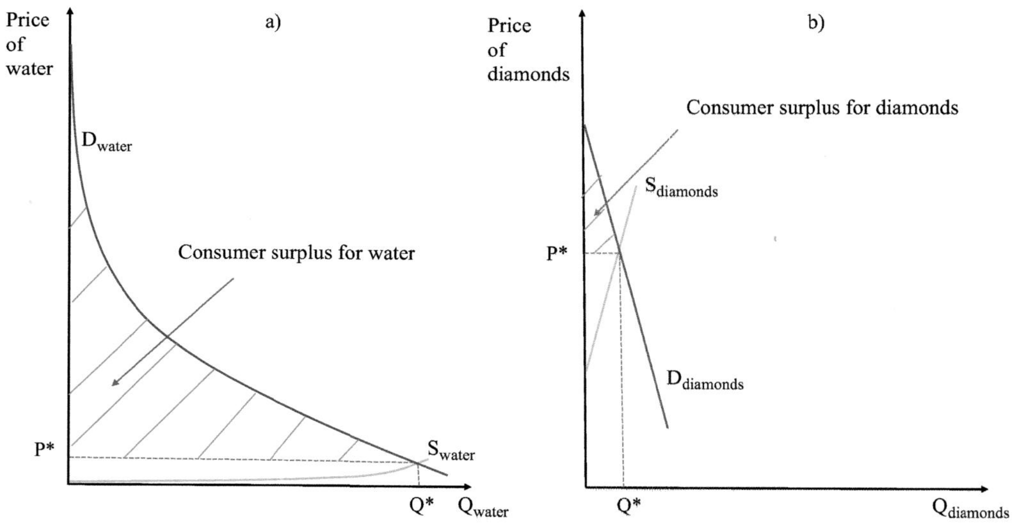

Figure 7.4 Diamonds and water – The difference between price and consumer surplus as measures of value.

consumer surplus, even if it doesn't affect price in a market where supply is plentiful, as illustrated in Figure 7.4. This exemplifies how, even if the price of water is very low, its value, as measured by the consumer surplus, can be very high. The opposite holds for diamonds.

7.3 Producer surplus

We are concerned not only with efficiency on the consumer side, and hence we want a measure of efficiency also for producers. We saw before that a price-taking firm is willing to supply a good at marginal cost. The difference between price and marginal costs can therefore be viewed as a measure of the value created on the supply side. Indeed, the corresponding measure to consumer surplus for the supply side is known as **producer surplus**. The producer surplus is defined as the difference between the price and the associated marginal cost (the price that it in principle would be willing to supply that unit for) aggregated over all the units produced by the firm. Figure 7.5 illustrates, where we have also included a set of numbers to allow calculation (price equal to 10 euros, an intercept of the marginal cost curve of 2 and 100 units supplied). With increasing marginal costs, the first units produced contribute much to producer surplus, and then additional units contribute successively less and less. We can calculate producer surplus as the area of the triangle between the price and marginal cost curve.[1] Thus the producer surplus in this case is given by $(10 - 2) \times 100/2 = 400$ euros.

In practice, there is a very simple way to calculate producer surplus. Note that the marginal cost for the first unit is 2, and then marginal costs are successively higher. What are total variable costs? Well, they are the sum of the marginal costs. We can thus think of the area below the marginal cost curve as the total variable cost.[2] Total revenue is given by price times quantity, which can be represented as the area of the rectangle outlined by price and quantity in Figure 7.5, in this case equal to $10 \times 100 = 1000$ euros. We can therefore express producer surplus as revenue minus variable costs. Knowing that profit is equal to revenue minus variable and fixed costs is also a useful relation in some applications:

$$\Pi = \underbrace{p \times q - \text{Variable cost}}_{\text{Producer surplus}} - \text{Fixed costs}$$

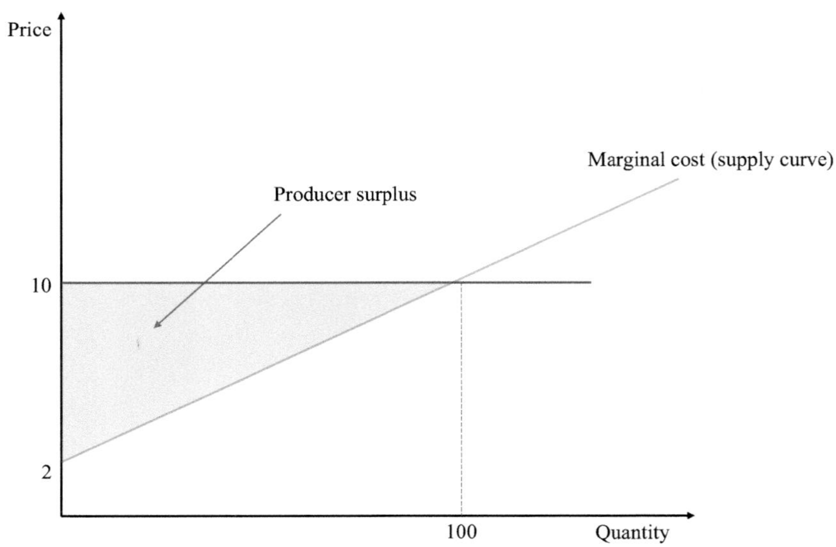

Figure 7.5 Producer surplus for a firm.

Thus, to estimate consumer surplus in real-world applications, we often rely on estimated demand curves. To gauge producer surplus, we instead use variable profit (revenue-variable cost) that we, for instance, measure with data from company annual reports or from data collected by national statistical offices.

7.4 Putting CS and PS together: Efficiency in partial equilibrium

We now have the ingredients needed to examine the efficiency of a perfectly competitive market. One potential measure of efficiency that directly takes "the size of the pie" as a starting point is the sum of consumer surplus and producer surplus. We thereby sum the value created on the consumer and producer sides of the market. Figure 7.6 illustrates one case, where supply is given by $p = 2 + 2Q^S$ and demand by $p = 23 - Q^D$. The market equilibrium quantity under perfect competition is given by equating supply and demand: $2 + 2Q = 23 - Q$, and thereby $Q^* = 7$, and equilibrium price equals $23 - 7 = 16$ euros. Consumer surplus is now $(23 - 16) \times 7/2 = 24.5$ euros, and producer surplus is $(16 - 2) \times 7/2 = 49$ euros. Welfare, measured as the sum of producer surplus and consumer surplus, is hence equal to $24.5 + 49 = 73.5$ euros.

To see that the perfectly competitive outcome maximizes welfare (when measured as CS + PS), we compare with alternative situations. First, consider the case where for some reason supply is constrained to be no higher than 5. If 5 units are supplied, the demand curve requires that $p = 23 - 5 = 18$ for the market to clear. Just by looking at the figure, it is clear that the shaded areas in Figure 7.7 are smaller than the shaded areas in Figure 7.6. Let us however consider the difference between the two figures in some detail. In the perfectly competitive case, consumer surplus is equal to areas A + B + C. In Figure 7.7, consumer surplus has fallen to A only. Area B represents a transfer to producer surplus; consumers are paying more for the units that are purchased. Area C represents a pure loss; these are

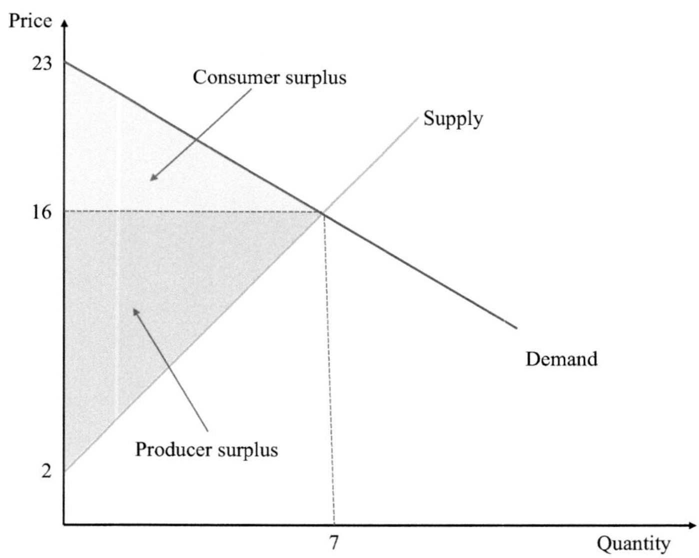

Figure 7.6 Consumer and producer surplus in a perfectly competitive market. Video link for Figures 7.6, 7.7 and Table 7.1: https://youtu.be/12-gu3LOR2w.

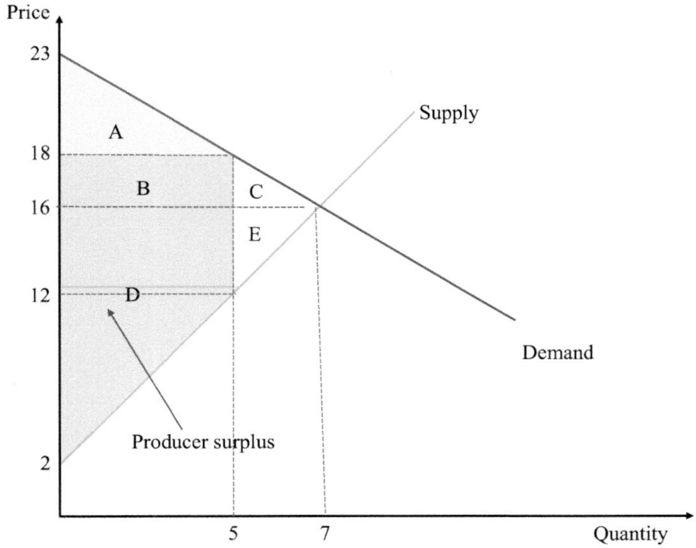

Figure 7.7 Lower welfare with an alternative price and quantity. Video link for Figures 7.6, 7.7 and Table 7.1: https://youtu.be/12-gu3LOR2w.

units that were consumed and added to consumer surplus in the perfectly competitive case but that are not consumed in the alternative situation. Producer surplus equals D + E in the perfectly competitive case and B + D in the alternative case. The area B is a transfer from consumers to producers, as already discussed, and area E represents a pure loss: units that were sold and added to the producer surplus in the perfectly competitive case that are now foregone.

The areas C and E represent what we term a **deadweight loss**. It is a monetary measure of the loss to society of a different quantity being produced than that which is efficient. Remember that all the areas in Figure 7.7 are in monetary terms, so with knowledge of the demand and supply curves, we can calculate the deadweight loss. A direct calculation of the area gives that it amounts to $(18 - 12) \times (7 - 5)/2 = 6$ euros. Alternatively, we can deduct the sum of CS and PS (67.5)[3] in this alternative situation from the total welfare estimate for the perfectly competitive situation and again reach a deadweight loss of 6 euros (73.5 – 67.5).

We can also present the situation in Table 7.1, which summarizes the previous discussion. The difference between the two cases, in this case areas C and E, represent the deadweight loss. This is loss in overall welfare in an alternative situation relative to an efficient situation. To take a specific example, think of apples in Figure 7.7. The welfare loss pertains to quantities between 5 and 7 kilos that would be traded in the perfectly competitive market but are not supplied in the alternative case. So there are consumers willing to pay, for instance, 17 euros for a kilo of apples, and producers willing to supply apples at a price of 13 euros per kilo. There are thus clear gains from trade, and it should be clear that it represents a loss of efficiency if such trades do not come about. We're not making the pie as large as possible if such inefficiencies exist.

Table 7.1 Market demand is the sum of individuals' demand

Welfare measure	*Alternative case*	*Perfect comp.*	*Difference*
CS	A	A+B+C	−B−C
PS	B+D	D+E	B−E
Welfare(CS+PS)	A+B+D	A+B+C+D+E	−C − E (Deadweight Loss)

Video link for Figures 7.6, 7.7 and Table 7.1: https://youtu.be/12-gu3LOR2w.

7.5 Policy and deadweight loss

7.5.1 Price cap

A price cap, or price ceiling, sets a limit on how high price can be. These have been commonly used in history, not seldom implemented in times of crisis and then not always easily abolished as conditions improve. We use Figure 7.8 to illustrate, using the same demand and supply functions as used earlier. Assume that there is a price cap at 12 euros such that price can be no higher than that. The price cap thus implies that price is 12, and at this price, supply will be given by 5 (since Q = 5 solves $2 + 2Q = 12$). There is clearly excess demand at this point (since $23 - Q = 12$ implies a quantity demanded of 11 units), and queues are a standard symptom of price caps. For the welfare analysis, the excess demand is not of importance however.[4] Relative to the perfectly competitive outcome, there is a shift from producer surplus to consumer surplus represented by the area B. Prices fall for the units consumed, and this benefits consumers at the expense of producers. In this case, the welfare transfer amounts to $(16 - 12) \times 5 = 20$ euros.

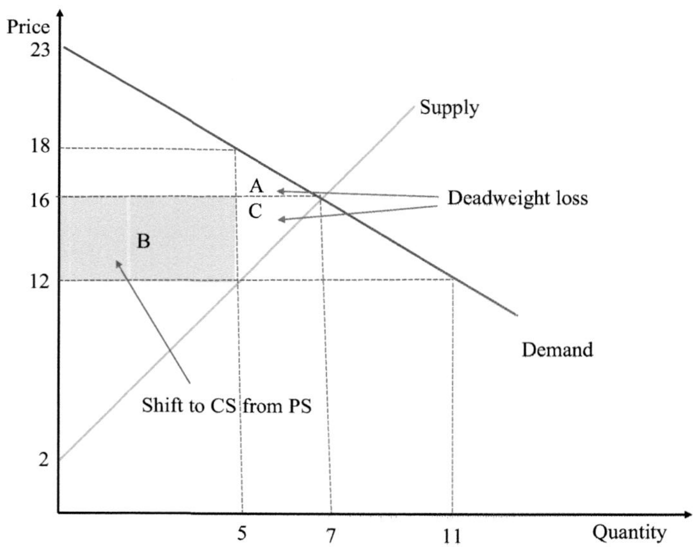

Figure 7.8 Welfare effects of a price cap. Video link for Figure 7.8: https://youtu.be/MZ73Wt7sSQI.

Relative to the perfectly competitive situation, there is also a pure loss from a loss of consumer surplus (area A) and producer surplus (area C). The deadweight loss amounts to $(18 - 12) \times (7 - 5)/2 = 6$ euros. From the consumers' side, they benefit from lower prices, but this is counterweighted by a loss of units that are not consumed as supply is held back. Indeed, the negative effect on supply is the key argument against price caps as a policy response to high prices in a given market. Also note that distributional aspects are important for the effects of price caps – some consumers may get to purchase at low prices, whereas others are not able to purchase at all (simply put, the people in B and A are not necessarily the same).

7.5.2 *Unit tax*

The analysis of taxes is an important topic in economics. Taxes are used to finance redistribution and insurance (in many countries, education and health care are, for instance, financed via taxes), as well as to finance a number of governmental tasks such as defense and other collectively supplied goods. They are also used to limit negative consequences of, for instance, environmentally harmful products (some of the motivations are discussed in Chapter 13). The simplest case to analyze is that of a **unit tax**, a tax that is a certain amount per unit sold. Common examples across countries is a tax per liter of gasoline, a tax per liter of alcoholic beverage, or a tax per cigarette.

We will again use the functional forms from earlier to illustrate. The key insight regarding a unit tax is that it creates a difference between the price that buyers pay and the price that sellers receive. Denote the first with p_b and the latter with p_s. Using t to denote the tax, we thus have $p_b = p_s + t$. To solve for the equilibrium prices and quantities with taxes, it is simplest to use demand and supply rather than their inverse forms (in this case rewriting $p = 2+2Q^S$ to $Q^S = -1+p_s/2$). Also assume that the tax is 3 euros per unit. We then have the following three relations that need to hold

$$\begin{cases} Q^D = 23 - p_b \\ Q^S = -1 + \frac{p_s}{2} \\ p_b = p_s + \underbrace{3}_{t}. \end{cases} \tag{7.1}$$

To solve this system, we can simply insert the price relation into the demand function and solve for the supplier price that equates quantity demanded and quantity supplied

$$23 - \underbrace{(p_s + 3)}_{p_b} = -1 + \frac{p_s}{2}.$$

We solve for p_s and find that, in steps

$$46 - 2p_s - 6 = -2 + p_s$$
$$p_s = \frac{42}{3} = 14.$$

With $p_s = 14$, we then know that $p_b = 14 + 3 = 17$ euros. The price that buyers pay is 3 euros higher than the price that the sellers receive. To find the quantity, we can simply use

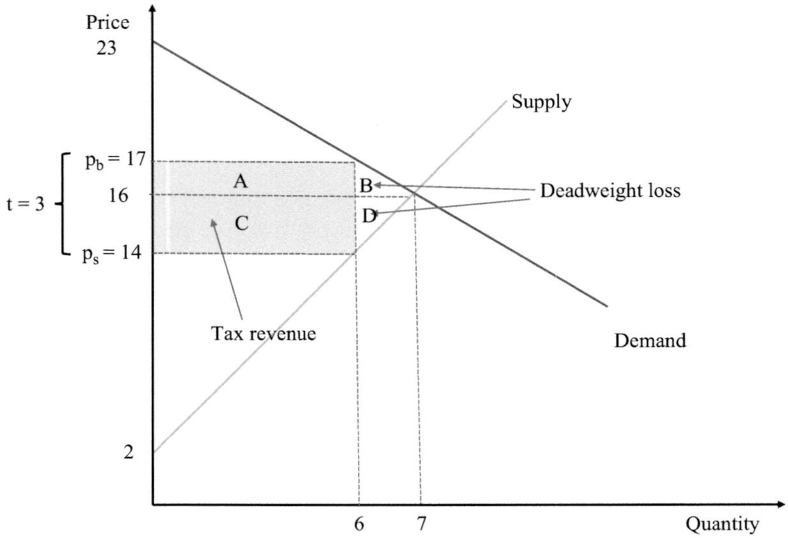

Figure 7.9 Calculating the effects of a unit tax. Video link for Figure 7.8: https://youtu.be/HaA7R2HS1a0.

the price that buyers pay in the demand equation to find that $Q = 23 - 17 = 6$. Figure 7.9 illustrates.

There are several things to note in the figure that hold generally. *The tax drives a wedge between the price that buyers pay and that sellers receive,* $p_b = p_s + t$. The tax raises the price that buyers pay and lowers the price that sellers receive (the extent to which this happens depends on the slope of supply and demand, as we examine next). The tax lowers consumer surplus (by A+B in Figure 7.9) and lowers producer surplus (by C+D in Figure 7.9). For society as a whole, these losses partly *represent a transfer to the government budget*; tax revenue is given by the unit tax times the quantity that is sold when taxes are implemented; in this case, the tax raises the equivalent of areas A and C: $3 \times 6 = 18$ euros. Areas B and D correspond to a *deadweight loss* however (in this case equal to $3 \times (7 - 6)/2 = 1.5$ euros).

A unit tax may be paid by producers (as is typically the case in Europe; for instance, as a buyer of gasoline, you do not directly observe the unit tax) or by consumers (as in the case of sales taxes in many US states, where you only learn about it at the cash register when the price is suddenly higher than that posted on the shelf or in the case of a tourist tax added to hotel bills in many countries). For the consequences of the tax – in terms of tax revenue, actual prices paid, and deadweight loss – *it doesn't matter who formally pays*. All that matters is that the tax drives a wedge between prices paid by buyers and those received by sellers.[5] What does matter, however, is the slope of demand and supply curves – these matter greatly for the effects. We use the term **tax incidence** to describe the effects of taxes on prices and quantities.

Tax incidence will depend on the relative slopes of supply and demand. The more price sensitive either supply or demand, the less will price to that side of the market be affected, but the more will quantity change. It is easy to play around with different combinations visually, and we exemplify with two cases in Figure 7.10. The left-hand panel shows the case where a tax is applied to a market with inelastic demand and elastic supply. As usual,

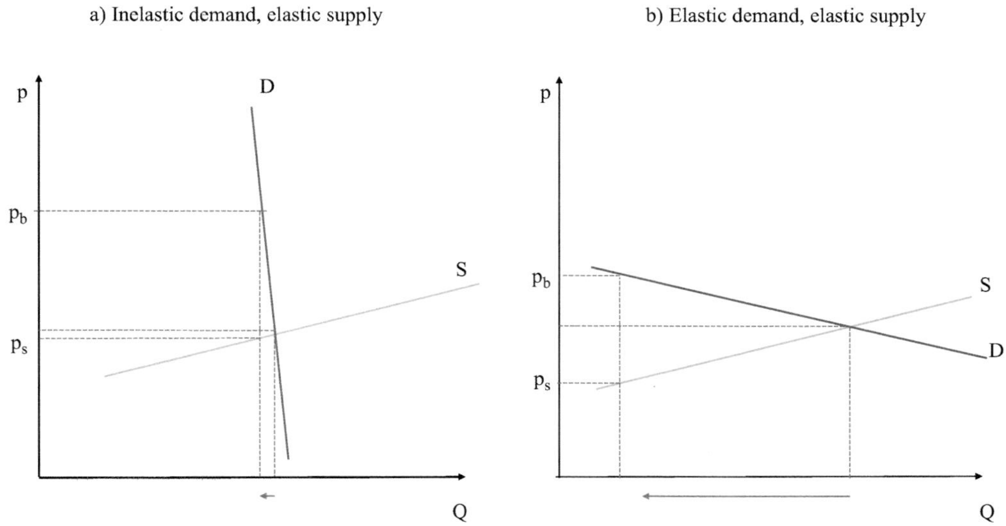

Figure 7.10 Tax incidence.

the intersection of supply and demand gives the perfectly competitive benchmark, and we depict the tax via the post-tax prices of p_b and p_s where, as before, $p_b = p_s + t$. So the combination of inelastic demand and elastic supply imply that the price that consumers pay increases by much. It also implies that since demand is insensitive to price, there is relatively little effect on quantities and a relatively small deadweight loss. As such, the tax doesn't distort choices much, and the takeaway that we prefer taxes on inelastic tax bases is a general one. The right-hand panel depicts a case where both demand and supply are relatively elastic. When elasticities are similar the effect on prices is more equally spread across buyers and sellers. With both supply and demand being relatively elastic quantities respond strongly to the tax, however, and there is a large deadweight loss.

The analysis of the impact of other taxes (e.g., income taxes and value-added tax) follows along the same lines as that of unit taxes but is typically left for more advanced courses.

7.5.3 Subsidies

Governments do not only tax; they also provide subsidies. In many cases, education and health care are provided at little or no cost to citizens. Another prominent example is the bread subsidy. In Egypt, for instance, bread is available at a heavily subsidized price, something that was also true for much of the time in ancient Rome. A subsidy can be examined in a similar fashion as a tax, and here as well, it is associated with a deadweight loss. Again, we keep track of p_b, the price that buyers pay, and p_s, the price that sellers receive. Using s to denote the tax, we thus have that $p_b = p_s - s$. Since $p_s > p_b$, the quantity demanded will be greater than the equilibrium quantity.

Using the same supply and demand functions from earlier, and assuming that there is a subsidy of 3 euros per unit, we then have the following three relations that need to hold:

$$\begin{cases} Q^D = 23 - p_b \\ Q^S = -1 + \frac{p_s}{2} \\ p_s = p_b + \underbrace{3}_{s} \end{cases} \tag{7.2}$$

To solve this system, we can simply insert the price relation into the supply function and solve for the buyer price that equates quantity demanded and quantity supplied:

$$23 - p_b = -1 + \underbrace{\frac{p_b + s}{2}}_{=p_s}$$

Solving this, we reach $p_b = 15$, and in consequence, $p_s = 15 + 3 = 18$. Quantity at this set of prices can be found by using p_b in the demand function, which yields $Q = 23 - 15 = 8$ units. Figure 7.11 depicts the effects of the subsidy. As an effect of the subsidy, producer surplus increases by the area A – the higher price that producers receive allows them to get a higher surplus for units sold, also without the subsidy, and in addition expand the number of units sold. Consumer surplus increases by area B, reflecting both lower prices and an increase in units consumed. It is clear that with a narrow view of welfare, both consumers and producers will find that the subsidy is a great idea. The subsidy has to be paid for, however, and the cost to government, the per unit subsidy × the number units sold, equals the areas A + B + C. Parts of the costs are offset by increases in producer and consumer surplus, but one part, C, is not offset by anything; it represents a deadweight loss. Return to the simple apple example to see the intuition. Here we have suppliers willing to supply additional apples at, for instance, a price of 17 euros per kilo, which represents their cost. Consumers are valuing these last apples at less, only 15.5 euros per kilo. So we are adding

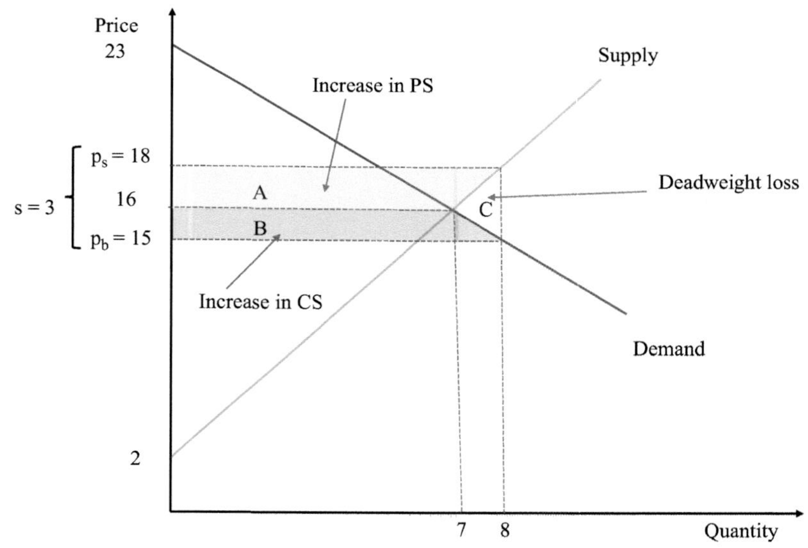

Figure 7.11 Effect of a subsidy. Video link for Figure 7.11: https://youtu.be/eFgpGRzQXRo.

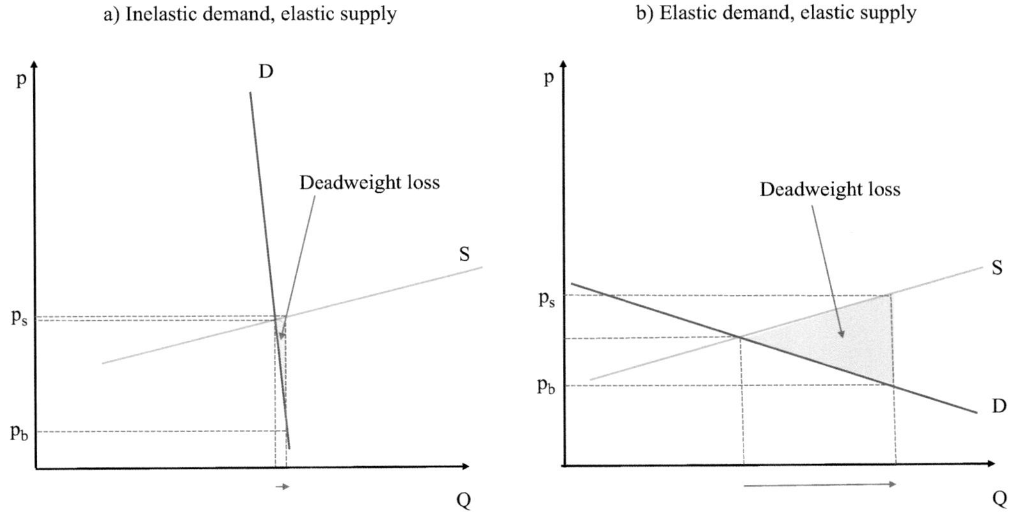

Figure 7.12 Subsidy incidence.

consumption that costs more than what it is valued at by consumers. In the case of subsidies as well, the deadweight loss and quantity effects depend on the relative slopes of supply and demand, as illustrated in Figure 7.12. If demand is inelastic, such as for emergency hospital care or primary education (where the number of children to be educated is mostly independent of price), the deadweight loss is limited. For cases where demand is elastic, on the other hand, quantities can expand sharply as a result of a subsidy and a sizable deadweight loss appears.

The previous discussion is not meant to show that taxes or subsidies cannot be motivated. As we discuss in the rest of the book, there are many reasons why we as a society may want to use taxes and/or subsidies to address distributional issues, provide insurance, or correct for market failures. The point of the analysis is to highlight how the framework allows us to make explicit the various costs and benefits of taxes and subsidies, helping guide decisions of how to best make use of scarce resources.

Notes

1 Clearly, the area is a triangle only in the case where the marginal cost curve is linear; more generally, producer surplus is given by the integral of the area between price and marginal cost.

2 To see this logic even more clearly, we may think of a firm with a stepwise marginal cost curve where the marginal cost for the first unit is 2, for the second unit 3, for the third unit 4, and for the fourth unit 5. What are total variable cost? They are simply the sum of the marginal costs $2 + 3 + 4 + 5 = 14$ euros.

3 Adding the different areas in Figure 7.7, we find CS = $(23 - 18) \times 5/2 = 12.5$ and PS = $(18 - 12) \times 5 + (12 - 2) \times 5/2 = 55$ euros. Hence welfare is $12.5 + 55 = 67.5$.

4 For simplicity, we disregard that time spent in queues has a value.

5 One way to see that is to note that if the tax is levied on consumers, the demand curve shifts down by t, whereas if it is levied on producers, it shifts up by t. In both cases, the quantities and prices will be as in Figure 7.9. This holds in theory, but in practice, psychological effects may lead to this playing some role, but such effects are typically expected to be limited, even if evidence in, e.g., Chetty et al. (2009) suggest that the impact of where the tax is levied may be non-trivial.

8 Efficiency in general equilibrium

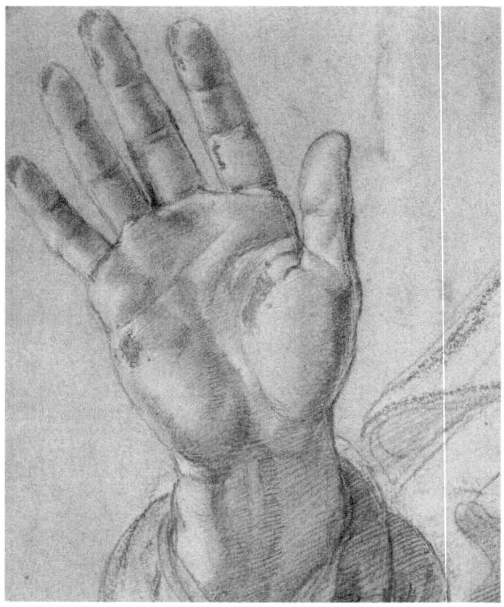

Illustration 8.1 A (visible) hand. *Upraised Right Hand, with Palm Facing Outward: Study for Saint Peter*, 1518/20, Raffaello Sanzio, called Raphael (detail from). Public domain, Art Institute Chicago.

8.1 How resources are allocated in an economy

So far in the book, we have examined one market at a time and disregarded interactions between markets. In this chapter, however, we take a broader view and analyze how markets interact. Studying only one market is referred to as **partial equilibrium** analysis, whereas an examination of several (or all markets in an economy) is known as **general equilibrium** analysis. Letting different markets affect each other makes the analysis more complicated, and in this chapter, the coverage will focus on providing examples and intuition, rather than solving questions step by step.

To introduce the issues, note that the type of question we pose in this chapter concerns how resources are directed in a market economy. We assume that all markets are **perfectly competitive**, and this is a good place to spell out the core assumptions behind a perfectly competitive economy in some greater detail. There are many firms and consumers in each market so that *everyone is a price taker*. There is *free entry*. In addition, a number of concerns

DOI: 10.4324/9781003623854-11

that we examine in later chapters are assumed to be mute. The perfectly competitive general equilibrium model that we examine in the following assumes that there are *no information asymmetries*, *no externalities*, and *no public goods*. Clearly, the real world differs from these assumptions, and in the coming chapters, we will examine how departures from the previous assumptions affect markets and how public policy can be used to improve outcomes.[1] It should also be emphasized that some additional assumptions underlie what we do in this chapter, even if they are often not stated. In particular, people engage in voluntary trade rather than stealing or use of force to get what they want. Nevertheless, insights that we develop in this chapter will be useful for also understanding real-world economies.

A useful conceptual idea in this chapter is to examine what a **social planner** would do – an unbiased decision-maker who wanted to achieve an efficient solution. Can the market equilibrium achieve the same outcome as the social planner? The central theme in this chapter is that *prices carry information*. We are concerned with what Adam Smith in the 1700s termed the "invisible hand." Well-functioning economies have various levels of government and laws, regulations, and social norms that shape the economy in many ways – redistribution, defense of national interests against other nations, and the kind of market failures that we examine later in the book are important motivations for this. As a starting point, however, economists often examine how resources are directed in an economy when everything works as well as possible for prices to send the right signals in terms of true costs and demand. We take a model of the type that we have examined in the previous chapters, where consumers only care about their own consumption and producers only maximize profits. How are resources allocated in this case?

In *Wealth of Nations* from 1776, Adam Smith noted, "It is not from the benevolence of the butcher, the brewer, or the baker that we expect our dinner, but from their regard to their self-interest. We address ourselves, not to their humanity, but to their self-love, and never talk to them of our necessities, but of their advantages." We saw in Chapter 5 that also among economists there is a widespread realization that we care about more than simply maximizing consumption and profit. Indeed, Adam Smith himself was remarkably profound in his thinking about the motivations for human behavior. That said, it is true that the butcher, brewer, and baker seem to be driven by profit motives, and we may ask: How are resources allocated?

To highlight a key intuition for the informational role of prices, let us revisit a case that we examined in Chapter 4, but now with some added commentary. Consider a market that is in equilibrium initially, and for concreteness, think of bread. Now assume that for some reason, consumers demand more bread – it can, for instance, be because of some health benefits of bread have been discovered or because some complementary goods to bread have gotten cheaper. A social planner would come to the conclusion that more bread should be produced. Does a social planner need to direct resources to achieve this, or can the market solve this redirection of resources on its own?

To illustrate the effects of a demand shock in a well-functioning competitive market, let us consider the left panel of Figure 8.1, which depicts a competitive market in equilibrium with price p_0 and quantity Q_0. The right-hand panel shows the situation for a representative firm, that, faced with the price p_0 supplies q_0. As above it supplies where $p = MC$, and we show a case where there are zero profits since $p = ATC$ at the profit maximizing point.

Assume now that there is a positive demand shock for bread. Demand shifts to D_1, which drives prices up to p_1. How do firms respond to the increased demand? Well, the supply curve is given by their marginal cost curve, and the representative firm supplies more in response to the rise in demand. Quantity for the representative firm increases to

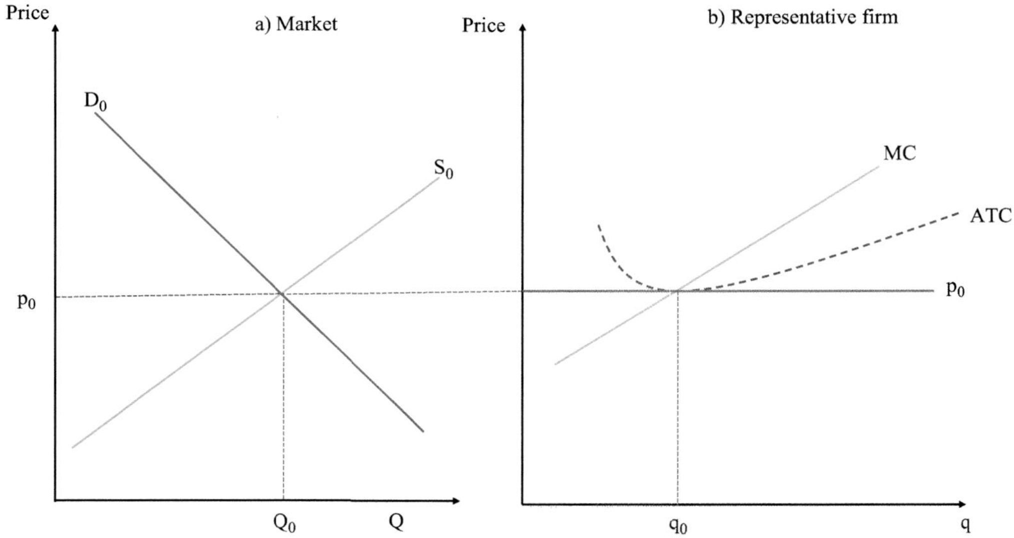

Figure 8.1 The relation between market supply and firm-level supply. Video link for Figures 8.1–8.3: https://youtu.be/tK-AM0T9OC4.

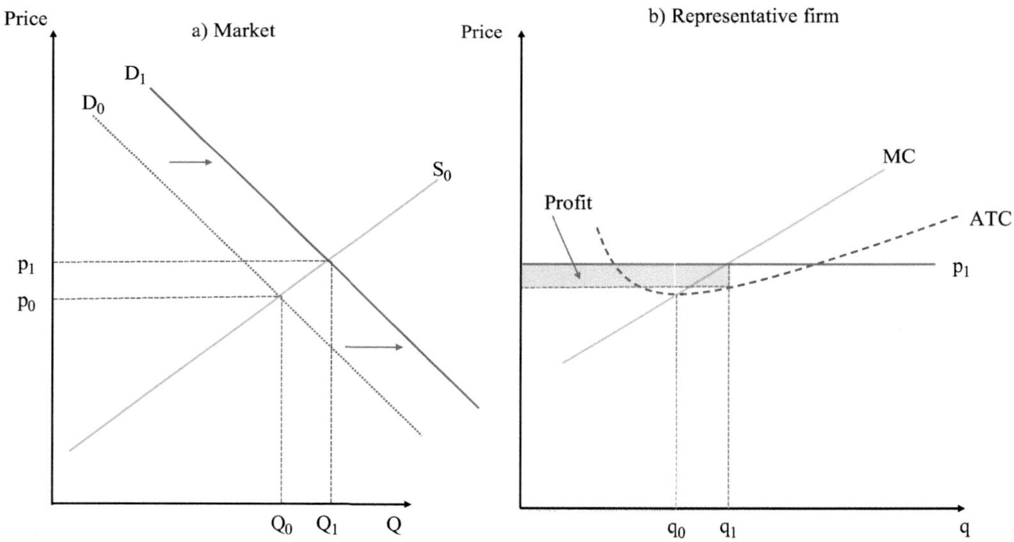

Figure 8.2 The relation between market supply and firm-level supply – Short run response to an increase in demand. Video link for Figures 8.1–8.3: https://youtu.be/tK-AM0T9OC4.

q_1, as shown in Figure 8.2. As price increases, the firm now makes a profit, as represented by the shaded area.

If there is free entry for bakeries, we expect that these profits will attract entering firms. The entry of these firms will be associated with an outward shift in the market supply

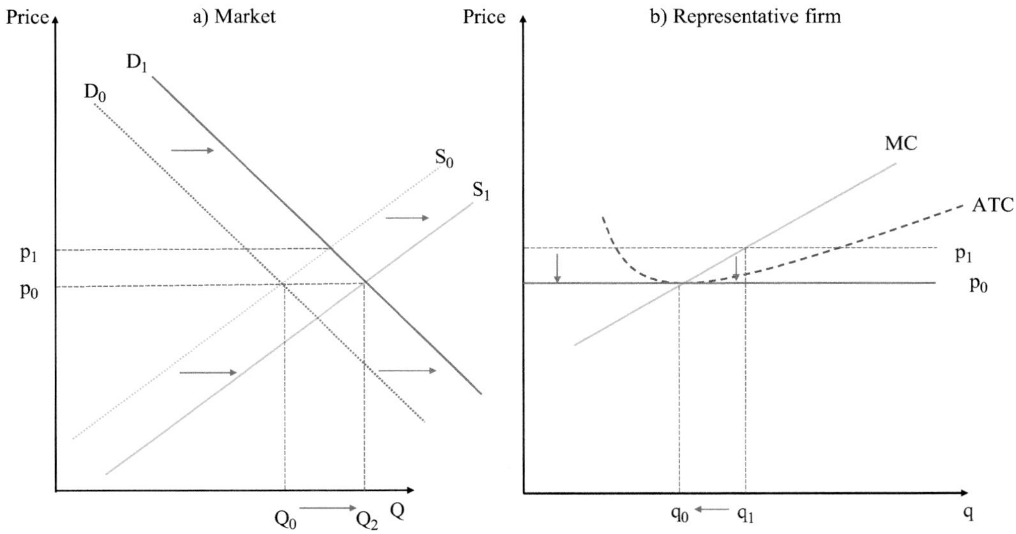

Figure 8.3 The relation between market supply and firm-level supply – An increase in demand triggers entry. Video link for Figures 8.1–8.3: https://youtu.be/tK-AM0T9OC4.

curve. At a given price, even more bread is supplied as now additional bakeries enter. The fundamental point here is that these entrants in principle do not need to know why demand shifted. No one needs to direct them to produce more bread. If they can understand the costs associated with making bread, they will be able to see that when the price has gone up, there are profits to be made from entering. The rising price sends a signal to responsive firms that in turn enter from a profit-seeking motive. They need not care about feeding people, but the profit-seeking motive effectively leads them to help satisfy demands.

At this point, it might be especially useful to think of economic models as stories. Not as full descriptions of everything that happens in the world, but as internally consistent stories that deepen our understanding of a certain class of problems.[2] The world is obviously much more complex than what the models in this chapter can possibly be expected to capture. But these models do capture central aspects – an inability to match supply and demand was pervasive in centrally planned economies in the 1900s, and long queues for goods were common. In contrast, such an inability of supply to meet demand is much less common in market economies. A core insight from economics is that in a market economy, individuals and firms respond to changes in price, and that behavior, to some degree, is shaped by the "invisible hand" of market prices.

An eloquent analysis for the role of prices in transmitting information – here in the context of a rising price of a raw material – is provided by Hayek (1945, p. 527): "The marvel is that in a case like that of a scarcity of one raw material, without an order being issued, without more than perhaps a handful of people knowing the cause, tens of thousands of people whose identity could not be ascertained by months of investigation, are made to use the material or its products more sparingly."

Thus, without further ado, let us examine the three different efficiency aspects that we typically focus on: efficient consumption, efficient use of inputs, and efficient output. We can solve for all of these in a single model, an intellectual project for which important groundwork was laid by French economist Léon Walras in the 1800s and which arguably reached its crowning glory in work by Nobel laureates Ken Arrow and Gerard Debreu.[3] A large number of consumers and firms interact in their trade of a large number of goods where, simply put, "everything depends on everything": all markets interact. How much consumers spend on one market affects how much they can spend on other markets. A full description remains outside the scope of an introductory book in microeconomics, and instead, we will present the intuition for core results in the case of two goods.

8.2 Efficiency in consumption

We commence with the case of two consumers who each has a given amount of two goods. These initial endowments are not reflecting their own choices, and we say that they are **exogenous**, given outside of our model. To provide a visual view, you could think of kids that have been given goody bags at a birthday party with different combinations of chocolate and sweets, or somewhat less frivolously, prisoners in a prisoner-of-war camp who have been given different combinations of goods. Indeed, in a highly readable article, Radford (1945) describes his experiences of trading, largely based on Red Cross packets, in a World War II prisoner-of-war camp.

Thus consider two people, Blue and Red, and two goods, Drinks and Food. We are concerned with efficiency; if we let people trade, are goods consumed by the people who value them the highest, or is there some way through which we can reshuffle the initial allocation and achieve a more efficient outcome? A first question regards how we should measure efficiency. The measure of consumer welfare that we used before, consumer surplus, takes prices of all other goods and incomes as given. In general equilibrium, "everything depends on everything;" all incomes and prices are endogenous, which makes an application of consumer surplus hard. In addition, we are tasked with comparing welfare across individuals, a highly complex issue. I may value the health and wealth of my family higher than I value the health and wealth of your family. Your position is likely to be the opposite.

Given the difficulties of comparing and adding up welfare across individuals, economists frequently rely on a notion of efficiency that largely sidesteps this comparison and aggregation: Pareto efficiency. We say that an allocation is **Pareto efficient** if there is no way of making someone better off without making someone else worse off.[4] This might seem like a confusing notion, but to understand the concept, think for a moment of a case where it didn't hold: Where we can make someone better off without making anyone else worse off. That clearly indicates that an allocation is inefficient – of course, you would want to make that change to a more efficient allocation. If we are at a point where there are no such moves that are possible, we have reached some level of efficiency. We assume that each individual only cares about their own consumption and disregards both altruism (where I get utility from someone else's consumption) and envy (where I get disutility from someone else's consumption).

To see how all this works, consider the allocation of Drinks and Food presented in Table 8.1. Blue initially has $2D$ and $8F$, whereas Red has $6D$ and $4F$. Assume that they trade such that Blue exchanges $1F$ for $1D$.

Can we say something about whether that trade improves efficiency? To further present ideas, we use a tool that traces its origins to British economist Francis Edgeworth (Edgeworth (1881)) and is termed an "Edgeworth box." Consider first Blue's situation in Figure 8.4, with D on the vertical axis and F on the horizontal. To evaluate efficiency, we

Table 8.1 Initial endowments and a trade

	Original allocation	*Trade*	*After trade*
Blue	2D, 8F	+1D,−1F	3D,7F
Red	6D, 4F	−1D,+1F	3D,5F

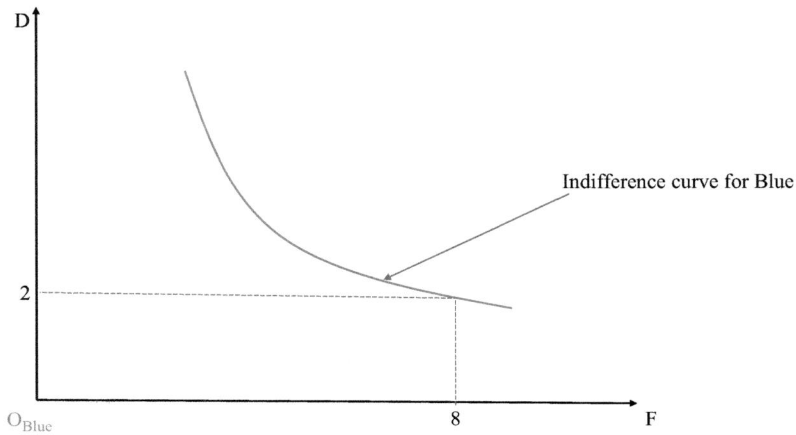

Figure 8.4 The initial allocation for Blue.

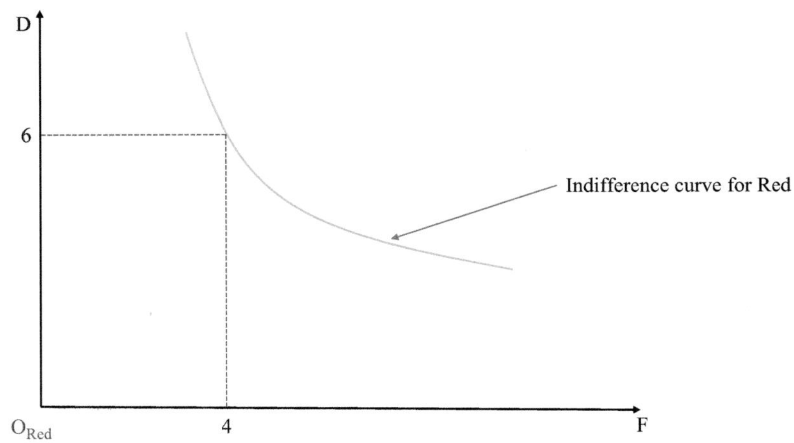

Figure 8.5 The initial allocation for Red. Video link for Figures 8.5–8.8: https://youtu.be/w08enns N4VM.

use indifference curves, and in Figure 8.4, we have drawn an indifference curve that passes through his original allocation.

Next, Red's situation is depicted in Figure 8.5, also with an indifference curve that passes through her original allocation.

We are interested in modeling trade between these two individuals and the welfare effects thereof. In a simple but clever realization, we flip one of the figures upside down so that they

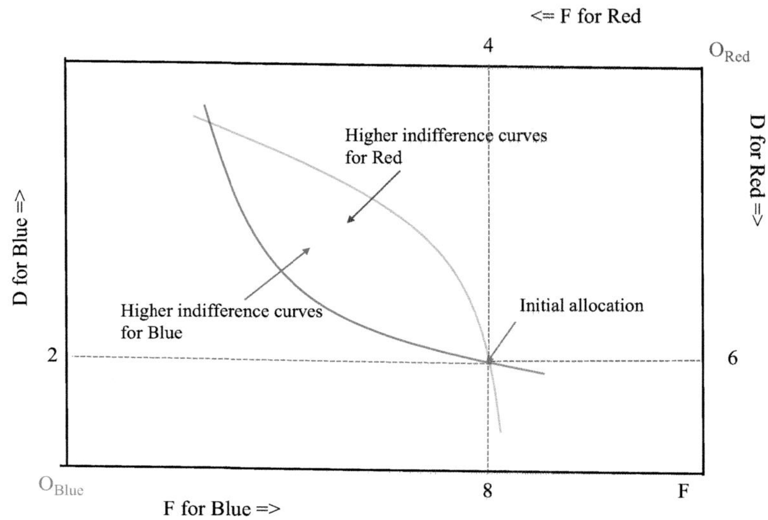

Figure 8.6 The initial allocation in an Edgeworth box. Video link for Figures 8.5–8.8: https://youtu.be/w08ennsN4VM.

together form a "box," as depicted in Figure 8.6. Thus, for Red, we measure the number of units of *F* moving leftward along the top line and units of *D* for Red moving downward along the right-hand axis. Just think of Red as a flipped version of Blue. All the goods in this little world belong to one of the people so that the width of the box is given by the number of units of *F* and the height by the number of units of *D*.

We are interested in modeling and understanding trade between individuals in this setting and whether it can raise utility. We measure utility by indifference curves, and we first consider the indifference curves that are associated with the initial allocation. Indifference curves for Blue that are further to the upper right, further away from the origin for him, are associated with higher utility. Likewise, indifference curves for Red that are further to the lower left right, further away from the origin for her, are associated with higher utility for Red.

Figure 8.7 illustrates the trade that we described in Table 8.1, with Red giving up one unit of *D* in exchange for one unit of *F*. We see that the new allocation, marked with an N in Figure 8.7, is associated with higher utility for both people as they reach higher indifference curves. Thus, since there was a possible trade where both could become better off, the initial allocation cannot have been Pareto efficient. Is the new allocation Pareto efficient? No. There are still trades left where at least one party can be better off without the other being worse off. At a point like A, for instance, Red would be no worse off, but Blue would be better off. At a point like B, Blue would be no worse off, but Red would be better off, and finally at a point like C, both parties would be better off. At a point like N, there thus remain Pareto improvements, and there is still scope for mutually beneficial trade.

Figure 8.8 shows an allocation, A, that is Pareto efficient, where there are no further mutual gains from trade. There are a few different ways to describe such an allocation.

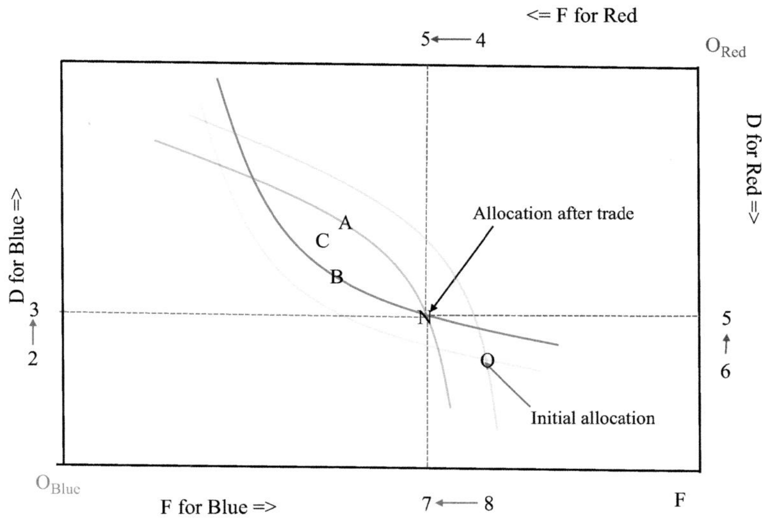

Figure 8.7 Trade in an Edgeworth box. Video link for Figures 8.5–8.8: https://youtu.be/w08enns N4VM.

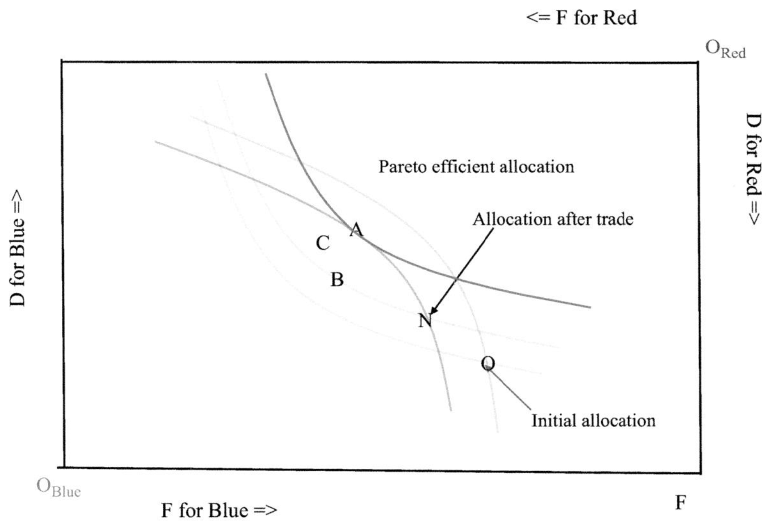

Figure 8.8 A Pareto efficient allocation. Video link for Figures 8.5–8.8: https://youtu.be/w08enns N4VM.

- *No one can reach a higher indifference curve without someone else needing to end up on a lower indifference curve.* This is a somewhat mechanistic way of describing the Pareto-efficient situation but nevertheless useful.
- There are *no more unexploited gains from trade*. The two parties are "done" trading.

- The two indifference curves are tangent to each other. Remember that the slope of the indifference curve could be interpreted as the ratio of marginal utilities (and we named it marginal rate of substitution (MRS)). Thus in this case

$$MRS_{Blue} = \frac{MU_F}{MU_D} = \frac{MU_F}{MU_D} = MRS_{Red}.$$

This is saying something rather deep; trading equalizes the ratio of marginal utilities. At this point, both people *value the goods equally on the margin.*

There can be very many points of tangency; many Pareto optimal points and a line that connects them is called a **contract curve**. At this stage, we may ask: How do we know where we end up? The initial endowment clearly matters, but in principle, both point A and point B in Figure 8.7 are possible outcomes, and we could speculate how various factors that influence bargaining matter. We could also consider a case where there are many individuals of type Blue and many individuals of type Red that interact on the market. How much each type would be willing to sell or buy depends on the market prices they face, their preferences, and their initial endowments. As in Chapter 5, the optimal choices imply that the indifference curve is tangent to the slope of the budget constraint. This holds for all individuals and hence

$$MRS_{Blue} = \frac{MU_F}{MU_D} = \frac{p_F}{p_D} = \frac{MU_F}{MU_D} = MRS_{Red}.$$

Using Figure 8.9 to illustrate, we would thus have a case where Red individuals would be selling D and using the revenue that they receive from these sales to buy F. Individuals of type Blue take the opposite side in this trade, and both are better off as we move from allocation O to allocation N.

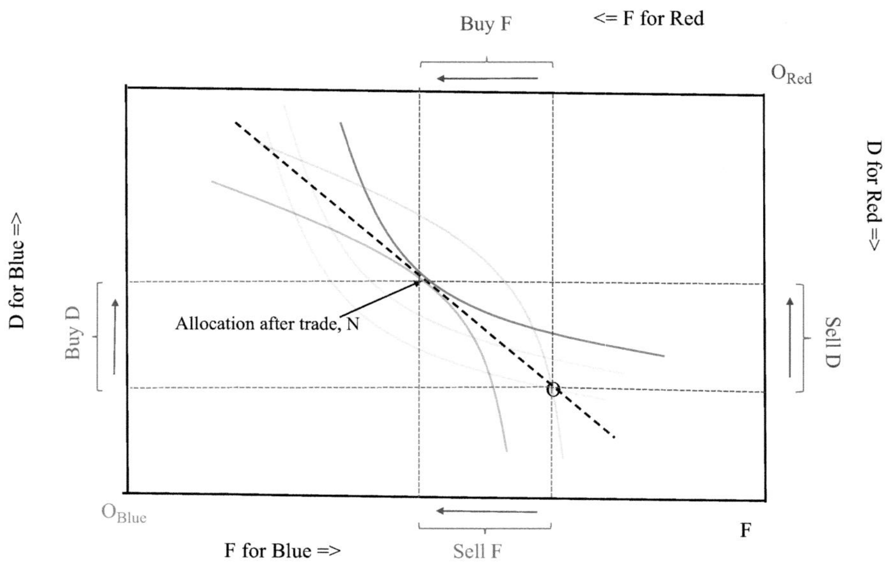

Figure 8.9 Trade in an Edgeworth box with many individuals.

In the case analyzed earlier, we could say that we've used a lot of machinery to make what is ultimately an almost trivial point: If we let people voluntarily trade, they might both be better off from trading. When at least one party has nothing more to gain from exchanging goods, the trading stops. However, while the point is trivial in this simple setting, it is far from trivial in a setting with many individuals, many goods, and many firms. The relation between relative prices and marginal utilities hold also in this more general setting, and the tools that we have examined are useful for seeing how the story is internally consistent. The result that we established earlier can be seen as an example of a general statement known as the

First welfare theorem: In general equilibrium with perfect competition, the allocation of resources is Pareto efficient.

The interpretation is that in a well-functioning market, individuals' choices will lead to an efficient outcome, in the sense that there are no unrealized mutual gains from trade. It would be common to give this a very "laissez-faire"[5] interpretation; the market is best left to its own devices, and there is no way that a social planner can improve upon the outcome without lowering the utility of some groups. Such an interpretation is going much further than needed, however, and gets us into a terrain of determining how far the real world is from the stylized assumptions of perfect competition. There is no consensus among economists on such an interpretation.

What there is broad appreciation of among economists however is a realization of the efficiency gains that are potentially realized by letting people trade. Let us use a goody- bag example to highlight some key intuition. Consider a birthday party where all the kids get goody bags stuffed with chocolate, gummi bears, and licorice. If all kids had the exact same preferences, and exact same content in their goody bags, there would be no point in trading. But as soon as preferences differ – someone likes gummi bears a lot but hates licorice, another likes them all equally and someone else doesn't like chocolate – there will be scope for beneficial reallocation. Similarly if preferences are the same, but there are differences in the initial allocation, there may be scope for beneficial reallocation. We could think that I, as a parent and social planner, would try to ask everyone of their preferences and based on that make up a list of who gets what.[6] Good luck with that. Some may overstate their preferences for some things and even if everyone is truthful it will be a pain to make sure that everything matches up. The first welfare theorem says: let the kids trade and the outcome will be such that I as a social planner/parent can't improve on the outcome that they will reach after trading without making some kids worse off.

The first welfare theorem says nothing about distribution and fairness. We could think of cases where someone has a lot and someone else almost nothing. Our preference as a society could clearly be that we want to redistribute in some way, as we discuss at the end of this chapter. To deepen our understanding of trade and equity in an Edgeworth box, let us however first explore an additional example of trading. Consider two goods, Müsli and Yogurt, and two people, Petter and Therese. Assume that Müsli and Yogurt are perfect complements for each of them. We depict the indifference curves and an initial allocation in Figure 8.10. Perfect complements imply L-shaped indifference curves, and we see that the original allocation, marked with O, is quite unequal. Petter has relatively little of both goods, whereas Therese has a lot. There are still gains from trade, but the set of allocations that we can expect after trade are bounded by the indifference curves that intersect the original allocation. No one wants to trade to be worse off than in this initial allocation.

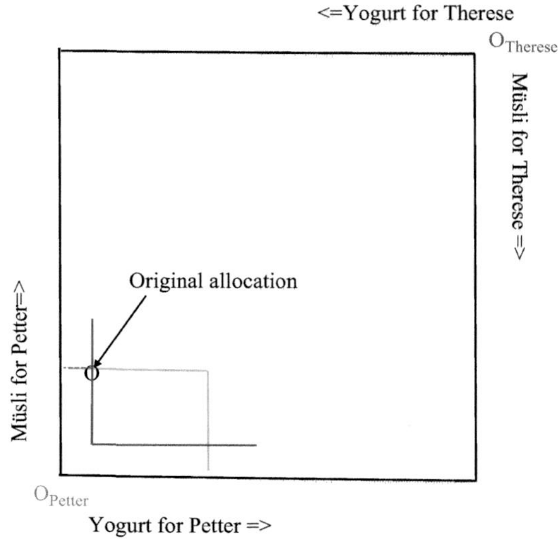

Figure 8.10 Trade in an Edgeworth box with perfect complements. Video link for Figures 8.10–8.12: https://youtu.be/CYA3fnLLuq0.

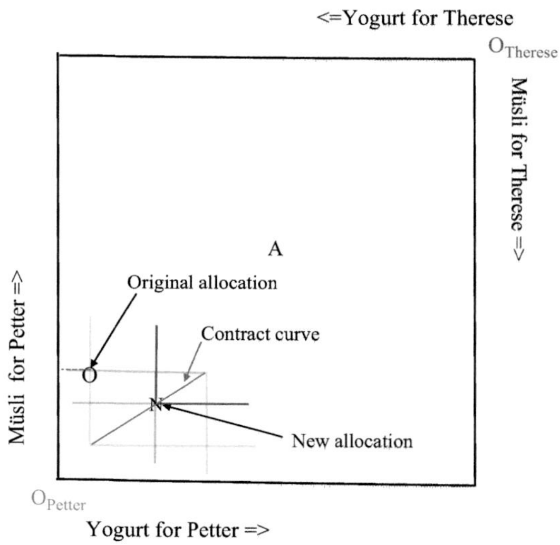

Figure 8.11 Trade in an Edgeworth box with perfect complements. Video link for Figures 8.10–8.12: https://youtu.be/CYA3fnLLuq0.

Figure 8.11 depicts one possible allocation together with the contract curve over the predicted range.[7] At the possible allocation N, both Petter and Therese have achieved higher indifference curves, and as such, trade is beneficial. Even if the initial allocation is very uneven, they can both gain from trading. However, the initial allocation determines the range of Pareto efficient allocations that are likely to be observed, and we do not expect trading to reach a point like A, for instance. In terms of the candy example earlier, if a kid

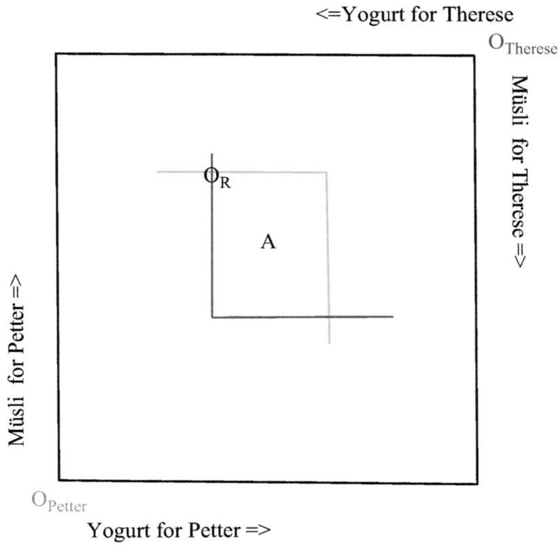

Figure 8.12 A Pareto efficient outcome with perfect complements. Video link for Figures 8.10–8.12: https://youtu.be/CYA3fnLLuq0.

likes licorice but has an initial endowment of only 2 gummi bears, he will be better off from trading but less happy than someone with the same preferences whose goodie bag contained large amounts different kinds of goodies.

Say that we are concerned with the distribution of goods across individuals and decided to redistribute the initial endowment to a point like O_R in Figure 8.12. Again, individuals could trade, and now the allocation A is within the set of allocations that we expect may emerge from trading.

The implicit lesson in comparing Figure 8.11 with Figure 8.12 is that, if we, as a social planner, are concerned with an unequal allocation of goods, we can simply reallocate initial endowments. We can achieve other allocations without sacrificing efficiency by choosing other initial endowments. This result is often summarized in what is known as the

Second welfare theorem: Every Pareto efficient allocation is a perfectly competitive equilibrium for some initial allocation of resources.

This is somewhat of a tongue-twister, but the interpretation is that there is no tension between wanting an even distribution of utility and efficiency – a social planner would simply redistribute initial endowments and allow people to trade to reach an efficient outcome. In political terms, we could view the first welfare theorem as supporting notions of minimal government involvement and thus quite right wing in some sense. The frictionless kind of environment that we examine here cuts both ways, however, and we can view the second welfare theorem as having a more left-wing flavor; there is no efficiency loss associated with redistribution.

Actual economies differ from the stylized setting of perfect competition in many ways – and in later chapters, we will examine motivations for government involvement due to *market failures*: imperfect competition in that some firms have monopoly power, externalities, and public goods, as well as cover various considerations regarding *equity*.

The theorems should not be seen as accurate descriptions of the world that we live in but as reflecting deep thinking on the logical possibility of various results in a stylized model. This is not to say that this deep thinking is without relevance for understanding the real world. The planned socialist economies of, for instance, the Soviet Union, Eastern Europe, and China during large parts of the 1900s were notoriously inefficient in many ways. For another example, I turn close to home. Sweden has long combined an ambitious welfare state with a lot of redistribution, with a level of government involvement in business and pricing that is surprisingly low to many outside observers. Such a combination fits well with the spirit of the first and second welfare theorems, and it is perhaps no coincidence that the policy of the welfare state saw engagement from strong economists like Nobel laureates Gunnar Myrdal (prominent in the Social Democratic Party) and Bertil Ohlin (chairman of the liberal party for more than 20 years).[8]

8.3 Efficient use of inputs

The next question that we pose to the perfectly competitive market is if it uses inputs in an efficient way. We could think of the question that we pose as the following: Is there some way that a social planner could reshuffle the use of production factors across industries and increase total production? After the analysis in the previous section, it will come as no surprise that the perfectly competitive equilibrium is efficient, and we cover the result relatively quickly. Think of a simple case with two factors of production, K and L, and

Illustration 8.2 Low marginal product of labor? *Hay-Makers*, 1791, George Stubbs (detail from). Public domain, Art Institute of Chicago.

two goods produced, F and D. Assume that the factors of production can be used in the production of either good.

From Chapter 3, we know from cost minimization of firms that the following holds for any firm

$$\frac{MP_L}{MP_K} = \frac{w}{r}.$$

This means that if all firms face the same wages and rental costs of capital, then firms in the production of F will have the same ratio of marginal product of labor to the marginal product of capital as firms in the D industry.

We can use an Edgeworth box to further illustrate the implications of cost minimization on the equilibrium allocation of production factors. To add some context to the discussion, consider a highly stylized version of Great Britain at the dawn of the Industrial Revolution. There are two factors of production (K and L) and two goods, agricultural products (A) and manufactured goods (M). Ways of producing can be described by isoquants. Consider an initial situation where labor predominantly works in agriculture, as shown in Figure 8.13. Remember from Chapter 3 that the slope of the isoquant is given by MP_L/MP_K.[9] At the original allocation of factors across firms, the marginal product of labor relative to capital is very high in manufacturing. Adding more workers to manufacturing would then imply that the marginal contribution of those workers was very high. In contrast, in agriculture, the marginal product of labor in relation to the marginal product of capital is very low. So we have a situation where a lot of people are employed in a sector where they make only very low contributions to output and another sector that is crying out for more people to match up with machines. A social planner who wanted to make better use of resources would therefore want to reallocate workers from agriculture to manufacturing. The questions that

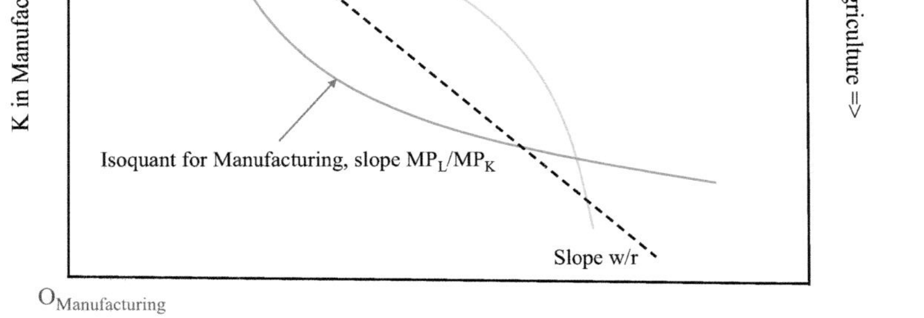

Figure 8.13 An initial inefficient allocation of inputs in an Edgeworth box. Video link for Figures 8.13–8.14: https://youtu.be/DxrXJ5zmJyU.

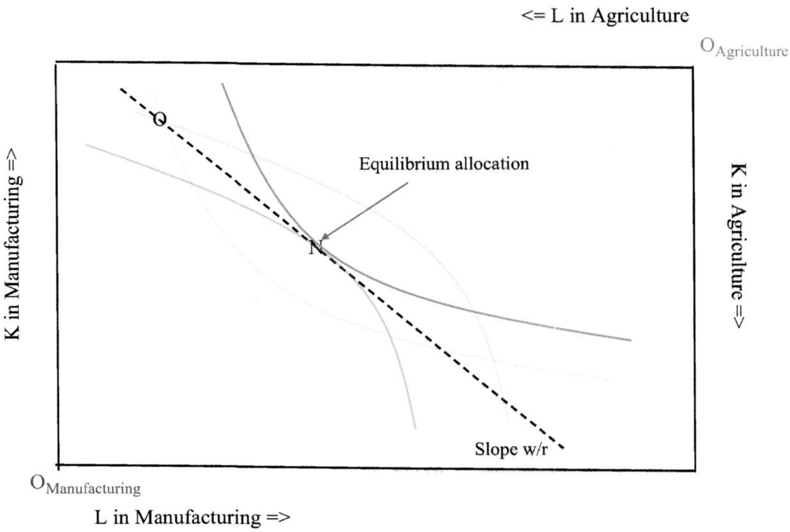

Figure 8.14 Efficient use of inputs in an Edgeworth box. Video link for Figures 8.13–8.14: https://youtu.be/DxrXJ5zmJyU.

a social planner would face are: How much labor should be moved from one sector to the other? How would the social planner know the contribution of changes in the use of factors in the different sectors?

In the perfectly competitive equilibrium, adjustment again comes via prices. If agriculture and manufacturing face the same wage and capital costs, profit-maximizing employers will adjust their use of inputs. At point O in Figure 8.13, the cost-adjusted (adjusted by the wage) contribution that the last workers make to output in agriculture is lower than the cost-adjusted contribution that capital makes ($MP_L/w < MP_K/r$). Agricultural firms will therefore want to use fewer workers. In manufacturing, on the other hand, the opposite holds, and manufacturing firms then want to increase the share of workers. Wages are thus playing a key role in the reallocation. Neither firms nor workers need to know all aspects of production functions in the economy – for firms, it is sufficient that they know their own production function and adjust optimally given the wages and costs of capital that they are facing. Figure 8.14 illustrates the adjustment to the competitive equilibrium at point N where the isoquants are both tangent to the isocost and to each other. By reallocating workers and capital between agriculture and manufacturing, firms in both sectors can reach a higher isoquant – by using resources more efficiently, the economy can produce more with given resources, and again, prices (in this case price of inputs) are central in steering how resources are used.

8.4 Efficient combination of goods

A point like N in Figure 8.14 is associated with a certain amount of agricultural goods and a certain amount of manufactured products being produced. Let us return to the example from earlier with Food and Drinks as the two goods. We can think of many tangency points between isoquants, as we illustrate with A_1, A_2, and A_3 in Figure 8.15. We can also use a

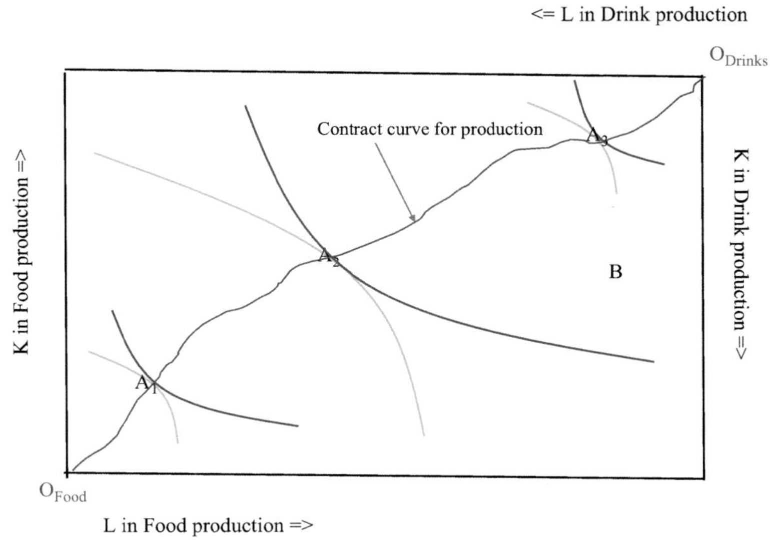

Figure 8.15 The contract curve in an Edgeworth box.

line to indicate all the efficient combinations, what is known as the production contract curve. Point B indicates an allocation that is not efficient, given the isoquants. Each point on the production contract curve is associated with a certain amount of each good being produced. What point will be chosen? That will depend on the demand for products, and it is time for us to turn to the third aspect of efficiency for perfectly competitive markets: an efficient combination of goods.

Clearly, if a point like A_1 in Figure 8.15 is chosen, very little capital and labor are used in the production of food; almost all resources are used in the production of drinks. As a society, this means that relatively little food is produced, whereas a lot of drinks are produced. In contrast at point A_3, the opposite holds; a lot of food is produced since the resources in the economy predominantly are used to produce food. We illustrate the amount of the different goods that can be produced in the economy if all resources are used efficiently in what is known as a **production possibility frontier** (PPF). If we are using inputs efficiently across sectors (such as at point A_1, for instance), we can only produce more F by producing less D. Note that this does not hold below the line; at a point like B, the production of both goods could increase by using inputs more efficiently. The PPF has a bowed shape. In principle, PPFs can be linear as well, but the bowed, strictly concave shape is typical – we analyze this in more detail in Chapter 18. The reason for the bowed shape is that we typically have decreasing returns to some inputs.

To provide intuition for what follows, it is common to simplify and think of the decision problem in what follows as that of one individual. Starting with Frédéric Bastiat in the 1840s, many have used Robinson Crusoe trapped alone on an island to provide a mental image. He can spend his time procuring food or producing drinks. For concreteness, think of food as fruits and of drinks as coconut milk. The more of the time he spends gathering fruit, the more difficult it will be to find even more fruit. He will have picked all the fruits close to his base, and he will be forced to make longer and longer expeditions in his hunt

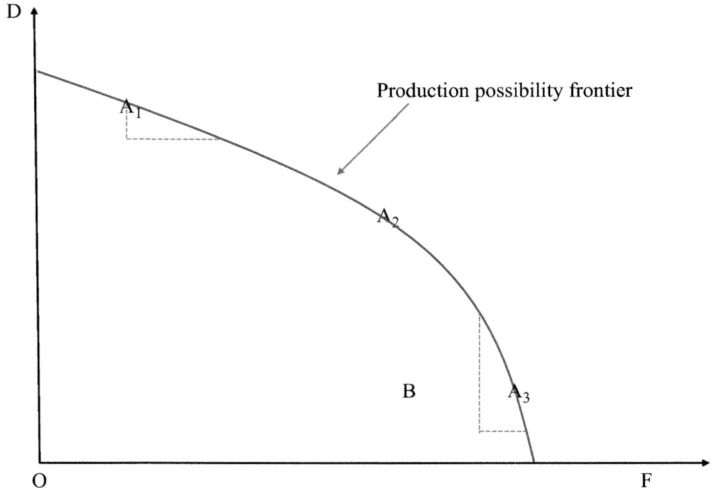

Figure 8.16 A production possibility frontier.

for additional fruit. On the other hand, if he spends almost all his time wandering about looking for fruit, he might have coconut trees closely available to him. Thus when he spends close to all his time hunting for fruit, the time thus used could instead have yielded a lot of coconut milk. This explains the increasing steepness of the PPF as he spends more and more of his time gathering fruit; the opportunity cost of food at a point like A_3 in Figure 8.16 is high; a lot of D is given up to get more F. The opposite is true at a point like A_1.

What combination of fruits and coconut milk should Robinson choose? That will partly depend on the opportunity costs, the shape of the PPF. But clearly, his preferences for consumption should also come into play, and we represent that with an indifference curve, as in Figure 8.17, where D_1 and F_1 indicate his optimal choices.

Of course, if Robinson knows his own preferences and his opportunity cost of gathering fruit at different points along the PPF, he can simply choose. Let us now turn to the case of a model with many firms and consumers. The slope of the PPF is known as the marginal rate of transformation (MRT). In a perfectly competitive market equilibrium, we will need to introduce prices as a way to steer the allocation. First, examining the slope of the PPF, we note that the opportunity cost of F in terms of D can be expressed as the marginal cost of F (MC_F) in relation to the marginal cost of D (MC_D). We also know that in perfect competition, firms set quantity so that marginal cost equals price: $p_F = MC_F$ and $p_D = MC_D$. For demand, we know from earlier that utility maximization implies that the ratio of marginal utilities equals the relative price. We therefore have that

$$\underbrace{\frac{MC_F}{MC_D}}_{\text{MRT}} = \frac{p_F}{p_D} = \underbrace{\frac{MU_F}{MU_D}}_{\text{MRS}}.$$

In typical wording, we thus say that the optimal solution implies that MRS equals MRT. While a useful shorthand for an economist, it clearly sounds like gibberish to untrained ears. More intuitively, we note that prices link the demand side (dependent on preferences)

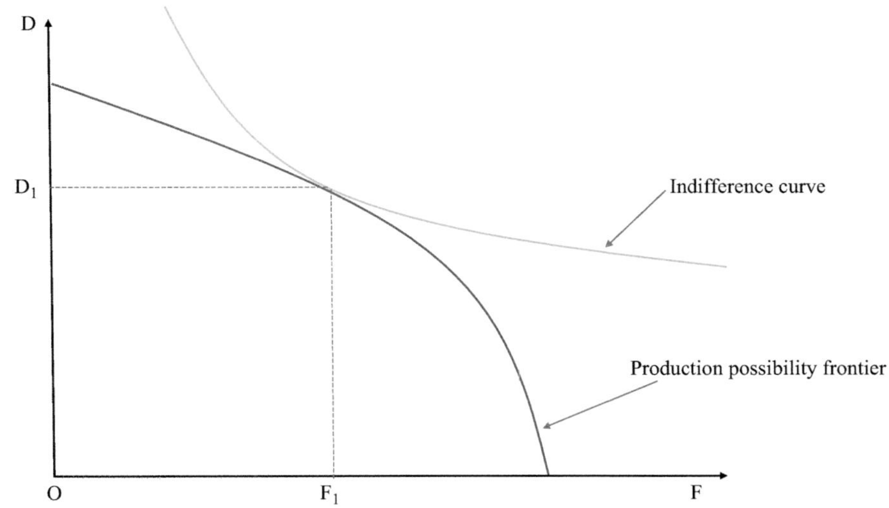

Figure 8.17 Optimal combination of goods.

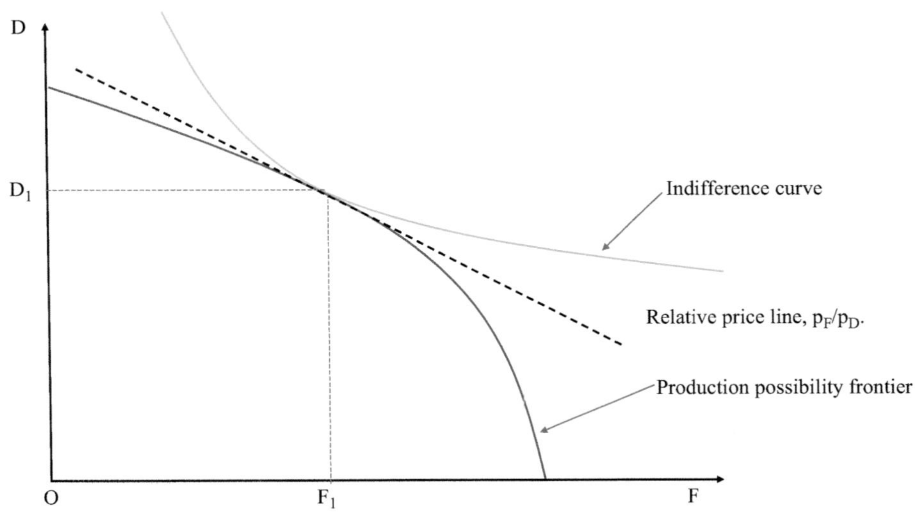

Figure 8.18 Optimal combination of goods with a relative price line.

to the supply side (dependent on marginal costs). This is where we started this chapter. If something raises the marginal costs of producing one good relative to the other, the price of that good will go up, and consumers will adjust.

8.5 Comparing different allocations: Equity

In teaching of questions regarding equity in microeconomics, the competitive equilibrium that we examined earlier is typically taken as a starting point, and it is noted that the distribution of resources may be very unequal. Different principles for how resources can be reallocated are then explained, and it is concluded that which way to organize society, and the extent of redistribution that is chosen, comes down to value judgments in which economics give little direct guidance. This is also the way that we will present it in the following since the terms and notions are part of what it means to be conversant with economic analysis.

Nevertheless, I can't *emphasize enough how limited a view* this is for the question of how to organize a real society. The broader question of what are the fundamental features of a society that determine its success – that allow its citizens to live healthy and happy lives – can't be successfully examined within such limited confines. A view to human history notes that different countries and groups have solved the question of how to organize societies in vastly different ways. Much of what goes as redistribution concerns insurance or redistribution across different stages of life – from the working population to the young and the old. When we think of equity and fairness, and the impact of various forms of redistribution in settings closer to actual economies, we are confronted with many issues regarding how to view equality.

As we saw in Chapter 5, it is well established that humans care about fairness. But what is fair? Are we concerned with *fairness* in terms of *outcomes* – that actual consumption levels be above a certain minimum or that we have some views on how much they can/should differ? Alternatively, we might think that fairness in terms of *opportunity* is most important – that the "playing field" should be level and that to the extent possible your life chances should be determined by your abilities and hard work. Or we might think that fairness in terms of *process* that generates inequality is key – that the process whereby goods and services are allocated is seen as fair. We might also think that fairness matters differently for different goods – that access to health care should be allocated in different ways than access to golf courses. Questions about what notions of fairness are important also tie into how we interpret various measures of, for instance, income inequality, social mobility, and health outcomes. In this book, we will not go deeper into these issues but instead stay with the standard curriculum that limits coverage to some various proposed measures for aggregating preferences.[10]

After those provisos, let us turn to a description of various ways that have been proposed to aggregate preferences. Before doing so, however, let us highlight the distinction between positive and normative uses of economic theory, something is especially important here.

8.5.1 Normative and positive economics

As we enter the topic of redistribution, we are making **normative statements**. We are saying how something should be; we are making value judgments. If we believe that equality of opportunity and among young people is good, that is a normative statement. If we believe that consumer surplus should be attached higher value than producer surplus, that is also a normative statement. Normative statements have no clear right or wrong. I might believe that all kids should start from as similar a position as possible, whereas you might believe that society has no right to try to neutralize efforts of previous generations to give their own kids as strong a starting position as possible. There is no scientific way to settle the argument. There is no evidence that we could look at and unequivocally say I'm wrong and you're right.

The other category is **positive statements**. Positive statements are statements about cause and effect, and much of economics has this purpose. How much will free education increase social mobility? How does public policy in terms of, for instance, taxes and safety nets affect labor supply? How much will consumption of alcohol decrease if alcohol taxes are raised? How will marijuana consumption change if it is legalized? What is the effect on prices of entry of an additional firm? These build on theory and on empirical work. As economists, we typically like to see ourselves as providing the answers to such positive statements – politicians and the democratic process can then weigh different aspects against each other in an analysis of costs and benefits. Simply put, we can think of positive economics as providing input into normative decisions. Positive economics helps quantify the trade-offs that go into normative decisions.

Milton Friedman was one of the key figures in the economics profession in the 1900s. He was somewhat of a double nature – combining deep scholarly work in some areas (in particular on the economics of money and central banking) with an active and highly rhetorical advocacy of deregulation and limits on government. He was also interested in methodological issues and had magnificent writing skills – his discussion of positive economics is worth citing at some length. Friedman (1953, p. 2) argues,[11]

> Positive economics is in principle independent of any particular ethical position or normative judgments. As Keynes [John Neville Keynes, father of the more famous John Maynard Keynes] says, it deals with "what is," not with "what ought to be." Its task is to provide a system of generalizations that can be used to make correct predictions about the consequences of any change in circumstances. Its performance is to be judged by the precision. scope, and conformity with experience of the predictions it yields. In short, positive economics is, or can be, an "objective" science.

Normative economics in contrast typically requires that we weigh utility of one individual against utility of another individual. These are value judgments that can't be decided by empirical evidence.

8.5.2 *Social welfare functions*

Remembering the caveats at the start of this section, let us then take the perspective of a social planner that somehow wants to make society as well off as possible, also taking equity into account. The question of course is how to operationalize that: What does it mean to make society as well of as possible? We're building from the ground up, so we are thinking of some way of aggregating up from individual preferences over different allocations and the use of a **social welfare function** is one way to aggregate. Arguably, the most straightforward way to aggregate is to simply let social welfare be the sum of individual utilities. We term such a social welfare function **utilitarian**. In the case of two individuals, as in the previous chapter, having utility level u_1 and u_2 of a particular allocation, the social welfare function (denoted by W) would simply be $W = u_1 + u_2$, and for n individuals, it is $W = u_1 + u_2 + ... + u_n$.[12] It is typically associated with British philosopher Jeremy Bentham, who was active in the late 1700s and early 1800s. At one level, it captures important features that many hold to be plausible ways to organize a society. A way to organize society where many are happier than in an alternative way where only a few are happy seems preferable to many of us. As often, however, both God and the Devil reside in the details. If someone gets tremendous pleasure out of truly extravagant consumption, should we prefer an allocation that gives more to her and less to others? How should we even try to measure, let alone compare, utilities as they are inherently unobservable? Or how should we view allocations where a few are punished to the benefit of many?[13]

Illustration 8.3 The "auto-icon" of Jeremy Bentham on display at University College London. For the background go to https://www.ucl.ac.uk/bentham-project/about-jeremy-bentham/auto-icon. Photo by the author.

One aspect of utilitarianism that is typically seen as promoting reallocation is worth highlighting. In the simplest case, assume that everyone has the same utility function. A standard assumption in economics would say that we have a diminishing marginal utility of income. Redistributing from person H to person L, as in Figure 8.19, would then have a relatively large effect on the utility of L but a relatively low effect on the utility of H.

Another social welfare function is associated with the American philosopher John *Rawls* (Rawls (1971)). In a famous thought experiment, Rawls imagines that all individuals meet and agree on a social contract – how utility should be allocated across individuals. Key is that we meet behind a **veil of ignorance**; we do not know our position in the society for which we are designing the rules. Will I be a prince or a pauper? Rawls concludes that this kind of situation should lead to a welfare function that only puts weight on the person least well off. Key for this result is that we do not know our place in the distribution of utilities and that we are very averse to risk, putting a lot of weight on this lowest possible outcome.

The two previous standpoints can clearly be interpreted as promoting rather large amounts of redistribution. In a contrasting view, often associated with Robert Nozick and partly written in response to Rawls, Nozick (1974), essentially argues that the state has no right to redistribute and demand resources from citizens above what is required to uphold law and order, what is sometimes known as the night-watchman state.

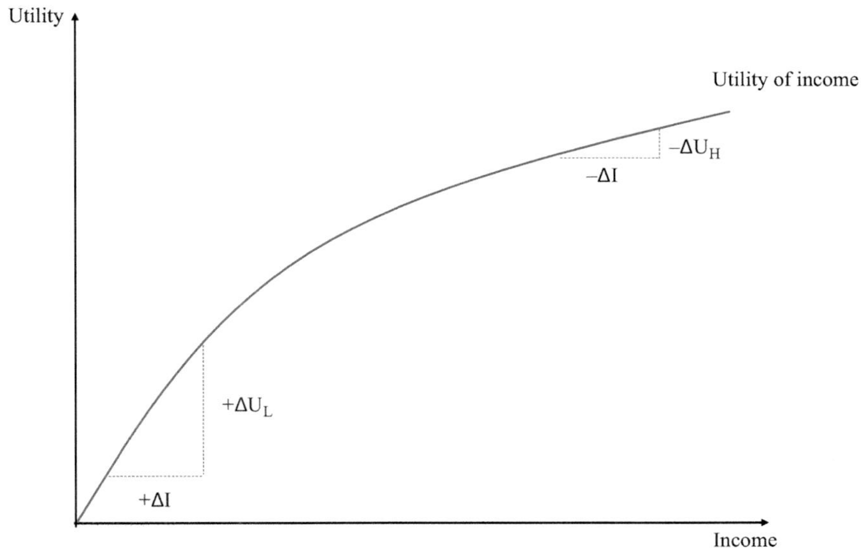

Figure 8.19 Diminishing marginal utility of income and redistribution.

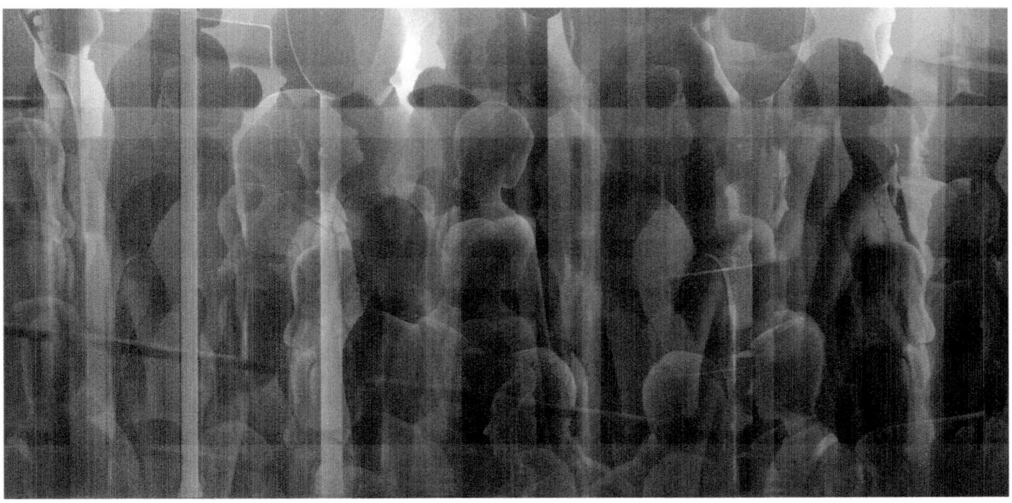

Illustration 8.4 The veil of ignorance. iStockPhoto by Getty Images, Jorm Sangsorn.

8.6 Final words

We have thus seen how under perfect conditions, a perfectly competitive equilibrium features efficient (in the sense of Pareto optimality) consumption, efficient use of inputs, and an efficient combination of goods being produced. As we shall explore in the following, these results are sensitive to a number of assumptions that underlie the perfectly competitive market: price-taking behavior by all, no externalities, and no information asymmetries. These will be examined in later chapters and are typically referred to as market failures.

In the efficiency results, we disregarded equity and relied on implicit assumptions that people engage in voluntary trade with no role for theft or coercion. In terms of a sports example, we can think of an analogy where a game of football is as good as can be when all the players strive to win the game but within the confines set by the rules of the game as upheld by the referee. Another limitation that is typically not explicitly discussed regards that we assume the set of products are fixed. The constant search for new products and innovations are key for well-functioning market economies in the real world.

That said, the framework outlined earlier is key to understanding the interaction of prices and optimizing behavior in a market economy. The United States has a tradition of asking how many people of some kind does it take to screw in a lightbulb. A variation of this is the following. Question: "How many free-market economists does it take to screw in a lightbulb?" Answer: "None, the market has already taken care of it." We find economists at many points of the political spectrum – from those who believe in a minimal state involvement to those who argue that market failures and redistribution necessitate a major role for government. Ideally, we would like to say that how important market failures are, and thus how much the earlier model should be seen as a description of actual markets, should be determined by empirical evidence. In practice, there is a strong element of personal conviction to this. As stated in the quote from Keynes in the introduction, "Economics is a science of thinking in terms of models joined to the art of choosing models which are relevant."

Notes

1 A somewhat subtle point to note is that an individual market may be workably defined as perfectly competitive, even if the whole economy is not – in this chapter, we consider the latter.
2 A concise argument for this view is presented in Rubinstein (2017).
3 Arrow and Debreu (1954) is one key reference.
4 The concept is named after the Italian economist and sociologist Vilfredo Pareto who developed its use, as we present it below, in the early 1900s.
5 From the French expression of "let do."
6 You might note that well-behaved kids might just generously share among themselves, but I choose to stick with this simple visualization rather than think of a more intricate exchange situation between strangers.
7 A minor point for those mathematically inclined: Here the indifference curves have a sharp corner at the "bend of the L," which means that the derivative of the indifference curve is undefined at this corner. Our definition of the contract curve for Figure 8.11 therefore relies on the logic of Pareto optimality, rather than on the result that tangents of the indifference curve are the same across individuals.
8 I'm probably overstating the case here for effect; similar thinking on the economics of the welfare state have been applied in many countries, see, e.g., Barr (2020).
9 Of course, this depends on what we measure on what axis, if capital was instead measured along the horizontal axis the slope would be MP_K/MP_L.
10 There are two reasons for this. One is that students at the Stockholm School of Economics, concurrently with the course in microeconomics, study a course devoted to the fundamentals of cooperation and conflict and empirical analysis of issues like inequality. To get a flavor of the theoretical grounding of that, see Ellingsen (2024). The second is that to do such an analysis in earnest would require a detailed analysis of issues like how redistribution works in practice with, for instance, taxes, social security, health care, child care, and education. The perspective from a Scandinavian welfare state will be very different from say India or a Latin American country. This is also something that would be very different from the main thrust of this book and the typical content of a microeconomics course, which focuses on understanding and learning to work with the key theoretical models of how prices and quantities are determined on markets.

11 The essay is perhaps most known for his defense of highly stylized assumptions in economics, arguing that the value of a theory should be judged by the accuracy of its predictions rather than if the assumptions seem to match up with experience or not.

12 At a deeper level, the utility levels used in social welfare functions can be defined both in terms of the utility of the overall distribution (where, for instance, your consumption level can enter my utility) or as only being defined by each individual's own consumption bundle, what is sometimes known as Bergson-Samuelson welfare functions. The distinction can safely be left for more advanced courses.

13 On a related note, you may have come across a thought experiment known as the Trolley problem: a runaway train is careening down the line and set to kill five people who are standing on the track. You have the possibility to pull a lever and divert the train so that only one person is killed but five are then saved. Various alternatives are often proposed to tease out where the moral limits lie in hurting some to save the many.

Part IV
Imperfect competition

Thus far in the book, we have studied the case of perfect competition, with a large number of firms selling identical products. We believe that to be a useful way of analyzing some fundamental properties of how prices and quantities are determined in markets when markets work under ideal conditions. We also believe that the framework provides a useful lens through which to analyze many real-world markets – an analysis based on supply curves forms the daily tools of analysis used in countless applications of how quantities and prices are determined in markets for raw materials and agricultural products. On the other hand, it is blatantly clear that not all goods and services that we consume are offered in this way. These other markets are termed imperfectly competitive, and we now turn to an analysis of such markets. Table 3.1 provides an overview.

One feature of perfectly competitive markets is that there is **free entry**; that is, it is "easy" for new entrants to come into the industry. In other markets, entry is not free, and we say that there are **entry barriers**. If I want to enter the market for wide-bodied aircraft, which at present is dominated by Airbus and Boeing, there are many barriers to entry. For instance, I need to enter on a very large scale and find funding that will support several years of technological development before I can make any revenues; I will further be at a disadvantage because many technologies will be secrets for the two existing firms, and long-standing links with the buyers of airplanes may further make it hard to enter this market. Markets where entry is not free can in consequence feature situations where only one or a few firms provide the good or service. The extreme case where entry is so hard that there is only one firm supplying the good or service, a monopoly, is the form of supply that we start out analyzing in Chapter 9. The reason for covering monopoly in detail is twofold: first, many real-world markets are indeed dominated by one firm only. Second, many of the features of imperfectly competitive markets are easiest to study in the case where there is only one firm.

The latter part of Chapter 9 examines where there are many independent firms selling differentiated goods and where there is free entry, **monopolistic competition**. Analytically, we can think of it as a combination of monopoly and free entry. Restaurant markets are an

Table 3.1 Different forms of market supply

	Perfect competition	*Monopoly*	*Oligopoly*	*Monopolistic competition*
Number of firms	Many	One	Few	Many
Barriers to entry	None	Very high	High	None
Type of product	Homogeneous	Only one	Homogeneous or differentiated	Differentiated

DOI: 10.4324/9781003623854-12

example of markets that we often model as monopolistically competitive. Restaurants are differentiated; for instance, the restaurants that I regularly go to for lunch differ in location, in what type of food they offer, and how well prepared it is, as well as in the ambiance and service level in the restaurant. There are also low barriers to entry; there will be some cost and possible permits involved, but in principle, it is straightforward to open a new restaurant, as evidenced by a large number of restaurants opening every year.

Chapter 10 then examines the case where entry barriers are such that there are only a few firms, **oligopoly**. When there are just a few firms in an industry, the optimal decisions of one firm depend on what its competitors are doing and vice versa. Markets where a few firms interact can feature homogeneous products, such as cement, but can also feature differentiated products, where the products offered by competing firms differ. Markets for many consumer products, such as beers, ready-to-eat cereal, and cars, are frequently modeled as oligopolies with differentiated products. As we shall see, the effects of competition on prices differs between differentiated and homogeneous products.

We say that there is **strategic interaction** in an oligopoly, in that the optimal course of action depends on the actions of others, and in Chapter 11, we examine how we can model strategic interaction in broader settings, expanding beyond applications to oligopoly markets.

Under perfect competition, each product has a per unit price (e.g., the price of one kilo of apples or one ton of wheat) with little leeway for more sophisticated pricing schemes like student rebates, differences in price across first and second class, or fixed fees like a monthly gym card that we frequently observe when there is imperfect competition. Chapter 12 covers some of the more prominent examples of such more sophisticated pricing schemes.

9 Monopoly and monopolistic competition

Illustration 9.1 John D. Rockefeller Sr. National Portrait Gallery, Smithsonian Institution, in the public domain.

In this chapter, we examine two types of markets that are closely related in the mechanics of how we analyze them. Both face downward-sloping demand curves and disregard strategic interaction with other firms. They are on the opposite sides of the spectrum when it comes to entry barriers, however – a monopolist is sheltered from entry by competing firms, whereas under monopolistic competition, there is free entry.

DOI: 10.4324/9781003623854-13

9.1 Quantity set by a monopolist

A **monopoly** market is one in which a firm sells a good or service for which there are no close substitutes. The perhaps clearest example is that of a pharmaceutical product that is alone in its ability to treat a disease and that is legally protected by patents. As is typical in economics, some judgment comes into play when we determine what we mean by "no close" substitutes. The Nordic countries Finland, Norway, and Sweden each has a retail monopoly on sales of alcoholic beverages. We say that they are monopolies, even if purchasing from abroad is a possibility. A ferry operating the only connection to an island has a monopoly even if people can in principle get to the island by their own boats. We would also say that monopoly is a useful way to describe the market if one firm is completely dominant, even if there is a small fringe of firms.

The key insight regarding how a monopolist sets quantity is that the *firm-specific demand curve* that it faces is downward sloping. Figure 9.1 illustrates the situation. Look first at panel (a) where we consider a firm that is only one of very many selling identical products and therefore has no effect on the price. If a potato farmer brings 1 more kilo to the market, she will assume that she has no impact on the price, as we've seen before. Assume that the price is 10 euros per kilo; if she sells 10 kilos, her revenue is 100 euros (10×10), and if she sells 11 kilos, her revenue is 110 euros (10×11). In other words, the *marginal revenue*, the change in revenue associated with a small increase in quantity, is equal to the price (revenue increases from 100 to 110, that is by 10, as 1 more unit is produced). This is the result that we used earlier to find the profit-maximizing supply of a price-taking firm.

In panel (b), we instead consider a monopoly. This firm meets the entire market demand for the good or service that it produces, and we expect market-level demand curves to slope downward. For simplicity, use the same starting point as in the left-hand panel such that if it sells 10 kilos, the price on the market is 10 euro, and consequently, its revenue is 100 euros (10×10). Now, if it instead produces 11 kilos, the heart of the matter is that, with a downward-sloping demand curve, the increase in quantity supplied is associated with a

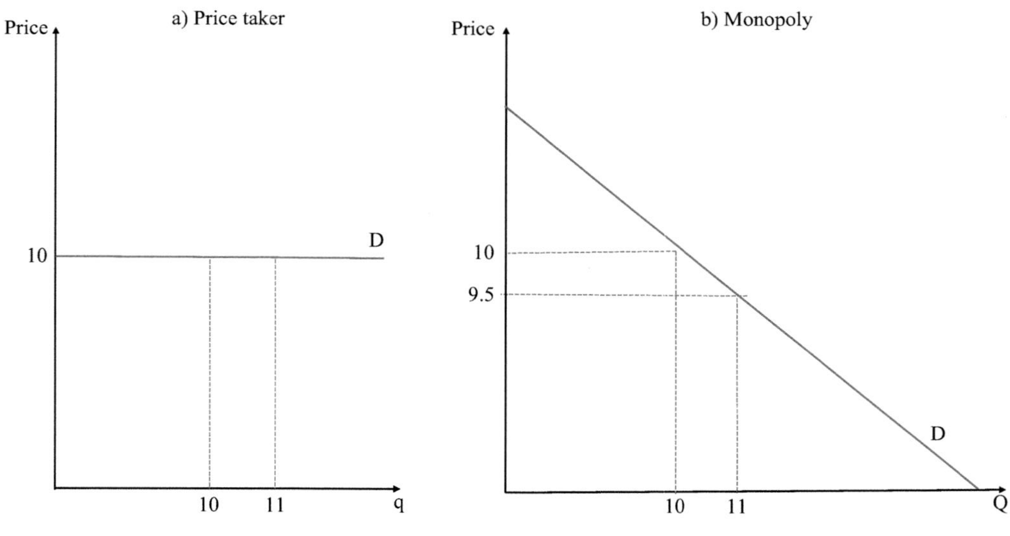

Figure 9.1 Demand curve facing a single firm: Price taker vs. monopolist.

lower price. To be concrete, assume that the demand curve is such that price falls from 10 to 9.5 euros as the quantity increases. Thus, its revenue at the higher quantity is 104.5 euros (9.5×11). In other words, the *marginal revenue*, the change in revenue associated with a small increase in quantity, is equal to 4.5 euros (revenue increases from 100 to 104.5). Thus the marginal revenue is lower than the price, the fundamental reason being that the greater quantity drives down the price. There is a mechanical increase in revenue from the sale of an additional unit, but this positive effect is counteracted by the increased sales coming at the cost of lower prices for all goods sold.

9.1.1 *Profit maximization for a monopolist – A numerical example*

With the aforementioned intuition for results, let us now consider a numerical example of monopoly profit maximization before we turn to present the more general case. Assume that the demand curve can be expressed as $p = 12 - Q$ and the cost function as $C(Q) = 3 + Q^2$. The profit-maximization problem facing the monopolist is to set quantity so as to maximize profit

$$\max_{Q} \underbrace{(12 - Q)Q}_{Revenue} - \underbrace{(3 + Q^2)}_{Cost}. \tag{9.1}$$

We want to identify the quantity at which profits are the highest; we want to find the top of the hill by differentiating profits with respect to Q and setting the derivative equal to zero. At the top of the hill, the tangent to the profit function has zero slope; this is the first-order condition for profit maximization.[1] To simplify the derivation, it may be useful to multiply in the quantity in Equation (9.1) and thus express profits as

$$\Pi(Q) = 12Q - Q^2 - 3 - Q^2. \tag{9.2}$$

Differentiating Equation (9.2) and setting the derivative equal to 0 – the first-order condition for profit maximization – yields that

$$\frac{d\Pi(Q)}{dQ} = \underbrace{12 - 2Q}_{MR} - \underbrace{2Q}_{MC} = 0. \tag{9.3}$$

Just as for the price taker, the firm maximizes profit by setting marginal revenue (MR) equal to marginal cost (MC). The only novelty compared to what we did before is that now the firm takes account of the downward-sloping demand curve and acknowledges that by producing more, it drives down price. Solving Equation (9.3) for Q yields $4Q = 12 => Q^* = 3$. To find the associated optimal price, we simply insert the profit-maximizing quantity into the demand function and establish the price of $p^* = 12 - 3 = 9$ euros. Figure 9.2 illustrates.

The figure has several things to tell. The firm finds it optimal to increase quantity as long as the increase in revenue from producing more is greater (MR) than the increase in cost (MC) from producing more. If quantity is below 3, each additional unit increases revenue more than what it increases costs and profits increase. In contrast, if quantity is above 3, each additional unit would increase revenue by less than what costs increase and profits decrease. At the point where MR = MC, profits are maximized. It may help the intuition to

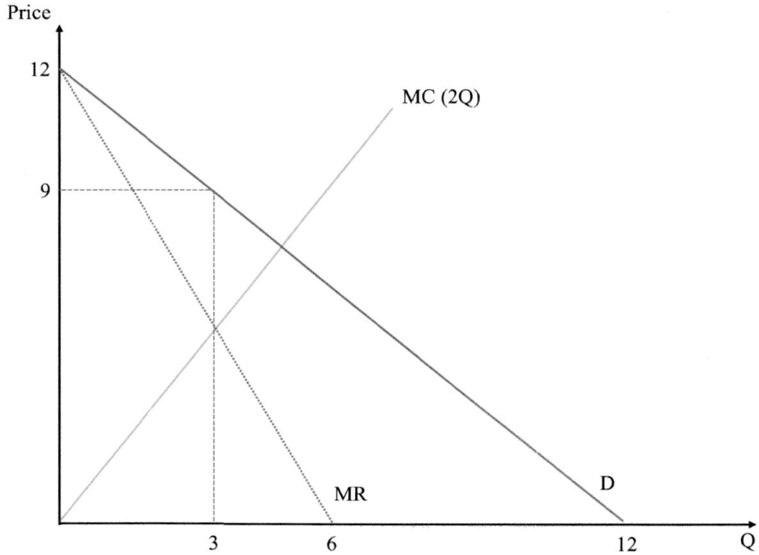

Figure 9.2 Profit maximization for a monopolist: Numerical example. Video link for Figures 9.2 and 9.3: https://youtu.be/xnrHDhq2mZE.

explore the exact numbers in this case. Moving from producing 3 to 4 units would increase revenue from 27 ((12−3)×3) to 32 ((12−4)×4). Thus marginal revenue for that change is 5 euros (32−27). That increase in quantity from 3 to 4 would increase cost from 12 $(3+3^2)$ to 19 $(3+4^2)$. Thus the marginal cost would be 7 euros (19−12). In short, cost increase more (7 euros) than revenue (5 euros), and it would be optimal to scale back.

An important point to realize is that the firm wouldn't necessarily make a loss even if it did not set quantity such that MR = MC. At the quantity of 4, profit would be $(12-4)\times 4-(3+4^2)=13$ euros, as opposed to $(12-4)\times 4-(3+4^2)=15$ euros at the profit-maximizing quantity. Just as in the case of perfect competition, we can express profit as $\Pi(Q)=(p-ATC)\times Q$, as depicted in Figure 9.3. Average total cost $(ATC=C(Q)/Q)$ is equal to 4 euros when $Q=3$ $((3+3^2)/3)$, and again, we find that profits are 15 euros since $(9-4)\times 3=15$ euros.

Before we move on, this may be a good spot to mention two points "by the way." First, many textbooks in economics do not use calculus (differentiating profits) to derive the optimal quantity and instead rely on a discussion of marginal revenue and marginal cost. While differentiation is slightly "technical," I believe that the beauty and simplicity of differentiation makes it well suited also for a course at the introductory level. Some textbooks also teach the "trick" that in a graph with a linear demand curve, marginal revenue is always twice as steep as demand. From inspecting revenue earlier, it is clear where this result comes from: Differentiating, Q^2 with respect to Q will always yield $2Q$. This does not necessarily hold for other demand functions, and there is no profound economic intuition for why the marginal revenue is twice as steep as demand in this case; its just a mechanical result of this particular functional form. Second, when a firm is a monopoly, it seems a bit roundabout to say that it takes account of the fact that it drives price down

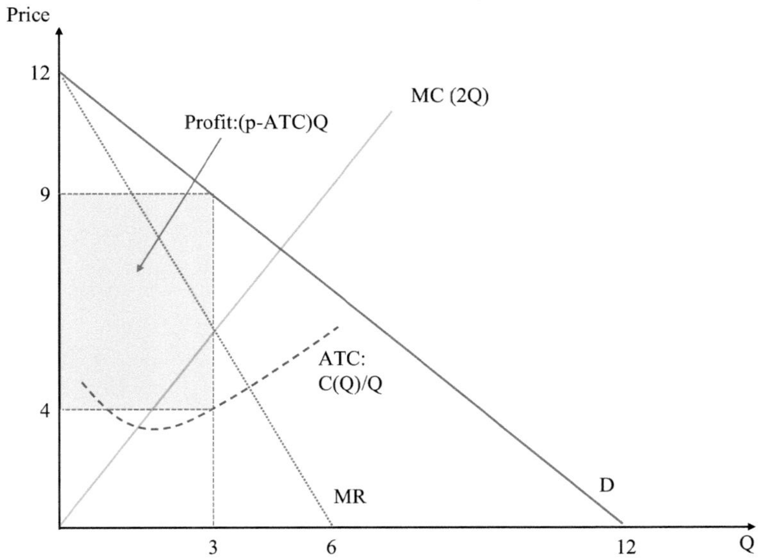

Figure 9.3 Profit at the optimal quantity for a monopolist: Numerical example. Video link for Figures 9.2 and 9.3: https://youtu.be/xnrHDhq2mZE.

when producing more. For most of us, it is more intuitive to say that only by lowering price can it sell more. In the case of a monopolist, these are the same, and in the appendix, we solve for the same optimization problem as earlier with respect to price setting instead. The reason why we, perhaps somewhat counterintuitively in the case of monopoly, focus on quantity setting is that it facilitates comparisons of outcomes across different market structures. We will return with a discussion of this in Chapter 10, where it, at first somewhat counterintuitively, matters a great deal for the outcomes whether we think of firms that are interacting strategically as setting prices or quantities.

9.1.2 Deadweight loss of a monopoly

The monopolist holds back on quantity to keep prices high and increase profits. This is detrimental to consumers in two ways: They pay a higher price for the units that they nevertheless purchase, and in addition, some units that would have been consumed with a lower price are not consumed. Since quantity is set at a point where price is above marginal cost, there is a deadweight loss associated with the monopoly quantity. In principle, consumers are willing to pay more (given by the demand curve) than what it costs the monopoly to produce those units (as given by the marginal cost curve). The core of the problem is that in order to sell these "last" units, a monopoly that sells all units at the same price will need to face a lower price on all units to sell these additional units. At the profit-maximizing quantity, there is thus some money left on the table in the sense that not all profitable trades are made; there is a deadweight loss.

Let us again use the numerical example from the previous section to discuss further. We use Figure 9.4 to examine the effects and calculate the deadweight loss. First, we need

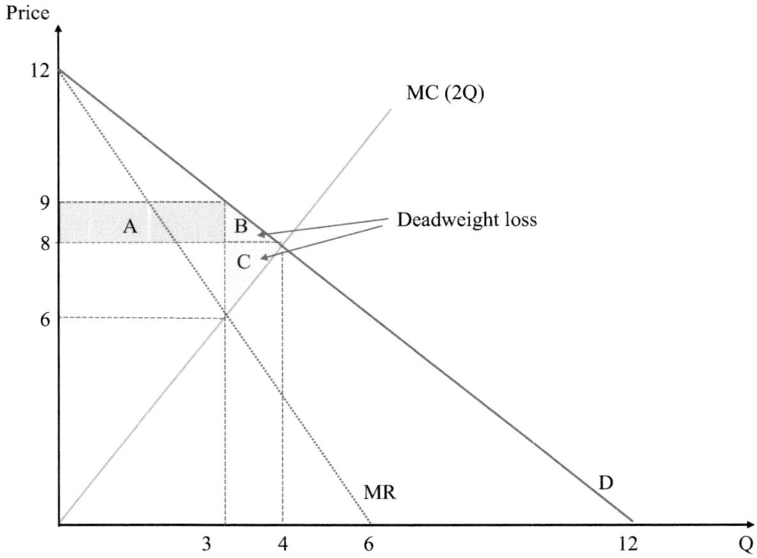

Figure 9.4 Deadweight loss of a monopoly: Numerical example.

to determine what the societally optimal outcome would be. We know that a price-taking firm will set quantity such that $p = MC$. In this case, the firm will thus let quantity be determined by

$$\underbrace{12 - Q}_{p} = \underbrace{2Q}_{MC} \tag{9.4}$$

and the quantity set by a firm acting as a price taker would be given by solving for Q in Equation (9.4), $3Q = 12$, which implies $Q^{pt} = 4$, where pt denotes price taker. At this quantity, price is $12 - 4 = 8$. So as a result of the higher price set by the profit-maximizing monopolist, consumer surplus decreases by areas A and B in Figure 9.4. Area A is a redistribution from consumer surplus to producer surplus – units that are purchased in both scenarios are sold at a higher price under monopoly. Consumers lose, and the monopolist gains, but, seen from the overall societal standpoint, there is no efficiency loss of this redistribution. For area B, this is not true; however, this is consumption that doesn't come about because of profit maximization, as just discussed. Similarly, area C represents the concomitant loss of producer surplus (clearly, area A is larger than C, so there is a net gain to the monopoly, however).

As before, a key point of the deadweight loss is that it is not only a conceptual measure but something that we can quantify. In this case, with linear functions, the area between the demand and marginal cost curves is simply given by a triangle, and we can use the relation that the area of a triangle is the base × height divided by 2. Think of the horizontal axis as the height of the triangle, which gives a height of 1 unit (4–3). For the base, which we measure on the vertical axis, we know that we will be interested in the difference between the price (9) and the point on the vertical axis at which MR and MC intersect (6). The latter value can be found by inserting 3 into the marginal cost function: $2 \times 3 = 6$ euros. In this case, we would thus have a deadweight loss given by

$$\frac{(9-6) \times (4-3)}{2} = 1.5 \text{ euros.}$$

9.1.3 *Profit maximization for a monopolist – The general case*

In Section 9.1, we solved for the profit-maximizing quantity for a monopolist under the assumption that costs and demand had particular functional forms. In the following, we redo the same exercise but for the general case where we simply assume that there is some arbitrary demand function $p(Q)$ and some arbitrary cost function $C(Q)$. The profit maximization problem is then

$$\max_{Q} p(Q)Q - C(Q).$$

In finding the optimal quantity, we make use of the product rule of differentiation and the first-order condition of profit maximization is given by[2]

$$\frac{d\Pi(Q)}{dQ} = \underbrace{\frac{dp(Q)}{dQ}Q + p(Q)}_{MR} - \underbrace{\frac{dC(Q)}{dQ}}_{MC} = 0. \tag{9.5}$$

Equation (9.5) clearly displays the two effects on marginal revenue of choosing to produce more: The first term captures that the monopolist is driving down price as it produces more and the second that it brings in additional revenue from selling an additional unit. As before, quantity is set so that marginal revenue is equal to marginal cost. We can also manipulate Equation (9.5) to yield a form that is particularly convenient for finding the intuition of how quantities are set in markets with different characteristics of demand. First, streamline notation and divide by p

$$\frac{dp}{dQ}\frac{Q}{p} + \frac{p - MC}{p} = 0. \tag{9.6}$$

We can then note that the first term is simply the inverse of the price elasticity of demand.[3] Thus, using that

$$E^D = \frac{dQ}{dp}\frac{p}{Q}$$

we can rewrite Equation (9.6) as

$$\frac{p - MC}{p} = -\frac{1}{E^D}. \tag{9.7}$$

The term on the left in Equation (9.7) sets the **markup**, the difference between price and marginal cost, in relation to the price. On the right hand side, we have minus 1 over the

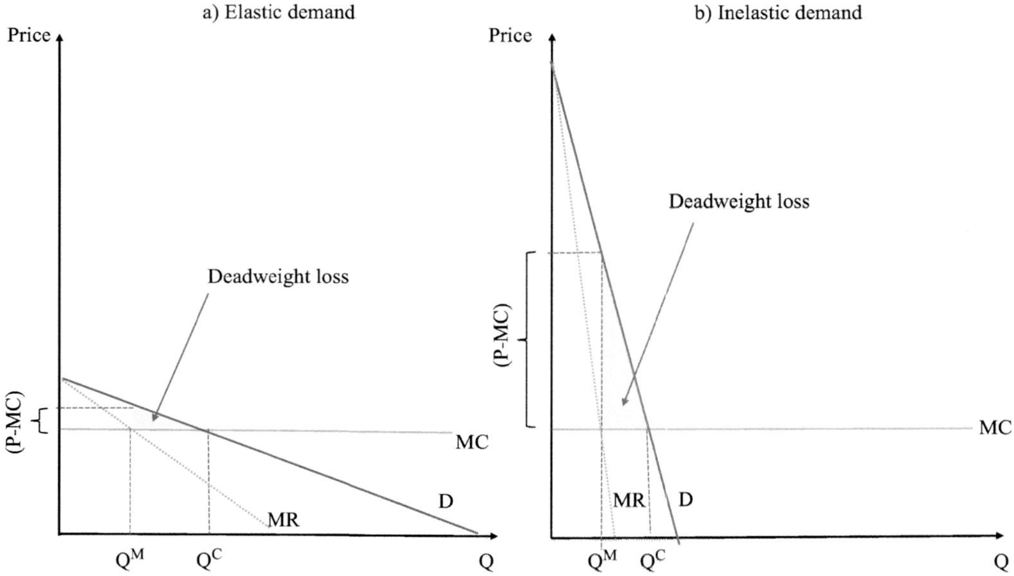

Figure 9.5 Lerner index for high and low elastictity of demand.

price elasticity of demand. The term on the left is also known as the Lerner index, named after the economist Abba Lerner. It is an index in the sense that it runs from 0 to 1. As price gets closer to marginal cost, as markups are lower, then the index tends toward 0. The equality teaches us that this happens when the elasticity of demand tends to negative infinity. Perfect competition is associated with a perfectly flat inverse demand, and this case is thus associated with a Lerner index of 0. The more elastic that demand is, the closer price is to marginal cost and the lower the Lerner index. At the other side of things, as markups become very large and marginal costs tend to become minuscule in relation to price, the Lerner index tends to 1 since $\frac{p-\text{something vanishingly small}}{p}$ will tend to 1. This happens when the elasticity of demand approaches -1 from below.

In Figure 9.5, we illustrate two cases. When demand is highly elastic, as in panel (a), the markup will be low, even if the product is supplied by a monopolist. The effect of monopoly power on the price that consumers pay is limited in this case, and we see a relatively small loss of consumer surplus as a result of monopoly. A limited price increase also pushes in the direction of a limited deadweight loss. If, on the other hand, demand is relatively insensitive, as in panel (b), the price increase associated with monopoly will be much higher, and there will be a substantial lowering of consumer surplus. The higher price will also push in the direction of higher deadweight loss, even if the overall effect is tempered by the demand responding relatively little to the price increase. Having a monopoly on products with a relatively low sensitivity of demand can clearly generate high profits. Swedish industrialist Ivar Kreuger gained a monopoly on match production in many countries during the 1920s. This kind of low-priced necessity clearly had a relatively low elasticity, and it comes as no surprise that these monopolies generated a lot of income for Kreuger.[4]

While we introduce the Lerner index in the context of monopoly, it should be noted that the study of differences between price and marginal cost, the markup, is of interest for any form of imperfect competition. The empirical measurement of Lerner indexes and markups are an important task in economics, and it is a type of exercise often conducted in analysis of actual markets and how they respond to changes in, for instance, entry barriers. How much are prices elevated above marginal costs in a particular industry or by a particular firm? This says something about the **market power** – the ability to in a profit-maximizing way set a price above marginal cost – that a firm has. The term **monopoly power** is also used as a synonym for market power, also in cases where the firm in question is not a monopolist. We as economists care about market power both for distributional reasons (a common preference in policymaking is to attach a greater weight to consumer surplus than to producer surplus) and because it results in a deadweight loss.

Before we move on, let us follow up on a final loose thread from the Lerner index. What if demand is inelastic? The term on the right-hand side in Equation (9.7) is then greater than 1, which would imply that the marginal cost would need to be negative for the relation to hold. Costs falling if a firm produces more is hardly a typical case, and instead, the case is typically highlighted to emphasize that a monopolist will not want to price at an inelastic part of the demand function.[5] We saw in Chapter 6 that for linear demand functions (and many other cases), demand becomes more elastic at higher price levels. If demand is inelastic, a monopolist can increase profit by increasing price since the change in price is greater then the change in quantity. In principle, this means that empirically, a firm that is charged with charging excessive prices in some way could defend itself by reporting that demand for its product is inelastic. If demand is inelastic, the firm can claim that it is not setting a monopoly price.[6]

9.2 Why do monopolies exist?

We saw that under perfect competition, there were forces pushing toward zero profits. The key explanation for that is free entry; if there are profits to be made in an industry, this is likely to attract entry, and these new entrants will tend to push prices and profits downdard. In short, monopolies exist because new entrants cannot come in and become efficient competitors. These barriers to entry can stem from a number of different sources, and we highlight a few particularly prominent reasons in the following.

9.2.1 Regulation

Historically, many monopolies have existed because laws and regulations banned competitors. The British East India company was granted a monopoly on trade between East Asia and Britain by Queen Elizabeth I, and the Hudson Bay Company was granted a monopoly for trading with parts of present-day Canada. **Patents** are a time-limited legal right to an invention. A firm that has a patent has a monopoly on products that build on that patent in a particular jurisdiction. The reason for granting such patents is that the profits during the monopoly period should act as a motivation for taking the costs of innovation. On the other hand, one does not want the inefficiency associated with monopoly to work in perpetuity, and hence, after the patent expires, other firms are able to observe the patented technology and enter as competitors. Monopolies may also exist because authorities for health, or other reasons related to consumer welfare, want to avoid a competitive situation in a market. For instance, a number of countries and some US states have retail monopolies on sales of alcoholic beverages. Pharmacies were a state monopoly in Sweden until 2009.

9.2.2 *Natural monopoly*

If the technology and costs of production are such that there are very important economies of scale when set in relation the the size of the market, we can be in a situation where one firm can operate profitably, but two firms would operate at a loss. The simplest example is one where there are large fixed costs and low marginal costs. Think of a railroad between two cities – the cost of building the rail is very high, partly because of physical construction costs, but potentially also because of costly bargaining with landholders whose permission one needs to build the rail. Another firm that would try to start competing with an already existing firm would first need to raise a lot of capital to build a second set of railway lines. In addition, prices under competition would be lower than prices under monopoly, which would also deter entry. Such large economies of scale are present in many industries that rely on infrastructure development, such as rail lines, electricity grids, or fixed telephone lines. Historically, and still today, electricity, telecoms companies, and railroads have often been monopolies where state ownership has been a way to avoid the loss of consumer surplus and deadweight loss associated with a profit-maximizing monopoly. A state-owned monopoly can be instructed to maximize social welfare rather than profit.[7] A mailman visiting all houses in a neighborhood rather than competing mailmen doing the same rounds similarly are associated with economies of scale, and postal services have been a public monopoly in many countries. In recent decades, these have in several cases been regulated in a way such that the government owns the key infrastructure (for instance, the actual railroad tracks) and one then attempts to have competition on the rail transport.

9.2.3 *Control of an important input*

In many industries, you need a certain input to be able to compete effectively. For instance, to extract oil, one needs access to oil wells. To sell diamonds, one needs access to diamonds. If such inputs are in scarce supply, whoever controls those inputs will be able to extract monopoly rents. Indeed, these two industries are prominent historical examples of monopolies. John D. Rockefeller gradually built up Standard Oil to control oil wells and oil production in the United States during the late 1800s and became one of the richest men in history. The concentration of this and other industries during the late 1800s and early 1900s were an important impetus to competition law, and Standard Oil was broken up by legal action in 1911. Similarly, South African diamond firm De Beers had a near-monopoly on supply of rough diamonds throughout the 20th century.

9.2.4 *Strategic behavior on the part of the incumbent*

The previous examples are mostly cases where entry is impossible or prohibitively expensive, even if the monopolist acts obliviously of potential entry. We can also think of other cases where entry in principle would be possible, but the current monopolist, the **incumbent**, acts in such a way so as to make entry unprofitable. Bain (1956) introduced a classification of responses by an incumbent to potential entry into the market where it is active. In Bain's classification, we say that entry is **blockaded** if it is not profitable to enter, even if the monopolist behaves without regard to potential entry. There might also be the case where entry is **deterred** – where the monopolist acts in such a way as to make entry unprofitable or in other ways unattractive. In illegal markets, this can take the form of threats of violence but more generally can concern actions such as the use of long-term contracts with customers or excess capacity to keep prices low. We explore such issues further in

Chapter 11, which models strategic behavior.[8] In a related vein, a firm might attempt to build a monopoly-like position through mergers and acquisitions, where Facebook's purchases of Instagram and WhatsApp are relatively recent examples. The extent to which strategic behavior and acquisitions can be used to build a monopoly position of course depends on the legal framework.

9.3 Monopolistic competition

We now turn to the case where firms face downward-sloping demand, and there is free entry – **monopolistic competition**. There are three key assumptions in this market structure:

- Firms produce differentiated products. Hence they face downdard-sloping demand. In other words, they can set price, and if they raise price a little, they typically lose some customers but not all.
- There are many competitors. This means that we disregard strategic interaction and don't try to model how what's optimal for one firm to do depends on what other firms are doing.
- There is free entry. It is easy for new firms to come into the market and replicate what the existing firms are doing.

Local services such as restaurants and hair salons are examples of markets that we often believe to be well described by models of monopolistic competition. To exemplify the assumptions, note that different restaurants tend to be imperfect substitutes; they offer

Illustration 9.2 Many restaurants. iStock Photo by Getty Images, Fani Kurti.

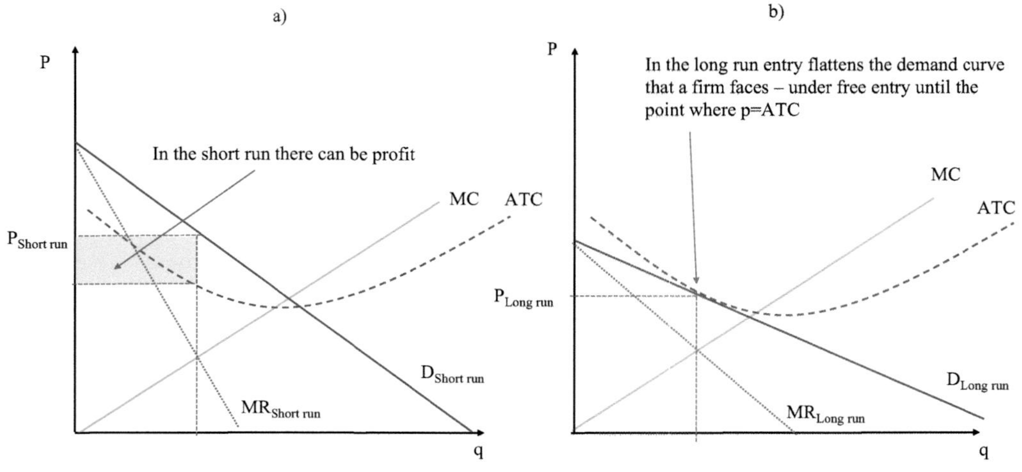

Figure 9.6 Monopolistic competition. Video link for Figure 9.6: https://youtu.be/_ugwjEnqojE.

different food, at different locations, and with differing staff. Two restaurants that are particularly close may engage in strategic reflections, but in a typical city-wide market, it is a natural simplifying assumption that not much is missed by disregarding such strategic interaction. Finally, restaurants frequently enter and exit the market in typical locations. An entrepreneur needs to find some financing, rent a location, and hire some staff, but the barriers to start operating are typically low. Compare that to the situation if I want to start competing in the market for producing jet engines or music streaming where there are likely too many entry barriers. Proprietary technology, complex legal arrangements with suppliers and customers, network effects where people prefer products that their friends are already using, all favor the already large firms. They are all examples of barriers to entry that we see in some industries but that have a low overall impact in industries that we analyze as monopolistically competitive.

Figure 9.6 illustrates the situation for a single firm under monopolistic competition. Panel (a) shows the situation in the short run. Say that a firm has opened up a restaurant in a new part of town. The restaurant sets quantity in a way such that marginal revenue equals marginal cost. So far, this could be a graph of a monopoly. In the short run, there may be some profit, but, just as in a perfectly competitive market, profits will trigger entry. From the perspective of a single firm already in the market, such entry then shifts the demand curve inward. For every price that the firm charges, it will sell fewer units since some customers go to competitors.

How long can entry occur? As long as there are profits that can be captured by entrants into the industry. In a long run, free-entry equilibrium, profits will be driven to zero. Remember that we can express profits as (price-average total cost)× quantity. Price is given by the demand curve evaluated at the quantity where marginal revenue equals marginal cost. Thus, for there to be zero profit, the demand curve has to be tangent to the average total cost curve, as illustrated in panel (b) of 9.6. Conversely, if firms are making losses, some will exit, shifting the firm-specific demand curve facing the remaining firms outward.

Just as oligopoly models that we examine in the next chapter are useful for understanding markets with few firms that interact strategically, the monopolistic competition model is useful for analyzing markets with differentiated products, free entry, and many firms. Say that there, for instance, is a change that raises the fixed cost of running a restaurant. We expect this to lead to the exit of some firms and an adjustment of overall quantities but that in the long run the market will return to a zero-profit equilibrium.

Another important use for monopolistic competition is to model markups where we consider the whole economy over time, as we do in macroeconomics. It was well understood for a long time that markups and economies of scale were important for issues related to international trade and general equilibrium effects of policy. However, generating models that we could conveniently work with represented a challenge, and models targeted to such analysis typically relied on perfect competition. Gradually convenient formalizations of monopolistic competition (in particular Dixit and Stiglitz (1977)) allowed researchers to, in a relatively tractable way, study differentiated product markets in general equilibrium. For instance, Paul Romer received the 2018 Nobel Prize in Economics for his modeling of how incentives for research and development could be incorporated into general equilibrium models to study the role of technological progress in economic growth (see, e.g., Romer (1990) for a key contribution). Similarly, as we shall see in Chapter 17, Paul Krugman received the 2008 Nobel Prize for introducing imperfect competition into general equilibrium models of international trade, relying heavily on monopolistic competition to do so.

9.3.1 Monopolistic competition when firms differ in productivity

Monopolistic competition as modeled earlier is convenient to examine markets characterized by free entry and differentiated products. Implicit in the earlier discussion, however is that firms are all the same or at least any differences between them are kept in the background. If we are interested in how preferences for differentiated products and economies of scale shape a market that may not be an important weakness. Work that tries to apply monopolistic competition models to policy questions, however, had to confront that in practice, the size and profitability differs widely across firms. If there, for instance, is a lowering of barriers to international trade, the evidence points to (as discussed in Chapter 17) the most efficient firms expanding, and the least efficient firms shrinking or exiting the market. To examine such issues, we need a workable model that can generate differences in efficiency across firms, and we now turn to such extensions of the monopolistic competition model, starting with a presentation of some empirical motivation.

9.3.1.1 Motivating evidence: Total factor productivity

What do we mean by more efficient firms? We can think of it as firms that are able to produce more with given inputs. In Chapter 3, we examined production functions and the marginal product of labor in detail. More broadly, we are frequently interested in how output is related to all the factors of production that are used, something that we turn to now. The Cobb-Douglas functional form (where all factors enter multiplicatively and raised to the power of an exponent), which we also examined in Chapter 3, is a common starting point for analysis. The output Q from firm i at time t can then be expressed as

$$Q_{it} = A_{it} L_{it}^{\alpha_L} K_{it}^{\alpha_K}. \tag{9.8}$$

This is a relation that we can take to the data, and a large empirical literature estimates the parameters of such production functions. The details of such estimation are beyond the scope of what we do here, but it may nevertheless be useful with a very brief example to understand the intuition behind estimates of production functions. Take the natural logarithm (ln) of Equation (9.8) to reach

$$lnQ_{it} = lnA_{it} + \alpha_L lnL_{it} + \alpha_K lnK_{it}. \tag{9.9}$$

So here Q_{it} can, for instance, be the number of units produced by a firm of a particular type in a particular year – such as the number of tons of cement produced or the number of patients operated. Firms themselves clearly will typically know this, but such data is also often reported to national statistical offices. The latter will typically also have a measure of the number of people who work in the firm, as well as some aggregate measures of the amount of capital used. With a large number of observations across firms and time, one can then use statistical techniques to relate changes in output (Q) to changes in inputs (K,L, and possible other inputs). As part of the estimation, one learns about the factor elasticity of different inputs, α_L and α_K. An estimated value of α_L of 0.5, for instance, says that if the amount of labor used increases by 10%, then the number of units produced increase by 5%. The first term in Equation (9.9), lnA_{it} captures the productivity – it is not something that we directly observe; rather, it is the difference in output across firms and time that we cannot relate to differences in firms' use of inputs. As we account for all factors of production, we term A_{it} total factor productivity (TFP).[9]

The empirical study of TFP has been a very active field in the last few decades and much is known. A few prominent stylized facts, as summarized by De Loecker and Syverson (2021), are the following:

- There are *large differences in TFP* across firms within the same industry and country. This is true even when we examine products such as plywood or cement where we believe that firms are using similar technologies and where products are comparable. De Loecker and Syverson (2021), for instance, summarize the evidence such that in a typical industry in Canada or the United States, the more productive firms have a TFP that is about twice that of its less efficient peers.[10] A simple numerical example may help our understanding: A factory of a given size with 100 workers produces 1,000 metal cans per year in one of the least productive firms and 2,000 cans in the most productive firms.
- Productivity is *highly persistent* – the most productive firms tend to stay the most productive. This indicates that the productivity differences are not just reflecting randomness.
- More productive firms tend to be *more profitable, larger, grow faster, as well as more likely to survive and pay higher wages*.

These differences can be due to many aspects of how firms combine inputs, manage processes, and the quality of inputs and output. An intuitive example is the transformation of automobile production associated with the introduction of mass production at Ford in the 1910s. Moving from a case where cars are built one by one to a moving assembly line where the chassis moves to successively new work groups that add certain highly standardized parts radically increased productivity. In recent decades, a culture of continuous improvement and attention to detail associated with Toyota have similarly been shown to greatly raise productivity. Little things, like always knowing where to find a particular tool, can in the aggregate have important consequences for output.

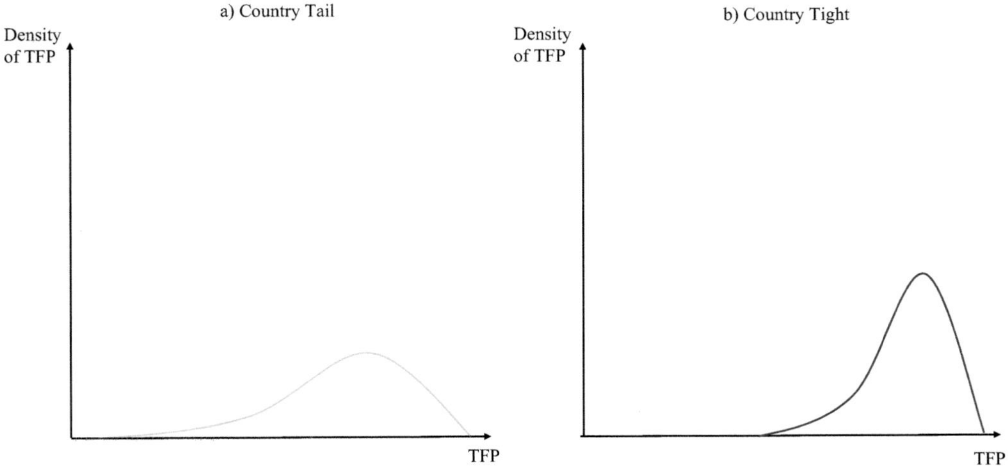

Figure 9.7 Two hypothetical TFP distributions. Video link for Figure 9.7: https://youtu.be/n9NZDdNH2MQ.

Not surprisingly, differences in TFP are large also across countries (see, e.g., Saliola and Seker (2011) or Bartelsman et al. (2013)). A useful way to summarize the dispersion of TFP is to present graphs of the TFP distribution in an industry, as we do in Figure 9.7. Conceptually, we can think of a histogram where bars denote the number of firms with a particular TFP level. The more firms that have a particular level, the higher the bar. The densities that we illustrate can then be thought of as a "smoothed curve" over the histogram. The figure panel (a), Country Tail, has a longer left-hand tail than what the country in panel (b), Country Tight, has.

As we now discuss in some detail, we expect competition to shape how the productivity distribution looks. We noted that the empirical evidence supported the intuitive result that more productive firms grow faster and are more likely to survive. If more productive firms compete with less productive firms, the latter are likely to be out-competed and be forced to exit unless they can improve their productivity. A long tail of firms with lower productivity can then be seen as a sign of "competitive reallocation" working less efficiently than is the case for a tighter distribution. In a well-cited paper, Hsieh and Klenow (2009) do a related exercise, using TFP distributions from China, India, and the United States, noting in particular that the TFP distribution for India looks more like Country Tail in Figure 9.7 and that of the United States, which looks more like Country Tight. They then use their model and estimates to quantify the effects of the counterfactual experiment, "What would average productivity be in India if the TFP distribution were as tight as in the United States?" and find predicted increases of around 50%.

The discussion in Hsieh and Klenow (2009) and related papers is very much focused on the question of what allows less productive firms to stay in business and, the flip side of the coin, why are more productive firms not growing faster? One thing to note is that product differentiation offers one reason – it is no mystery that a maker of luxury T-shirts can stay in business if able to charge a price 10 times higher than a maker of more generic, low-quality T-shirts. This offers a partial explanation, but the empirical literature documents very large differences also in cases where differentiation can't be the main explanation (see Foster et al. (2008) for an analysis). A long host of issues in how markets work can potentially affect competition and reallocation, ranging from how well do capital markets work (so that entrepreneurs can access funds) to how well do the legal and political systems work so that a level playing field is provided?

An example of work that tries to explore cross-country (and across-firm) differences is a string of high-impact papers that show how management practices in a firm help explain productivity differences (see, e.g., Bloom and Van Reenen (2007) or Bloom and Van Reenen (2010)). Management practices here being policies regarding if the firm, for instance, works in systematic ways with tracking performance, actively works to retain top talent, and continually seeks to improve production processes. Bloom et al. (2013), for instance, offered aid on efficient management practices to a random sample of Indian textiles firms and observed large positive effects on productivity when comparing a set of "control firms" (that did not receive such aid). Bloom et al. (2013) also point to a lack of trust leading to a hesitancy to bring in managers from outside the owner's family as a constraint on the growth of more productive firms, thus pointing to how the general level of trust in a society and the functioning of the legal system can affect productivity.

Before moving on to discuss what kind of models we can use to analyze TFP distributions, we should note that the literature that examines international trade has been at the forefront of developments in the productivity literature – documenting patterns of size and productivity differences across firms (see, e.g., Bernard et al. (2007)), as well as examining competitive redistribution in response to trade policy changes (e.g., Trefler (2004) on trade liberalization in North America and Pavcnik (2002) on trade liberalization in Chile).

The recent literature on competitive reallocation from which we've just referred to a few key empirical investigations does remarkably well in describing patterns of productivity, growth, and size of firms in markets. This clearly presents a challenge to models of perfect competition, as well as to a baseline monopolitistically competitive model where all firms are symmetric. This is not to say that those models are useless; as discussed they capture many important facets of how markets work and how shocks affect them. The evidence discussed in this section nevertheless points to the value of having models that are more aligned with the facts across a broad range of markets. Clearly, such models also become more challenging to work with and teach. As they already today are important in policy discussions, and are likely to become even more influential in the future, it is therefore useful to provide an overview of monopolistically competitive models with heterogeneous firms, as we do in the following.

9.3.1.2 *Modeling monopolistically competitive models where firms differ in productivity*

Models that build on monopolistic competition and allow for differences across firms are the foundation of recent work on competitive reallocation and productivity. The first and most influential in a new generation of such models was applied to international trade and presented in Melitz (2003). Next, we present a simplified exposition of some key insights from this type of model, building more closely on follow-up work in Melitz and Ottaviano (2008) and Melitz and Trefler (2012).

We assume that there is:

- Monopolistic competition – goods are differentiated, and there is free entry.
- Differences in marginal costs across firms.

Illustration 9.3 What do the dies show? *The Last Throw*, painting by Charles Robert Leslie. Metropolitan Museum of art, public domain.

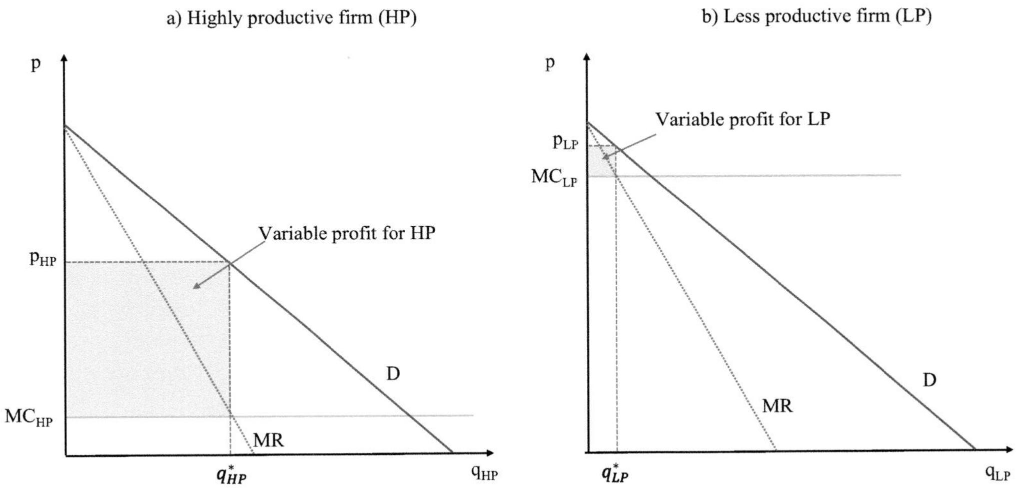

Figure 9.8 Variable profit of firms with two different levels of marginal costs. Video link for Figures 9.8 and 9.9: https://youtu.be/7ddF9PX1HKg.

Let us first examine the assumption of differences in marginal costs across firms, which is the key novel assumption relative to the model of monopolistic competition that we examined earlier. In Figure 9.8, we consider two firms that meet identical firm-level demand curves but with different marginal costs. Firm *HP* (as in High Productivity) has lower marginal costs than firm *LP* (as in Low Productivity), as seen by $MC_{HP} < MC_{LP}$. In consequence, *HP* produces a greater quantity and sets a lower price. Firm *HP* also has higher variable profit than firm *LP*. By assuming differences in marginal costs in a case with monopolistic competition, we can thus easily capture that a more productive firm is larger, more profitable and sets lower prices, as documented empirically. In a situation where competition increases, we clearly also expect *HP* to be more likely to survive.

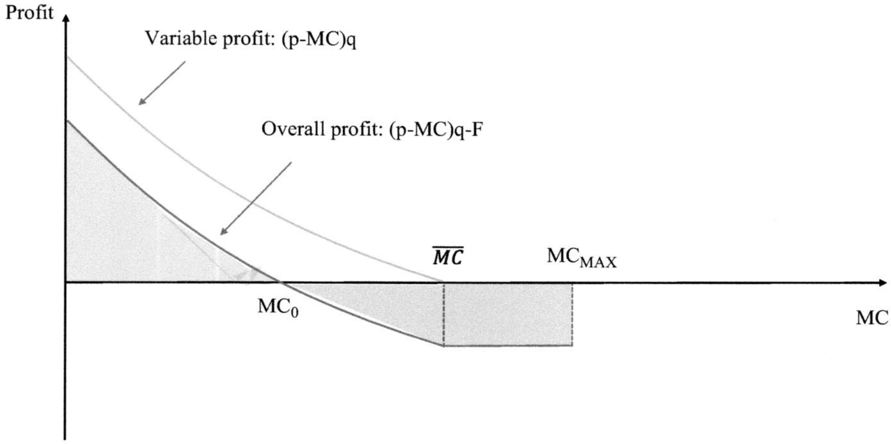

Figure 9.9 Profits of firms at different realizations of marginal costs. Video link for Figures 9.8 and 9.9: https://youtu.be/7ddF9PX1HKg.

We now come to the key conceptual issue in monopolistically competitive models with differences across firms: How can we combine free entry with differences in variable profits across firms? If fixed entry costs are low enough that firm *LP* can profitably enter, then firm *HP* would be making a substantial profit. Why is entry of similarly efficient firms not leading to zero profit for firm *HP*? The key modeling "trick" in this class of models is to assume that the fixed cost of entry is taken first and then, *after* having paid the entry cost, the firm learns about the marginal cost that it will have.[11] While it is a convenient modeling device, the assumption also captures an important element of reality. A lot of firms enter, and many of them fail. Had they known that they would fail, they clearly would not have entered. Only upon entering and actually being active do firms learn if they are efficient enough to be able to stay alive.

Figure 9.9 depicts the relation between profits and marginal cost for firms in this type of model. You can think of this as a lottery. The fixed entry cost is the price of the lottery ticket, and your winnings will be determined by the marginal cost that you draw. Start with the upper curve, variable profit $(p - MC)q$. The higher realization of marginal cost that a firm has, the further to the right along the horizontal axis it is and the lower is its variable profit. The lower curve gives profit, also taking account of the fixed entry cost, that is sunk at the stage when marginal cost draw is realized. The lowest possible marginal cost draw is 0, and the highest possible draw is MC_{MAX}. For very high cost draw, $MC > \overline{MC}$, the firm will not start producing and will just walk away. If marginal cost is higher than the demand intercept, there is clearly no point in producing and throwing good money after bad (as examined in Chapter 4, this corresponds to a case where "$AVC > p$"). $\overline{MC}$ denotes the highest possible marginal cost at which variable profits are 0, and MC_0 denotes the marginal cost at which overall profits, including the fixed entry cost, are 0.

For marginal costs that are between MC_0 and $\overline{MC}$, the firm will produce even if it overall makes a loss. At the time that the firm realizes that the investment was bad, the entry cost is already sunk. It lowers the loss by actually producing, just as we saw in Chapter 4, where a firm will operate as long as it covers the variable costs. Finally, firms with low enough realizations of marginal costs, below MC_0, make a profit, also after having taken account

Table 9.1 A simple example with free entry: Zero profit in expectation

Die shows	*Variable profit if operate*	*Overall profit*
1	48	28
2	36	16
3	24	4
4	12	−8
5	0	−20
6	−12	−20 since firm will shut down

of the fixed cost. From an ex ante perspective, a zero profit condition implies that firms make *zero profit in expectation*. The expected profit from low marginal cost realizations (given by the area above the horizontal axis, marked shaded), balances the loss from high marginal cost realizations (given by the shaded area below the horizontal axis).

To capture the intuition between expected and realized profits on the one hand, and entry on the other, let us do a little digression. Consider a simple game of dice where profits are decided by the toss of a die with the variable profits, as described in Table 9.1, and the entry cost set to 20.

So here, the firm pays the cost 20 first, which plays the role of sunk entry cost. If the die comes up with a 6 (the equivalent of MC_{MAX}), the variable profits would be -12 if the firm actually produced. This clearly is unattractive, and the firm limits its loss to the sunk cost 20 by not producing. If the die comes up with a 5, the firm is indifferent between producing or not (the equivalent of $\overline{MC}$). If the die is equal to 4, the firm makes a variable profit and clearly produces, even if with the benefit of hindsight it would have preferred not to enter: The variable profit of 12 is less than the sunk entry cost of 20. But it limits the overall loss by producing. These disadvantageous draws are balanced by the lucky shots 1, 2, or 3. If any of these come up, the firm makes a variable profit that more than compensates for the sunk entry cost. Zero profit in expectation here simply notes that $-20 + 1/6 \times 48 + 1/6 \times 36 + 1/6 \times 24 + 1/6 \times 12 + 1/6 \times 0 + 1/6 \times 0 = 0$.

In terms of policy analysis, a model of this type is quite similar to the standard monopolistic competition model that we examined in the previous chapter. The main difference is that it allows the model to match the facts of how markets behave much more closely. Economies of scale and product differentiation drive welfare effects of markets also in the case of heterogeneous firms. In models with differences in marginal costs, average TFP in an industry can increase for several reasons: individual firms investing to become more productive, more productive firms entering, less productive firms exiting, and more productive firms increasing their market share whilst less productive firms decrease their market share.

As noted, these models were first developed in the context of international trade. As markets become larger when countries open up for trade, the demand curve facing a firm rotates and becomes flatter. A firm loses more customers at higher prices, but access to a larger market implies that with low prices, more customers can be reached. Opening up for trade means that the most productive firms gain and expand, less productive firms shrink, and the least productive firms exit from the market.

We cover international trade in Chapter 17, but for now, note that the models that we have covered can be embedded in a general equilibrium model as, is indeed done in much of modern trade analysis.[12] The latest round of trade models that build on monopolistic competition have two implications that partly modify implied lessons from earlier generations of models. First, perfectly competitive models often center on the question of manufactured goods vs. agricultural products or raw materials. During much of the 1900s, we also saw rich countries producing manufactured products and poorer countries often reliant on raw materials and agriculture. Policy aiming at industrialization was common. Models with monopolistic competition instead place the emphasis on productivity and markups for welfare. Exporting high markup products like premium Ethiopian coffee beans, Spanish Pata Negra ham, or French Champagne is not necessarily less attractive than churning out industrial products. A second point is that the models of trade with monopolistic competition where there were no differences in marginal costs might easily be interpreted as implying a very strong competitive advantage from economies of scale. The 1990s, for instance, saw a large number of mergers in Europe with the given motivation that a more integrated common market in the European Union will be associated with a greater need to be large and gain scale economies. Scale economies are, of course, an important factor for success for firms, but the models with heterogeneous firms emphasize productivity rather than size as a success factor; this seems to be in line with the empirical evidence, as discussed earlier.

9.3.2 *Appendix*

Setting price instead of setting quantity

As discussed in Section 9.1, the optimal prices and quantities for a monopolist are the same irrespective of whether the firm optimizes over price or quantity. Let us illustrate this for the specific case examined earlier with demand $p(Q) = 12 - Q$ and the cost function $C(Q) = 3 + Q^2$. The first step is to express these as functions of price instead so that we have $Q(p) = 12 - p$ and $C(Q(p)) = 3 + (12 - p)^2$. The profit-maximization problem facing the monopolist is now to set *price* so as to maximize profit:

$$\max_p (12 - p)p - (3 + (12 - p)^2).$$

We want to identify the price at which profits are the highest; we want to find the top of the hill by differentiating profits with respect to p and setting the derivative equal to zero. At the top of the hill, the tangent to the profit function has zero slope, this is the first-order condition for profit maximization. The first-order condition for profit maximization is hence

$$\frac{d\Pi(p)}{dp} = 12 - 2p + 2(12 - p) = 0,$$

which, solving for p, yields $4p = 36$ or $p^* = 9$ euros, which is the same solution, as we established under quantity setting.

Notes

1 First order, as in the first derivative. To determine that we have identified the top of the hill, we also should examine the second derivative, what is known as the second-order condition. If this is negative, the function is concave, and it is indeed a maximum point. In the current case,

differentiating Equation (9.3) with respect to Q (differentiating the first derivative), we get that $\frac{d^2\Pi(Q)}{dQ^2} = -4$. This is taking us further into calculus than typical for intermediate microeconomics, and for the purposes of this course, this can be disregarded – all the examples that we will use are going to be "well behaved."

2 The product rule says that if a and b are both functions of x such that $f = a(x) \times b(x)$, then $\frac{df}{dx} = \frac{da}{dx} \times b + a \times \frac{db}{dx}$.

3 We use the general rule that $\frac{a}{b} = \frac{1}{\frac{b}{a}}$.

4 He was also involved in a number of complex financial dealings with governments, and his business empire crumbled in connection with the Great Depression of the 1930s.

5 In Chapter 4, we examined some cases where the long-run supply curve was downward sloping. In principle, it is possible that a monopolist similarly faces a downward-sloping marginal cost also in the time frame that is relevant for quantity setting. It clearly would be an unusual case, however.

6 In practice, such claims will easily revolve around a discussion of the time horizon; as also noted in Chapter 6, we expect long-run demand to be more elastic than short-run demand.

7 On the other hand, a state-owned monopoly often has weaker incentives to keep costs low than when there is competition. We revisit the issue of government or private provision of various goods and services in Chapter 14.

8 The third and final way to act in Bain's classification is to **accommodate**, the entrant does indeed enter the market, but the incumbent acts in such a way as to maximize any advantage that it has from its incumbency.

9 Here we just use two factors for simplicity, but in practice, additional factors such as electricity and intermediate inputs are also included. The logic of estimation is the same, however, and TFP is whatever we can't explain by changes in observed use of input factors.

10 National statistical agencies report data at different levels of aggregation where more digits represent less aggregated levels. The figure of twice as productive refers to the "6-digit" level where firms typically can be assumed to be quite comparable. An example of a 6-digit level is"metal can manufacturing"; moving up to "3-digit," these firms are part of "fabricated metal products manufacturing."

11 This way of modeling entry was introduced in Jovanovic (1982).

12 While differences across firms may be important for matching the details of trade, the simpler perfectly competitive models that we examine in Chapter 17 still provide valuable insights (results in, e.g., Arkolakis et al. (2012) also suggest that the overall welfare effects of trade are similar between the older and newer models).

10 Oligopoly

Illustration 10.1 Different bottled waters. iStock by Getty Images, TPopova.

10.1 Overview of oligopoly markets

We have now considered both markets where there are a very large number of competing firms, as well as markets where there is only one firm. In between these extremes lie many market forms where entry barriers are nontrivial but nonprohibitive. Prices and quantities in such markets will be shaped by the number of competing firms, the nature of strategic interaction, and the extent to which products differ from one another. Clearly, these kinds of markets are common in our daily lives, where a typical consumer product or service is offered to us by a limited set of sellers.

One important aspect of the analysis in microeconomics is that "one size doesn't fit all." We need to pay attention to the market situation to determine what the appropriate model is. For instance, as we will see in the following sections, in some cases, different models have sharply differing predictions on how prices respond to entry of new firms. In the following, we first consider competition between firms when there is no product differentiation; that is, the products of different firms are perfect substitutes. In other words, competition when products are **homogeneous**. Several examples of this kind of market are found in suppliers to other firms – cement and paper pulp are examples of markets where supply is often modeled in this way. Later on in this chapter, we turn to the case where differentiated products are

DOI: 10.4324/9781003623854-14

offered by competing firms, as would be the case, for instance, for most products that we choose between in a supermarket.

10.2 Oligopoly with homogeneous products

When few firms compete, there will typically be strategic interaction. We explore this in further depth in the next chapter, but for now, we can note that this implies that my optimal action will depend on your action and vice versa; your optimal action will depend on my action. The interplay between such actions depends on what the strategic variable of choice is – are firms setting prices, or are they setting quantities? While this may appear puzzling at first, the differences are perfectly natural once we understand their reasons. We first consider the case of firms setting quantities.

10.2.1 Quantity competition: Cournot

To keep things as simple as possible, we first consider two competing firms that offer a homogeneous product and decide on the quantities that they are to produce simultaneously. The case was first analyzed by the French economist and philosopher Augustin Cournot already in 1838. His book was remarkably ahead of its time and received virtually no attention back then but is nowadays seen as the fundamental starting point for oligopoly models. Reading Cournot (1838) is like reading a modern micro-book. Cournot used two firms producing bottled water as his example, and let us utilize the same example to honor his pioneering analysis.

The decision problem of the firms is the following: how much water should they put in bottles and bring to the market? The firms decide at the same time how much to produce. Consumers are indifferent between the two firms' products, and thus the price on the market will depend on the joint quantities offered. How much to put in bottles and bring to the market depends on how much you expect the competing firm to bring. The more bottles the other firm brings to the market, the lower the price will be and the less you will want to bring to the market. But how much will the other firm bring? What it does will depend on what it expects you to do, and what you do depends on what you expect it to do. How can we solve this without just getting stuck in an endless loop? Cournot's brilliant solution to this conundrum is to essentially do the analysis in two steps. First, we pinpoint precisely how my optimal quantity depends on your optimal quantity. We then place ourselves in your shoes and see what is optimal for you to do in the same manner. Then look for a solution that is consistent with both of our best responses to the other's choice. This may still appear puzzling; let us therefore work through an example in some detail.

Let the two firms be called Blue and Red, where Blue produces q_B units, and Red produces q_R units. Market demand is given by $p = 70 - Q$, where quantity depends on the quantity of both firms: $Q = q_B + q_R$. The cost for Blue is given by $C(q_B) = 10q_B$ and symmetrically for Red. Thus, there are no fixed costs, and marginal costs are constant and equal to 10 for each of the firms. As usual, we assume that firms maximize profit. How many bottles should firm Blue fill up and bring to the market? Its maximization problem is given by

$$\max_{q_B} \underbrace{(70 - q_B - q_R)}_{=p(Q)} q_B - 10q_B.$$

As for any company, the profit for Blue is given by revenue minus cost. Revenue in turn is given by its own quantity times the price. In contrast to the case for a monopolist, the price depends not only on Blue's quantity but also on the quantity produced by Red. As Blue differentiates the profit function with respect to the variable that it controls, q_B, it needs to make an assumption about Red's quantity. Does Blue conjecture that Red will produce less if it produces more, and if so how much? Cournot's insight is to first treat Red's quantity as a constant in the differentiation. Blue, when maximizing, takes Red's quantity as given and only later puts herself in Red's shoes. Thus, Blue's first-order condition for profit maximization is given by

$$\frac{\partial \Pi_B}{\partial q_B} = \underbrace{(70 - 2q_B - q_R)}_{\text{MR}} - \underbrace{10}_{MC} = 0. \tag{10.1}$$

We can now solve Equation (10.1) for the optimal quantity for Blue as a function of Red's quantity.

$$q_B = 30 - \frac{q_R}{2}$$

We term this the **best-response function** – it gives the profit-maximizing response of Blue to Red's quantity. The more Red produces, the more Red drives down price and the less Blue will want to produce. The intercept on the vertical axis in Figure 10.1 is the quantity that Blue would want to produce if it believed that Red produced nothing; this is the monopoly quantity.

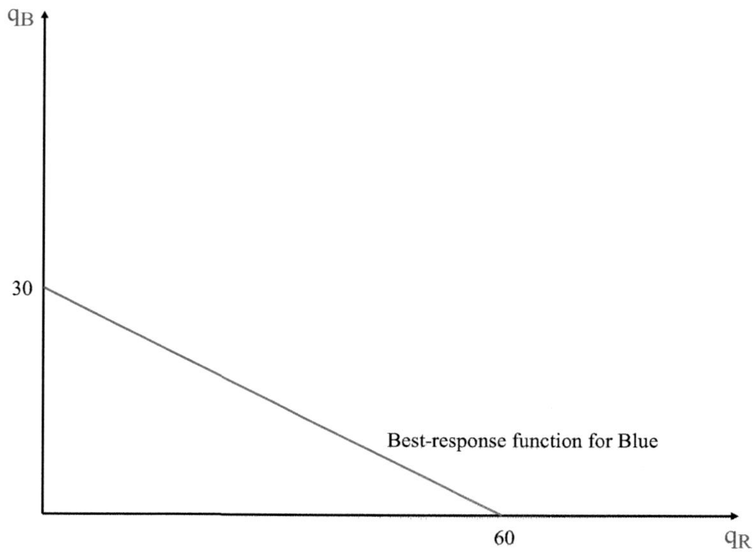

Figure 10.1 The best-response function for a Cournot firm. Video link for Figures 10.1 and 10.2: https://youtu.be/xqQsHJk9PAI.

But where on the best-response curve should Blue expect that Red chooses to produce? It may of course wish that Red produced nothing, but wishful thinking is typically not a sound foundation for strategy. Instead, we assume that Red will also try to maximize profits, similarly taking Blue's quantity as given. Hence, Red's maximization is given by

$$\max_{q_R} \underbrace{(70 - q_R - q_B)}_{=p(Q)} q_R - 10q_R. \tag{10.2}$$

The first-order condition for Red is thus given by

$$\frac{\partial \Pi_R}{\partial q_R} = \underbrace{(70 - 2q_R - q_B)}_{\text{MR}} - \underbrace{10}_{MC} = 0,$$

and we can solve for Red's best-response function:

$$q_R = 30 - \frac{q_B}{2}.$$

In this case, with the same marginal costs, it is simply the mirror image of Blue's best-response function, and we could have used that as a shortcut, rather than explicitly working through the maximization problem.

So now we have Blue's optimal quantity as a function of Red's optimal quantity and vice versa. A Cournot equilibrium is the set of quantities where the best-response functions cross. Blue is then doing as well as Blue can, given that Red is doing as well as Red can. If we want to draw Red's best-response function in the same graph as we drew Blue's, we need to reshuffle Red's best-response function so as to have q_B on the left-hand side. Remember that a function is just relating one variable to another, and we can express q_R as a function of q_B or q_B as a function of q_R – these are two equivalent ways of describing the equilibrium relations between the two variables. Red's best-response function can hence also be written as

$$q_B = 60 - 2q_R.$$

Figure 10.2 graphs the two best-response functions and solves for the Cournot equilibrium – the set of quantities that we expect firms to choose. There are two equations, the best-response functions, that we solve for two unknowns, q_B^C and q_B^C, where we use the superscript C to denote the Cournot equilibrium quantities. We can solve the equations, for instance, via inserting Red's best-response function (Equation 10.2) into Blue's best-response function (Equation 10.1) and then solving for the Cournot quantity

$$q_B = 30 - \frac{1}{2}\underbrace{\left(30 - \frac{q_B}{2}\right)}_{q_R}. \tag{10.3}$$

Solving Equation (10.3) for q_B, we find $q_B^C = 20$, which we can insert into Red's best-response function (Equation 10.2) as well and equally find a Cournot equilbrium quantity for Red of 20 bottles.

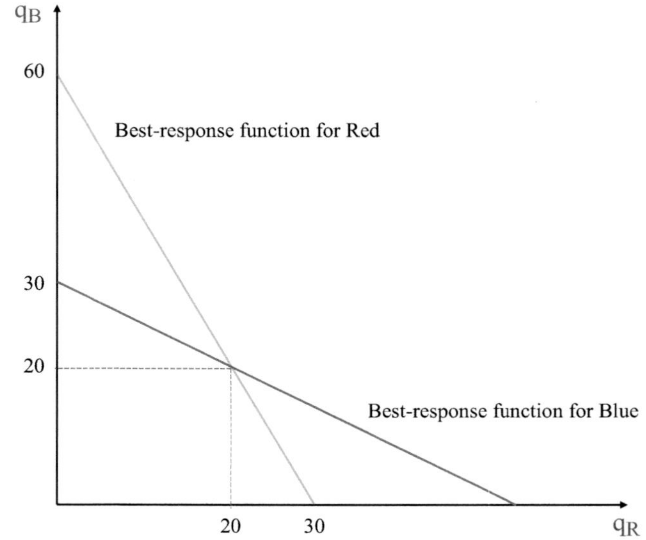

Figure 10.2 The Cournot equilibrium quantities. Video link for Figures 10.1 and 10.2: https://youtu.be/xqQsHJk9PAI.

Thus total quantity supplied by these two firms is $20 + 20 = 40$ bottles and the Cournot equilibrium price is given by $p = 70 - 40 = 30$ euros. Profits for the two firms are equal and given by $\pi = 30 \times 20 - 10 \times 20 = 400$ euros.

The Cournot equilibrium is a conceptually rather deep concept but one that, once understood, remains with you, so let us spend some time in the following to make sure that we really understand the concept and its implications. We do so in several steps. (i) comparing the Cournot outcome to that of monopoly and price-taking behavior, (ii) thinking hard about the sense in which it is an equilibrium, (iii) examine the case where one firm decides quantity first, and (iv) examine the case when firms differ in marginal costs.

10.2.1.1 A Comparison between Cournot and other market forms

If the two firms had acted as a monopolist, they would have maximized the joint profit. In this case, such a joint profit-maximizing entity would set quantity to maximize

$$\max_{Q} \underbrace{(70 - Q)}_{=p(Q)} Q - 10Q.$$

The first-order condition is then

$$70 - 2Q - 10 = 0$$

with a monopoly quantity of $Q^M = 30$ and a price of $70 - 30 = 40$ euros. The resulting monopoly profit would be equal to $40 \times 30 - 10 \times 30 = 900$ euros.

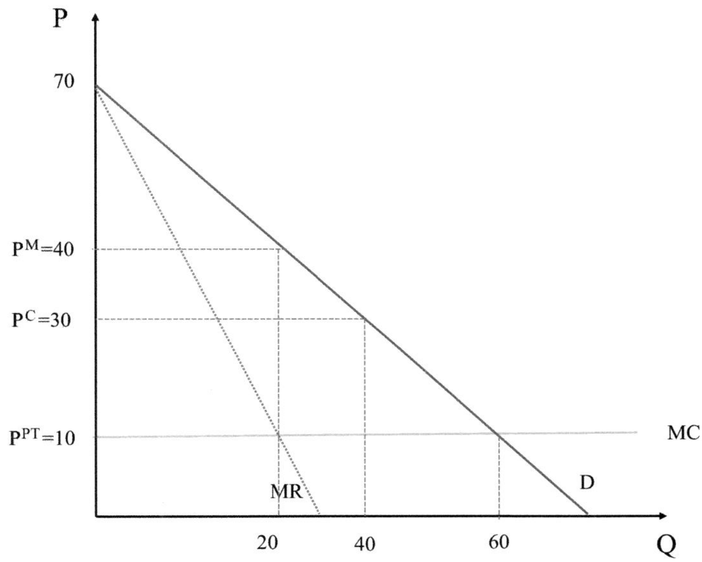

Figure 10.3 Prices and quantities under different assumptions about how firms compete. Video link for Figure: https://youtu.be/3M29o3cKxLM.

If a joint firm in contrast acted as a price taker, it would instead set quantity at the point where $p = MC$, that is the point at which

$$\underbrace{70 - Q}_{p} = 10$$

such that $Q^{PT} = 60$ and the price in this case is 10. Figure 10.7 illustrates. We see that the Cournot quantity is between the monopoly and price-taking outcomes. Thus having two competitors rather than a monopoly is beneficial for society in the sense that prices fall, consumer surplus increases, and the deadweight loss decreases. However, just having two Cournot competitors still leaves the market with substantially lower quantity (and hence higher price and higher deadweight loss) than is the case where firms act as price takers.

10.2.1.2 The deeper intuition behind the Cournot equilibrium

In presenting the Cournot outcome as the intersection of best-response functions, we somewhat glossed over the question of why it is an equilibrium. Here we dig deeper and will do so in two ways. It is a static game where the two firms decide how much water to put in bottles at the same time, and we think of them only meeting once (this of course is a simplification, and we will revisit the question of repeated interaction in the next chapter). Nevertheless, an interpretation of interaction over time (or in terms of iterative thinking) is useful for understanding the intuition, and this is indeed how Cournot motivates the equilibrium in his brilliant text from 1838. Figure 10.4 illustrates.

If profit-maximizing firms could write a binding agreement on what quantities to produce, they would jointly choose to produce the monopoly quantity. For simplicity,

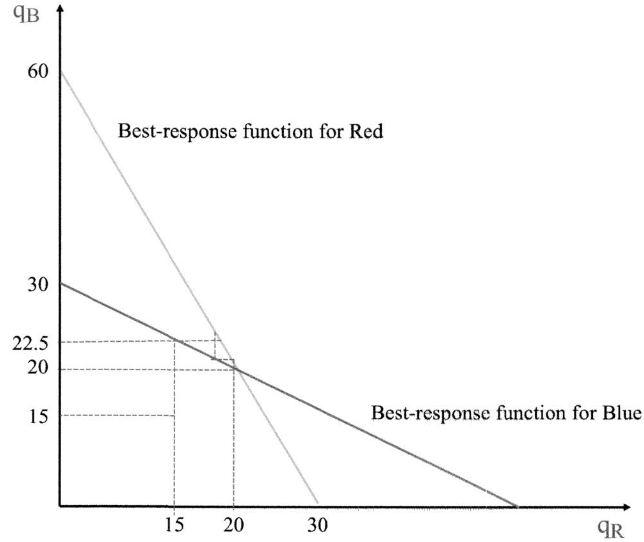

Figure 10.4 One intuition for why the intersection of best-response functions is an equilibrium set of quantities. Video link for Figure: https://youtu.be/evoIiB8AR7M.

assume that they would each produce half the monopoly quantity in that case, thus producing 15 each. Such agreements are illegal, but as a starting point, we could consider if Red chose to produce 15, would we expect Blue to produce 15 as well? No. Blue's best response to the quantity 15 from Red is given by Blue's best-response function in this case, 22.5 (30−15/2). But if Red is also thinking through this, what would her best response to 22.5 be? Well, that is given by Red's best-response function evaluated at 22.5, which is 18.75 (30−22.5/2). But then Blue's best response to 18.75 is given by Blue's best-response function, 20.625 (30−18.75/2), and so forth. Each successive thought experiment brings us closer to the Cournot equilibrium quantities of 20 for each firm. This set of quantities is the only one where each firm's quantity is a best response to the other firms' quantity. It is the only set of quantities where none of the firms has an incentive to unilaterally deviate from the chosen quantity.

In the next chapter, we will examine game theory, so you may want to revisit the rest of this subsection after studying game theory. The Cournot equilibrium is namely an example of what is termed a Nash equilibrium, a set of strategies such that none of the players has an incentive to unilaterally deviate. Table 10.1 illustrates. To simplify further, consider two firms A and B that each can choose between quantities 1, 2, or 3 tons (for concreteness, we may think of cement [pun intended]). The first number in each cell is the profit for firm A, and the second number is the profit for firm B. Clearly, maximization of joint profits and splitting the gains equally would lead us to predict each firm to produce 2 and achieve profit 10. But again, in this case, each of the firms has an incentive to deviate; if A believes that B will produce 2, A would earn more from choosing to produce 3. A situation where each firm produces 3 tons is the unique Nash equilibrium, as well as the unique Cournot equilibrium. This can be easily seen if we walk through the table following the technique that we later explain in the next chapter.[1]

Table 10.1 Cournot equilibrium in a payoff matrix

		Quantity for firm B		
Quantity for firm A		1 ton	2 tons	3 tons
	1 ton	*8* , 8	*6* , 12	*5* , 15
	2 tons	*12* , 6	*10* , 10	*6* , 12
	3 tons	*15*, 5	*12* , 6	*8* , 8

Video link for table: https://youtu.be/Cu-CAIMfd2Y.

10.2.1.3 Letting one firm decide first

In the Cournot equilibrium, both firms decide quantity simultaneously. Now we consider the case where one firm gets to decide quantity first, and the other firm after having observed the first choice gets to decide. The case is typically seen to be useful to understand strategic behavior in some lines of business where one firm has a leadership position, and it is also useful to, in even further depth, see what the best-response functions capture. The game is typically called Stackelberg, after German economist Heinrich von Stackelberg's work in the 1930s.

Let us return to the previous example with p = 70–Q and firm Blue and Red each having a fixed marginal cost of 10. Assume that firm Blue gets to decide quantity first and wants to choose quantity so as to maximize profits. In the Cournot equilibrium, decisions were simultaneous, and Blue would treat Red's quantity as a constant in its optimization problem, put itself in Red's shoes to see how Red would set quantity, and then solve for the equilibrium. But now, Blue decides first, and Red can see Blue's quantity. Blue comes with a number of water bottles to the market and, having observed this quantity, Red makes its decision. What will be Red's best response to Blue's quantity? Well clearly that is given by its best-response function. Foreseeing this, Blue will use Red's best-response function in its own maximization problem. Blue thus solves the following maximization problem

$$\max_{q_B} \underbrace{\left(70 - q_B - \underbrace{\left(30 - \frac{q_B}{2}\right)}_{=q_R(q_B)}\right)}_{=p(Q)} q_B - 10q_B.$$

The first-order condition is now

$$\frac{d\Pi_B}{dq_B} = \underbrace{(70 - 2q_B - 30 + q_B)}_{\text{MR}} - \underbrace{10}_{MC} = 0.$$

Note that now Red's best-response function is already taken account of in Blue's maximization problem so that we can solve the first-order condition directly for Blue's optimal quantity; $q_B = 30$. Inserting 30 into Red's best-response function yields $q_R = 30 - 30/2 = 15$. We illustrate the situation in Figure 10.5. Total quantity under the Stackelberg outcome

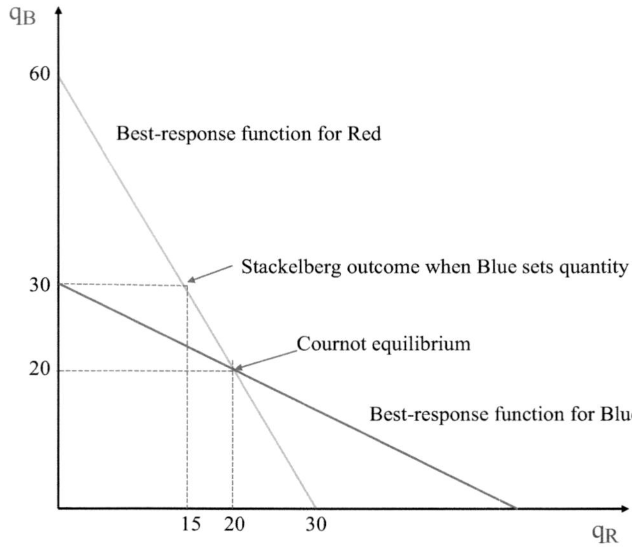

Figure 10.5 Quantities when blue decides quantity first. Video link for Figure 10.5: https://youtu.be/T4diMqbyzRI.

is thus $30 + 15 = 45$ bottles and price is $p = 70 - 45 = 25$ euros. Compared to the Cournot equilibrium, quantity is thus greater and price lower in the Stackelberg case. Using the optimal quantities, it is easy to calculate the leader's profit to be $\pi_B = 25 \times 30 - 10 \times 30 = 450$ euros and the follower's to be $\pi_R = 25 \times 15 - 10 \times 15 = 225$.

A final point that makes the Stackelberg outcome instructive is that it illustrates one important aspect of competition: What is bad for competitors is not necessarily bad for consumers. Compared to the Cournot outcome, the leader's profit increases, and the follower's decreases. Thus one firm gains, and the other loses from this strategic behavior by the leader. Higher equilibrium quantities and lower price implies that consumers gain relative to the Cournot outcome, however.

10.2.1.4 Differences in marginal costs

The Cournot model is a quintessential example of a "rich" model. It is simple in appearance but offers deep insights about why competition lowers price and increases quantity. The extension to a leader/follower situation showed us how we can learn something about differential effects on competitors and consumers from the model. Now let us turn to asymmetries between firms and in particular situations where one firm is larger than the other. One might think that a case where one firm is larger is "closer" to a monopoly situation and hence that this is automatically bad for consumers. In the Cournot model with different marginal costs, however, this is not true – in this situation, one of the firms would be larger because of lower marginal costs. It is clearly more efficient from a societal perspective, and associated with lower price, if the low cost firm produces a larger share of the output.

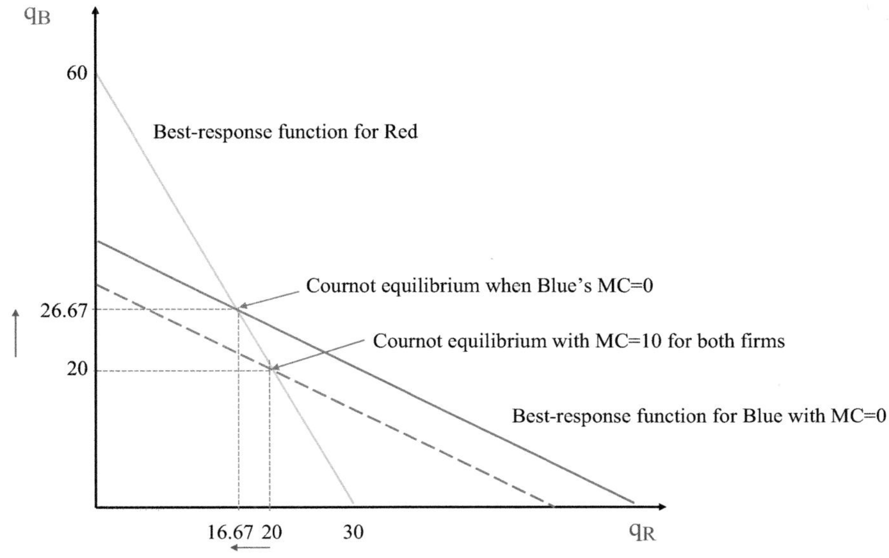

Figure 10.6 Cournot equilibrium with differences in marginal costs across firms.

Looking at this in some more detail, we again use our best-response functions from earlier. Assume that Blue has a marginal cost of 0 but that Red's marginal cost is as before (constant and equal to 10 euros). To highlight the role of the marginal cost, we write MC in the best-response function instead of using the value for marginal cost in the earlier example, which was 10. The intercept of Blue's best-response function thus shifts up from 30 ((70−10)/2) to 35 (70/2) as MC drops from 10 to 0. The slope is unchanged, and Red's reaction function is also unchanged.

$$q_B = \frac{70 - MC}{2} - \frac{q_R}{2}$$

Figure 10.6 illustrates the situation where the low-cost firm's reaction function is shifted upward – which results in higher quantities for the low cost firm and lower quantities for the firm with relatively higher cost. Again, using the two reaction functions to solve for equilibrium quantities, we find that Blue will in this case produce approximately 26.67 bottles and red approximately 16.67, thus together producing slightly more than 43 bottles. The asymmetric market shares in this case is the result of cost asymmetries, and it is beneficial to consumers that the larger firm supplies more. Clearly, this does not mean that asymmetric market shares are always beneficial; moving beyond this specific model, they may, for instance, reflect various entry barriers that make it hard for new competitors to reach customers.

10.2.2 Price competition: Bertrand

Cournot was way ahead of his time, and his book had next to no impact at the time of publication. After 45 years, in 1883, a review finally appeared, however! It was penned by another French mathematician, Joseph Bertrand (Bertrand (1883)). In Bertrand's short verbal review, he argued that firms set prices and not quantities, and if firms set prices, the outcome is very different with price equal to marginal cost. The intuition for results is perhaps easiest seen by referring back to the previous example. We saw that the monopoly outcome was a quantity of 30 bottles and a price of 40 euros per bottle. We also saw why this was not a noncooperative equilibrium outcome, each of the firms had a unilateral incentive to deviate and produce more. Now if firms set prices, consider a situation where each firm in isolation irrevocably commits to a price and comes to the market with a sign of its price. Goods are homogeneous, so all consumers will choose to purchase from the producer with the lowest price. We assume that if prices are equal, the consumers split themselves equally between the two firms. So, what if Blue would choose to write 40 euros on the sign? Would the best response from Red be to also write 40 euros? No, if Red were to believe that Blue would set the price at 40, Red's best response would be to set price just slightly lower than 40. Red would then get all the customers and make almost the monopoly profit. But presumably, Blue would foresee this and want to charge an even lower price, undercutting Red. And so one can go on, as long as price is above marginal cost, there is an incentive to charge a lower price and undercut the other firm. The only set of prices where no one has a unilateral incentive to deviate are when each firm sets price equal to marginal cost.[2]

The Bertrand analysis under homogeneous products clearly point to extremely strong effects of just one competitor entering a monopoly market. The results could further seem somewhat disconcerting – under monopoly, we saw that it did not matter for results if firms set quantity or price. Now, what might seem as an almost semantic change has a huge effect on outcomes. What is going on at a deeper level? In the following, we dig into this question in two ways: first, we contrast the predictions vis-à-vis Cournot further and discuss in more detail when one description is more likely to fit a market than the other. Second, we move on to cover models of price competition that feature positive markups.

10.2.2.1 A comparison between Cournot and Bertrand

The Cournot model can easily be extended to include additional firms. To avoid a sense that this is voodoo, let us briefly show how this is done in the simple case where there are a number of n firms that are identical. Assume that the demand intercept is given by a parameter a and that all firms have constant marginal costs of c. Consider the maximization problem of one firm; for simplicity, we consider firm 1. In a simple extension to what we showed earlier, the maximization problem for this firm is then

$$\max_{q_1}(a - Q)q_1 - c_1 q_1 \text{ where } Q = q_1 + q_2 + ...q_n.$$

Let us use the simple notation where the quantity for each of the j other firms is denoted by $q_{j\neq 1}$. Since there are n firms in total, there are going to be $n - 1$ such other firms. The first-order condition for firm 1 is then

$$\frac{\partial \Pi_1}{\partial q_1} = a - 2q_1 - (n - 1)q_{j\neq 1} - c_1 = 0.$$

Since all firms are symmetric, they will produce the same quantity in equilibrium, and we can now use q to denote this quantity. We can thus express the first-order condition as

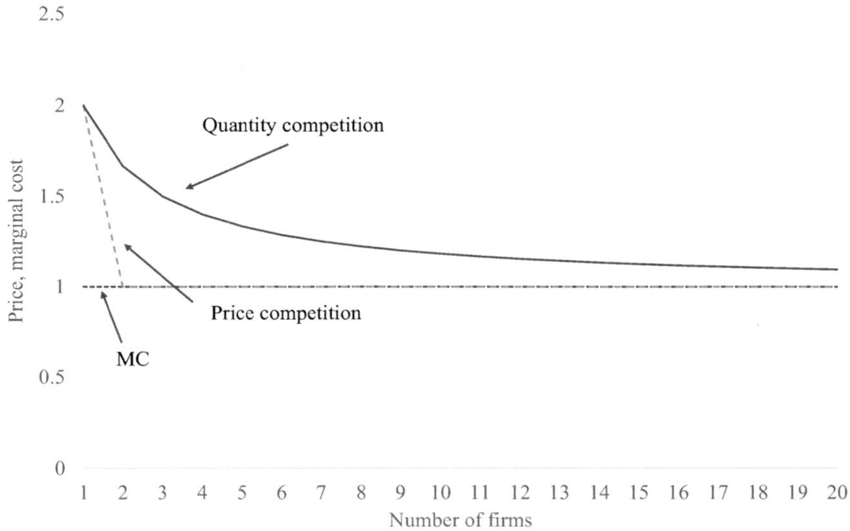

Figure 10.7 The relation between price and marginal costs for homogeneous goods as the number of firms change: Bertrand (price setting) vs. Cournot (quantity setting).

$a - 2q - (n - 1)q - c = 0$ and solve this expression for q to reach the profit-maximizing quantity for each firm

$$q = \frac{a - c}{1 + n}.$$

Inserting these equilibrium quantities into the demand function, we get

$$p = \frac{a}{1 + n} + \frac{n}{1 + n}c.$$

Hence, as the number of firms grows, price gets closer and closer to marginal cost (this is easy to convince yourself of, consider, for instance, what price is in the case of n=2 and the case where n = 20). In Figure 10.7, we present a stylized comparison of how the equilibrium price relates to the number of firms in a market for price-setting (Bertrand) and quantity-setting (Cournot) competition. If there is only one firm, it does not matter if it sets price or quantity. If there are two firms, the differences are stark, however. Under price setting, price falls to marginal cost, whereas under Cournot, prices only gradually tend to marginal cost. The pattern is an additional reason why Cournot is a popular workhorse model. The general pattern of how prices relate to marginal costs as the number of firms vary across markets rhymes well with patterns across a lot of studies that consider competition on local markets.[3]

10.2.2.2 Which model provides the best description: Bertrand or Cournot?

As we shall see shortly, the prediction of such strong competitive effects as in the Bertrand case is often seen as implausible. At the same time, it is easy to think that many firms choose price rather than quantity. How can we reconcile these observations? Two explanations are especially prominent:[4]

- A first important aspect to note is that the extreme differences in outcomes hinges on that under price competition the firm with the lowest price has no problem supplying the entire market. There are no constraints in terms of capacity. Again, it is worth highlighting that under oligopoly, one size doesn't fit all, and if we consider markets with very little product differentiation where it is very easy to expand quantity, we can expect very strong competition. Competition where goods are delivered digitally is one example (and indeed, many goods sold digitally have prices close to zero). Another is procurement auctions where firms put a price in a sealed envelope, and then whoever wins the auction gets to supply the entire market (which also means that there are strong incentives to collude on price setting, more on that in the next chapter). In contrast, if it is hard to adjust quantities, Cournot is a better description. Indeed, in an important paper, Kreps and Scheinkman (1983) show that if firms in a first stage decide capacity and then in a second stage compete in prices, the equilibrium outcomes are the same as if they competed in quantity.
- Perhaps the most important reason why price competition does not lead to price falling all the way to marginal costs is that many products (that are supplied by only a few firms in markets and where there are entry barriers) are differentiated. They are different. Consumers care about which product they buy. Having a slightly higher price than your competitor does not imply that all consumers disappear. In a somewhat silly but memorable analogy, we can think of a situation where each shoe size was sold by one firm. If size 40 had a slightly higher price than other sizes, it would lose some customers – some would squeeze into 39s, and some would waddle around in size 41s, but some would also stick to 40. The extreme result that a slightly lower price captures the entire market is what drives the stark result in Bertrand competition with homogeneous products; if products are differentiated, this extreme result disappears. We return to this question in the following section.

10.3 Oligopoly with differentiated products

Now assume that firms are selling **differentiated products**. Thus different products are not perfect substitutes for each other. The reasons why products are seen as differentiated from the perspective of a consumer can be several. One reason is that the physical characteristics differ. Compare two different bikes; for instance, they can differ in size, in the number of gears, in weight, in color just, to name a few dimensions. Different brand names may also appear to different consumers, and some brands will have built up an image via advertising, for instance. Indeed, the case of mineral water is a good example where in a country where tap water is of high quality, a lot of consumers would not be able to differentiate tap water from a high-priced, branded still water, but still the high-priced bottled waters are able to find some buyers.

Sometimes we distinguish between vertical and horizontal product differentiation. **Vertical product differentiation** is the case where one product is objectively better in some dimension, for instance (keeping other characteristics fixed), a faster computer, a lighter bike, or a more comfortable train ride. **Horizontal product differentiation** concern the case where different consumers differ in their valuation of the product because of taste differences. Movies, novels, and music are some clear examples. Reading one particular book is not a perfect substitute for reading another particular book, and we may differ in how much we like the book.[5] Geographical differentiation is another form of horizontal product differentiation. A restaurant that requires substantial travel to get to for me is not a perfect substitute to a restaurant close by. In many cases, we will have elements of both vertical and horizontal differentiation that combine to make products different from each other in the eyes of consumers.

10.3.1 Price competition with differentiated products

Again, we consider a simple example with two firms that we denote with Blue and Red. We can think of the product as two different forms of fruit juices, and Blue produces Blueberry juice and Red produces Raspberry juice. The goods that these firms produce are thus differentiated, and they compete by setting prices. We thus want to express demanded quantity as a function of prices, rather then price as a function of quantities as before. So assume that quantity demanded of Blueberry juice and Raspberry juice are given by, respectively

$$\begin{cases} q_B = 85 - p_B + \frac{p_R}{2} \\ q_R = 85 - p_R + \frac{p_B}{2}. \end{cases} \tag{10.4}$$

Thus, the quantity demanded for Blueberry juice depends on an intercept, negatively on the price of Blueberry juice and positively (but to a lesser extent) on the price of Raspberry juice. In a close analogy to the Cournot case noted earlier, we assume that the firms select prices to maximize profits. Prices are chosen noncooperatively. Assume that each firm has a constant marginal cost at 11. The profit-maximization problems become slightly more involved than in the quantity setting case, as marginal costs are now capturing how a change in price leads to a change in quantity that in turn leads to a change in cost.[6] For Blue, the profit-maximization problem then becomes

$$\max_{p_B} \underbrace{\left(85 - p_B + \frac{p_R}{2}\right)}_{q_B} p_B - \underbrace{\left(85 - p_B + \frac{p_R}{2}\right)}_{q_B} \underbrace{11}_{MC}.$$

Collecting terms, the profit-maximization problem for Blue can then be written as

$$\max_{p_B} \underbrace{\left(85 - p_B + \frac{p_R}{2}\right)}_{q_B} (p_B - 11).$$

Blue maximizes profits, which, as usual, are given by price times quantity minus costs. As in the case of Cournot, it treats the decision variable of the other firm (p_R) as a constant in the maximization problem, and the set of optimal prices are found by combining the best-response functions. The intuition is the same for best-response functions in quantities, and the Bertrand solution is also an example of a Nash equilibrium. The first-order condition for profit maximization is given by

$$\frac{\partial \Pi_B}{\partial p_B} = 85 - 2p_B + \frac{p_R}{2} + 11 = 0,$$

which we rewrite to find the best-response function

$$p_B = \frac{96}{2} + \frac{p_R}{4}.$$

Firm Red faces the symmetric problem and sets its price to maximize profit

$$\max_{p_R} \underbrace{\left(85 - p_R + \frac{p_B}{2}\right)}_{q_R}(p_R - 11),$$

and we can rewrite its first-order condition as a best-response function as well

$$p_R = \frac{96}{2} + \frac{p_B}{4}.$$

As in the case of Cournot, we want to plot both best-response functions in the same graph and therefore reshuffle Red's best-response function so as to have p_B on the left-hand side.[7]

$$p_B = -96 \times 2 + p_R 4.$$

Figure 10.8 graphs the two best-response functions. They are now upward sloping, a higher price of one firm is associated with a higher price by the other firm. Again, we have a system of two equations and two unknowns, and we can insert one function into the other

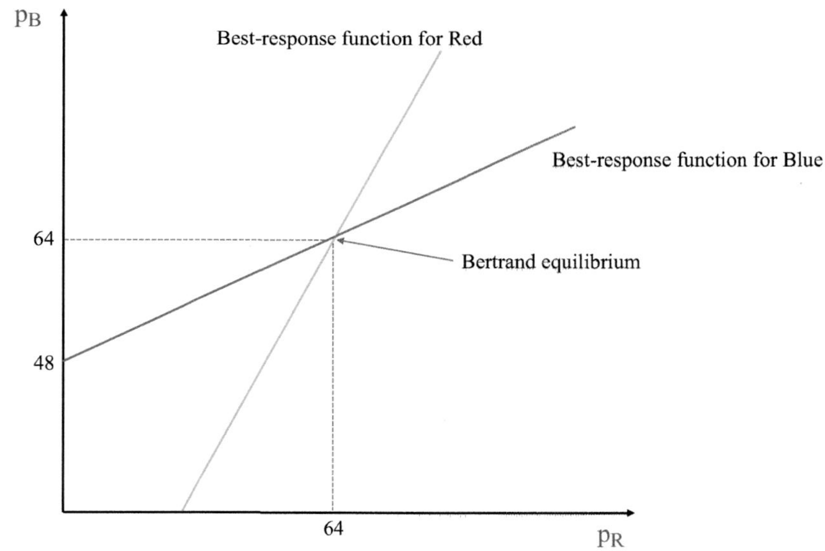

Figure 10.8 Best-response functions: Price competition with differentiated products (Bertrand). Video link for Figure 10.8: https://youtu.be/q6gb_gdearg.

to find the equilibrium prices. For instance, insert Red's best-response function into Blue's best-response (and simplifying by using that $96/2 = 48$) function to find

$$p_B = 48 + \frac{1}{4}\underbrace{\left(48 + \frac{p_B}{4}\right)}_{p_R}.$$

Solving for p_B, we find that $p_B = 64$ bottles. Inserting this into the best-response function for Red, we find $p_B = 64$ bottles as well (or in this where firms are symmetric, we could simply have noted that the symmetry gives the same profit-maximizing price).

A key point to note is that price (at 64) is above marginal cost (at 11). Thus, once we introduce product differentiation, price competition no longer leads to marginal cost pricing.

10.3.1.1 Several different products

The framework with price competition with differentiated products can also be extended to more than two products. Such extensions are beyond the scope of introductory courses in microeconomics, but for the curious, let us just sketch how such models provide a natural extension to the kind of framework that we considered earlier. Just to take an example, the kind of products that you see when you enter a grocery store are often differentiated products with firms competing by setting prices. There are often many products, and one important feature of such markets is typically that a few producers control many different products. Say that you look at various fruit juices and consider a firm like Pepsi that owns the Tropicana set of brands. As a consumer, you would typically encounter a large number of differentiated fruit juices, several of which are controlled by Tropicana/Pepsi: Orange juice with bits, orange juice without bits, apple juice, grapefruit juice, and so forth. Tropicana/Pepsi would then set prices to maximize profits of all the products that it controls. Similarly, the market for sunglasses contain a large number of brands, but a single firm, EssilorLuxotica, is controlling Oakley, Ray-Ban, and a host of other brands giving it a large combined market share in many countries.

To illustrate how the models that we covered earlier can be extended to cover such cases, consider a simple case with a market with four products and three firms. The firms are Blue, Green, and Red. Blue controls two products, 1 and 2, whereas Green controls product 3 and Red product 4. For simplicity, assuming that marginal costs are constant and denoting the quantity of each product by q, we can then express the profits for each of the firms as

$$\begin{aligned}\pi_B &= (p_1 - MC_1)q_1 + (p_2 - MC_2)q_2 \\ \pi_G &= (p_3 - MC_3)q_3 \\ \pi_R &= (p_4 - MC_4)q_4.\end{aligned}$$

Just as in the two-product case, there will be one first-order condition associated with each product. Just as before, the price of competing products are treated as a constant in the optimization problem, and one then uses all the best-response functions to solve for the set of prices that constitute a Bertrand equilibrium. An important point is that the firm that controls several products will set price so as to to take account of the effects on all the products that it controls.

The four first-order conditions in this market will be given by

$$\frac{\partial \pi_B}{\partial p_1} = q_1 + (p_1 - MC_1)\frac{\partial q_1}{\partial p_1} + (p_2 - MC_2)\frac{\partial q_2}{\partial p_1} = 0 \tag{10.5}$$

$$\frac{\partial \pi_B}{\partial p_2} = q_2 + (p_1 - MC_1)\frac{\partial s_1}{\partial p_2} + (p_2 - MC_2)\frac{\partial q_2}{\partial p_2} = 0 \tag{10.6}$$

$$\frac{\partial \pi_G}{\partial p_3} = q_3 + (p_3 - MC_3)\frac{\partial q_3}{\partial p_3} = 0 \tag{10.7}$$

$$\frac{\partial \pi_R}{\partial p_4} = q_4 + (p_4 - MC_4)\frac{\partial q_4}{\partial p_4} = 0. \tag{10.8}$$

The last two first-order conditions are of the same format as in the two-product case. Blue's first-order conditions, Equations (10.5) and (10.6), are also similar but take account of the effect of a change in each price on both the products that it sells. Consider Equation (10.5). If the firm raises the price somewhat on good 1, there will be one positive effect of this from increased sales. By how much? Well, by the amount that it sells, q_1, the first term. Raising the price of p_1 will also lead to a loss of some sales, $\frac{\partial q_1}{\partial p_1}$. How much those lost sales will affect profits depends on the difference between price and marginal cost of product 1. The last term captures that by raising the price of p_1, the demand for product 2, which is also controlled by Blue, will be affected, as seen in the last term of Equation (10.5). If the goods are substitutes, the derivative, the "cross-price effect," $\frac{\partial q_2}{\partial p_1}$ will be positive. Demand for good 2 will increase and how much this matters to profits will be proportional to the difference between price and marginal cost on good 2. Often, we express those effects as the effects of a lower price, and we talk of **cannibalization**: When a firm lowers price for one product, some of the new sales will be drawn from other products that the firm controls. For instance, by setting a low price of a budget brand a firm may be hurting itself by replacing high margin sales (say on good 1) with lower margin sales (say on good 2). Such effects tend to keep prices higher for goods that are controlled by the same firm.

10.3.1.2 Empirical applications of price competition with differentiated products

Price competition with differentiated products matches well with what we intuitively think of in many consumer markets. Cars; ready-to-eat cereals, such as Kellogg's Corn Flakes; beers; and carbonated soft drinks are just a few of the types of products that have been analyzed through this lens. We will not attempt to do justice to this line of research here but include a few pointers for future reference. First of all, note that there are many reasons why we might be interested in analyzing competition in a market for differentiated products. For instance, two firms propose to merge, and competition authorities need to make a decision on whether to accept the merger as proposed or not. Typically, fewer firms will be associated with higher prices. As a regulator or central bank, we may be interested in modeling and understanding how cost changes for some firms affect the prices that we observe in the market. Or we might be interested in studying the welfare effects of new products.

Key to empirical applications are estimated own-price $\frac{\partial q_i}{\partial p_i}$ and cross-price effects $\frac{\partial q_j}{\partial p_i}$ for $i \neq j$. Estimating demand patterns in markets with many goods presents a number of challenges and is the subject of active research. An important article in launching the later applications was work by Berry et al. (1995) who estimated demand for cars in the United States.[8] To get a flavor of this kind of work, it can be useful to highlight an article by Nevo (2001) that examines price-cost margins in ready-to-eat cereal in the United States.

The starting point for Nevo's investigation is that outside observers have noted that the industry seems to be making high profits, be dominated by a few firms, and have a very large number of products. It has, for instance, been argued that one reason for why the large brands have so many different products is to "fill up" the shelf space, making it hard for new entrants to come in and challenge the established brands.

Nevo (2001) estimates demand and then combines this estimation with different assumptions on the supply side to back out markups. Demand estimation relies on the techniques introduced and popularized by Berry et al. (1995). Using data on cereal sales for 25 different products, he estimates demand as a function of observable product characteristics, such as advertising, calories per serving, fiber content, and whether the cereal tends to get mushy in milk. If firms set price on each product independently, profit maximization would imply certain marginal costs for each firm. If accounting data on price-cost markups matched well with these backed-out markups, we could argue that product differentiation in itself can largely explain markups in this market. In another supply side scenario, he assumes that all firms jointly maximize profits. If this scenario fit accounting profits best, clearly we would be interested in pursuing any evidence that may point at collusion. A third scenario is the actual market structure where price-cost markups reflect both product differentiation and that the same firms own many products (the effect that we discussed earlier in connection to "cannibalization"). Nevo finds that the third assumption fits the data best. For the purposes here, however, the key point is to exemplify how the combination of this class of models and data from markets can be used to shed light on important issues.

Notes

1 As we shall see later, Nash equilibrium is named after Nobel laureate John Nash, subject of the film *A Beautiful Mind*. If Cournot modeled this lucidly in 1838, is this just a case of Stigler's law (Stigler (1980))? Stigler's law states that no scientific discovery is named for its original discoverer (true to form, Stigler argues that the sociologist Robert K. Merton is the originator of the law). I'd argue no – Cournot was way before his time and must have had a beautiful mind of his own, and indeed the concept of Nash equilibrium is clearly discussed in his work. However, John Nash's 1950 PhD dissertation has been absolutely fundamental for the development of game theory and proved several results surrounding games that showed the generality of the solution concept.

2 If marginal costs differed, the incentives to undercut would stop at the level of marginal costs for the high cost producer. For instance, in the case where Red had a marginal cost of 10 and Blue a marginal cost of 0, the Bertrand equilibrium would be a price just a sliver below 10, and Blue would be the only firm present in the market and making some profit.

3 This is true, for instance, in Bresnahan and Reiss (1991), who consider competition between, e.g., tire dealers in isolated local communities in the western United States or in prices of gas stations across Greek islands (Genakos and Pagliero (2022)).

4 Two additional explanations have been proposed: One is to note that firms may collude and hence avoid the pressure of competition. We return with a discussion of this case in the next section. A second explanation focuses on patterns over time. In what is known as "Edgeworth cycles," we can have a situation where firms sequentially undercut each others' prices until at some point, one of the firms relents and raises the price. The easiest way to model this is to assume that two firms each get to change price in every second period (Maskin and Tirole (1988)). Such patterns have been found in some markets, in particular, a number of studies document Edgeworth-style cycles in gasoline markets (see, e.g., Noel (2007)).

5 As an aside, some of these are also what we term "experience goods"; you only know your valuation after consumption. Only after reading the book do you know if you liked it or not. Some of these goods are only consumed once (for a typical consumer), whereas others can see repeat use, such as going to your favorite restaurant.

6 The study of differentiated product markets typically assume price setting, largely because this seems to be the way that a typical firm in those industries operate. We can also model quantity setting with differentiated products; the demand functions ($q(p)$) are then inverted and expressed as $p(q)$ and maximization proceeds following the same steps as below: solve for best-response functions and determine the equilibrium quantities. Prices and quantities differ somewhat between price and quantity competition under differentiated products, with price competition typically being associated with somewhat lower prices, see, e.g., Belleflamme and Peitz (2015) for an analysis.

7 Again, remember that a function is just a relation between x and y and expresses the same relation no matter what we have on the left hand side. We can express temperature in Fahrenheit as a function of temperature in Celcius or temperature in Celcius as a function of temperature in Fahrenheit – they both express the same relation.

8 Davis and Garcés (2009) provide an accessible introduction to many of the issues regarding demand estimation; Gandhi and Nevo (2021) contains an advanced treatment.

11 Games and strategies

Illustration 11.1 A game of shogi. *A Young Woman and Man Playing Shogi; Chunagon Kanesuke, from a Games and Series Alluding to the Thirty-Six Poetic Immortals*, Suzuki Harunobu, Metropolitan Museum of Art, in the public domain (detail from).

11.1 Overview

The previous chapter examined strategic interaction in the setting of quantity and price. In the current chapter, we describe a set of tools that can be used to describe strategic interaction more generally, often described under the heading of game theory and that has many applications in economics, political analysis, international conflicts, biology, and beyond.

There are three basic ingredients that describe a **game** in the following. There are a set of **players** that can each take different **actions** (also termed strategies) and finally there are **payoffs** that depend both on each player's own action and on the actions of the other players. We begin our analysis with a stylized setting where players meet only once and take their

DOI: 10.4324/9781003623854-15

decisions of what strategy to play simultaneously, not knowing the actions taken by other players. Such games are also known as **static games**, reflecting that there is no important time dimension in this theoretical setting. The Cournot game that we studied in Chapter 10 was an example of such a game. There were two players: firms Blue and Red; their strategies were the different quantities that they could choose, and payoffs were their profits, which depended on the strategies chosen by both firms.

After that, we move on to **repeated games**. Here we allow for a static game of the type just discussed to be played several times. Applications are again many; for instance, how do we motivate countries to follow international agreements on environment? We will, however, mostly focus on the study of cartels and collusion, something that is the subject of intense study in economics.

Finally, we consider **sequential games** – where one player gets to select strategy first, after which others follow. The Stackelberg game that we studied earlier is an example of a sequential game. Chess is another example.

Before we move into the material, let us also note that we're moving into more modern theory than previously in the book. Much of what we've covered so far was developed during the 1800s or early 1900s. Clearly, thinking about strategic moves is as old as humankind itself. Teaching military strategy in, for instance, the 1700s would draw on rich historical roots. We also saw that the concept of Nash equilibrium, which we will cover in the following, saw an insightful application in 1838 by Augustin Cournot. Nevertheless, the way that we formalize game theory in the following depends crucially on developments from the 1940s and onward. As part of the efforts surrounding World War II, many leading mathematicians and thinkers were active at Princeton. They worked on strategic problems related to the war, such as how to organize the convoys of ships that plied the sea between the United States and Europe. Clearly, one could view the interaction between convoys and German submarines as one with "players," strategic choices, and where the very dire payoffs depended on the strategies that both parties chose. At the same time as these sharp minds were thinking of such problems, they were also thinking about strategies in games like poker. John Von Neumann, a brilliant all-round mathematician, who also provided important groundwork for computers, collaborated with economist Oskar Morgenstern on developing various sets of topics in the new field of game theory, and in 1944, the first edition of *Theory of Games and Economics Behavior* was published (Von Neumann and Morgenstern (1944)). Another landmark progress was represented by John Nash's 1950 PhD thesis. At all of 26 pages (with only two references) and written at the age of 21, it set the stage for the noncooperative game theory that we shall present in the following.[1]

11.2 Simultaneous games

11.2.1 Dominant strategies and the prisoner's dilemma

We start with describing noncooperative games with simultaneous moves. A particularly useful tool for describing such games is to use what is known as a payoff matrix. Consider the following game situation.

> Two firms, Black and Orange, can choose to cooperate or to play aggressive. If both firms cooperate, they each earn 5 million. If Black cooperates but Orange plays aggressively, Black earns 1 million while Orange earns 8 million. If Orange cooperates but Black plays aggressively, Orange earns 1 million while Black earns 8 million. If both play aggressive, they each earn 2 million.

Table 11.1 A simultaneous game depicted in normal form

		Orange's strategy	
		Cooperate	Play aggressively
Black's Strategy	*Cooperate*	*5* , 5	*1* , 8
	Play Aggressively	*8* , 1	*2* , 2

Video link for Table 11.1: https://youtu.be/Pd3vUgrsO6s.

It is clearly a game; there are 2 players (Black and Orange)[2], which each have 2 strategies that they can play (cooperate or play aggressive), and there are payoffs that depend on own actions, as well as the actions of the other player. As players of the game, or as outside observers, we are interested in making predictions – what strategies do we expect players to choose? Clearly, the text that describes the game is somewhat impenetrable, even in this simple case with only 2 players and 2 strategies. To simplify analysis, we use a payoff matrix to describe the game, as we do in Table 11.1.

The rows of the **payoff matrix** describe the strategies of one of the players (Black) and the columns describe the strategies of the other player (Orange). Here the strategies available are symmetric, but the possible strategies can differ across the players. The first number in each cell gives the payoff of the row player, and the second gives the payoff of the column player. The payoff matrix is a useful tool, even in this "simple" case with only 2 players and 2 actions each. There are 8 potentially different payoffs whose internal ranking all potentially matter for the predicted outcome. Finding some way to represent these different choices simplifies the analysis a lot relative to just keeping all the combinations in your head. The payoff matrix provides such a way.

One way to solve for the predicted outcomes is to look for the best responses. We essentially walk through the table, successively putting ourselves in each player's shoes and considering the payoffs from each combination of strategies. So let's start with considering Black's choices. We call her the row player since her choice is restricted to what row that she chooses. Her payoffs partly depend on her own choice, but importantly, her payoffs also depend on what Orange does. Let us consider the different payoffs in turn. First, *if* Orange were to cooperate, then Black's payoff from playing cooperatively would be 5, whereas the payoff from playing aggressively would be 8. Players are assumed to compare payoffs and choose whatever is the highest. Since 8 is higher than 5, we expect Black to play aggressively in this case. To keep track of that, we can underline the best response, hence underlining 8 for Black in this first column (check or circle are other common ways of marking the best response).

We continue, now considering Black's payoffs *if* Orange were to play aggressively. If Black cooperates, Black gets 1, whereas if Black plays aggressively, she gets 2. Since 2 is greater than 1, we again expect Black to play aggressively.

Table 11.2 A simultaneous game depicted in normal form where best responses have been underlined

		Orange's strategy	
		Cooperate	Play aggressively
Black's Strategy	*Cooperate*	*5* , 5	*1* , 8
	Play Aggressively	*8* , 1	*2* , 2

Video link for Table 11.2: https://youtu.be/13sV5xkn3uo.

Now turn to Orange. First, we consider the case if Black were to cooperate. For the column player, we compare payoffs across columns, and Orange thus compares her payoff from the left cell in the top row (payoff of 5) to the payoff in the right-hand cell of the top row, which carries a payoff of 8. Since 8 is greater than 5, we expect Orange to play aggressively. And finally, we let Orange consider the bottom row, now comparing the payoffs of 1 (cooperate) to 2 (play aggressively), where the latter is higher.

Table 11.2 presents the same payoff matrix as in Figure 11.1, but where we have now underlined the best response for each player in each case. We see that this particular game has what we term **dominant strategies** – a strategy that is optimal no matter what the other player does. For each of these players, payoffs are always higher when she plays aggressively. So the predicted equilibrium outcome in this case is that both players play aggressively, and each receive a payoff of 2.

In the movie *A Beautiful Mind* actor Russel Crowe, depicting John Nash, is supposed to get his key insights into game theory in a bar. In the purported Eureka moment, he states, "Adam Smith needs revision" – which presumably is a reference to a game with this kind of payoffs.[3] As analyzed earlier, Adam Smith's analogy of the invisible hand, expanded upon in Chapter 8, points to a situation where everyone simply maximizes their own individual utility can yield an outcome that is Pareto efficient. But in Figure 11.2, everyone is maximizing their utility individually, yet there exists a possible Pareto improvement. If the two players could agree to cooperate, they could each get a payoff of 5 instead of each getting a payoff of 2. Thus, the equilibrium set of strategies is such that the players could both be better off without anyone being worse off. In this sense, Adam Smith would need "revision."

What is going on here? At one level, the problem is that the players do not trust each other. If they completely trust each other, or could sign a binding agreement, then clearly they could do better. In a game with these kinds of payoffs, dominant strategies lead to a set of payoffs that are worse than what could be achieved by coordination. Examples of situations that have been interpreted in these terms is doping in sports, the general level of trust in a society, and choice of regulations to limit pollution. Competition between firms also has important elements of such a situation when seen from the perspective of the firms themselves. Competition between firms is good for consumers, but the firms would clearly make higher profits if they could act as a monopoly rather than each following a dominant strategy of competing more aggressively.

Games of the type that we have now discussed are known as **Prisoner's dilemma** games – it is a dominant strategy not to cooperate, but all players could achieve higher payoffs if they would be able to coordinate on cooperating. The origin of the name stems from the US plea bargaining system where a suspect in a criminal case can bargain for a lower punishment if she confesses and provides information that helps the prosecutor. In the typical setup of such a game, it is dominant strategy to confess even though collectively the suspects would get off with a lower punishment if they didn't confess. The example also illustrates that applications typically exist in a context with social norms that may be hard to incorporate into the payoff matrix. "Nobody likes a snitch" is a message that we've seen play out innumerable times in movies, for instance. Therefore it is probably more useful to have cases like advertising choices between firms in mind when thinking of the canonical example of a "prisoner's dilemma." Advertising can be seen as a "prisoner's dilemma" game in cases where advertising is costly and advertising mostly "steals" market share from competitors, rather than expand total sales. Two firms that spend a lot of resources on combative advertising – that essentially only neutralizes the advertising of the competing firm – are following dominant strategies that lead to an unattractive equilibrium.

11.2.2 Nash equilibria

As we have hinted at before, a highly useful concept in analyzing games is that of **Nash equilibrium**: A set of strategies such that no one player can achieve a higher payoff by unilaterally changing strategy. The set of strategies examined earlier was an example of a Nash equilibrium, as were the Bertrand and Cournot equilibria in the previous chapter. If Orange plays aggressively, Black has no incentive to switch to cooperate on her own – that is, unilaterally. She would only decrease her payoff from 2 to 1 by doing so. For predicting the outcome of the prisoner's dilemma game, we could use dominant strategies, but other games may not feature dominant strategies and thus require a more subtle analysis.

Table 11.3 presents the same game as noted earlier with the simple change that payoffs where both players cooperate are now higher. Doing the same walk-through of comparing payoffs, and underlining the best responses in each case, we now, mechanistically speaking, have two cells where both payoffs are underlined. In a mechanistic sense, such cells are Nash equilibria. And the game thus has two Nash equilibria: two sets of strategies where no player can achieve a higher payoff by a unilateral deviation. Clearly, with the kind of payoffs that

Table 11.3 A simultaneous game with two Nash equilibria

		Orange's Strategy	
		Cooperate	Play Aggressively
Black's Strategy	*Cooperate*	*<u>10</u>* , <u>10</u>	*1* , 8
	Play Aggressively	*8* , 1	*<u>2</u>* , <u>2</u>

Video link for Table 11.3: https://youtu.be/ddBkoW79XJI.

we have in this game, we might expect the players to be able to coordinate on the strategies where both cooperate, as this is the outcome where they both have the highest payoff. But, if for some reason Black expects Orange to play aggressively, Black has no reason to deviate from this strategy. The set of payoffs that are illustrated in Figure 11.3 are an example of a **coordination game** – the key aspect is that the players want to coordinate. Examples of coordination games are which side of the road to drive on, what social media platforms to use, or when two firms are to decide on which products to develop – ones that are somewhat differentiated or ones where competition is more fierce and profits lower.

The payoffs in Table 11.3 are also representative of what is sometimes called a stag hunt game, following discussions by Rousseau and others about the origins of cooperation in society. There are gains to be had if we can coordinate on cooperating, but that coordination also relies on trust and that the other player sees the game the same way that I do. The lowest possible payoff if Black plays aggressive is 2, whereas the lowest possible payoff if Black cooperates is 1. With 2 being larger than 1, we then say that playing aggressively is the **maximin strategy** in this game, the strategy that maximizes the minimum payoff. Maximin is an alternative solution concept to Nash equilibrium. While the risk in this case seems limited, we can think of cases where your family's survival hinges on the choice or where issues of war and peace are at stake.

11.2.3 Cases where there are no equilibria in pure strategies

Earlier, we considered the case where there are one or several Nash equilibria. Next consider a game where there are 3 strategies that each player can take, depicted in Table 11.4. The figure depicts the game of rock, paper, scissors between two players, Blue and Red. This is a useful example to highlight that payoff matrixes, what is also known as the normal form representation of a game, can have more than 2 strategies for each player. Whether the number of strategies differ across the players, and whether the different players have different strategies, will depend on the details of the situation to be described. It is also an example of what we term a **zero-sum game**, when the one player's gain is the other player's loss and the sum of payoffs in each cell is zero.

Our main reason for including Table 11.4, however, is to highlight that not all games need to have a Nash equilibrium in what we term **pure strategies**. In the discussion earlier,

Table 11.4 A simultaneous game with no Nash equilibria in pure strategies: Rock, paper, scissors

		Red		
		Rock	Paper	Scissors
Blue	*Rock*	*0,0*	*−1,1*	*1,−1*
	Paper	*1,−1*	*0,0*	*−1,1*
	Scissors	*−1,1*	*1,−1*	*0,0*

Video link for Table 11.4: https://youtu.be/N1sIME1uTfE.

we left out the qualifier pure strategies, something that we indeed often do. If I just say Nash equilibrium, I mean Nash equilibrium in pure strategies. Walking through the payoff matrix in Figure 11.4 and underlining the best response shows that there is no cell where both payoffs are underlined. Mechanically, we're then saying that there is no Nash equilibrium in pure strategies. The deeper insight is that there is no combination of strategies where not one of the players would want to unilaterally change. Take the case where Blue plays Rock and Red Paper, for instance. The paper bag catches the Rock, and Red would not want to change. But Blue would like to unilaterally change to Scissors (which cuts the paper bag). Here though, Red would like to unilaterally change, and so forth. There is no combination of strategies where not at least one of the players would like to change, while keeping the strategy of the other player fixed.

As anyone who has played rock paper scissors knows, the key to playing successfully is to be unpredictable. Simply put, you will want to randomize and play each strategy with probability 1/3. If you, for instance, were more likely to choose scissors, your opponent would take advantage of this and increase her probability of choosing rock, thus making her more likely to win. We term a strategy where each of the players chooses probabilities so as to best respond to the probabilities chosen by the opponent as a **mixed strategy**. The intuition is important, but the formal derivation is usually saved for more advanced courses. A common application of mixed strategy equilibria are in sports where questions such as where to put the serve in tennis or where to target penalty kicks in football are prominent examples.

11.2.4 Nash Equilibria with continuous strategies

The normal form representation of Nash equilibria can easily give the impression that Nash equilibrium only applies to variables where the strategic choices are discrete (e.g., cooperate or not) rather than continuous (such as how much will you cooperate on a continuous scale from 0 to 100). This is not the case, and remember from Chapter 10 that the profit-maximizing choices in Bertrand and Cournot games (with prices and quantities as strategic variables) were examples of Nash equilibria. Let us take a final example of a simultaneous move noncooperative game to show how Nash equilibrium strategies can be applied to a simple continuous case. The game is sometimes termed the ice-cream vendor game and its origins go back to Harold Hotelling (1929).

Think of a beach with consumers spread out uniformly along the length of the beach, which is 1,000 meters wide. Consumers each value an ice cream and will buy one if their utility of the ice cream is greater than the cost, which is the price that they pay together with their "transport cost," the disutility associated with walking to get the ice cream. The longer they walk, the higher the transport cost. Now consider two ice-cream vendors and a case where prices are fixed, and the two vendors offer the same ice creams. If I were a social planner, I would place one vendor, Westie, 250 meters from the left-hand end of the beach and the other, Eastie, 250 meters from the right-hand end of the beach, as depicted in the top panel of Figure 11.1. This minimizes the average transport cost.

Is the situation in the top panel a Nash equilibrium however? No. At least one of the vendors has a unilateral incentive to change strategy. To see this, we may hold the location of Westie fixed and allow Eastie to relocate. Where would she want to relocate if she maximizes profit? Just to the right of Westie. All the consumers on the 750 meter stretch to the right of Westie would have her as their closest ice-cream vendor. Only the consumers on the 250 meters to the left of Westie would have her as their closest ice-cream vendor. Clearly,

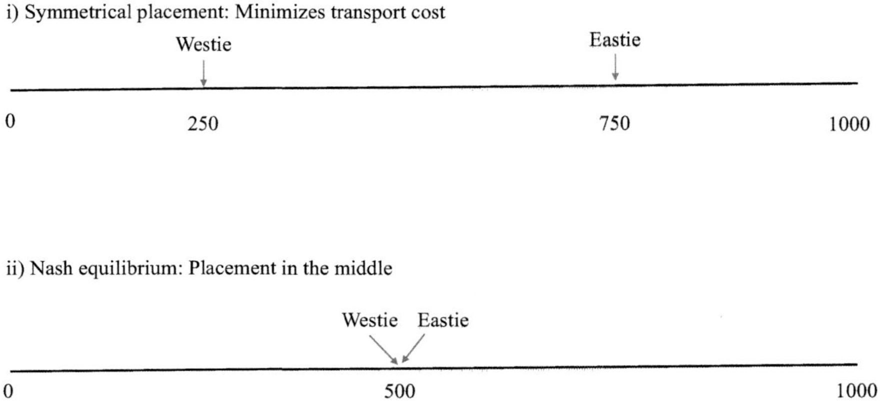

Figure 11.1 A simultaneous game with continuous variables: The ice-cream vendor problem. Video link for Figure 11.1: https://youtu.be/9lpQM_ONoJY.

Westie would have an incentive to relocate to just the other side of Eastie, who in turn would relocate. And so forth. Of course, we don't expect to observe this moving carousel; we expect the firms to contemplate and then choose a location based on their reasoning once and for all. Is there a Nash equilibrium in this game? Yes. The unique Nash equilibrium in this game is that both firms locate right next to each other in the middle of the beach. All the consumers from the 500 meters to the left of Westie come to her, and all the consumers from the 500 meters to the right of Eastie come to her, as illustrated in the lowest panel of Figure 11.1. None of the firms has an incentive to unilaterally relocate in this case. In other words, we have established a Nash equilibrium.

The unique equilibrium is sensitive to assumptions; for instance, if there are three vendors, there is no Nash equilibrium in pure strategies. Nevertheless, many people find the analysis useful for understanding why there is often so little product differentiation – streaming services providing very similar shows, stores or gas stations locating right next to each other, or political parties adopting very similar political platforms.

11.3 Repeated games

> People of the same trade seldom meet together, even for merriment and diversion, but the conversation ends in a conspiracy against the public, or in some contrivance to raise prices.
>
> (Adam Smith, The Wealth of Nations)

The case where players meet only once is a useful analytical tool for understanding many cases of strategic interaction, as suggested by the previous coverage. However, it is clear that many important cases of strategic interaction involve repeated play. A seller on a local market is likely to meet the same customers again – even though it may be a dominant strategy for an unscrupulous seller to provide low quality in a one-shot game, the loss of reputation may well hamper profitability in the long run. More generally, the ability to use future payoffs as reward for "good" behavior can impact the equilibria that players are able to sustain in repeated games. Again, applications range far and wide, and some of the more important concern international environmental agreements or agreements on international trade rules. Much attention has, however, been given to understand a case

Table 11.5 The payoffs in a one shot game: Can repeated play sustain cooperation?

		Orange's Strategy	
		Cooperate	Defect
Black's Strategy	*Cooperate*	*5* , 5	*1* , 8
	Defect	*8* , 1	*2* , 2

where, from the societal perspective, cooperation is not beneficial. That of collusion between firms.

Consider again the payoffs that we used to illustrate the prisoner's dilemma, but now instead, think of Black and Orange as symbolizing two firms that each can choose to "cooperate" or to "defect," as illustrated in Figure 11.5. Cooperate means to abide to a cartel agreement – that could be explicit as in an international cartel such as that between oil producers within OPEC. It could also be a case of tacit collusion, where, for instance, based on mutual understanding, both firms set a high price, or avoid competitive advertising, etc. If the game is only played once the dominant strategy for each firm is to defect.

But now assume that the same two firms will meet again and that the same game is repeated in each future period. Then, in principle, gains from cooperating tomorrow can work as a reward for cooperating today. To highlight this, we assume that firms start out following what is known as a **grim trigger strategy**. Under this strategy, we assume that both firms start out by choosing to cooperate. If one firm defects, however, we enter a punishment face where firms play noncooperatively ("defect") for all future. Since cooperative profits are higher, this provides a clear incentive to keep cooperating. In this case, the incentive to cooperate is given by the expectation that the player will get a payoff of 5 instead of 2 (which is the equilibrium in the one shot game) in all future periods. The incentive for defection is given by the higher profit achieved in the first period for the firm that defects (a profit of 8 instead of 5 in this first period for the defecting firm). We assume that it takes one period for the opponent to trigger the "punishment" face. In this setup, the incentives to cooperate thus depend on the difference between the payoffs under the different cases. The one period payoff of a unilateral deviation is higher than the payoff from continued cooperation, which in turn is higher than the noncooperative payoff. Writing this in general terms (which we will use next), we write that

$$\pi_{i,nash} < \pi_{i,cooperate} < \pi_{i,defect}.$$

To compare the choice of whether to continue to cooperate or to defect, we also need to take account of how each firm values the present relative to the future. Seen from the perspective of today, profits in the future are worth less than profits today, and we use δ (Greek letter "delta") to denote the firms' **discount factor**, how future profit is valued today.

Let us first clarify how a discount factor works in relating payoffs tomorrow to payoffs today before turning to the case of many periods. Consider an investment whose value grows by 5% in one year. The 5% here can be regarded as the interest rate r (or sometimes as the discount *rate*, which, as we shall see is not the same as the discount *factor*). A 100 euro investment today is therefore worth $100 \times 1.05 = 105$ euros in one year's time. Thus future value (FV) equals the present value (100 in this case) times the interest term

$$\textit{Future Value} = \textit{Present Value} \times (1 + r).$$

Turning this around, the present value of a future payoff is given by

$$\textit{Present Value} = \textit{Future Value} \times \underbrace{\frac{1}{(1+r)}}_{\text{Discount Factor}}.$$

Thus, if the discount factor is 1, future payoffs are valued the same as today's. Typically, however, we expect the discount factor to be less than 1. There are several reasons for this – one is that if we use the discount factor to value an investment, we could typically expect some positive return (r) on alternative investments against which the current investment should be measured. The discount factor can also be used to capture that circumstances change, maybe the future payoff may not materialize at all, and this possibility lowers the discount factor, making me attach a lower value today to future payoffs.

Thus, the present value of a payoff in the next period is future value $\times\delta$. The present value of a payoff two periods ahead is future value $\times\delta \times \delta$ or, more compactly, future value$\times\delta^2$. Under the grim trigger strategy, we expect that the game will continue without a known final period and continue indefinitely into the future (even though the weight of those future payoffs become smaller and smaller in today's valuation).[4]

If $V_{i,cooperate}$ is the discounted sum of profits in case the collusion is stable, and $V_{i,defect}$ is the discounted sum of profits for a firm that defects, a firm will be indifferent between defecting and cooperating if $V_{i,cooperate} = V_{i,defect}$.

First note that the present value of cooperating is given by (where the last equality follows from the formula for the sum of an infinite series)

$$V_{i,cooperate} = \pi_{i,cooperate} + \delta\pi_{i,cooperate} + \delta^2\pi_{i,cooperate} + \delta^3\pi_{i,cooperate} + \ldots = \frac{\pi_{i,cooperate}}{1-\delta},$$

and the present value of defecting is given by

$$V_{i,defect} = \pi_{i,defect} + \delta\pi_{i,nash} + \delta^2\pi_{i,nash} + \ldots = \pi_{i,defect} + \frac{\delta}{1-\delta}\pi_{i,nash}.$$

Thus for the payoff from adhering to the collusive strategy to be at least as great as the payoff from defecting, the following must hold

$$V_{i,cooperate} \geq V_{i,defect} \Rightarrow \delta \geq \frac{\pi_{i,defect} - \pi_{i,col}}{\pi_{i,defect} - \pi_{i,nash}} = \delta_{min}.$$

So collusion is sustainable only if sufficient weight is put on the future, if the discount factor is high enough. For instance, with the payoffs that we assumed in Figure 11.5, collusion is sustainable if

$$\delta \geq \frac{8-5}{8-2} = \frac{1}{2}.$$

The framework thus suggests a number of cases where it is more difficult to sustain collusion.[5]

- The greater $\pi_{i,defect}$, the greater is δ_{min} and therefore the more difficult is it to sustain collusion. The greater the temptation to defect, the more do firms need to value the future in order to keep cooperating. If the payoff when defecting in the example would increase from 8 to 10, the discount factor would need to be at least 0.625 ((10 – 5)/(10 – 2) to sustain cooperation. Competition authorities often take a skeptical view of measures that increase the possibility of competitors to observe each others' prices, and the framework presented here gives the intuition for why. If a firm is able to act more competitively (setting lower prices through secret rebates, for instance) without the other firms reacting, the period when it is able to achieve the defection payoff is likely to be longer. Rapid detection thus limits the incentives to defect.
- The greater $\pi_{i,col}$ the lower is δ_{min} and the easier it is to sustain collusion. If the payoff from cooperating is high, this clearly promotes cooperation. If the payoff when cooperating in the example, for instance, would increase from 5 to 6, the discount factor would only need to be at least 0.33 ((8 – 6)/(8 – 2) to sustain cooperation. One example of an application comes from a consideration of tacit collusion with only two firms compared to tacit collusion between many firms. To see this starkly, consider a situation with homogeneous products and price competition. If the colluding firms split collusive profits equally, a firm's share of the collusive profit would be 1/2 if there are two firms but only 1/10 if there are 10 firms. This is one foundation for the presumption that we are more likely to see collusion in cases where just a few firms are (repeatedly) interacting.
- The greater $\pi_{i,nash}$ the larger is δ_{min} and the more difficult is it to sustain collusion. The greater the profits in the case of noncooperation, the less of an incentive to cooperate there is, the less of a concern it is if cooperation breaks down. If the payoff when not cooperating in the example, for instaance, would increase from 2 to 4, the discount factor would need to be at least 0.75 ((8 – 5)/(8 – 4) to sustain cooperation. One implication of this is that collusion will be particularly valuable, and hence easier to sustain, in industries that sell relatively homogeneous products. Indeed, formal cartels have often been documented among raw material producers (such as the oil producers' cartel OPEC), thus relatively homogeneous products where price is likely to be relatively close to marginal cost in the absence of collusion. More differentiated products are less likely to be subject to collusion.

In the preceding discussion of repeated games we focused on tacit collusion between firms – a setting where, from a societal perspective, cooperation is bad. If our focus is on consumer welfare and overall efficiency, we want to make it hard for firms to cooperate on prices. Policy does this first and foremost by making it illegal to participate in a cartel. For instance, in the United States, the Sherman act from 1890 made anticompetitive agreements illegal, and similarly, in the European Union, article 101 of the Treaty on the Functioning of the European Union also makes such agreements illegal. Policy also strives to make cartels harder by vigilantly working against what are seen as facilitating practices, various forms of working in an industry that tend to facilitate tacit collusion, for instance, ways that make it easier to signal intentions of price increases or that make it easier to detect defection.

In many other cases, cooperation is beneficial to society, and the logic of repeated games can be used as an instrument to promote cooperation. When enforcement of contracts by legal means is costly or difficult, the loss of future gains from cooperation can be used as a stick to promote cooperative behavior. As we shall see later, a platform such as Airbnb has an interest in that users correctly describe quality, for instance, and will work with mechanisms whereby a failure to correctly describe quality of the product offered ("defection") triggers a loss of reputation and the thereby associated profits ("punishment via lower future profits"). Similarly, contracts between countries are hard to enforce, and using the benefits from future cooperation to deter defection today is a way to enforce cooperation.[6]

11.4 Sequential games

In the games that we covered earlier, players chose their action at the same time. Sequential games, whereby one player chooses action first and then the other player chooses after having observed the first player's choice, are a final important category of game-theoretical analysis that we cover. To frame ideas, it may be useful to first consider a simultaneous game in normal form, this time the type of game that is known as "chicken," as described in Table 11.6.

The archetypal story is that of two studs that strive to be the top dog, and the game is often associated with the 1950s US movie *Rebel without a Cause* where Jim (played by James Dean in an iconic performance) faces off in a race against his protagonist named Buzz. For the visuals, think of them sitting in their respective cars at each end of a straight piece of road. At a given signal, they drive toward each other, and each has a choice between staying the course – driving straight ahead – or swerving.[7] Staying the course while the other swerves establishes the latter as a low-status loser, "chicken," whereas the one that stays the course establishes himself at the top of the hierarchy. If both swerve, they get to walk away with honor intact, whereas if no one swerves, they crash with nasty consequences for both.

Table 11.6 A game of chicken with best responses in the simultaneous game underlined

		Jim's Strategy	
		Drive Straight	Swerve
Buzz's Strategy	*Drive Straight*	*−10* , −10	<u>5</u> , <u>−5</u>
	Swerve	<u>−5</u> , <u>5</u>	*0* , 0

Video link for Figures 11.6–11.3: https://youtu.be/oj2XTQN8p3E.

If this were played as a simultaneous game, it is an asymmetric coordination game, and we underline the best responses in Table 11.6. For each player, it is a best response to swerve if he expects the other to stay the course, but clearly, you would want to convince the other that you will not swerve.

If this were a sequential game where Buzz got to choose first, he would clearly like to commit to drive straight, thereby in effect blocking out the lower part of the payoff matrix in Table 11.6. Welding the steering wheel fixed, placing a large stone onto the gas pedal, and climbing into the back seat, he would commit to driving straight ahead, forcing Jim to only choose between a certain crash and swerving.

The game of chicken is used to understand aspects of many games. One example is for entry into markets, or market segments, by firms that can only profitably hold one firm, such as entry by a really large hypermarket grocery store in a small town. Competition between Airbus and Boeing in the segments with the largest airplanes have also been seen in this light as has nuclear conflict between the United States and Soviet Union during the Cod War.

As noted, we could in principle examine a sequential game, where Buzz gets to choose first in the payoff matrix by reasoning what he would want to choose and then letting Jim as second choose. For more complex sequential games, the tool of a game tree is useful, and let us introduce that here. A **game tree** (the term **extensive form** of a game is also used) starts from the left with a node where all the different strategic choices that are possible for that player at that stage are illustrated by lines. Moving rightward, we then get to the next nodes where the strategic choices for the second player are illustrated. Figure 11.2 illustrates with a game of chicken from Table 11.6. Assume that Buzz gets to decide strategy first and choose to (irrevocably commit to) drive straight or to swerve, choices that are illustrated by the first two branches in Figure 11.2. After having observed Buzz's choice, it is Jim's turn to choose. Since the payoffs associated with Jim's choices depend on the strategy chosen by Buzz in the first stage, the game tree represents Jim's decision nodes at the end of each line depicting Buzz's strategic choice. After Jim has chosen, this simple game ends, and the payoffs are illustrated at the end of the branches, with the payoffs of the last player written last.

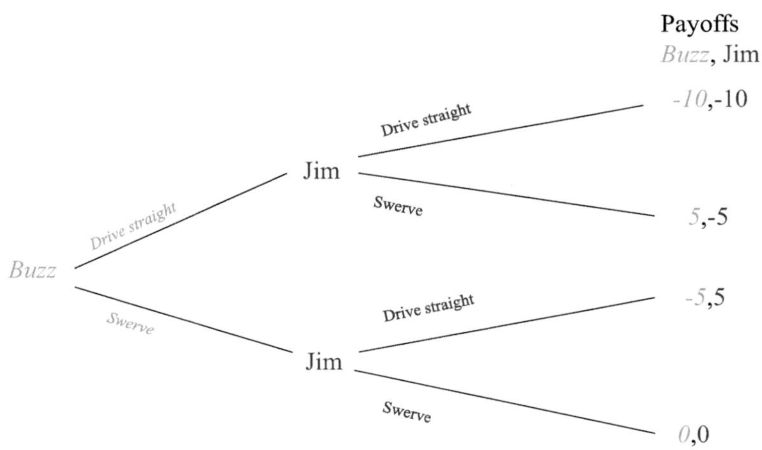

Figure 11.2 A sequential game of chicken depicted with a game tree. Video link for Figures 11.6–11.3: https://youtu.be/oj2XTQN8p3E.

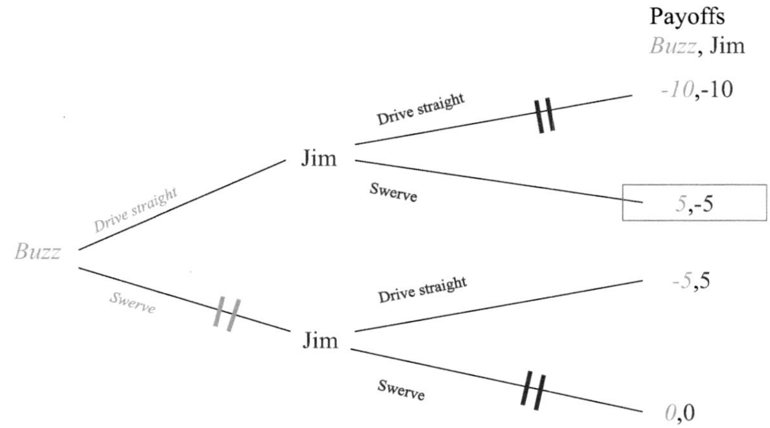

Figure 11.3 A sequential game of chicken depicted with a game tree solution using backward induction. Video link for Figures 11.6–11.3: https://youtu.be/oj2XTQN8p3E.

To solve sequential games, we use **backward induction** – "look ahead and reason back." First examine the actions of the player making the last moves and assume that he chooses so as to maximize his payoff. The second to last to move takes as a given that the last mover will choose this way and, conditional on that belief, chooses the action that maximizes his payoff. So the process goes on until one reaches the first stage of the game. The equilibrium that we find from such reasoning is referred to as a **subgame perfect Nash equilibrium**.

Thus, starting from the back, we first place ourselves in the shoes of the last player (Jim in this case) and evaluate his choices at each node. If Buzz in the first stage has chosen to drive straight, Jim faces the choice between driving straight with a payoff of -10, or swerving with a payoff of -5. While a payoff of -5 is unappetizing, it is still higher than -10, and Jim will choose to swerve. We mark this in the graph by "closing" the branch where Jim drives straight, as shown by the two vertical bars on the top branch in Figure 11.3. Another common way of indicating best responses is to use arrows to show the predicted action that is chosen. Similarly, if Buzz in the first stage has chosen to swerve, then Jim is faced with the choice between 5 (when driving straight) and 0 (when swerving), choosing the former and again using vertical bars to mark the strategy not chosen. Turning now to Buzz in the first stage, he makes a comparison between the strategies, taking into consideration what he expects Jim to do at the different nodes. He thus compares the payoff 5 (drive straight) to the payoff -5 (swerve), choosing the former. The predicted set of equilibrium strategies is that Buzz drives straight, and Jim swerves.

The game of chicken, and an analysis of possible moves in a first stage, are a common example of the value of strategic commitment. If you could convince your opponent that you will not swerve, you'll come out on top. So why not brace your steering wheel straight ahead, put a rock on the gas pedal, and climb into the back seat? Doing so would amount to a commitment not to swerve. Altering your opponent's beliefs about what you will do should lead him to swerve. In such a case, limiting your options by taking away your flexibility to act will benefit you. A **credible commitment** of this kind, however, must be *observable* and *irreversible* in order to play a commitment role. If you have an automatic release for the steering wheel in the back seat, and your opponent knows so, there is little point to rigging the wheel.

The classic example of strategic commitment is that of an army blocking its ability to retreat. In game-theory terms, this is typically seen as a move to make the enemy back down because, knowing that you must fight your way out, the enemy knows that fleeing is not an option for you. It will therefore be tempting for the enemy to back down and avoid a fight at present, hoping for a better situation sometime in the future. This strategy reportedly was used in Xiang Yu's battles against Qin around 200 B.C., by Tariq Ibn Ziyiad when Muslim forces invaded Spain around 700 A.D., by William the Conqueror when invading Britain in 1066, and by Hernán Cortés in the early 1500s as he challenged the Aztec Empire. "Burning your ships" or "burning the bridges behind you" are some of the names attached to this strategy.

The value of commitment is an important insight. It should be noted, however, that in teaching, all too often, there has been an almost exclusive focus on the upside of commitment. This may be because the idea that it can be profitable to limit your options is so counterintuitive that it needs to be explained at length. Yet, it deserves to be stressed that the benefit of commitment is not a general property of strategic games. In some game situations, it is useful to commit and in others not. Think of the simple game of rock paper scissors, for instance. Making your move first and being committed is clearly not a good way to play that game. Furthermore, in teaching, we are often presented with the case where one party exogenously is given the role of being able to act first. If several parties are vying to be the first to commit, the analysis becomes significantly more complex. That said, let us consider two applications related to the study of commitment.

11.4.1 Credible commitments

Illustration 11.2 The ship and the lighthouse. Wojciech Wrzesien/Shutterstock.com

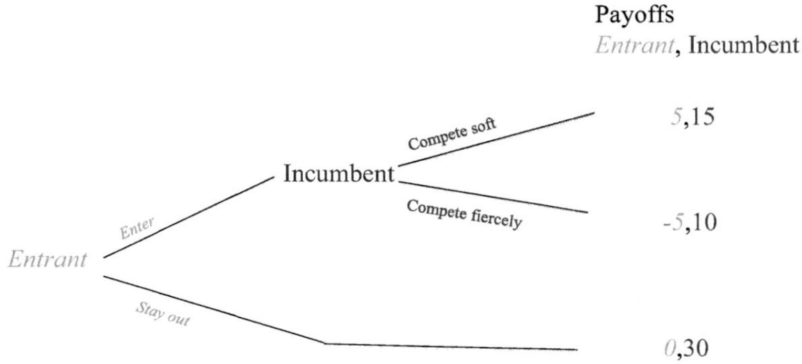

Figure 11.4 An entry game. Video link for Figures 11.4 and 11.5: https://youtu.be/133OJ2bRLIE.

What is a picture of a warship and a lighthouse doing here? An example often used in teaching, a purportedly true intercepted radio communication between parties A and B, goes as follows: "A: Please divert your course 20 degrees to the North to avoid a collision. B: Recommend you divert YOUR course 20 degrees to the North to avoid a collision. A: This is the aircraft carrier USS Nimitz accompanied by our full battle group. I demand that you divert your course 20 degrees to the North to avoid a collision. B: This is a lighthouse. Your call." Its doubtful whether such an event actually has happened, and it is a classic urban legend, but nevertheless useful for understanding the value of commitment. The lighthouse has a credible case that it is committed to staying put.[8]

Commitments are often discussed in a business context. Remember the discussion of why monopolies exist in Chapter 9 – we there considered the case where entry was deterred. A firm already present in the market – *the incumbent* – might take actions that keep the potential entrant out. Consider the setup in Figure 11.4. Looking at the payoffs for the incumbent, they are clearly the highest if the entrant stays out. The incumbent could make statements to the effect that "if you enter I will compete fiercely" – if these are credible the expected payoff for the entrant is −5, and this is clearly lower than 0, which is the payoff if she stays out.

However, and this is a big however, is the threat to compete fiercely credible? If the entrant does indeed establish herself on the market, the incumbent is faced with a choice of competing softly (with a payoff of 15) or of competing fiercely (with a payoff of 10). At this node, the situation that the incumbent wanted to avoid has already materialized – the incumbent is in this case confronted with a fait accompli, and if she maximizes payoffs, she will in this case act as a soft competitor. Foreseeing this, the entrant would indeed establish herself on the market and entry followed by soft competition is the predicted outcome if we solve this game by backward induction. Just as in the game of chicken a reputation for being reckless and aggressive can have a value in these kinds of situations – as they may raise doubts in the entrant that the incumbent will follow the payoff-maximizing strategy. Note, however, that in a wider game, it is not clear that a reputation for being reckless is useful – neither employees nor suppliers are likely to appreciate such behavior.

Another way to solve the commitment problem for the incumbent is to take actions that modify the payoffs. It could, for instance, choose to invest in a technology that has higher fixed costs but lower marginal costs. In the case where competition is soft, or it is alone on the market, this suboptimal cost structure would hurt profits.

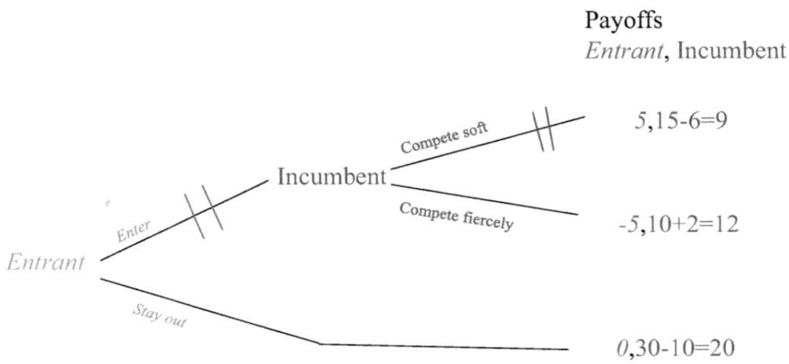

Figure 11.5 An entry game, solution using backward induction. Video link for Figures 11.4 and 11.5: https://youtu.be/133OJ2bRLIE.

Figure 11.5 presents a numerical example of such modified payoffs.[9] The equilibrium now is that the entrant stays out and that the incumbent makes a payoff of 20. At one level, it seems as though the incumbent is just pointlessly hurting her own profits – why have a suboptimal cost structure? The point here is that the change in cost structure makes it optimal for the incumbent to compete fiercely if the entrant should come in – it serves as a *credible commitment* – the investment is irreversible and affects the optimal strategy in later stages of the game.

11.4.2 Hold-up problems

The preceding analysis illustrated a case where a commitment to be aggressive was useful. In the same way a commitment not to be aggressive can be useful in many situations – the blushing emoji can be a useful way to remember this. Blushing when one lies can potentially be seen as something that is disadvantageous – it makes it harder to bluff your way out of situations and get a good deal at the expense of others. But, if people know that you blush if you lie, this "weakness" becomes a strength; people are more likely to trust you.[10]

An important class of examples of where a commitment not to be aggressive may the way out of a suboptimal equilibrium are known as **hold-up problems**. Hold-up problems concern cases where a party makes a relation-specific investment, which puts them at risk of being taken advantage of ex post. A firm that chooses a specialized supplier rather than a more general technology may have given up outside options if the specialized supplier ex post wants to raise the price. A firm that rents its facilities may have little possibility to move if the landlord wants to increase rents sharply. If one could write contracts that specified what would happen in all eventualities, the hold-up problem would be mute – but that is typically not the case.[11]

To illustrate with a specific example, consider the case of a firm, denoted Buyer, that wants to invest in a computer system to organize its operations. It can choose a generic

Illustration 11.6 Blushing. iStock Photo by Getty Images, calvindexter.

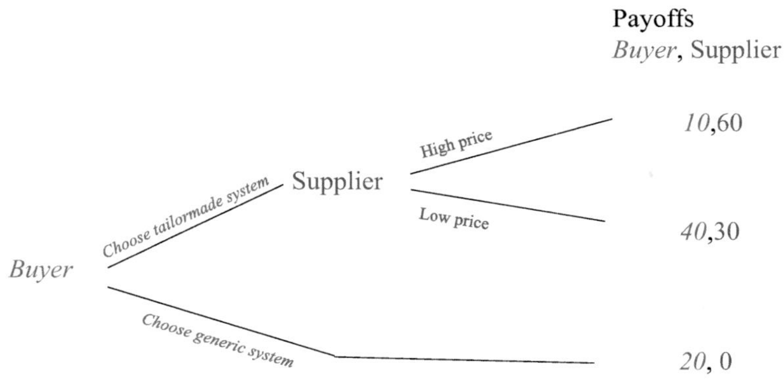

Figure 11.6 A hold-up problem. Video link for Figure 11.6: https://youtu.be/MChZSfz8xe0.

system that is available on the market from several different suppliers, or it can choose to purchase a tailor-made system from a firm that we call the Supplier. Assume that there are large efficiency gains from the tailor-made system as reflected by the payoffs in Figure 11.6 – joint payoffs are 70 with the tailor-made system rather than 20 with the generic system. The Supplier realizes a payoff of at least 30 if she sells the tailor-made system rather than 0 if the Buyer instead purchases a generic system. The hold-up problem consists of that once the Buyer has chosen the tailor-made system, she has locked herself into this line of action. There is then a temptation for the Supplier to set a high price and get a payoff of 60 rather than 30. Foreseeing this risk of ex-post opportunistic behavior – the hold-up problem – the Buyer may instead choose the generic system. The lack of trust thereby hurts both parties.

There are several potential ways to solve the hold-up problem, which may be more or less relevant depending on the setting – for instance, sometimes combining the two into one firm is a solution, and long-term contracts may work in some other situations. We may also note that in some cases, there are different ways through which the supplier can effectively tie her hands as to what course of action she can take. Committing to a low-price strategy may appear foolish, but maybe its what it takes to get a deal – otherwise, a forward-looking buyer might opt for the general technology.

11.5 Game theory – Some concluding thoughts

The game theoretical models that we covered in this chapter are by many seen as highly useful tools in describing strategic interaction. That said, let us end with a few provisos regarding their application to decision-making. One is that in the simple games that we examined, we saw clear predictions. In real-world settings, game theory is a useful guide, but clearly, many aspects will be unmodeled – for instance, in cooperation between students we see much less of a breakdown in cooperation than would be predicted by prisoner's dilemma-type games. This reinforces that we need to be cognizant of the social setting in which interaction takes place.

Another point to highlight is there is often many different ways to specify a game situation, and your opponents may see the game differently. Setting up a game tree of a situation is often a very useful way to provide an analytical approach to a decision situation, see what the crucial assumptions are and what worst-case scenarios offer. In the examples in this chapter, we assumed that both parties had a common understanding of the game and of the payoffs of different sets of strategies. This is relatively likely to hold true in chess or poker but not necessarily in military conflict between nations. Game theory is a useful tool also in broader applications – but be alert that in settings more complex than board games, the other players may well see the game and payoffs very differently.[12]

Notes

1 Presumably, some readers will have seen the movie *A Beautiful Mind*, which that depicts both his early struggles with making a contribution worthy of his abilities, his long struggle with schizofrenia, and the Nobel Prize in 1994. If you haven't seen the movie, it comes highly recommended, having won the Oscar for best movie in 2002.

2 The colors are the colors of Princeton and see it as a small tribute to that university's role in the beginnings of game theory.

3 I find it a great movie but, of course, not flawless. That the scene in question is sexist may perhaps reflect the state of the world in the late 1940s. More worrying from a game theory perspective is that contrary to impression, the scene does not depict what we call a Nash equilibrium – a setting in which there will be no unilateral incentives to change strategy.

4 The assumption that the game continues indefinitely is an important one. In theory, if there is a known final period, then clearly in that last period, future payoffs cannot be used to incentivize cooperation. Then the prediction is that firms will not cooperate in the last period which means that in the penultimate period the firms will not cooperate either, and there is an unraveling where the cooperative equilibrium fails to be supported. Arguably, however, situations where there is a known final period are rather rare, and it is sufficient that there is a positive probability that the game continues into the future for cooperation to be sustainable, given a high enough discount factor.

5 In the list below, we focus on a few of the more prominent predictions. See, e.g., Ivaldi et al. (2003) for a comprehensive examination of different aspects using this kind of framework. Note also that sometimes the empirical evidence on these types of issues is not clear-cut; see, e.g., Levenstein and Suslow (2006) for an overview. One complicating factor is that if collusion is harder to sustain (for instance, if there are more firms), this also strengthens the incentives to invest in mechanisms, such as information exchange, that make collusion easier to maintain. There is also evidence that, rather than use the extremely harsh punishment associated with reversion to competitive behavior forever, firms try to find mechanisms whereby it will be possible to forgive and forget but still maintain some bite in the threat of punishment. A particularly fascinating description of the mechanisms used to stifle defection, that in the case of cartel in sugar market in the early 1900s, is given by Genesove and Mullin (2001).

6 In Chapter 13, we will consider cooperation between individuals who jointly use a common resource, such as fishing in a local lake, and the design principles associated with Elinor Ostrom can also be related to the repeated game setting presented above.

7 In *Rebel wihout a Cause*, they drive toward a cliff edge rather than against each other – Buzz gets entangled in the door and dies as he drives over the cliff. I find it a more striking thought experiment with them driving toward each other, however.

8 For references to the urban legend see, e.g., https://en.wikipedia.org/wiki/Lighthouse_and_naval_vessel_urban_legend. Remains amusing and illustrative of the value of commitment anyway – see, for instance, https://www.youtube.com/watch?v=EPqtwV5utUY.

9 The numbers here are just examples. They nevertheless capture the basic premise, as described, of choosing a technology with higher fixed cost and lower marginal cost than optimal if competition was not an issue. The cost benefit of this alternative technology is greatest when competition is fierce and quantity is high and lowest when quantities are low and there is no competition.

10 A lot of work in psychology and evolutionary biology is devoted to blushing – and Charles Darwin took considerable interest in why we blush (Black (2002)). I'm way out of my depth in the medical and biological aspects of blushing – for me, it nevertheless provides a useful thought experiment for appreciating why something that can appear as a weakness can serve as a strength.

11 Indeed, the hold-up problem is an important starting point for a literature on "incomplete contracts," see, e.g., Hart (2017) for an overview.

12 An example sometimes used in teaching of game theory to highlight this point is a scene from the movie *The Princess Bride*. The scene is loaded with clichés – but if you can see beyond those there lies a lesson in that the game and payoffs may be different than what they first appear to be. The scene is available at e.g. https://www.youtube.com/watch?v=rMz7JBRbmNo.

12 Price discrimination

12.1 Overview of price discrimination

Table 12.1 shows a small excerpt of the price list in an Austrian climbing gym. All in all, there are 54 different prices listed for the same basic service, access to the climbing wall, with different combinations of duration of access, as well as age, employment status, and membership in Alpine clubs of the customer. As for many goods and services that we consume, there is not only a simple price per visit, but the pricing menu also offers a number of different rebates, monthly tickets, and closely related products sold at different prices. We refer to the practice of selling different units of the same good at different prices as **price discrimination**. We observe this in many guises: Student rebates or coupons in the grocery store are two examples. Different consumers pay different prices for the same good. Price structures where consumers pay a fixed fee and then no price per additional unit consumed (e.g., many mobile subscriptions, a monthly card on a gym or on public transport) and quantity discounts are other examples of price discrimination. Here the per-unit price differs across consumers and depends on how much they consume. Price discrimination can also refer to cases where products are not identical (for instance, first and second class on trains), but where the logic for the price differences can be clearly linked to price discrimination.

Following Arthur Pigou (1920), we distinguish between 3 different forms of price discrimination, and let the dividing line be how much the firm knows about the customer's willingness to pay: (1) when willingness to pay is perfectly observed (perfect price

Table 12.1 Price of entry at Innsbruck climbing gym

	Price in euros
Single ticket entry – regular	16
Single ticket entry – student	13.60
Single ticket entry – children	8.4
3-month card	267
12-month card	683

https://www.kletterzentrum-innsbruck.at/en/, accessed February 2, 2024

DOI: 10.4324/9781003623854-16

discrimination), (2) when different groups have different willingness to pay and what group that a person belongs to (e.g., student) can be observed, and (3) when willingness to pay of an individual is not observed, but the firm knows that differences in willingness to pay exist and are correlated with valuation of properties of the goods offered – high-income consumers are, for instance, more likely to have a higher opportunity cost of time and therefore less liable to spend time redeeming coupons.

Price discrimination is seen in markets characterized by different forms of imperfect competition. To introduce the basic concepts, it is easiest to analyze the motivations for and effects of price discrimination under monopoly, and that is our focus in this chapter. Broadly, similar logic holds also for other market forms.[1] One key ingredient for price discrimination to be a viable strategy is that price is above marginal cost. Thus we don't expect to see price discrimination in perfectly competitive markets. Another key ingredient is that resale should be hard – the firm that is price discriminating typically doesn't want whoever buys the product to be able to just sell it on to other consumers. We don't expect student discounts on purchasing stocks in the stock market.[2]

12.1.1 Perfect price discrimination

In this most "extreme" form of price discrimination, **perfect price discrimination**, the monopolist knows the highest price that a given customer is willing to pay for a unit of the good or service.[3] The perhaps simplest way to understand the situation is to consider a market where there are 100 consumers who either buy one unit or none. The person with the highest reservation price is willing to pay a maximum of 99 euros; the next person is willing to pay max 98 euros, and so forth. We can then express demand as $p = 100 - Q$. Assume that the cost of serving each customer is 10 euros. If the monopolist was *not* able to price discriminate, it would set quantity to maximize profit with

$$\max_{Q}(100 - Q)Q - 10Q,$$

Illustration 12.1 Perfect price discrimination: Monopolist knows the buyer's valuation. TeBe Photography/Shutterstock.

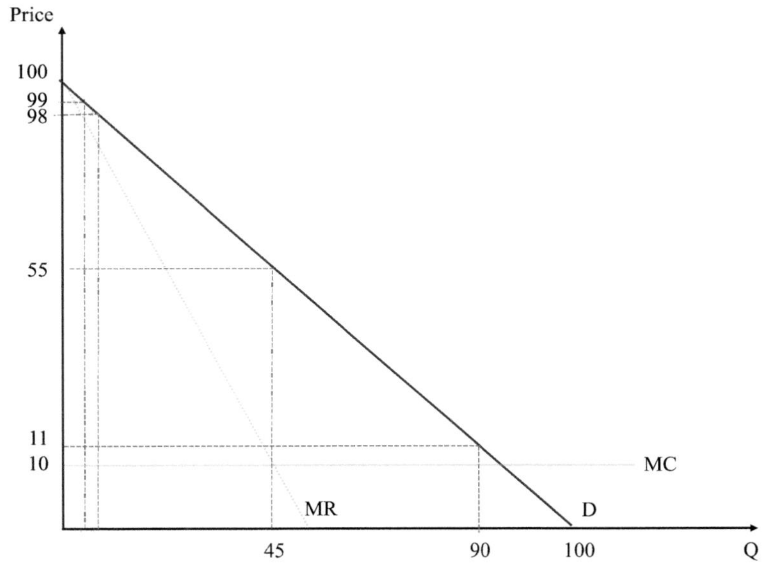

Figure 12.1 Perfect price discrimination – An illustration.

which yields a first-order condition for profit maximization

$$100 - 2Q - 10 = 0$$

that we can use to solve for profit-maximizing quantity $Q^* = 45$ and a price of $100 - 45 = 55$ euros. Inserting the profit-maximizing quantity into the profit function, we find the profit to be 2,025 euros under this policy. From the perspective of the monopolist, this solution leaves money on the table, however. A number of consumers are willing to pay more than 55 euros but get away with paying this lower price. The monopolist thus offers these consumers some surplus. There are also a number of consumers who have a maximum willingness to pay below 55 euros but above the cost of serving these customers (10 euros). Thus there is a deadweight loss.

Under perfect price discrimination, the monopolist knows the maximum willingness to pay for each consumer. In a common visual image, we say that the willingness to pay is stamped on the forehead of each consumer. The perfectly price discriminating monopolist will then charge 99 euros to the person willing to pay a maximum of 99 euros, 98 to the person willing to pay 98 euros, and so forth, all the way down to the person who is willing to pay 10 euros, which is the last person to which it can profitably sell. There will be no consumer surplus since it is all soaked up into profit by the monopolist. On a more positive note, there will be no deadweight loss either. Without price discrimination, it was not worth it to try to sell to the weaker consumers with a willingness to pay less than 55 euros since the firm would have had to lower the price for all consumers to do so. Instead, these consumers can now be charged a lower price without lowering the price for the ones willing to pay more. The simplest way to calculate profits in this situation is to simply see that profit corresponds to the area between the demand curve and the marginal cost curve up to the last unit sold. In this case, it will thus be equivalent to the triangle bounded by 100 (demand intercept) and 10 (marginal cost) on the vertical axis and 90 on the horizontal (given by 10 = 100 – Q) axis: $90 \times 90/2 = 4\,050$ euros. The profits of the monopolist thus increase sharply relative to the case where all consumers paid the same price, something we at times call uniform pricing.

It is clear that perfect price discrimination as construed here is an abstraction – we rarely see people paying their reservation price in a situation such as this.[4] Important flavors of this kind of pricing are nevertheless present in the real world. Pigou originally exemplified with a country doctor who knew all his patients and their economic circumstances well. He could charge a high price to the local baron and a low price to the coal miner's widow. For many goods and services sold online, sellers might have a very precise knowledge about the maximum willingness to pay, given that so many choices by individuals are observable. Auctions may also be a way of trying to get customers to pay a price close to their reservation wage (as we examine in detail in Chapter 18). That said, perfect price discrimination is rare, and our main reason for covering it in introductory microeconomics courses is that it starkly illustrates key points of price discrimination in a simple model: It is (i) profitable for a monopolist, (ii) can lower deadweight loss, and (iii) different customers are affected differently; some win and some lose relative to the case of a uniform price.

12.1.2 Different prices to different customer groups based on observable criteria

The next form of price discrimination that we cover is one where the firm knows that there are different consumer categories that are somehow identifiable, and in addition, there are systematic differences in demand across these different groups.[5] Discounts to students and retired people are two examples of this common form of price discrimination. This type of price discrimination is especially common on personal services such as travel, gym cards, and hair salons. Identification is straightforward with, for instance, a student ID, and there is little scope for the customer to resell the service – good luck with trying to resell a haircut. Another common application of this type of pricing is different prices in different countries – charging lower prices in poorer countries.

If markets can be segmented, this type of price discrimination entails setting the optimal price to each group according to the standard markup formula where markup is lower, the more elastic that demand for that group is such that the price to group i satisfies the following condition.

$$\frac{p_i - MC}{p_i} = -\frac{1}{E_i^D}$$

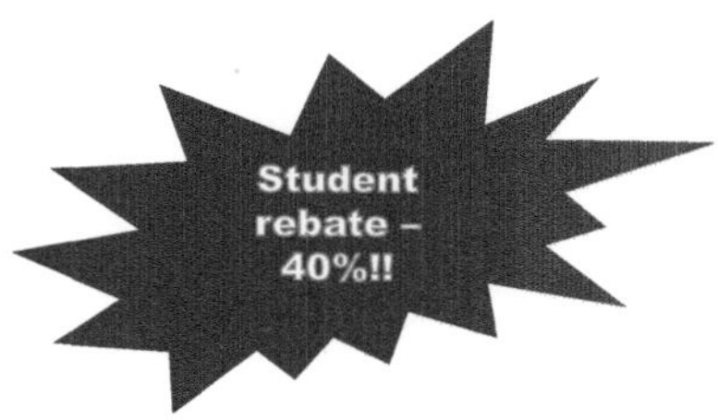

Illustration 12.2 Prices to different groups: Monopolist knows the group you belong to.

To explore this form of price discrimination in detail, it may be instructive with a numerical example. Consider a market where there are two groups: Lowies and Highies. For concreteness, we may think of Lowies as being students and Highies as nonstudents (and hence typically having higher incomes). For simplicity, we assume that the marginal cost is equal to zero to sell to both groups (we may, for instance, think of a service that is delivered digitally). Just to keep calculations as simple as possible, we also disregard fixed costs. First, we assume that the two groups can indeed be segmented such that the firm can set a lower price to Lowies without them being able to resell the service to a higher price to Highies. Assume that Lowies demand is given by

$$p_L = 1 - \frac{1}{2}Q_L.$$

Setting quantity to maximize profits to Lowies,[6] gives the first-order condition $1 - Q_L = 0$, and we get that $Q_L^* = 1$, which, inserted in the demand function, gives a price $p_L = 1/2$ and profit $\pi_L = 1/2$.

Assume that Highie demand is given by

$$p_H = 2 - Q_H,$$

Setting quantity to maximize profits to Highies gives the first-order condition $2 - 2Q_H = 0$, and we get that $Q_H^* = 1$, which inserted in the demand function gives a price $p_H = 1$ and profit $\pi_H = 1$. Figure 12.2 illustrates. Since marginal cost is equal to 0 in both cases, the profit maximization condition simplifies to setting quantity such that marginal revenue is equal to 0 for each group. As seen, Lowies are paying a lower price, reflecting their flatter inverse demand curve, which we associate with more price-sensitive demand.

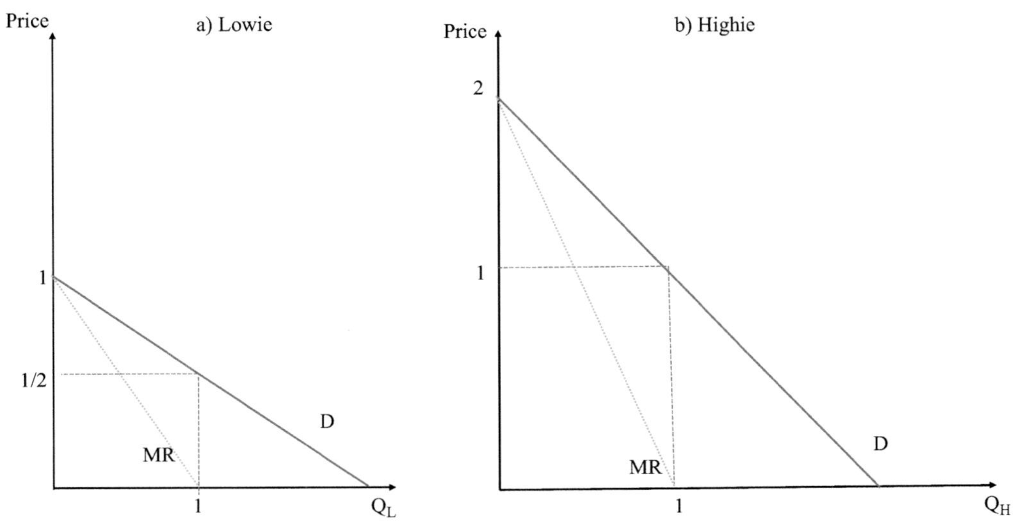

Figure 12.2 Price discrimination – Different prices to different groups. Video link for Figures 12.2 and 12.3: https://youtu.be/yaC6zOvZF9M.

A useful comparison can now be made to the case where the two markets cannot be segmented. The relevant profit-maximization problem then involves choosing the optimal quantity based on the combined demand from both groups, the aggregate demand curve. To find this, we first note from Figure 12.2 that if price is above 1; Lowie demand is zero, whereas for prices below 1, $Q = Q_L + Q_H$. Adding demand functions, as in Chapter 6, we want to combine the quantity demanded by each of the groups at a particular price and get that for $p \leq 1$, $Q = Q_L + Q_H = 2 - 2p + 2 - p = 4 - 3p$. Hence demand is given by

$$Q = \begin{cases} 2 - p & \text{if } p > 1\text{: Only Highies purchase} \\ 4 - 3p & \text{if } p \leq 1\text{: Both groups purchase.} \end{cases} \tag{12.1}$$

Figure 12.3 depicts the inverse demand curve for the aggregate market, where the part below a price of one is given by solving $Q = 4 - 3p$ for p to get $p = 4/3 - Q/3$. The profit-maximization problem when the two groups can't be segmented is given by

$$\max_{Q} \left(\frac{4}{3} - \frac{Q}{3}\right) Q,$$

with first-order condition

$$\frac{4}{3} - \frac{2}{3}Q = 0.$$

Again, since marginal cost is 0, the optimal quantity is determined by the point where marginal revenue intersects the horizontal axis.[7] Hence $Q^* = 2$, which, when used in the demand and the profit function, produces $p = 2/3$ and $\pi = 4/3$.

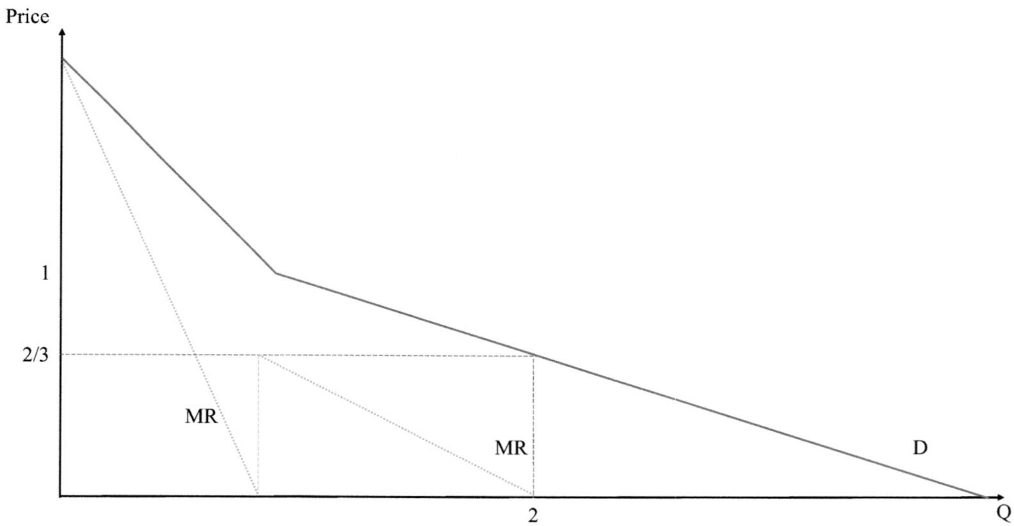

Figure 12.3 The case where the two consumer groups cannot be segmented. Video link for Figures 12.2 and 12.3: https://youtu.be/yaC6zOvZF9M.

There are several things to note in this example that hold generally for monopoly price discrimination with different prices to different groups.[8]

- The price under uniform pricing lies between the prices offered to the different groups under price discrimination – in this case, $1/2 < 2/3 < 1$. This is intuitive – the price when the firm can't separate the groups is a weighted average of the prices that the firm would optimally like to set to the different groups.
- Price discrimination raises consumer surplus for Lowies lowering whereas consumer surplus for Highies decreases. This is a simple consequence of price discrimination lowers price for Lowies and raising it for Highies.[9]
- Profit is higher when the monopolist can price discriminate. Intuitively, by having different optimal prices for different groups, the monopolist does better than if it is constrained to offer the same price to everyone.

Higher prices when markets are segmented imply that it may be valuable for firms to take additional measures to hinder the reselling from Lowies to Highies. In international settings, such reselling is sometimes known as parallel imports or gray markets. A large number of court cases in the European Union testify that firms often actively try to hinder such resale (blocking this is illegal within the European Union).

An additional point to note is that in some cases, the profit associated with only selling to Highies may be greater than the profit that would be achieved by setting a price that accommodates both groups. If the profit is higher when the monopolist only targets Highies is greater than the profit when it also accommodates Lowies the monopolist is liable to set a price high enough that the Lowies are excluded. Consider, for instance, the case from earlier but let demand from Lowies instead be given by $p = 1/2 - 1/2Q$. Following the same steps, the optimal quantity in the case when groups can't be segmented is then $Q = 3/2$, and profit would be given by $\pi = 3/4$. But this profit is lower than if the monopolist only sets price to accommodate Highies, which was 1. In cases such as this, price discrimination may have an additional benefit for the Lowies in that they get access to a good that they otherwise would not be able to purchase. Sales of pharmaceuticals in different countries is one area where such issues have been particularly prominent. Marginal costs are low and ability to pay may differ massively across rich and poor countries. If resale from poor to rich countries can be prevented, such that price discrimination is possible, this may have very large welfare effects in the poor country.

12.1.3 Price discrimination under self-selection constraints

In the final "major" form of price discrimination, the monopolist knows even less about the consumers and their willingness to pay. It knows that there are consumers with different willingness to pay out there, but it can't observe a given individual's willingness to pay or what group that a consumer belongs to.[10] Firms have found a large number of ways to price under such conditions that would increase profit for a monopolist – next, we examine a few particularly noteworthy examples.

12.1.3.1 Offering different versions of the good

One way for a firm to try to charge a high price from those with a high willingness to pay, even if it can't directly observe their type is to design different "versions" and let consumers

Illustration 12.3 What train ticket will you buy – first, second, or third class? *Arrival of the Normandy Train, Gare Saint-Lazare, 1877*, Claude Monet, Courtesy Art Institute Chicago. Public domain.

self-select among these versions. The most classic example is that of first and second class, first analyzed in the 1800s by Jules Dupuit.[11] He noted:

> It is not because of the few thousand francs which would have to be spent to put a roof over the third-class carriage or to upholster the third-class seats that some company or other has open carriages with wooden benches. ... What the company is trying to do is prevent the passengers who can pay the second-class fare from traveling third class; it hits the poor, not because it wants to hurt them, but to frighten the rich. ... And it is again for the same reason that the companies, having proved almost cruel to the third-class passengers and mean to the second-class ones, become lavish in dealing with first-class customers. Having refused the poor what is necessary, they give the rich what is superfluous.

To make the ideas somewhat more precise, assume again that there are two types: Highies and Lowies. The monopolist creates two different "versions," B_H and B_L, targeted to the respective customer group. These could be first (B_H) and second class (B_L), as in Dupuit's example, or different quality seats in a concert venue. Different timing of consumption is another example (e.g., different times of travel). Use of coupons to get a rebate is another one; consumers with a lower willingness to pay are likely to have a lower valuation of time and be more willing to invest time in administering coupons. Let the two different groups have utility functions U_H and U_L, respectively, and let the monopolist charge p_H and p_L, respectively, for the different versions. The goal of the monopolist is then to maximize profits subject to two constraints: first, it wants the Highies to select the version that is targeted to them.

$$U_H(B_H) - p_H \geq U_H(B_L) - p_L.$$

In words, the utility for a Highie of choosing first class and paying the first-class ticket must be at least as high as the utility of a Highie to choose the second-class ticket and pay the second-class ticket price. In choosing this, the monopolist can adjust both the qualities of the versions and the prices. We refer to this constraint as the **self-selection constraint** or **incentive compatibility constraint** (IC) – the monopolist wants the Highies to select the "right" version.

The second constraint is what we call the **participation constraint**, or **individual rationality constraint** (IR).[12] The monopolist wants to decrease the attractiveness of the Lowie bundle to steer away Highies from choosing it. But it can't make it too unattractive if it still wants to keep Lowies in the market. Thus the second constraint is given by

$$U_L(B_L) - p_L \geq 0.$$

A particularly stark example to understand the logic of price discrimination with versioning is that of "damaged goods" (Deneckere and McAfee (1996)). To take a simple example, consider the case of a software program targeted to do statistical analysis. Assume that it has been developed to deal with many estimation routines and virtually unlimited capacity of dealing with a large number of observations. This would be the B_H version that a monopolist would be aiming to sell to users with a need for sophisticated analysis. To these, it can charge a high price. Can it offer the program to users with a lower willingness to pay, even if it can't observe who's who? Yes it can, but it needs to make the version targeted to such users less attractive. Making it less attractive in this case would involve some cost in blocking out parts of the code to, for instance, make the program slower, able to deal with fewer estimation techniques or fewer variables. The monopolist would thus take an additional cost to sell a "damaged" version of its good. Can this increase profits? Yes, if it means that it can sell additional units without lowering price to the customers who have a high willingness to pay.

Price discrimination under self-selection constraints thus implies that we are not considering different prices for literally the same good as the most narrow definition of price discrimination would stipulate. Here the question of whether we see a case of price discrimination or just a case of different goods being priced differently is partly in the eye of the beholder and boils down to the following: Does an analysis based on price discrimination offer important insights into the problem at hand or not? In the cases discussed earlier, it arguably does.

12.1.3.2 Bundling

Bundling refers to the practice of selling several products together as part of a package. **Pure bundling** is the case where a set of products are *only* offered as a bundle – as in the case of a package resort where you can only purchase an all-inclusive option that includes both food and lodging or a Netflix subscription where you get access to all content for a fee rather than

Table 12.2 Willingness to pay for dinner and a room for different types of customers: Negative correlation between types

	Dinner	*Room*	*Bundle (dinner+hotel room)*
Gourmets	100	50	150
Snoozers	80	70	150

renting or purchasing movies individually. One may ask, Why not let everyone pay just for the series and movies that they want to watch rather than pay a single price and get access to the full set of series and movies? Knowledge that there are different, unobservable types provides a profit-maximizing explanation in some cases.[13] To see what drives this result, consider the following example of a hotel.

The hotel foresees two types of customers, Gourmets and Snoozers, in about equal numbers. It knows that these types exist but can't observe if a given person is a Gourmet or a Snoozer. The willingness to pay for dinner and a hotel room for each of these types are given by Table 12.2. The hotel can sell a bundle, where both dinner and a hotel room are included for one price, or it can sell dinner and room separately such that a person, for instance, can choose to buy a hotel room but not buy dinner.

To see what is profit maximizing, we see that one group has the highest willingness to pay for one good (Gourmets for dinner), whereas the other group has the highest willingness to pay for the other good (Snoozers for hotel rooms.) For simplicity, assume that there is one of each type of customer. Selling the goods separately, then, generates revenue of $2 \times 80 = 160$ from dinners (which is more than the alternative of charging 100 and only selling to Gourmets) and of $2 \times 50 = 100$ from hotel rooms (since $2 \times 50 > 70$). Note that a profit-maximizing firm would not set a price lower than the minimum willingness to pay for a particular good. If the hotel sets prices of goods separately, it thus has revenue of $160 + 100 = 260$ euros. In contrast, if it only sells package deals, it has revenue of $2 \times 150 = 300$ euros. Since costs are the same across the two ways of selling, profits are higher under bundling. The reason why bundling yields higher profits is that the two consumer groups differ in their ranking of the goods in terms of willingness to pay – we say that there is a *negative correlation* of willingness to pay across the consumer types: A relatively high willingness to pay for a good for one type is associated with a low willingness to pay for the other type. If goods are sold separately, the price is constrained by the group with a lower willingness to pay; Snoozers would hurt profits from dinners, and Gourmets would hurt profits from hotel rooms. By bundling, this effect is avoided.

The negative correlation is important in driving the previous result. In Table 12.3, we've changed the ranking for rooms (and relabeled the types since in this case one type has the highest willingness to pay for both goods, we label this type High and the other Low). Applying the same logic as earlier, we see that profits are the same under bundling and when goods are sold separately if valuations are as in Table 12.3: Profits in the bundled case is $2 \times 120 = 240$ euros and profits when goods are sold separately are $2 \times 80 + 2 \times 40 = 240$ euros. The Low type's valuation is the binding constraint on prices in both these pricing schemes. In the case where it is not profitable to sell to all types, however, profits under separate prices are higher than under bundling if willingness to pay is positively correlated. If the willingness to pay for a room, for instance, was equal to 90 for the high types in Table 12.3, then the hotel would increase profits by not bundling and setting price for rooms equal

Table 12.3 Willingness to pay for dinner and room for different types of customers: Positive correlation between types

	Dinner	*Room*	*Bundle (dinner+hotel room)*
High	100	50	150
Low	80	40	120

to 90. Its profit under separate prices would then be $90 + 2 \times 80 = 250$ euros but only $2 \times 120 = 240$ in the case of bundling.

Many goods are also sold under what is known as **mixed bundling**: The case where a consumer can choose to purchase a bundle but can also purchase the goods separately. A value meal at a fast-food restaurant is a bundle that, for instance, offers one price for the combination of burger, fries, and a soda, but a customer can also choose to purchase any of these separately. Examinations of whether mixed bundling is profitable or not follow the same logic as the comparisons noted earlier and determine profits under the different hypothetical prices whilst being mindful of how consumers with a lower willingness to pay constrain prices that the monopolist can charge those with a higher willingness to pay. Mixed bundling may, for instance, allow the sale to additional customers who have a high valuation for just one of the products. To exemplify, let's again consider Table 12.2 but now assume that there are 10 Gourmets and 10 Snoozers and one additional customer, Lucullus, with a valuation of the dinner of 120 euros and 0 for the hotel room. Offering the bundle at 150 euros plus the dinner separately at a price of 120 – mixed bundling – now yields profits of 3,120 ($10 \times 150 + 10 \times 150 + 120$).

12.1.3.3 Two-part tariffs

The analysis of pricing in most of the book concerns the situation where there is a price per unit, such as a price per kilo of apples or a price for a meal at a restaurant. However, many services and some goods are sold via a combination of a fixed and variable fee: a practice known as **two-part tariff**. For instance, a subscription for mobile communication may entail a monthly subscription fee and then a variable fee per megabyte of communication. An amusement park may use an entrance fee and then an additional payment per ride. We also analyze goods where there is only a fixed fee, and the variable price is zero using the same tools – a gym card, an all-you-can-eat buffet at a restaurant, a monthly pass for public transport weekly or a week pass at a ski resort are examples of such pricing. When there are different consumer types, combinations of fixed fees and variable fees can be used to maximize profits, making use of self-selection constraints and participation constraints, as in the case of different versions. Such an analysis is outside the scope of an introductory course in microeconomics but uses similar tools, as we've examined so far. We can also think of two-part tariffs as price discrimination in another, simpler, way: The price that you pay per unit is not the same across units. Important insights into two-part tariffs can be gotten even in the simplest case where all consumers are of the same type, and this is our focus in the following.

Consider an old-style subscription model for minutes of talk on a telephone. The demand for a representative individual is given by $p = 10 - Q$, where Q is hours talked. This reflects that some calls have a higher valuation (as in "Hi, Dad. I'm alive") than others, where you're just idling time away together with a friend. The phone company has a constant

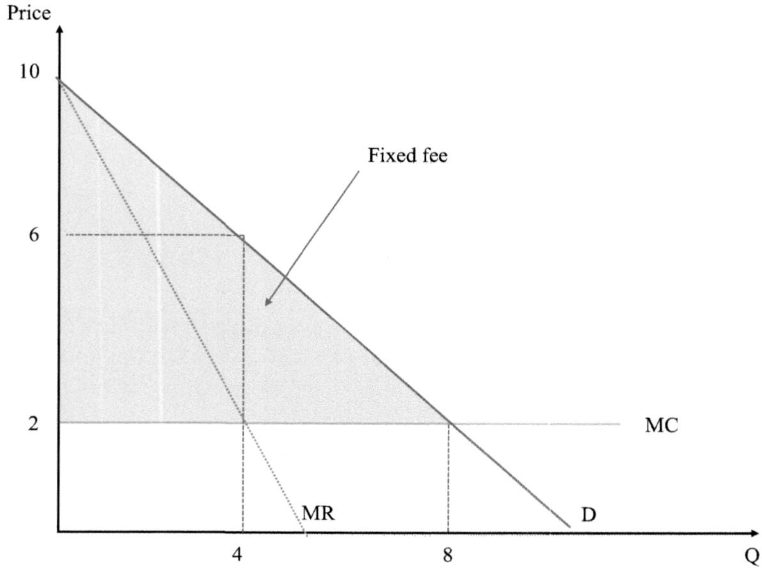

Figure 12.4 Two-part tariff. Video link for Figures 12.4 and 12.5: https://youtu.be/lSy_HUeAHN4.

marginal cost of 2 euros per hour. Figure 12.4 illustrates the setup. If the phone company were to set a regular monopoly price per hour, it would set quantity where marginal revenue equals marginal cost, 4 hours, and a price of 6 euros per hour. Profit in this case would be $(6-2) \times 4 = 16$ euros. There are two sources of "lost profit," in this case for the monopolist. First, the first few hours of talk are valued at more than the price 6; the consumer gets a positive consumer surplus from these. There is also a deadweight loss from only 4 hours of talk, even if willingness to pay is above marginal cost up to 8 hours of talk. Is there some way for the monopolist to convert these areas into profit? Yes, two-part tariffs offer such an alternative.

Consider the following two-part tariff: Offer a price per unit equal to 2 euros, the same as the marginal cost. Since $p = MC$, this is the efficient quantity, following the arguments in Chapter 7. Consumer surplus from one consumer in this case is equal to $(10 - 2) \times 8/2 = 32$ euros. What then is the highest fixed fee that the monopolist could charge if it charges $p = 2$ per unit? Clearly, the monopolist can charge up to 32 euros in fixed fee. As it makes 0 profit on the per-unit price (since $p = MC$ for all units), this is also the profit, 32 euros – much greater than the regular monopoly profit of 16 euros. The monopolist here succeeds in capturing both the consumer surplus from the first units where there is a very high willingness to pay and to monetize the deadweight loss.

As noted, a perhaps even more common form of pricing is that where there is only a fixed fee, such as for a gym card or a monthly card for public transport. Let us again use the same demand and cost curves to illustrate in Figure 12.5. If price per time that you go to the gym is 0, the consumer surplus is $10 \times 10/2 = 50$ euros, and this is the maximum fixed fee that can be charged. However, to calculate profit, costs have to be deducted from this,

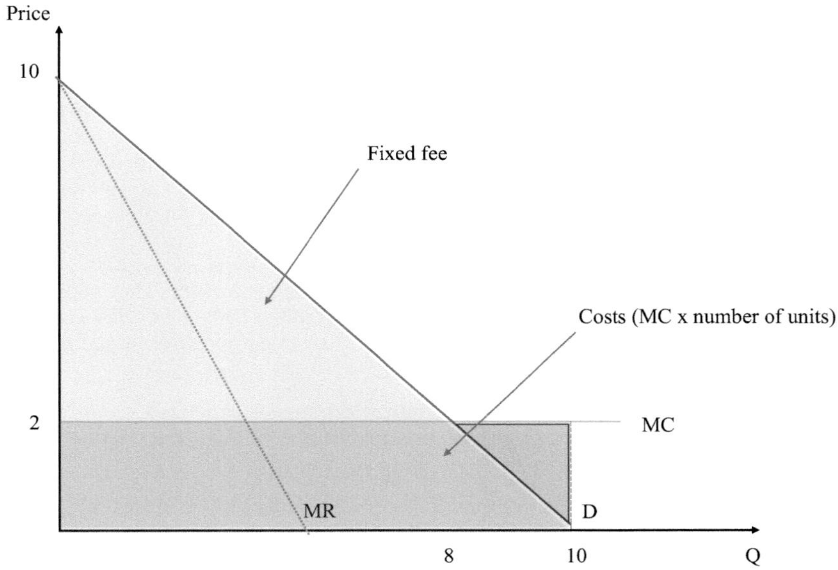

Figure 12.5 Two-part tariff. Video link for Figures 12.4 and 12.5: https://youtu.be/lSy_HUeAHN4.

and in the case of constant marginal costs, the total cost is 20 euros: 2 (marginal cost) × 10 (number of gym visits when per visit price is 0). Profit from the representative consumer is thus 50 − 20 = 30 euros. This is slightly lower than the optimal two-part tariff, but on the other hand, the case where there is only a fixed fee may in real applications be valuable because of its simplicity; this may save on staffing costs, and simplicity may be attractive to consumers. We also see why the case with a fixed fee and no additional price per unit is often seen in cases where there are low marginal costs: gym visits, ski lifts, public transport, or internet use.[14]

12.1.3.4 Freemium

Many goods and services sold digitally follow what is known as a freemium pricing strategy: The product is free to download and use, but additional features can be purchased. Spotify, for instance, comes in a free advertising-funded version, but for a monthly fee, the user can have a access to a premium version that has no advertising and includes valuable features, such as the ability to listen offline or save playlists. Dropbox offers a free version with limited storage, but to have additional storage and capabilities, you need to pay. The word freemium is a combination of free and premium. Many games and mobile apps also feature this way of pricing. Again, it is a form of price discrimination.[15] Users with a high valuation pay and thereby directly generate revenue from sales, and those that only consume the free service can still add value to the firm by generating advertising revenue, and in many cases, the value of a service is greater the more that are using it – a concept that we term network effects that we return to in Chapters 13 and 18.

Notes

1 A statement that logic carries over from monopoly to various oligopoly markets clearly must come with a number of provisos and exceptions, see, for instance, Corts (1998) for a particularly elegant demonstration of some conditions under which results from monopoly can be overturned when there are two firms that compete. Such issues are typically left for more advanced courses, however.
2 Again, some provisos may be in order – for instance, concert tickets are frequently sold under price discrimination and sometimes resale is possible. This is enough of a puzzle to give rise to a separate literature, however, see, e.g., Connolly and Krueger (2006) for an introduction to some of the issues.
3 This form is also known as first-degree price discrimination.
4 Even if it were observed, a monopolist would also be well advised to study some behavioral economics – the ultimatum game that we discussed in Chapter 5 shows that people are willing to say no to transactions that in principle would give them utility if they perceive a split too unfair.
5 This form of price discrimination is also known as third-degree price discrimination.
6 As familiar by now, we set quantity Q_L to maximize $\left(1 - \frac{1}{2}Q_L\right) Q_L$.
7 Clearly, if marginal costs were positive, profit maximization would instead, as usual, require that marginal revenue equals marginal cost. For instance, if the profit-maximization problem were instead given by $\max_Q \left(\frac{4}{3} - \frac{Q}{3}\right) Q - \frac{1}{3}Q$ first-order the first order condition would be $\frac{4}{3} - \frac{2}{3}Q - \frac{1}{3} = 0$.
8 This form of price discrimination is common also in markets that are not monopolies, such as gyms and transport markets. The results below do not always generalize to markets where there is competition – for instance, if one firm's high price market is another firm's low price market, price discrimination can lead to stronger competition and lower profits overall, see Corts (1998).
9 One may be curious whether aggregate consumer surplus increases or not as a result of price discrimination. Here there are no general results, and depending on functional forms (e.g., whether the demand curve is linear or has some other form), it can increase or decrease. This is explored in Varian (1985).
10 Nowadays, this is also referred to as second-degree *price discrimination*. In Pigous's original classification, which predated many of the tools that economists now use to deal with these kinds of situations, second-degree price discrimination only referred to quantity rebates, lower prices when you buy several units such as when a six pack of beers is cheaper than buying six cans individually.
11 The quotation is from Ekelund Jr (1970).
12 We here introduce IC and IR constraints in a particular setting, but they are a pervasive tool of analysis when we consider design of pricing and other mechanisms when people's types are not directly observable. Such more general study, of what is known as mechanism design, is left for more advanced studies and was the topic of the 2007 Nobel Prize in Economics, https://www.nobelprize.org/uploads/2018/06/advanced-economicsciences2007.pdf.
13 There may be additional explanations based on costs – a bicycle, for instance, is made up of many different parts that you in principle could buy separately – only a true aficionado would be willing to spend the time and have the knowledge to do that, however, and most of us are happy to just buy the ready product that we can think of as a bundle.
14 In addition, these are cases where resale is difficult – having consumers pay a fixed fee and then wander off with all the shirts that they want in a given month is not a great business idea.
15 See, e.g., Enache et al. (2023) for a simple model and empirical analysis.

Part V

Market failures

Externalities and asymmetric information

In the first part of the book, we showed how markets allocated resources when prices were sending the right signals about costs and demand. The following two chapters examine market failures where that is not the case. In Chapter 13, we examine externalities, when all the relevant costs and benefits are not reflected in prices. In Chapter 14, the reason why prices are not right is that asymmetries in the information that different agents have distort prices and markets. In both chapters, we are interested not only in understanding why markets run into problems in the face of these features but also how policies can work to improve the outcomes.

DOI: 10.4324/9781003623854-17

13 Externalities

Illustration 13.1 The great stink. *Mist on the Thames*, 1903, Joseph Pennell, Art Institute of Chicago (detail from). Public domain.

13.1 Externalities

Many actions taken by individuals and firms affect others, even if such side effects don't directly feature in benefits or the costs of the decision-maker. We term such effects on third parties **externalities**. The name stems from that which is external to the decision-maker – not part of the decision problem. The effects on others can be negative or positive. Environmental pollution is a key example of **negative externalities**, where the effect on third parties is negative. Most countries have a set of regulations meant to limit pollution, but to fix ideas, think of a factory in the early 1800s when regulation was minimal and, for instance, the River Thames flowing through London had more resemblance to an open sewer of industrial and human waste than to a river. A factory owner, acting as a profit maximizer in the manner examined in previous chapters, would maximize the difference between revenue and costs of production. But a number of costs associated with pollution would affect others rather than the factory owner. These costs can take on many aspects. Pollution would create health problems among local residents – some of these health effects might entail

DOI: 10.4324/9781003623854-18

direct costs, such as lost income because of sick days or cost of medical treatments. Other negative health effects may manifest themselves as a lower quality of life as we are sick or troubled by asthma. External effects can also affect other businesses negatively – with fishermen or local tourist companies losing incomes. External effects can in addition affect property values – a house next to a river known for the Great Stink as the Thames in the 1850s will be worth less than if it were next to a pristine river.[1]

Negative externalities related to pollution can come from production, as in the case of a factory, but can also come from consumption, as in the case of emissions from cars. As anyone who has lived in Mexico City, New Delhi, or Shanghai knows, these cases of pollution are not only a thing of the past. Externalities can be local in nature, such as when your neighbor is burning garden waste or when they get started with an afterparty at 2 am, keeping you awake. Externalities can also be global, as in emissions that contribute to climate change.

There are also cases of **positive externalities**, where positive side effects on others do not enter fully into the decision-maker's maximization problem. My university being located where it is means that local businesses benefit from a lot of students raising demand for local services. This was not something considered by the university when it decided where to start operations. **Network externalitites** are another example of positive externalities, capturing cases where the more people use a particular good or service, the greater is the benefit for an additional user. For instance, if I'm choosing to work with a particular statistical program, more people will be able to make direct use of my code and I help increase the market for others providing code. The more of my friends who use a particular social media app for communicating, the greater is the value of that social media app for me. Education is often seen as a positive externality as well – there are some private benefits to education, but there are commonly perceived to be additional benefits to society, as a more educated society can function better in many ways. Similarly, if I get vaccinated, there is a private benefit, but I also help limit contagion, a positive externality.

If a decision-maker does not take account of all the costs, too much will be produced in the case of negative externalities, whereas too little will be produced in the case of positive externalities. Let us expand on this statement in the following.

13.1.1 *Too much is produced when there is strong competition and negative externalities*

Consider the market for paper and assume that paper mills are price takers. Assume that demand for paper is given by $p = 100 - Q^D$ and supply, given by the marginal cost curves of firms is given by $p = 10 + Q^S$. This marginal cost curve reflects the **private costs**, the type of costs that we have examined so far in the book: costs for labor, capital, and various inputs needed in production. In addition, there are external costs, as exemplified in the previous section. Costs that harm consumers and firms exposed to the pollution. Assume that the **marginal external cost**[2] equals Q.

First, consider the quantity and prices in the market if firms do not take account of the external effect in their production decisions. We term this the "private solution," highlighting that only the producers' own costs, their **private costs**, are taken account of. Equating supply and demand thus implies solving $100 - Q = 10 + Q$ and a quantity of $Q_{private} = 45$ and an associated price of $p = 100 - 45 = 55$ euros, as illustrated in Figure 13.1.

The figure also shows the marginal external costs of pollution – these are the costs that affect the rest of society. They are low at very low levels of production, but as more is produced, the additional costs imposed on the rest of society keep increasing. The marginal

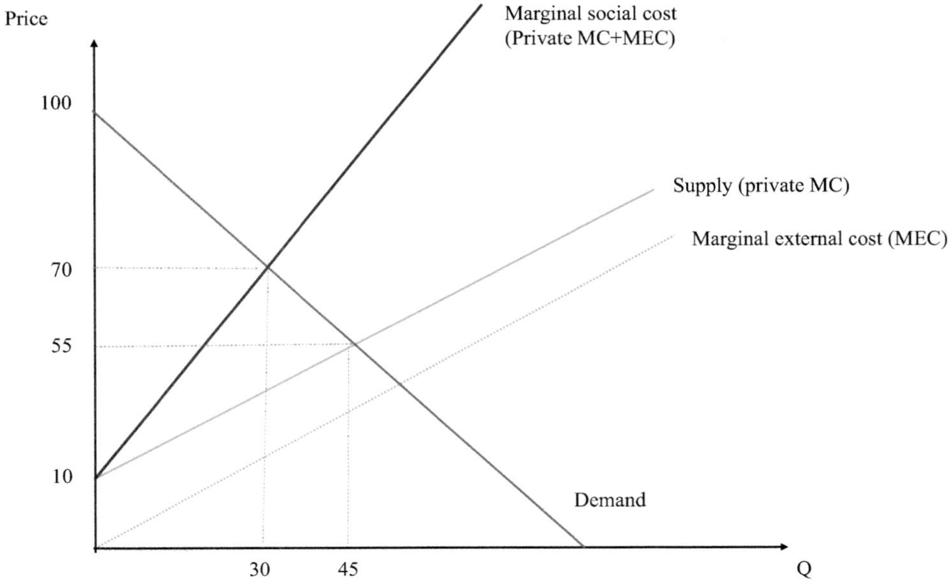

Figure 13.1 Overproduction in the case of negative externalities: Quantities and prices. Video link for figures 13.1–13.4: https://youtu.be/apDS8R9RCjc.

social cost, the total marginal cost to society, is given by the sum of the private and external marginal costs: 10 + Q + Q. If the marginal social cost is taken account of, we would thus again equate demand with a supply based on marginal cost, but this time, the full marginal cost that is relevant to society and solve $100 - Q = 10 + 2Q$ with $Q_{opt} = 30$ and an associated price of $p = 100 - 30 = 70$ euros.

The example illustrates that with a negative externality, the private solution implies that too much is produced. We want producers to take account of the full costs, also including the externality; in other words, we want them to **internalize** the externality. Think of it as incorporating the external costs into the internal costs that a producer takes account of.

There are several important observations associated with a comparison of the social optimum with the private solution. A first point to note is that quantity of paper is lower, and the price is higher in the social optimum. This lowers the consumer surplus, as seen in Figure 13.2.

Next, to understand the effects on producers, and on the costs associated with the negative externality, it is useful to consider a simple extension to producer surplus: the **societal producer surplus**. Remember from Chapter 7 that producer surplus measures the area between price and marginal cost curve. The societal producer surplus does the same but takes account of the full social marginal costs, rather than just the private marginal cost, as illustrated in Figure 13.3. For low levels of production, price is greater than the social marginal cost and production on balance makes a contribution to society, despite the fact that there are negative externalities associated with production. At quantities above 22.5 (given by $10 + 2Q = 55$), however, the marginal cost to society is greater than the price (55), and each additional unit produced lowers the societal producer surplus. To some extent,

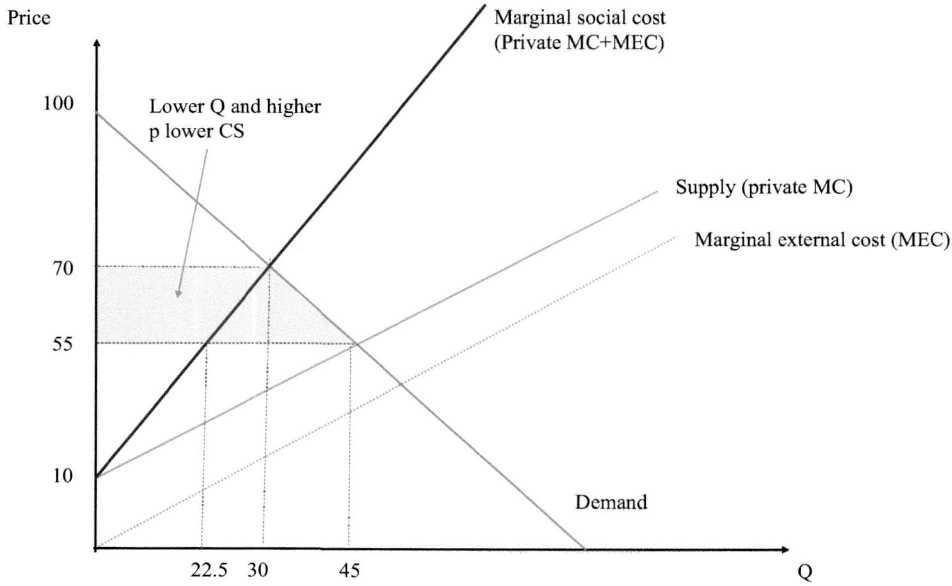

Figure 13.2 Overproduction in the case of negative externalities: The effect on consumer surplus. Video link for figures 13.1–13.4: https://youtu.be/apDS8R9RCjc.

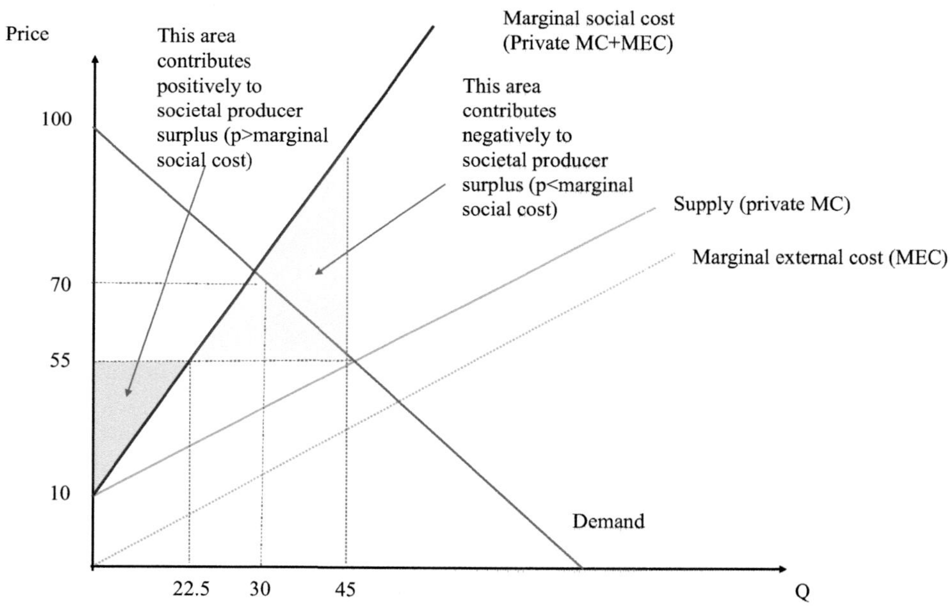

Figure 13.3 Overproduction in the case of negative externalities: The effect on societal producer surplus. Video link for figures 13.1–13.4: https://youtu.be/apDS8R9RCjc.

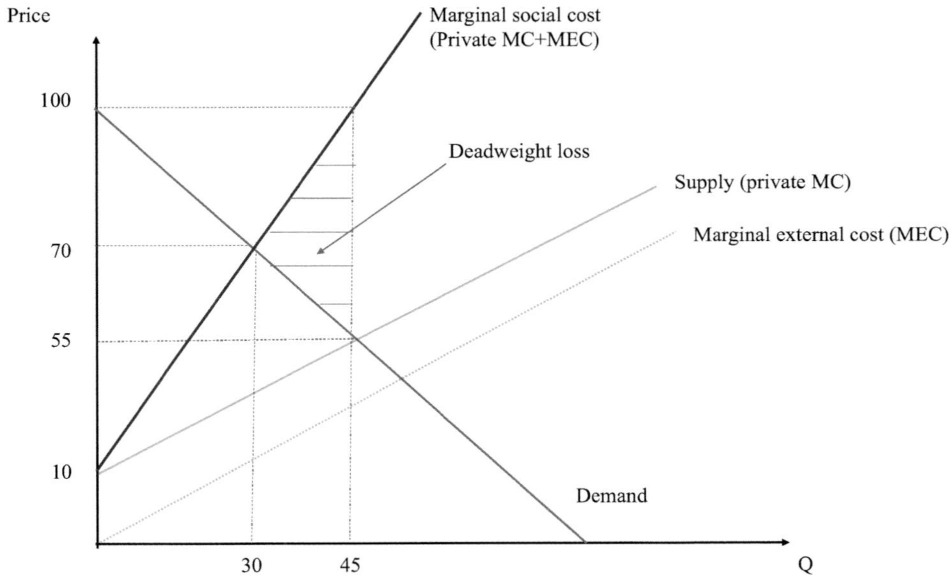

Figure 13.4 Overproduction in the case of negative externalities: The deadweight loss. Video link for figures 13.1–13.4: https://youtu.be/apDS8R9RCjc.

this loss is balanced by the higher consumer surplus, as seen by a comparison of Figures 13.2 and 13.3.

Part of the loss in societal producer surplus is not counteracted by a higher consumer surplus, however, and this appears as a deadweight loss, as illustrated in Figure 13.4. These are units where the increase in costs is greater than the valuation of additional units of paper. At Q = 40, for instance, consumers' valuation of additional units of paper is 60 euros (given by 100 − 40), whereas the increase in costs to society is 90 euros (given by 10 + 2 × 40). The loss is greater than the gain, and these additional units create a loss relative to the efficient situation. As in other cases, the deadweight loss can also be calculated explicitly. Using values from Figure 13.4, the value associated with the area is given by $(100 - 55) \times (45 - 30)/2 = 337.5$ euros.

If there is a positive externality, the case is the opposite; too little is produced in a competitive market, as producers don't reap the full rewards of their efforts. Provision of education is often given as an example of a service that is associated with positive externalities – more education is associated with many aspects of what we believe makes a modern society work well, and public policy aimed at promoting education (free and compulsory primary schools, support for university education in the form of publicly funded universities) is commonplace. We use Figure 13.5 to illustrate. Competitive supply is given by the supply curve and demand by the private demand curve. We can think of this demand curve as summarizing the private marginal benefit. A positive externality can be thought of as something that yields additional benefits at the societal level, and we capture that by the marginal external benefit curve labeled MEB. Marginal social benefit is given by the sum of the private demand, and the external effect as depicted by the MSB curve. Social optimum occurs when the full benefits are incorporated into decision-making with quantity

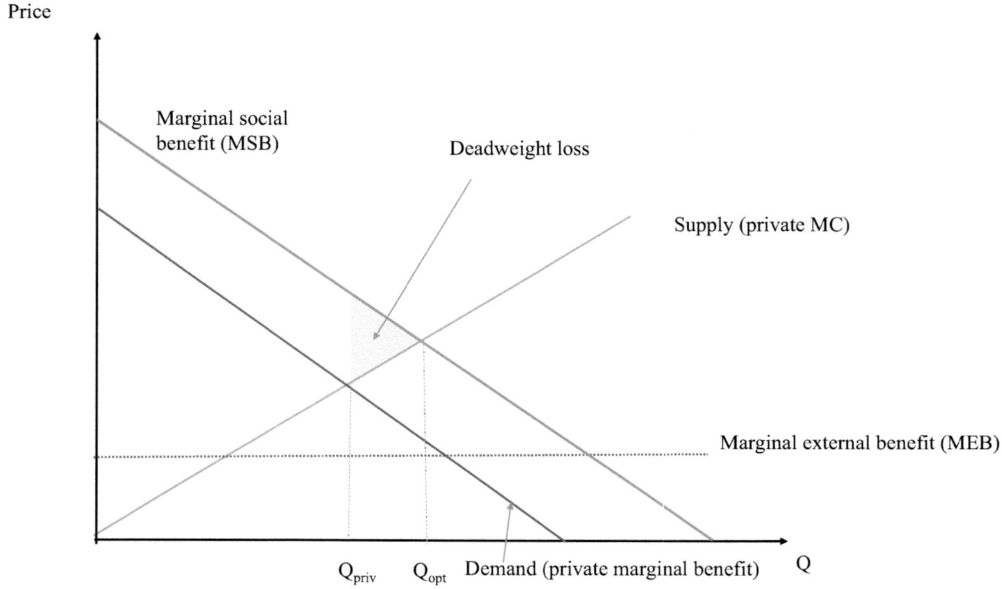

Figure 13.5 Underproduction in the case of positive externalities. Video link for figure 13.5: https://youtu.be/heg_Enxo6K0.

Q_{opt} rather than Q_{priv}. There is a deadweight loss associated with the competitive situation – additional education is valued higher for society than its cost in the private solution, but because the external effect is not internalized, these gains are forgone. In the following, we examine how policy can deal with the issue that too much or too little is produced in markets when externalities are not sufficiently taken account of. That focuses on negative externalities, partly for ease of exposition and partly because some of the problems, such as pollution, are so pervasive. It is also the case that many positive externalities are linked to what we term "public goods," a topic that we examine later in this chapter.

13.1.2 *Public policy to deal with externalities*

Thus, when there is strong competition and a negative externality, too much is produced. The next question is clearly what can be done about it? How can we limit the negative consequences of pollution? As we explain in detail next, a range of different policy options can be used. A first important issue to point out, however, is that it is not the production of paper per se that is the problem – the problem is the negative externality, and this is key to what we want to limit. Sometimes it may be practically difficult to directly target the externalities, and then a limit on the production of the good in question (paper in this case) may be motivated, but otherwise, we want to target the problems at their source.

Thus, we turn to another type of diagram, Figure 13.6, where we examine emissions directly. The marginal external costs are as before but are now measured as a function of the amount of pollution, rather than as a function of the amount of goods produced. The marginal cost of limiting pollution is the private cost to producers of taking actions so as to limit pollution. This may, for instance, involve installing filters, collecting hazardous waste,

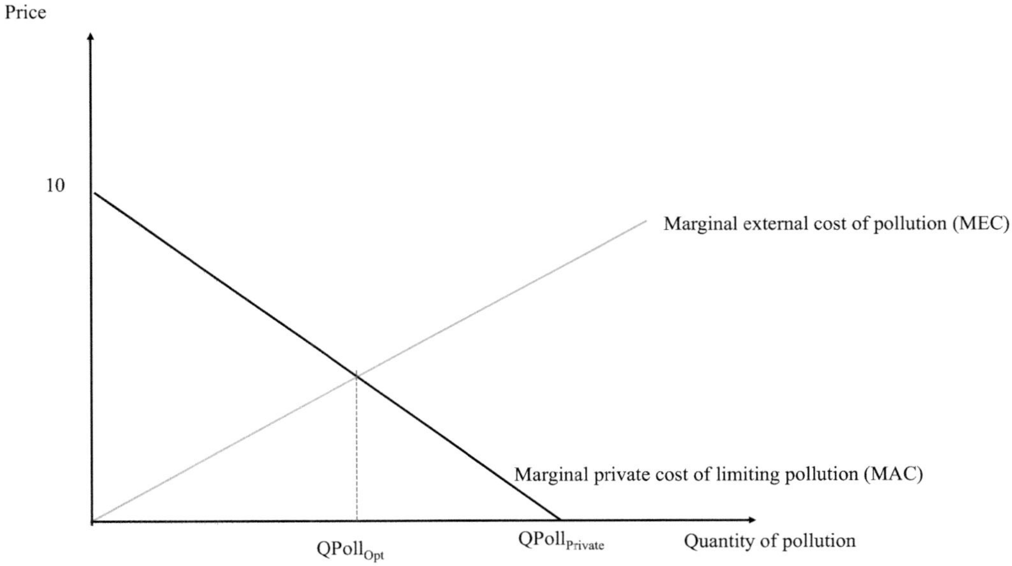

Figure 13.6 Private and external costs of pollution. Video link for Figures 13.6 and 13.7: https://youtu.be/Vn4YQk6wYlI.

or using processes that involve less toxic inputs. The curves in Figure 13.6 have slopes that we believe characterize many situations. The marginal external costs of pollution are low at very low levels of pollution but then increase – many pollutants need to be present in sufficient quantities before serious adverse effects on nature and others appear.

We take as given that a social planner wants to maximize welfare and in doing so takes two effects into account when deciding on how much pollution to allow: the private savings from not limiting pollution and the external costs of pollution.[3]

The private solution in Figure 13.6 is $QPoll_{Priv}$, and the social optimum is $QPoll_{Opt}$ – given at the point where the marginal cost of limiting pollution equals the marginal external cost. For concreteness, assume that the marginal cost of limiting pollution, which we term marginal abatement cost (MAC) is given by $MAC = 10 - QPoll$, and the external marginal cost is given by $MEC = QPoll$. The two curves intersect when $10 - QPoll = QPoll$, and hence the regulated solution is for 5 units of pollution to be emitted. How can this solution be achieved?

A first way to steer producers to the regulated solution is to use a tax. Such a tax, which aims at making agents internalize an externality, is often referred to as **Pigouvian tax**, named after Cambridge economist Arthur Pigou, who in the early 1900s made fundamental contributions to our understanding of externalities and other aspects of welfare economics.[4] At the socially optimal quantity of 5 units, the marginal cost of lowering pollution is equal to $MAC = 10 - 5 = 5$ euros. We set the Pigouvan tax equal to 5 then, which is the marginal external cost at the social optimum and also equal to the marginal cost of lowering pollution.[5] To see its effect, put yourself in the shoes of a producer and start at the privately optimal quantity. Since the MAC is given by $10 - QPoll$, the marginal cost of limiting pollution by one unit from this starting point is only 1 euro (moving from a cost of 0 to a cost of $(10-9) = 1$ euro).[6] It is thus cheaper to limit pollution

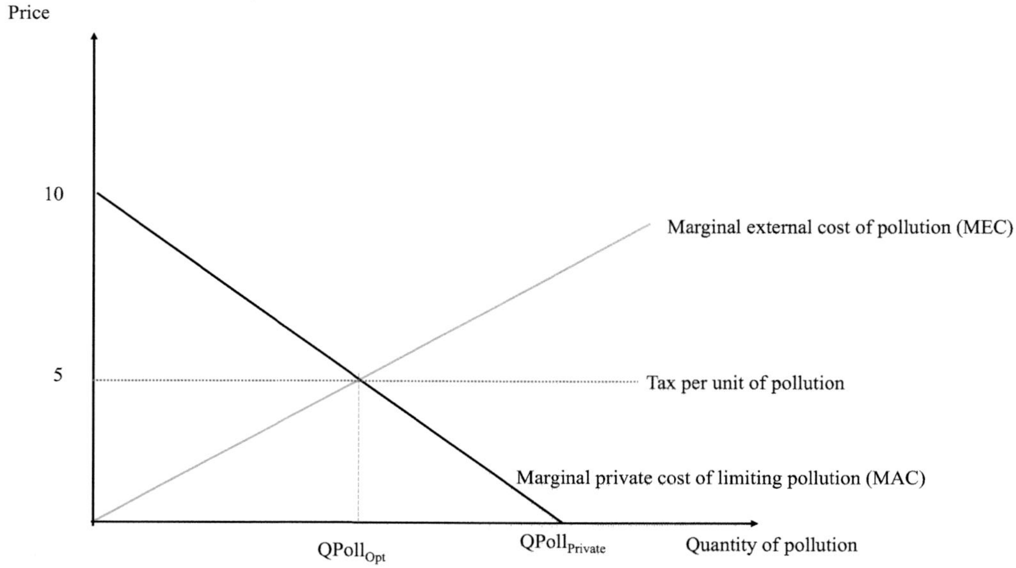

Figure 13.7 A pollution tax as a way to limit emissions. Video link for Figures 13.6 and 13.7: https://youtu.be/Vn4YQk6wYII.

by one unit rather than pay the tax of 5 euros for emitting this unit. Indeed, as long as it is cheaper to limit pollution than to pay the tax, we expect firms to do so – this leads to predicted emissions of 5 units. Clearly, for even lower emissions than 5 units, the firms would find it cheaper to simply pay the tax than to try to further limit emissions.

Another possible policy response is to impose a **quantity control**. In this case, the social planner would simply say that at most 5 units of pollution may be emitted.

Both taxes and quantity controls are common in practice. In the early 1990s, Sweden, for instance, introduced a unit tax that applies per ton of fossil carbon dioxide emitted. This is an example of a Pigouvian tax directly linked to emissions (as in Figure 13.7). Other Pigouvian taxes are linked to quantities of a good that in turn is linked to negative externalities – unit taxes on gasoline, nitrogen fertilizer used in farming, and cigarettes are all examples of this.[7]

Quantity restrictions on emissions are also commonly used. In the example we used, the social planner simply set the maximum total level of emissions. Other quantity-based tools include regulations as to which type of equipment that can be used and how much of various emissions, for instance, a car produces.[8]

Taxes and quantity controls each have their strengths and weaknesses as ways of regulating emissions. A benefit of taxes is that they provide tax revenue, something that quantity controls in the baseline case do not. Taxes may also be easier to implement, in particular when there are many users. For instance, a gasoline tax is easier to implement than a regulation focusing on how much a given car can emit in a year. Benefits of quantity restrictions is that they typically give more control of total emissions – something that is especially important if the marginal external costs are sharply increasing (something emphasized in an influential analysis by Weitzman (1974)).

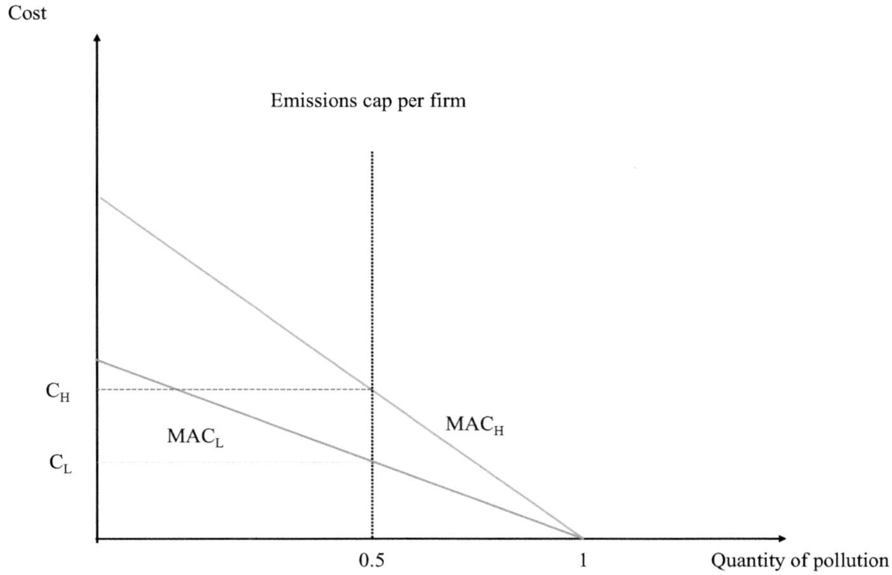

Figure 13.8 Firm-level emission quota with differences in marginal costs of abatement. Video link for Figures 13.8 and 13.9: https://youtu.be/ZFA9QXH0XRM.

One complication of a quantity restriction imposed on a market is that the social planner needs to decide how to allocate emission rights across different producers. Consider again the case represented in Figure 13.7. A Pigouvian tax at 5 euros applies to all producers and in this way is simple to implement. But say that there are 10 producers: How should a total emissions cap of 5 units of pollution be split up among firms? A simple way would be to just split them equally among the 10 firms, with a pollution allowance of 0.5 per firm. We have illustrated the situation for 2 firms in Figure 13.8, where we also assume that the two firms differ in their marginal abatement cost. Firm *H* has a relatively high cost of limiting pollution, and firm *L's* cost is lower. If they each are allowed to emit a maximum of 0.5 units, firm *H*'s marginal cost of limiting pollution is higher than firm *L*'s at this point. Society is clearly not minimizing the cost of limiting a given amount of pollution, as it is cheaper for *L* to limit pollution than for *H* to do so.

Since *L* can limit emissions at a lower cost than *H*, there are gains from trade here. If *H* could buy rights to pollute from *L*, they could both gain from the transaction, as illustrated in Figure 13.9. Society can achieve a given level of emissions reduction at a lower cost if firms are allowed to trade.

That the right to pollute should be something that is traded can be seen as highly cynical, but as explained, there are potentially substantial efficiency gains. Tradeable emission permits also offer flexibility in other ways. To explain some of the benefits, consider a highly stylized example. Think of a situation where taxis had a limit of 10,000 kilometers that they could drive per year. Suppose that there is a large positive demand shock in one area and a large negative demand shock in another area. For taxis in the high demand area, the quantity restriction would bind, and they would be standing idle while some customers would find themselves without a taxi. For taxis in the low demand area, they might as well be cruising around for customers, having little incentive to limit driving. If they instead could

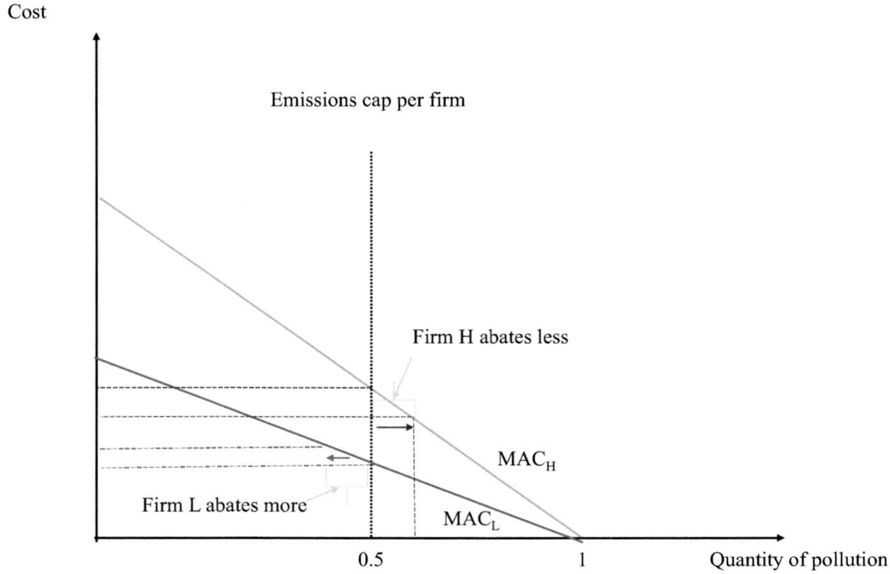

Figure 13.9 Tradeable emission permits. Video link for Figures 13.8 and 13.9: https://youtu.be/ZFA9QXH0XRM.

sell the right to drive to taxis in the high demand area, we could increase efficiency. A further advantage of tradeable emission permits relative to a fixed quota is that they give additional incentives for investment in more efficient technology – someone who saves emissions is able to gain from selling the right to the unused emission rights and so get revenue from them. The arguments for tradeable emissions permits have been sufficiently convincing so that, for instance, the European Union has a market for tradeable emission permits for CO_2.[9]

Before ending this discussion, let us also note that there are additional ways of limiting negative externalities that are sometimes used. We know that a monopoly has weaker incentives to expand quantity, and in some jurisdictions, alcohol is sold via government monopolies, with this as a motivation. Subsidies to clean technology (e.g., a subsidy for installing solar panels or insulating houses) are other options. As in many cases in microeconomics, whole books, courses, or indeed large government agencies and international cooperative efforts are devoted to what we cover in one chapter. The mechanisms outlined earlier nevertheless contain the key elements needed to be conversant in this area.

13.1.3 Property rights and bargaining as a solution to externalities

At a deep level, one might ponder, Why aren't the external effects incorporated into decision-making without the use of quotas, taxes, and so forth? Why aren't firms and individuals able to work out a solution by themselves? Nobel laureate Ronald Coase did indeed think deeply about this, and in the following, we explain his conceptual framework. In Coase's (1960), *The Problem of Social Cost*, he examines a number of court cases with the theory of externalities as a starting point. He notes that many of the court cases are of a reciprocal nature – of the type that a dentist has a claim against a factory owner because the factory's noise hurts the dentist's business. But the factory owner in turn notes

Illustration 13.2 White water kayaking in a forest. Pexels, Tom Kilpatrick. Public domain.

that he was there first, and if the dentist hadn't moved his practice next to his factory, the problem wouldn't have occurred. Simply put, one can argue that the factory exerts a negative externality on the dentist, and the dentist exerts a negative externality on the factory owner.

Let us take a prominent Swedish court case as an example to explain Coase's analysis in more depth.[10] A simplified summary runs as follows: A company organized white water rafting in rapids that were on land (and water...) owned by someone else. The landowner argued that there were substantial negative externalities associated with the rafting: The rafting hurt fishing and hunting, and many of the rafters would hike back up on land, which in turn hurt forestry. The rafting company, on the other hand, argued that because of Sweden's "all man's right" – essentially guaranteeing everyone's access to nature irrespective of who owns the land – the business could not be banned.

Coase's answer to this kind of situation, in what is sometimes referred to as the **Coase theorem**,[11] is that if property rights are well-defined and there are no bargaining costs (costs of negotiating and writing binding contracts), then the efficient solution will be realized. This may appear puzzling, but we'll take the argument step by step. First, a key insight is that if the landowner also owned the white water company, there would be no externality. Since he would own both the land (with its associated income from forestry, hunting, and farming) and the white water company (with its associated income from rentals), he would naturally internalize the effect of the one on the other. But if the landowner and the white water company are separate, why are they not able to bargain and come to an agreement? Assuming that the profits from white water rafting more than well made up for the negative effects on the landowner, there are clearly gains from trade.

Let us discuss the role of property rights and transaction costs in turn and apply them to the Swedish court case. First, in this case, the property rights were unclear. **Property rights** are rights that come with ownership and that allow the owner to decide what she does with the property: use it, earn income from it, or sell it. Here, the legal situation was unclear because of the all man's right. That right assures access for individual's enjoyment of nature but not for commercial activities on others' land. The rentals to private persons, but clearly benefiting from access to the rapids, thus had an unclear legal status.

Assume that the payoffs are as described in Table 13.1. The white water rafting company can totally abstain from renting boats and then have a payoff of 0. They can rent an amount $Q_{Moderate}$ and have a payoff of 10 or rent many at Q_{High} and get a payoff of 14. Renting affects the landowner negatively with his payoffs being 12, 10, and 2, respectively. The white water company looks to its own costs when renting, and it is clear that the table illustrates a negative externality. If property rights are not well-defined, as indeed they were not prior to the court case, the white water company would maximize its profit by going for Q_{High}, and the payoffs would then be 14 and 2, respectively. The last column gives the social surplus; in this simple case, it is simply the sum of the two payoffs, and we see that $Q_{Moderate}$ maximizes social surplus. As noted earlier, a negative externality that is not internalized leads to excessive production. It also exemplifies that there are gains from the activity that carries a negative externality; simply banning white water rafting is not efficient in this situation.

Now *assume that the landowner has the property right over the water*. He can of course ban the white water company from business and thus get a payoff of 12. However, we see in Table 13.1 that the social surplus is the highest at $Q_{Moderate}$ – the size of the pie is greatest here, and this is what a profit-maximizing joint owner of both businesses would choose. Now that the landowner has the property right (and under conditions that it is cheap to bargain), he can, for instance, offer to allow the white water company to run $Q_{Moderate}$ if it pays 9 to the landowner and Q_{High} if it pays 14 to the landowner. The size of the pie is greatest with $Q_{Moderate}$, and with the property right, the landowner can steer the bargaining toward this and extract enough of the surplus to make it attractive, as illustrated in Table 13.2.

Table 13.1 Coasian example: Payoffs when no bargaining

Quantity of rentals	*Payoff white water co.*	*Payoff landowner*	*Social surplus*
None	0	12	12
$Q_{Moderate}$	10	10	20
Q_{High}	14	2	16

Table 13.2 Coasian example: Example of payoffs when landowner has property right

Quantity of rentals	*Payoff white water co.*	*Payoff landowner*
None	0	12
$Q_{Moderate}$	1 (10–9)	19 (10+9)
Q_{High}	0 (14–14)	16 (2+14)

Table 13.3 Coasian example: Example of payoffs when the white water company has property rights

Quantity of rentals	*Payoff white water co.*	*Payoff landowner*
None	0	12
$Q_{Moderate}$	17 (10+7)	3 (10−7)
Q_{High}	14	2

Next, let's look at the case where the *white water company has the property right*. It can earn 14 by choosing Q_{High}, as we see in Table 13.1. But again, the size of the pie is greatest at $Q_{Moderate}$. The white water company can, for instance, offer a deal to the landowner where it says if the landowner pays 7, the company will limit itself to $Q_{Moderate}$, as illustrated in Table 13.3. If they do not agree, the landowner would get 2 since the white water company then chooses Q_{High}. With the deal, the landowner thus does better than otherwise, and again, we reach the social optimum. In this simple example, the key to efficiency is thus that someone has the property right – for social efficiency, it doesn't matter which of the parties has the property right. It does clearly matter for the income distribution; however, it is valuable to control an asset.

As noted earlier, clear assignment of property rights is one element of the Coase theorem, another is costless bargaining. In practice, **bargaining costs** can take many forms:[12] one is the actual costs of time and involving legal experts to actually formulate a contract. In cases where one side consists of many agents, there are also important difficulties in coordinating action between these. Factory emissions that hurt many would, for instance, require that all those hurt were able to coordinate – something that is inherently difficult, as we discuss below. Say that a factory's emissions hurt a thousand people. If they are to bargain with the factory, they need to agree on a lot of things, in particular how to divide gains or costs. Emotions and views on what is fair, as discussed in Chapter 5, can also affect bargaining, and the social norms in many societies would characterize several Coasian deals as strange if not downright offensive. A simple case of a negative externality would be that burning leaves in your garden, which affects neighbors negatively. In Sweden, the property rights in this dimension differ across municipalities, but assume that I live in a municipality where I have the right to do this (so that property rights are well assigned).[13] If I ask my neighbor for money in return for me abstaining from burning leaves in my garden, he'd most likely think me deranged.

One possible interpretation of the Coase theorem is that if property rights are well assigned, the bargaining takes care of many externalities, and we do not need to rely on states to use taxes, quotas, and so forth. For many externalities, the evidence does not support such a stance, but a Coasian-style analysis is useful in clarifying the nature of the problem at hand, nevertheless. The discussion of bargaining costs also lead us to believe that the theorem is a better guide in some cases than in others: When there are few parties and externalities are positive, we are more likely to see private solutions to externalities. For instance, a common example of a positive externality is that of a beekeeper next to an orchard, where bees pollinate the trees. But this simple-enough case generates plenty of deals where orchards pay beekeepers to locate close by (see, e.g., Johnson (1973)).

Another possible interpretation of the Coase theorem is that bargaining costs are high, and this, incidentally, is the position often advocated by Coase himself.[14] Note that one may think of governments as solving some of the problems associated with bargaining costs.[15]

13.2 Different types of goods

The goods that we have discussed so far in the book are what we call **private goods.** They are the kind of goods and services that we would naturally think of when we purchase something: an apple, a shirt, a haircut, a meal at a restaurant. But what about listening to the radio – isn't it special that a lot of other people can listen to the same show at the same time? Is it like we're all wearing the same shirt? And what about a good like national defense? How does that fit in?

In the following, we see how we can get a lot of insights from distinguishing whether goods are what we call rival or not and whether they are excludable or not. Goods are **rival** in consumption if one person's consumption means that another person cannot consume that same good. If I eat an apple, you can't eat the same apple. If I wear a shirt at a certain time, you can't wear that same shirt at the same time. The opposite, when goods are **nonrival**, describes goods where my consumption doesn't hinder you from consuming the same good. We can both listen to the same radio broadcast at the same time, and we can both be protected by the same national defense.

A good is **excludable** if people can be excluded from consumption. If I own the apple, I can say no to others taking it instead. A good is **nonexcludable** if people cannot be barred from consumption. A lighthouse that warns against a shallow reef will warn everyone; no one can be excluded from seeing a lighthouse perched on top of a cliff. The characterization implies that we can identify different types of goods, resulting from the different combinations of characteristics, as described in Table 13.4.[16] Underlying the different economic effects are externalities – costs and benefits of different actions not being fully internalized.

In the lower right-hand corner, we have what we term **public goods**. Goods that are nonrival in consumption and nonexcludable. National defense is the perhaps most prominent example. It is nonrival in consumption – just because I'm included in the set of people defended by a national defense doesn't mean that you are defended less. It is also nonexcludable. It is hard to think of a case where the national defense defends the whole country and its citizens against invasion except for person X. The whole judicial system

Table 13.4 Different types of goods

	Excludable	*Nonexcludable* *Nonrival*
Rival in consumption	Private goods	Common resource
Non-rival in consumption	Club goods	Public good

with police and courts are also often thought of as a public good. Eradication of malaria in an area is a public good. A lighthouse is a particularly straightforward example – it is nonexcludable, as discussed earlier, and it is also nonrival; you being warned of a reef from a flashing light doesn't hinder me from being warned from the same reef.

In the lower left-hand corner, we place **club goods** that are nonrival in consumption but excludable.[17] Broadcast media that are protected by login details are a clear example – that you watch a football game on some streaming platform doesn't affect anyone else's opportunity to watch the same game, so the streaming is nonrival. Streaming services can require a log-in and payment, however, so they are excludable. Another example comes from the name "club" – a member club that is not full is nonrival, but club managers can exclude people who do not pay. Concerts, spectator sports events, a golf club, a toll road, or public transport are other examples of club goods. As long as they are not congested, they are nonrival. Here we can also point out that someone who provides a good that is excludable can choose to make it available at no charge – a bridge can, for instance, be provided for free, but it would also be straightforward to set up a toll booth (as opposed to the case for a public good like defense, a lighthouse, or a malaria-free environment where it is very hard to see how they can be made excludable).

The final category is a *common resource*. These are rival in consumption but non-excludable. Many natural resources, such as ocean fishing, are of this type. Applications also concern situations where free access generates congestion, such as with traffic in large cities. Again, whether a good is excludable or not partly depends on choices made by society.

Let us discuss the different goods in turn – see in what sense they constitute market failures and how various policies can ameliorate problems.[18]

13.2.1 Common resource

Common resources are goods that are rival in consumption and nonexcludable. Note that we here bundle together two different, but related, situations with respect to non-excludability. One is where a limited set of agents repeatedly interact regarding a common resource. A fruit basket by the company coffee machine with free fruit, three firms drilling oil from the same oil well, or a set of fishers surrounding a small lake are some examples of this type. In all of these cases, a limited set of agents interact. Common resource problems are sometimes referred to as **tragedy of the commons** – remember that a "commons" in old times was an area commonly owned by a village where villagers, for instance, could let their livestock graze. A slightly different case concerns a good that really is nonexcludable in a broader sense, such as fishing in the world's oceans or people taking the car and adding to congestion in large cities. The first setting often entails some form of repeated interaction and a different set of possible solutions than the case where access is open to anyone. The latter case is sometimes referred to as open access resources, and in terms of nonexcludability, it is thus broader.

Many situations will also contain elements of both of the aforementioned types. For instance, many readers are likely to have seen images or videos of people waiting to get up to the summit of Everest.[19] Access is limited in the sense that a limited set of permits are sold, but on a clear day, more people want to summit than what is practical, and long lines appear with people literally dying in line. Most people only attempt the summit once, and there is limited scope for long-term cooperation to appear.

The key underlying mechanism creating difficulties of common resources is that there is a negative externality – when someone uses the common resource, they lower the payoff for

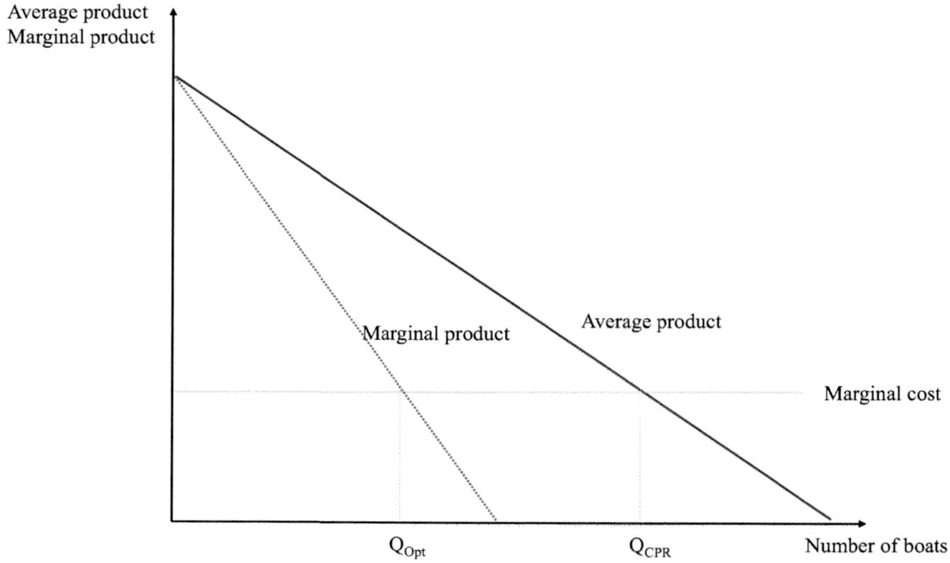

Figure 13.10 Overuse of a common resource.

other users. Figure 13.10 exemplifies the case of fishing in a lake where there are a number of fishermen around the lake. First, consider the case where they maximize surplus jointly (or alternatively think of it as the case where one fisherman has the property rights). Let $F(b)$ denote the amount of fish caught, which depends on the number of boats b used to catch fish and the cost of running a boat, c. The maximization problem is then

$$\max_{b} F(b) - cb$$

with associated first-order condition

$$\underbrace{\frac{dF(b)}{db}}_{\text{Marginal Product}} = c.$$

We illustrate the solution that maximizes the surplus with Q_{Opt} in Figure 13.10.

In contrast, if it is a common property that is nonexcludable, there is effectively free entry. As long as the surplus from adding an additional boat is non-negative, additional fishers will be attracted. Thus, there will additional fishing as long as

$$F(b) - cb \geq 0.$$

At the point where the equality holds with equality, we thus have

$$\underbrace{\frac{F(b)}{b}}_{\text{Average Product}} = c.$$

There will be entry until the average product is equal to the cost, and we denote this with Q_{CPR} in Figure 13.10. Thus, from the perspective of the people around the lake, there will be overuse. A single owner, or a village acting jointly, has an incentive to limit outtake.[20] For the common resource without cooperation, the logic is instead, "If I don't take it, someone else will." How can we then work with policy to achieve better outcomes? As in any case involving externalities, we want agents to internalize them, to take the full social costs and benefits into account when making decisions. The kind of solutions that we analyzed earlier are then again relevant; let us exemplify.

- *Quantity restrictions*. Fishing quotas are a prominent example. Within national jurisdictions there can be quotas for how much each fishing boat can land of different types of catch. Other restrictions limit the time of year that there may be hunting or fishing. American national parks and wilderness areas issue a limited number of so-called backcountry permits that allow users to backpack and hike outside the main areas with the intent to keep down environmental impact of excessive use. Another case of crowding relates to anything that relies on sending information via air – mobile networks or radio stations. If transmission is on frequencies too close, they interfere with each other, and typical policy is again to issue a limited set of permits.
- *Raising costs* Another way of dealing with overuse relies on raising the cost of using the common resource. Congestion charges on car traffic are a clear example. If I were to take my car to the office in the morning, a number of aspects affect that decision, but the fact that I'd be contributing to congestion is not one of them – I would incur a negative externality on others. A congestion charge, which raises my cost, is one way to try to get me to internalize this cost. As an aside, we might also note that there are other ways to raise the cost besides fees or taxes – restrictions on the type of tools allowed to be used in hunting and fishing are examples of this.
- *Property rights* The Coase theorem indicated that property rights had a key role in understanding externalities. In practice, the bargaining costs are too high, in many cases involving externalities for Coasean bargaining to solve the issues. In terms of natural resources, it may nevertheless be a way to solve the problems due to nonexcludability. A simple example may provide some intuition. Assume that demand for some rare mushroom that grows wild in the forest increases sharply.[21] We would be fearful of overuse and, in the end, depletion of the mushroom in parts of the land. If, on the other hand, demand for corn increased sharply, we would not worry about the extinction of corn – we would just expect farmers to increase corn production. For "whatsoever a man soweth, that shall he also reap," as the saying has it when property rights are well-defined – sow and someone else shall reap is the case for a common resource.

  Finally, note that it is not just a matter of formal property rights; they also need to be upheld in practice. Illegal logging of tropical forests on public land or rogue gold miners on tribal lands in today's South America or the United States in the 1800s are two prominent examples.
- *Local rules and social norms* In a case where there is a limited set of users who interact, various customs and social norms can work to limit overuse. Much of our understanding of the way that local communities can sustainably manage common resources stems from Nobel laureate Elinor Ostrom. Based on detailed empirical studies, she and her coauthors established a number of design principles that support sustainable use of a common property resource.[22] Importantly, however, as noted earlier, these can be seen as applying more to a group of people who jointly manage a common resource rather

Illustration 13.3 Buffalo hunt. *After the Chase*, North Montana Range, Laton Alton Huffman. Getty Museum Collection, public domain.

than the free-for-all that would come in a situation where literally there is no possibility to exclude. For instance, the design principles proposed by Ostrom include clear boundaries between legitimate users and nonusers, as well as a set of sanctions against people who break the rules.

Let us end this section by noting that overuse of common resources in nature not only risks overuse in the current period but also critically hurts the future stock. In particular, in the oceans, we can see the history of whaling and much of fishing in general as examples of how nonexcludability can very rapidly run a species into extinction or close to it. A local community may have created norms and institutions that allow for its sustainable use, but when there is literally open access, there may be massive overuse. As a striking example of this, Taylor (2011) documents how the American buffalo was hunted to near extinction. By the mid 1800s, it is estimated that some 15 million buffalo lived in the United States. By 1880, it is estimated that only about 100 buffalo remained. Taylor (2011) finds support that the combination of new techniques that allowed buffalo hides to be used in industrial-scale tanning in Europe, a lack of price response to the large increase in export of hides from the United States, and, for our purposes, nonexcludability set the stage for the near-extinction in just a few decades with much of the impact happening during the 1870s. This serves as a reminder of how the combination of a valuable resource and virtually open access can be devastating.

13.2.2 Public goods

Illustration 13.4 The Lighthouse. *The Lighthouse at Honfleur*, Georges Seurat, Metropolitan Museum of Art, public domain.

The key mechanism behind our interest in common resources is negative externalities – for our next focus, public goods, it is instead positive externalities that are at the core. Since public goods are nonexcludable and nonrivalrous in consumption, agents have the opportunity to consume irrespective of whether they have contributed or not – something that gives rise to a **free-rider problem**. The opportunity to gain the benefits without contributing creates a temptation to free ride on the efforts of others.

Let us first examine how much of the public good would be efficient to produce. As noted, national defense is a key example, which highlights that important applications concern a very large number of individuals. However, as is often the case, it is easier to understand the concepts in a simpler setting, and we commence with a public good demanded by two apple growers, H and L. Their small orchards are right next to each other but far from everyone else, and apple theft is a concern. To stave off thieves, they can hire a guard service that patrols the orchards. We assume that guards in one of the orchards deters apple thieves in both orchards (nonexcludable) and that the guard services are not diminished by the guard watching 2 rather than just 1 orchard (nonrivalrous). Let h be the number of hours that guards patrol the area. Assume that the willingness to pay for guard services, the marginal benefit of an extra hour, is $p_L = 10 - h$ for L and $p_H = 20 - h$ for H. We illustrate the situation in Figure 13.11.

Consider 1 hour of guarding, L's willingness to pay for this is 9 euros, and H's willingness to pay for this is 19 euros. Since this is a public good, they are effectively consuming the same amount. The relevant question is therefore how much they together are willing to pay for one hour. In this case, $9 + 19 = 28$ euros. To find their total valuation for different number of guard hours, we simply sum their valuations, taking care to note that L's valuation crosses the horizontal axis at 10 hours (since p = 10 – h). Only H is willing to pay for additional guard hours above 10. Below 10 hours, however, their combined willingness to pay is given by $10 - h + 20 - h = 30 - 2h$. Thus the combined willingness to pay from these two individuals is

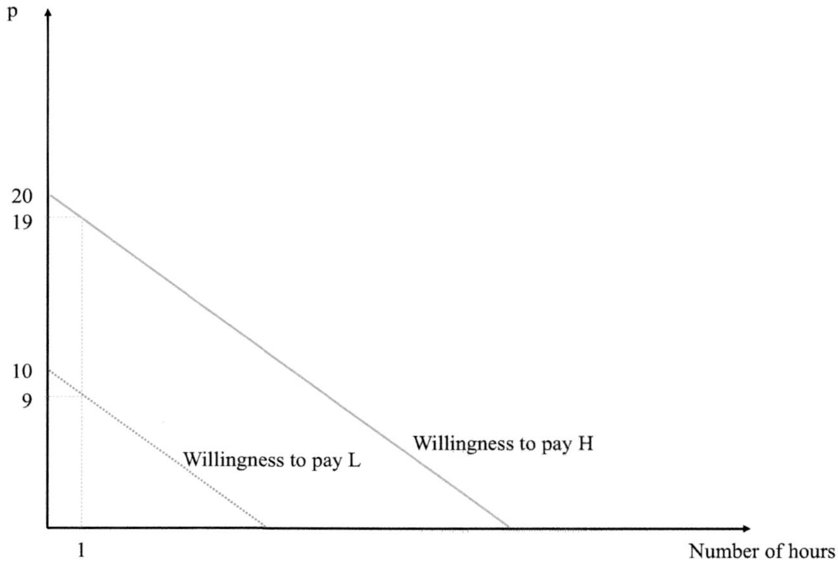

Figure 13.11 Willingness to pay for a public good. Video link for Figures 13.11 and 13.12: https://youtu.be/Z5wVGcMrykY.

$$p(h) = \begin{cases} 20 - h & \text{if } h > 10 \text{ and } h \leq 20 \\ 30 - 2h & \text{if } h \leq 10. \end{cases} \tag{13.1}$$

Figure 13.12 illustrates and also considers two alternative levels of hourly price for guard services. First, we see the combined willingness to pay given by the kinked curve. We can think of this as the aggregate demand curve, and as usual, for an optimal outcome, we want demand to equal supply. Consider first a price per hour of 26 euros. The optimal solution is then to hire a guard for 2 hours (solving for the h in 30 – 2h = 26). Next, consider a lower price of guard services, alternative (b) in the figure where p = 14. In this case, the efficient solution is 8 hours of guard services (solving for h in 30 – 2h = 14).

It is important to note that it is not straightforward to get each of the agents to reveal their willingness to pay. Consider the case where p = 14, for instance. They are effectively consuming the same amount, and L gets access to guard services even if she doesn't pay anything. If she doesn't pay, she will get 6 hours instead of 8 hours but gets to enjoy the benefits of consuming the good even if she doesn't pay; that is, she can act as a *free rider*. There are two concerns with this – one is the situation illustrated with the price of 14 – the good is provided but at an inefficiently low level. If H pays, she effectively provides a positive externality for L. The other concern is the one illustrated by p = 26; the good may not be provided at all if not all agents truthfully reveal their willingness to pay.

Another important application of public goods is new knowledge and ideas. Recipes, ideas, and innovations are often nonrival. My making a Tiramisu dessert following a recipe does not hinder anyone else from making their dessert following the same recipe.[23] Me using the Pythagorean theorem to complete a proof does not hinder anyone else from using the same theorem. Many innovations and much of research and development have this

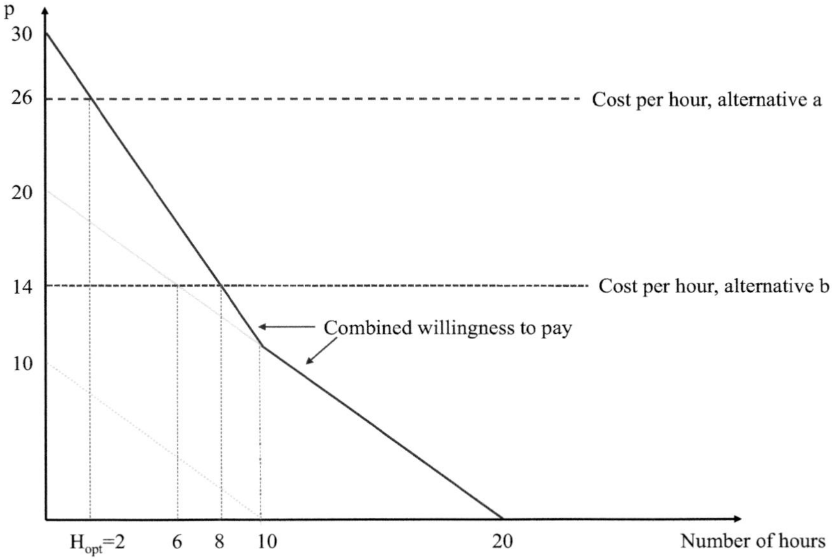

Figure 13.12 (In-)efficiency of outcomes in demand for a public good. Video link for Figures 13.11 and 13.12: https://youtu.be/Z5wVGcMrykY.

nonrival flavor. The fact that many can make use of innovations suggests that the social benefits of many innovations are much greater than their private benefits to the inventor, indicating a positive externality and that innovations are underprovided. A lot of research in economics tries to understand the driving forces behind research and development and how new products shape economic growth – the research of Nobel laureate Paul Romer was key in generating a deeper understanding of these relations.[24] If the innovation is excludable, then the innovation in practice becomes a club good; otherwise, it will be a pure public good.

Again, let us end with an overview of some of the ways that public good provision can be solved, essentially drawing on the same kind of mechanisms as noted earlier.

- *Taxation* As noted, key examples of public goods were defense and other goods typically provided by the state. Typically, taxes finance such expenses – since the payment of taxes is mandatory, this solves the free-rider problem.
- *Quantity mechanisms*. Another way to provide a public good is to have mandatory requirements of delivery. A mandatory military service is one example. Rwanda's nationwide process of Umuganda is another example – on the last Saturday of every month, everyone between 18 and 65 is required to engage in mandatory community work.
- *Local rules and social norms* In cases where a small number of individuals interact over time, cooperation may be sustained and public goods provided, much in the same way we discussed in relation to common resources.

13.2.3 Club goods

In line with most microeconomic textbooks at this introductory level, we will only cover club goods briefly. The main reason for doing so is that they are excludable. This implies that a

Illustration 13.5 An example of a club good as discussed in the text. *Pexels*, Sami Aksu. Public domain.

provider of them can restrict provision to those who pay and overuse (common resources) or underprovision (free riding) are much easier to deal with. In this sense, the inefficiencies and issues raised are much closer to the analysis that we pursue in the rest of the book. One of the key issues with club goods is instead that since the good is nonrival, the marginal cost of an additional user is likely to be close to zero. With price above marginal cost, there would be an inefficiency because of this. An illuminating example is that of a largely empty toll-financed highway running parallel to a congested smaller toll-free road.

Notes

1 Various ways to attach monetary values to the external costs exist, but covering them in detail would bring us to far afield. Also note that we have taken a very human-centered approach to externalities. In principle, one can also try to quantify effects on nature per se. An early prominent example of this regarded the effects on Alaskan sea life, for instance, sea otters, after an oil tanker leak (Exxon Valdez in 1989), see for instance Carson (2012). Similarly, many externalities regarding the environment have long-term consequences and an important set of questions regard how we should factor in future generations into decisions.

2 As with supply, this is the marginal cost, total external cost are in this example equal to $C(Q)_{ext} = \frac{Q^2}{2}$ with $\frac{dC(Q)_{ext}}{dQ} = Q$.

3 This goal is not self-evident, and you might ask, Why should the social planner take account of the private cost of limiting pollution? Exactly where the trade-off should be drawn is a value judgment, but it seems appealing that we would like to take the private cost savings into account at least to some extent– if costs of further limiting pollution were astronomically high at the same time as the benefit was low, this seems wasteful.

4 I really like the title of a recent biography of Pigou: *The First Serious Optimist* (Kumekawa (2017), reflecting that he thought deep about these kinds of problems and how they could be solved.
5 We could also have used a tax on output (rather than on pollution as here) to limit production in the situation depicted in Figure 13.4. Such a tax is also termed Pigouvian; again, it incentivizes agents to internalize the externality.
6 We're simplifying the discussion here somewhat, as it is the whole industry that limits pollution by one unit, but the comparison of the marginal cost of limiting pollution and the tax is true also at the level of an individual producer.
7 Cigarettes, of course, do not only have negative external effects – harming health through passive smoking but also through harming the smoker herself. Taxes motivated by a desire to limit people's consumption of goods that are harmful to themselves is sometimes referred to as taxing to deal with "internalities." Taxes on alcohol and sugar-sweetened beverages are other examples.
8 A prominent example of this comes from attempts to cheat on the tests of emissions by Volkswagen, which were at the center of what became known as Dieselgate, see, e.g., Schiermeier (2015). We can also see bans of certain substances or methods of production as a quantity restriction. For instance, DDT, heavily used as an insecticide after its discovery in the 1940s, is banned for most uses in most countries after its adverse environmental effects came to the fore – partly as a result of Rachel Carson's highly impactful book *Silent Spring* (Carson (1962)).
9 See https://climate.ec.europa.eu/eu-action/eu-emissions-trading-system-eu-ets_en for a description.
10 Decision in Sweden's supreme court in 1996, T3615-95.
11 While the term "theorem" would make you expect that this is a highly precise mathematical statement, Coase's argument in Coase (1960) is quite informal.
12 We only scratch the surface here. The related concept of transaction costs is fundamental to how we understand, for instance, the limits of firms – what is done within firms and on the market? Should a firm produce a particular input in-house, or should it buy it on the market? Coase has seminal work here as well (Coase (1937)), and, among others, Nobel laureate Oliver Williamson has deeply increased our understanding of transaction costs. His Nobel lecture, published as Williamson (2010), provides an accessible overview.
13 In some municipalities, it is banned; in others, it is always allowed, and yet others allow it on specific days only.
14 Coase was not only a very influential economist 102-year-old he also had a very long life. A to me fascinating interview about externalities with a 102-year old Ronald Coase is available here: https://www.econtalk.org/coase-on-externalities-the-firm-and-the-state-of-economics/.
15 On a related note, another highly impactful article by Ronald Coase (1937) proposes that firms exist to economize on transaction costs. There are costs and benefits to using the market to do a transaction rather than doing that same transaction within a firm.
16 We follow a common practice in teaching here and view each characteristic as binary – for instance, excludable or nonexcludable. Alternatively, one could think of this as a continuum and characterize along a scale with goods being more or less excludable.
17 They are sometimes also known by the name of excludable public goods.
18 We do not cover private goods, as the analysis in the rest of the book is directly applicable to them.
19 See, e.g., this video https://www.youtube.com/watch?v=Fh-kHohMRe8.
20 As seen by the example, this kind of common property resource has a close intellectual connection with the question of monopoly vs. perfect competition. Why is competition good there but not here? A simple reason is that competition in the standard model is good for consumers, whereas it lowers profit for the firms. Here only the second effect matters. In other variants of common resources, there may in addition be costs due to congestion.
21 Like when it was recently discovered that a Swedish mushroom is the same as the highly priced Japanese matsutake mushroom – with the Swedish all man's right, anyone can pick these irrespective of who owns the land.
22 Her Nobel Prize lecture is a good place to start reading for the curious: https://www.nobelprize.org/uploads/2018/06/ostrom_lecture.pdf. If you read it, you will also note that she proposes some different nomenclature compared to what we use above – for instance, naming club goods toll goods. Above I stick with what I perceive to be the most common terminology, and differences between uses are minor. One great appeal of economics to me, as opposed to some other social sciences, is the focus on using a few sets of tools repeatedly and seeing the exceptional mileage that

we get out of those in terms of analytical sharpness. Minor differences in how researchers define different concepts can arguably be left for more advanced studies.

23 The origins of the Tiramisu recipe appear to be somewhat mysterious – but the invention is typically dated to the late 1960s.

24 See, e.g., Romer (1994) for an accessible overview.

14 Asymmetric information

Illustration 14.1 Asymmetric perspectives. *Pexels*, Magda Ehlers. Public domain.

14.1 Different forms of asymmetric information

We now turn to another class of market failures: those linked to **asymmetric information**, where parties involved in a transaction differ in their knowledge of the good or service being sold. This can have pervasive effects on how markets function. For instance, a buyer who knows little about the good she is buying may be taken advantage of by a more informed seller. This can affect how much is traded and at what prices, and, as we shall see, markets may shut down as a result of asymmetric information.

One set of applications of asymmetric information concerns markets for insurance. Assume for a moment that you have a business idea to sell insurance that pays out a sum if the insured person fails a test to qualify for a driving license. You look at the statistics and see that on average, 50% of the takers of these tests fail. Would you on average expect to have to pay 50% of the insured? A little thinking suggests you should expect to pay more than 50% of the insured, and the insurance industry has two terms that lay bare two fundamental mechanisms:

DOI: 10.4324/9781003623854-19

- **Adverse selection**. This concerns the situation where there are different characteristics of a good or a service, and one part of the transaction knows more about those characteristics than the other party does. In insurance markets, there is asymmetric information in that the party looking to buy insurance typically know much more about their risk than the insurance company does. In the example of insurance against a failed driving test, people with a higher probability of failing are more likely to want to buy the insurance. If you have poor motor skills, you are more likely to fail the test and want to buy insurance. The pool of insured is likely adversely selected; high-risk customers are likely to be over-represented since low-risk customers are less likely to purchase the insurance. More generally, we apply the term "adverse selection" to situations where different goods, services, or people have different levels of quality (or risk), and one party knows much more than the other about the quality. *Hidden information* is another term sometimes used as a synonym for adverse selection – reflecting that the information about characteristics is partly hidden from some parties.
- **Moral hazard**. This concerns the situation where parties differ in their ability to observe actions taken by one of the parties. The insured can act in different ways that the less informed party (the insurance company in this case) can't observe. In the example of insurance against a failed driving test, people are likely to act less carefully if they know that they are insured. The term originally comes from maritime insurance – a ship sent on long voyages was subject to a lot of hazards. There were, for instance, hazards due to bad weather or piracy, but there was also a hazard due to (lack of) morals – if insured, the captain would be less diligent. *Hidden action* is a term sometimes used as a synonym for moral hazard – reflecting that it is the actions of one party that is partly hidden from other parties.

Many situations will feature aspects of both adverse selection and moral hazard, but for analytical purposes, it is useful to treat them separately. In terms of intellectual history, we are now dealing with younger theories than much of the other material in an introductory microeconomics book. Much of what we cover in this chapter was developed in the early 1970s and onward, with the 2001 Nobel Prize honoring three of the key contributors: George Akerlof, Michael Spence, and Joseph Stiglitz.

This may also be a good place to briefly reflect on the role of theory in economics. How can discovery rest with these people when insurance terms for these concepts have been around for a long time? The concerns have been with us humans for ages, and solutions have been sought – for instance, Roman law contained elements of being allowed to return livestock if quality was revealed to be lower than could be expected at the time of purchase, one type of regulation that helps limit the negative consequences of adverse selection (Lavan (2021)). Taking of hostages to ensure behavior in line with a treaty can be seen as a way to deal with moral hazard and the taking of hostages to ensure obedience was a standard modus operandi for Julius Ceasar some 2,000 years ago during his campaigns in present-day France (Moscovich (1979)). Nothing new under the sun, but what theories like those that we examine in the following allow us to do is to pinpoint what precisely is the problem. This allows us to examine large classes of solutions and learn across different fields by seeing analogies.

14.2 Adverse selection

The modern analysis of adverse selection issues in economics was pioneered in a seminal article published by George Akerlof: "The Market of Lemons" (Akerlof (1970)). Lemon was slang for a low-quality used car at the time. Fresh out of his PhD program, the 26-year-old Akerlof had just started a position at UC Berkeley and was thinking deeply about differences between the market for new cars and used cars. He identified asymmetric information as a key problem in the used car market. He also continued working on the paper during a later visit to India for the Peace Corps, where he found that similar kinds of asymmetric information problems were hampering markets, which further stressed the importance of the ideas.[1]

To understand the concept, consider the simple example presented in Table 14.1. To provide a visual image, you can think of a field where a large number of used cars are parked, each with a seller and where a large number of buyers are also present. The used cars can be either of a high quality or of a low quality, where the latter would have problems that increase the likelihood of costly repairs and breakdowns. Buyers are willing to pay at most 150 euros for a high-quality car and at most 50 euros for a low-quality car. Owners of a high-quality car are willing to sell it for a price of at least 130 euros, and owners of a low-quality car are willing to sell it for a price of at least 30 euros. To understand how information asymmetry affects this market, we will sequentially consider different assumptions regarding the information buyers and sellers have.

Symmetric information with observable quality

In the first case, assume that there is full information. Both parties can see if a car is of high or low quality, and with these valuations, there are gains from trade, with high-quality cars trading for a price between 130 and 150 euros and low-quality cars trading for a price between 30 and 50 euros. From a buyer's perspective, a low-quality car can clearly

Illustration 14.2 Lemons. iStockPhoto by Getty Images, Skodonnell.

Table 14.1 An example to illustrate adverse selection

	High quality	*Low quality*
Valuation Buyers	150	50
Valuation Sellers	130	30

be attractive, as the lower quality also comes with a lower price. The standard analysis that we presented in the previous chapters applies here.

Symmetric information with unobservable quality

Now consider the polar case where neither party knows the quality. Judging the quality of a used car is difficult, and it takes no great leap of faith to assume that buyers can't ascertain the quality. Assume for now that the same applies to the seller. We assume that both sides try to calculate the expected quality, however. For the sake of the argument, assume that each side assumes that there is a 50% probability that a given car is of high quality and a 50% probability that it is of low quality.[2] A risk-neutral[3] buyer would value a car of unknown quality using her estimated probabilities of the different qualities. In this case, she would be willing to pay at most $0.5 \times 150 + 0.5 \times 50 = 100$ euros for a car.

The key mechanism is that the higher the probability that the product is of low quality, the lower is the willingness to pay. If, for instance, the probability that the car was of low quality was increased to 0.7, the willingness to pay would drop to only $0.3 \times 150 + 0.7 \times 50 = 80$ euros.[4] Intuitively, think of someone pondering to purchase an expensive Swiss watch. You know that it can be original (= high quality) or a copy (= low quality). Buying it on high street in Geneva, potential buyers would assign a probability of it being an original as close to 1 and be willing to pay 10,000 euros, for instance. There has also been a long history of copies being sold in, for instance, Southeast Asia. So, if the same potential watch buyer were offered a watch on a beach in Southeast Asia, the assigned probability that it was a copy would on the other hand be high, and willingness to pay would be much lower at, for instance, 30 euros. The probability that the product is of low quality is pulling down the willingness to pay and hence the price.

In the case where sellers do not know whether the quality is high or low, they are similarly willing to accept a lower price. In this case, they would be willing to sell their car for $0.5 \times 130 + 0.5 \times 30 = 80$ euros. Since the buyers are willing to pay a higher price (100 euros) than what the sellers require in order to part with their car (80 euros), there are mutual gains from trade. Some sellers will be selling a high-quality car for a low price but will be (happily) unaware that they are parting with a high-quality car.

Asymmetric information: Sellers know quality but buyers' don't

In this last case we will see how the *asymmetry of information* can have drastic effects. Take the previous case as a starting point and note that buyers are willing to pay 100 euros if they don't know the quality. But the sellers of high-quality cars require at least 130 euros to sell. Thus the price buyers are willing to pay is not sufficiently high to motivate sellers of high-quality cars. High-quality used cars disappear from the market, and, of course, if buyers update their probability taking account of this, the effect will be even stronger. In the end, we would expect only low-quality used cars being traded at a price between 50 and 30 euros.

At a deep level, what is going on here? Buyers are willing to pay less since the probability that the product is low quality lowers their willingness to pay. Sellers, who know the quality of their product, find this price too low to motivate them to sell, and they withdraw from the market. If you had an original high-quality Swiss watch to sell, you would not do it on the beach alluded to earlier – the perceived high probability that it was a copy would make it hard for you to get the desired price.

The result is important – asymmetric information can shut down a market. There are clear gains from trade but because of information asymmetries, the market breaks down. Adverse selection need not only have the consequence that a market totally shuts down (after all, used cars are traded) but can also have other important consequences for how markets work. Let us consider a few examples of prominent applications in the following – a thing to note in several of these cases is that institutions and regulations have appeared that partly solve the problems with adverse selection. We will examine those solutions in greater detail later in the chapter, but let us first look at the examples.

14.2.1 Examples of situations with scope for adverse selection

14.2.1.1 Insurance markets

As noted, the term "adverse selection" stems from insurance markets, and they remain a prominent example. To take a simple example, consider health insurance (see, for instance, Geruso and Layton (2017) for a survey of the literature). In most countries, there is an important public involvment in health insurance, but suppose that this was not the case. Out of a large group of people, most would have no health issues in a given year, a few would have some accidents or health concerns and even fewer would have really serious health conditions. The latter could easily generate skyrocketing costs – the cost of a cancer treatment, for instance, can easily outstrip the ability to pay, and without an insurance solution, many people would die for lack of treatment. It is clear that a functioning insurance scheme can be attractive under such circumstances. Everyone pays an insurance premium every year – the people who get sick get treated, with payment coming from the insurance, and the people who don't get sick end up subsidizing the sick, but only in hindsight. Now assume that people know more about their risk of needing costly medical attention than what the insurance company can see or verify. That is, there is asymmetric information. A 20-year-old student with no known medical conditions may be tempted not to get insured, whereas a 60-year-old smoker is less likely to be so tempted. As low-risk patients opt out of insurance, the pool of insured will be increasingly dominated by high-risk patients, patients who on balance are going to be more costly for the insurance company. To cover the cost, an insurance company would then most likely charge a higher premium to cover the costs, which will trigger further adverse selection. Such a "death spiral" can lead to private health insurance not being offered at all. It can also lead to other distortions; for instance, only people below 60 can take up health insurance or there are a large number of exceptions as to what is covered. Think of two insurance companies that compete that both have caps on the costs they cover up to 10,000 euros per year. Do the thought experiment that one of the companies took away the cap – it would likely get more customers, but they are likely to be skewed toward customers who believe themselves to be at more serious risk of needing costly treatment.

14.2.1.2 Credit markets

Credit markets are another example where adverse selection can play a large part. If you want to buy a house or start a business and, like the rest of us, don't have sufficient savings to do so out-of-pocket, you need to borrow from a bank or from other givers of credit. For simplicity, think of relatively safe and relatively risky projects. On the relatively safe side, two 45-year-olds with high wages, permanent employment, and a substantial amount of their own capital may find it straightforward to find a bank willing to lend them money with their home acting as security. A 22-year-old entrepreneur with a novel business idea that sounds brilliant is clearly something that ends up on the risky side. The problem for someone lending to such an entrepreneur is that if things go well, she can pay back the money with some interest, and all is fine and well. If the project fails, however, there will be no way to get the money back. The latter type of investment is risky – if you lend to many such entrepreneurs, there are likely to be many cases where the borrower can't pay back. The lender could compensate for this by raising the interest rate ("the price"), but then the lender is likely to attract an adversely selected pool of high-risk borrowers, and again, we are at risk of a death spiral.[5]

Many also assign an important role to adverse selection in the financial crisis of 2008. As anyone who has seen the movie *The Big Short* knows (if you haven't, it comes highly recommended), the early 2000s saw lending expand to many households with relatively weak ability to pay back loans – known as subprime lending. Simply put, these loans were often lumped together and resold to other investors (think of the asset "here is an income stream from 100 loan payments across the country"), and from the way the loans were packaged together and assigned a credit rating, a risk grade, were seen as safe assets. As failures to repay loans increased, the realization that these asset-backed securities were not so safe after all gained traction. With additional problems and bankruptcies in the financial sector, trade in many of these securities came to a complete standstill – the fear of lemons completely shut down the market (see, e.g., Kacperczyk and Schnabl (2010) for an overview).

14.2.1.3 Personal services

Many personal services (babysitter, dentist, car repair, carpenter, etc.) are such that it is hard for the buyer to evaluate quality. Again, these are markets prone to problems associated with adverse selection. Not that these markets don't exist, but how they operate are partly shaped by information asymmetries. Many people rarely change supplier and choose supplier via long chains of recommendations, which tends to make the market more rigid than what it would be if information were more evenly distributed.

14.2.1.4 Ethical production

Other applications concern cases where the physical quality of the good in itself is independent of the supplier, but production can take place in different ways. Fish can, for instance, be caught in relatively noninvasive ways (e.g., by hook) or by dragging nets along the bottom, bottom trawling, that has a great negative environmental impact. Say that consumers value a relatively noninvasive way of fishing but can't see how fish are caught. For a given size of the catch, the private cost of fishing by hook is much higher than the private cost of bottom trawling. In a case such as this, low-cost production can drive out high-cost production, again a form of adverse selection. If we are willing to call fishing by hook ethical, one could argue that maybe a number of fishermen will value ethical production and that this will then be supplied on the market. Note, however, that if there is free entry into the business, profits will be driven to zero for low-cost producers. In this kind of setup, an ethical, high-cost fisher would need to be willing to operate at a loss to remain in the business – if they have a choice, clearly many would choose to work in another line of business instead – the products that remain in the market will be adversely selected.[6]

14.2.2 Ways of limiting effects of adverse selection

A number of ways have evolved that limit negative effects of adverse selection on markets. In some cases, the problem is largely solved – in other cases, the market remains heavily distorted. At a broad level, you could argue that many of the problems would be solved if people were simply honest and truthful. This is true – and we will offer some reflections on this when concluding this chapter. Awaiting that, note that the ways through which we can limit problems due to adverse selection can be classified in different ways. Next, we highlight three mechanisms – group policies, avoiding one-shot games, and equalizing information.

14.2.2.1 Group policies

Consider the health insurance example from earlier. At one level, we can think of the problem as being that the low-risk customers opt out of insurance. A potentially straightforward way to avoid adverse selection leading to an unraveling of the market is to create **group policies**, institutions that keep the low-risk customers in the pool of insured. Mandatory health insurance, possibly provided by the government as in many countries, is a way to do this. Another way is to purchase health insurance via the employer. A single individual looking to buy health insurance on her own faces an adverse selection problem, and insurers may be hesitant to let her enroll and/or have severe spending caps. If, in contrast, an employer approaches the insurance company with say 100 employees, it seems highly likely that the insurance company will assume that there is a mix of risk types among those employees such that they are likely to get a bundle of low- and high-risk types. The insurance company is thus likely to be able to offer a better deal for the group, and there is a partial solution to the adverse selection issue.

Another example of group policies comes from third-party liability insurance – for instance, insurance that covers costs associated with you hitting another person whilst driving a car. In many cases, third-party liability insurance is mandatory for cars, maritime shipment, and air transport. Note that in these cases, the concern is typically not that high-risk customers not be able to get insurance. The standard argument is instead related to what we studied under ethical production earlier, that firms with an undue cost advantage should not out-compete responsible firms.

14.2.2.2 Avoid one-shot games

In the car example that we started with, we implicitly assumed that buyer and seller only met once. However, if the same people interact over time, we know from game theory in Chapter 11 (and from experience) that repeated interaction can be used to motivate cooperative and truthful behavior. While it may be difficult to estimate, for instance, the quality of a car prior to purchase, we typically learn quality over time. A seller who provides us with bad quality is not likely to get repeat business.

Brand names and public reviews can be a way to transfer the discipline on behavior from a punishment for bad behavior against one customer to many. Online marketplaces like Airbnb, where we interact with strangers, may be prone to adverse selection issues, and it comes as no surprise that such firms invest a lot in designing a review system that incentivizes good behavior.[7] Similar problems have been faced throughout history and, for instance, Greif (1993) shows how reputational mechanisms promoted good behavior among long distance traders in the Mediterranean in the 11th century, and Milgrom et al. (1990) document the role of institutions to create a role for reputation at medieval trade fairs.

14.2.2.3 Equalizing information

The asymmetry of information is at the root of the problems associated with adverse selection, and we may adress the problem at its heart in various ways.

Government regulation Some forms of officially mandated policies have the effect of lowering the scope for asymmetric information. Requirements that products or services conform to certain minimum standards is a way to avoid the risk of very low quality blocking the functioning of a market.[8] Safety standards when it comes to electrical equipment, fulfillment of hygiene requirements for restaurants, minimum standards when it comes to aircraft maintenance are but a few examples. Regulations regarding how information is presented is another way to limit the scope for low-quality products to taint the demand for high-quality products – looking at different investments, I know that all firms are required to fulfill the same basic rules regarding accounting, for instance. Similarly, if we go to a medical doctor, an accountant, or a lawyer, we know that they have gone through a particular form of training and may be stripped of their right to practice if they violate basic requirements of professional conduct.

Policy may also be targeted to make use of the fact that in many cases, you learn quality over time. A legally mandated right to return a product within a certain amount of time is a way to equalize information. Similarly, many places with laws that make it difficult to fire a worker have laws that allow for a trial period of, for instance, six months, during which information asymmetries between the worker and the employer about ability diminish.

Private standard setting and information sharing In some cases, standards may also appear by nongovernmental initiatives – or as a mix of public and private initiatives. When we examined perfect competition in the first part of this book, we took for granted that a large buyer of, e.g., wheat could place an order of a, for instance, 5 tons of a particular quality grade of wheat for delivery in 6 months. How can that buyer be sure that the quality is sufficient – that it is not rotten or mixed up with sand? In a small market, personal and repeated interaction can function as a check on adverse selection, but in large global markets, such mechanisms are weaker for homogeneous products. Various certification agencies and standards are then important.[9]

Similarly, firms that keep track of credit history help keep credit markets open and credit accessible. We noted earlier how low-cost producers could crowd out high-cost producers if consumers could not observe details of the production process that they cared about. Labeling of products to signify ecological production or sustainable fishery, for instance, are then ways to avoid adverse selection in this particular dimension.

14.2.2.4 Signaling

The two previous classes of equalizing information feature third parties that help find a solution. However, the more informed party can also work to equalize information. A firm that credibly transmits quality reviews from previous customers is in effect attempting to equalize information. A particular way of thinking of information-sharing is what is known as **signaling**. We ask ourselves, is there some "signal" of quality that a high-quality supplier will find attractive to send that a low-quality supplier will not. The formalization of these ideas was originally made by Michael Spence in a labor market setting, and in the following, we present a simple example.[10] Assume that there are two types of job seekers only – that we term ambitious (A) and slackers (S). Each job seeker knows their own type, but potential employers can't see the type of a given individual. Trial periods and references from previous employers are ways through which problems due to adverse selection can be lowered, but now we ask, is there any way that the job seeker can credibly show that she is ambitious? Simply saying that I'm ambitious may have some effect, but if sufficiently many slackers don't mind bending the truth a bit (or live in the happy illusion that they are ambitious),

Illustration 14.3 Watch me jump. iStockphoto by Getty Images, Johan63.

simply stating that one is ambitious doesn't do it. Anyone can say that. In game theoretical terms, we would say that such communication is cheap talk. Similarly, dressing up nicely for the interview is also easy for anyone to do. The question then is, is there anything that the ambitious can do to show that they are indeed ambitious that slackers would not find attractive to do? Spence notes that education can fulfill such a role.

A simple (and popular) way to frame the question is to start by assuming that there is no direct use for an employer of what you learn at university. None. All these hours spent on problem sets, late-night coding, and struggling to understand an idea teach you absolutely nothing of value. In such a world, could there still be a value to education? Yes, if the two types differ in their perceived cost of university education, then education can act like a signal that is worth it to send for an ambitious person but not for a slacker. Assume that the monetary costs of going to university are the same for everyone but that there is a private cost associated with the effort that you spend. If you're a slacker, the mental cost of sitting with an assignment Sunday night and long hours doing calculations is higher than for someone who's ambitious and finds joy in the challenge. Let the costs of a university education then be C_S and C_A, respectively. Assume that the value of hiring motivates a salary of 100 euros for A and of 60 euros for S. Further assume that the employer offers a wage of 100 for those with a university degree and 60 for others.[11] Can university education work as a signal under these conditions? For a slacker to go to university, and thus try to send a signal that she is ambitious, the following would need to hold

$$100 - C_S \geq 60,$$

whereas for someone who is a ambitious, the following would need to hold

$$100 - C_A \geq 60.$$

Since $C_A < C_S$, there are values where university is worth it for someone ambitious but not for a slacker. For instance, if $C_A = 30$ and $C_S = 50$, we would have a situation where going to university is a signal that is worth sending for someone ambitious but not for a slacker (since $100 - C_S = 50$, which is less than 60, whereas $100 - C_A = 70$, which is greater than 60). We say that such a signal is credible, and we have a **separating equilibrium** where agents of different types take different actions – in equilibrium, we can see who's of what type depending on their actions.[12] Clearly, if differences in costs between the two types of agents are small enough, the types will not be separated, and we would instead have a **pooling equilibrium** where both types take the same action. For instance, if $C_A = 30$ and $C_S = 35$, both types would find it attractive to go to university, and the value of the signal would be lost.

Signaling has also been invoked as a reason to understand warranties for durable goods – only suppliers who know that they have a high quality find it attractive to offer an ambitious warranty, the thinking goes. Similarly, research that applies similar reasoning to evolutionary biology has, for instance, suggested that the practice known as stotting – high jumps by grazing animals like antelopes – can be seen as a signal of speed to predators.[13]

14.2.2.5 *Equalizing information due to efforts from the less informed party*

The less informed part in a setting with asymmetric information may also make investments with the aim to learn more about quality or risk. Insurance companies may require health checks; a buyer of a car may use a car inspection service; an employer will ask for references. In a process known as **screening**, the less informed party can also try to set up a set of choices such that the more informed agent reveals her type. A case of this that is sometimes mentioned concerns work conditions in law firms (or consulting firms) where young associates are faced with very long hours of work at relatively low pay. Just like the signalling story noted earlier, where the ambitious could send a costly signal by going to university, a law firm could work under the assumption that only someone ambitious would accept such a work contract. The benefit presumably comes in later stages as a partner at the firm where pay becomes very high. Only people who believe that they have the characteristics that it takes to make partner will be willing to slog those long hours at the beginning of their careers.[14]

14.3 Moral hazard

Now we turn to the other main class of situations where asymmetric information plays a role: moral hazard. To recapitulate, adverse selection concerned the case where there were different types, and the type was not observed by the less informed party. In the case of moral hazard, it is the **actions** of the more informed party that are not observable to the less informed. A standard example is that of insurance – a driver of a rental car that is fully insured is likely to be less careful than someone who has no insurance.[15]

To introduce the issues let us consider a specific form of moral hazard type situations, a **principal-agent** problem. This refers to a situation where a less informed party (the principal) hires another more informed party (the agent). The key question in moral hazard concerns how contracts should be designed to provide the right incentives to act. To take a specific example, consider the case of a wealthy landowner and a poor farmworker.[16] Key to the moral hazard dilemma is that the worker can act in different ways that are not observable to the landowner. To be concrete, the worker can provide high effort (H) or low effort (L). Providing high effort comes with a private, unobservable for the landowner, cost to the

Illustration 14.4 Lots of hazards for a captain – also a moral hazard. *Landscape with a Ship and Jonah and the Whale*, Lucas Gassel. Metropolitan Museum of Art, public domain.

worker. Think of this as going the extra mile, being extra diligent to take care with weeding, watering at the right moments and doing all those extra things that are associated with doing your best. A low effort can be thought of as slacking off and doing the minimal only (shirking is a term often used) – "just doing my job." Assume that the private cost of working hard is 10. The harvest depends on two things: the level of effort from the worker (H or L) and whether growing conditions were good (G) or bad (B). The latter essentially captures luck – with good weather, rain at the right time, absence of pests, and little weeds leading to the G outcome and B the outcome of bad weather, stray deer that eat part of the harvest, or a number of other possible causes for bad luck. Table 14.2 presents the payoffs associated with the different combinations of effort and luck.

First, we consider what would be optimal to do if there was no moral hazard issue – we can think of this as the case when the landowner and the worker are the same person. Unobservable actions by one party are at the core of the problem, and if there is only one party, the problem goes away. We term this the *efficient solution*, as it would take account of all the costs and benefits. The decision here is simple: It is only to provide H or L effort. It is efficient to provide H effort if the expected benefits of doing so are higher than the expected benefits of providing L effort. Thus, H is efficient if

$$\underbrace{0.5 \times 40 + 0.5 \times 100}_{\text{Expected revenue if H effort}} - \underbrace{10}_{\text{Effort cost}} \overset{?}{\geq} \underbrace{0.5 \times 20 + 0.5 \times 40}_{\text{Expected revenue if L effort}},$$

Table 14.2 Payoffs in a principal-agent problem

	Bad conditions (probability 0.5)	*Good* conditions (probability 0.5)
High effort by agent (private cost for agent 10)	40	100
Low effort by agent (cost for agent 0)	20	40

Table 14.3 A comparison of different contracts under moral hazard

	Fixed wage	*Sharecropping*
Expected payoff worker	w	25
Expected payoff landowner	30-w	35
Efficient effort	No	Yes
Who bears risk	Landowner	Split

which holds in our case since if we do the calculation, we see that the condition requires that $70 - 10 \geq 30$, which indeed is true.

Thus we want to think of contracts lead to high effort. We consider two forms of contracts: (1) a fixed wage contract and (2) a sharecropping contract where the harvest is split 50/50 between the worker and the landowner. Since the worker is the party with the private information, we want to examine her incentives.[17] Consider the incentives under a fixed wage. The worker would provide H effort if

$$\underbrace{w - 10}_{\text{Expected net income H effort}} \overset{?}{\geq} \underbrace{w}_{\text{Expected net income L effort}},$$

which clearly doesn't hold. Under the fixed wage contract, her effort will be L under the assumptions made.

Now consider instead a situation where the payoffs are split equally between the landowner and the worker. In this case, the comparison becomes

$$\underbrace{0.5 \times \underbrace{(0.5 \times 40 + 0.5 \times 100)}_{70} - \underbrace{10}_{\text{Effort cost}}}_{\text{Expected net income H effort}} \overset{?}{\geq} \underbrace{0.5 \times \underbrace{(0.5 \times 20 + 0.5 \times 40)}_{30}}_{\text{Expected net income L effort}}.$$

In this case, the expected benefit of high effort is greater than that of low effort since $35 - 10 > 15$. The landowner in this case receives an expected payoff of 35 (0.5×70) and also prefers this to $30 - w$. Let us summarize this simple comparison in Table 14.3.

The downside in this setting of a fixed wage is that it doesn't provide the incentive to exert high effort; it doesn't provide incentives to make the cake as large as possible. The upside of the wage contract on the other hand is that it lays the risk on the landowner, who presumably has more wealth and finds it easier to deal with the consequences of a shortfall. This tradeoff between efficiency and risk-bearing is common in moral hazard problems, as we shall expand upon further next.

Also note that the topic of moral hazard and how we behave are much more complex than what the simple models we present can capture. Our motivation to exert effort in the workplace is a complex web depending on expectations, social norms, standing in the workplace, and many others factors. A brief look at military history is sufficient to highlight that monetary compensation is far from everything when it comes to what motivates humans. That said, economic incentives can be very powerful in directing behavior.

The simple model noted earlier can, for instance, help explain why sharecropping has been prevalent in large parts of the world, also in cases where workers are close to subsistence level and hence should be very averse to taking on risk. It can also provide insights into the extreme productivity gains seen in Chinese agriculture, as China in the early 1980s transferred from agriculture mainly being in collective farms to a case where households were delegated a lot of decision power and got to keep part of the proceeds in what has key aspects in common with the sharecropping system discussed earlier. The system was known as the "household responsibility system," see, e.g., Deakin and Meng (2022) for a discussion and overview. You may also wonder why there is a picture of two cats in Illustration 14.5: It alludes to the saying associated with Deng Xiaoping and taken as a motivation for the pragmatic approach to reforms at the time: "It doesn't matter if a cat is black or white, as long as it catches mice its a good cat."

Illustration 14.5 Black cat, white cat. *The Cats' Rendezvous*, 1868, Edouard Manet (detail), Courtesy of Art Institute Chicago. Public domain.

14.3.1 Further examples of moral hazard

Moral hazard appears in many situations – and the following present a few important applications.

14.3.1.1 Cases where the public picks up the bill

An important class of moral hazard situations concern cases where someone gets private benefit of an action if a project is successful, and society at large gets the negative consequences if the project fails. As the rather apt quip has it, "Heads I win, tails you loose." The core problem in such cases is that in the case of failure, others cannot claim the full damages because a company that created the problem simply goes bankrupt. Or because managers of a company simply change jobs before the negative consequences materialize. One potential area for such cases concern investments with environmental risks.

Consider, for instance, the case of offshore oil drilling. Assume that a firm has gained the right to extract oil and can do so in one of two ways: a cheaper way with a higher probability of oil spill or a costlier way that has a lower probability of an oil spill. The authorities cannot directly observe which way to extract oil that the firm chooses. Assume that the cheap technology gives a profit for the firm of 10 million euros with a probability of 0.9, and with probability 0.1 profit is 0. If the firm chooses the costly technology, profit is 5 million euros with probability 0.99, and with probability 0.01, profit is 0. The case of 0 profit reflects a situation when the oil platform has a major breakdown, and there is a large oil spill. The costs that accrue to the rest of society are then valued at 100 million euros. If the firm has full insurance, that is correctly priced, or very deep pockets so that it can pay to compensate for the full negative effects on others, the firm would face the societally correct incentives.[18] If **limited liability** protects the owners of firms from downside risk: if the firm can't cover its losses, it will go bankrupt, but owners' and managements' private assets are not at risk if the company fails. The amount that they stand to lose (their liability) is limited.

With limited liability in this simple case, the expected profit with the expensive technology is $5 \times 0.99 + 0 \times 0.01 = 4.95$ million euros. With the cheap technology, expected profit is $10 \times 0.9 + 0 \times 0.1 = 9$ million euros. We would therefore expect a profit-maximizing firm to produce in the cheap way. The costs that affect the rest of society are an externality, and we don't expect a firm to fully internalize these, unless given incentives to do so.

Cases where large banks engage in risky lending and then need to be bailed out by governments that want to avoid a financial collapse are another example of this kind of situation. The term "too big too fail" captures the heart of the moral hazard problem in this case, and this application of moral hazard was particularly relevant in the aftermath of the 2008 financial crisis.[19]

Financing of firm-level investments Moral hazard is also important for understanding many aspects of how businesses are financed. In general, asymmetric information is an important factor in credit markets – the borrowing and lending of funds. At one level, this is not surprising – a lender provides funds to a borrower (or an investor provides funds to an entrepreneur) in the hope of getting the funds back, plus some interest in the future. There is a gap in timing, and there are many ways in which a borrower can act without them being observable by the lender. A large literature in corporate finance takes moral hazard as a starting point to understand how investments can be financed (see Tirole (2010) for an advanced text book). Let us sketch a simple stylized situation to capture some fundamental

Table 14.4 A investment problem with moral hazard

	Investment cost	*Payoff if success*	*Probability success*	*Payoff if fail*	*Private benefit*
Entrepr. chooses H	20	40	0.8	0	0
Entrepr. chooses L	20	40	0.4	0	B

facets of the situation. Assume that an entrepreneur has an investment project. The cost of the investment is 20 euros, and we first assume that the entrepreneur has no funds so that she needs to borrow it all. If the project is successful, earnings are 40 euros, and if it fails, earnings are 0. The entrepreneur can work in a way that gives a high probability of success (denoted by H) or in a way that gives a lower probability of success (denoted L). The latter is typically thought to capture a number of potential mechanisms: It can be because she takes it easy and works less hard, because she spends the time and resources in developing another parallel project, or because she engages in activities that give power and prestige but lower the probability of success (fancy office, expensive travel, empire building etc.). We let the variable B capture these private benefits of choosing L. Whether H or L is chosen is not observed by investors – we thus have a moral hazard problem and summarize the setup in Table 14.4.

Suppose first that the entrepreneur has no funds and is offered a contract in which she borrows 20 and pays back 25 in case the investment is a success, and 0 otherwise. For the investor, the expected payoff under H is then $0.8 \times 25 - 20 = 0$, so the investor is just indifferent *if* the entrepreneur chooses H.[20] To see if the entrepreneur would be expected to work hard, we again look at her incentives; she would work hard if the following holds:

$$\underbrace{0.8 \times (40 - 25)}_{\text{Expected gain if H}} \overset{?}{\geq} \underbrace{0.4 \times (40 - 25) + B}_{\text{Expected gain if L}}.$$

$$12 \overset{?}{\geq} 6 + B$$

Thus, as long as the private benefit B is no greater than 6, we can expect the entrepreneur to choose H. Let us highlight three points that can be examined with the kind of framework just explained:

- Private benefit and moral hazard can shut down the supply of capital to investments. The investor can accept no payback less than 25, and if B is greater than 6, the entrepreneur will not be incentivized to choose H.
- We cover ways of limiting moral hazard–related problems next, but for now, note that it is indeed typically very hard to finance a new firm with bank loans – often, entrepreneurs instead sell parts of the firm to outside investors that take seats on the board and in other ways improve both their information and ability to act upon it – which is limiting the amount of information asymmetry.
- If the entrepreneur has some of her own funds to invest in the project, this helps slacken the constraint on her incentives – it will be less tempting to risk default if she has her own funds invested in the project, "skin in the game," as it is commonly referred to.[21] The idea that having one's own funds is key for being able to borrow and invest has empirical

support and is key to a large literature on credit constraints – limits to borrowing because of information asymmetries.

Insurance As noted, the term "moral hazard" stems from the insurance business, and insurance remains an important application. It is often referred to as you're more likely to "play with fire" if you're insured. Sometimes people retort that even if your house is insured, its a big negative shock if your house burns down. You'd want to avoid that. Similarly, you want to avoid a car accident even if the rental car is insured. So isn't moral hazard in insurance a mute issue? Here there are three things to point out. First, clearly an analysis of a specific case needs to take factors that affect the harm to the insured into account. As a driver of a fully insured rental car, you may continue to avoid a crash but may be less careful about how you park the car, for instance. Similarly, business insurance against low performance may be more prone to moral hazard than personal injury insurance. Second, while we in teaching often consider simple examples where decisions are binary (as in the examples, effort is either high or low), many moral hazard problems affect decisions on the margin, as is common in economics; many are likely to drive a little less carefully if their rental car is fully insured. Third, the magnitudes of response may differ across people – if a sufficiently large share of the potentially insured respond strongly to moral hazard–related incentives, this is enough to have a major effect on the functioning of the insurance.

As we shall see in the following, insurance companies try to limit moral hazard by using checks and using deductibles – typically, the insured needs to cover some of the cost herself – again some skin in the game as a solution to moral hazard. Note that moral hazard affects not only private insurance companies but also social insurance. In many European countries and beyond, much of what the state does can be seen as insurance rather than redistribution per se: unemployment insurance and sick pay where you as an employee receive wages even if you're sick are two examples. For the latter, different mechanisms that limit moral hazard are often in play, as we cover in some detail next.

Procurement when quality is hard to measure Some services paid for by government are almost always provided by governments themselves (such as police and courts), whereas others are frequently provided by private firms, which are paid to provide the service (such as garbage collection or snow removal). When government purchases from private providers, we term this "public procurement," and as documented in, e.g., Bosio et al. (2022), the sums involved are large in most countries. In many cases, the sums allocated to public procurement in a country corresponds to more than 20% of that country's gross domestic product. Again, these are situations where moral hazard potentially plays a large role. To analyze some of the core issues, Hart et al. (1997) present a model where government can choose to provide a service itself, "in-house," or choose to buy the service from private providers, public procurement. Their model involves a trade-off where private providers have lower costs of producing the product (which thus favors procurement), but this is balanced against quality being hard to observe.[22] A private contractor may then be tempted to cut down on quality to save on costs. Key to their modeling framework is that some issues are easy to observe and contract on and others difficult – as the balance of these differ across goods, some activities lend themselves well to procurement (cases where costs are much lower in private and quality easy to contract on) and others badly (smaller cost differences and quality hard to contract on).

To capture parts of the intuition, consider the following simple model. Assume that a government cares about the quality of a service provided to households and achieves a utility of $12q$, where q denotes quality of the service. Further, assume that the cost of producing quality for the government is $2q^2$ such that if the government provided the service itself, it would set quality to maximize $12q - 2q^2$. The optimal quality level in case the government provides the service itself is thus $q^G = 3$ at a total cost of 18 (2×3^2).[23] By assumption, the private firm has a lower cost of providing quality, specifically assume that this is q^2. *If* government could perfectly observe quality, it could offer a contract where it paid 9 if quality is at least 3: The private provider would then maximize profit by providing a quality of 3 at a price of 9 (and precisely break even since profit is then $9 - 3^2$). By procuring, the government could then offer the same quality at a lower cost.

But now suppose that government can't observe quality, at least not in way that would be verifiable in court. If it in this case were to offer a fixed payment of 9, a profit-maximizing firm would provide a quality of zero since the firm would then solve the profit-maximization problem by setting $q = 0$, which maximizes $9 - q^2$. Unobservability of quality then clearly promotes in-house production, again the consequence of a moral hazard problem.

The way that we set up the problem is extremely simplified, but the predictions of this type of model have some support in empirical studies: Looking at around 30 different services provided by local government, for instance, Levin and Tadelis (2010) find that services that are judged to be more difficult to contract are more likely to provided in-house by local government. To get a feel for the kind of characteristics that determine contract difficulty, examples of services that are deemed to be relatively easy to contract on are vehicle towing and garbage collection, whereas those that are hard to contract on are crime prevention, drug/alcohol treatment programs, and fire prevention. Typically, services where quality resides in the quality of human interaction and in bad things not happening. "We prevented 1 out 3 possible crimes" is a harder case to measure than "we emptied 97% of garbage cans on time." Similarly, in a detailed study of private and public ambulances in Stockholm, Knutsson and Tyrefors (2022) find that private providers reduce costs and perform better on contracted measures (for instance, response time) but perform worse on noncontracted measures (such as mortality). Their results are consistent with the kind of trade-off between cost and quality savings as modeled by Hart et al. (1997).

14.3.1.2 Other applications

In some markets like car inspection or accounting, a lax enforcement of legally mandated rules can be a way of increasing demand and what is known as the Enron scandal, when massive accounting wrongdoings at Texas energy firm Enron was eventually uncovered, is a prominent example of this. The accounting firm Arthur Andersen, one of the leading in the world at the time, was effectively shut down as a result of the affair. A related case notes that a pharmacy will increase sales of prescription drugs if it is less diligent in checking whether prescriptions are correct and issued by discerning doctors. Such behavior is likely to be more tempting for a small independent pharmacy where the owner gets to keep the profit, and the probability of detection and punishment may be lower. Janssen and Zhang (2023) documents behavior in line with this prediction for sales of opioid painkillers in the United States – highlighting a contributing role of (some) retail pharmacies in the US opioid epidemic.

Other important fields of study, for instance, examine the kind of contracts that owners of firms can use to get management to act in the owners' interest rather than in management's own interest.[24] The rulers of a country (or local jurisdiction) also have an incentive to act in their own interest rather than for the public good – privatizing state assets to friends in a way that is hard for others to trace, for instance. How the rulers and upholders

Illustration 14.6 Who guards the guardians? *A Soldier in Ancient Roman Costume with Pike and Shield*, Lattanzio Gambara. Smithsonian Institute, public domain.

of public regulations should be steered away from moral hazard is a key question in political science. To highlight the perennial nature of this question, it is not seldom introduced by a 2,000-year-old Latin quote "quis custodiet ipsos custodes?" – who guards the guardians?[25]

14.3.2 *How to limit consequences of moral hazard*

We have partly covered examples of how to limit problems related to moral hazard but let us in the following collect some key points.

Incentives vs. sharing of risk A first important point is that, as discussed in connection to Table 14.3, there is in many cases a trade-off between placing stronger incentives on the more informed agent and sharing risk. Deductibles in an insurance lowers the risk of moral hazard but places more risk on the more informed party. In many situations, the less informed party has a greater ability to take on risk as in the case of (wealthier) landowner vs. a (poorer) sharecropper, a (large and diversified) insurance company rather than an individual user or the government-funded social insurance rather than the individual. On the other hand, the more of the risk that is placed on the informed party, the more incentives aligned for efficiency. As in many cases, economics does not necessarily point to a "correct" level, which will partly be a normative issue, but aid decision-making by clearly spelling out the trade-offs involved. Consider, for instance, the case of sick pay. If coverage is 100% from day 1 with no controls, the sick pay provides incentives for moral hazard, in this case to stay at home even though one is not sick and perhaps only hungover or tired from watching a sporting event in the wrong time zone.[26] On the other hand, the insurance then provides full insurance for someone who really is sick. Decreasing the replacement rate and letting sick pay kick in only after several days of sick leave are ways through which the moral hazard problem can be lessened – but at the cost of providing less insurance (see, e.g., Palme and Persson (2020) for a survey of the literature and practices across European countries).

Make information more equal Attacking the information asymmetry at its heart is another way of managing moral hazard. In the case of sick leave discussed earlier, one can, for instance, have sick pay come from the employer for a first limited period rather than from social insurance. As the employer knows the situation better, this in effects delegates (and motivates) the decision to a more informed party. Requiring a doctor's certificate is another way of lessening the information asymmetry. Putting investor representatives on company boards is another example of moves to limit the information asymmetry, in this case when it comes to financing of start-up firms.

Efforts at equalizing information can also come from the more informed party – having an open kitchen at a restaurant where consumers can see the chefs at work is one way to signal that the restaurant is committed to avoiding moral hazard in the kitchen.[27]

Rules and social norms on acceptable behavior A final point to highlight is that while behavior is not necessarily observable in the short term, we often learn over time. Having delayed rewards is one response, another is to establish and maintain social norms on acceptable behavior, as we discuss next.

14.4 Concluding discussion

Let us conclude with some reflections on how we respond to asymmetric information. Much of the behavioral economics analysis on deviations from the simple selfish materialist behavior that we presented in Chapter 5 has focused on deviations at the individual level – regarding, for instance, overoptimism or letting our choices be influenced by how information is presented. However, when we enter topics of what is morally acceptable behavior in interactions with others, the scope for deviations from a simple model where we only care about our own consumption of goods and services is even larger. Even the most superficial look at human behavior across time and space shows that, under different circumstances, humans are capable of both spectacular selflessness and prosocial behavior, as well as exceptional selfishness. As discussed earlier, there is substantial empirical evidence for adverse selection and moral hazard playing a role for behavior – but the extent to which this is true needs to be sensitive to the context that we examine and the institutional rules and social norms that are relevant.

Would higher morals and more honest behavior solve problems related to asymmetric information? Yes, in an idealized world where everyone was fully truthful toward everyone that is indeed true. Note, however, that many of the adverse effects of asymmetric information do not necessarily rely on outright lies and deception. Take the car example that we started this chapter with as an example. The equilibrium where the market breaks down in essence relies on all the owners of low-quality cars do not explicitly state that the car is of low quality. Terms from sellers like "I don't know," "it has worked well for me" imply that there will be a lack of knowledge on the buyer's part. This lowers price, and sellers of high-quality cars rationally pull back from the market. One also gets into moral dilemmas – pretty much everyone would agree that deceiving friends and family is unacceptable. But what about bending the truth against a large insurance company to help me get medical treatment so that I can see my kids grow up? Biases like overoptimism can

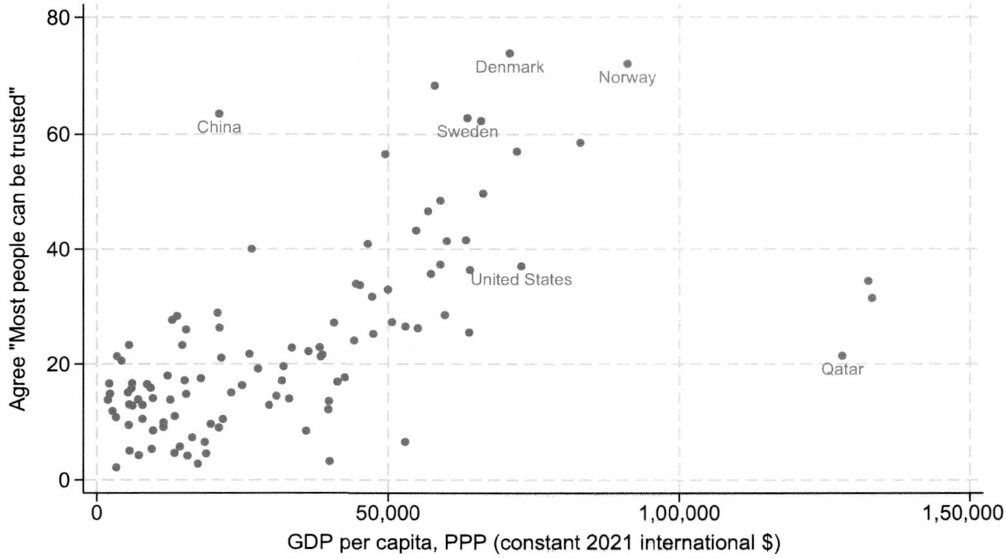

Figure 14.1 Trust and GDP per capita. OurWorldinData.org/trust. Integrated Value Surveys (2022). Data compiled from multiple sources by World Bank. For each country, trust data is shown for the latest survey wave in the period 2009–2022. GDP per capita is expressed in international US dollars at 2021 prices.

also lead to people perceiving themselves as truthful when they report themselves as being highly efficient and ambitious. Thus full truthfulness would also require full truthfulness to ourselves.

While the previous provisos are important, it is also clear that social norms and institutions shape our own behavior in terms of honesty and the expectation of how others will behave, and these can vary over time and place. A variable that captures the general level of trust in society is, for instance, very correlated with how well an economy functions. A number of surveys examine the level of trust across countries and individuals – one variety is, for instance, to ask how much people agree with a statement such as "most people can be trusted."[28] Figure 14.1 illustrates the relation across countries between the share of people who agree to the statement that most people can be trusted (on vertical axis) and gross domestic product per capita (the value of all goods and services sold in a country divided by the number of inhabitants). The latter has a number of well-known weaknesses as a general measure of how well a country functions, but we also know that it is positively correlated with a number of outcomes that are clearly linked to well-being, such as health outcomes.[29]

Broadly speaking then, it seems that trust in a society has several benefits. The deeper question then becomes how do you increase trust and trustworthiness? A huge and important topic that will have to remain outside the scope of an introductory textbook in microeconomics, but see, for instance, Ellingsen (2024) for an analysis that relies on many of the tools that we also use in introductory microeconomics.

Notes

1 A personal history of the article is available at https://www.nobelprize.org/prizes/economic-sciences/2001/akerlof/article/.

2 You may reasonably ask where the prior of 50% comes from. The exact number is not important for the story; however, the key point is that a nonzero probability that a product is of low quality lowers the willingness to pay. A simple motivation for the equal probabilities is what is sometimes known as the principle of indifference: If there are several possible events, give them equal probabilities. This works well for coins or dice but not necessarily for buying a used car; anyway, it is just a starting point.

3 Attitudes toward risk are covered in Chapter 16. For now, just note that someone who is risk-neutral cares only about the expected value. A risk-averse buyer would put a higher weight on the negative outcome.

4 Remember that with only two possible outcomes, the probabilities of the car being of high and of low quality sum to 1; a probability of a low quality of 0.7 thus implies a probability of 0.3 (from 1 to 0.7) of it being of high quality.

5 But there is financing for entrepreneurship nevertheless – how does that work? We return to this below but note that financing of start-ups typically doesn't mainly operate via banks but via investors buying parts of the company, taking a seat on the board, and so forth, various ways of limiting the information asymmetry.

6 Shleifer (2004) contains a discussion of other related examples.

7 See, for instance, Ert and Fleischer (2019) for a case study of Airbnb and references to other work in this area.

8 See, e.g., Dranove and Jin (2010) for a survey.

9 To get a glimpse into some of these processes, you may, for instance, want to check out the website of the International Organization for Standardization, iso.org.

10 Spence (1973). Again, for a slight deviation into the role of models in economics, we note that in connection to the Nobel awards, the laureates typically come to the Stockholm School of Economics and engage in informal discussions. On his visit, Spence was reflecting on the need for models against the backdrop of having had another laureate, Thomas Schelling, as a supervisor. Schelling largely worked in a verbal style and is a joy to read, also for someone who hasn't studied economics. Spence noted that Schelling was highly inspirational, but as a student, it was sort of like looking at Yo-Yo Ma playing the cello and wondering, "Where do I start?" A model is a way to clearly transmit an idea and allow others to work and build on it.

11 Clearly, the model is super simple as presented here; there is, for instance, no time dimension.

12 We also encountered separating equilibrium in the context of second-degree price discrimination – if customers with a high willingness to pay travel first class and others do not, we have a separating equilibrium.

13 For another application of signaling in evolutionary biology, note that it has been proposed that only a specimen with very high biological fitness can "afford" to develop what appears to be a handicap like the feathers of a peacock (Zahavi (1975)). This hypothesis is far from generally accepted, however – the details of whether this latter hypothesis holds depend on how traits are inherited and their benefits, and a discussion would bring me far out of my depth in biology. One of the giants of evolutionary biology, John Maynard Smith, is one of those who has criticized the applicability of the "handicap theory" to evolutionary biology (Smith (1976)).

14 See, e.g., Landers et al. (1996) for a simple model and an empirical study.

15 Of course, that doesn't mean that the a driver of a fully insured car will not care at all. Most of us have some sense that we don't want to destroy property and risk the health of ourselves and others – but on the margin, the fully insured are expected to be less careful, as indeed found in, for instance, Weisburd (2015) that studies links between the extent of insurance coverage and accident rates for drivers.

16 The example also follows the historical development of the analysis of moral hazard in economics. The third Nobel laureate from 2001, Joseph Stiglitz, has been extremely prolific, and the prize cited several works as central – but the Stiglitz (1974) examination of sharecropping was prominent among those.

17 In formal terms, this is again the incentive compatibility constraint that we examine, which we also analyzed in connection to price discrimination under self-selection constraints.

18 The example has taken some inspiration from the Deepwater Horizon oil spill in 2010. The expectation of what liability BP was responsible for was less clear-cut than in this example. The official US investigation of what happened points to corners being cut when it came to safety, see https://www.govinfo.gov/content/pkg/GPO-OILCOMMISSION/pdf/GPO-OILCOMMISSION.pdf.
19 See, e.g., Duffie (2019) for an accessible discussion of moral hazard issues in the run-up to the 2008 crisis.
20 If the entrepreneur chooses L, the investment is a bad deal in expectation since $0.4 \times 40 - 20 = -4$.
21 The saying may appear a bit strange and its origins seem unclear – online searches turn up everything from southern horse racing, golf tournaments at IBM, and a popularizing role by legendary investor Warren Buffet (William Safire in the *New York Times Magazine* tries to find the roots but with no definitive answer https://www.nytimes.com/2006/09/17/magazine/17wwln_safire.html. I intuitively think of a somewhat rough sport event where if you're out on the field, you can get bruised and battered (having skin in the game) – as opposed to if you're just a spectator at a safe distance.
22 Note that we can further differentiate between observability and contractability. Consider a case where you hire a babysitter. You're not likely to be at home when the babysitter takes care of your kids, so you don't perfectly observe how she acts – quality here being things like being kind and stimulating so that your kid has a joyful, stimulating, and safe time. But you can talk to your kids (given that they are not literally babies) and let the babysitter try out when you are also at home to see the kid-sitter interaction. So there may be partial observability. For public procurement, however, note that you would typically need to specify ex ante what you mean by quality. If you are to break the contract or demand penalty payments from the provider, you would need to be able to argue that quality has been low in a way that can hold up in court and be written into a contract. Doing this for a task like babysitting is nontrivial.
23 As in previous chapters, we optimize (in this case over q) and reach the first-order condition $12 - 4q = 0$.
24 Jensen and Meckling (1976) is a central reference in the literature applying modern models of asymmetric information to the relations between a firm's owners and its managers.
25 One inroad to the questions of how country decision-making is organized and essentially how moral hazard on the part of the ruler can be controlled is found in Acemoglu and Robinson (2012).
26 As indeed documented in Thoursie (2004).
27 If you've seen the movie *Fight Club* you may remember Tyler Durden's guerilla terrorist in the food industry – open kitchens minimizes that risk for a restaurant.
28 See, for instance, World Value Survey at https://www.worldvaluessurvey.org/wvs.jsporhttps://ourworldindata.org/trust for an overview.
29 See, e.g., Jones and Klenow (2016).

Part VI

Applications

Partly drawing on the set of tools that we have developed so far, a number of different topics can be analyzed – topics that are often the basis for a full course in themselves. Such applications typically draw on a combination of institutional detail and theory that pays careful attention to the key issues in the questions at hand. In the next four chapters, we cover four such applications. For many of us, the labor market is the single-most important market for our well-being, and Chapter 15 expands on some key mechanisms of relevance for labor markets. Chapter 16 introduces some of the basic concepts of how we can model and manage uncertainty. Chapter 17 then uses the tools of microeconomics and some institutional detail to understand the welfare effects of international trade and how trade policy works. Finally, Chapter 18 examines some topics from digital markets. Digitalization has a huge impact on how many markets function, from how we consume movies and TV series to how people are dating. In this chapter, we in particular focus on the economic logic behind platforms and also some of the basics of auctions, which are particularly prominent in online markets.

DOI: 10.4324/9781003623854-20

15 Labor supply and demand

Illustration 15.1 In the textile factory. *The Interior of a Textile Factory*, unknown artist. In the public domain, Smithsonian Institute.

Once you've finished studying, many of you are likely to enter an employment relation and get paid a wage in return. How the matching takes place between employers and employees, how we choose an occupation, and how wages and other conditions at work are determined is clearly hugely important. Both at a personal and at a societal level. The functioning of labor markets, such as how unemployment develops over economic booms and recessions, and links between wage setting and inflation are a central feature in many textbooks and courses in macroeconomics. For that reason, this chapter is not a comprehensive examination of the vast question of how labor markets function. A few of the key mechanisms at play however – governing the supply and demand for labor do fit in well in a course in microeconomics, and this chapter focuses on giving you the tools to understand these mechanisms.

DOI: 10.4324/9781003623854-21

15.1 Firm-level demand for labor under perfect competition

We get considerable insights on how much labor to hire for a firm already in the simplest case where all potential employees are equally well suited, and the firm is a price taker on the input market, meaning that changes in how much labor it hires doesn't affect the wage. Consider the case of a firm that has a production function given by $Q = f(K, L)$, so that, just as in, e.g., Chapter 3, the number of units produced depends on how much of the inputs capital (K) and labor (L) that is used. Assume that the amount of capital is fixed at $\bar{K}$ so that we examine the choice of how many workers to hire in the short run. A firm that wants to maximize profits would want to choose L so as to maximize the profits, maximizing the difference between revenue (which depends on L as this determines the quantity produced) and costs (which clearly depend on how much L the firm is paying wage for):

$$\max_{L} pf(\bar{K}, L) - wL - r\bar{K}. \tag{15.1}$$

The resulting first-order condition for the profit-maximizing choice of labor is then

$$\underbrace{p \underbrace{\frac{\partial f(\bar{K}, L)}{\partial L}}_{MP_L}}_{\substack{\text{Marginal value of} \\ \text{an additional worker}}} - \underbrace{w}_{\substack{\text{Marginal cost of} \\ \text{an additional worker}}} = 0.$$

The first term captures the increase in profits from hiring an additional worker. If the firm is a price taker on the market for its output, it sells whatever it produces at a price of p. Hiring an additional worker increases the amount of goods produced by the marginal product of labor, denoted by MP_L. As noted in Chapter 3, the typical assumption is that the marginal product of labor is diminishing, each additional worker adds less and less. The profit-maximizing firm hires labor up to the point where the increase in profit from the last worker hired ($p \times MP_L$) equals the cost of the last worker hired (w). Figure 15.1 illustrates a particular case where, at the wage of 50 euros, 10 workers are hired.[1] For fewer than 10 workers, the value of adding an additional worker is higher than the cost of hiring an additional worker, whereas if more than 10 workers are hired the last workers hired don't contribute enough to make up for the cost of hiring them.

In this simple setting, we can examine how demand for labor for this firm changes as conditions change. A higher wage implies that less labor is demanded, whereas a higher price of the output implies that the value of additional workers increase and more are hired.

Similar logic applies for the demand of other inputs as well – and sometimes the markets for inputs into production are referred to as factor markets, the markets for input factors. We expect decreasing marginal products also of other inputs such as capital. As long as the value (price $\times$ marginal product) of using more of an input exceeds its cost, we expect a firm to use more of that input. Clearly when all inputs are variable, the situation is a bit more complex than what we examined in Figure 15.1 since marginal product of, e.g., labor, also depends on how much of other inputs that are used. With two inputs, the conditions become $p \times MP_L = w$ for labor and $p \times MP_K = r$, which implies that, just as we saw in Chapter 3, the equilibrium choices of K and L are such that $\frac{w}{r} = \frac{MP_L}{MP_K}$.

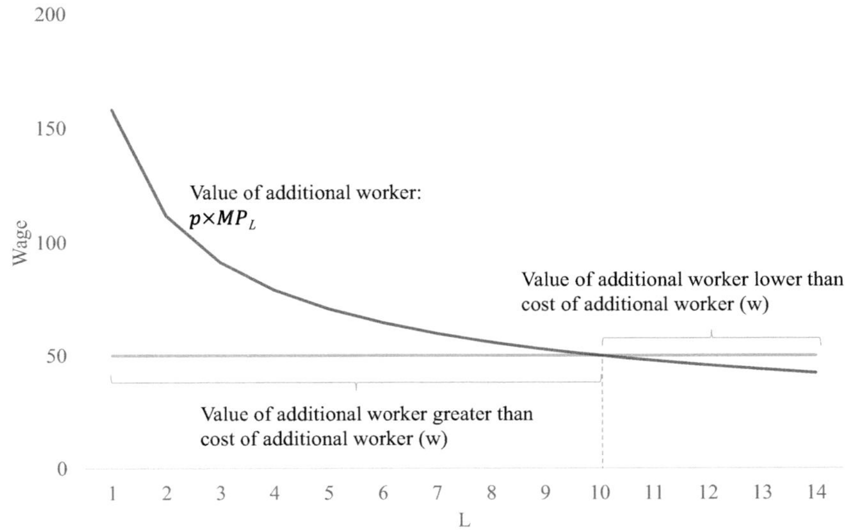

Figure 15.1 Demand for labor from a price-taking firm. Video link for Figure: https://youtu.be/g5DewBVc9tM.

15.2 Supply of labor

As we examine in this section, the mechanisms underlying labor demand and labor supply are substantially more complex than for many goods. Think of a price-taking producer of wheat; the amount of wheat that it is willing to produce is likely to a very large degree to be determined by a the price of wheat. If we instead think of the amount of labor that we supply, there are a large number of factors that determine how much we work, in what occupation for what employer and in what location. Each grain of wheat is not likely to care a lot about where it ends up, whereas for each of us, a large part of our life satisfaction is likely to be tied to where we work and under what conditions. We will scratch the surface on some of those issues next, but first we focus on a simple application of the supply of goods that we examined in Chapter 4 to the supply of labor: How do the number of hours I am willing to work depend on the wage (or in other words, on the price of labor)?

Consider the case where an individual gets utility from two sources; from consumption of goods (G) and from time spent not working, that is from leisure (nonwork, denoted by N). The utility function of this individual can thus be written as $U(G, N)$. Assume that consumption of goods and leisure are imperfect substitutes. Further assume that an indifference curve that captures the willingness to trade off one against the other has the downward-sloping convex shape that we remember from Chapter 5.

How will the individual choose? As usual in economics, the optimal choice depends on preferences, costs, and income. A novel feature compared to what we did in Chapter 5 is that income now is partly chosen by the individual: By determining how much to work, she partly determines her income. Put yourself in the shoes of this individual, and let the hourly wage equal w. There are only 24 hours to a day, so this puts a hard upper limit to how much you can work in a day. Time not spent in leisure is spent working, and the number of hours

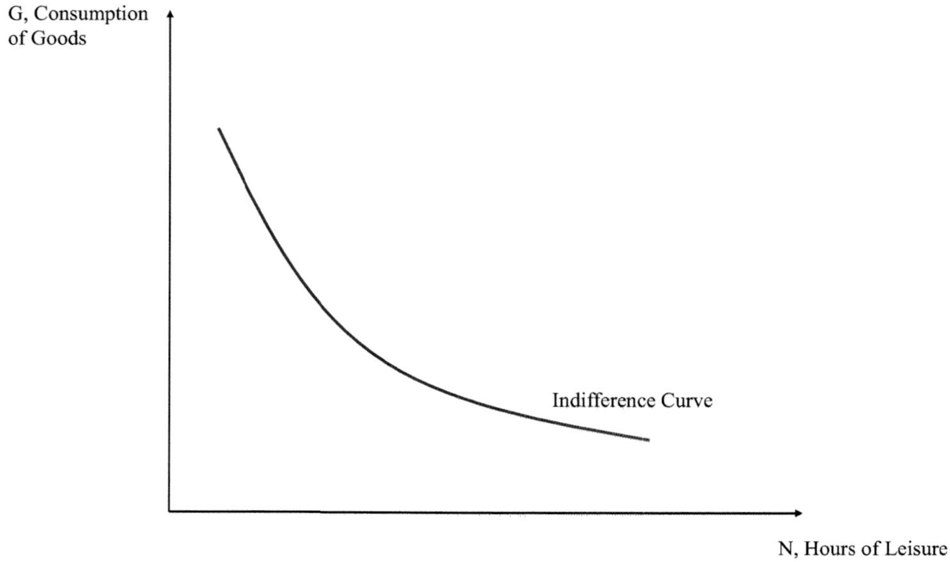

Figure 15.2 Indifference curve capturing preferences for goods and leisure. Video link for Figures 15.2 and 15.3 : https://youtu.be/aWCo_rJJqWU.

worked per day, H, is thus determined as $24 - N = H$. For simplicity, setting the price of goods as $P_G = 1$, we can thus write the budget constraint as

$$G = w \underbrace{(24 - N)}_{\text{Hours of work (H)}}$$

$$G = w24 - wN.$$

If it were possible to work 24 hours, you would be able to consume all the goods G that 24 hours of work at a wage w could buy.[2] If you also want some leisure, you are giving up some consumption of goods in order to do this. For each hour that you choose to spend on leisure rather than working, your income and thereby your ability to purchase goods decreases by w. The slope of the budget constraint is $-w$. The wage is the opportunity cost of your time. Figure 15.3 depicts the utility maximizing choice. We assume that you choose to maximize utility subject to the budget constraint. At the optimal solution, the highest possible indifference curve is attained given the hourly wage you face, resulting in you spending N^* hours on leisure and the remaining $24 - N^*$ hours working, the remuneration for those hours worked allow you to purchase G^* amounts of goods.

To examine the effects of changes in the wage on the supply of hours worked, we can use the framework represented in Figure 15.3. Changes in the wage will rotate the budget constraint, and an optimizing individual will choose the combination of leisure and consumption that maximizes her utility; the combination of goods and leisure that lets her reach the highest attainable indifference curve given that budget constraint. At a higher wage, the budget constraint gets steeper. The intersection with the vertical axis is given by the consumption of goods that you would have if you worked for wage literally all the time ($w \times 24$) and spent all the earnings on goods. If you want to also have some leisure, you

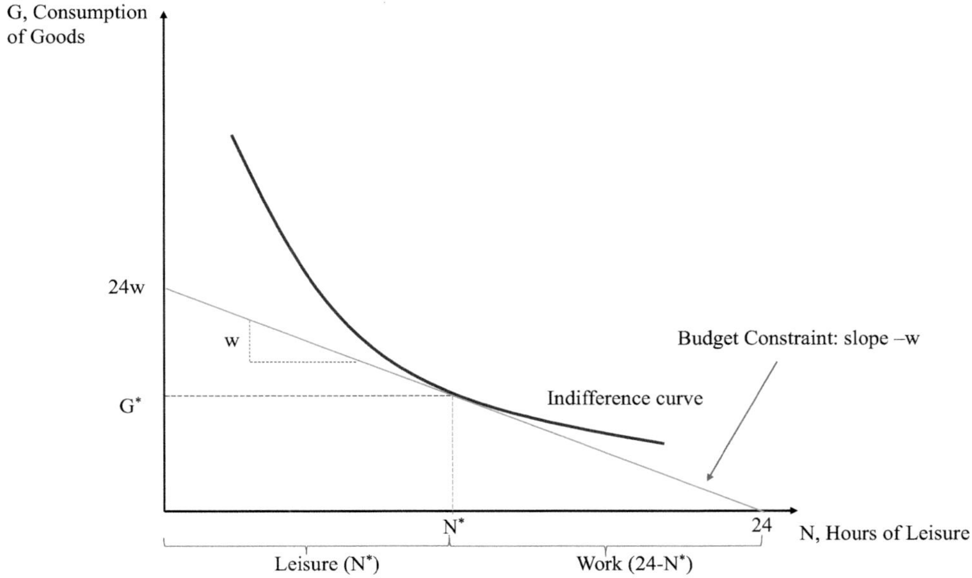

Figure 15.3 Utility maximizing choice of consumption and leisure. Video link for Figures 15.2 and 15.3 : https://youtu.be/aWCo_rJJqWU.

give up some consumption; for each hour less that you work and instead spend on leisure, your consumption of goods decreases by w. The opportunity cost of leisure is greater at a higher wage.

Figure 15.4 shows optimal choice of goods and leisure at two different levels of wage, one lower w_L and one higher, w_M. Since time is spent either working or in leisure, the choice of leisure directly implies a choice of how many hours to work. Figure 15.4 depicts a case where, as wage increases, an individual chooses to spend less on leisure and more time working. Thus, the points of tangency between the indifference curves and budget constraints in the left panel of Figure 15.4 each represent a combination of wage and hours worked. The two points indicated in the left panel thus give us two points on the labor supply curve depicted in the right-hand panel. The labor supply curve gives the relation between wage and the number of hours supplied for work by this individual. Here it is upward sloping; as wage increases, you are willing to put in more hours.

The upward slope of the labor supply curve is not the only possibility, however. Figure 15.5 illustrates a case where at an even higher wage of w_H; the individual wants to use some of the gains from the higher wage to have more leisure. A case where the slope of the labor supply curve is positive at first and then becomes negative at even higher wages is known as a backward-bending labor supply curve, and Figure 15.5 clearly illustrates where the name comes from.

To understand what drives the possibility of a backward-bending supply curve at a deeper level, remember back to our analysis of income and substitution effects in Chapter 6. In Figure 15.6, we zoom in on the shift from w_M to w_H that we examined in Figure 15.5. This is the case where a higher wage (w_H) is associated with more leisure and therefore fewer working hours: $N_H > N_M$. Analogously, as for the case of price changes of a good, the response to a change in the price of leisure (the wage) can be decomposed into a substitution

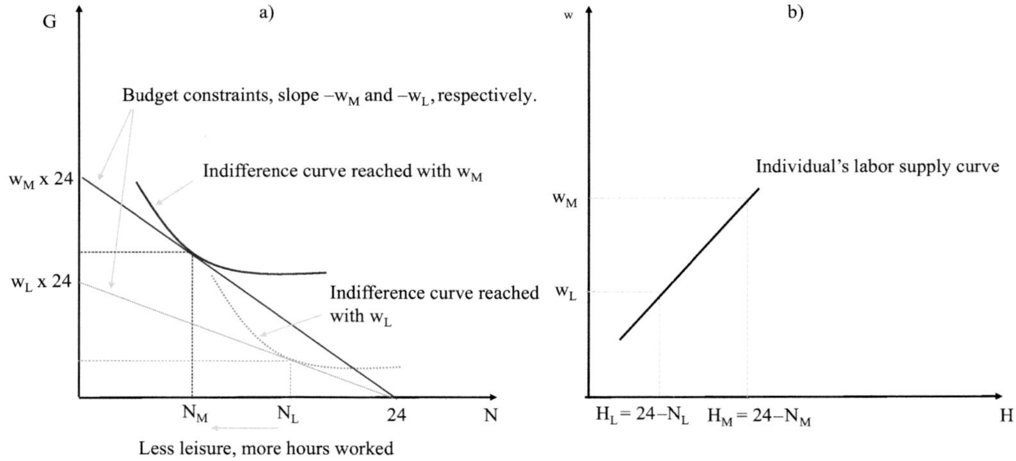

Figure 15.4 From utility maximizing choice of consumption and leisure to the labor supply curve. Video link for Figure 15.4: https://youtu.be/3z1UI_RXkbw.

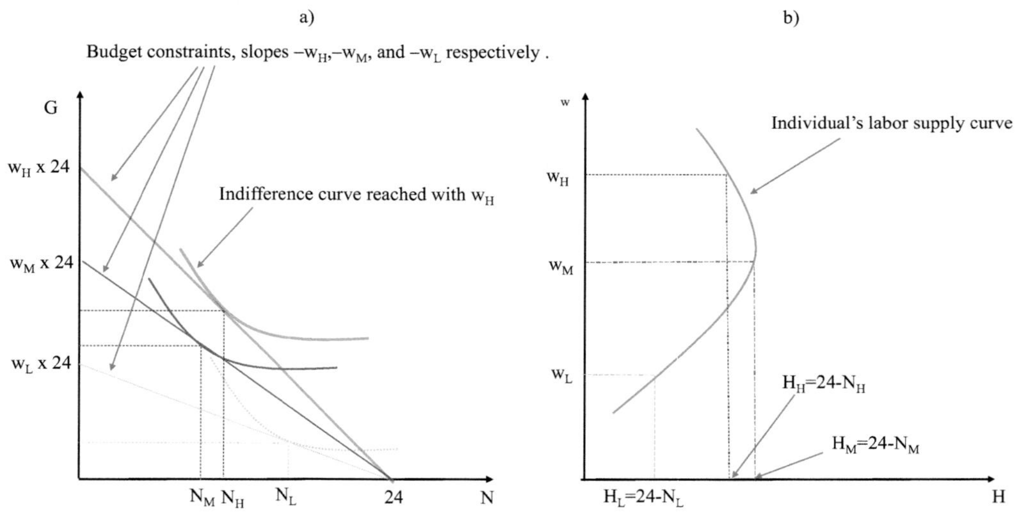

Figure 15.5 A backward-bending labor supply curve: An example. Video link for Figures 15.5 and 15.6: https://https://youtu.be/lUVUAsurIB0.

effect and an income effect. The substitution effect measures the response in hours worked as we move from the initial situation (N_M) to one where the individual is at the same indifference curve as initially (U_M), but facing the new relative price (w_H). The steeper slope of this hypothetical budget constraint implies a point of tangency that involves less leisure and more work. Leisure has become more expensive; you give up more consumption to have leisure when wages are higher. One part of the response is to have less leisure, leading to the hypothetical and unobserved choice of N_S hours of leisure. The difference between N_S and N_M is the substitution effect. This is not all that is going on however. With the higher wage,

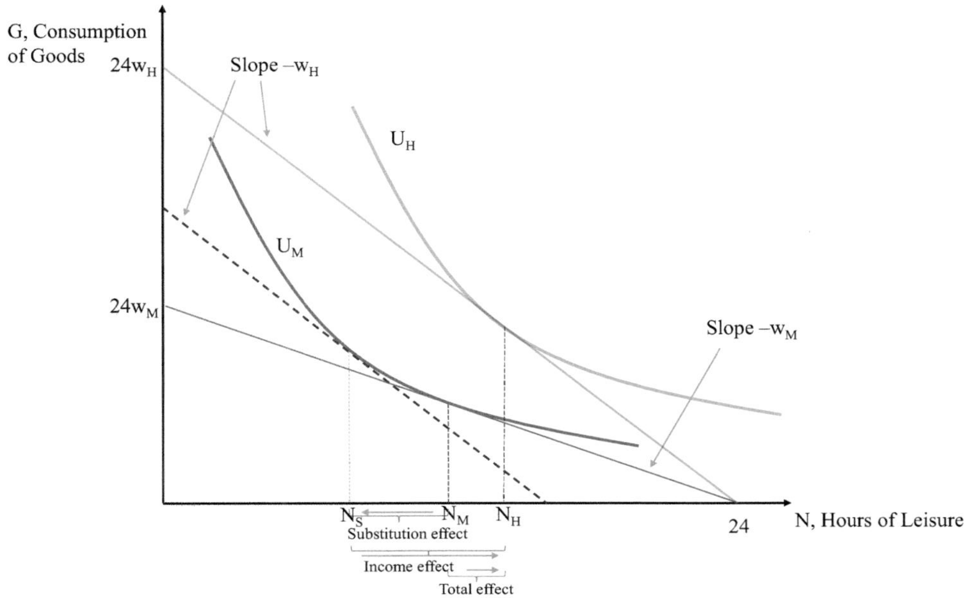

Figure 15.6 A backward-bending labor supply curve: The role of income and substitution effects. Video link for Figures 15.5 and 15.6: https://https://youtu.be/lUVUAsurIB0.

it is as if you had a higher income, which we can think of as a parallel shift in the budget constraint from the hypothetical one to the actual budget constraint at a higher wage. If leisure is a normal good – that is, we want more leisure at higher incomes – then the income effect counteracts the substitution effect. If the income effect is sufficiently strong, it will outweigh the substitution effect, and an individual will choose to have more leisure as the wage increases, as is indeed shown in Figure 15.6.

While simple, the previous framework forms one conceptual basis for understanding the effect of changes in wages on the supply of labor. This is a key factor in many areas of economics, useful in making predictions for how labor supply will respond to changes in taxes and how the labor market evolves over recessions and booms. As is in many other applications of microeconomics, the empirical evidence often measures the outcome of interest as an elasticity. The **labor supply elasticity** measures the percentage change in hours worked in response to a percentage change in the wage.[3] Broadly speaking, much of the empirical evidence points to that for men in their prime working age, the elasticity is close to zero; that is, the supply curve is approximately vertical. At one level, this is not surprising; having a full-time job with a fixed monthly wage is the way many of us make sure that we can pay our bills, and there is not a lot of leeway in adjusting in the short run from such a position, even if we wanted to.

Before moving on, let us also elaborate somewhat on the income effect of a higher wage. If the income effect is positive, as in Figure 15.6, then a higher income is associated with a greater demand for leisure. On the other hand, it is easy to think of many high-income individuals who work very long hours – just look at many management consultants or managers. However, the hourly wage is not the only thing that differs between the incentives, constraints, and expectations facing a McKinsey consultant and someone with a more ordinary career. To get at the causal effect of higher income on labor supply, we would ideally want to examine cases where some people at random receive a higher income. This is precisely what a lottery does. Whoever wins a lottery receives a higher income, and we can compare a winner's labor supply relative to a "control group" that didn't win on the lottery. My next-door neighbor at the Stockholm School of Economics has together with coauthors examined what happens to the labor supply of Swedish lottery winners (Cesarini et al. (2017), see also Imbens et al. (2001) for an influential precursor using US data). Winning a lottery causes a winner to work less, consistent with a positive income effect, such that at higher income leads, you to have more leisure. The effect is rather small, however; also, a winning as large as 20% of lifetime earnings leads to a cutback of after-tax labor income of only some 3.5%. Overall, their findings are consistent with a near-vertical labor supply curve such that the income and substitution effects are of similar magnitude.

15.2.1 Bringing in the real world: The intensive and extensive margins of labor supply

Thus for people in full-time employment, the number of hours worked are relatively unresponsive to changes in the wage. But just as the supply of goods is made up of the supply from many different producers, the supply of labor is made up of a large number of people, and people may move in and out of work. In many economic applications, it is useful to distinguish between the intensive margin and the extensive margin. The **intensive margin** refers to the effect of someone doing more or less of what they already are doing. A firm producing more units or, in the case of labor supply, a worker choosing to work more hours. The **extensive margin** refers to the effect of someone doing something new or stopping to do something altogether. It reflects a binary decision: Either you do something or you don't. It concerns firm entry or exit into markets or, in labor supply applications, individuals moving, e.g., from being a housewife into paid work.

Official statistics define a person as part of the **labor force** if she is either **employed** or **unemployed** – that is, actively looking for a job. Also, for people in the ages when we typically work for pay (between childhood and retirement), not all people will be part of the labor force. Some will be full-time students; some may be married women taking care of the home; some will be in early retirement; some may be just trying to scrape by in the informal sector, and yet others might be living off of their parents playing video games. The share of the population that is in the labor force differs both across time and across countries, as shown for a selection of countries and geographical regions in Figure 15.7. Scandinavian countries like Sweden typically exhibit high labor force participation.

The differences in labor force participation indicate that there is room for the extensive margin to affect labor supply, even if there is little action on the intensive margin. Three important drivers of the extensive margin of labor supply that have been examined by economists are the following.

- *Changes in female labor force participation.*[4] Focusing on Europe and the United States, one might present a highly stylized view whereby female labor force participation was high in the preindustrial era with everyone working on the farm, then low in the early 1900s when women stayed at home taking care of the home and children, into one where also a large share of married women with children work. The 2023 Nobel Prize to Claudia Goldin largely centered on the forces that shaped this development. Broadly speaking, a focus on the extensive margin of female labor force participation widens the scope of labor supply to include many other factors than just the wage rate. Factors that

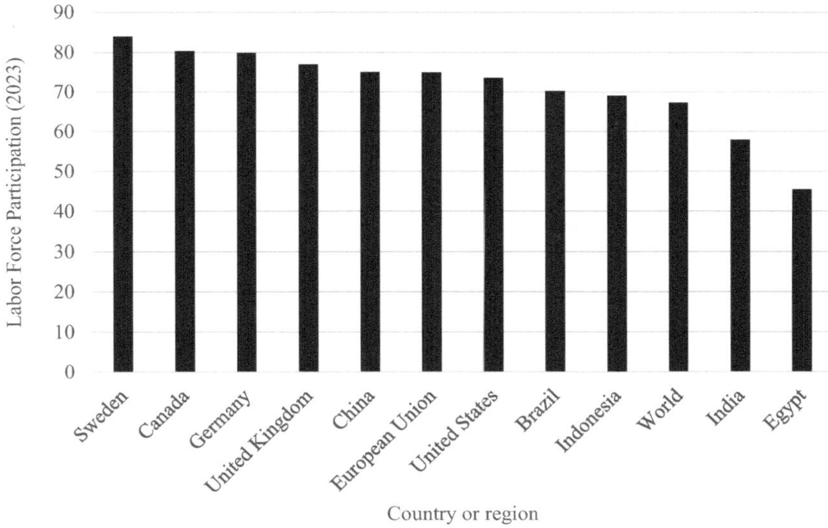

Figure 15.7 Labor force participation in selected regions: Share of population 15–64 years of age that are in the labor force. Labor source participation rate for 2023, total (% of total population aged 15–64) https://data.worldbank.org/indicator/SL.TLF.ACTI.ZS.

affect the ability to combine work and children such as subsidized and widely available childcare, norms regarding who does what in the home and with children, an ability to steer the number of children and the timing of their births, expectations regarding the labor market outcomes of educational investment, and rules regarding what marginal tax rates married couples pay (e.g., will someone married to a high-income earner also pay a high marginal tax rate based on the spouse's high income) may each have substantial effects.[5]

- *Policies that affect when people start working and retirement.* This is another potentially important aspect of the extensive margin – what are the economic incentives to continue working? Factors that affect the income from pensions, as well as the possibility to make sure that older workers continue to have up-to-date skills, are potentially important in this dimension.[6]
- *Migration.* When a large number of people move in or out of a local labor market, this is clearly another important driver of the extensive margin of labor supply. Rules regarding factors such as international migration and validation of licences (e.g., is a qualification as a nurse accepted in other countries) matter for the response of the extensive margin of labor supply.[7]

15.3 Analysis of equilibria in labor markets

As for many markets, a model of supply and demand under conditions of perfect competition may be useful for generating a first shot at the effects of changes in conditions on prices and quantities also in labor markets. Many older microeconomic textbooks would at this stage show graphs of the labor market as a perfectly competitive market and illustrate the effect of various shifts in costs or demand. Such an analysis still has its place; we, for instance, expect a marked shift in demand for a particular type of worker in an area that is not fully open to immigration to drive up wages. We might see such an analysis as a special case of the supply and demand analysis that we examined in the first chapters.

Applying the perfectly competitive model to a real-world market always comes with caveats. For modern labor markets, such qualifiers and cautions should be especially strong. Different workers are not perfect substitutes. We differ both by our innate abilities, education and previous experiences, and work contracts may be partly shaped by concerns regarding asymmetric information. The extent to which this matters will differ across positions; a lot of us will have similar productivity for mowing a lawn, but we will differ hugely in our ability to score goals if we were to play for Real Madrid or to design an airplane engine. Similarly, different employers are not perfect substitutes. If I want to keep working as a university professor, there are a large number of universities around the world, but within commuting distance, there are just a handful, and they differ by travel time and how closely the research interests of their faculty align with mine. The matching of employers and employees is a drawn-out procedure that requires substantial resources. In addition, the institutional details surrounding unions and bargaining processes are important for outcomes. In my native Sweden, for instance, wages are typically set in bargaining between employer organizations and unions in so-called collective bargaining agreements – typically setting wage levels for several years at a time and regulating not only wages but also many aspects of the relation between employers and employees.[8]

The effects of minimum wages have become perhaps the most important cautionary tale for using a perfectly competitive model to analyze a labor market. Minimum wage is a regulation that exists in many countries, where political decisions determine a floor for the hourly wage that employers may offer.[9] One might be tempted to use an analysis like that in Figure 15.8 to evaluate the effect of a minimum wage. *If* the labor market is perfectly competitive, a minimum wage that is above the market clearing wage lowers demand, raises supply, and leads to excess supply, which in a labor market takes the form of unemployment.

However, a string of highly influential papers in the early 1990s examined the effects of minimum wages in different areas of the United States and found essentially no evidence for important negative effects of the type represented in Figure 15.8 – key early references are found in, e.g., Card (1992), Katz and Krueger (1992), Card and Krueger (1994). These were pioneering works in using naturally occurring variation in policy across different regions to trace out effects of those policies. In an analogy to testing of new pharmaceutical products, we can think of a "treated" group (for instance, employers affected by minimum wage, such as fast-food restaurants in one state) and a "control" group (e.g., employers across the border in another state not affected by the policy change but otherwise affected by similar shocks).[10] A large subsequent literature, also examining other countries, by and large confirms the lack of large negative effects on employment from minimum wage increases of the magnitudes that are observed empirically; see Manning (2021a) for an accessible overview.

A comprehensive analysis of equilibria in labor markets will have to await specialized courses in labor economics and in macroeconomics, where, for instance, the development of unemployment and wages during economic booms and recessions is of key interest. Let us, however, develop the theoretical understanding of one mechanism, whereby it would not be surprising if there are small or no negative effects of a minimum wage on employment:

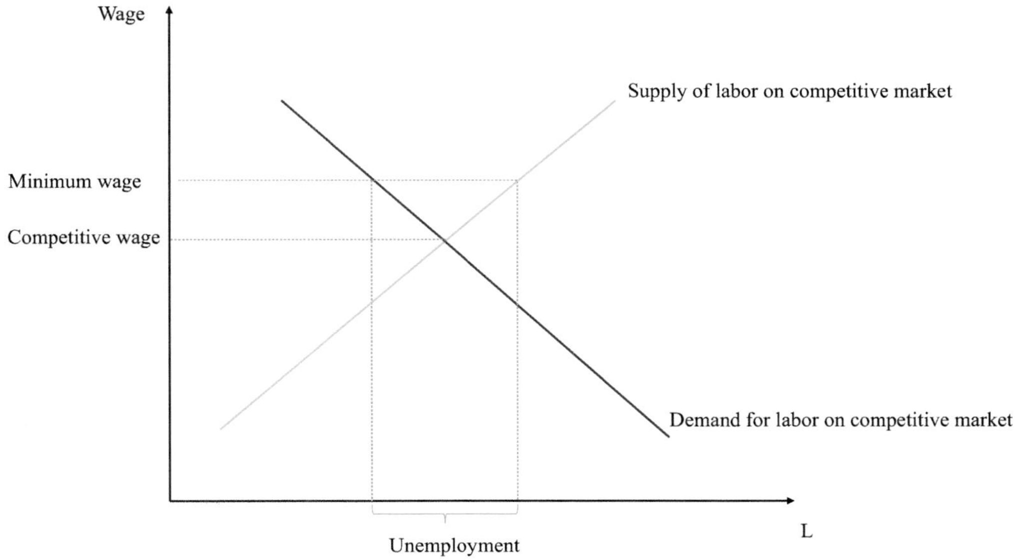

Figure 15.8 Supply and demand on a perfectly competitive labor market: Regulation above market clearing wage.

that of market power on input markets. Monopoly refers to the case where there is a sole seller on a market; its mirror image monopsony refers to the case where there is a single buyer on the market. Under monopsony, an increase in the minimum wage can even increase employment; in the following, we examine the mechanism.

15.3.1 Market power on input markets: Monopsony

Under **monopsony**, there is a single buyer of a product. Similarly, if there are a few buyers of a product, we term this **oligopsony**. This can be relevant to several types of product markets (e.g., large supermarket chains or where many independent farmers sell to one dairy).[11] Demand for labor is an especially relevant application. At the outset of this chapter, we examined labor demand for a firm that was a price taker on the labor market. The wage that it paid to a worker was independent of how many workers it employed – the wage is constant just as the price of the output is constant for a price-taking firm. In contrast, a monopsonist is not a price taker on the local labor market. For a visual image, you can think of a "company town," a small isolated city where a large factory totally dominates the labor market. If labor supply (including both intensive and extensive margins) is upward sloping, then the firm meets this upward-sloping supply curve. The maximization problem facing the monopsonist, when deciding how much labor to hire, is essentially the same as in Equation (15.1) at the outset of the chapter, but with the new added twist that w is not constant but instead depends on L so that the cost of hiring is given by $w(L)L$ rather than just wL. The analogy to monopoly on the output market should be clear; there we compare $p(q)q$ for the monopolist to pq for the price taker. The maximization problem with respect to the amount of labor to hire for the monopsonist is hence given by Equation (15.3).

Illustration 15.2 The only game in town. *The Factory Village*, 1897, Julian Alden Weir, Courtesy of Metropolitan Theory of Art. Public domain.

$$pf(\bar{K}, L) - \underbrace{w(L)}_{\text{Wage depends on L}} L - r\bar{K} \tag{15.2}$$

Let us consider a numerical example to illustrate how the incorporation of market power on the labor market impacts the hiring decision. Assume that $pf(\bar{K}, L)$ is given by $30L - L^2$ and that $w(L) = 2L$. The maximization problem for the monopsonist is then

$$\max_L \underbrace{(30L - L^2)}_{pf(\bar{K},L)} - \underbrace{2L}_{w(L)} L - r\bar{K}, \tag{15.3}$$

and the first-order condition for profit maximization with respect to L is then given by

$$30 - 2L - 4L = 0,$$

which we solve for the profit maximizing choice of $L = 5$, which gives the associated wage of $2 \times 5 = 10$ euros. Figure 15.9 illustrates the situation, where we use the subindex M to denote the profit-maximizing choice of labor L_M and the associated wage, w_M. If the firm instead had acted as a price taker on the input market (denote the solution with subindex C),

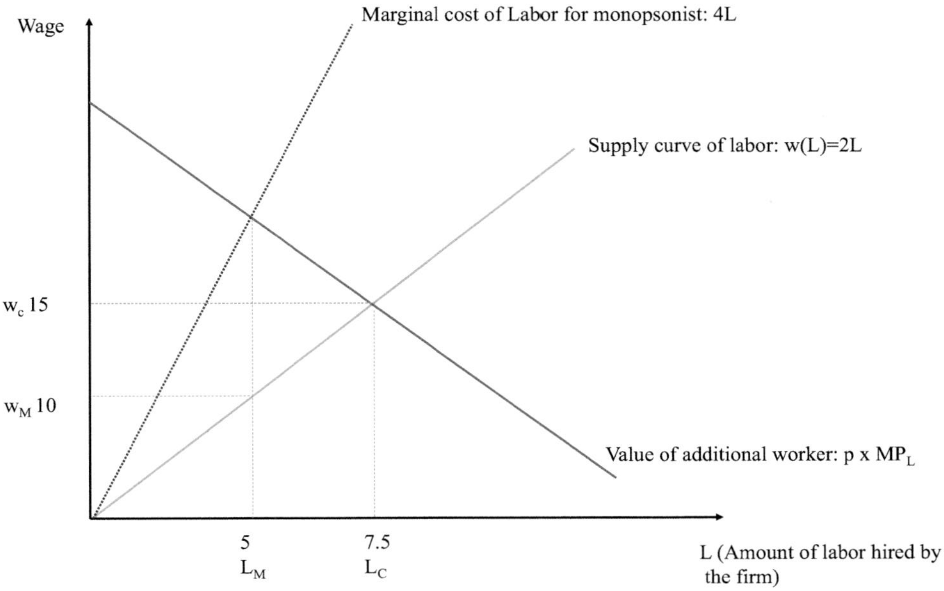

Figure 15.9 Labor demand by a monopsonist. Video link for Figure 15.9: https://youtu.be/VDNlB8YxQB8.

it would have set L such that the marginal benefit of an additional worker ($30 - 2L$) was equal to supply curve ($2L$) at the optimal point, leading to $L_C = 7.5$ and an associated wage equal to $2 \times 7.5 = 15$ euros. As a flip side of the coin, where a monopolist on the output market holds back on quantity to drive up price, the monopsonist holds back on hiring to avoid driving up the wage. Relating to the discussion of a minimum wage earlier, we now see that if the wage is between w_M and w_C, a minimum wage can actually be associated with an increase in employment: The monopsonist's incentive to hold back on hiring in order to avoid driving up wages is then muted. Also note that while a clear monopsony situation is likely to be uncommon, this mechanism is likely to play some role in many situations (just as we are interested in market power, also outside of a textbook monopoly case). The key element is that by hiring more, the firm needs to increase wages; the supply curve for labor faced by the firm is upward sloping.[12]

15.3.2 Market power on the supply side: Unions and wage bargaining

There can also be market power on the supply side of labor markets – in particular, employees can organize into labor unions.[13] Wage setting in many countries is done in negotiations between two sides with market power – employers (or association of employers) and labor unions. An additional feature is that regulations in many countries imply that unions bargain on behalf of all workers in a firm – something known as **collective bargaining agreements**. Many textbooks are written with a focus on the United States situation – a country with low participation in labor unions and relatively few employees covered by collective bargaining agreements. In many other countries, in particular in Europe, collective bargaining is the dominant way through which wages are set. Figure 15.10

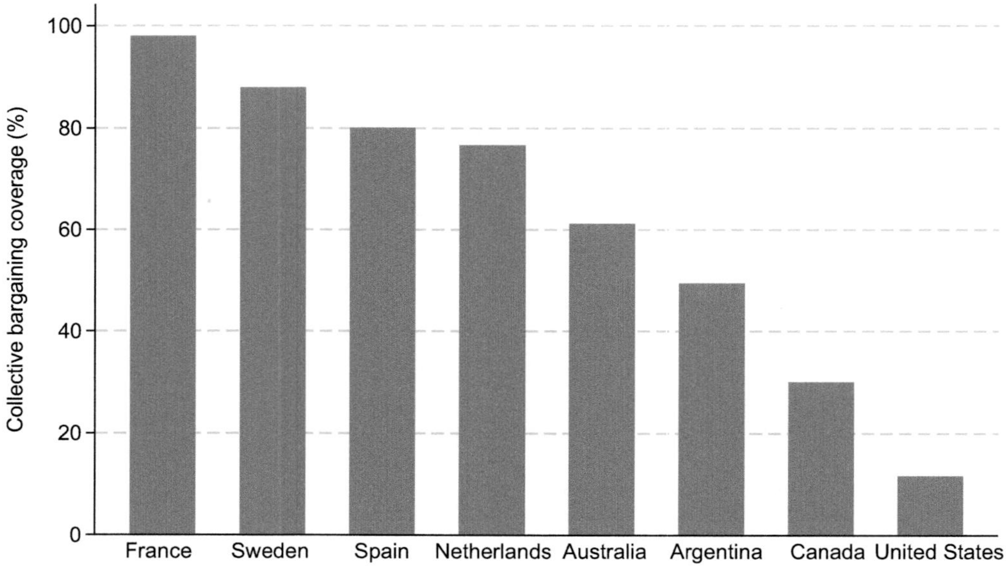

Figure 15.10 Share of employees covered by collective bargaining agreements, selected countries 2018. OECD, https://www.oecd.org/employment/ictwss-database.htm

provides an illustration of this, showing the share of workers who are covered by collective bargaining agreements for a selection of countries. In France, it is close to 100%, but also in many other European countries, more than three quarters of employees are covered by collective bargaining agreements.

The wage contracts negotiated in such collective bargaining agreements often cover several years, but as emphasized in overviews of collective bargaining practices, there is substantial cross-country variation in practices (see Bhuller et al. (2022) or Jäger et al. (2024)). Practices differ across countries regarding how *centralized* wage bargaining is – for instance, at the level of the plant or at industry level (e.g., all firms in the paper and pulp industry bargaining with the unions that are represented in their establishments). Practices also differ with respect to *coordination* – the extent to which different union and employer organizations coordinate their bargaining strategies. In several European countries, sectors that are important for the country's performance on export markets bargain wages first in every wage-setting cycle (a cycle might, for instance, refer to that wage contracts are bargained over three years in relatively rapid sequence for different industries).

Underlying factors that affect the supply and demand for labor will typically be pushing employment and wages in the same direction, irrespective of whether wages are set by bargaining or in a decentralized fashion. What we have emphasized in this section, however, is that precisely how those forces play out depend on how wages are set, and in many countries, the process is very different from perfect competition.

Notes

1 This particular figure is created by assuming that price of the output is 100 euros and $Q = \sqrt{K \times L}$. In this case, $MP_L = \frac{1}{2}\sqrt{\frac{K}{L}}$, and in the figure, we assume that K is fixed at 10 units.

2 You also need some sleep, whether we include a minimum level for sleep or not in the amount of hours that you can allocate for work can safely be left for more advanced work.

3 Advanced treatments also examine different versions of these elasticities, see e.g. Keane (2022). The labor supply elasticity that is associated with Figure 15.6 lets both income and substitution effects play a role and is referred to as the Marshallian elasticity (after Alfred Marshall that was discussed in early chapters). Other versions try to isolate the substitution effect (the associated elasticity is named after British Nobel laureate Sir John Hicks) and to measure the effect of a temporary change in wages (the associated elasticity is named after Norwegian Nobel laureate Ragnar Frisch, see e.g. Elminejad et al. (2023)).

4 See, e.g., Attanasio et al. (2018) for an investigation of the intensive and extensive margins of female labor supply in the United States.

5 For quantitative investigations of some of these margins see, e.g., work by another colleague in a next-door office Domeij and Klein (2013) or Bick and Fuchs-Schündeln (2017).

6 Continuing with references to close colleagues see, e.g., Rogerson and Wallenius (2013) or Laun and Wallenius (2015).

7 As one inroad into the relevant literature, see the classic study of Card (1990) that examined the impact of a large number of Cuban refugees on the Miami labor market. For an overview see, e.g., Hanson (2009).

8 See, for instance, the home page of the governmental agency tasked with mediating in terms of labor conflict, https://www.mi.se/english/about-us/.

9 Many but not all. Sweden, for instance, does not have a politically determined minimum wage – instead, wages are determined by industry-level wage bargaining; see, for instance, Bustos (2023) for an analysis of its effects.

10 Indeed, the cited papers were important in the motivation for the 2023 Nobel Prize in economics given to Josh Angrist, David Card, and Guido Imbens on the use of "natural experiments" to identify causal effects in social sciences.

11 See, for instance, Rogers and Sexton (1994) or Lopez and You (1993).

12 See Manning (2021b) for an overview.

13 Clearly, there can be market power on both sides of the markets also in other input markets. For instance, large retail chains on one side of the market meet producers with market power such as Nestlé, Procter & Gamble, or Unilever. When there is market power on both sides of a relation, we talk of bilateral monopoly, even if strictly speaking neither side is a monopoly.

16 Uncertainty

Illustration 16.1 The fog of uncertainty. Etching by James McNeill Whistler *Nocturne Shipping*, Public domain, via Smithsonian Institute. Thanks to Amar Bhidé for opening my eyes to this source of naval illustrations.

The etching in Illustration 16.1 shows ships weakly discernible through a nighttime fog. For much of history, seafaring has been associated with opportunities, as well as with the "fog of uncertainty" in the form of storms, navigational errors, and pirates. Similarly, the outcomes of many decisions that we make are uncertain – both for us as individuals and for the organizations that we work for. Outcomes can be affected by others' unexpected behavior, by changes in prices, by weather, by technology mishaps, or by other surprising developments. Following the adage that we want an analysis to be "as simple as possible, but not simpler than that," economists often disregard uncertainty. However, sometimes the uncertainty is important enough that we want to put its consequences in the limelight,

DOI: 10.4324/9781003623854-22

and this chapter explains some of the key tools that we use to describe choice in the face of uncertainty.[1]

To set the stage, consider the following situations, which all involve a decision before we know the realizations of variables that affect the outcomes.

1 A bet on a roll of the die
2 Choosing what profession to study at university
3 Choosing how to invest an inheritance that you received – for instance, buying stocks
4 Choosing what crop to plant for a farmer
5 Choosing to start a restaurant

What side of the die that comes up is purely random and follows a known probability distribution. The uncertainty affecting the other choices is less clear-cut. For instance, the value of pursuing education as an economist depends on what jobs you will be able to get in the future and the overall developments of the supply and demand for economists. It also depends on personal developments, where will you be living, and will you be healthy? How can we find a structured way of reasoning around choice in the face of uncertainty? That is what we will be introducing in the following.

16.1 States of the world, risk and uncertainty

To model our choices when there is uncertainty, it will be useful to introduce some structure. First we use **states of the world**, or states for short, to describe the world under different conditions. In the case of the die toss, there are typically just six states of the world, capturing which side of the die that comes up. However, the description of the state of the world is inextricably linked to your role as a decision-maker. For most of us, there would be no point distinguishing between "the die shows a 2, and the sun is shining" from the "the die shows a 2, and it is dark," but if you were a vampire, it would clearly be crucial, as in the former, you would be pulverized by the sun. For a choice of what crops to grow, the states of the world might importantly reflect the prices of the crop at harvest time and climate conditions during the growing season, such as amount of rainfall and whether there has been a frost at sensitive times.

The purpose of listing states is to provide a useful guide to decision-making, not to make comprehensive lists of everything that possibly can happen. As noted already by a key developer of the framework presented here, Leonard Savage, it is even utterly beyond our capabilities to plan a picnic if the approach of describing all possible states is taken to the extreme (Savage (1954, p. 16)). For instance, the two states "rain" or "not rain" are likely to be the two key states to take into account for planning a typical picnic.

Our focus is on various decisions that we can take, and we use the term **actions** to describe our choices. Examples of actions are to bet 10 euros on the die toss, to bet 20 euros on the die toss or not to bet at all. Sowing your fields with wheat is one action and sowing them with corn is another action. Crucially, and this is what makes it a choice under uncertainty, is that we chose action before we know the state, before uncertainty has been resolved. I need to make my bets before I know which side of the die that comes up.

Finally, we are interested in **outcomes** – the value that you attach to different combinations of actions and states. For the action "bet 10 euros" and the state "the die comes up with 2," your outcome will be your winnings if you indeed bet on 2, but −10 if you instead bet on another state. Depending on the relevant problem, the outcome can be a monetary value, or it can be your utility associated with a combination of the action that you've taken and the state.

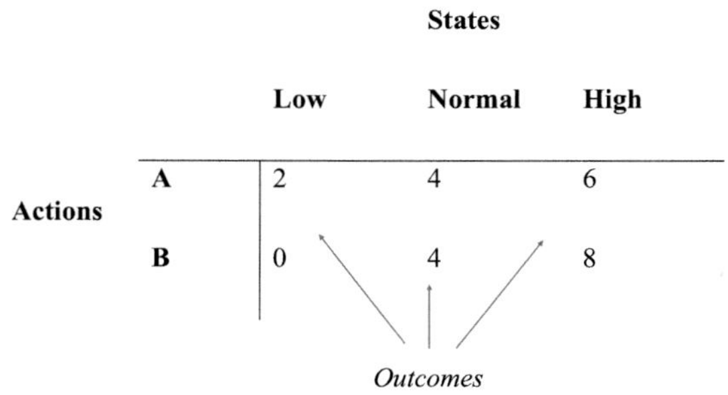

Figure 16.1 Describing a choice under uncertainty: States, actions, and outcomes.

Figure 16.1 illustrates a stylized view of one decision problem under uncertainty. In this case, there are two possible actions to choose between (A and B), and there are three possible states (Low, Normal, and High). Outcomes depend on both the state and on the actions taken. If you chose Action A before the resolution of uncertainty, and state Low is realized, then your outcome is 2. If you instead had chosen Action B, your outcome would be 0 in that same state.

Consider, for instance, the choice between two different investments. Let states Low, Normal, and High reflect the general level of demand in the economy, with Low reflecting little demand, whereas High would reflect strong. Let Action A be investing in something that is not so sensitive to the overall state of the economy (such as a grocery chain, people buy food also in downturns), and let Action B be investing in something that is more affected by the general level of demand (such as a car manufacturer). The outcomes represent the monetary return that depends on both the state and your actions taken. Here we have chosen the values such that they are equal (at 4) in the Normal state, but Action A clearly results in a better outcome in the Low state ($2 > 0$), whereas Action B gives a better outcome in the High state ($8 > 6$).

How should the individual choose between the two actions? Apart from the values of the outcomes that will depend on two things; how likely the different states are and the individual's preferences toward risk. First, let us examine how likely the different states are before turning to preferences toward risk in Section 16.2. Sometimes, as in the case of a single die toss, we know the probabilities from logic and/or previous experience. Unless there is something fishy going on, the probability is 1/6 that each of the sides of the die come up. We sometimes use the term **objective probabilities** to describe such likelihoods; there is no room for disagreement between reasonable people, and we can turn to science and statistics to find the relevant probabilities. In many other cases, such as weather, stock prices, and interest rates, the probabilities of different states may not be as unambiguous, but we can still use data series across time and place to establish reasonably accurate estimates.

In yet other cases, it is hard to have any objective evidence at all to guide the view on likelihoods. Julius Ceasar allegedly said "alea iacta est" – the die has been cast – when he crossed the river Rubicon into Rome at the head of his troops, setting off on an irreversible attempt to overthrow the Roman republic. Clearly, this is largely a one-off event, and there is little scientific basis on which to gauge the probability of different states (succesful coup-d'êtat vs. defeat). Still, his action showed that he was willing to take the bet, and we talk of **subjective probabilities**, as the probabilities reflected in the bets that you are willing to take. Presumably, they represent your best guesses, but for many cases, there is no scientific way to determine if your subjective probabilities are closer to an objective truth than mine.

Following Chicago economist Frank Knight (1921), we sometimes distinguish between the following:

- **Risk** – Strictly speaking, this is the case where the probabilities of different states are known, as in the case of roulette or throwing of dies. Somewhat more broadly, we can also let risk capture cases where statistics and previous data give us a reasonably clear view of the relevant likelihoods of different states.[2]
- **Uncertainty** – Capturing the case where statistics and previous data give limited guidance as to the relevant likelihoods of different states. To distinguish this from "uncertainty" as used in everyday language (and in the title of the chapter), we often refer to this as **Knightian uncertainty**.

Knightian uncertainty here refers to a wide range of cases from those where we are reasonably sure, but we may disagree if the probability of a certain state is 0.10 or 0.20 to cases where we struggle to even describe the relevant states ex ante. We sometimes refer to the latter as choice situations in the face of "unknown unknowns"; we don't know what we don't know. To consider a decision under uncertainty, think of Columbus's decision to sail west to discover a new sea route to India. Clearly, the probability of success was not something for which he could have had a scientific basis, and the possible states would have been hard to specify ex ante. Indeed, it took a number of trips before Europeans realized that it was not the eastern part of India that they had come to but a whole different continent. As evidenced by the discussion so far, it is often relevant to think of the distinction between risk and uncertainty as one where different situations are somewhere on a scale as being more or less amenable to analyse with the help of probability distributions and statistics. The preference relations that we discuss in the following are formalized by referring to risk, with known probability distributions, but are widely taken to be of relevance also for more amorphous cases involving at least some uncertainty.

16.2 Risk preferences

As just noted, the most clearly formulated rules for how we describe choice when the realized state is unknown concerns choice under risk; that is, with known probability distributions. In terms of preferences toward risk, we can distinguish between three main types: You are indifferent; you don't like risk (risk averse); you like risk (risk loving). We cover each of these in turn in the following. Let us first provide an intuitive introduction to the concepts, however. Assume that you are given a choice between receiving 50 euros for sure and a lottery where you either get 100 euros or 0 with equal probabilities. The expected value of the lottery is thus also 50 euros (since $1/2 \times 0 + 1/2 \times 100 = 50$). If you are indifferent between receiving 50 euros for sure and the lottery with the same expected outcome, you are risk neutral. If you prefer receiving the sure outcome of 50 over the lottery with the same expected value, you are risk averse, something that a lot of individuals are. Note that you could also have different degrees of risk aversion; would you choose a sure outcome of 45 over the lottery with expected value of 50? Would you choose a sure outcome of 25 over the lottery with an expected value of 50? A sure outcome of 5 over the lottery with an expected value of 50? The lower the value that you would be willing to accept, the more risk averse you are. If you prefer the lottery with expected outcome of 50 euros over receiving 50 euros for sure, you are a risk lover.

Now, having some understanding of the concepts, let us turn to a more detailed run-through of preferences toward risk. Return to the situation depicted in Figure 16.1 and assume that the probability of each of the states is 1/3. We assume that the decision problem covers all the possible states such that the sum of probabilities of the different states is 1.

16.2.1 Risk neutrality and defining an increase in risk

First, consider the case where the decision-maker is **risk neutral** – she only cares about the expected values of the alternative actions and will choose the action that has the highest expected value. We therefore examine the expected value of the different actions, using $E(A)$ to denote the expected value of action A and equivalently for B

$$E(A) = \frac{1}{3} \times 2 + \frac{1}{3} \times 4 + \frac{1}{3} \times 6 = 4.$$
$$E(B) = \frac{1}{3} \times 0 + \frac{1}{3} \times 4 + \frac{1}{3} \times 8 = 4.$$

Both actions yield the same expected value, and this is what matters to a risk neutral decision-maker – she is thus indifferent between these two actions.

It may also be useful to illustrate the results in a graph, which will also allow us to depict a more general case with more states and consider some additional aspects. Assume now that the state being able to take on any value between 1 and 3, where 1 corresponds to state Low, 2 to Normal, and 3 to High. Using x to denote the state, we can thus express the outcome for A as $A = 2x$ and for B as $B = -4 + 4x$. Figure 16.2 illustrates this case. We see that for realizations of the state lower than Medium, A gives a higher outcome, whereas for realizations of the state higher than Medium, B gives a higher outcome. In a case like the one depicted in Figure 16.2, when the functions linking the state and the outcomes are linear, only the expected value matters for choice and an increase in risk does not affect choice.

To examine the effect of changes in risk, we need to clarify what we mean by an "increase in risk," and for that purpose, we introduce the concept of a **mean-preserving spread**. A

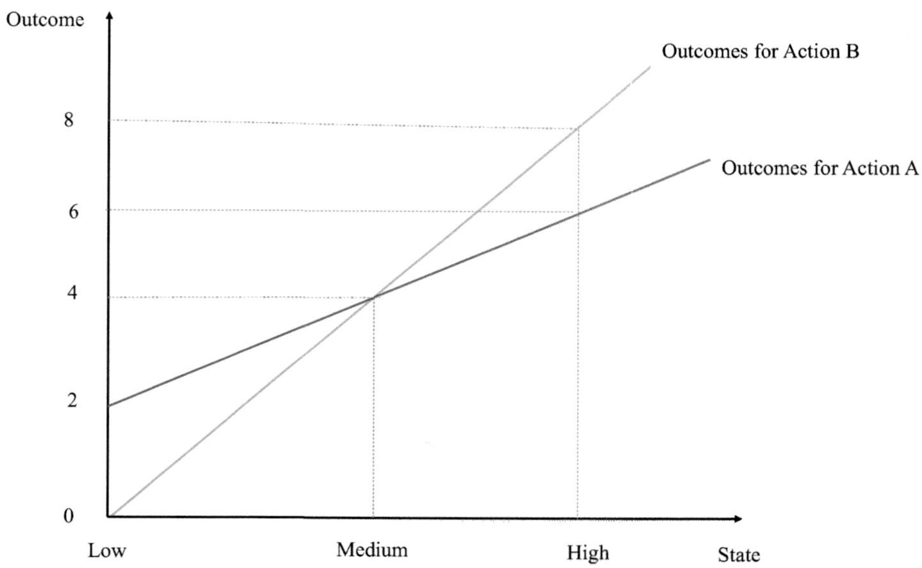

Figure 16.2 Outcomes of two different actions: Risk neutral decision-maker. Video link for Figure 16.2: https://youtu.be/JywFUWtWr2E.

mean-preserving spread is a change in probabilities such that the expected value of the state variable is the same (hence "mean-preserving"), but there are higher probabilities of results in the tails of the probability distribution (hence the "spread"). To exemplify, consider first the case where the distribution of probabilities is 1/3 on each of the states such that the expected value of the state variable is 2 (since$E(x) = \frac{1}{3} \times 1 + \frac{1}{3} \times 2 + \frac{1}{3} \times 3 = 2$). An example of a mean-preserving spread in this case is thus a case where instead of a probability of 1/3 for each of the states, there is a probability of 1/2 for the Low state and a probability of 1/2 for the High state. This is a mean-preserving spread of the state variable: mean preserving since the expected value is the same (since$E(x) = \frac{1}{2} \times 1 + \frac{1}{2} \times 3 = 2$) and since there is now a wider spread of the probability mass. If we think of a histogram depicting different probabilities more weight is in the tails in the riskier case.

For a risk-neutral individual, this increase in risk does not affect choice, and we can easily verify that also in this case both actions still give an expected outcome of 4

$$E(A) = \frac{1}{2} \times 2 + \frac{1}{2} \times 6 = 4$$
$$E(B) = \frac{1}{2} \times 0 + \frac{1}{2} \times 8 = 4.$$

This is an example of a general result: if the variable of interest is a linear function of a random variable, then the expected value of the variable of interest is unaffected by a mean-preserving spread in the random variable. In intuitive terms, the amount of risk does not matter for your valuation of different actions. Some states are better; others are worse, but in expectation, they make up for each other. The decision-maker is thus indifferent toward-risk.

16.2.2 *Risk-averse preferences*

Risk neutrality may clearly be relevant in some situations. Say that you are a firm, and the outcomes from Actions A and B are just a small part of your overall operations. It does not seem puzzling that you would only care about expected value. But think instead that the actions represent harvests for a self-sufficient farmer, and the actions correspond to different crops. The harvest of 0 in the Low state could be devastating, and there would be little consolation that if the state instead had happened to be High, you would have had a great harvest. Avoiding the risk of starvation seems prudent, and the higher outcome in the Low state under Action A would make A more attractive. On the other hand, even if you like the better outcome under A in the Low state, you also want to take account of the higher gains associated with B in the High state when evaluation overall policy. To take account of such issues, we make use of utility functions.[3] In Chapter 8, we illustrated a utility function that had decreasing marginal utility of income, higher incomes were associated with a higher utility but at a decreasing rate as incomes increased further. An extra euro gives you more additional utility if you're living on 2 euros a day than if your living on 100 euros a day. Formally, we say that the utility function is concave. If we use such a utility function to evaluate the different choices, we naturally give a higher weight to low realizations and downplay the high realizations. A marginal increase in the harvest in the Low state is valued more than a marginal increase in the harvest in a High state. Use y to denote the outcome, examples of concave utility functions are then for instance one that takes the square root of the outcome $U = \sqrt{y}$ or the natural logarithm of the outcome, $U = ln(y)$.[4] An individual that cares about risk weighs the *utility of* different outcomes rather than the outcomes themselves. For instance, with $U = \sqrt{y}$, the expected utility of the two actions A and B are

$$U(A) = \frac{1}{3} \times \sqrt{2} + \frac{1}{3} \times \sqrt{4} + \frac{1}{3} \times \sqrt{6} \approx 1.95,$$
$$U(B) = \frac{1}{3} \times \sqrt{0} + \frac{1}{3} \times \sqrt{4} + \frac{1}{3} \times \sqrt{8} \approx 1.61.$$

So now Action A gives higher utility than B since $1.95 > 1.61$. Intuitively, a decreasing marginal utility of income gives a greater weight to relatively good outcomes in the Low state, which pushes in the direction of making A more attractive. A mean-preserving spread, assigning a probability of $1/2$ to each of the extreme outcomes further decreases expected utility for a risk-averse individual, as seen by

$$U(A) = \frac{1}{2} \times \sqrt{2} + \frac{1}{2} \times \sqrt{6} \approx 1.93,$$
$$U(B) = \frac{1}{2} \times \sqrt{0} + \frac{1}{2} \times \sqrt{8} \approx 1.41.$$

To gain additional insights, we graph the situation in Figure 16.3, which comes from applying the utility function $U = \sqrt{y}$ to the choice situation illustrated by Action A in Figure 16.2. The utility function for a risk-averse individual is concave, increasing but becoming successively flatter. The weighing of outcomes is such that the *increase* in utility is especially high for low realizations. We here examine the "extreme case" where the state can be either Low (associated with an outcome of 2 and hence $U = \sqrt{2} \approx 1.41$) or High (associated with an outcome of 6 and hence $U = \sqrt{6} \approx 2.45$). Multiplying the utility levels associated with each of these outcomes with $1/2$ (their probability) and summing gives the expected utility of around 1.93. We are looking at a combination of two outcomes – multiplying by two shares that sum to 1 – which means that we can illustrate

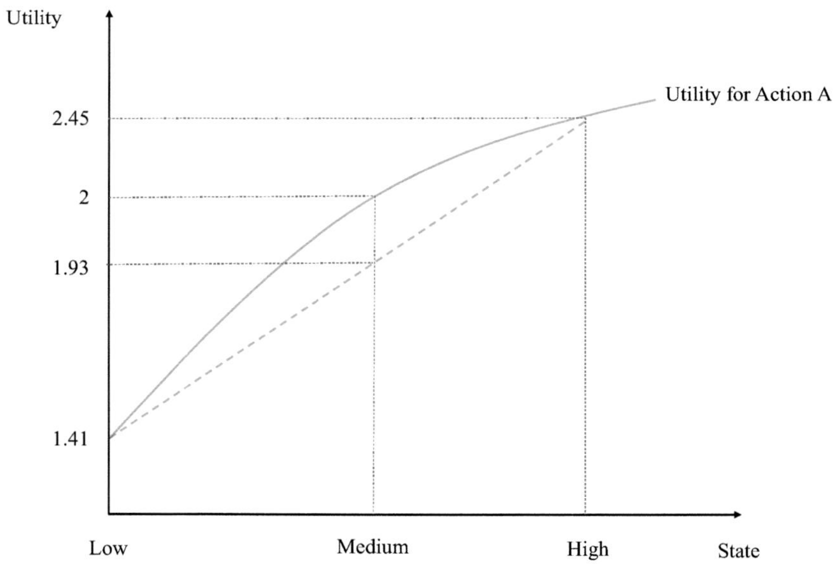

Figure 16.3 Utility for risk-averse decision-maker. Video link for Figure 16.3: https://youtu.be/4q_EbRfkuqg

the combinations by the dashed line. With weights of 1/2, we read off the expected utility at the midpoint of the dashed line.

An important point to note is that if there were no risk, if we were certain that the state Normal would be realized, the utility would instead be given by the function evaluated at the state Normal, where $U = \sqrt{4} = 2$. This is higher than the expected utility of the lottery associated with ending up in either of the extreme states (1.93). Indeed, the definition of a strictly concave function is that the value of the function at a point is always higher than the value of a string that connects two points on the function. In a thought experiment, you can move the dashed line upward, reflecting a decrease in risk and see how the individual's utility increases as risk decreases. She is risk averse.

16.2.3 Risk-loving preferences

To complete the run-through of preferences toward risk, we note that an individual might also prefer more risk to less; she could be a **risk lover**. You might be in a situation where you value upside possibilities more and put less weight on low realizations. Let us again examine Actions A and B. A risk lover would attach extra importance to high realizations, like that offered by the outcome of 8 under Action B in state High. In the same fashion as above, we can again use the curvature of the utility function to capture risk preferences, but for a risk lover, utility weights are increasing. An example of such a utility function is $U = y^2$. Redoing our exercise from above with this utility function then yields expected utility of the two actions A and B as

$$
\begin{aligned}
U(A) &= \frac{1}{3} \times 2^2 + \frac{1}{3} \times 4^2 + \frac{1}{3} \times 6^2 \approx 18.67, \\
U(B) &= \frac{1}{3} \times 0^2 + \frac{1}{3} \times 4^2 + \frac{1}{3} \times 8^2 \approx 26.67.
\end{aligned}
$$

So now Action B gives higher utility than A since $26.67 > 18.67$. The quadratic utility function gives a greater weight to relatively good outcomes in the High state, which pushes in the direction of making B more attractive. A mean-preserving spread, assigning a probability of 1/2 to each of the extreme outcomes, further increases utility for a risk-loving individual, as seen by

$$
\begin{aligned}
U(A) &= \frac{1}{2} \times 2^2 + \frac{1}{2} \times 6^2 = 20, \\
U(B) &= \frac{1}{2} \times 0^2 + \frac{1}{2} \times 8^2 = 32.
\end{aligned}
$$

Figure 16.4 depicts the utility for Action A in the case where probabilities of either of the two extreme states (Low or High) are equal to 1/2. The expected utility of 20 is given by the average of the utility at the two endpoints ($U = 2^2 = 4$ and $U = 6^2 = 36$). Again, if we are to lower risk and in a thought experiment move the dashed line lower, reflecting that the end points come closer, we see that the expected utility of the action is lowered. This individual likes risk, and expected utility decreases if risk is lowered. This individual's utility function is strictly convex; it becomes steeper at an increasing rate. A strictly convex function is defined by that the value of the function at a point is always lower than the value of a string that connects two points on the function. If we were certain that the state Normal

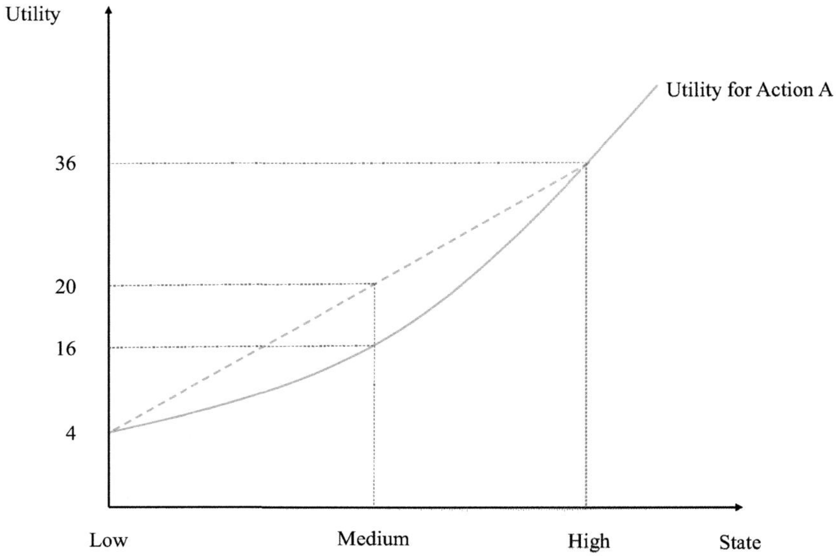

Figure 16.4 Utility for risk-loving decision-maker. Video link for Figure 16.4: https://youtu.be/-WzsI3zBtu4.

would be realized, the utility would instead be given by the function evaluated at the state Normal, where $U = 4^2 = 16$, which is lower than the utility of the lottery associated with ending up in either of the extreme states.

In economic applications of decisions under risk, we frequently assume risk aversion (for individuals) or risk neutrality (for firms).[5] Risk-loving preferences are more rare. It is not uncommon to encounter situations where we prefer more risk to less however, but then the pattern might not driven by preferences toward risk per se but the underlying distribution of outcomes. An important example of this is real options, which we examine in the following.

16.2.3.1 Real options

In finance, an option is a financial instrument that gives the right, but not the obligation to, for instance, buy a stock at at given price at a future date. Similarly, a **real option** gives the right but not the obligation to take a particular action. The value of a real option is typically increasing in the amount of risk for the same reason that a risk lover prefers risk: The expected value of a strictly convex function is increasing in the amount of risk. While that may sound overly mathy for an introductory course in microeconomics, let us illustrate with a simple example. Assume that you are a manager at a gold mine, and let the price of gold s be the relevant state. The outcome of interest is profit π, which depends on s. For simplicity, assume that profit is a linear function of the price of gold if the mine is in operation but that if the price of gold is too low, you keep the mine closed in which case $\pi = 0$. Figure 16.5 depicts the situation.

Think of the firm in a period 0 looking ahead at the value of the gold mine in a future period 1 when the profit from the mine operation will depend on the as of a yet unknown level of the price of gold. Assume that the price of gold follows a probability distribution such that its expected value is $E(s)$. As shown, if the price of gold would happen to be at

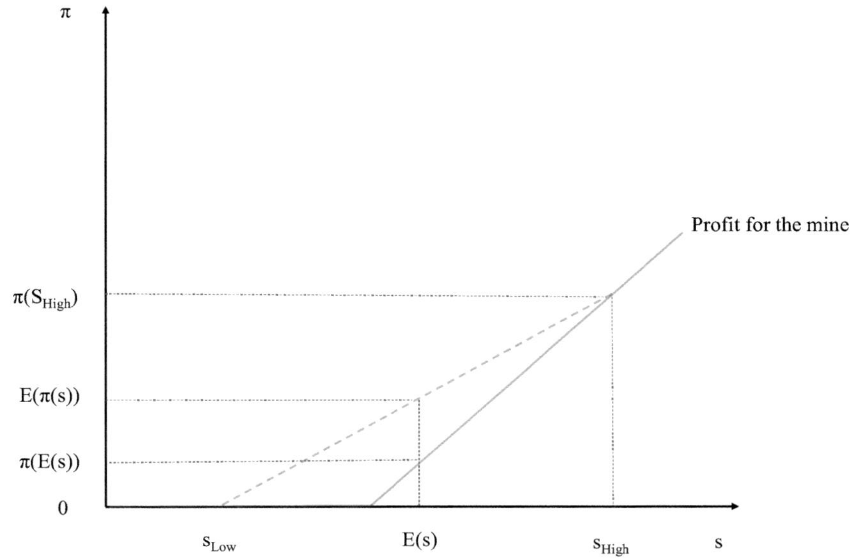

Figure 16.5 A real option. Video link for Figure 16.5: https://youtu.be/M2_FFPSINhI.

this point in period 1, the profit could then be expressed as $\pi(E(s))$. Now consider risk. For simplicity, make the same assumption that the price of gold can only take one of two extreme values, s_{Low} or s_{High}, with a probability of 1/2 for each of these outcomes. The expected profit under this situation equals $E(\pi(s))$, which is higher than $\pi(E(s))$. If we were to examine the effect of a mean-preserving spread, symmetrically increasing risk by shifting down s_{Low} and shifting s_{High} up, the difference would be even greater. Expected profits are increasing in risk in the case of a real option. As depicted, a higher s_{High} increases expected profit, but there is no concomitant decrease in profits from the lower s_{Low}: Profits are 0 for both these levels of s_{Low}. Just as in the case of risk-loving preferences, it is the strict convexity of the function that we use to evaluate the effects of risk that drives the result that the expected value is increasing in the amount of risk. In the case of the real option, the strict convexity stems from the option to keep the mine closed.

The real option effect implies that a risk-neutral firm might act as if it were a risk lover. Similarly, a risk-averse individual might be acting as a risk lover if evaluating a real option with a sufficiently low degree of risk aversion in her preferences.[6] Conversely, there could also be effects that make profits a strictly concave function of some underlying state (e.g., some capacity constraints becoming binding after a certain level), implying that a risk-neutral firm might act as if it were risk averse.

16.3 Strategies for dealing with risk and uncertainty

The previous analysis of preferences toward risk was strictly speaking valid only for risk. The extent to which such results extend also to the wider domain of Knightian uncertainty will have to be left for later studies (with some self-promotion, a good place to start may be Friberg (2015)). One important point is that the concepts of actions, states, and outcomes are useful tools also in cases where we find it hard to assign probabilities. For instance, think back to the decision problem in Figure 16.1. It will typically to be useful to describe the decision situation in this way also if there is ambiguity surrounding the relevant probabilities. The worst-case scenario of a 0 outcome under Action *B* would, for instance, motivate a self-sufficient farmer to choose Action *A*, even if she didn't know the associated probability. Let us therefore turn to some common ways of dealing with risk (and uncertainty) with a somewhat broad focus. This list is not meant to be exhaustive, and there are many different ways to split the pie. Arguably, some of the most important ways of managing risk are the following, however.

16.3.1 Diversification

Diversification entails combining different actions with the intent to lower the amount of overall risks faced. Not putting all the eggs in one basket is the proverbial example. For the strategy to work, the outcomes must differ across the states, putting eggs in two baskets has little effect if the baskets are going to be carried by the same person. In terms of savings, it would amount to investing in several different stocks (or a fund that invests in many stocks) rather than just picking one stock and investing all your savings in that stock. For a firm, it might mean operating in several markets or in several market segments, such as in a conglomerate. If one part of the business is facing tough times, the overall impact will be muted if you also operate in another segment that is not likely to face tough times at the same time.

To illustrate the key trade-offs, consider the simple example depicted in Figure 16.6. The first two rows give the outcomes of two state-contingent payoffs – the payoffs depend on the realized state. The first corresponds to the now familiar Action *A*. The second *C* has another set of outcomes; in particular, the outcome in *C* is high in the Low state and low in the High state. We now compare two different actions: Assume that the decision-maker can choose to "focus" – an action equivalent to achieving 2 × *A* or "diversify," to combine Actions *A* and *C*. We see that the outcome under the "focused" action remains risky, whereas the outcomes under "diversification" are independent of the state.

That the diversified outcomes are independent of the states reflects the exact numbers chosen, and is not a general result. If the outcomes under *C* had, for instance, been 3, 2, and 1 instead, the diversification outcomes would instead have been 5, 6, and 7 – with a positive slope but flatter than the case under "focus." Key in driving the effects of diversification is the extent to which the outcomes jointly develop in different states. Statistically speaking, we would say that outcomes under *A* and *C* are negatively correlated – they move in opposite directions. One way to capture correlations, as explained in standard textbooks in statistics,

			States	
		Low	**Normal**	**High**
Underlying state-contingent outcomes	**A**	2	4	6
	C	4	2	0
Actions	**Focus (2 x A)**	4	8	12
	Diversification (A+C)	6	6	6

Figure 16.6 Diversification: A simple example.

is by a correlation coefficient that ranges from −1 to 1. If two random variables move together perfectly, the correlation coefficient is 1; if they perfectly move in the opposite direction, the correlation coefficient is −1, and the further away from 0, the stronger is the comovement. Intuitively, the more negative the correlation, the greater the benefits from diversification.

The numerical example in Figure 16.6 is chosen such that the expected value under diversification is lower than under focus. This corresponds to what many empirical studies point to when, for instance, examining firm behavior – a diversified firm is likely to offer more stable but lower returns.[7] For further intuition, we can think of a bank – if you only lend to a few big borrowers, the bank's fortunes are going to be very dependent on the fortunes of those few borrowers.[8] If you instead lend to many small borrowers, and shocks to their ability to repay are not to highly correlated, diversification is going to shield the bank. Several observers point to an underestimation of the correlation in defaults on housing debt as a co-contributor to the depth of the financial crisis of 2008; the diversification benefit of large lender portfolios were lower than thought since the positive correlation in default rates was higher than anticipated.[9]

16.3.2 Insurance

Insurance is a state-contingent payment. If your house is insured, you receive a payment in case the state is Fire and you pay in the state Not Fire. In terms of our running example, you would thus pay in states Normal and High, and receive some support in state Low. Insurance may be especially valuable when there are large negative outcomes (such as a house burning down, very costly medical treatments) that occur with a low probability and not very correlated across the insured – offering insurance will then allow many to mitigate large downside risks at a relatively modest cost. Note that much of what the government does in a welfare state can be seen as insurance – for instance, subsidized health care and caps on health-care costs and unemployment insurance.

16.3.3 Buffers

Another way of managing risk is to have some buffers or stockpiles: The proverbial precautionary savings for a rainy day. This can show up in many guises. At an individual level, there is a value to having some savings that can be used to deal with unexpected costs, such as emergency dental care or car repair. As discussed in Chapter 2, national buffer stocks of rice in Japan were important in ultimately smoothing out the response to high rice prices in 2008–2009. Having a second pilot on a commercial airline if something happens to the first pilot is another example. Firms managing risk by, e.g., holding more cash as a form of precautionary savings in the face of risk and production plants having more excess capacity when they face more variable demand.[10]

16.3.4 Flexibility

The last major class of ways to manage risk and uncertainty that we cover is flexibility, the ability to adapt and make the best of circumstances. We use Figure 16.7 to illustrate some key aspects of the concept, thinking of a firm. Again, think of a state that is captured by a variable s, and let a baseline set of outcomes (profit in this case) be captured by the dashed

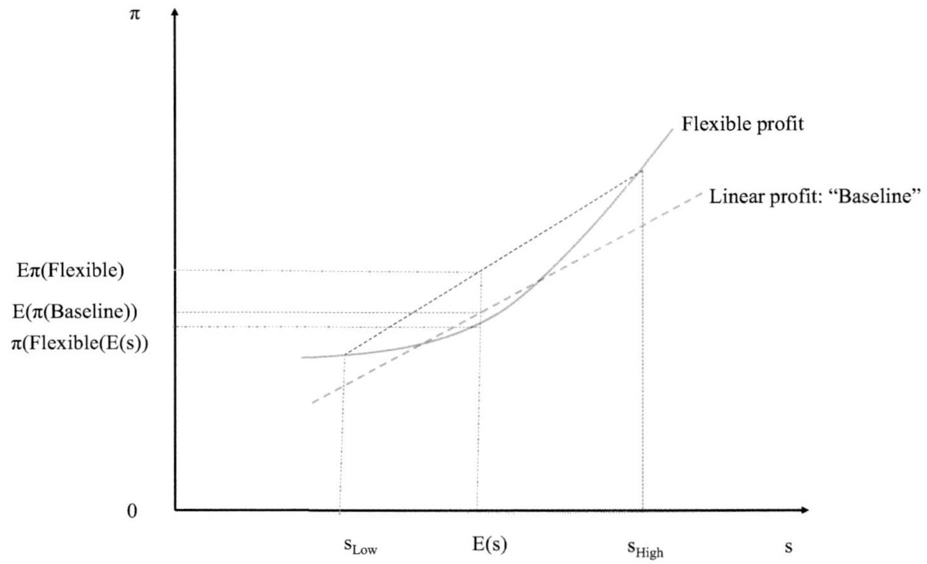

Figure 16.7 Investing in flexibility. Video link for Figure 16.7: https://youtu.be/gWeznFArL8w.

line. It is drawn as linear and increasing in s: A risk neutral firm would thus be indifferent between different levels of risk.

What does flexibility mean – it means adapting to circumstances and making the most of each state. The upward-sloping and curved (strictly convex) profit implies that for, e.g., s_{High} the firm expands when conditions are profitable and the higher profits associated with s_{Low} are associated with cutting back and limiting the harm of adverse states. Standard assumptions in economics imply that nothing comes for free, and here we assume that the firm pays a fixed cost to achieve this higher flexibility – this implies that if there is little risk (such that realizations of s are likely to be close to the expected value $E(s)$), it will not be profitable to invest in flexibility.[11] The strict convexity of profits under the flexible strategy implies that expected profit will increase if we take a mean-preserving spread of s. For instance, in the case where the probabilities of s taking on one of the endpoint values of s_{Low} or s_{High} are both 0.5, then the expected profit under the flexible strategy is given by $E(\pi(\mathit{flexible}))$, which, summarizing our previous discussion, is higher than expected profit under the baseline. In terms of policies for a firm, a flexible policy might, for instance, imply working with a costlier but easier-to-adjust technology. Think of s as the price of the output of a price-taking firm – if the firm were to produce the same amount irrespective of the price, profit would be a linear function of s; if the firm instead expands production when price is high and contracts to limit the harm when price is low, its profit function becomes a strictly convex function, and the expected profits are increasing in risk.[12]

In closing, let us highlight two aspects of risk management. First, risk management typically comes at some cost – the increased safety that it buys in adverse conditions are typically paid for by somewhat lower utility or profits in more favorable conditions. The higher the risk, the more valuable it is typically to engage in risk management. Second, the ways of managing risk that we discussed earlier can clearly be combined. A farmer in a premarket economy might, for instance, combine diversification by having several different crops with buffers, in the form of some stored supplies, and with insurance in the form of neighbors and friends helping each other when one is hit harder by a shock than others.[13]

Notes

1 Tools for managing risk and uncertainty has been an interest throughout my career, see, e.g., Friberg (2015) for a textbook treatment.

2 Not everyone agrees that the distinction between risk and uncertainty is useful; some argue that we can always have a best guess, and there is not this kind of clear dichotomy; we just have different cases with more or less clear prior expectations. Also note that many reserve risk for the case mentioned as "strictly speaking": where probabilities are known. I would nevertheless argue that for many applications, it is useful to cast a slightly wider net as in the broader definition, see Friberg (2025) for a further discussion.

3 Utility functions that are used to evaluate choice under risk are sometimes known as von Neumann-Morgenstern utility functions. The name stems from all-around genius John von Neumann and economist Oskar Morgenstern who formulated the axioms ("sufficient foundations") for utility functions to work in a setting where we are choosing between different actions whose outcomes are random). For the purposes of this book, you can think of them as "regular" utility functions.

4 As noted before, the formalization of choice under risk goes back to the work by von Neumann and Morgenstern that was also central to the development of game theory (Von Neumann and Morgenstern (1944)). The deeper realization that a weighing of outcomes was potentially important for choice under risk was elaborated on already by members of the famous Bernouilli family of mathematicians in the early 1700s under the name of St. Petersburg paradox – the problem they identified was that if there is potential for infinite winnings in a lottery, this will dominate expected values since something infinite becomes infinite even if multiplied with a low probability. Evaluating lottery winnings under a decreasing marginal utility of income is a way out of the "paradox" offered by such games with a potential for infinite winnings; see a republication of the remarkably modern original work of Bernouilli (1954).

5 Such a general statement summarizes a vast literature sweeping many finer details under the rug. Implicitly, it also implies that the risk preferences are similar across domains, which may not always hold – a person might engage in rock climbing without protection in the form of a rope (putting little weight on adverse possible outcomes) at the same as her financial portfolio indicates great caution. See Einav et al. (2012) for an introduction to some of the issues.

6 See, e.g., Friberg (2015, Ch. 4) for a further analysis.

7 A well-cited study of Berger and Ofek (1995) provides one entry point to the relevant literature.

8 As captured by the saying, "If you owe the bank $100, that's your problem. If you owe the bank $100 million, that's the bank's problem."

9 See, e.g., Zimmer (2012).

10 See, e.g., Bates et al. (2009) on cash holding or Amberg et al. (2025) on excess capacity.

11 This way of thinking about flexibility can be traced back to at least Stigler (1939).

12 Linking to our discussion above, we can also think of a choice to invest in being more flexible as a real option, paying a cost for the option to adjust more.

13 An important empirical literature examines risk management in poor farming communities, see, e.g., Townsend (1994) for one illustrative example.

17 International trade

Illustration 17.1 Ships in the port of Venice. *Venice, from the Port of Madonna della Salute*, ca. 1835, Joseph Mallord William Turner. Courtesy of Metropolitan Museum of Art. Public domain.

17.1 International trade – Some background

Trade between different regions has affected societies throughout history. It has expanded choice of consumer products and inputs for production, and lowered prices of many goods. Early on, expanded choice might mean having access to flint, metals, or salt that were not available locally. Nowadays, it also implies access to a wider range of differentiated products than what would otherwise be the case. Specialization has allowed for a more efficient use

DOI: 10.4324/9781003623854-23

of resources. Trade is also associated with an openness to ideas that historically has been a driver of development. There are thus many reasons to expect that international trade increases welfare.

On the other hand, a policy of lowering trade barriers is sure to generate intense debate. Trade reshapes economies and that reshaping can create losses for some groups and introduce a dependency on other countries. International shipment may be associated with environmental costs. Furthermore, a well-functioning market economy relies on regulation to avoid, e.g., dangerous products and harmful work practices. International trade may be a way to circumvent such regulation.

On balance, it is fair to say that many economists have a very favorable view of international trade. This is partly based on the empirical evidence that we discuss in some detail further in this chapter. The favorable view is also based on an appreciation for the theoretical underpinnings of the welfare effects of trade. In the following, we cover three different models of international trade. They accord to different stages in the development of our theoretical understanding of trade and are useful for highlighting three different aspects of trade. We first rely on insights from David Ricardo from the early 1800s to show that trade can be a win-win proposition when everyone specializes in production of the good for which they have a low opportunity cost. We then move on to a general equilibrium model with perfect competition to highlight how some groups may lose from opening up for trade, even if there are overall welfare gains. Finally, we explore a model with monopolistic competition where product differentiation and economies of scale are important drivers of the welfare effects of trade.

It should be emphasized at the outset that we, in keeping with the focus of a textbook in microeconomics, focus on developing an understanding of the key theoretical mechanisms involved in determining who trades what and the welfare effects of trade and only briefly touch upon the empirical analysis of trade. Following the historical development of ideas – and to present the key ideas as simply as possible, we focus on trade in finished goods rather than some other aspects that are important in the current era: trade in services (such as a call center for European customers located in South Africa) and global value chains, the splitting up of production of one product across many destinations so that it is hard to think of export of a bicycle from Italy as export of an "Italian" bicycle.[1]

17.2 The mechanisms that drive trade – Three classes of models

17.2.1 Comparative advantage and the gains from trade – An example

In an effort to clarify the effects of trade policy, David Ricardo in the early 1800s produced one of the first examples of mathematical models in economics. Intellectually, Ricardo's work represented a break from a previous, mercantilistic approach where, simply put, exports were seen as good and imports as bad. The model highlights how both parties of a trade can benefit if they each specialize in doing what they are relatively efficient in. Ricardo assumes that there are exogenous differences in productivity in the time that it takes to complete a particular task (his original example involved England and Portugal and wine and cloth). For a full-fledged model, we want a labor market and prices to be determined by supply and demand. To focus on Ricardo's key insight, we hold off on those elements, however, and instead consider trade and specialization in a two-person example.

Table 17.1 Productivity differences: Hours needed to produce a given quantity of goods

	Blueberries	*Raspberries*
Speedy	1	2
Dud	6	3

Consider two people called Speedy and Dud. They can allocate their time to harvest two goods that they both like, Blueberries and Raspberries. They differ in their productivity, and Table 17.1 details the hours needed for each of them to pick 1 liter of the respective goods.

As seen, Speedy is quicker in the production of both goods since $1<6$ and $2<3$. The question we pose is, can they both gain from trade here? Can Speedy, who is more efficient at both tasks, benefit from trade? Can Dud, who is less efficient at both tasks benefit from trade?

The answer will be yes to both questions. Intuitively, first think of the case where they each want 1 liter of each type of berries. If they each pick their own, Speedy spends 3 (1 + 2) hours picking and Dud spends 9 (6 + 3) hours picking. Contrast this with the case where they instead specialize such that each picks one type of berry, and then they split the harvest such that each again gets one liter of each type of berry. In that case, Speedy picks 2 liters of blueberries in 2 hours, and Dud picks 2 liters of raspberries in 6 hours. So by specializing, they can achieve the same output by working 2 instead of 3 hours (for Speedy) and 6 instead of 9 hours (for Dud).

What is going on here at a deeper level? First, we note that Speedy has an absolute advantage in producing both goods since the labor requirement is lower for both goods for her. The two people differ in their *relative* efficiency, however. Every hour that is spent on picking raspberries is an hour not spent on picking blueberries. In other words, the opportunity cost of raspberries is the amount of blueberries that you give up. Figure 17.1 illustrates the production possibility frontiers for a case where they each have 12 hours to allocate between the two different tasks.

If Speedy only picks blueberries, she has 12 liters to show for her effort, and if she only picks raspberries, her output is 6 liters (since it takes two hours to pick 1 liter). The production possibility frontiers in this simple case are straight lines, as the labor requirements are independent of how the time is split. The slope of the production possibility frontier shows the opportunity cost. For 1 liter of raspberries picked by Speedy, she gives up 2 liters of blueberries. Dud only gives up 0.5 liters of blueberries to pick 1 liter of raspberries. In other words, Dud has a lower opportunity cost of picking raspberries, and therefore Dud has a comparative advantage in picking raspberries.

More generally, the Ricardian logic implies that trade between two countries can benefit both if they each specialize in the production of goods in which they have comparative advantage. Country A has **comparative advantage** in producing good A if it needs to give up less of other goods to produce an additional unit of A. In other words, country A has a comparative advantage in producing good A if country A has a lower opportunity cost of producing good A.

The concept of comparative advantage is far from trivial, and wrapping your head around the result can take some time. Thus, it may be useful to note that we can think of three different ways to determine who has a comparative advantage in an example like the aforementioned.

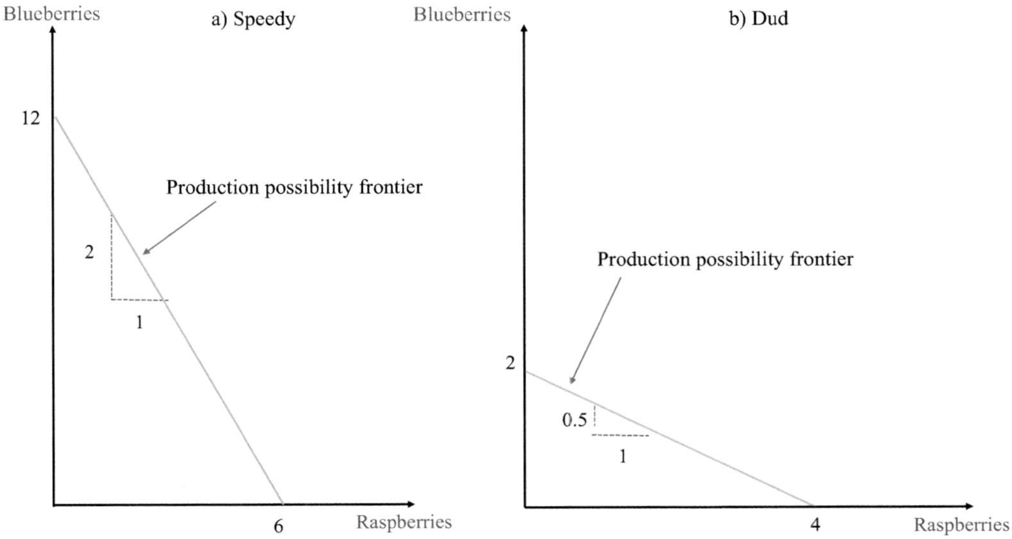

Figure 17.1 Production possibility frontiers. Video link for figure: https://youtu.be/wsm9yxNbsC8.

A first way is to simply reason as follows. It takes Speedy two hours to pick 1 liter of raspberries. What could she instead do with those two hours? She can pick blueberries. With the two hours that Speedy frees up by not picking 1 liter of raspberries, she can pick 2 liters of blueberries (since it takes her one hour to pick a liter of blueberries). In other words, her opportunity cost of 1 liter of raspberries is 2 liters of blueberries. Similarly, Dud can use three hours to pick 1 liter of raspberries. If she were to free up those three hours, they would only give her 0.5 liter of blueberries (since she needs six hours to pick 1 liter of blueberries). Hence, her opportunity cost of a liter of raspberries is 0.5 liters of blueberries.

A second way to determine who has a comparative advantage is to draw the production possibility frontiers as noted earlier and compare the slopes; a flatter line indicates a lower opportunity cost of the good on the horizontal axis. A third way is to use a "trick," noting that the opportunity cost of a good A = (the number of hours needed to produce one unit of A)/(the number of hours needed to produce one unit of B). The last way is clearly the quickest, but the others are more enlightening about the underlying mechanisms.

Before moving on, we may note that we can think of comparative advantage as describing division of labor in general in an economy. Rather than being self-sufficient farmers, many of us have chosen to specialize in one line of work and buy what we need from others. Others might be more efficient in any activity that we can think of, but both they and I can gain from everyone specializing in doing activities in which they are relatively efficient and have a low opportunity cost.

As a final point, we can also use a joke to understand the concept.[2] Think of a medical doctor who is superefficient at everything that she does and has the opportunity to work extra hours at the hospital at a high hourly wage rate whenever she wants. She has just repainted her house and a friend asks, "Was it expensive?", to which she replies, "Yes, I did it myself." The point being that her opportunity cost is high – the hours that she spent painting could instead be spent making a high wage from work.

17.2.2 Trade under perfect competition with specific factors

Illustration 17.2 Export of a commodity – loading wheat on a ship. Shutterstock/Elena Larina.

The simple Ricardian example highlighted how differences in opportunity costs can generate gains from trade. We now turn to describing a full model of trade where the use of production factors and prices are endogenous. The benchmark model of trade under perfect competition is known as the Heckscher-Ohlin model. It features perfect competition on all markets and countries where preferences and production technologies are identical. The difference across countries lies in factor endowments, where one country, for instance, has more capital in relation to labor than its trading partner. It is a very natural extension of a one-country general equilibrium model of the economy to an international setting. Despite the apparently simple structure, it is somewhat hard to work with in an introductory textbook, and we instead present the closely related "specific-factor model," which is slightly easier to work with and that can be used to develop some key results that have close relatives in Heckscher-Ohlin and other models of international trade.[3]

Consider a setting with 2 countries, 2 goods, and 3 factors of production. Assume perfect competition on all markets. One good, which we call Food (F), is produced using labor (L) and land (J). The other good, Stuff (S) for short, is produced using capital (K) and labor. Labor is mobile between sectors, while capital can only be used in the production of Stuff and land only in the production of Food. Let the countries differ in their relative endowments such that we assume that one country, which we call Agraria, has relatively more land than capital, and the reverse holds for the other country, Capitalia. Preferences and technology are the same in both countries.

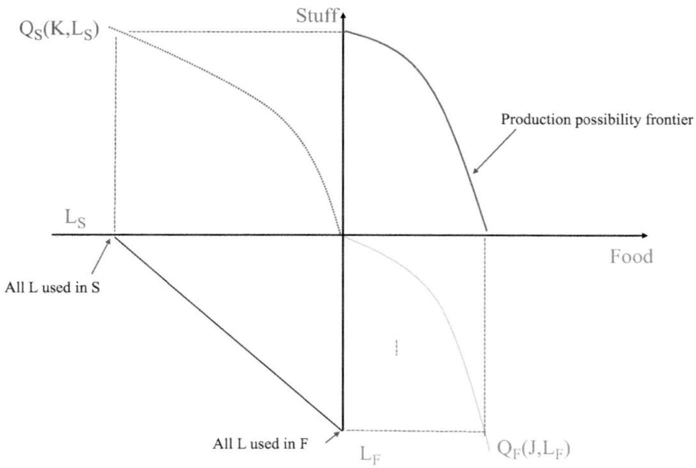

Figure 17.2 Derivation of the production possibility frontier in Capitalia. Video link for figure: https://youtu.be/mtZxDAscEK4.

Just as in the Ricardian model, differences in the opportunity cost of producing goods, comparative advantage, will be key to trade patterns and generating gains from trade. We therefore start with the production possibility frontiers and now note that they will not be straight lines, as output depends on the proportion of inputs. Figure 17.2 illustrates the production possibility frontier for Capitalia. While perhaps looking somewhat overloaded, it is, I hope, a useful tool for understanding the shape of the production possibility frontier.

First, look in the lower left-hand corner. Measure labor used in the production of Stuff on the horizontal axis going left and labor used in producing Food moving down on the vertical axis. Having more labor in Food production means having less labor in Stuff production, as depicted by the line in the lower left-hand corner. Thus, each point on that line corresponds to a certain amount of Labor working in the production of Food and a certain amount of Labor working in the production of Stuff. Labor is combined with land to produce Food. How much Food is produced is determined by the production function $Q_F(J, L_F)$, as drawn in the lower right-hand corner. As the amount of land is given, the production function displays decreasing marginal product of labor in Food production. Each additional unit of labor contributes less and less to the production of Food. Similar reasoning gives decreasing marginal product of labor in the production of Stuff.

Thus the figure relates the distribution of labor across sectors to the production of the two goods and thereby traces out the production possibility frontier. It has a curved shape because of decreasing marginal product of labor in the respective sector.

A standard thought experiment in international trade models is to compare the situation when there is no trade (which we refer to as **autarky**[4]) to the case where there are no barriers to trade, "free trade." Figure 17.3 presents production possibility frontiers in Agraria and Capitalia. The shape of the production possibility frontiers reflects the underlying resources, with production possibilities of Agraria shifted toward Food and those of Capitalia toward Stuff.

In autarky, consumption equals production in each country. If we're not trading, we can't consume more than we produce. We can think of the combination of goods as given by the

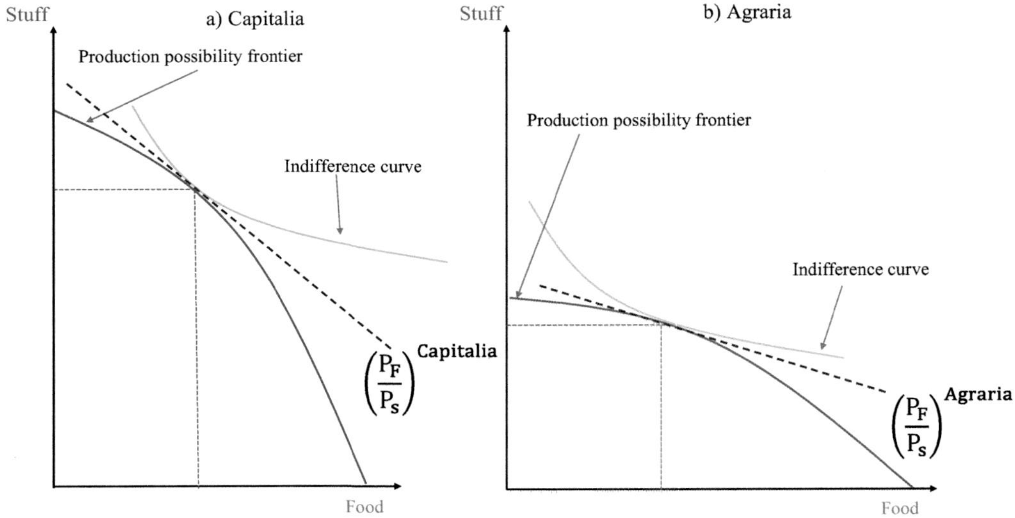

Figure 17.3 Production and consumption in autarky.

point where the indifference curve of a representative consumer is tangent to the production possibility frontier. How does this allocation come about? In a perfectly competitive setting, prices are in essence transmitting information about valuation and costs, and in equilibrium, we know that on the consumer side, $p_F/p_S = MU_F/MU_S$, where p denotes prices and MU marginal utility. From the producer side $p_F/p_S = MC_F/MC_S$, where MC are marginal costs of producing the respective good. The differences in factor endowments between Agraria and Capitalia imply that the equilibria, and hence consumption bundles, will look different across the two countries in autarky. More land relative to labor in Agraria imply that Food will be cheaper in Agraria. Since Food is relatively cheap in Agraria, people there will consume relatively more Food in Agraria, even though preferences are identical across countries. Intuitively, if Argentina and Japan existed in autarky, land-abundant Argentina would have a lower price of food than the mountainous and densely populated Japan.

Now consider what happens if we let the two countries trade. The downward-sloping relative demand curve in Figure 17.4 shows the relationship between *relative demand* (how much Food is demanded relative to how much Stuff is demanded, Q_F/Q_S) and *relative price* p_F/p_S. As preferences are equal, the relative demand curve is the same in both countries. Relative supply, however, differs; with more capital than land, price of Food will be relatively high in Capitalia. If countries open up for trade, disregarding transport costs, prices will be equalized across the two countries. With perfect competition, Food from one country is a perfect substitute for Food from the other country, and their prices will be equal. Price equalization implies that if we allow the countries to trade, the relative price of Food will fall in Capitalia and rise in Agraria.

We now come to the heart of the analysis. Production and consumption in both countries will change in response to the new equilibrium prices that are associated with free trade. Figure 17.5 shows the adjustment in Capitalia – Food becomes relatively cheaper, and production responds by shifting away from Food and into the production of Stuff.

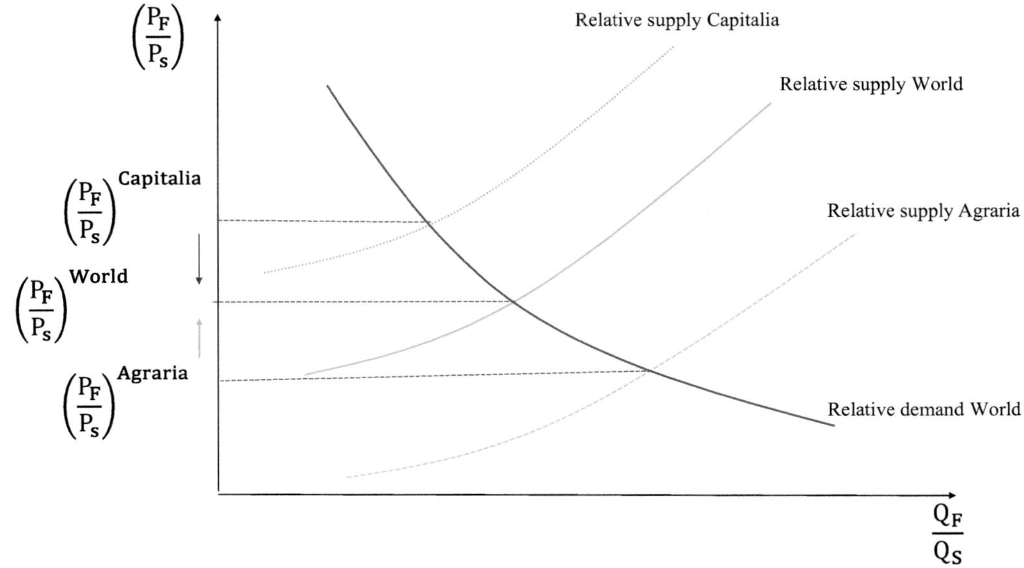

Figure 17.4 Adjustment of relative prices to trade.

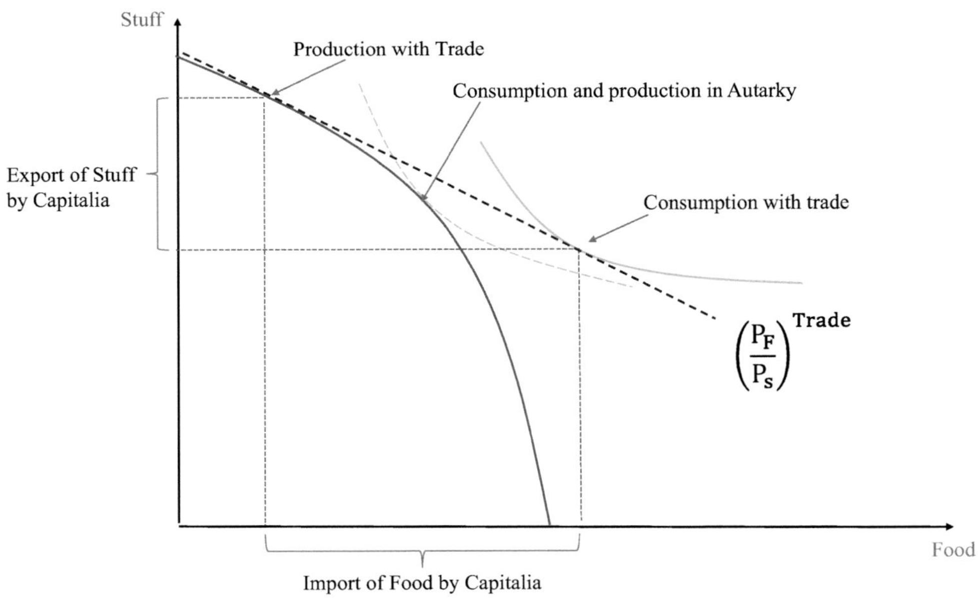

Figure 17.5 Opening up for trade in Capitalia.

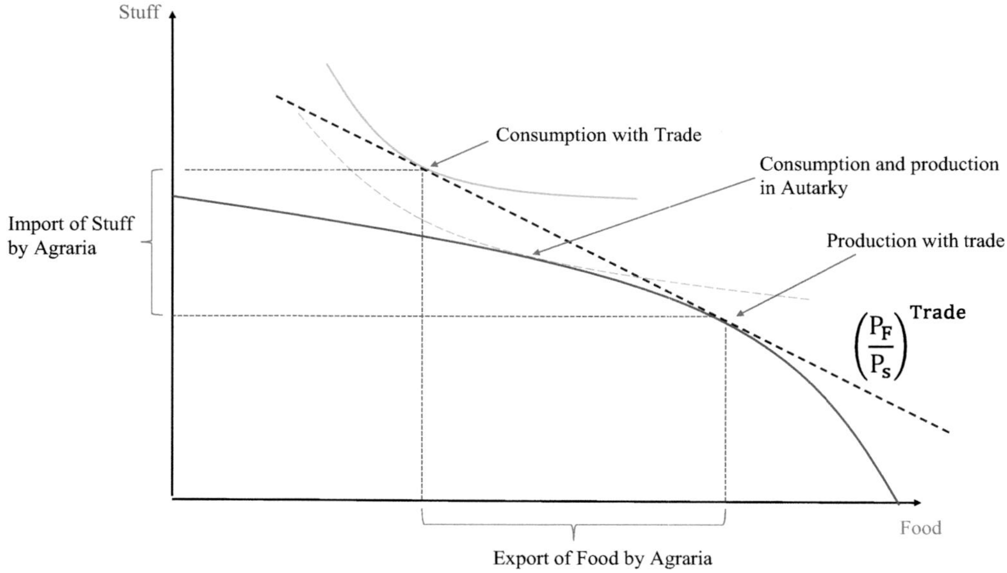

Figure 17.6 Opening up for trade in Agraria.

A key difference from autarky is that in an open economy, consumption and production need not match at the national level. By exporting some of the Stuff, and using the revenue from those sales to import Food, Capitalia can consume more Food than it produces. The new set of prices are associated with changes in both production and consumption and a new, higher indifference curve can be reached. Trade thus increases welfare of the representative consumer in Capitalia.

Turning to the flip side of the story, in Agraria, relative prices there move in the opposite direction, and Agraria's adjustment is depicted in Figure 17.6. Here the relative price of Food increases as they open up to trade, and labor will shift toward Food production. Agraria will end up exporting Food and importing Stuff. It will also achieve a higher utility.

Wrapping up, what we've seen so far is that *trade raises welfare in both countries.* We also see that differences between countries imply differences in the opportunity cost of producing different goods and that trade induces countries to *specialize*. How do they specialize? They increase production of goods in which they have a *comparative advantage.* How does the adjustment take place? Via prices reflecting relative valuations and production costs. While we illustrated the results in this paragraph in a particular setting, these results hold very broadly across the different types of trade models that economists work with.

The model has even more to say. If we think of a country as one individual, we saw that trade raised utility in both countries. However, the overall pattern hides differential impacts on different factors of production. To first see the intuition, think of Argentina and Japan as the two countries. If a land-abundant country like Argentina were to move from autarky to free trade, Argentinian farmers would be likely to gain as they now can export to land-scarce Japan. On the other hand, Argentinian manufacturers would face import competition from Japan and lose out. The welfare gains from trade arise because relative prices and production patterns change. These changes affect different agents differently.

To move beyond the broad intuition, we therefore want to examine the returns to capital, land, and labor. In perfectly competitive markets, each production factor will earn returns according to how much value it produces, as we examined in Chapter 15. Let us first examine the effect on *capital*. How much revenue will using an extra unit of capital in the production of Stuff in Capitalia give? Well, firms that produce Stuff will want to increase the use of capital up to the point where the revenue increase from employing more capital (the price of Stuff times the marginal product of capital (MPK_S)) equals the cost of using capital, r_K. Thus in equilibrium $r_K = MPK_S \times p_S$. To look at the welfare effect, we need to set returns to production factors in relation to prices. In Capitalia, p_S increases relative to p_F. For owners of capital in Capitalia, trade raises welfare since r_K increases both from a higher p_S and from that MPK_S increases. A shift of labor toward the production of Stuff implies that each unit of capital is matched with more labor, thereby increasing the marginal product of capital. So rents increase in relation to both p_S and p_F. The opposite is true in Agraria, there owners of capital lose.

The flipside of the coin is that for landowners in Capitalia the move from autarky to free trade unambiguously lowers welfare. The return on land r_J (given by $r_J = MPJ_F \times p_F$) falls since p_F falls, and in addition, each unit of land is combined with less labor, which decreases the marginal product of land, MPJ_F. In Agraria, the effects are the opposite – landowners gain.

For labor, the effects are ambiguous, unless we make additional assumptions on how people weigh consumption of Food vs. consumption of Stuff. Following the same logic as above, $w = MPL_S \times p_S$, wage increases in Capitalia as p_S increases, but the lower MPL_S moderates the upward pressure on wages. So in terms of p_S, wage decreases in Capitalia. In terms of Food, wage increases in Capitalia, however, since p_F falls.

This last analysis highlights a final important aspect that carries over also into more elaborate models. Some people gain, and some lose from trade liberalization, which is an important aspect of understanding the political economy of how trade policy is determined. Trade increases welfare at the national level, but some groups may lose. The increase in utility at the national level implies that in principle, the losers could be compensated by those who gain, with the latter still having a net gain. There is thus scope for what is sometimes known as a potential Pareto improvement: Those who gain from a change gain more than what is lost by those who lose. So, if redistribution could be accomplished, there would be a Pareto improvement. Simply put, in these models, the gains are sufficient for the winners to be able to pay off the losers and still have some gains left.

17.2.2.1 Does the empirical evidence support the predictions from trade under perfect competition?

We now turn to a brief overview of which countries a country typically trades with and how what is exported and imported relates to the characteristics of the trading countries. Table 17.2 shows the main export markets for two examples – Sweden and Thailand. Sweden's largest export market is Norway, with only 5 million inhabitants. The United States comes in at spot number 3. For both of these countries, we can discern a pattern where trading partners are close (like Norway in the case of Sweden and Malaysia in the case of Thailand) and/or large (like Germany and the United States for Sweden and China and the United States for Thailand).

The pattern suggested by Table 17.2, where trade increases with size and proximity, is pervasive. Statistical examinations of this are often referred to as **gravity models**, as there is an analogy to Newton's law of gravity, where the gravitational pull between two objects

Table 17.2 Largest export markets for Sweden and Thailand

Sweden *Export market*	*Share of exports*	*Thailand* *Export market*	*Share of exports*
Norway	10.7	United States	16.6
Germany	10.0	China	12.0
United States	8.9	Japan	8.6
Denmark	7.4	Vietnam	4.6
Finland	7.3	Malaysia	4.4

Data for 2022 https://wits.worldbank.org/.

depends positively on their mass and negatively on distance. Simply put, just observing how close two countries are and how large their respective economies are (as measured by GDP) allows us to make a remarkably well-fitting prediction of their bilateral trade volume (see, e.g., Head and Mayer (2014) for a survey). Transport costs are an obvious explanation for the strong performance of gravity models. For simplicity, transport costs are excluded in the simple stylized model that we examined earlier, but the main insights continue to hold also when transport costs are included.

Researchers who take account that comparative advantage is determined both by differences in labor productivity and by relative endowments of production factors find that trade patterns to an important degree line up with predictions once important frictions such as transport costs have been taken account of (see, for instance, Davis and Weinstein (2001)). A look at the trade data for many countries indicates that there is an intuitive match between the endowments of resources, education levels, economic institutions, and trade patterns. As we shall see in the next section, there are also important features of the international trade of goods that can't be explained by perfectly competitive models, which leads us to a examine trade with monopolistic competition in the following.

17.2.3 *Trade with monopolistic competition*

Models of trade with perfect competition are useful in highlighting the intuition behind some important results of opening up for trade. There are also important aspects unexplained by perfectly competitive trade models, however. If trade were only determined by comparative advantage, a prediction is that trade should be the most intense between countries that differ widely in technology or endowments. We also expect that there is no simultaneous exporting and importing of the same good. Ukraine selling wheat in exchange for textile garments from Bangladesh is an example of the kind of trade that springs to mind.

In contrast, much of world trade is in similar goods between countries with similar endowments and productivity. For instance, Japan sells cars to Germany, and Germany sells cars to Japan. In the late 1970s and early 1980s, the theoretical models that could explain such a pattern were developed. In particular, the models of Paul Krugman (Krugman (1979), Krugman (1980)) were widely adopted. These models assumed *monopolistic competition* in differentiated products and economies of scale. We like both Mercedes and Toyota, which accounts for German consumers liking to drive both of these. Similarly, Japanese consumers like to drive both of these. If we are allowed to trade with each other, we will observe trade between the two countries in these types of goods.

Illustration 17.3 Trade in differentiated products. Shutterstock/GreenOak.

Krugman and others developed models that could be used to explain the bulk of trade and that were simple and flexible enough to allow for extensions and policy analysis. Working through an international trade model, where there is monopolistic competition, is outside the scope of an introductory textbook in microeconomics, but it is straightforward to convey the key intuition. In essence, think of two national markets that are initially in autarky, and assume that there is monopolistic competition (as we modeled in Chapter 9) in each national market. Thus, a large number of firms are producing differentiated products, and free entry keeps equilibrium profits at 0.

Assume now that we move to a situation of free trade. Each firm gains access to a larger market – instead of only selling on the national market, a firm now also has access to an export market. On the other hand, it also faces competition on the home market. This implies that the firm-specific demand curve rotates – the intercept shifts down, but it becomes flatter. In this class of models, economies of scale are an important aspect of the welfare gains from trade, and the easiest way to model economies of scale is to assume that there is a fixed cost of production and then constant marginal costs, which together imply a falling average total cost (ATC). We illustrate in Figure 17.7.

Free entry in monopolistic competition imply that there will be entry until profits are zero, which happens when $(p - ATC) \times q = 0$ or, in other words, when the demand curve that is faced by the individual firm is tangent to the average cost curve. In autarky, a firm then produces q_A and charges price p_A. Opening up for trade implies intercept of the demand curve shifts down at the same time as the slope of the demand curve becomes flatter. The lower intercept comes from foreign competition that now makes it impossible to sell a positive number of units at very high prices. The flatter demand curve reflects that a successful firm can now also sell to foreign customers. Again, in a free-entry equilibrium, production would be where the average cost curve is tangent to demand, which occurs at a larger quantity and lower price, q_T and p_T.

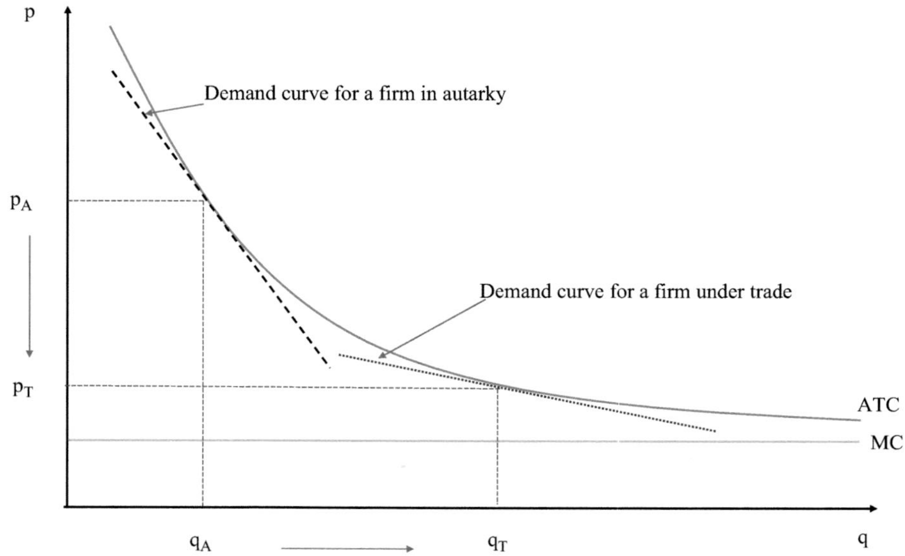

Figure 17.7 Production of one firm under monopolistic competition in autarky and under trade.

There are two sources of gains from trade in a framework that relies on monopolistic competition: *increased variety* and *lower production costs* because of economies of scale. To help with the intuition for first effect, note that models feature what is sometimes known as "love of variety." Its as if on your cheese tray you prefer to have 10 different cheeses with different characteristics than just 1 or 2. Trade allows access to Stilton, Appenzeller, and other cheeses rather than just your local variety. Decreasing trade barriers leads each consumer to face more varieties, which is welfare enhancing in this class of models.

For the lower production costs, note that combining previously separated national markets allows producers to spread fixed costs over more units; these economies of scale imply lower prices. Falling prices also force the exit of some firms. Thus, if in autarky country A supported 10 firms and country B 10 firms, the combined market supports, for instance, 15 firms. An implication of these two effects is that there can be important welfare gains from trade liberalization between similar countries.

In the Krugman-style models, firms are symmetric – theory is silent on which firms are forced to exit if trade is liberalized, and all firms are exporting. The Krugman-style models might easily be interpreted as implying a very strong competitive advantage from economies of scale and being large. The 1990s saw a large number of mergers in Europe with the given motivation that a more integrated common market will be associated with a greater need to be large and gain scale economies.

Theory necessarily builds on simplification, but during the early 1990s and early 2000s, it was increasingly stressed that firms are heterogeneous; they differ in productivity and within a given industry, only a small fraction of firms are exporters. More recent models of trade also take into account that firms are different. These models with heterogeneous firms, with Melitz (2003) as a central reference, emphasize efficiency rather than size in itself as a success factor; this seems to be in line with the empirical evidence, as we see in the following.

Models of this type are discussed in Chapter 9, but we leave the application to international economics for more advanced textbooks.

17.3 Trade policy

The models that we outlined earlier examined the motivations for, and welfare effects of, international trade, starting from a position of autarky. If there are no obstacles to foreign products and firms competing on the domestic market, we say that there is free trade. In practice, there are a number of policies in place in almost all countries with the aim of limiting foreign competition and sometimes strengthening domestic production at the expense of foreign competitors. Some of the key examples of trade policy are as follows:

- **Tariffs**. A tariff is a tax on imported goods. For example, a tariff of 10% on imported oranges will raise the price of imported oranges.
- **Import quota**. An import quota is a legally mandated limit on the amount of particular goods from a particular origin that can be imported. An example of an import quota would be that 100 tons of oranges can be imported from Spain during a given year.
- **Export subsidies**. A subsidy on exports or, more generally, actions that aim to encourage exports and strengthen exporting firms. A prominent example is a long-standing dispute between US-based Boeing and European Union–based Airbus and the extent to which public policy in the two regions has been geared toward strengthening the "own firm."
- **"Red tape."** Bureaucratic obstacles that place foreign producers at a disadvantage.
- **Many domestic policies contain a trade policy dimension**. Intellectual property laws (such as patents), for instance, exists to strike a balance between incentivizing the creation of new products on the one hand and gaining the benefits of competition on the other hand. If innovation mainly takes place in other countries but domestic producers easily copy foreign products, it becomes clear that, for instance, intellectual property laws can be seen as a part of trade policy. Similarly, clamping down on foreign cartels but tolerating domestic firms to form cartels on their export markets can be used to exemplify that competition policy can have a trade policy dimension.

As seen earlier, the theories of international trade highlight global welfare gains from trade. Why then do we see trade policy that aims to restrict trade? One way to group the arguments is as follows:

Reasons for restrictive trade policy that favor some groups, or firms, but are overall harmful for national welfare

Trade creates welfare gains from restructuring economies – some activities and firms shrink while others grow. This clearly creates incentives for the harmed groups or firms to try to limit foreign competition, even if it is detrimental for the country as a whole. In the model of trade under perfect competition that we examined earlier, landowners in Capitalia, for instance, would see a decrease in their incomes as a result of free trade. A concern might be that the losers from lower trade barriers may be few and well organized (say a couple of firms), whereas those who gain may be dispersed and with a weak voice. Typically, other ways to redistribute and provide support are preferable.

Reasons for restrictive trade policy that are potentially welfare enhancing for one country but hurt other countries

In markets where there is imperfect competition, there are gains to be had from domestic firms having a strong position in global markets. This is sometimes termed "beggar-thy-neighbor" policies – policies that aim to promote national welfare at the expense of other countries. From a European perspective, it is more attractive if Europe-based Airbus has a near monopoly on the global market for a segment of the aircraft market than if US-based Boeing has that position.

Reasons for restrictive trade policy that are potentially welfare enhancing globally

Finally, there are a number of reasons for trade policy that are arguably welfare enhancing on a global level. Perhaps, most importantly, we note that there are a number of instances where externalities and other market failures motivate public policies in the form of, e.g., regulations. Some aspects of trade policy can be seen as maintaining such rules. These kinds of concerns are often mentioned in terms of avoiding "a race to the bottom" regarding, for instance, environmental protection and labor standards. These concern issues where global welfare may be higher because of restrictive trade policy.[5]

In particular, the second of the motivations for trade policy – that it may increase welfare at the expense of other countries and hurt overall welfare – suggests that there is great value to having internationally agreed-upon rules and regulations for trade policy. The main governing body for international trade has been the World Trading Organization (WTO). Its beginnings are in the General Agreement on Tariffs and Trade (GATT) that started after World War II as cooperation between 23 countries with the United States in the lead that then gradually expanded to become the WTO in 1995 with ultimately almost all countries becoming members. Arguably, China's accession to the WTO in 2001 was an important factor in shaping China's increasing role in world trade. At the time of writing, there is great uncertainty as to institutional rules concerning international trade, and I therefore refrain from including information that can quickly become outdated. A central guiding principle of the WTO has been that all members should be treated the same. The policy of equal treatment may be waived when groups of countries have more far-reaching agreements, including **free trade areas** (where a group of countries remove trade barriers between themselves) and **customs unions** (a free trade area that also has identical tariffs toward the rest of the world).

17.3.1 Partial equilibrium analysis of trade policy

The general equilibrium model of trade that we examined earlier captures important aspects of trade, as it reshapes economies by shifting resources from the production of some products toward others. The drawback from a general equilibrium analysis is that it tends to become complex and somewhat unwieldy to work with. To examine the welfare effects of tariffs and other forms of trade policy, we therefore consider a partial equilibrium analysis and apply tools of supply and demand analysis.

Before we turn to tariffs supply and demand it is instructive to model trade in a supply- and demand-analysis framework. We consider a **small open economy** that takes prices on the world market as given. For instance, if Sweden were to limit imports of rice, this would have little long-run effect on the world market price of rice. Figure 17.8 displays

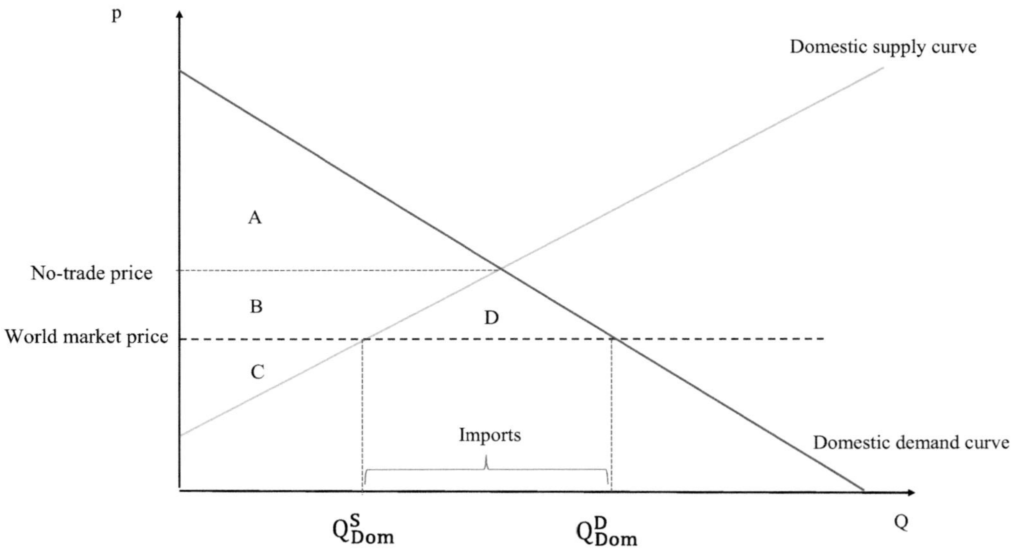

Figure 17.8 Partial equilibrium analysis of an importing country opening up for trade.

the domestic demand and supply coming from domestic firms of a good. If there is no trade,[6] equilibrium prices and quantities are given by the intersection of domestic supply and demand. Now assume that the country opens up to trade in this good and that the world market price is lower than the domestic price. Let the world market price be given by the horizontal line. Domestic supply will then be Q^S_{Dom} and domestic demand Q^D_{Dom}. Use consumer surplus and producer surplus as measures of welfare. Moving from no trade to trade implies that consumer surplus increases by the areas B + D, whereas domestic producer surplus decreases by the area B. The net welfare effect is positive and captured by the area D. Just as in the analysis earlier, there are overall positive welfare effects from trade but distributional conflicts – here consumers gain and producers lose, but consumers gain more than what producers lose.

Figure 17.9 shows the flip side of the coin – the case of a country where domestic price is lower than world market price. Here opening up to trade implies that price increases. Producer surplus increases by areas B + D, whereas consumer surplus decreases by area B. Overall gain is thus D, but again, there is a distributional issue in that some firms or individuals lose. To examine a concrete case, consider a country with a high supply of cheap electricity. Opening up for exports of electricity by developing transmission capacity increases the domestic price, to the detriment of consumers, but the gain in profits for firms more than makes up for the loss at a national level. In principle, policy could make producers compensate consumers and still be better off than without the possibility to export. In principle, producers could transfer B to consumers and still keep the area D.

We are then ready to consider how a tariff affects welfare. Figure 17.10 illustrates the welfare effects of an import tariff. A tariff of t euros per unit increases price by t euros. The reason why we have this perfect pass-through of tariffs onto price is that we assume that the importing country is "small" in the sense that it meets a perfectly elastic supply curve. We assume that world market price does not respond to the tariff.[7]

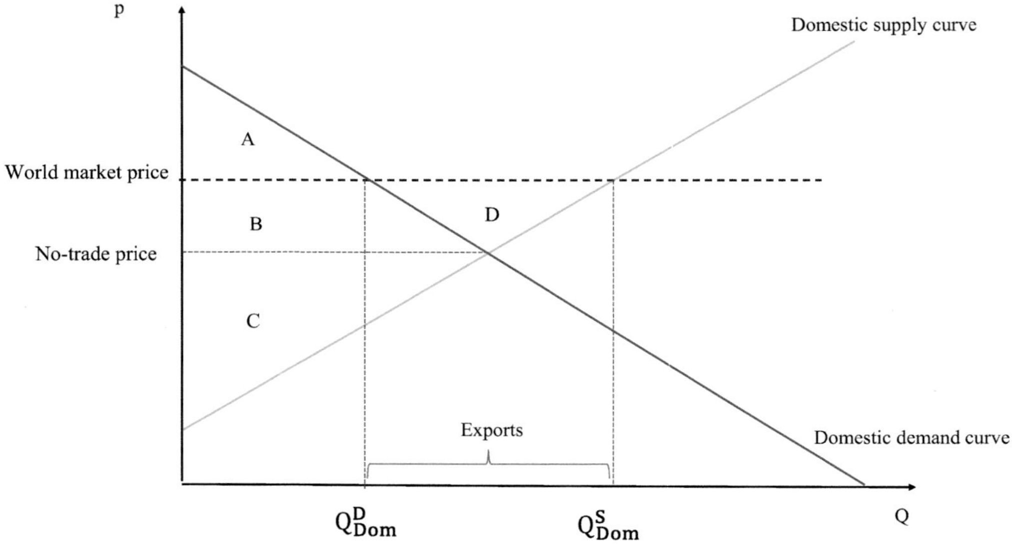

Figure 17.9 Partial equilibrium analysis of an exporting country opening up for trade.

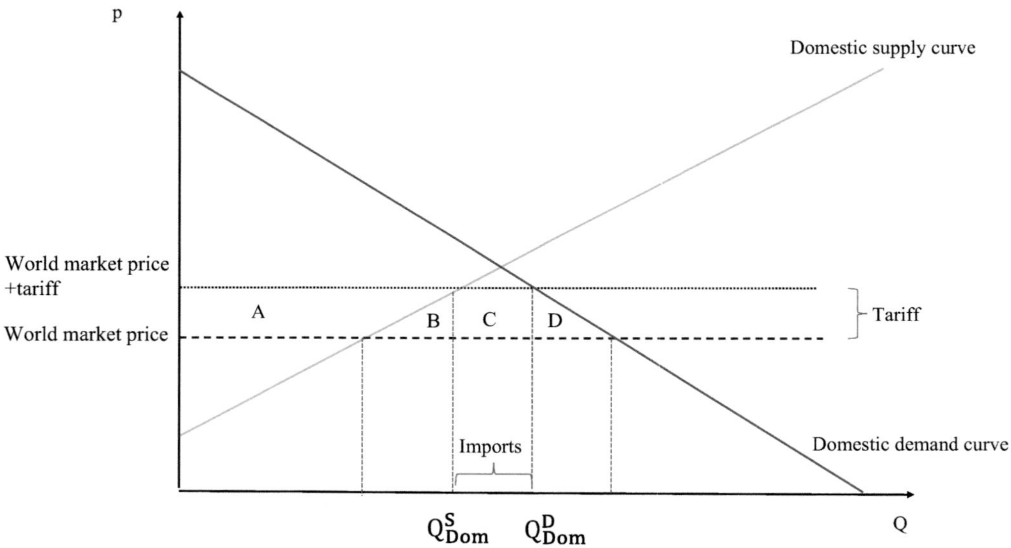

Figure 17.10 Partial equilibrium analysis of welfare effect of a tariff. Video link for figure: https://youtu.be/OAelllHGolc.

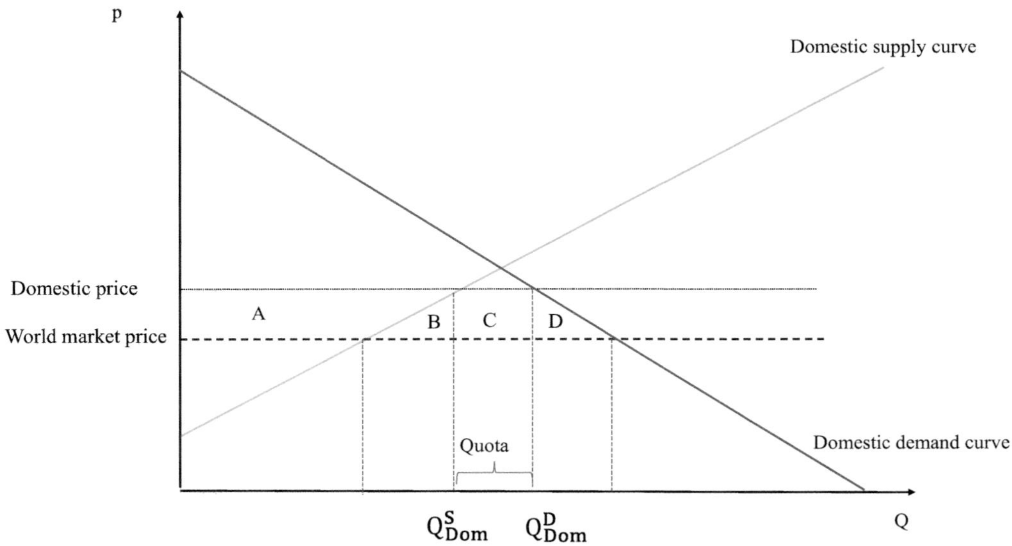

Figure 17.11 Partial equilibrium analysis of welfare effect of a quota.

A tariff thus raises price in the importing country, increasing domestic supply and decreasing domestic demand. The loss in domestic consumer surplus corresponds to the areas A + B + C + D. The gain in domestic producer surplus is area A. Tariff revenue corresponds to the area C, the imported amount times the tariff. If, for instance, 100 tons of bananas are imported at a tariff of 2,000 euros per ton, then tariff revenue would be 200,000 euros. The deadweight loss of a tariff is equivalent to the areas B and D. These are the losses to consumer surplus and producer surplus that are not offset by any gains elsewhere. This tariff thus hurts domestic welfare, but domestic producers gain, and government revenue is increased.

Figure 17.11 shows the case of an import quota. In terms of welfare effects, the analysis is very similar to that of a tariff. Domestic producer surplus increases by A, and consumer surplus decreases by area A + B + C + D. Here there is no revenue from tariffs, and hence there is no government revenue to counterweigh the loss of consumer surplus. The net effect is thus to lower domestic welfare by the equivalent of the areas B, C, and D.

17.3.2 *The welfare effects from trade integration – A very brief overview of the evidence*

Questions regarding the welfare effects of trade continue to take the center stage in policy debates in many countries. Broadly speaking, the evidence supports the notion that trading and being integrated with the world economy raises national incomes (see, e.g., Irwin (2019) for a survey). As always, when interpreting the evidence, it is important to recognize that correlation need not imply causation. The prediction from the theoretical models covered earlier is that trade raises welfare and national income. It could reflect that lower trade barriers increase trade, which in turn increase incomes, which is the direction of causality that theory focuses on. It could, however, also reflect that causality goes in the other direction, in which it is the higher incomes that lead to increased trade. Consider a simple illustrative example: If I have middle income, I might only consume local cheese, but if my income grows, I might start buying imported Swiss Appenzeller cheese, Basque goat cheese, and Italian buffalo mozzarella. Then my rising income would raise trade, rather than the other way around. Nevertheless, studies that carefully try to address the causality support the notion that more trade causes higher incomes (Irwin (2019); Frankel and Romer (1999) provide a much cited study).

It is also worth pointing out that the type of thought experiment that we focus on when comparing autarky to free trade, is not what we typically see in the world. Even countries that we today think of as mostly closed engage in substantial international trade. History provides some examples that are closer to the thought experiment of moving from autarky to free trade, and results support a pattern of specialization according to comparative advantage and that welfare increases as a result of trade: Bernhofen and Brown (2005) and Bernhofen and Brown (2004) study the effect of Japan opening up from autarky in the mid-1800s, and Donaldson (2018) examines the effects of railroads allowing interregional trade in India in the late 1800s and early 1900s.

It must also be stressed that, while we on average believe that international trade is beneficial for both trading countries, the specifics of cases might change conclusions. In a simple analogy, we might feel confident that paracetamol is useful in alleviating pain, but we also know that for patients with liver problems, paracetamol can be harmful. The history of colonization is replete with examples of how gains from trade all accrued to one party, as in the colonization of Congo, and weak regulation can imply that national resources are squandered as exemplified by the near extinction of the American buffalo in the 1800s, as discussed in Chapter 13 (Taylor (2011)). History also shows many examples where a large foreign power has used trade to create a dependency that can then by used for wider issues related to power and control. Hirschman (1945) documents how Nazi Germany systematically used trade to dominate countries in Southeastern Europe, and McLaren (1997) provides additional examples and a theoretical analysis (the hold-up problem that we examined in Chapter 11 is a useful way to think about such issues).

The evidence is also supportive of the notion that trade impacts different people differently, and a large literature examines links between incomes of different groups and trade. There is support for lower trade barriers that are linked to lower demand for intermediate-skill work and that, e.g., increased competition from China hurt workers and regions in the United States who were most directly in competition with Chinese products (Autor et al. (2013)). Demand for different factors of production, including workers of different skill levels is, however, affected by many changes with a particularly important role for technological changes. Overall, the evidence suggests that technological changes have played a larger role in developments and stress that the overall impact depends importantly on other factors that impact inequality such as educational systems and broader labor market policies (see, e.g., Helpman (2016) or Pavcnik (2017) for overviews).

Notes

1 Intermediate inputs come from so many countries; one part of the assembly might be done in one country, another part in another country, and different tasks that are needed to bring a product to market – also including marketing, coordination, and research and development may also be located in different regions.

2 As with many economics jokes, it is not particularly funny but maybe instructive.
3 Being a professor at the Stockholm School of Economics, it feels somewhat unsatisfactory not to cover the Heckscher-Ohlin model, as they were both professors here as well. Bertil Ohlin received the Nobel Prize in 1976 for his contribution to the theory of international trade. Eli Heckscher was the first professor of economics (and economic history) at the school and Ohlin's supervisor for his doctoral thesis. Within the school, Heckscher is also known for having given out the highest grade in a course only five times during his entire career – one of those times was to Ohlin.
4 Note that it is not spelled autharchy, which instead refers to governance rather than trade rules.
5 There are also instances where concerns related to national security motivate trade policy. This may not be necessarily beneficial to other countries, but harm is limited, and the motivation is clear.
6 We here say no trade rather than autarky since the country in principle could be open to trade in many other products than the specific one that we consider in the partial equilibrium analysis.
7 If we instead were to assume that the world market price is affected, the world market price would be lowered by the tariff, which tends to reduce the welfare loss from a tariff for the country that imposes it.

18 Topics in digital markets

Illustration 18.1 Alan Turing – An early pioneer. flickr, parameter_bond. Public domain.

18.1 Digitalization

Computer chips are contained in an ever-increasing set of goods. Services are increasingly not only purchased online but also delivered electronically. Costs of transportation, of search, of matching are all falling sharply as a result of digitalization.[1] Labor and product markets are profoundly affected by this. By and large, such developments lie beyond the scope of an introductory textbook in microeconomics. That is not to say that the theories presented in this textbook are irrelevant for digital markets; instead, I would argue that the tools that we have seen before in the book are extremely useful. A cost structure with large fixed costs and near-zero marginal costs are important for understanding many digital markets. Similarly, substitutability between man and machine are central for

DOI: 10.4324/9781003623854-24

understanding the labor market impact of automation (see, e.g., Autor (2019)). Indeed, the idea that fundamental notions from microeconomics are key for navigating digital markets is something that has been repeatedly stated by one of the more prominent economists that work with digital markets: Hal Varian. Varian authored the microeconomic textbooks (at undergraduate and PhD levels) that I first learned and taught economics from. He moved to Google to become its chief economist as early as 2002 – a position he still holds at the time of writing more than 20 years later. He also wrote early influential texts on digital markets – for instance, co-authoring Shapiro and Varian (1999)) whose fundamental message was "Technology changes, economic laws do not." This is well in line with our focus on the fundamental models of economics in this textbook. That said, this chapter raises two types of topics that have gained in prominence as digitalization has progressed. The first is platform markets – we explain the concept later, but for now, think of a website like Airbnb that connects buyers and sellers on a market.

The second topic is auctions. Auctions have been used for several thousands of years but have gained in importance as digitalization makes their implementation easier. For instance, every time you run a search on a site like Google or Facebook, an auction is run that determines what ads that you will see and in what ordering the sponsored result will appear. These auctions have a turnover of several hundreds of billions of dollars. An early article in *Wired* on the topic that reports on a speech by Varian at the annual meeting of the American Economic Association:[2] "During the question-and-answer period, a man wearing a camel-colored corduroy blazer raises his hand. 'Let me understand this,' he begins, half skeptical, half unsure. 'You say that an auction happens every time a search takes place? That would mean millions of times a day!" Varian smiles. 'Millions,' he says, 'is actually quite an understatement.'" We thus also provide a brief overview of some topics and key results regarding auctions.

18.2 Platform markets

Increasingly, goods and services, as well as interactions with other people, are mediated via platforms. A **platform** (two-sided market, multisided market) is one in which (1) two (or more) sets of agents interact through an intermediary and (2) the decisions of each side of agents affects the other set of agents. Figure 18.1 illustrates. Key to platforms are **network effects**; the value of using the platform depends on how many users of the platform there are and their characteristics. Let us exemplify with one platform before expanding. Airbnb matches houses and apartments from owners (sellers) with renters (buyers) for short-term stays. **Network effects between the two sides** are key to making such a platform attractive. The more sellers there are on the platform, the more attractive is it for prospective buyers, as they can expect to find a better match for their needs. Similarly, the more buyers there are, the higher the value to a seller as it increases the probability that a property will be rented out, and the better the match, the higher price you can command.

Within-side network effects can also be important; for instance, the more reviews of an object, the more certain of the quality a consumer can expect to be. While in principle pretty much any business could be thought of as a platform, we believe that in many cases, the simplifying assumptions that we use to study firms that buy inputs and sell them to consumers to be a convenient way of capturing the key elements of the economic decisions. But in some situations, as we explore next, one can argue that the key economic issues revolve around platform economics and taking account of network effects.

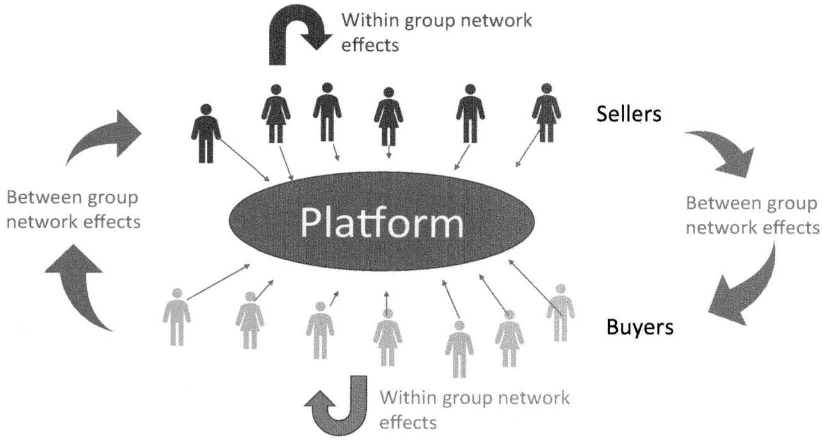

Figure 18.1 A schematic illustration of a platform.

Platforms have been present in human history for a long time – we can think of a market in a village square at the time of Aristotle in Greece as a platform – but digitalization from the early 2000s and onward have marked a stupendous increase in their role.

Rather than define platforms further in the abstract, it may be useful to give examples and enumerate some of the more prominent forms of platforms. One type of platform is the *exchange*. These can be stock exchanges, which have been around for a long time, but also a market platform such as Apple's App Store and the Android App Store. Such exchanges can be focused on connecting sellers to private consumers, such as Booking.com and Airbnb ("B2C" in common parlance) or for connecting commercial buyers and sellers ("B2B") with Alibaba as a prominent example. *Matchmaking* platforms with dating platforms such as Tinder, or job-market platforms such as Linkedin are other examples of platforms. *Advertising supported media* are another form of platform that has been prominent for a long time. Newspapers and commercial television channels bring together advertisers and viewers/readers. They also provide a service beyond the matching of sellers and buyers by producing or distributing content, but clearly, a key role for the content is to attract enough readers to be attractive as a platform for advertisers. Social media such as Instagram and Facebook are more recent examples. *Transactions systems*, such as credit cards, are another type of platform where it is crucial for the credit card firm to get enough retailers to sign up. Finally, let us also mention *software platforms* – a gaming platform such as Xbox is reliant on both sides of the market being there – game developers creating games for the platform and consumers buying the hardware.

Network effects are associated with a self-reinforcing situation; the more users that a product has, the more is it valued, which in turn attracts even more users. In the case of a platform, there are, as noted, also network vis-à-vis the other side. Many renters use Airbnb because there are many offerings and vice versa. One implication, which we will get back to, is that popular products tend to stay popular. Another implication is that getting a platform started can be difficult: No one uses the platform because no one uses the platform. A classic kind of chicken or the egg problem, what comes first, the chicken or the egg?

18.2.1 Issues when designing a platform

In creating a successful platform, a number of issues come into play. Broadly speaking, a successful platform will *promote positive network effects and limit negative effects*. An example of positive network effects on the consumer side is product reviews: The more users, the more reviews there can potentially be, which potentially allows for reviews to become more informative. Platforms can also try to increase interaction and value creation among users, with mechanisms such as an ability to share computer code. Of course, network effects can also be negative – more users can create congestion, and norms of conduct may deteriorate in free-entry settings, as seen by hate speech on some social media. More generally, we can in many cases think of platforms as creating a market – maintaining quality will often be a key concern. Many platforms are *subject to asymmetric information issues* where adverse selection and moral hazard can both affect supply and demand. Again, in the case of Airbnb, how do I know that the apartment that looks great on the web is as great in reality and even that it exists? Similarly, as an owner, if I entrust my apartment to a total stranger, how can I be reassured that it is not a person who will trash the apartment? Manual monitoring by the platform is one mechanism. A platform can also rely on reviews to incentivize good behavior and weed out rotten apples. Designing mechanisms that promote truthfulness in reviews are an important facet of platform design.

Digital platforms easily attract very many users and products. Just to take an example, several million apps are available on Apple's App Store. Even apart from quality issues, it is clear that platforms have a need for efficient ways of presenting the most attractive alternatives for a user. So, methods for *search and matching* are another key aspect of platform design.

A final important design issue regards how to *design price structure*. Many of the platforms that we are familiar with, and that we discussed earlier, are free to use for consumers. There is some truth to the saying that "if you're not paying anything, you're the product." The value of a platform partly depends on the number of users on the other side – if they are valuable, it is easy to see that one may want to charge little or zero to one side if the platform can more than make up for it with higher profits on the other side. In the following, we explore this idea formally.

18.2.1.1 Pricing by a monopolist platform with two sides

The details of how prices are set on platforms depend on many aspects, and the empirical literature, against which predictions can be evaluated, is still very limited in scope, see, e.g., Belleflamme and Peitz (2021) for an overview. The following model, based on Armstrong (2006), is however often taken as a starting point and offers intuitively appealing results. The important takeaways from the model will largely be gained by just understanding the setup and the trade-offs that it highlights.

Figure 18.2 presents the outline of the model. There is a monopoly platform that has two sides. There are n_b buyers and n_s sellers. The platform sets membership fees to each side, p_b

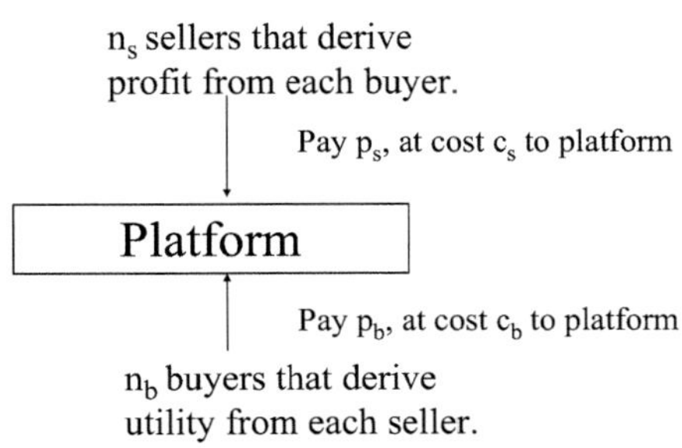

Figure 18.2 Set up for a monopoly platform with two sides – Armstrong model.

and p_s, respectively. These membership fees need not be strictly positive but can be zero or even negative (a subsidy) to one side. Let buyers value each seller with f_b and sellers each buyer with f_s.

Given the aforementioned setup, the net utility for a buyer is $v_b = f_b n_s - p_b$, and the net utility for a seller is $\pi_s = f_s n_b - p_s$. First, note that the key element that we want a model of platforms to capture is that the value of being on the platform depends on how many users are on the other side. The more sellers on the platform, the higher the value to a buyer of being on the platform. Similarly, the more buyers on the platform, the higher the value of a seller of being on the platform. A simple and transparent way to capture such effects is to simply include the number of agents on the other side of the market that are present on the platform – value for buyers is increasing in n_s, and value for sellers is increasing in n_b.

Let us pause for a moment and elaborate on the different variables that play a role in the analysis. First, the prices p_b and p_s are the prices for having access to the platform, they are not prices for the good or service traded on the platform. Intuitively, as a consumer, it is the price that you pay for having access to Airbnb, Netflix, or Spotify. It is not the price of an apartment on Airbnb but the access price to the platform. The cost of serving a member for the platform is c_b and c_s, respectively. These are the costs for the platform – in the case of a music streaming platform, for instance, c_b would be the data-processing costs of having an additional user and broadly interpreted would include the royalty fees that the platform needs to pay to artists. Finally, f_b and f_s capture the between-group network effects that are central to the platform logic. In the model, these are just parameters (just like a is a parameter in a demand function given by $Q = a - 2p$). At a deeper level, we can think of them as capturing the attractiveness of the platform. Broadly interpreted, if the buyers on the platform, for instance, are high-income consumers with a high willingness to pay, and the matching process on the platform works well, these are factors that would be associated with a higher f_s, increasing the value of an additional buyer to the seller side of the market.

Profits are generated from both sides – on each side given by the number of users on that side times the profit per user (price minus marginal cost for access to the platform for agents from that side) and are given by

$$\Pi_p = n_b(p_b - c_b) + n_s(p_s - c_s). \tag{18.1}$$

The platform sets prices to maximize profits, taking into account that a lower price to one side will attract more users on that side and hence increase attractiveness of the platform to the other side. While the intuition behind the results is important, the derivation of the optimal prices are more difficult than what you can be expected to be able to work with in a first textbook in microeconomics – hence, they are included in the appendix for completeness rather than in expectation that you will follow all the steps.

From the framework explained earlier, we reach expressions for the optimal prices for buyers and sellers, respectively, as

$$p_b = (c_b - n_s f_s)\left(\frac{\epsilon_b}{\epsilon_b - 1}\right) \tag{18.2}$$

and

$$p_s = (c_s - n_b f_b)\left(\frac{\epsilon_s}{\epsilon_s - 1}\right). \tag{18.3}$$

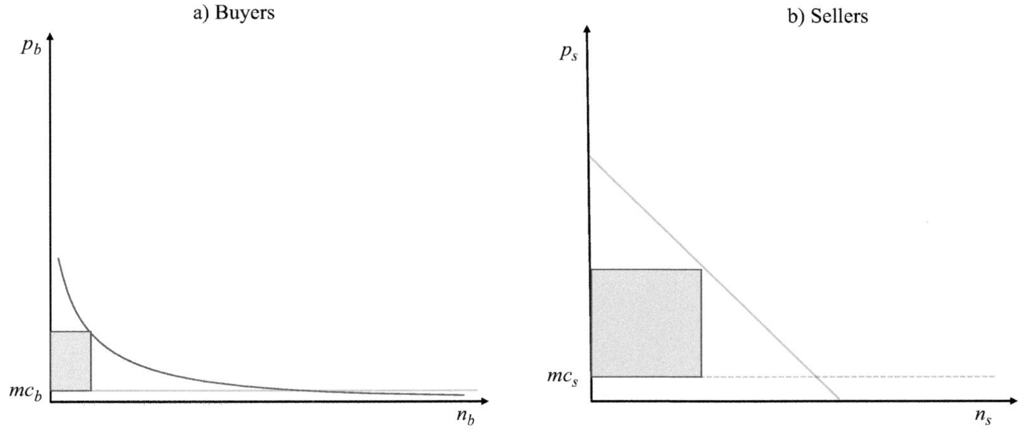

A case where monopoly price to each side of the market separately (MR=MC) yields profits as in the boxes

Figure 18.3 Prices on a platform without taking account of between-group network effects.

Thus the optimal price charged by the platform for a buyer, p_b, depends on the cost of serving a buyer c_b but, crucially, is lowered by the benefit that an additional buyer offers to sellers ($n_s f_s$). This is the key reason why many platforms offer their products for free to one side of the market – users on that side are valuable enough to the other side of the market to make it profitable. In addition, many goods and services have low marginal costs, which contributes to keeping prices low. As in standard models, the elasticity of demand (here expressed as the absolute value of the elasticity) from each side also matters for price (ϵ_b and ϵ_s). More elastic demand is associated with a lower price.

It may also be instructive to graphically illustrate the key mechanism in why it is attractive to lower price to one side in order to raise revenue from the other side. In Figure 18.3, we illustrate a case where the platform were to simply set standard monopoly prices where MR = MC on each side. The profits from each side are illustrated by the shaded areas.

In Figure 18.4, we instead illustrate the case where the platform takes account of the network effects between groups. Lowering the price toward buyers lowers the profits made directly from buyers; the grey area representing profits in the previous case is replaced by the darker area, which is lower. On the other hand, the lower price is associated with a large increase in the number of buyers, which shifts the value of being present on the platform for the sellers, and the increase in profits from this side (illustrated with the darker area) more than outweigh the lost profits on the buyer side. These figures thus give the intuition for the pricing on a monopoly platform market, and the expressions noted earlier give the actual optimal solutions as a function of the demand elasticities, the extent of between-group network effects and marginal costs.

18.2.2 Competition issues raised by platforms

Platforms have been at the center of much attention in competition policy. The network effects that we highlighted earlier, where self-reinforcing dynamics make popular products

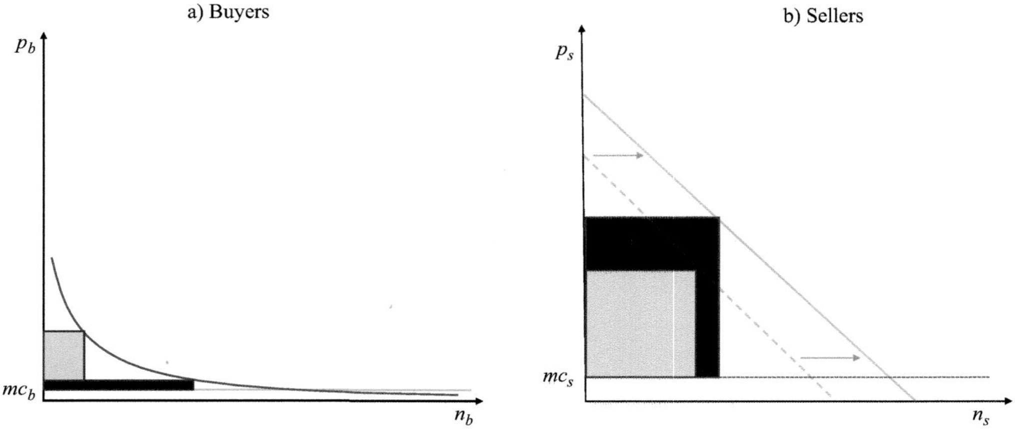

Can increase profit overall by lowering price to one side, which shifts demand curve on other side which can increase overall profit

Figure 18.4 Prices on a platform when between-group network effects are taken account of. Video link for table: https://youtu.be/f26Umw8VAUs.

even more popular, are a strong force in the direction of concentration, leading to relevant market being dominated by just one or a few firms. For instance, in many countries, Android and Apple are virtually a duopoly on operating systems for smartphones. Brands like Airbnb and Uber have strong roles in many markets. While we may think of Amazon as a retailer, it also has important platform features, for instance, via its use of third-party sellers on its sites under what is known as Amazon Marketplace. Also, in previous eras, most cities were dominated by one or two newspapers, and credit cards have been dominated by just a few firms such as Visa and Mastercard. The logic of network effects can have the effect that "a platform is large because it is large." A new entrant may thus find it very hard to attract a sufficient number of agents on both sides to be competitive. Another aspect of the advantage of large platforms is that large amounts of consumer data make it easier to predict what products will be attractive; algorithms that are used to predict what consumers will choose and guide in what order they see search results can be trained on larger datasets, become more accurate, and, likewise, on the other side of the market more targeted advertising can be sold.

One aspect that matters for the concentration is whether it is easy for users to be on several competing platforms or not. If users only use one platform for a particular good or service, we say that they **singlehome**, whereas if they use several they **multihome**. Smartphones are an example of a product where consumers singlehome. Very few customers find it worth it to have both an Android and an Apple smartphone – they singlehome. On the other hand, streaming services such as HBO or Netflix are examples of platforms where many consumers multihome. An ability to multihome and platform product differentiation are forces that push in the direction of several platforms being able to coexist, whereas singlehoming pushes in the other direction. In short, it is often hard to compete with a platform, and many of the large global brand names that have rapidly grown to be among the world's largest firms are platform-based. A ranking of the world's largest firms in spring 2025,[3] for instance, has four out of the five top companies with important platform characteristics (Apple, Microsoft, Alphabet (Google), and Amazon; the closely related tech company Nvidia is the odd man out in this group).

Many of the leading platforms have also been very active in acquiring potential competitors. Facebook's purchases of WhatsApp and Instagram are two prominent examples. Such purchases are especially hard to evaluate for competition authorities since merger regulation in many jurisdictions is focused on potential price effects of mergers and acquisitions, something that is clearly less of an issue when the product is offered for free to consumers.

Another set of competition policy issues concern platforms that are often active as competitors, as well as owners and rule-setters of the same platform. This opens up for the concern that platform owners are both "umpire and player." Google operates the price comparison site Google Shopping, but consumers also use Google to search for other price comparison sites. Apple hosts Spotify in its App Store but also competes with Spotify via Apple Music. Platforms have opportunities to favor themselves by, for instance, presenting their own products higher up in the order of search results (key in a European court case known as "Google shopping" for instance),[4] by charging high fees for competitors, or by using its position to gain advantage by observing data that is shrouded from competitors, as has been at the center of European Union investigations against Amazon.[5]

18.3 Auctions

In an auction, a good or service is allocated based on bids that have been submitted, and then, based on those bids, the auction procedure determines who gets the good and at what price. The example that comes to mind for many people is an art auction where the auctioneer stands on a podium, repeating the bids, and then when only one bidder remains pointing to that person, repeating the highest bid, and sealing the deal with the loud knock

Illustration 18.2 The art auction. *Christie's Auction Rooms*, various artists, 1808. Courtesy Metropolitan Museum of Art. Public domain.

of the auction hammer. Examples of this kind of auction range from when Leonardo Da Vinci's painting *Salvator Mundi* was sold for $450 million to high-speed cattle auctions.[6] But auctions are used to sell many goods and services: They are common in financial markets where government bonds are sold via auctions and when the right to transmit electronic signals on the airwaves via so-called spectrum auctions. Similarly, rights to natural resources are often assigned via auctions, and Sweden houses and apartments are sold via auctions. As mentioned in the introduction, auctions are also used to sell ads on the internet. Auctions have been used for a long time, with slave auctions in ancient Rome as an early prominent but sad example.[7] However, digitalization has transformed the ease with which auctions can be run – vastly expanding their range.

18.3.1 Valuations and bids

There are two basic elements of an analysis of auctions. First, the **valuations** of the item by different prospective buyers (v_1 and v_2 in the case of two buyers), which is the most that each of them would be willing to pay. Second, the **bids** (b_1 and b_2), which are the proposed payments they each submit to the auctioneer. Crucially, each individual's valuation is known only to herself; it is private information unless it is revealed during the bidding process (as when someone drops out in an art auction). Historically, auctions were typically used when a seller had great uncertainty about the value of the object to be sold, for instance, when the object is novel or unique – that's why there's an auction for Leonardo da Vinci paintings but not for apples at your local grocery store. To capture this intuition, it is sometimes stated that auctions are a machine for "price discovery." The seller needs to think about a setting that maximizes the expected revenue from the auction whilst taking into account that valuations may look very different depending on which bidders show up. Similarly, several auction formats imply that you as a bidder need to make guesses about the valuations of the other bidders.

For analyzing auctions, we distinguish between two types: private-value and common-value auctions. In a **private-value** auction, the valuations are independent of each other. The value of a concert ticket that you are not able to resell solely depends on how much you value going to that concert. In contrast, in a **common-value** auction, all bidders in principle attach the same value to the item. If you are bidding for the rights to operate a mine in a particular area, the value of that asset hinges crucially on the volume of mineral in that area. A key component of the value of the mining right is the expected market value of that unknown quantity of minerals – something that should be essentially the same for all bidders. In practice, most auctions contain elements of both: Your valuation of a house would, for instance, depend on where you happen to work, where your kids' friends live, your tastes regarding appearance of the house, and how much of a handy(wo)man that you are. These are factors that push in the direction of making a real estate auction a private value auction. On the other hand, the value that you will be to sell it for later (a common value component) is also important. Similarly, for mining, the costs of setting up operations may differ across bidders, where, for instance, one bidder may have operations close by and hence a higher valuation because of a lower cost of developing the mine, as it can draw benefits from nearby resources.

In the following discussion, we focus on private-value auctions for simplicity, but before doing so, we point out an important aspect of common-value actions: the **winner's curse** – the tendency for whoever wins a common-value action to pay more for the item than what its worth. Who ever overestimates the value the most will win the auction. Think of the mineral rights from a mine where the true value is V, but there is uncertainty about this true value. All bidders form their own estimate, given by $V + \epsilon$, where ϵ can be thought of as a random variable. For concreteness, assume that bidders on average are right so that the expected value of ϵ is zero – some will overestimate and some will underestimate, but these balance out so that the average valuation is correct. Who will win the auction however? Not the one who is closest to the true valuation but the one who has the highest ϵ; the one who overestimates the value the most. Clearly, this is something that you want to take account of in a common-value action and adjust your bid downward to avoid overpaying.[8]

18.3.2 Various auction formats

Auctions come in several different formats; let us first describe the most prominent mechanisms.

- **Ascending-bid auction** (also known as "English auction"). Starting from a lowest acceptable bid, bidders announce subsequently higher prices, and when at the end no one is willing to pay more than the currently highest bid, the object is sold to the person who gave that bid at the bid that she gave. The bids of the others are known, and you may or may not know their identity. This the classic art auction.
- **Descending-bid auction** (also known as "Dutch auction"). The auctioneer starts at a very high price, lowering bids until the first bidder says yes, at which point, she gets the good at this price. The Aalsmer flower auctions in Holland where many millions of flowers are auctioned off every day is the classic example of a descending bid auction. Historically, one advantage of the descending-bid auction was that it was very quick – there is only one bid, and the highest bidder gets the good; the auctioneer can rapidly move on to the next item.
- **First price sealed-bid auction**. Each bidder submits a bid without observing other bids, and the good is then sold to the highest bidder. Note that for simplicity, we, for the most part, frame our discussion in terms a good being sold via an action to the highest bidder. More generally, an auction can also be used to, for instance, buy a service from the lowest bidder. Public procurement of infrastructure is often run as first price sealed-bid auction, but the government then selects the lowest bid – who is willing to build a particular tunnel for the lowest price? We can think of the bidders as putting their bids in an envelope and sending these to the auctioneer.
- **Second price sealed-bid auction**. This is also known as a Vickrey action, after Nobel laureate William Vickrey in honor of his pioneering theoretical analysis of such auctions. This is similar to the first price sealed-bid auction, but the winner pays the second-highest bid rather than her own bid. While this may sound like an odd rule, note that this is how it works if you bid via an automated proxy bidder. For instance, in many online auctions, I can enter my maximum willingness to pay, my reservation price. This price is not observed by other bidders. The auction then incrementally raises the price, and when I'm the only bidder remaining, I win the object, but the price stops at the second-highest bid (plus a small increment). As we shall see next, second price auctions have some attractive properties from the perspective of the auctioneer, and auctions of this type are used in selling ads by, for instance, Google and Facebook.[9]

Table 18.1 A schematic view of some main auction formats

		Price that winner pays is essentially given by:	
Type of bidding process:		*Second price*	*First price*
	Open	Ascending bid auction ("English auction")	Descending-bid auction ("Dutch auction")
	Sealed-bid	Second price sealed-bid auction ("Vickrey auction")	First price sealed-bid auction

Schematically, we can think of these four auction formats as reflecting different characteristics in two dimensions. The first dimension is whether bidding is **open** or **sealed-bid**. If bidding is sealed, each bidder just submits one bid, and bids of others are not observed at the time of the bid. There is no opportunity to learn about the bids and valuations of others during the auction process. In contrast, in an open auction, the different bids are played out over time and observed as bids are placed. The open setting provides an opportunity to learn about the bids of others as one input into your decision of what to bid.[10]

The second dimension concerns what price you will end up paying. Your own bid (first price) or the price of the second-highest bid (second price). In the case of an ascending auction, the winner pays her own bid, but we think of it as a second price auction, as the winner will typically pay just a small increment over the price when the second-highest bidder drops out. If two bidders remain, one with a valuation of 100 euros and one with a valuation of 500 euros, we expect the latter to win at a price of say 110 euros, the valuation of the second-highest bidder plus some relatively small increment.

18.3.3 Evaluating the different auction formats

To evaluate the different auction mechanisms, we are typically interested in two questions: *Who gets the item*, and *how much revenue is generated*? From the perspective of efficiency, we typically want the item to go to whoever values it the most, and a natural goal for the seller is to maximize revenue.[11]

Start with evaluating the *ascending auction* with the two previous questions in mind. The auction starts from a reserve price r, which is lower than v_1 and v_2, assuming that $v_1 > v_2$. The reserve price is the lowest price that the seller is willing to accept; if no bid is above the reserve price, the good isn't sold. As the auctions starts, both bidders will be active, submitting sequentially higher bids. As the bidding reaches v_2, buyer 2 will stop, and buyer 1 will win the auction. So the item goes to the bidder who values the item highest. How much revenue is generated? The winning bid will essentially be equal to v_2; bidder 1 pays whatever the price had escalated to at the point where bidder 2 dropped out (plus some additional increment that is assumed to be small in relation to the price). Two important lessons that follow from this for setting up an auction, from the perspective of the seller, is that it is often useful to have many bidders and to use a reserve price. Selling a Matisse painting at a local farm auction with no reserve price is a bad idea. If valuations among two bidders are 1 million euros and 100 euros, respectively, the painting would go to the one who values it the most, but the auction would only raise 100 euros – setting a reserve price, the lowest price the seller is willing to accept, is important.

Consider now the *first price sealed-bid auction*. In the ascending auction, all the bids were observed, and the valuation of the second-highest bidder was learned during the bidding process. In the case of a first price sealed-bid auction, that is not the case. Put yourself in the shoes of bidder 1. You know that your valuation is v_1, but you do not know the valuation of bidder 2, nor what bid that bidder 2 makes. The higher your bid b_1, the higher the probability that you win the auction, but the drawback is, of course, that the higher your bid, the lower your surplus $(v_1 - b_1)$ if you win the auction. If you guess wrong about 2's valuation, you could easily end up losing the auction and bidder 2 would get the item – at a price that may well be below v_2. In this case, the first price sealed-bid auction would thus not allocate the item to the bidder with the highest valuation and not maximize revenue.

Do not from this small example draw the conclusion that an ascending auction is always preferable – what auction performs best is a complex topic that blends both theoretical analysis and empirical evidence. For instance, the first price sealed-bid auction can also result in the winning bid being much higher than the second-highest bid and thus raise more revenue than an ascending auction. More systematically, the revenue and efficiency of allocations under various auction formats also depend on a number of issues, in often subtle ways, that we have disregarded in our discussion. Examples of such issues are whether several objects are auctioned and whether they are substitutes or complements (a telecommunications operator will, for instance, have a higher value of owning spectrum licenses in two adjacent regions), how the bidders' information about the value of the object are related across bidders, the costs associated with entering an auction (to place a serious bid on mineral rights, for instance, you need to spend time and money to make an estimate of the value), and how the number of bidders influences results. The ability of bidders to collude, and in various ways signal their intentions to each other, is also a topic that is of great practical importance. All of this is left for more advanced texts.[12] Furthermore, under certain conditions, theory predicts that different auction formats give the same expected revenue – the so-called revenue equivalence theorem. This is more advanced than what is typically seen as relevant to teach at an introductory or intermediate level, but for completeness, we offer a brief description in the appendix.

Before closing this chapter, let us highlight one attractive aspect of a second price sealed-bid auction from the perspective of a seller. Using the same notation as earlier and putting yourself in the shoes of bidder 1, think of the expected payoff from a bid in a first price sealed-bid auction – it is given by the probability of winning the auction (which depends on your own bid b_1) times the surplus that you get if you win (your valuation minus what you paid, which is your own bid in this case):

$$\text{Probability } (b_1 > b_2) \times (v_1 - b_1).$$

So a higher bid raises the probability that you win but is also associated with paying a higher price, which tempers your desire to bid high. You will thus tend to bid lower than your valuation. If you value an item at 100 euros, you would prefer to get it for less than 100 euros. Indeed, if you were to bid your valuation, you would be assured to get a payoff of zero (since if you loose, you get zero, and if you win, you get $v_1 - b_1$, which is then also zero).

In contrast, in the expected payoff from a second price sealed-bid auction, you do not pay your own bid but the bid of your competitor, so there is no incentive to hold back.

Probability $(b_1 > b_2) \times (v_1 - b_2)$

In fact, in the simplest case, it is a dominant strategy to truthfully bid your valuation in a second price sealed-bid auction. The second price auction format decouples your bid from your payment. To see that you would want to bid your true valuation in this case, compare the different payoffs from letting your bid be the same as your valuation $b_1 = v_1$ with overbidding $(b_1 > v_1)$ or underbidding $(b_1 < v_1)$. The key concerns that keep you truthful is that by overbidding, you risk ending up with paying more than what you value the item at (if $b_1 > b_2 > v_1$), and by underbidding, you risk losing the auction, for instance, even if the price is lower than your valuation (if $v_1 > b_2 > b_1$).

18.4 Appendix – Further details on profit maximization on a platform

This appendix spells out the steps that take us from the profit-maximization problem in Equation (18.1) to the expressions for markups in Equations (18.2) and (18.3). They are beyond the scope of an introductory microeconomics course and just here for the sake of completeness. To solve the model, we follow Armstrong (2006) and first express prices as functions of net utility and then express platform profits as functions of these net utilities.

$$\Pi_p = N_b(v_b)(\underbrace{f_b N_s(\pi_s) - v_b}_{p_b} - c_b) + N_s(\pi_s)(\underbrace{f_s N_b(v_b) - \pi_s}_{p_s} - c_s).$$

We assume that the platform maximizes profits by choosing net utilities offered to the two sides. Letting the platform maximize profits by choosing v_b and π_s yields the following two first-order conditions:

$$\frac{dN_b(v_b)}{dv_b}\left(\underbrace{f_b N_s(\pi_s) - v_b}_{p_b} - c_b\right) - N_b(v_b) + \underbrace{N_s(\pi_s)}_{n_s} f_s \frac{dN_b(v_b)}{dv_b} = 0$$

$$\underbrace{N_b(v_b)}_{n_b} f_b \frac{dN_s(\pi_s)}{d\pi_s} + \frac{dN_s(\pi_s)}{d\pi_s}\left(\underbrace{f_s N_b(v_b) - \pi_s}_{p_s} - c_s\right) - N_s(\pi_s) = 0$$

Using the expressions for prices and number of members on each side given in the brackets, we can express optimal prices as

$$p_b = c_b - n_s f_s + \frac{N_b(v_b)}{\frac{dN_b(v_b)}{dv_b}}$$

and

$$p_s = c_s - n_b f_b + \frac{N_s(\pi_s)}{\frac{dN_s(\pi_s)}{d\pi_s}}.$$

Thus, the optimal price for buyers, p_b, depends on the cost of serving a buyer, c_b, but, crucially, it is lowered by the benefit that an additional buyer (f_s) offers to sellers (of which there are n_s). The last term denotes the number of buyers, divided by the derivative of the number of buyers with respect to net utility of buyers. An increase in net utility for buyers is positively associated with the number of buyers, so this term is positive. The more sensitive the number of buyers is to the net utility, however, the greater will the denominator be and the lower will the price be.

We can also take this one step further to reach an expression for the markup that lines up well with the standard formula for monopoly prices. We rewrite the fraction and multiply and divide by p_b. Further, note that N_b is a function of v_b, which in turn is equal to $f_b n_s - p_b$. Thus, for a given number of sellers, the change in N_b, the number of buyers, depends on p_b only, and we can think of the denominator as the equivalent of the demand elasticity. Since we are differentiating with respect to v_b, net utility, the denominator will be positive, and we can think of it as the absolute value of the demand elasticity, ϵ_b.

$$\frac{N_b(v_b)}{\frac{dN_b(v_b)}{dv_b}} = \frac{p_b}{\underbrace{\frac{dN_b(v_b)}{dv_b}\frac{p_b}{N_b}}_{\epsilon_b}}.$$

18.5 Appendix – The revenue equivalence theorem

As mentioned in the main text, a celebrated result in auction theory is what is known as the **revenue equivalence theorem**, first proposed by Vickrey (1961). It states that under a set of assumptions, the expected revenue from different types of auctions are the same. Thus, if you're a seller, you need not give much thought to whether to use, e.g., an ascending bid auction or a first price sealed-bid auction. They both yield the same expected revenue. The key assumptions needed for this result is that bidders are risk neutral, each bidder's valuation is drawn from a "well-behaved" probability distribution, and the auction format is such that the highest bidder wins, and the lowest bidder has zero expected payoff.[13]

The theorem is a key point of reference in the theoretical literature that examines auctions and is therefore worth mentioning also in an introductory text. That said, the takeaway from this is *not* that if you're a seller it does not matter which format you choose. As always, you also need to examine empirical evidence on whether theoretical predictions hold. A theorem such as this also has implicit assumptions on, e.g., optimizing behavior, whether the set of bidders are the same across the different formats and the ease of collusion between bidders. A number of cases have been documented where the auction format does matter for revenue (see, e.g., Lucking-Reiley (1999), Athey et al. (2011) or Hortaçsu and Perrigne (2021) for a survey). It is also the case that for a given seller and a given type of good, we often see little variation in auction formats. Art, for instance, is typically sold with an ascending auction rather than a first price sealed-bid auction. This gives empirical researchers few cases to compare – and may also suggest that there is something in the, e.g., setting when art is sold that makes an ascending auction particularly attractive (this point about lack of variation in auction formats for a given good is highlighted in, e.g., Maskin and Riley (2000)).

Deeper examination of revenue equivalence and bidding strategies in auctions requires more mathematical machinery than what is reasonable to cover in an introductory or intermediate textbook in microeconomics. Let us nevertheless provide a brief example of bidding in two different auction formats.[14] Consider a case where there are n bidders who all play the same strategy and have independent private values of the good to be auctioned off. These valuations are drawn from a uniform distribution over the interval from 0 to 1. As discussed in the main text, in the first price sealed-bid auction, each bidder trades off two opposing incentives when deciding how much to bid: A higher bid increases the probability of winning the auction but also leads to a lower surplus if you actually win. The predicted equilibrium strategy will in this case be given by bidder i placing a bid that is lower than her valuation by a term that depends on the number of bidders, as specified in Equation (18.4). We say that she "shades" her bid and more so the fewer bidders who there are.

$$b_i = v_i \times \frac{n-1}{n} \tag{18.4}$$

If, for instance, a bidder's valuation is 0.8, and there are 4 bidders, then her bid is predicted to be

$$b_i = 0.8 \times \frac{4-1}{4} = 0.6.$$

The higher the number of bidders, the closer to your own valuation you bid. The precise relation between the "shading" and number of bidders is specific to this particular setup, but the general intuition that more bidders produce higher bids is not. The winning bid is expected to be the highest value of $v_1 \times (n-1)/n$, $v_2 \times (n-1)/n$ and so forth, where the valuations, the v_i's, are drawn from a uniform distribution. Under these assumptions, it can be shown that the winning bid, and hence the expected revenue in the first price sealed-bid auction $E(R_{fpsb})$, is expected to be given by

$$E(R_{fpsb}) = \frac{n-1}{n+1}.$$

Thus, if $n = 4$, for instance, $E(R_{fpsb}) = (4-1)/(4+1) = 3/5$, whereas if $n = 11$ $E(R_{fpsb}) = (11-1)/(11+1) = 10/12$. More bidders generate higher revenue since the highest expected valuation is higher when there are more draws[15] and bidders shade their draws by less.

Under the same set of assumptions, it can be shown that the expected revenue in an ascending auction, $E(R_a)$, is also given by

$$E(R_a) = \frac{n-1}{n+1}.$$

Here, the revenue will be given by the second-highest bid, the second-highest valuation. The more bidders there are, the higher a draw can we expect the second-highest valuation to be. In this setup, the expected revenue is thus equivalent for these two different auction formats.

Notes

1 See, e.g., Goldfarb and Tucker (2019) for an overview.

2 Levy, Steven (2009) Secret of Googlenomics: Data-Fueled Recipe Brews Profitability, *Wired*, https://www.wired.com/2009/05/nep-googlenomics/.

3 https://companiesmarketcap.com/, accessed March 26, 2025.
4 see, e.g., https://ec.europa.eu/commission/presscorner/detail/en/MEMO_17_1785.
5 See, e.g., https://www.nytimes.com/2022/07/14/business/amazon-europe-antitrust.html
6 See, e.g., https://www.youtube.com/watch?v=3orkmMlSpmI and https://www.youtube.com/watch?v=Ea7gn8hhEFA
7 Famously, the imperial guard in Rome also auctioned off the emperorship in A.D. 193. Cassady (1967) is one classic reference to the use of auctions through history.
8 It is also the case that the more bidders who enter the auction, the more dispersed are the estimates likely to be, implying that the winner's curse gets worse as more bidders enter. This is indeed the pattern found in, e.g., Ebay auctions (Bajari and Hortaçsu (2003)).
9 See, e.g., Edelman et al. (2007) or Varian and Harris (2014) for detailed descriptions of ad auctions.
10 This is particularly true for the ascending bid auction, where you see the bids of others and eventually only one bidder remains. It is less clear-cut for the descending auction, where by the time someone calls out that they are willing to pay at a given level, it will be too late for others to act.
11 Exceptions are possible. Consider, for instance, an auctioning of the right to operate some service to the public where one efficient nonprofit provider is bidding against a profit-maximizing monopolist. Clearly, the latter has a higher valuation of winning the right, but this is associated with lower overall welfare.
12 Classic textbook treatments are found in for instance Klemperer (2004) and Milgrom (2004).
13 The above provides an intuitive presentation of the key assumptions and follows Tadelis (2013). A more complete, and technical, presentation is found in Milgrom (2004).
14 See Tadelis (2013) for a full description of the reasoning and mathematical background.
15 Just as when you're throwing a die – the more tosses you have, the more likely is it that you get at least one six.

19 Mathematical appendix

This appendix presents a set of key concepts and definitions related to the use of functions in microeconomics. It is not intended to give a completely general treatment for students who have never worked with functions, graphs, and calculus, but its aim is instead to provide an intuitive refresher and point of reference for the parts of mathematics that you covered in secondary school but where recollection is somewhat hazy. In my experience, many students easily remember that the derivative of $3x^2$ is equal to $6x$ but are somewhat perplexed when asked to take the derivative of the cost function $C(q) = 10 + q^2$ with respect to q and interpret the result. This is for you.

19.1 Functions of one variable and their slopes

A **function** is a mathematical rule that relates one variable to one or several other variables. For example, in $y = f(x)$, the function f describes how variable y depends on the variable x. In some way, y depends, as specified by the function f, on the values of x. For every value of x that you give, the function specifies one value for y. We refer to y as the **dependent variable** and x as the **independent variable**. The letters used are clearly only examples, and what letters we use in different applications will depend on what is convenient and ideally self-explanatory. For instance, in $Q^D = g(p)$, quantity demanded Q^D depends on price p in a way specified by the demand function g.

We can work with functions in a general form, not being more specific than noting that $y = f(x)$. For instance, we can say that how many pages I write, (y), depends on the number of hours spent writing, (x), in some way as captured by f that could represent very many different forms of that relation. This may allow a conceptual analysis that incorporates many cases and thus is very general. Often, we are however interested in a specific form, pinpointing exactly what values of y different values of x imply. To illustrate particular functional forms, we can use a **graph**, representing the function as a curve in a diagram with x on the horizontal axis and y on the vertical axis.

One type of relation is where the function is **linear** such that, for instance,

$$y = a + bx,$$

where we term a the **intercept** and b captures the **slope** of the function. For every increase in x, y increases at a constant rate, as captured by b. We illustrate the curve for this function in Figure 19.1. Clearly, if the term b is negative, the function is downward sloping.

A second type of relation is where the function is increasing at an increasing rate, as depicted in Figure 19.2 such that, for instance,

$$y = a + bx^2. \tag{19.1}$$

DOI: 10.4324/9781003623854-25

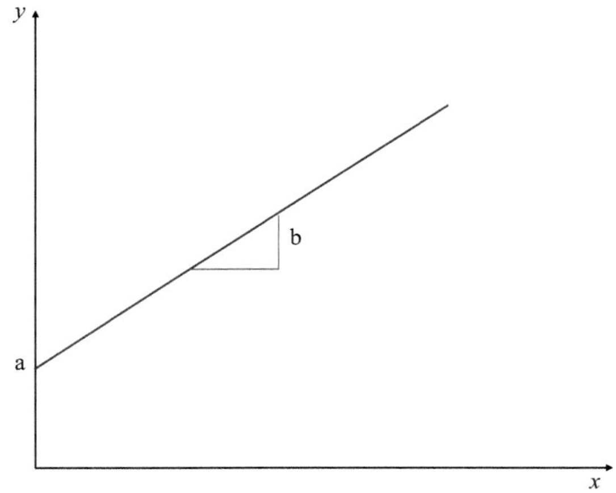

Figure 19.1 A linear function.

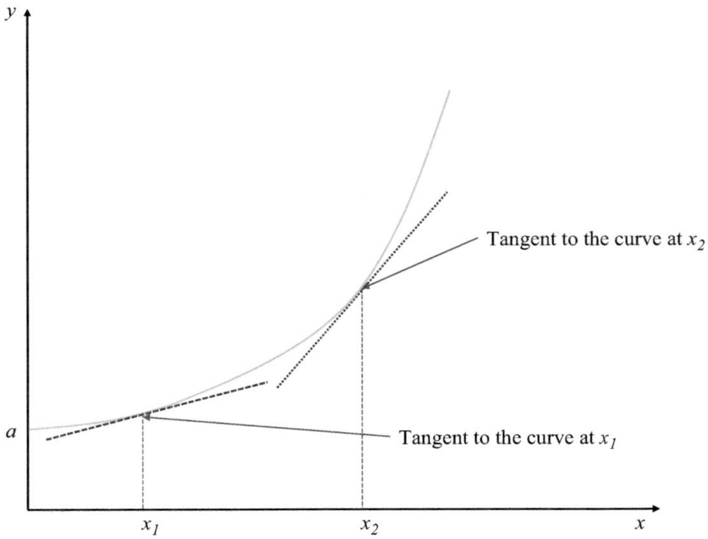

Figure 19.2 A curve that is increasing at an increasing rate: strictly convex.

The term a is again the intercept, but the slope of the curve is now not constant. It depends both on a coefficient b and on the particular way that x enters, in this case, in the form of a quadratic term. Another example of where x has successively greater impact on y for greater values of x would be x^3. To describe the slope, it is useful to introduce an additional concept: We say that a **tangent** to a curve in a specific point is a line that just touches the curve at that point as shown by the tangents at x_1 and x_2 in Figure 19.2. The tangent at x_2 has a steeper slope than the tangent at x_1, and thus the curve is becoming increasingly steep.

To find the tangent of a curve at different points, we can **differentiate the function** f, take the derivative, to determine the change in y in response to a change in x. The branch of mathematics known as *calculus* specifies the rules and concepts for how we can differentiate functions. Taking the derivative of y with respect to x in Equation (19.1), we establish that

$$\frac{dy}{dx} = 2bx^{2-1}. \tag{19.2}$$

We remind ourselves of the rules of differentiation next, but for now, note that the apparatus for taking derivatives was developed independently by two spectacularly smart scholars in the late 1600s, Gottfried Leibniz and Isaac Newton. In this book, we use the notation associated with Leibniz and denote the **derivative** of the function y with respect to x as $\frac{dy}{dx}$, where d denotes a "small" change. Another, perhaps more common form of notation, is associated with Newton, and the derivative of y with respect to x is then denoted by y'. They only differ in notation, and I have chosen to use the Leibniz notation in this book, as I find it to be the clearest when we extend the analysis to functions of more than one variable, but clearly, the notation you use is a matter of taste – it is just two different ways of expressing the same thing.

From inspection of Figure 19.2, it is clear that the tangents are steeper the higher the value of x. We can also use calculus to explore this, differentiating the first derivative in Equation (19.2) with respect to x to find the second derivative of the function and establish that

$$\frac{d^2y}{dx^2} = 2b > 0. \tag{19.3}$$

For a function that is increasing at an increasing rate, the second derivative is positive. More generally, we say that a function is **strictly convex** if, figuratively speaking, a string tied between two points on the function is always above the function. Clearly, the curve in Figure 19.2 satisfies this condition. A curve that is downward sloping, where the downward slope becomes flatter and flatter, also satisfies this condition.

A third type of relation is where the function is increasing at an decreasing rate, as depicted in Figure 19.3 such that, for instance,

$$y = a + b\sqrt{x}. \tag{19.4}$$

The term a is again the intercept, and again, the slope of the curve is not constant. It depends both on a coefficient b and on the particular way that x enters, in this case in the form of $\sqrt{x}$. Visually, the pattern looks like that in Figure 19.3. The tangent at x_2 has a flatter slope than the tangent at x_1, and thus the curve is becoming less steep at higher values of x.

We can again take the derivative of the function with respect to x to find the slope of the curve at different points, in this case

$$\frac{dy}{dx} = \frac{1}{2}bx^{\frac{1}{2}-1} = \frac{b}{2\sqrt{x}} > 0, \tag{19.5}$$

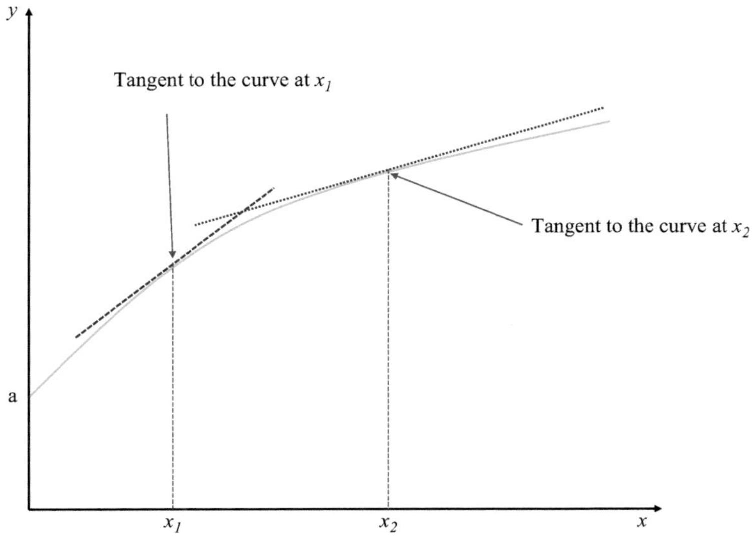

Figure 19.3 A curve that is increasing at a decreasing rate: strictly concave.

where we use $\sqrt{x} = x^{\frac{1}{2}}$ and $1/x^k = x^{-k}$. The function is increasing, and to find the rate at which it increases, we differentiate the function a second time, seeing that the derivative of Equation (19.5), or the second derivative of Equation (19.4), is

$$\frac{d^2y}{dx^2} = -\frac{1}{2}\frac{1}{2}bx^{-\frac{1}{2}-1} = -\frac{1}{4}bx^{-\frac{3}{2}} < 0. \tag{19.6}$$

For a function that is increasing at a decreasing rate, the second derivative is negative. We say that a function is **strictly concave** if, figuratively speaking, a string tied between two points on the function is always below the function. Clearly, the curve in Figure 19.3 satisfies this condition. A curve that is downward sloping and where the downward slope becomes increasingly steep also satisfies this condition.

A key point to emphasize for the strictly convex and concave functions is that the slope of the curve depends on where we evaluate it. The effect of a change in x on y is not everywhere the same. As discussed in the main text, this is important for the interpretation of changes in a large set of topics in microeconomics – marginal costs and marginal revenue are but two examples. Anytime we are using the term **marginal** in economics, we are in effect thinking of the tangent to a curve – referring to the slope at a particular point. An example of an application in (almost) everyday language is that of a marginal tax rate, as illustrated in Figure 19.4. Say that for income up to 5,000 euros, you pay an income tax of 0.3 for every euro that you earn, and for incomes above 5,000 euros, you pay a higher rate; your marginal tax rate jumps to 0.5 at that point. In terms of total tax payments, this does not mean that you pay a tax rate of 0.5 on all your earnings. The higher rate only applies to earnings above 5,000. If you earn 6,000 euros, for instance, your total tax payment is then $5,000 \times 0.3 + (6,000 - 5,000) \times 0.5 = 2,000$ euros and *not* $6,000 \times 0.5 = 3,000$ euros.

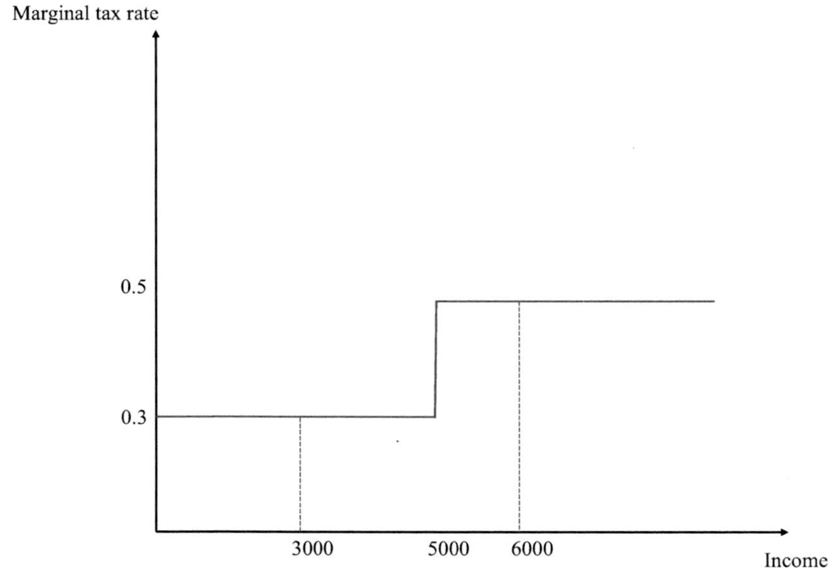

Figure 19.4 An example of marginal analysis: Marginal tax rate.

19.2 Finding the optimum of a function of one variable in the absence of constraints

Often, we are interested in finding the value of x that leads to the highest or lowest value of y. For instance, what is the quantity at which a firm's profit is the highest? When searching for the value that gives the highest value, we say that we are looking for the **maximum** of the function, and when we are searching for the lowest value, we are looking for a **minimum**. For the maximization problem, we express this as

$$\max_x f(x).$$

We can use the results to find such a point. The tangent of a curve gives the slope of the curve at that point, and clearly at the highest value of the curve, at the top of the hill, the slope is 0, as illustrated in Figure 19.5.

We term this the **first-order condition** for a maximum

$$\frac{dy}{dx} = 0$$

and often use a * to denote the optimal value of x. We further say the first-order condition (often abbreviated to f.o.c.) is a **necessary** condition for a maximum. It needs to hold at a maximum, but it is not **sufficient** for a maximum, as the slope of the function will be 0, also at a minimum. To determine if a point is a minimum or a maximum we can examine the second derivative. If the function is concave, has a negative second derivative, the first-order condition is associated with a maximum, as in Figure 19.5. This is known as the **second-order condition**. When examining maximization problems in this book, we only consider cases where the second-order condition holds, and we do not explicitly verify it. In general this

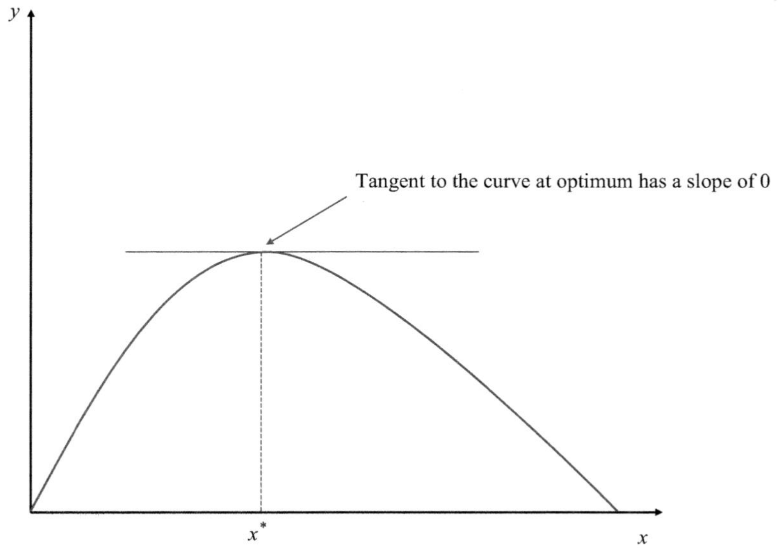

Figure 19.5 Finding the maximum of a function.

book, as is typical of introductory- or intermediate-level microeconomic textbooks, only considers functions that are "well-behaved," as economists would say. For instance, when the first-order condition holds in a profit-maximization problem, the function is such that we have found a maximum rather than a minimum. We also only examine cases where the maximum or minimum is unique; there is only one value of the independent variable that is associated with the optimal value for the dependent variable rather than several potential candidates.[1]

For completeness, Figure 19.6 illustrates the case of a minimum of a curve. Here the second-order condition relies on the function being strictly convex, and the second derivative is negative.

19.3 Some rules of differentiation

We here recapitulate some rules of differentiation that are used in the book. Three useful results if we differentiate a function with respect to x are that (i) the derivative of an additive constant is 0; (ii) a constant multiplying x remains; (iii) the power rule is such that an exponent to x is brought in front of x and the exponent decreased by 1. While this may sound complicated, the end result should be familiar. If the function is given by

$$y = a + bx^s,$$

the derivative is

$$\frac{dy}{dx} = sbx^{s-1}.$$

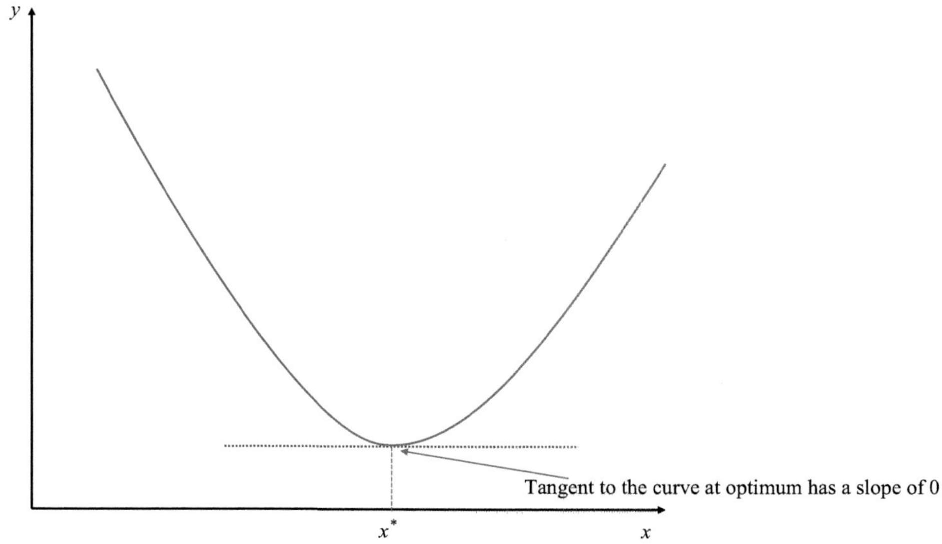

Figure 19.6 Finding the minimum of a function.

In the derivative, a drops out, b remains, and s "moves down." If we also remember that

$$\frac{1}{x^s} = x^{-s},$$

we have all we need to apply the rules of differentiation that we use in this book. For instance, if $y = 1/x$

$$\frac{dy}{dx} = -\frac{1}{x^2}$$

since we can write $1/x$ as x^{-1}, and applying the power rule to $y = x^{-1}$ gives us

$$\frac{dy}{dx} = -1x^{-1-1} = -\frac{1}{x^2}.$$

The **product rule of derivatives** is also used in some cases in the book: If $y = f(x)g(x)$ such that y depends on two functions of x that enter multiplicatively, then

$$\frac{dy}{dx} = \frac{df(x)}{dx}g(x) + f(x)\frac{dg(x)}{dx}.$$

This is what we use when examing the marginal revenue of a monopoly, for instance, where revenue is determined by the multiplication of two functions that depend on q: $p(q)$ and q. In some cases (for instance, if we want to solve for the minimum of an average cost curve is given by $C(q)/q$), we are also interested in the derivative where the variable we are differentiating over appears both in the nominator and denominator of a quotient. Thus if $y = f(x)/g(x)$, then the **quotient rule of derivatives** establishes that

$$\frac{dy}{dx} = \frac{\frac{df(x)}{dx}g(x) - f(x)\frac{dg(x)}{dx}}{g(x)^2}.$$

If, for instance, the average cost curve is given by $ATC = (16+q^2)/q$, then the first-order condition for the minimum is given by

$$\begin{aligned} \frac{dATC}{dq} &= \frac{2q \times q - (16+q^2)}{q^2} = 0 \\ q^2 &= 16 \\ \sqrt{q^2} &= \sqrt{16} \\ q &= 4, \end{aligned}$$

where the last line relies on that of the two roots of 16 (4 and −4); we can discard −4, as it does not make sense for a quantity of production.

19.4 Inverse functions

When examining demand, we use both the demand function $Q(p)$ and its mirror image, the inverse demand function $p(Q)$. More generally, if the function $y = f(x)$ is such that for each value of y there is only one value[2] of x, we can also represent the relation between y and x with the **inverse function** $x = f^{-1}y$. Intuitively, for each value of temperature, as measured in Fahrenheit, there is a unique value for temperature in Celsius. We can express temperature in Fahrenheit as a function of temperature in Celsius, or, equivalenently, temperature in Celsius as a function of temperature in Fahrenheit. For example, consider the function $y = 4x^2$ and its inverse below:

$$\begin{aligned} y &= 4x^2 \\ x^2 &= \frac{y}{4} \\ x &= \frac{\sqrt{y}}{2}. \end{aligned}$$

Thus if $x = 2$, then $y = 4 \times 2^2 = 16$, or using the inverse function, if $y = 16$, then $x = \sqrt{16}/2 = 4/2 = 2$, as also depicted in Figure 19.7.

19.5 Functions of two variables

In several cases, we are interested in functions where there are more than one independent variable – for instance, the production functions f pins down the relation between quantity produced (Q) and the amounts of labor (L) and capital (K) that are used as inputs. Several results regarding optimization of such functions are outside the scope of an introductory or intermediate course in microeconomics, and we will contend ourselves with highlighting a few properties that are useful in the book. First, we note that we can differentiate a function

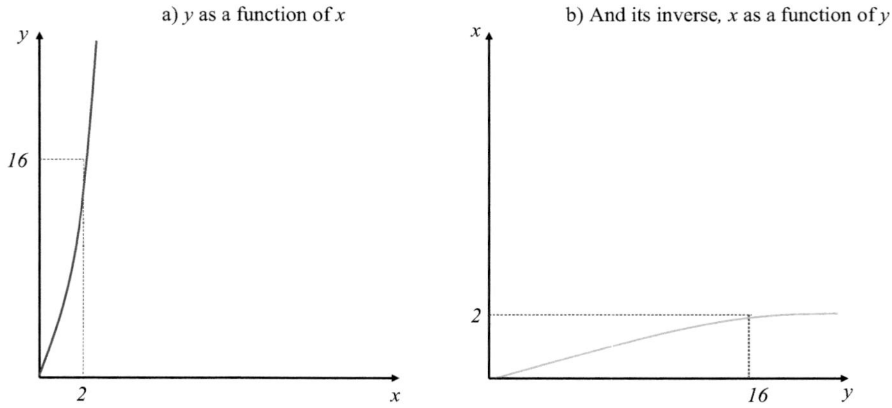

Figure 19.7 A function and its inverse function.

to see how the value of the dependent variable changes, as we change only one of the independent variables. The derivative where we let only one independent variable change and keep other independent variables constant is known as **partial derivative**, and we use the greek letter ∂ (lowercase "delta") to denote the partial derivative of f with respect to x. For instance, the partial derivative of the production function with respect to L is denoted as

$$\frac{\partial f(K, L)}{\partial L}. \tag{19.7}$$

Other forms of notation are also sometimes used; f'_L is perhaps the most common. Again, I find the notation associated with Leibniz that we show in Equation (19.7) to be the clearest.

For a partial derivative, the rules of differentiation (e.g., the factor rule) are the same as when we are differentiating a function of one variable. We let one independent variable change and treat the other independent variables as constants. For instance, the partial derivative of the production function $Q = K^3L^2$ with respect to L is given by

$$\frac{\partial f(K, L)}{\partial L} = 2K^3L^{2-1} = 2K^3L.$$

K is simply treated as a multiplicative constant in this partial differentiation. We use the term "marginal" to denote such a derivative, as in the previous case the *marginal product of labor*. The partial derivative with respect to capital will similarly be given by

$$\frac{\partial f(K, L)}{\partial K} = 3K^{3-2}L^2 = 3K^2L^2.$$

When we examine the slope of the indifference curve or isoquant in the text, we use *total differentiation* – we examine the effects of changes in both the independent variables on the dependent variable. Examine the function $y = f(x, z)$ and use d to denote a small change. Total differentiation then relates the change in y to the change in x and the marginal impact of that change $\frac{\partial f(x,z)}{\partial x}$, as well as the change in z and the marginal impact of that change $\frac{\partial f(x,z)}{\partial z}$. We let "everything change."[3] Thus, the total differential of the function f is given by

$$dy = \frac{\partial f(x, z)}{\partial x}dx + \frac{\partial f(x, z)}{\partial z}dz.$$

We are also sometimes interested in finding the values of x and z that maximize (or minimize) the value of y, possibly also subject to a constraint. The intuitive coverage of such analysis is presented in Chapters 3 and 5; a complete rigorous treatment is outside the scope of a book such as this. Nevertheless, an example of such analysis is presented in the appendix to Chapter 5.[4]

Notes

1 More generally, there can also be local maxima or minima where the first-order condition holds but where a higher value exists elsewhere – as when you're hiking in the mountains and there is a small summit (local optimum), leading you to lose some altitude before reaching the true summit (the global optimum).

2 The one-to-one mapping holds for a function that is everywhere increasing or everywhere decreasing but not for a parabola, for instance.

3 We focus on small changes here – for (somewhat) larger changes, we also want to take account of interaction effects between x and z, but that is left for more advanced courses.

4 Several comprehensive textbooks exist that require little prior knowledge. For instance, Simon et al. (1994) or Hoy et al. (2022).

Bibliography

Acemoglu, D. and Robinson, J. A. (2012). *Why nations fail: The origins of power, prosperity and poverty*. Profile London.

Akerlof, G. A. (1970). The market for "lemons": Quality uncertainty and the market mechanism. *The Quarterly Journal of Economics*, 84(3):488–500.

Allcott, H., Lockwood, B. B., and Taubinsky, D. (2019). Regressive sin taxes, with an application to the optimal soda tax. *The Quarterly Journal of Economics*, 134(3):1557–1626.

Amberg, N., Friberg, R., and Syverson, C. (2025). Have we got news for you: Firm-level evidence on the optimal choice of expected capacity utilization. *NBER Working paper No. 33400*.

Arkolakis, C., Costinot, A., and Rodríguez-Clare, A. (2012). New trade models, same old gains? *American Economic Review*, 102(1):94–130.

Armstrong, M. (2006). Competition in two-sided markets. *The RAND journal of economics*, 37(3):668–691.

Arrow, K. J. and Debreu, G. (1954). Existence of an equilibrium for a competitive economy. *Econometrica*, 265–290.

Ashraf, N., Camerer, C. F., and Loewenstein, G. (2005). Adam Smith, behavioral economist. *Journal of Economic Perspectives*, 19(3):131–145.

Asplund, M., Friberg, R., and Wilander, F. (2007). Demand and distance: Evidence on cross-border shopping. *Journal of Public Economics*, 91(1–2):141–157.

Athey, S., Levin, J., and Seira, E. (2011). Comparing open and sealed bid auctions: Evidence from timber auctions. *The Quarterly Journal of Economics*, 126(1):207–257.

Attanasio, O., Levell, P., Low, H., and Sánchez-Marcos, V. (2018). Aggregating elasticities: intensive and extensive margins of women's labor supply. *Econometrica*, 86(6):2049–2082.

Autor, D., Dorn, D., and Hanson, G. H. (2013). The China syndrome: Local labor market effects of import competition in the United States. *American Economic Review*, 103(6):2121–2168.

Autor, D. H. (2019). Work of the past, work of the future. *AEA Papers and Proceedings*, 109, 1–32.

Bain, J. S. (1956). *Barriers to new competition: The character and consequences in manufacturing industries*. Harvard University Press.

Bajari, P. and Hortaçsu, A. (2003). The winner's curse, reserve prices, and endogenous entry: Empirical insights from eBay auctions. *RAND Journal of Economics*, 329–355.

Barr, N. (2020). *Economics of the welfare state*. Oxford University Press, USA.

Bartelsman, E., Haltiwanger, J., and Scarpetta, S. (2013). Cross-country differences in productivity: The role of allocation and selection. *American Economic Review*, 103(1):305–334.

Bates, T. W., Kahle, K. M., and Stulz, R. M. (2009). Why do US firms hold so much more cash than they used to? *The Journal of Finance*, 64(5):1985–2021.

Becker, G. S. (1976). *The economic approach to human behavior*, volume 803. University of Chicago Press.

Bell, C. R. (1988). Economies of, versus returns to, scale: A clarification. *The Journal of Economic Education*, 19(4):331–335.

Belleflamme, P. and Peitz, M. (2015). *Industrial organization: Markets and strategies*. Cambridge University Press.

Belleflamme, P. and Peitz, M. (2021). *The Economics of Platforms*. Cambridge University Press.

Benjamin, D. J., Laibson, D., Mischel, W., Peake, P. K., Shoda, Y., Wellsjo, A. S., and Wilson, N. L. (2020). Predicting mid-life capital formation with pre-school delay of gratification and life-course measures of self-regulation. *Journal of Economic Behavior & Organization*, 179:743–756.

Benkard, C. L. (2000). Learning and forgetting: The dynamics of aircraft production. *American Economic Review*, 90(4):1034–1054.

Berger, P. G. and Ofek, E. (1995). Diversification's effect on firm value. *Journal of Financial Economics*, 37(1):39–65.

Bernard, A. B., Jensen, J. B., Redding, S. J., and Schott, P. K. (2007). Firms in international trade. *Journal of Economic Perspectives*, 21(3):105–130.

Bernhofen, D. M. and Brown, J. C. (2004). A direct test of the theory of comparative advantage: The case of Japan. *Journal of Political Economy*, 112(1):48–67.

Bernhofen, D. M. and Brown, J. C. (2005). An empirical assessment of the comparative advantage gains from trade: evidence from Japan. *American Economic Review*, 95(1):208–225.

Bernouilli, D. (1954). Exposition of a new theory on the measurement. *Econometrica*, 22(1): 23–36.

Berry, S., Levinsohn, J., and Pakes, A. (1995). Automobile prices in market equilibrium. *Econometrica*, 841–890.

Bertrand, J. (1883). Théorie des richesses: revue des théories mathématiques de la richesse sociale par Léon Walras et reserches sur les principes mathématiques de la richesses par Augustin Cournot. *Journal des Savantes*, 499–508.

Bhuller, M., Moene, K. O., Mogstad, M., and Vestad, O. L. (2022). Facts and fantasies about wage setting and collective bargaining. *Journal of Economic Perspectives*, 36(4):29–52.

Bick, A. and Fuchs-Schündeln, N. (2017). Quantifying the disincentive effects of joint taxation on married women's labor supply. *American Economic Review*, 107(5):100–104.

Black, J. (2002). Darwin in the world of emotions. *Journal of the Royal Society of Medicine*, 95(6): 311–313.

Bloom, N., Eifert, B., Mahajan, A., McKenzie, D., and Roberts, J. (2013). Does management matter? Evidence from India. *The Quarterly Journal of Economics*, 128(1):1–51.

Bloom, N. and Van Reenen, J. (2007). Measuring and explaining management practices across firms and countries. *The Quarterly Journal of Economics*, 122(4):1351–1408.

Bloom, N. and Van Reenen, J. (2010). Why do management practices differ across firms and countries? *Journal of Economic Perspectives*, 24(1):203–224.

Bosio, E., Djankov, S., Glaeser, E., and Shleifer, A. (2022). Public procurement in law and practice. *American Economic Review*, 112(4):1091–1117.

Boysen, O., Ferrari, E., Nechifor, V., and Tillie, P. (2023). Earn a living? What the Côte d'Ivoire–Ghana cocoa living income differential might deliver on its promise. *Food Policy*, 114:102389.

Bresnahan, T. F. and Reiss, P. C. (1991). Entry and competition in concentrated markets. *Journal of Political Economy*, 99(5):977–1009.

Bustos, E. (2023). The effect of centrally bargained wages on firm growth. *IFN Working Paper*.

Card, D. (1990). The impact of the Mariel boatlift on the Miami labor market. *Industrial and Labor Relations Review*, 43(2):245–257.

Card, D. (1992). Do minimum wages reduce employment? A case study of California, 1987–89. *Industrial and Labor Relations Review*, 46(1):38–54.

Card, D. and Krueger, A. B. (1994). Minimum wages and employment: A case study of the fast-food industry in New Jersey and Pennsylvania. *The American Economic Review*, 84(4):772–793.

Carson, R. (1962). *Silent spring*. Getty Publications.

Carson, R. T. (2012). Contingent valuation: A practical alternative when prices aren't available. *Journal of Economic Perspectives*, 26(4):27–42.

Cassady, R. (1967). *Auctions and auctioneering*. University of California Press.

Cesarini, D., Lindqvist, E., Notowidigdo, M. J., and Östling, R. (2017). The effect of wealth on individual and household labor supply: evidence from Swedish lotteries. *American Economic Review*, 107(12):3917–3946.

Chai, A. and Moneta, A. (2010). Retrospectives: Engel curves. *Journal of Economic Perspectives*, 24(1):225–240.

Charness, G. and Rabin, M. (2002). Understanding social preferences with simple tests. *The Quarterly Journal of Economics*, 117(3):817–869.

Chetty, R., Looney, A., and Kroft, K. (2009). Salience and taxation: Theory and evidence. *American Economic Review*, 99(4):1145–1177.

Coase, R. H. (1937). The nature of the firm. *Economica*, 4(16):386–405.

Coase, R. H. (1960). The problem of social cost. *The Journal of Law and Economics*, 3:1–877.

Connolly, M. and Krueger, A. B. (2006). Rockonomics: The economics of popular music. *Handbook of the Economics of Art and Culture*, 1:667–719.

Cooper, A. C., Woo, C. Y., and Dunkelberg, W. C. (1988). Entrepreneurs' perceived chances for success. *Journal of Business Venturing*, 3(2):97–108.

Corts, K. S. (1998). Third-degree price discrimination in oligopoly: all-out competition and strategic commitment. *The RAND Journal of Economics*, 306–323.

Cournot, A.-A. (1838). *Recherches sur les principes mathématiques de la théorie des richesses par Augustin Cournot*. chez L. Hachette.

Davis, D. R. and Weinstein, D. E. (2001). An account of global factor trade. *American Economic Review*, 91(5):1423–1453.

Davis, P. and Garcés, E. (2009). *Quantitative techniques for competition and antitrust analysis*. Princeton University Press.

Dawe, D. and Slayton, T. (2010). The world rice market crisis of 2007–2008. In Dawe, D., editor, *The Rice Crisis*, pages 15–28. The Food and Agriculture Organization of the United Nations.

De Loecker, J. and Syverson, C. (2021). An industrial organization perspective on productivity. In *Handbook of Industrial Organization*, volume 4, pages 141–223. Elsevier.

Deakin, S. and Meng, G. (2022). Resolving Douglass C. North's 'puzzle'concerning China's household responsibility system. *Journal of Institutional Economics*, 18(4):521–535.

Deneckere, R. J. and McAfee, P. R. (1996). Damaged goods. *Journal of Economics & Management Strategy*, 5(2):149–174.

Diamond, J. (2005). *Collapse: How societies choose to fail or succeed*. Penguin.

Dixit, A. K. and Stiglitz, J. E. (1977). Monopolistic competition and optimum product diversity. *The American Economic Review*, 67(3):297–308.

Domeij, D. and Klein, P. (2013). Should day care be subsidized? *Review of Economic Studies*, 80(2):568–595.

Donaldson, D. (2018). Railroads of the raj: Estimating the impact of transportation infrastructure. *American Economic Review*, 108(4–5):899–934.

Dranove, D. and Jin, G. Z. (2010). Quality disclosure and certification: Theory and practice. *Journal of Economic Literature*, 48(4):935–963.

Dubois, P., Griffith, R., and Nevo, A. (2014). Do prices and attributes explain international differences in food purchases? *American Economic Review*, 104(3):832–867.

Duffie, D. (2019). Prone to fail: The pre-crisis financial system. *Journal of Economic Perspectives*, 33(1):81–106.

Edelman, B., Ostrovsky, M., and Schwarz, M. (2007). Internet advertising and the generalized second-price auction: Selling billions of dollars worth of keywords. *American Economic Review*, 97(1): 242–259.

Edgeworth, F. Y. (1881). *Mathematical psychics: An essay on the application of mathematics to the moral sciences*, volume 10. CK Paul.

Einav, L., Finkelstein, A., Pascu, I., and Cullen, M. R. (2012). How general are risk preferences? Choices under uncertainty in different domains. *American Economic Review*, 102(6):2606–2638.

Ekelund Jr, R. B. (1970). Price discrimination and product differentiation in economic theory: An early analysis. *The Quarterly Journal of Economics*, 268–278.

Ekelund Jr, R. B. and Thornton, M. (2011). Galileo, Smith and the paradox of value: The 'connection' of art and science. *History of Economic Ideas*, 85–101.

Ellingsen, T. (2024). *Institutional and organizational economics: A behavioral game theory introduction*. Polity Press.

Elminejad, A., Havranek, T., Horvath, R., and Irsova, Z. (2023). Intertemporal substitution in labor supply: A meta-analysis. *Review of Economic Dynamics*, 51:1095–1113.

Enache, A., Friberg, R., and Wiklander, M. (2023). Demand for in-app purchases in mobile apps–A difference-in-difference approach. *International Journal of Industrial Organization*, 102945.

Ert, E. and Fleischer, A. (2019). The evolution of trust in Airbnb: A case of home rental. *Annals of Tourism Research*, 75:279–287.

Foster, L., Haltiwanger, J., and Syverson, C. (2008). Reallocation, firm turnover, and efficiency: Selection on productivity or profitability? *American Economic Review*, 98(1):394–425.

Frankel, J. A. and Romer, D. H. (1999). Does trade cause growth? *American Economic Review*, 89(3):379–399.

Friberg, R. (2015). *Managing risk and uncertainty: A strategic approach*. MIT Press.

Friberg, R. (2025). A Knight for the modern age – some reflections inspired by Amar Bhidé's uncertainty and enterprise. *Critical Review: A journal of Politics and Society*.
Friedman, M. (1953). *Essays in positive economics*. University of Chicago press.
Galor, O. and Weil, D. N. (2000). Population, technology, and growth: From Malthusian stagnation to the demographic transition and beyond. *American Economic Review*, 90(4):806–828.
Gandhi, A. and Nevo, A. (2021). Empirical models of demand and supply in differentiated products industries. In *Handbook of Industrial Organization*, volume 4, pages 63–139. Elsevier.
Genakos, C. and Pagliero, M. (2022). Competition and pass-through: Evidence from isolated markets. *American Economic Journal: Applied Economics*, 14(4):35–57.
Genesove, D. and Mullin, W. P. (2001). Rules, communication, and collusion: Narrative evidence from the sugar institute case. *American Economic Review*, 91(3):379–398.
Geruso, M. and Layton, T. J. (2017). Selection in health insurance markets and its policy remedies. *Journal of Economic Perspectives*, 31(4):23–50.
Gilboa, I. (2009). *Theory of decision under uncertainty*, volume 45. Cambridge University Press.
Goldfarb, A. and Tucker, C. (2019). Digital economics. *Journal of Economic Literature*, 57(1): 3–43.
Greif, A. (1993). Contract enforceability and economic institutions in early trade: The maghribi traders' coalition. *The American Economic Review*, 525–548.
Güth, W., Schmittberger, R., and Schwarze, B. (1982). An experimental analysis of ultimatum bargaining. *Journal of Economic Behavior & Organization*, 3(4):367–388.
Hanson, G. H. (2009). The economic consequences of the international migration of labor. *Annual Review of Economics*, 1(1):179–208.
Hart, O. (2017). Incomplete contracts and control. *American Economic Review*, 107(7):1731–1752.
Hart, O., Shleifer, A., and Vishny, R. W. (1997). The proper scope of government: Theory and an application to prisons. *The Quarterly Journal of Economics*, 112(4):1127–1161.
Hayek, F. (1945). The use of knowledge in society. *The American Economic Review*, 35(4):519–530.
Head, K. and Mayer, T. (2014). Gravity equations: Workhorse, toolkit, and cookbook. In *Handbook of International Economics*, volume 4, pages 131–195. Elsevier.
Helpman, E. (2016). Globalization and wage inequality. Technical report, National Bureau of Economic Research.
Henrich, J., Boyd, R., Bowles, S., Camerer, C., Fehr, E., Gintis, H., and McElreath, R. (2001). In search of homo economicus: Behavioral experiments in 15 small-scale societies. *American Economic Review*, 91(2):73–78.
Hirschman, A. O. (1945). *National power and the structure of foreign trade*. University of California Press.
Hortaçsu, A. and Perrigne, I. (2021). Empirical perspectives on auctions. In *Handbook of Industrial Organization*, volume 5, pages 81–175. Elsevier.
Hotelling, H. (1929). Stability in competition. *The Economic Journal*, 39(153):41–57.
Hoy, M., Livernois, J., McKenna, C., Rees, R., and Stengos, T. (2022). *Mathematics for Economics*. MIT Press.
Hsieh, C.-T. and Klenow, P. J. (2009). Misallocation and manufacturing TFP in china and india. *The Quarterly journal of economics*, 124(4):1403–1448.
Imbens, G. W., Rubin, D. B., and Sacerdote, B. I. (2001). Estimating the effect of unearned income on labor earnings, savings, and consumption: Evidence from a survey of lottery players. *American Economic Review*, 91(4):778–794.
Irwin, D. A. (2019). Does trade reform promote economic growth? A review of recent evidence. Technical report, National Bureau of Economic Research.
Irwin, D. A. and Klenow, P. J. (1994). Learning-by-doing spillovers in the semiconductor industry. *Journal of Political Economy*, 102(6):1200–1227.
Ivaldi, M., Jullien, B., Rey, P., Seabright, P., and Tirole, J. (2003). The economics of tacit collusion. *IDEI Working Paper*.
Jäger, S., Naidu, S., and Schoefer, B. (2024). Collective bargaining, unions, and the wage structure: An international perspective. *NBER Working paper No. 33267*.
Janssen, A. and Zhang, X. (2023). Retail pharmacies and drug diversion during the opioid epidemic. *American Economic Review*, 113(1):1–33.
Jensen, M. C. and Meckling, W. H. (1976). Theory of the firm: Managerial behavior, agency costs and ownership structure. *Journal of Financial Economics*, 3(4):305–360.

Jensen, R. T. and Miller, N. H. (2008). Giffen behavior and subsistence consumption. *American Economic Review*, 98(4):1553–1577.

Johnson, D. B. (1973). Meade, bees, and externalities. *The Journal of Law and Economics*, 16(1):35–52.

Jones, C. I. and Klenow, P. J. (2016). Beyond GDP? Welfare across countries and time. *American Economic Review*, 106(9):2426–2457.

Jovanovic, B. (1982). Selection and the evolution of industry. *Econometrica*, 649–670.

Kacperczyk, M. and Schnabl, P. (2010). When safe proved risky: Commercial paper during the financial crisis of 2007–2009. *Journal of Economic Perspectives*, 24(1):29–50.

Kahneman, D. (2017). *Thinking, fast and slow*.

Kahneman, D., Knetsch, J. L., and Thaler, R. H. (1990). Experimental tests of the endowment effect and the Coase theorem. *Journal of Political Economy*, 98(6):1325–1348.

Kahneman, D., Knetsch, J. L., and Thaler, R. H. (1991). Anomalies: The endowment effect, loss aversion, and status quo bias. *Journal of Economic Perspectives*, 5(1):193–206.

Kahneman, D. and Tversky, A. (1979). Prospect theory: An analysis of decision under risk. *Econometrica*, 47(2):263–292.

Katz, L. F. and Krueger, A. B. (1992). The effect of the minimum wage on the fast-food industry. *Industrial and Labor Relations Review*, 46(1):6–21.

Keane, M. P. (2022). Recent research on labor supply: Implications for tax and transfer policy. *Labour Economics*, 77:102026.

Keynes, J. M. (1920). *Economic consequences of the peace*. Harcourt, Brace and Howe.

Keynes, J. M. (1921). *A Treatise on Probability*. Macmillan.

Keynes, J. M. (1924). Alfred Marshall, 1842-1924. *The Economic Journal*, 34(135):311–372.

Keynes, J. M. (1936). *The General Theory of Employment, Interest and Money*. Macmillan.

Klemperer, P. (2004). *Auctions: Theory and practice*. Princeton University Press.

Knight, F. H. (1921). Risk, uncertainty and profit. *Hart, Schaffner and Marx*.

Knutsson, D. and Tyrefors, B. (2022). The quality and efficiency of public and private firms: Evidence from ambulance services. *The Quarterly Journal of Economics*, 137(4):2213–2262.

Kreps, D. M. and Scheinkman, J. A. (1983). Quantity precommitment and Bertrand competition yield Cournot outcomes. *The Bell Journal of Economics*, 326–337.

Krugman, P. (1979). Increasing returns, monopolistic competition, and international trade. *Journal of International Economics*, 9:469–479.

Krugman, P. (1980). Scale economies, product differentiation, and the pattern of trade. *The American Economic Review*, 70(5):950–959.

Kumekawa, I. (2017). *The first serious optimist*. Princeton University Press.

Labandeira, X., Labeaga, J. M., and López-Otero, X. (2017). A meta-analysis on the price elasticity of energy demand. *Energy Policy*, 102:549–568.

Landers, R. M., Rebitzer, J. B., and Taylor, L. J. (1996). Rat race redux: Adverse selection in the determination of work hours in law firms. *The American Economic Review*, 329–348.

Laun, T. and Wallenius, J. (2015). A life cycle model of health and retirement: The case of Swedish pension reform. *Journal of Public Economics*, 127:127–136.

Lavan, M. (2021). Asymmetric information and adverse selection in the roman slave market: The limits of legal remedy. *Managing Information in the Roman Economy*, 179–202.

Levenstein, M. C. and Suslow, V. Y. (2006). What determines cartel success? *Journal of Economic Literature*, 44(1):43–95.

Levin, J. and Tadelis, S. (2010). Contracting for government services: Theory and evidence from us cities. *The Journal of Industrial Economics*, 58(3):507–541.

Lewis, M. (2016). *The undoing project: A friendship that changed the world*. Penguin UK.

Lopez, R. A. and You, Z. (1993). Determinants of oligopsony power: The Haitian coffee case. *Journal of Development Economics*, 41(2):275–284.

Lucking-Reiley, D. (1999). Using field experiments to test equivalence between auction formats: Magic on the internet. *American Economic Review*, 89(5):1063–1080.

Malmendier, U. and Taylor, T. (2015). On the verges of overconfidence. *Journal of Economic Perspectives*, 29(4):3–8.

Manning, A. (2021a). The elusive employment effect of the minimum wage. *Journal of Economic Perspectives*, 35(1):3–26.

Manning, A. (2021b). Monopsony in labor markets: A review. *ILR Review*, 74(1):3–26.

Marshall, A. (1890). *Principles of Economics*. Macmillian.

Maskin, E. and Riley, J. (2000). Asymmetric auctions. *The Review of Economic Studies*, 67(3): 413–438.
Maskin, E. and Tirole, J. (1988). A theory of dynamic oligopoly, ii: Price competition, kinked demand curves, and edgeworth cycles. *Econometrica*, 571–599.
McClure, S. M., Laibson, D. I., Loewenstein, G., and Cohen, J. D. (2004). Separate neural systems value immediate and delayed monetary rewards. *Science*, 306(5695):503–507.
McLaren, J. (1997). Size, sunk costs, and judge bowker's objection to free trade. *The American Economic Review*, 400–420.
McMillan, J. (2003). *Reinventing the bazaar: A natural history of markets*. WW Norton & Company.
Melitz, M. J. (2003). The impact of trade on intra-industry reallocations and aggregate industry productivity. *Econometrica*, 71(6):1695–1725.
Melitz, M. J. and Ottaviano, G. I. (2008). Market size, trade, and productivity. *The Review of Economic Studies*, 75(1):295–316.
Melitz, M. J. and Trefler, D. (2012). Gains from trade when firms matter. *Journal of Economic Perspectives*, 26(2):91–118.
Milgrom, P. (2004). *Putting auction theory to work*. Cambridge University Press.
Milgrom, P. R., North, D. C., and Weingast, B. R. (1990). The role of institutions in the revival of trade: The law merchant, private judges, and the champagne fairs. *Economics & Politics*, 2(1):1–23.
Miller, N. H., Sheu, G., and Weinberg, M. C. (2021). Oligopolistic price leadership and mergers: The united states beer industry. *American Economic Review*, 111(10):3123–3159.
Mischel, W. (2014). *The marshmallow test: Understanding self-control and how to master it*. Random House.
Moscovich, M. J. (1979). Obsidibus traditis: Hostages in Caesar's De bello Gallico. *The Classical Journal*, 75(2):122–128.
Nevo, A. (2001). Measuring market power in the ready-to-eat cereal industry. *Econometrica*, 69(2):307–342.
Noel, M. D. (2007). Edgeworth price cycles: Evidence from the toronto retail gasoline market. *The Journal of Industrial Economics*, 55(1):69–92.
Nozick, R. (1974). *Anarchy, state, and utopia*, volume 5038. Basic Books.
Oosterbeek, H., Sloof, R., and Van De Kuilen, G. (2004). Cultural differences in ultimatum game experiments: Evidence from a meta-analysis. *Experimental Economics*, 7:171–188.
Palme, M. and Persson, M. (2020). Sick pay insurance and sickness absence: some european cross-country observations and a review of previous research. *Journal of Economic Surveys*, 34(1):85–108.
Pavcnik, N. (2002). Trade liberalization, exit, and productivity improvements: Evidence from Chilean plants. *The Review of Economic Studies*, 69(1):245–276.
Pavcnik, N. (2017). The impact of trade on inequality in developing countries. Technical report, National Bureau of Economic Research.
Pigou, A. (1920). *The economics of welfare*. Macmillan.
Rabin, M. (1993). Incorporating fairness into game theory and economics. *The American Economic Review*, 1281–1302.
Radford, R. A. (1945). The economic organisation of a pow camp. *Economica*, 12(48):189–201.
Rawls, J. (1971). *A theory of justice*. Harvard University Press.
Rodrik, D. (2015). *Economics rules: Why economics works, when it fails, and how to tell the difference*. OUP Oxford.
Rogers, R. T. and Sexton, R. J. (1994). Assessing the importance of oligopsony power in agricultural markets. *American Journal of Agricultural Economics*, 76(5):1143–1150.
Rogerson, R. and Wallenius, J. (2013). Nonconvexities, retirement, and the elasticity of labor supply. *American Economic Review*, 103(4):1445–1462.
Romer, P. M. (1990). Endogenous technological change. *Journal of Political Economy*, 98(5, Part 2):S71–S102.
Romer, P. M. (1994). The origins of endogenous growth. *Journal of Economic Perspectives*, 8(1):3–22.
Roth, A. E. (2007). Repugnance as a constraint on markets. *Journal of Economic Perspectives*, 21(3):37–58.
Rubinstein, A. (2017). Comments on economic models, economics, and economists: remarks on economics rules by Dani Rodrik. *Journal of Economic Literature*, 55(1):162–172.
Ruttan, V. W. (2002). Productivity growth in world agriculture: sources and constraints. *Journal of Economic Perspectives*, 16(4):161–184.

Saliola, F. and Seker, M. (2011). Total factor productivity across the developing world. Technical report, The World Bank.

Sarpong, D. B. (2002). *Farm size, resource use efficiency, and rural development: Technoserve and small-scale pineapple farmer groups in Ghana*. Winrock International.

Savage, L. J. (1954). *The foundations of statistics*. John Wiley & Sons, Inc.

Schiermeier, Q. (2015). The science behind the Volkswagen emissions scandal. *Nature*, 9:24.

Seabright, P. (2010). *The company of strangers: A natural history of economic life*. Princeton University Press.

Shapiro, C. and Varian, H. R. (1999). *Information rules: A strategic guide to the network economy*. Harvard Business Press.

Shleifer, A. (2004). Does competition destroy ethical behavior? *American Economic Review*, 94(2): 414–418.

Simon, C. P., Blume, L., et al. (1994). *Mathematics for Economists*, volume 7. Norton New York.

Skidelsky, R. (2009). *Keynes: The return of the master*. Allen Lane.

Smith, J. M. (1976). Sexual selection and the handicap principle. *Journal of Theoretical Biology*, 57(1):239–242.

Smith, V. L. (1962). An experimental study of competitive market behavior. *Journal of Political Economy*, 70(2):111–137.

Spence, M. (1973). Job market signaling. *The Quarterly Journal of Economics*, 87(3):355–374.

Stigler, G. (1939). Production and distribution in the short run. *Journal of Political Economy*, 47(3):305–327.

Stigler, S. M. (1980). Stigler's law of eponymy. *Transactions of the New York Academy of Sciences*, 39(1 Series II):147–157.

Stiglitz, J. E. (1974). Incentives and risk sharing in sharecropping. *The Review of Economic Studies*, 41(2):219–255.

Tadelis, S. (2013). *Game theory: An introduction*. Princeton University Press.

Taylor, M. S. (2011). Buffalo hunt: International trade and the virtual extinction of the North American bison. *American Economic Review*, 101(7):3162–3195.

Thaler, R. H. and Shefrin, H. M. (1981). An economic theory of self-control. *Journal of Political Economy*, 89(2):392–406.

Thompson, P. (2001). How much did the Liberty shipbuilders learn? New evidence for an old case study. *Journal of Political Economy*, 109(1):103–137.

Thoursie, P. S. (2004). Reporting sick: Are sporting events contagious? *Journal of Applied Econometrics*, 19(6):809–823.

Tirole, J. (2010). *The theory of corporate finance*. Princeton University Press.

Townsend, R. M. (1994). Risk and insurance in village India. *Econometrica*, 539–591.

Trefler, D. (2004). The long and short of the Canada-US free trade agreement. *American Economic Review*, 94(4):870–895.

Tversky, A. and Kahneman, D. (1981). The framing of decisions and the psychology of choice. *Science*, 211(4481):453–458.

Varian, H. R. (1985). Price discrimination and social welfare. *The American Economic Review*, 75(4):870–875.

Varian, H. R. (2016). How to build an economic model in your spare time. *The American Economist*, 61(1):81–90.

Varian, H. R. and Harris, C. (2014). The VCG auction in theory and practice. *American Economic Review*, 104(5):442–445.

Vickrey, W. (1961). Counterspeculation, auctions, and competitive sealed tenders. *The Journal of Finance*, 16(1):8–37.

Von Neumann, J. and Morgenstern, O. (1944). *Theory of games and economic behavior*. Princeton University Press.

Weisburd, S. (2015). Identifying moral hazard in car insurance contracts. *Review of Economics and Statistics*, 97(2):301–313.

Weitzman, M. L. (1974). Prices vs. quantities. *The Review of Economic Studies*, 41(4):477–491.

Williamson, O. E. (2010). Transaction cost economics: The natural progression. *American Economic Review*, 100(3):673–690.

Zahavi, A. (1975). Mate selection—A selection for a handicap. *Journal of Theoretical Biology*, 53(1):205–214.

Zimmer, D. M. (2012). The role of copulas in the housing crisis. *Review of Economics and Statistics*, 94(2):607–620.

Index

Pages in *italics* refer to figures, pages in **bold** refer to tables, and pages followed by n refer to notes.

accounting: costs 76–77, 78n13; profits 77, 203
Adam Smith 3, 27n2, 95, 97–98, 139, 208, 212
adverse selection 266–272, 274, 283, 341
agriculture 44–47, 60n8, 151–152, 184, 277; production 34, 44, 151; productivity 46; products 8, 22, 27n1, 151, 163, 184
allocation 9, 117, 123, 141–149, 151–154, 157, 324; economy, in 138; efficiency of 123, 142, 349; health care 156' initial 142–144, *145*, 147–149; Pareto efficient 145, 149; resources 155–156; unequal 149
altruism 7n6, 95, 142
American Economic Association 7n3, 339
asymmetric information 239, 265–269, 271–275, 277–279, 281, 283, 285, 286n24, 298, 341
auctions 198, 228, 287, 339, 345–348, 351, 353n7–353n8
autarky 323–327, 329–331, 336, 337n6
automation 34–35, 38, 41–43, 50, 339, 347

backward induction 218, 220, *221*
Bain, J.S. 174, 185n8
bargaining costs 251, 253–254, 257
Beautiful Mind, A (movie) 203n1, 208, 223n1
behavioral: bias 96; biases 94, 96, 99; economics 93–94, 101n11, 238n4, 283
Bentham, Jeremy 157, *158*
Bertrand, Joseph 195–201, 203n2, 209, 211; analysis 195–196; equilibrium *200*, 201, 203n2
bidders 2, 345–349, 351–352, 353n8, 353n10
bidding 345–346, 348–349, 351–352, 353n11
Big Short, The (movie) 270
budget constraints 87–91, 103–108, 116–117, 120, 121n11, 146, 292–295
bundling 233–235; mixed 235
business: cycles 6, 7n5, 115; insurance 280

cannibalization 202–203
capacity 68, 174, 198, 233, 313, 315, 317n10, 333
capital 34, 37–38, 48; intangible 34; intellectual 34
cartels 206, 215–216, 331
ceteris paribus 24; *see also* other things equal
charity 92, 95
choice 4, 92, 97; optimal 64, 79, 87, 100, 104–106, 291, 293; rational 79, 81, 85, 92–93, 98, 101n1; *see also* preferences
club goods 254–255, 261–262, 263n22
Coase, Ronald 250–251, 253–254, 257, 263n11–263n12, 263n14; theorem 251, 253–254, 257
Cobb-Douglas production function 59, 60n18, 99, 177
collective bargaining 298, 301–302; agreements 298, 301–302
collusion 203, 206, 213–216, 223n5, 351
commodities *9*, 10, 22–23, 27n1, 28n3, 34, 77, 322
common resources 223n6, 254–259, 261–263n20
comparative advantage 319–321, 323, 326, 328, 336
compensation 105–106, *107*, 117, 277
competition 31; authorities 114, 202, 215, 345; imperfect 149, 163–164, 173, 177, 226, 332; perfect 130, 147, 149, 154, 163–164, 168, 172–173, 177, 180, 263n20, 272, 290, 297, 302, 319, 322, 324, 327–328, 331; policy 331, 343, 345; substitutes 41, 84–86, 116, 175, 291
constrained optimization 99, 103
consumer surplus 125–134, 136, 142, 156, 170, 172–174, 191, 227, 231, 236, 238n9, 243–245, 333, 335
consumption 87, 93, 127, 156; bundles **82**, 324; constraints on 97; efficient 141; food 91, *325*, 327; goods 291–293; individual 94; nonrivalrous 259; patterns 91; rival 254; utility 95
contract curve 146, 148, 153, 160n7

cooperation 7n5, 95, 160n10, 210, 213, 215–216, 222, 223n4, 223n6, 255, 257, 261, 332
coordination games 210, 217
corner solution 51–53
corporate social responsibility (CSR) 62
cost function 47, 53–57, 69, 167, 171, 184, 354
costs 48, 61, 75, 77; digitalization and 338; economic 77, 78n13; fixed 54–56, 65, 69, 71, 129, 174, 177, 182–183, 187, 220, 223n9, 229, 316, 329–330, 338; long-run 57–58; marginal 54–56; minimizing 48–49, 51, 53, 57, 151; opportunity 4, 48, 76–77, 78n13, 154, 226, 292–293, 319–321, 323, 326; short-run 57; staffing 237; structure 31, 220–221, 338; variable 54–55, 65, 69–71, 129, 182
Cournot, Augustin 187–200, 203n1, 206, 209, 211; equilibrium 189–195; model 194, 196; quantity 189, 191
COVID-19 15
credible commitment 218, 221
credit: constraints 280; markets 269, 272, 278
cross-price elasticity of demand 110–111, 114–115, 171–172
curves: demand 9–19, 22, 24, 26, 28n6–28n9, 28n10, 74, 90, 102–103, 105, 107, 109–113, 115–117, *119*, 121n11, 130, 165–166, 181; supply 9, 17–18, 22, 24, 31, 56, 72–73, 77, 79, 131, 134, 163
customs unions 332

deadweight loss 131–137, 169–174, 191, 227–228, 236, 245–246, 335
death spiral 269–270
defection 213–216, 223n5
defensive stocks 115
demand 10–14; excess *20*, 21–22, 132; increased 24, 74, 139; individual 110; inelastic 112, 134–135, 137, 172; patterns 202; price and 22; shock 24, 26–27, 57, 74, *75*, 77, 139, 249; unmet 21
demand curves 9–19, 22, 24, 26, 28n6–28n9, 28n10, 74, 90, 102–103, 105, 107, 109–113, 115–117, *119*, 121n11, 130, 165–166, 181
demand function 10–11, 15–16, 28n5, 28n8, 107, 109–110, 113, 126, 133, 136, 167, 171, 173, 197, 229, 342, 354, 361
dependent variable 10, 17, 354, 359, 362
Diamond, J. 60n10
diamonds 9, 22, 127–128; selling 174
diamond-water puzzle 9
differentiated: products 10, 22, 28n4, 79, 113, 164, 175, 177, 186, 198–202, 204n6, 215, 318, 328–329; profits 167–168, 184
differentiation 5, 37, 42, 63, 78n2–78n3, 86, 168, 171, 179, 183, 186, 188, 198–199, 201, 203, 212, 319, 344, 356, 359–360, 362; geographical 199
digital markets 287, 338–339, 341, 343, 345, 347, 349, 351, 353
digitalization 287, 338–340, 346; costs and 338
discount factor 213–215, 223n4
discrimination 93, 225–229, 231, 233, 235, 237, 238n2–238n3, 238n5, 238n8–238n10, 285n12, 285n17
diseconomies of scale 58
diversification of risk 314–316
domestic: producers 331–335; supply 29n13, 333–335
dominant strategies 206, 208–209, 212–213, 350
drink production *153*
drugs 5–6, 97, 281
Dubois, P. 91
duopoly 344
Dupuit, Charles 232

economic: costs 77, 78n13; decisions 98, 339; rent 77
economies of scale 57–59, 60n16, 174, 177, 183–184, 319, 328–330
Edgeworth box 142, *144–146*, 147, *148*, 151–153
education 1–2, 4–5, 6n1, 34, 62, 97, 133–137, 156, 160n10, 242, 245–246, 273, 297–298, 305, 328, 336
efficiency 125, 142; allocation, of 123, 142, 349; consumption 141; equilibrium 125; gains 147, 222, 249; loss 149, 170
efficient solutions 139, 251, 260, 275
Einstein, Albert: models 4
elastic supply 134–135, *137*, 333
elasticity 99, 102, 110–116, 120, 171–172, 178, 295, 303n3, 343, 351; demand, of 110–115, 120, 171–172, 343; estimates 112
emissions regulations *23*, 24
endowment effect 98
Engel curves 115
entry barriers 163–165, 173, 176, 186, 195, 198
equality 2, 156, 172, 214, 256; opportunity, of 156
equilibrium 74, 77, 133, 151, 208, 221; associated 19, 24; Bertrand *200*, 201, 203n2; choices 290; competitive 150; Cournot 189–195; free-entry 176, 329; general 138–139, 141–143, 145, 147, 149, 151–161, 177, 183, 319, 322, 332; market 19–21, 23, 28n10, 93, 130, 139, 154; model 139, 183, 319, 322, 332; Nash 192, 199, 203n1, 206, 209–212, 218, 223n3; partial 123, 125, 127, 129–131, 133, 135, 137–138, 332–335, 337n6; pooling 274; price 19–22, 24, 28n10, 130, 190, 28n10, 333; separating 274, 285n12; shifts 22, *25*, *27*; trade model 332
equity 123, 147, 149, 155–157, 160
ethical production 270–271
European Union 6n1, 184, 215–216, 231, 250, 331, 345

excess: demand *20*, 21–22, 132; supply 21–22, 298
expected revenue 275, 346, 349, 351–352
export 26, 29n13, 112, 184, 258, 302, 319, 322, *325*, 326–331, 333, *334*; bans 29n13; subsidies 331
extensive margins 296–299, 303n4
externalities 78n1, 139, 149, 159, 239, 241–251, 253–255, 257, 259, 261–264, 332

fairness 95, 123, 147, 156
farmers 10, 77, 78n2, 257, 299, 321, 326
farming 3, 73, 248, 251, 317n13; communities 3, 317n13
female labor supply 296
Fight Club (movie) 286n27
financial crisis 26, 270, 278, 315
first welfare theorem 147, 149
fixed: costs 54–56, 65, 69, 71, 129, 174, 177, 182–183, 187, 220, 223n9, 229, 316, 329–330, 338; fees 164, 225, 235–237, 238n14
fixed wage contract 276
food: consumption 91, *325*, 327; production 153, 323, 326
free entry 73–74, 77, 78n1, 123, 138, 140, 163, 165, 173, 175–177, 180, 182, **183**, 256, 270, 329
free trade 323–324, 326–327, 329, 331–332, 336; areas 332
Friberg, Richard 313, 317n1–317n2, 317n6
Friedman, Milton 157

game theory 192, 203n1, 205–206, 208, 222–223, 224n12, 271, 317n4
game tree 217–218, 222
games: coordination 210; excludable 254; repeated 206, 212, 215–216; sequential 206, 216–218; static 206; ultimatum 95, 238n4; zero-sum 210
General Agreement on Tariffs and Trade (GATT) 332
general equilibrium 138–139, 141–143, 145, 147, 149, 151–161, 177, 183, 319, 322, 332; model 139, 183, 319, 322, 332
geographical differentiation 199
Giffen, Robert 28n6, *119*, 120, 120n4; goods 28n6, 120, 120n4
goods 34; club 254–255, 261–262, 263n22; consumption 291–293; homogeneous 22, *197*; inferior 12, *13*, 108, 115–116, 120; manufactured 151, 184; nonexcludable 254; nonrival 254; normal 12, *13*, 108, 115–116; rival 254
goods and services 3–4, 6, 34, 61, 82, 87, 93, 156, 163, 185n7, 225, 228, 237, 254, 283–284, 339, 343, 346; allocation of 4; bundles 82
government: regulation 272; revenue 335
gravity models 327–328
gray markets 231
green revolution 46, 60n10
grim trigger strategy 213–214

handicap theory 285n13
health care 115, 133, 135, 156, 160n10, 315
Heckscher-Ohlin model 322, 337n3
heterogeneous firms 180, 183–184, 330
heuristics 97
Hicks, Sir John 59n6, 121n11, 303n3; Hicksian substitution 121n11
hidden: action 266; information 266
historical trends 3
hold-up problems 221–222
homogeneous: goods 22, 196, *197*; products 10, 12, 28n4, 73, 78n2, 79, 123, 164, 186–187, 196, 198, 215, 272
horizontal product differentiation 198–199

imperfect: competition 149, 163–164, 173, 177, 226, 332; substitutes 41, 84–86, 116, 175, 291
import: parallel 231; quota 331, 335; tariff 333
incentive compatibility constraint (IC) 233, 238n12, 285n17
income 4; effects 116–117, *118*, 120, 294–296; resource, as a 4
income elasticity of demand 114–115, 120
income statement, firm 76
increased demand 24, 74, 139
incumbent 174, 185n8, 220–221
independent variable 354, 359, 361–362
indifference curves 83–92, 103–106, *107*, 117, 120, 121n11, 143–148, 154–155, 160n7, 291–294, 324, 326, 362
individual demand 110
individual rationality constraint (IR) 233, 238n12
industrialization 184
inelastic demand 112, 134–135, *137*, 172
inequality 156, 160n10, 336
inferior goods 12, *13*, 108, 115–116, 120
information asymmetries 123n1, 139, 159, 267–272, 279–280, 283, 285n5; sharing 272
initial allocation 142–144, *145*, 147–149
inputs 34; relative prices of 50
insurance 97, 133, 137, 156, 265–266, 269, 271, 274, 278, 280, 282–283, 285n15, 315, 317; business 280; group policies 271
intangible capital 34
intellectual capital 34
intensive margin 296
interior solution 51
intermediate inputs 35, 185n9, 336n1
internal prices 77

international: shipment 319; trade 177, 180, 183, 212, 287, 318–319, 321–323, *325*, 327–329, 331–333, 335–336, 337n3
inverse demand function 10, 28n5, 28n8, 109–110, 361
inverse supply curve 17
investment 61, 77, 182, 214, 221, 250, 270, 279, 286n20, 297
investor representatives 283
invisible hand 139, 141, 208
isocosts 49–53, 57, 60n14, 88, 152; line 49
isoquant 39–43, 48–52, 57, 83, 87, 152

Kahneman, Daniel 96–98, 101n8, 101n13
Keynes, John Maynard *1*, 5, 7n5, 29n12, 94, 157, 160
Knightian uncertainty 307, 313
Krugman, Paul 177, 328–330

labor 34, 38, 48, 51–52, 76, 290; markets 287, 289, 297–298, 301; microeconomics and 289; productivity 46–47, 328; supply of 291, 295–296, 299; unions 301
labor force 296, *297*; female 296
labor supply 157, 289, 291, 293–297, 299, 301, 303n3–303n4; elasticity 295
Lagrange: function 99; method 49, 99
land 34, 38, 44, 46, 59n3, 73, 76–77, 78n11, 251–252, 257, 263n21, 322–324, 326–327; organization of 46; supply and demand for 289
leisure 82, 291–296
Lerner index 172–173
Levitt, Stephen 91
limited liability 278
lottery 2, 182, 296, 307, 311–312, 317n4

macroeconomics 6, 177, 289, 298
Malthus, Thomas 44, 46, 59n3, 60n9–60n10; Malthusian trap 46, 60n9
management practices 180
manufactured goods 151, 184
marginal abatement cost (MAC) 247
marginal costs (MC)54–56, 63–77, 78n4, 78n8, 129, 137n1–137n2, 139–141, 154–155, 167–174, 176, 180–190, 193–203, 215, 220, 223n9, 225–231, 236–237, 238n7, 242–249, 256, 262, 263n6, 290, 301, 324, 329–330, 338, 342–344, 357
marginal external benefit (MEB) 245–246
marginal external cost *243–244*, 245, 247–248
marginal product 36–38, 42, 44–47, 50, *150*, 151, 177, 256, 290, 323, 327, 362; capital, of 37, 42, 50, 151, 327; labor, of 36–38, 42, 44–47, 50, *150*, 151, 177, 290, 323, 362
marginal rate of substitution (MRS) 87, *88*, 91, 146, 154
marginal rate of transformation (MRT) 91, 154
marginal revenue (MR) 63, 166–172, *181*, 188–189, 191, 193, *227*, *229–230*, 236–237, 238n7, 343, 357, 360
marginal social benefit (MSB) 245–246
marginal utilities 87, *88*, 90, 146–147, 154, 158, *159*, 309–310, 317n4, 324
market clearing: price 19, 22; wage 298–299
market power 173, 299–301, 303n13; *see also* monopoly power
markets *8*, 9, 16; demand 72, 109–110, 126–127, 132, 166, 187; equilibrium 19–21, 23, 28n10, 93, 130, 139, 154; failures 6, 137, 139, 149, 159–160, 239, 255, 265, 332; interaction 123, 138, 142; online 287; operation 6; platform 339; prices 9–10, 19, 22, 64, *75–76*, 78n2, 140–141, 332–335, 337n7; secondhand 22; supply 71–75, *76*, 140, *141*, 163
markups 171–173, 177, 184, 196, 203, 228, 350–351
Marshall, Alfred 5, 22–23, 94, 303n3
materialism 92
maximin strategy 210
maximization of utility 5, 89
maximizing profits 4, 61–62, 139, 167, 184, 187, 189, 193, 199–203, 226, 229, 233, 235, 281, 290, 342, 350
mean-preserving spread 308–311, 313, 316
microeconomics 3, 5, 201, 295; labor and 289; models 5
migration 297
military strategy 206
minimizing costs 48
minimum wage 298, *299*, 301, 303n9
models 6; Cournot 194, 196; economics 5, 97; Einstein, Albert 4; equilibrium trade 332; general equilibrium 139, 183, 319, 322, 332; gravity 327–328; Heckscher-Ohlin 322, 337n3; intellectual appeal 90; microeconomics 5; oligopoly 177; rational 98
money 3, 6, 62, 69–70, 77, 78n12, 81, 84, 92, 95, 105, 117, 125, 157, 169, 182, 227, 253, 269–270, 349
monopoly 163, 166; competition, monopolistic 163–165, 167, 169, 171, 173, 175–177, 179–185n7, 319, 328–330; power 149, 172–173; profit 167, 190, 196, 236;
monopsony 299, 301
moral: hazard 266, 274–283, 285n16, 286n19, 286n25, 341; views 6
Morgenstern, Oskar 206, 317n3–317n4
MRS 87, *88*, 91, 146, 154
mutual gains 144, 147, 268

Nash, John 192, 199, 203n1, 206, 208–215, 218, 223n3; equilibrium 192, 199, 203n1, 206, 209–212, 218, 223n3

navigational tools 5
negative externalities 241–246, 248, 250–251, 259
network: effects 176, 237, 339–344; externalities 242
Nevo, A. 202–203, 204n8
noncooperative payoff 213
nonexcludability 255, 257–258
normal goods 12, *13*, 108, 115–116
normative statements 156
Nozick, Robert 158

objective probabilities 306
oligopoly **163**, 164, 177, 186–187, 189, 191, 193, 195, 197–199, 201, 203–204, 238n1; markets 186, 238n1; models 177, 187
online markets 287
operating at a loss *71*
opportunity costs 4, 48, 76–77, 78n13, 154, 226, 292–293, 319–321, 323, 326
optimization 99, 103, 169, 193, 201, 361; choices, of 64, 79, 87, 100, 104–106, 291, 293; outcomes, of 170, 260; quantities, of 49, 63, 65–66, 104–106, 168–169, 171, 187–189, 193, 230–231, 247
organic products 92
organized exchanges 22
other things equal 24, 104, 106, 116; *see also* ceteris paribus
outlays 61, 76, 87–88
output 33, 35–39, 42, 44, 47, 59, 141, 151–152, 177–178, 194, 263n5, 290, 299, 301, 302n1, 316, 320, 323
overconfidence 98
overoptimism 283
overproduction *243–244*, 245
ownership 98, 174, 252

palladium 23–26, 35
parallel imports 231
Pareto, Vilfredo 160n4; efficient 142, 144–145, 147–149, 208; efficient allocation *145*, 149; improvement 208, 327; optimal points 146; optimality 159, 160n7
partial derivative 36–37, 42, 59n5, 362
partial equilibrium 123, 125, 127, 129–131, 133, 135, 137–138, 332–335, 337n6
participation constraint 233
patents 34, 166, 173, 331
payoffs 76, **193**, 205–223, 224n12, 252–255, 275–276, 279, 314, 349–351; matrix **193**, 206–209, 211, 217; noncooperative 213
perfect: complements *40*, 41, 84–85, *86*, 147–148, *149*; substitutes 22, 39–41, 51, 64, 84–85, 186, 198, 298
perfect competition 130, 147, 149, 154, 163–164, 168, 172–173, 177, 180, 263n20, 272, 290, 297, 302, 319, 322, 324, 327–328, 331
perfectly competitive: economy 123, 138; markets 64, 73–74, 123, 130–131, 150, 153–154, 159, 163, 176, 226, 297, 327
philosophy 7n5, 27n2, 41, 97–98
physical products; *see* goods
Pigou, Arthur 225, 228, 247, 263n4; Pigouvian tax 247–249
platform: economics 339–340; markets 339
Polynesians 5
pooling equilibrium 274
population 38, 44, 46, 59n3, 156, 296, *297*; growth 44, 46
positive: externalities 242, 245–246, 259; statements 156–157
predictions 3–4, 24, 28n10, 79, 93, 101n7, 157, 161n11, 186, 196, 207, 222, 223n4–223n5, 281, 295, 327–328, 341, 351
preferences 91–93; social 94–95; stable 93; transitive 82, 101n2; *see also* choice
price 5–6, 13–14, 16, *17*, 48, 318; cannibalization 202–203; cap 21–22, 132; changes 8, 18, 79, 110, 112, 116, 293; competition 195–202, 204n6, 215; demand and 22; differences 91, 225; discovery 346; discrimination 225–229, 231, 233, 235, 237, 238n2–238n3, 238n5, 238n8–238n10, 285n12, 285n17; downward pressure 21–22; equilibrium 19–22; internal 77; quantity and 11; relation 133, 136; structures 225, 341; transfer 77; uniform 228, 231; upward pressure on 21–22
price ceiling; *see* price cap
price elasticity 110–111, 114–115, **116**, 120n7, 171–172; demand, of 110–111, 114–115, 171–172
price takers 10, 17, 28n10, 110, 123, 191, 242
pricing schemes 164, 234; *see also* price structures
Principles of Economics (Marshall) 22
Prisoner's dilemma 206, 209, 213, 222
private: costs 242; solutions 242–243, 246–247, 253
probabilities: distribution of 305–308, 312, 351 objective 306; subjective 306
Problem of Social Cost, The (Coase) 250
producers 5, 9–10, 22–24, 28n4, 57–58, 64, 123, 125, 129–132, 134, 136, 137n1, 137n5, 139, 201, 213, 215, 242–243, 245–247, 249, 270, 272, 296, 303n13, 330–331, 333, 335; domestic 331–335; surplus 129–134, 136, 137n1, 156, 170, 173, 243–245, 333, 335
product: differentiation 5, 78n2, 179, 183, 186, 198–199, 201, 203, 212, 319, 344; marginal 36–38, 42, 44–47, 50, 150–151, 177, 256, 290, 323, 327, 362; organic 92; substitute *14*, 114

production 34, *45*, 88; drinks, of 153; ethical 270–271; factors 34; food, of *45*, 153, 322–323; functions 35–37, 41–45, 50, 58–59, 60n7, 60n18, 152, 177–178, 290, 323, 361–362; processes 180; trade and 323–324, *325*
production possibility frontier (PPF) 153–155, 320–321, 323–324
productivity 44–47, 60n8, 177–181, 184, 277, 298, 319–320, 328, 330; developments 47, 60n8; differences 178, 180, 320; gains 44, 46, 277; improvements *45*, 47; literature 180; patterns 180
profit 4, 31, 68, 129, 173, 227; lost 236, 343; maximization 61–69, 139, 167–168, 170–171, 184, 188, 199, 203, 227, 229, 233–234, 238n7, 281, 290, 300, 313, 350; motives 139; variable 71, 130, 181–183; zero *70*, 74–75, 77, 123, 139, 173–176, 182–183
property rights 250–253, 256–257
prosocial behavior 283
psychological motivations 62
public: economics 6; procurement 280, 286n22, 347
punishment 209, 213, 216, 223n5, 271, 281
pure: loss 130–131, 133; pure strategies 210–212

quantities 6; competition 187, 197, 204n6; mechanisms 261; price and 11; restrictions 248–249, 257, 263n8

rational: behavior 94, 96–98; choice 79, 81, 85, 92–93, 98, 101n1; model 98; utility 92
raw materials 34, 163, 184
real options 312–313, 317n12
recessions 289, 295, 298
redistribution 133, 139, 149–150, 156, 158–160, 170, 180, 280, 327
regulations 6, 21, 23, 173, 241, 248, 266, 272, 298, *299*, 319, 336, 345; changes 23; emissions *23*, 24; government 272
religion 41
repeated: games 206, 212, 215–216; interaction 191, 255, 271–272
research and development 177, 260–261, 336n1
resources 61, 137, 152, 318–319; allocation 2, 9, 138–139, 151, 155–156; common 223n6, 254–259, 261–262, 263n20; income 4; time 4; *see also* scarcity
responses 97, 106, 174, 187, 207–209, 216–218
returns to scale 58–59, 60n18
revenue 61, 290
revenue equivalence theorem 349, 351
rice 6, 8–10, 22, 26, 28n6, 29n13, 57, 62, 111, *119*, 120, 315, 332
riots 8
risk 313–314; buffers 315; decisions 312; diversification 314–316; flexibility 315–316; lovers 307, 311–313; neutral 307–308, 316, 351; sharing 282
Robinson Crusoe analogy 153–154
Romer, Paul 177, 261, 264n24, 336

scarcity 2–4, 43, 77, 137, 141, 174, 326; *see also* resources
school 62; choice 5; secondary 2, 354
screening 274
second welfare theorem 149
secondary effects 24
secondhand market 22
selection 2; adverse 266–272, 274, 283, 341; methods 2
self-selection constraint 231, 233, 235, 285n17
sellers 5, 9–10, 16, 19, 21–22, 28n10, 133–135, 186, 228, 267–268, 283, 339–344, 351
separating equilibrium 274, 285n12
sequential games 206, 216–218
services 34
sharecropping 276–277, 285n16; contract 276
shocks 23–24, 26, 110, 112, 180, 298, 315
signaling 26, 272, 274, 285n13
singlehome 344
small open economy 332
Smith, Adam 3, 27n2, 28n10, 82, 95, 97–98, 101n11, 139, 208, 212, 285n13
social: class 2, 4; mobility 156–157; optimum 243, 245, 247, 253; preferences 94–95
social costs 243–245, 250; marginal 243
social norms 93, 95, 139, 209, 253, 257, 261, 277, 283–284
social planners 139, 147, 149–152, 157, 211, 247–249, 262n3
social welfare function 157–158
socialism 150
societal producer surplus 243–245
solutions: corner 51–53; efficient 139, 251, 260, 275; interior 51; private 242–243, 246–247, 253
Stackelberg outcome 193–194
staffing costs 237
starvation 22, 46, 309
states of the world 305
static games 206
stick charts 5
stockpiling 15
stocks 19, 78n12, 115, 226, 258, 304, 306, 312–315, 340; defensive 115; unsold 19
strategic: interaction 164–165, 175–176, 186–187, 205, 212, 222; reflections 176
students 2, 68; housing 4; loans 4
subjective probabilities 306
subsidy 105–106, 135–137, 250, 331, 342; incidence *137*

substitutability 120, 338
substitutes 14, 22–23, 39–41, 51, 64, 84–87, 110–111, 113–114, 116, 166, 175, 186, 198, 202, 291, 298, 349; imperfect 41, 84–86, 116, 175, 291; perfect 22, 39–41, 51, 64, 84–85, 186, 198, 298; product *14*, 114
substitution: ease of 113; effects of 116–117, *118*, 120, 121n11, 294–295, 303n3
supply: domestic 29n13, 333–335; excess 21–22, 298; shocks 110, 112
supply and demand 123, 133, 136; analysis 9, 11, 22, 24, 27n2, 298, 332; labor 289; shocks 23, 26
supply curve 9, 16–18, *19*, 21–27, 31, 56, 64, 66, 71–74, 77–79, *129*, 130–131, 134, 139, 163, 185n5, 245, 293–296, 299, 301, 333–335; inverse 17
supply of labor 291, 295–296, *299*
symmetric information 267–268

tariff 235–237, 331–336, 337n7; two-part 235–236
tax 261; incidence 134–135; planning 62; tourist 134
technology 31, 33, 79; progress 47, 177
Theory of Games and Economics Behavior (Von Neumann and Morgenstern) 206
Thinking, Fast and Slow (Kahneman) 96
total differentiation 42, 86, 362
total factor productivity (TFP) 177–180, 183, 185n9
total variable costs 129, 137n2
tourist tax 134
trade 319; international 177, 180, 183, 212, 287, 318–336, 337n3; policy 180, 287, 319, 327, 331–332, 337n5; production and 323–324, *325*
tradeable emissions 249–250
tragedy of the commons 255
transaction costs 252, 263n12, 263n15
transfer prices 77
transitive preferences 82, 101n2
transitivity 82–83, 101n2
Trolley problem analogy 161n13
trust 284
two-part tariff 235–236

ultimatum game 95, 238n4
uncertainty 7n5, 78n2, 287, 304–307, 309, 311, 313–315, 317n1–317n2, 332, 346–347
underproduction 246
unemployment 280, 289, 298–299, 315
unequal allocation 149
uniform pricing 228, 231
unit tax 133–134, 248
university revenue 2
unmet demand 21
utility: consumption, of 95; functions 85–86, 89–92, 95, 99, 103, 120n1, 158, 233, 291, 309–311, 317n3; long-term 96; maximization 5, 89, *90*, 96, 99, 103, 154; rational 92

valuations 28n10, 81, 234, 259, 267, 326, 346, 348, 352
variable: costs 54–55, 65, 69–71, 129, 182; profits 71, 130, 181–183
Varian, Hal 238n9, 339, 353n9
vertical product differentiation 198
violence 2, 174
volume 34, 38, 69, 328, 346
voluntary trade 139, 147, 160
Von Neumann, John 206, 317n3–317n4

wages 4, 18, 36, 38, 48–51, 53, 60n14, 75, 93, 151–152, 178, 228, 269, 273, 276–277, 280, 289–296, 298–302, 303n3, 303n9, 321, 327; bargaining 302; market clearing 298–299; minimum 298–299, 301, 303n9; upward pressure on 298, 301, 327
Walras, Léon 28n10, 142
Wealth of Nations (Smith) 3, 97–98, 139, 212
welfare 326–327, 331; gains 319, 326, 329–331
welfare theorems: first 147, 149; second 149
willingness to pay 10, 126–127, 225–228, 231–236, 259–261, 268, 285n2, 285n12, 342, 347
winner's curse 346, 353n8
workers 36–37, 39, 43, 60n14, 151–152, 178, 277, 290, 297–299, 301–302, 336; allocation 151–152
World Trading Organization (WTO) 332
World War I 7n5
World War II 7n5, 78, 332

yield 17, 26, 43, 46, 64, 68, 72, 78n11, 86, 105, 112, 136, 157, 167–171, 184, 193, 208, 227, 234–235, 245, 308, 311, 343–351

zero profit *70*, 74–77, 123, 139, 173–176, 182–183, 270; equilibrium 177